Major Problems in
American History Since 1945

MAJOR PROBLEMS IN AMERICAN HISTORY SERIES

GENERAL EDITOR

THOMAS G. PATERSON

Major Problems in
American History Since 1945

DOCUMENTS AND ESSAYS

SECOND EDITION

EDITED BY

ROBERT GRIFFITH

AMERICAN UNIVERSITY

PAULA BAKER

UNIVERSITY OF PITTSBURGH

HOUGHTON MIFFLIN COMPANY
Boston   New York

Editor in Chief: Jean L. Woy
Senior Associate Editor: Frances Gay
Associate Project Editor: Heather Hubbard
Associate Production/Design Coordinator: Lisa Jelly
Senior Marketing Manager: Sandra McGuire
Senior Manufacturing Coordinator: Priscilla Bailey

Cover image: Davis Cone, "Plaza/Twilight," 1988. Acrylic on canvas, 30 × 30 in.
 Private Collection. Courtesy Forum Gallery, NYC.
Cover design: Deborah Azerrad Savona

Library of Congress Catalog Card Number: 98-72035

ISBN: 0-395-86850-5

3456789-CRS-05 04 03 02

For Our Students

Contents

C H A P T E R   1 2
The Reagan Revolution and After: Politics and Political Economy in the New Era
Page 449

C H A P T E R   1 3
The Empire Strikes Back: Ronald Reagan and the End of the Cold War
Page 498

C H A P T E R   1 4
*Brave New World: The United States
and the Global Era*
Page 531

Preface

If it is true that historians interpret the past through the prism of their own times, it is especially true when they try to understand America's recent past. Consider how the world has changed since the first edition of this book was assembled in the early 1990s. The sudden and unexpected collapse of the Soviet Union had just occurred, and the outlines of the new post-Cold War world were difficult to discern. The United States was in economic recession, prompting worried debates about America's productive capacity. The arrival of new immigrants was reconfiguring the nation's demographics, prompting worried, sometimes nativist-tinged debates over the future of American national identity. Here, as in so many other areas, Americans were just beginning to grapple with the economic, political, and cultural impact of globalization. And though the revolution in new information technologies was underway, the Internet itself existed only in outline, still largely dominated by scientists and technicians. The new edition of *Major Problems in American History Since 1945* is thus designed to address both the new issues that Americans face at the beginning of the new century, as well as changing interpretations of older issues.

Like the earlier version, this one covers classic issues raised by America's rise as a global economic and military power in the wake of World War II. Early chapters cover American policymakers' debate about using atomic weapons against Japan, the origins of the Cold War, and how the conflict between the United States and the Soviet Union played out around the world. If America's place in the world was one important debate in postwar public life, civil rights and race relations was the other. One chapter traces civil rights directly; others deal with race relations as part of debates about radicalism, feminism, and the welfare state. Many chapters touch the transformation in American society and culture in the years between World War II and the present. The closing chapters focus on the last decades of the twentieth century: on the changes in American politics and political economy in the "post-liberal" world of Ronald Reagan and Bill Clinton; on the dilemmas of foreign policy in the new, post-Cold War era; and on ideas about citizenship and the nation in a world in which national boundaries seem to mater less and less.

The present volume takes a measure of new developments both in American life and in the work of historians, social scientists, and other commentators since the last edition. Two-thirds of the essays are new for this edition, and the chapters on social issues in the 1950s (Chapter 4) and the women's movement in the 1960s and 1970s (Chapter 10) are essentially new, with mostly new documents and all new essays. The final chapter on globalization is also new for this edition. Other chapters that include new essays are Chapter 1, designed to present the significant themes of the volume; Chapter 2 on the decision to drop the atomic bomb; Chapter

3 on the Cold War; Chapter 5 on the Cuban Missile Crisis; Chapter 7 on the civil rights movement; Chapter 9 on the politics of the 1960s; Chapter 12 on the Reagan Revolution; and Chapter 13 on the end of the Cold War.

New documents include recently released material from Soviet archives that add insight to Cold War controversies; documents that touch on the history of political conservatism and illuminate its later ascendancy in the 1980s; documents that give new views of underlying social issues during the 1950s; and personal experiences of the Vietnam war, the 1960s, and the feminist movement.

Like other volumes in this series, *Major Problems in American History Since 1945* approaches its subject in two ways: documents introduce historical problems and highlight key issues, while the essays reveal how different interpretations can result from reading the same documents or observing the same phenomena. We invite readers to analyze the diversity of viewpoints and approaches on critical issues and arrive at their own conclusions. The chapter introductions and head-notes to the documents and the essays sections place the readings in historical and interpretive perspective. Suggestions for further reading at the end of each chapter provide additional resources for students who want to continue their study of particular issues and areas.

We would like to thank again the many readers who provided helpful suggestions and comments on the first edition. We would also like to thank the following reviewers who gave us helpful suggestions and comments for the second edition: Laura A. Belmonte, Oklahoma State University; Mark S. Byrnes, Davidson College; Cheryl Greenberg, Trinity College; Frank C. Costigliola, University of Connecticut; Gregory Field, University of Michigan at Dearborn; Richard M. Fried, University of Illinois at Chicago; Norman Markowitz, Rugers University; Gary May, University of Delaware; Chester Pach, Ohio University; and David F. Schmitz, Whitman College. And we wish to thank especially all those with whom we have worked at Houghton Mifflin: Thomas G. Paterson, the general editor of the Major Problems in American History series; Frances Gay, whose patience and perseverance helped assure the project's completion; Heather Hubbard, who managed the sometimes tricky task of copyediting; and Teresa Buswell, who tracked down permissions. We owe a special debt to our colleagues at the University of Massachusetts at Amherst, the University of Maryland at College Park, the University of Pittsburgh, and American University; and to our students, to whom this volume is dedicated.

As with the first edition, we look forward to hearing suggestions as to what should or should not be included in future editions, and invite students and teachers alike to write us in care of our respective institutions.

R. G.

P. B.

*Major Problems in
American History Since 1945*

CHAPTER

1

World War II and the Origins
of Postwar America

✖

In the spring of 1945, the new president of the United States, Harry S Truman, anxiously surveyed a world in turmoil and transition. In Europe more than three decades of economic crisis and violent upheaval not only had inflicted an enormous toll in lives and material but had irreparably weakened the old, European-led world system that had organized international affairs for more than a century. Germany, which had dominated the continent economically and militarily during much of the twentieth century, now faced virtual annihilation as Allied armies closed in on Berlin from east and west. France and Great Britain, once mighty imperial nations and now ostensibly victorious, were only little better off than the vanquished. By contrast, the Soviet Union had emerged from the war a battered but nevertheless major new world power. In Asia the imminent defeat of Japan promised to alter the balance of power in the Pacific radically. Throughout the colonial world of Asia, Africa, and the Middle East, the collapse of imperial Europe released powerful revolutionary stirrings among peoples seeking self-determination and economic development.

The United States, which alone of the great powers had escaped the war's physical destruction, was now the strongest nation in the world. In victory, however, Americans and their leaders confronted many difficult questions involving how, toward what ends, and in whose interest their enormous resources would be deployed. What would be the character of America's postwar relations with its allies, especially the Soviet Union; with its vanquished enemies, Germany and Japan; with the war-devastated nations of Europe; and with the peoples of Latin America, Africa, Asia, and the Middle East? What role would the United States play in the recovery of shattered foreign nations and in the reconstruction of a stable postwar system of international relations? How would the costs and burdens of that role be distributed, and with what consequences at home and abroad?

In domestic affairs, President Truman and other Americans faced a second, equally daunting set of problems. The depression decade that had preceded World War II had produced enormous, if piecemeal and at times contradictory, changes in U.S. politics and the American political economy. The New Deal had sought to impose social discipline on American capitalism, to protect individuals from arbitrary and impersonally inflicted deprivation, and to mobilize ordinary men and women in pursuit of a more democratic social and economic order. But the New Deal at the same

1

time had aroused fierce opposition from U.S. business leaders, who were determined if not to destroy reform, then at least to turn it to their own purposes. The power and reach of the federal government had grown enormously during the depression and war, but the question of how and in whose interest that power would be used remained largely unanswered. Could the American economy be harnessed to democratic and egalitarian goals, or would it serve as a great engine of inequality and special privilege? Would the New Deal's supporters succeed in constraining the autonomy of private property through progressive taxation, vigorous proconsumer regulation, and public ownership? Or would government be used instead to secure and defend patterns of privilege? Would the federal government seek to redistribute power by encouraging the organization of the powerless, or would its authority now be used to restrain organized workers, farmers, and urban minorities?

A third set of postwar issues concerned the day-to-day lives of ordinary citizens. In 1945 a great metamorphosis in American society was under way as the continued spread of industrial organization, mass consumption, mass communication, and secular values transformed the nation from a patchwork of local village cultures into an increasingly interdependent, national culture. Both the Great Depression and the Second World War, moreover, powerfully reshaped American lives. "The great knife of the depression . . . cut down through the entire population, cleaving open the lives of rich as well as poor," wrote Robert and Helen Lynd upon their return in the 1930s to "Middletown," the midwestern city of Muncie, Indiana, which they had studied a decade earlier. "The experience has been more nearly universal than any prolonged recent emotional experience in the city's history; it has approached in its elemental shock the primary experiences of birth and death." The impact of war was even more profound and far-reaching. More than 12 million men and women had entered the armed forces, nearly a million of whom had been killed or wounded. More than 15 million others had taken work in the humming defense industries. In 1945, as the war drew to a close and the nation began its conversion to peacetime, Americans anxiously faced a future over which they had only partial control. Would they secure jobs in the transformed postwar society, and if so, on what terms? Would they find decent housing, and if so, where and at what costs? How would Americans confront the deep and potentially explosive divisions of race, class, and gender? What would be the character of relationships between husbands and wives, parents and children, friends and neighbors? How would balances be struck between private and public consumption, between development and preservation, between competition and community?

The way in which all these questions—foreign and domestic, political and economic, social and cultural—were answered; the way in which the conflicts of nations and classes and interests were resolved or institutionalized; the myriad compromises, arrangements, accommodations, bargains, and truces that were struck; and the balances of power that resulted, all would mark the emergence in the late 1940s of a fundamentally new era in American and world history. The essays that follow explore the origins of this new postwar era.

✖ E S S A Y S

In the first essay, excerpted from *On Every Front: The Making of the Cold War* (1979), diplomatic historian Thomas G. Paterson of the University of Connecticut examines the impact of World War II on world politics and the early efforts of U.S. leaders to shape the emerging new international system. In the second essay, political sociologist Alan Wolfe of the New School for Social Research argues that in the 1940s the older, conflict-ridden and redistributionist politics of the New Deal era gave way to a new politics of growth and social consensus. The subsequent collapse of this politics of growth in the 1970s, he argues, would usher in the changes of the Reagan era. In the final essay, Alan Brinkley of Columbia University explores the complicated legacies of World War II that would help shape the lives of ordinary Americans in the years that followed.

The Origins of the Postwar International System

THOMAS G. PATERSON

Winston S. Churchill wore his usual bulldog visage. The ever-present cigar and hunched gait, other familiar trademarks of the British prime minister, also drew the crowd's attention on that very hot day of July 16, 1945. He was surveying the dusty remains of the Nazi capital—"That rubble heap near Potsdam," murmured one Berliner. This time a preoccupied Churchill evinced little interest in his curious onlookers. What captured Churchill's attention in Berlin was the grisly aftermath of heavy Allied bombing and artillery fire and stout German resistance. He and the passengers in his motorcade grew sick, utterly stunned by the stark display of carnage in the humbled German city.

The prime minister entered what was left of Adolf Hitler's Chancellery. The Führer's marble-topped desk lay in a thousand pieces. Iron Crosses, military ribbons, and papers littered the floor. The British visitors picked up souvenirs; one pocketed a fragment of Hitler's world map. The descent into the damp hideaway carried great moment for Churchill, who uncharacteristically, said little. Shaken by what he saw, General H. L. Ismay hurried away to his villa to take a hot bath and a strong drink. That night Churchill finally talked about his visit to the Chancellery. "It was from there that Hitler planned to govern the world," he mused. "A good many have tried that; all failed." Savoring the Allied victory, the prime minister smiled contentedly and went to bed.

The president of the United States, Harry S Truman, surveyed Berlin that same day. After reviewing the American Second Armored Division, the president led his entourage down the Wilhelmstrasse to the Chancellery of the Third Reich, all the while growing more awestruck by the destruction of the city. "That's what happens," he remarked, "when a man overreaches himself." For two hours Truman rode through Berlin's streets. "I was thankful," he noted later, "that the United States had been spared the unbelievable devastation of this war."

At the time 65 to 75 percent of Berlin was leveled or damaged. General Lucius Clay, who was soon to become the military governor of the American zone, found that "the streets were piled high with debris which left in many places only a narrow one-way passage between mounds of rubble, and frequent detours had to be made where bridges and viaducts were destroyed. . . . It was like a city of the dead." The once-prized chariot of victory on the Brandenburg Gate had been reduced to a

Selections from *On Every Front: The Making and Unmaking of the Cold War,* Revised Edition by Thomas Paterson. Copyright © 1992, 1979 by W. W. Norton & Company, Inc. Used by permission of W. W. Norton & Company, Inc.

gnarled mass of molten metal, the Reichstag to a hollow shell. Some "Nicht Für Juden" signs remained, ugly reminders of the Nazi extermination of European Jews. Factories that had escaped bombing raids now stood hull-like, stripped as war booty by the conquering Soviets, who tore industrial equipment from their foundations.

"There is nothing to do here," sighed a dispirited Berliner. Old men, women, and children trudged along, aimlessly pushing wheelbarrows. More than a million people lived in cellars, ruins, and makeshift suburban shacks, trading what they could for precious scraps of food to support their meager diets. In the western zones of Germany alone, two million crippled people hobbled about. Thirty-four percent of the Germans born in 1924 were badly mutilated in some way by 1945. "The people seem so whipped," wrote an American official to a friend back home, "that you can never believe that they had nursed Storm Troopers among them." Partially buried corpses lay rotting in the sun. As Berliners, under the stern guidance of Soviet and other Allied soldiers, began to stack bricks and shovel ashes, thousands of bodies were unearthed. The American diplomat Robert Murphy smelled "the odor of death" everywhere. Indeed, "the canals were choked with bodies and refuse." Lord Moran, who traveled with Churchill through Berlin, "felt a sense of nausea." Worse, "it was like the first time I saw a surgeon open a belly and the intestines gushed out."

From urban center to rural village, Germany looked charred and ravaged. Bomb-gutted Cologne and Nuremberg were hardly recognizable. Ninety-three percent of the houses in Düsseldorf were totally destroyed. Hamburg, Stuttgart, and Dresden had been laid waste by fire bombs and fire storms. In Dresden mounds of bodies had to be bulldozed into mass graves or burned on huge makeshift grills, so great was the toll and the fear of epidemic disease. An American army air corpsman flying low over the country at the end of the war could not spot streets or homes in Mannheim—only tossed dirt. "Aachen," he observed, "lay bleaching in the sun like bones on a desert." A disbelieving companion gazed at the pulverized land below and asked, "Where do the people live?" . . .

In Churchill's once-mighty island nation the war also claimed a frightful toll. Some observers after V-E Day grimly observed that the Germans looked better fed and less ragged than many British. The air blitz, which struck London, Coventry, and other cities in 1940–1941, and then subsided, began anew in 1944 with German V-1 and V-2 rockets that indiscriminately pounded buildings and people. Major districts of London were badly mangled, turning that regal city into a shabby, battered replica of itself. The Foreign Office building lost most of its windows and doors, and the prime minister's residence at No. 10 Downing Street looked racked as well. After one attack it took workmen six hours to free a woman from a tumbled row house on Stepney High Street. The rescuers asked if she had a husband. "Yes," she snapped. "He's at the front, the dirty coward."

Few Europeans escaped the marauding armies and death-dealing bombers of the Second World War. In Greece in 1945 a million people were homeless; one-quarter of the nation's buildings were damaged or destroyed. . . .

In neighboring Yugoslavia the retreating Germans had devastated the country-side, causing starvation in some regions. Upon liberation only one of Yugoslavia's seven large power stations was operating, and the rails running through the Danube Valley, which linked the nation to other European states, were inoperable. In the Hungarian capital of Budapest, the splendor of the Hapsburgs had given way inelegantly to the specter of death. All the bridges over the Danube were demolished, houses were flattened, and the 860-room royal palace of Maria Theresa and Franz Josef survived only as a maze of walls. During the winter of 1944–1945, near the war's end, the cold, hungry people of Budapest huddled in basements as Soviet bombs pummeled suspected German positions. One citizen described his apartment as a "ghostly castle, inhabited by a few scarcely living shadows." In Austria, German fires and Allied bombs had gutted 70 percent of the center of Vienna, not even sparing the seven-hundred-year-old St. Stephen's Cathedral. Women searched for sticks in the Vienna Woods, there being no coal for fuel. Elderly Viennese men and women looked pallid; listless young people begged for GI rations.

In Czechoslovakia and Italy, Prague and Rome had mercifully escaped large-scale devastation, but such blessings were rare in those otherwise-trampled nations. Italy's agricultural production was down 50 percent, and the government lacked foreign currency to pay for essential imports of food and raw materials. People in Naples clawed like cats through garbage cans for tidbits of food. Before abandoning that city, the Germans had wrecked the gas, electric, and water systems and put the torch to the university. In the Netherlands, 540,000 acres were flooded and Rotterdam was battered. As for France, Paris had largely been spared, but almost 20 percent of the buildings in the entire country were destroyed—twice the number demolished in the First World War. As many as 90 percent of French trucks were out of action, and much of the French fleet rested on the bottom of the harbor at Toulon. . . .

To the east, the Union of Soviet Socialist Republics tallied the greatest losses of all. More than 21 million soldiers and civilians had died—one-ninth of the total population. More than 30,000 industrial plants and 40,000 miles of railroad track were destroyed. Thousands of towns and cities had been leveled. Agricultural production was half of what it had been in 1940. Coal mines were flooded; bridges were down. The oil industry suffered shortages of steel pipe. As if the war had not done damage enough, a killer drought struck farming regions in 1946. The Ukraine ranked high in the gruesome record of war losses. Before the war a mainstay of the Soviet economy with its large production of coal, pig iron, steel, and manganese, as well as farm goods, the region now lay denuded by the Soviet scorched earth policy and the German rampage. Mines were blown up and flooded, the Dnieper Dam blasted, whole farm villages razed, tractors wrecked, and livestock massacred or driven off. The modern Zaporozhal steel plant near the Dnieper Dam was reduced to acres and acres of tangled debris. Famine and starvation hit the Brovary district, where 12,099 out of 16,000 prewar farm buildings were destroyed. The Soviet Socialist Republic of Byelorussia fared no better. Outside Minsk, thirty-four pits held the corpses of 150,000 people murdered and buried by the Germans. The much fought-over province of Vitebsk counted 300,000 dead.

Elsewhere in the Soviet Union, correspondent Harrison Salisbury called Sevastopol "a city of the dead." Of the city's fifteen thousand houses, only five hundred remained standing after the German retreat. "If a room has three walls and a ceiling," the mayor told Salisbury, "we count it in good shape." As for Stalingrad, American Ambassador W. Averell Harriman viewed "a desert of broken brick and rubble, the survivors huddling in cellars or tar-paper shanties." Another reporter, Alexander Werth, passed through Istra, west of Moscow, and saw nothing but a "forest of chimneystacks." The people of Moscow looked haggard as they piled their rubble. Shortly after the war British visitors entered a Moscow trade school and began asking students about their economic problems. Did their homes have heat and water? The school's director interrupted. There were more important questions. He asked pupils who had lost fathers at the front to stand up. All but one rose. The lone student who remained seated explained that his father had also fought against the Germans but had lost both his legs rather than his life.

The Second World War claimed the lives of some 55 million—*55 million*—people, and at least 35 million of them were Europeans. The grisly statistical gallery ranked the Soviet Union an uncontested first. The exact numbers are not known, but Poland and Germany (and Austria) shared second place with about 6 million dead each; Yugoslavia lost at least 1.6 million; France, 600,000; Rumania, 460,000; Hungary, 430,000; Czechoslovakia, 415,000; Italy, 410,000; Britain, 400,000; and the Netherlands, 280,000. . . .

As for the living, they had to endure food shortages, closed factories, idle fields, cold stoves, currency inflation, festering wounds. Displaced persons (DPs) provided another picture. "The wind will tell you what has come to us; / It rolls our brittle bones from pole to pole," went "The Refugees' Testament." Many dazed refugees wandered helplessly through Europe, searching for relatives, for friends, for a livelihood, for a ride home. . . .

Asia had its own sobering chronicle of the living and the dead. As the imperial Japanese went down to stubborn defeat, they took other Asians down with them. The lush vegetation of the Philippines and numerous Pacific islands was singed and burned, whole jungles disappearing. Some 120,000 Filipinos died, and Manila lay in ruins. Nobody counted exactly, but probably 4 million Indonesians died under Japanese occupation. In 1945, 1 million Vietnamese died of starvation; the war also took the lives of 150,000 natives of Okinawa, 70,000 Koreans, 40,000 Indians, and 30,000 Australians.

China had known population pressure, hunger, and epidemics before the war. But Japanese plunder, destruction of cities, and disruption of vital agricultural production increased the burdens that the Chinese had to bear in the postwar period. The provinces of Hunan, Guangxi, and Guangdong, like others, were visited by famine; millions suffered malnutrition and outright starvation. Cholera, plague, tuberculosis, smallpox, and malaria struck a population that had only twelve thousand physicians—one for every forty thousand people. In 1938 the Japanese had blown up the key dikes along the Huang Ho (Yellow) River—"China's Sorrow"—killing thousands and flooding three million acres of fertile land. China's rivers now rampaged in the spring and summer through vulnerable villages. Manchuria's industrial plants were destroyed or dismantled, and China's small railroad network hardly functioned.

The Chinese counted ten million war dead, many of them in 1945–1946 from starvation or disease caused by Japan's end-of-the-war devastation of rice-producing areas. People in Harbin suffered a peculiar calamity: in 1947 thirty thousand of them died from bubonic plague; two years earlier, at war's end, Japanese military researchers experimenting with germ warfare techniques had released infected rats into the city. . . .

For defeated Japan, the bitter results of imperial dreams could be measured in the loss of 2.5 million lives. American planes had dropped napalm-filled bombs on Tokyo, engulfing residential districts in fire storms which generated intense temperatures that reached 1,800° F. The odor of burning flesh drifted upward, sickening the pilots who delivered the horrible punishment. After a savage March 1945 raid that killed 84,000 people in what observers described as a mass burning, a Japanese reporter wrote that Tokyo was "like a desert, in a drab and monotonous panorama of hopelessness." The fifteen-mile stretch between Yokohama and Tokyo, remarked an American officer who accompanied American General Douglas MacArthur to Japan, had become a "wilderness of rubble." A light dust hung in the air, staining visitors' clothing. Wood and paper houses had been reduced to powdered ashes, factories to twisted metal. A shantytown of rusted, corrugated sheets and other junk ringed the capital city, its inhabitants reminding some observers of the Okies who trekked to California during the Great Depression—except that the Japanese scene was more shocking. One of the first American naval officers to arrive in Tokyo wrote to a friend that "I feel like a tramp who has become used to sleeping in a graveyard."

Hiroshima and Nagasaki became special cases, sharing and enduring a special fate, giving unique meaning to the most familiar postwar word: "rubble." Hiroshima was Japan's eighth-largest city, a residential, commercial center of 250,000 people. But until 8:15 A.M. on August 6, 1945, Hiroshima had not witnessed large-scale American bombing raids. On that cloudless day the crew of the *Enola Gay,* a custom-outfitted B-29, unleashed "Little Boy," an atomic device packing the power of twenty thousand tons of TNT. The bomb fell for fifty seconds and exploded about two thousand feet aboveground. A blinding streak of light raced across the sky; a tremendous boom punctuated the air. Then a huge purplish cloud of dust, smoke, and debris shot forty thousand feet into the atmosphere. At ground level the heat became suffocating, the winds violent. Buildings instantly disintegrated. Shadows were etched in stone. Trees were stripped of their leaves. Fires erupted everywhere, and the sky grew dark. Survivors staggered toward water to quench their intense thirst. Skin peeled from burned bodies. A maimed resident, Dr. Michihiko Hachiya, noted that "no one talked, and the ominous silence was relieved only by a subdued rustle among so many people, restless, in pain, anxious, and afraid, waiting for something else to happen."

The toll: 140,000 dead, tens of thousands wounded, and 81 percent of the city's buildings destroyed. Three days later the nightmare was repeated in Nagasaki, where at least 70,000 died. Two weeks before the slaughter President Truman told his diary that the atomic bomb "seems to be the most terrible thing ever discovered, but it can be made the most useful." Upon hearing of the success of the world's first nuclear destruction of a city inhabited by "savages," as the president had recently called the Japanese, he allowed that "this is the greatest thing in history." Truman's words did not necessarily mean that he was pleased that so many Japanese civilians had been killed but rather that he was marveling over the new, spectacularly deadly weapon in America's possession—a weapon that might bring the long war to a close and boost U.S. power in the postwar era.

The Hiroshima tragedy was but one chapter in the story of massive, war-induced destruction. This story, with all its horrid details, must be recounted not because it shocks or sensationalizes but because it illustrates how massive and daunting were the problems of the postwar world, how shaky the scaffolding of the international order. Hitler had once said about his warmongering pursuits that "we may be destroyed, but if we are, we shall drag a world with us—a world in flames." Because he largely satisfied his prophecy, the Second World War, like any war of substantial duration, served as an agent of conspicuous international changes. The conflagration of 1939–1945 was so wrenching, so total, so profound, that a world was overturned—not simply a material world of crops, buildings, and rails, not simply a human world of healthy and productive laborers, farmers, merchants, financiers, and intellectuals, not simply a secure world of close-knit families and communities, not simply a military world of Nazi storm troopers and Japanese kamikazes, but all that and more. The war also unhinged the world of stable politics, inherited wisdom, traditions, institutions, alliances, loyalties, commerce, and classes. . . .

Leaders of all political persuasions, as they witnessed the immensity of the destruction, spoke of a new age without knowing its dimensions. "The world was fluid and about to be remade," remembered the American journalist Theodore H. White. The normal way of doing things now seemed inappropriate, although as creatures of the past the survivors remained attached to ideas and institutions that seemed to provide security through familiarity. They sensed the seriousness and the enormity of the tasks of cleaning up the rubble, of putting the broken world back together again, of shaping an orderly international system. But imponderables abounded. Would peoples in the long-restive colonized countries, for example, rebel against their foreign masters at the very time that the once-mighty imperial nations themselves suffered internal political upheavals? Few people could say with confidence that they knew the configuration of the postwar world. What lay ahead was a tortuous time of experimenting, of trial and error, of stumbling and striving, of realized and dashed hopes, of contests among competing formulas for a stable world order.

Few nations or individuals had the material resources, talent, and desire—the sheer energy, guts, and money—to mold a brave new world out of the discredited and crumbled old. If the reconstruction tasks seemed Herculean, however, the opportunities appeared boundless for the ambitious, the hearty, and the caring. One vigorous, optimistic, well-intentioned, competitive voice sounded above the rubble that constituted London, Berlin, Warsaw, Minsk, and Tokyo. That voice echoed with power from the United States, the wartime "arsenal of democracy."

At war's end President Truman declared a two-day national holiday. Horns, bells, and makeshift noisemakers sounded across the nation. Paraders in Los Angeles played leapfrog on Hollywood Boulevard; farther north, jubilant sailors broke windows along San Francisco's Market Street. In New York City office workers tossed tons of paper from the windows of skyscrapers on cheering crowds below. Stock market prices shot up. A five-year-old boy recorded the August 1945 moment: "This is the best year. The war is over. Two wars are over. Everyone is happy. Tins cans are rolling. Everything is confused. And little pieces of paper." Not only had the dying subsided, but also the United States had emerged from the global conflict in the unique position of an unscathed belligerent. No bombs had fallen on American cities. No armies had ravaged the countryside. No American boundaries had been redrawn. Factories stood in place, producing goods at an impressive rate. In August, at the General Motors plant in Moraine, Ohio, shiny new Frigidaire refrigerators and airplane propeller blades moved along parallel assembly lines. Farm fields were rich in crops, and full employment during the war years had buoyed family savings.

"The American people," remarked the director of the Office of War Mobilization and Reconversion, "are in the pleasant predicament of having to learn to live 50 percent better than they have ever lived before."

Whereas much of Europe and Asia confronted a massive task of "reconstruction," the United States faced "reconversion"—adjusting the huge war machine to peacetime purposes. Automobile plants had to convert production from tanks to cars, a delightful prospect for auto manufacturers, who knew that Americans were eager to spend their wartime earnings on consumer goods once again. With great pride Americans applauded their good fortune. They were different. They had no rubble to clear. The Soviets knew, said Joseph Stalin in a grand understatement, that "things are not bad in the United States."

Actually Americans had worries. Some feared that the sparkling prosperity of the war years would dissipate in a postwar economic disaster. They remembered that military production, not Franklin D. Roosevelt's New Deal reform program, had pulled the United States out of the Great Depression of the 1930s. Would there be enough jobs for the returning GIs? Americans also suffered temporary shortages of many goods, sugar and gasoline among them, and resented the rationing that limited their economic freedom. "Hey, don'tcha know there's a war on?" said clerks to anxious consumers. There were not enough houses to meet the needs of an expanding and mobile American population, which grew from 131 million to 140 million during the war years and was entering a "baby boom" period. The national debt skyrocketed from $37 billion to $269 billion. The war cost the federal government $664 billion. Inflation threatened economic stability. At least 10 million American families still lived in poverty in this land of plenty. Although these national pains aroused grumbles, they seemed bearable and soluble, were played down, or were ignored. As *Fortune* magazine commented two months after V-J Day: "August 14, 1945, marked not only the war's end but the beginning of the greatest peacetime industrial boom in the world's history."

Americans read charts brimming with impressive data that justified such enthusiasm. The gross national product of the United States expanded from $90.5 billion (1939) to $211.9 billion (1945). Steel production jumped from fifty-three million tons in 1939 to eighty million tons at the close of the war. Cut off from rubber imports from the Dutch East Indies during the war, Americans developed synthetic rubber, launching a new industry. New aluminum plants went up, and the aircraft industry, in infancy when Germany attacked Poland, became a major new business as well. In 1939 only 5,856 military and civil airplanes were turned out; but in 1945 the figure reached 48,912, a decline from the peak of over 95,000 in 1944. All told, over 300,000 aircraft rolled from American factories during the war—a figure far surpassing that of any other nation, including Germany and Japan combined. Employment in the aircraft industry swelled 1,600 percent. With its numerous aircraft factories, Southern California bustled, becoming a mecca for dreamers of wealth and adventure. During the war 444,000 people moved to Los Angeles.

Workers' wages kept up with inflation during the war years. Women took jobs once held by men who were called to military duty. Unable to spend their abundant incomes on the shrinking supply of consumer items during the war, many Americans visited their banks. Total personal savings increased from $6.85 billion to $36.41 billion. Americans continued to spend for pleasure as well. The baseball World Series played on, and films whirred at local theaters. Beaches beckoned vacationers. In the summer of 1944, as Europe and Asia reeled from the blasts of war, Americans flocked to resorts and racetracks. Betting on horse racing totalled a record-breaking $1.4 billion in 1945, even though the tracks were closed from January to May. Farmers enjoyed some of their best years of the twentieth century. Whereas in 1939 they counted sixty-six million head of cattle, by 1945 that figure reached eighty-three million. Agricultural output rose 15 percent. American universities also made wartime advances. Government contracts for scientific research went to the California Institute of Technology for rocket studies; Princeton University received grants for ballistics research. In mid-1945 the Massachusetts Institute of Technology held government contracts worth $117 million. The GI Bill, which offered money to veterans for their college educations, promised higher enrollments. Wartime musicals like *Oklahoma!* and *Carousel* caught the optimistic mood, and sluggers Joe DiMaggio and Ted Williams were heading home to reclaim their baseball fame. Despite uncertainties about the future, life looked good to Americans, and after the hardships and setbacks of the depression decade, "the old self-confident America is coming into its stride again."

When foreign delegates journeyed to San Francisco for the United Nations Conference in April of 1945, many crossed the territorial United States and could not help but notice the stark contrast with war-torn Europe and Asia. Soviet Foreign Minister V. M. Molotov once referred to statistics in the *World Almanac* to remind Americans about their uniqueness as prosperous survivors of the Second World War. During a conversation with Stalin in 1944, the president of the United States Chamber of Commerce, Eric A. Johnston, citing the American example, lectured the Kremlin leader on the need for a better distribution of goods in the Soviet Union. No doubt wondering how so knowledgeable a man as Johnston could be misreading reality, Stalin replied that in order to distribute, there must be something to distribute." Months before, at the Teheran Conference, Stalin had toasted the United States as a "country of machines," applauding its great productive capacity for delivering victory to the Allies. Truman's words also bear repeating: "I was thankful that the United States had been spared the unbelievable devastation of this war." Even the death count for Americans in uniform, about four hundred thousand, appeared merciful when compared with staggering figures elsewhere. Indeed, the *Saturday Evening Post* editorialized in 1945 that "we Americans can boast that we are not as other men are." The war had overturned a world, and many Americans believed that they were now on top of it. A new international system for the postwar era was in the making, and the United States intended to be its primary architect. . . .

Two nations with quite different ideologies emerged from the rubble of World War II to claim high rank. The United States and the Soviet Union, eager to realize their universalist visions of the postwar world and to seize opportunities for extending their respective influence, tried to fill vacuums of power. With the old barriers to American and Soviet expansion gone, Washington and Moscow clashed over occupation policies in German, Italy, Japan, Austria, and Korea. They squabbled over which political groups should replace the Nazi regimes in Eastern Europe. The competitive interaction between the United States and the Soviet Union— "like two big dogs chewing on a bone," said Senator J. William Fulbright—shaped the bipolarism or bipolarity of the immediate postwar years. "Not since Rome and

Carthage," Dean Acheson claimed, "had there been such a polarization of power on this earth." This new bipolar structure replaced the multipolar system of the 1930s, wherein at least six nations had been active, influential participants. By the late 1940s decisions made in the imperial capitals of Washington and Moscow often determined whether people in other nations voted, where they could travel, how much they ate, and what they could print.

To say that the world was bipolar, however, is not to suggest that the two poles were equal in power. They were not. An asymmetry—not a balance—of power existed. In fact, the United States held preponderant power and flexed its multidimensional muscle to build even more power. As the only major nation not devastated by the war, the United States so outdistanced other nations in almost every measurement of power—from industrial production to domestic political stability—that it enjoyed hegemony. Hegemony exists when one nation possesses superior economic, military, and political power in the world system. The first ingredient is a prerequisite for the other two. No nation can aspire to hegemony or achieve that Olympian status unless its economy is strong—and stronger than any other's. More than statistics established American supremacy. World conditions did so. The United States was powerful because almost every other nation was war-weakened.

Both the United States and the Soviet Union emerged from the war as powers, but only one at that time was a superpower—the United States. The Soviet Union was certainly not weak. Although handicapped by its economic wreckage, the huge nation held predominant postwar power over its neighbors in Eastern Europe. Still, the Soviet Union was a regional, not a global, power before the early 1950s. The characteristic of hegemony meant that the United States had more opportunities and resources than other nations to shape the postwar system. By exercising their preponderant global power—through military occupations, foreign aid and loans, and domination of the World Bank and United Nations Organization, for example— U.S. officials pushed the world toward the American postwar goal of a nonradical, capitalist, free trade international order in the mold of domestic America. . . .

Another prominent characteristic of the international system that unleashed conflict was the destruction of economies in many parts of the world. The war cut an ugly scar across Europe and Asia. "If Hitler succeeds in nothing else," mused Office of Strategic Services officer Allen Dulles, "like Samson, he may pull down the pillars of the temple and leave a long and hard road of reconstruction." The postwar task was forbidding. Not only did cities have to be rebuilt, factories opened, people put back to work, rails repaired, rivers and roads made passable, and crop yields increased, but the flow of international commerce and finance had to be reestablished if nations were to raise through exports the money needed to buy the imports required for recovery. Many old commercial and financial patterns had been broken, and given the obstacle of economic disarray, new exchanges were difficult to establish. Where would Germany's vital coal and steel go? Would industrial Western Europe and agricultural Eastern Europe re-create old commercial ties? Would the restrictive trade practices of the 1930s, especially the tariff barriers, continue into the 1940s? Would colonies continue to provide raw materials to their imperial lords? Could international cooperation and organizations like the General Agreement on Tariffs and Trade (1948) curb economic nationalism? Would trade be conducted on a multilateral, "open door" basis, as the United States preferred, or by bilateral or preferential methods, as many others, such as Britain and the Soviet Union, practiced? Would the economic disorders spawned by the Great Depression be repeated to produce political chaos, aggression, and war?

The answers to these questions helped define the international system of the post-1945 era. The new international system, it was hoped, would enjoy stable economic conditions to ensure pacific international relations. Yet the very effort to reconstruct economies and create economic order engendered conflict because different models and formulas—Communist? socialist? capitalist? mixed economy?—competed to define the future. At the same time the asymmetrical distribution of power persuaded weaker nations that they faced the danger of economic coercion.

The Second World War also bequeathed domestic political turmoil to the new international system. The governments of the 1930s, now discredited, vied with insurgent groups for governing power in many states. Socialists, Communists, and other varieties of the political left, many of whom had fought in the underground resistance movements and had thus earned some popular respect and following, challenged the more entrenched, conservative elites, many of whom had escaped into exile when the German armies goose-stepped into their countries. In Poland the Communist, Soviet-sponsored Lublin Poles successfully undercut the political authority of the Poles who had fled to London. The conservative Dutch government-in-exile watched warily as leftist resistance groups gradually rallied political support. Political confusion in the Netherlands was heightened by the wartime loss of voting lists. In Greece a coalition of leftists in the National Liberation Front (EAM) fought the return to power of a British-created government and the unpopular Greek monarchy of King George. The civil war that rocked Greece until fall 1949 claimed some 158,000 lives and ended in an American-backed conservative government. In France Charles de Gaulle gained ascendancy after vying for power with the Communists. The Chinese civil war, which had raged for years between the Communists of Mao Zedong and the Nationalists of Jiang Jieshi (Chiang Kai-shek), flared up again at the close of the war. That internecine struggle ended in a Communist victory in 1949. Yugoslavia was also the scene of political battle between Josip Borz Tito's ultimately successful Partisans and a group headed by Dr. Ivan Šubašić of the London émigré government, which in turn suffered strained ties with King Peter. In the occupied nations of Germany, Austria, and Korea, moreover, the victors created competitive zones, postponing the formation of central governments. In the defeated countries of Japan and Italy, American officials decided who would rule, whereas in parts of Eastern Europe, Soviet officials placed Communists in strategic positions of power.

The major powers, in short, intervened abroad to exploit the political opportunities created by the destructive scythe of World War II. The stakes seemed high. A change in a nation's political orientation might presage a change in its international alignment. The great powers tended to ignore local conditions, especially nationalism, which might and often did mitigate against alignment with an outside power. Americans nonetheless feared that a leftist or Communist Greece would look to the East and permit menacing Soviet bases on Greek territory or open the door to a Soviet naval presence in the Mediterranean. Moscow dreaded a conservative anti-Soviet Polish government led by the London faction, for it might prove so weak and so hostile to Moscow as to permit a revived Germany to send storm troopers once again through the Polish corridor into the heart of Russia or block the Soviet Union's efforts to contain a resurgent Germany. A Communist China, thought Americans, might align with the Soviet Union; a Nationalist China would remain in the American camp. All in all, the rearranging of political structures within nations drew the major powers into competition, accentuating the conflict inherent in the postwar international system.

Just as the war threw politics into chaos, it also hastened the disintegration of empires. The Japanese movement into French Indochina and drive for Dutch East Indies oil had led to Pearl Harbor in 1941. The initially successful Japanese expansion demonstrated to many Asian nationalists that their white imperial masters could be defeated. In a spirit of Pan-Asianism, some nationalists collaborated with Tokyo during the war. The Japanese, in need of administrators to manage occupied areas, trained and armed some indigenous leaders. Japan granted Burma considerable autonomy in 1942, for example, and after the war the Burmese became determined to push the British out. Other nationalists gained organizational unity, élan, and experience by battling the Japanese invaders. At the end of the war the European powers, exhausted and financially hobbled, had to struggle to reestablish mastery over rebellious colonies. The appeal of the self-determination principle, still echoing from the days of Woodrow Wilson and given new emphasis by the Atlantic Charter (1941) and the United Nations Charter (1945), became far-reaching. The long process of "regime collapse" in what became known as the Third World gained momentum. "There are many peoples who are clamoring for freedom from the colonial powers," American Undersecretary of State Sumner Welles remarked during the war. He predicted "trouble" unless these peoples got what they wanted. Failure to plan for the transfer of power to them, he warned "would be like failing to install a safety valve and then waiting for the boiler to blow up." There were too many boilers and too few safety valves.

No empire was immune to decolonization. The United States granted the Philippines independence in 1946, but that new nation became a client state where U.S. officials helped the government resist a peasant revolt led by the Huks. The British, worn low by the war and by the challenges of nationalist groups demanding independence, retreated in 1947 from India, which then descended into civil war between Hindus and Muslims. The two new nations of India and Pakistan were thus born amid massacres and a massive uprooting of people. The following year Britain also relinquished Burma (Myanmar) and Ceylon (Sri Lanka). Israel, carved out of British-governed Palestine, became a new independent state in 1948. The British also found it difficult to maintain their sphere of influence in Iran, Greece, and Egypt and began retreats from those politically unsteady states. The French clung to Indochina, where nationalist forces led by Ho Chi Minh had declared an independent Vietnam by quoting the American Declaration of Independence. "If those gooks want a fight," boasted French General Étienne Valluy, "they'll get it." Bloody battle ensued, ultimately forcing French withdrawal in 1954. The French empire also came under siege in Africa; in early 1947 Malagasy insurgents in the island colony of Madagascar rebelled. Ninety thousand people died as French troops crushed the insurrection the next year (France finally granted the Malagasy Republic independence in 1960). The Dutch also decided to fight, but after four debilitating years of combat they pulled out of Indonesia in 1949. The defeated Japanese were forced to give up their claims to Formosa and Korea, as well as to Pacific island groups. Italy departed from Ethiopia and lost its African colonies of Tripolitania (Libya) and Eritrea. In the Middle East, Lebanon, Syria, and Jordan, areas once managed by Europeans, gained independence in 1943, 1944, and 1946, respectively.

The world map, as after World War I, was redrawn. The emergence of so many new states, and the instability associated with the transfer of authority, shook the very foundations of the international system. Power was being redistributed. In varying degrees, the United States and Soviet Union competed for the allegiance of the new governments, meddled in colonial rebellions, and generally sought to exploit opportunities for an extension of their influence. In the case of Vietnam the powers supported different sides: Washington, without relish, backed the ruling French, and Moscow endorsed the Vietminh insurgency. The stakes seemed high. President Roosevelt told an adviser near the end of the war that more than one billion "brown people" yearned for independence—and "1,100,000,000 potential enemies are dangerous." The emerging nations could serve as strategic bases, markets for exports, sources of vital raw materials, sites for investments, and votes in international organizations; conversely, they could deny powerful nations such assets. As a Central Intelligence Agency report emphasized, the resource-rich Third World and the reconstruction of hobbled Western Europe were intricately linked: "The continuance of unsettled conditions [in colonial or former colonial areas] hinders economic recovery and causes a diversion of European strength into efforts to maintain or reimpose control by force."

To the angry frustration of the great powers, some new nations, like India, chose nonalignment in the developing Cold War. Asian countries, asserted Indian nationalist leader Jawaharlal Nehru, "can no longer be used as pawns by others; they are bound to have their own policies in world affairs. . . . We do not intend to be the playthings of others." To U.S. officials, neutralism meant not only that some nations were not with them but also that they stood against them—that the nonaligned countries were forming "a power bloc against us," as the American ambassador to Burma put it. Indeed, Americans feared that Nehru championed a "third force" that, if it developed to the stage of a bloc of like-minded states, could shift the world from bipolar to tripolar form. Avowedly neutral states thus ultimately became targets for Cold War conversion through American and Soviet foreign aid, subversion, and propaganda campaigns.

As one U.S. government study noted, the disintegration of empires, especially the withdrawal of the British from their once-vast domain, created an "over-all situation of near chaos" in the international system. In some areas, such as Southeast Asia, it meant a "new balance of power." The upheaval was fundamental: "Old values are being changed and new ones sought. New friendships are being formed." The international system creaked and swayed under this unsettled burden.

Conflict over and within the new United Nations Organization also disturbed the system. At the Dumbarton Oaks Conference in 1944 the Allies initiated plans for a United Nations Organization to replace the defunct League of Nations. The United States, Britain, and Soviet Union became its chief architects, and the institution they created at the San Francisco Conference of April–June 1945 reflected their insistence on big-power domination. They instituted a veto power for the five "permanent members" of the Security Council (the United States, Britain, U.S.S.R.,

France, and China) and assigned the General Assembly, the forum for smaller nations, a subordinate status. Because each member recognized that the new international body could become an instrument, through bloc voting, of one nation's foreign policy, they feuded. Churchill crudely complained that China, hardly a "great" power, would be a "faggot vote on the side of the United States," and the Soviets protested that France would simply represent a British vote. "China was a joke," remarked State Department veteran John Hickerson, "a FDR joke." For a time Roosevelt pushed Brazil as a veto power member; Brazil, he said, was "a card up his sleeve." Because Britain could marshall the votes of several of its Commonwealth countries and the United States could muster most of the Latin American nations, the conferees at the Yalta Conference of early 1945 acknowledged the glaring imbalance by granting the Soviet Union three votes in the General Assembly.

At the San Francisco Conference membership applications from Argentina and Poland produced heated differences. Against vehement Soviet objections, Argentina, which had declared war against Germany only at the last minute and which some critics considered a "fascist" nation, gained membership after the United States backed its application and the nations of the Western Hemisphere voted yes as a bloc. Yet when Lublin-led Poland, not yet reorganized according to the American interpretation of the Yalta accords, applied for entry, the United States voted no, and the conference denied Poland a seat. Moscow railed at this rebuff, charging a double standard. The United Nations Organization, which held its first session in January 1946, thus made its debut amid controversy. Rather than serve as a stabilizing force in the postwar international system, the largely U.S.-dominated United Nations early became a source of conflict, a competitive arena of power brokers, a verbal battleground for the allegiance of world opinion, a vehicle for condemnatory resolutions, a graveyard for idealistic hopes—in short, part of a "masquerade peace."

The new atomic bomb and the ensuing nuclear arms race further destabilized the postwar international system. As the two bickering major powers groped for ways to deal with "the bomb" and spurred their atomic development programs, people everywhere held their breaths, harboring thoughts about doomsday. Nuclear weapons were not simply dangerous to enemies; they threatened apocalypse for humankind. Cartoonists sketched pictures of uncontrollable monsters that the scientists had created. "All the scientists are frightened—frightened for their lives—and frightened for *your* life," a Nobel Prize-winning chemist wrote in early 1946 in a popular magazine. About the same time a French radio station broadcast a make-believe story about an atomic storm engulfing the earth after radioactive atoms had escaped from a U.S. research laboratory. Many Parisians thought they heard truth and panicked. One observer suggested that a Soviet-American war "might not end with *one* Rome but with *two* Carthages."

The atomic bomb, uncontrolled, envied, copied, and brandished, became a major obstacle to a peaceful postwar international system. The "most terrible weapon ever known in human history," Secretary of War Henry L. Stimson quietly told the president, unsettled the world community, for it was an agent of massive human destruction, and "in a world atmosphere already extremely sensitive to power, the introduction of this weapon has profoundly affected political considerations in all sections of the globe." Nations that possessed *the* bomb seemed to hold an advantage in international politics, for it could serve as a deterrent against an adversary as well as a means to annihilate an enemy. When combined with air power and a long-range delivery capability, the atomic bomb also hurdled geographical boundaries, rendering them useless as protective elements in a nation's security shield. With the perfecting of air warfare in World War II, "the roof blew off the territorial state."

The question that dogged the peacemakers was: How were they to control the development, spread, and use of atomic energy? There had been arms races before, and disarmament conferences in the 1920s and 1930s, but the postwar nuclear race moved at a far different and more dangerous level. The atomic bomb was the "absolute weapon," not only more violent but also capable of speedy delivery, rapid retaliation, immediate cataclysm, and lingering death-dealing radioactivity. Americans worried that they would lose their monopoly—that nuclear proliferation would leave them vulnerable, too. Such fears intensified when the Soviet Union successfully produced its own bomb in 1949. While from the start some people appealed for a world government to put the atomic genie back in the bottle—"world state or world doom"—others began to marvel over the new armament's potential value as a diplomatic weapon to pry concessions from adversaries or as a deterrent to keep them at bay. . . .

Such was the postwar international system—with its opportunities and constraints, with its many characteristics that generated conflict. The makers of the postwar order grappled with immense, new problems, and they strove to reduce the systemic instability. Their decisions, however, exacerbated conflict. The reason why the leaders of the postwar world made bad conditions worse is clear: Sensing danger from the volatile international system to their domestic systems, they sought to build their nations' power, to enlarge their spheres of influence. The conflict inherent in any international system, especially one struggling to make the transition from full-scale war to postwar peace, hardened into a four-decade-long Cold War.

The Roots of Postwar Politics

ALAN WOLFE

The United States came out of World War II facing extremely important decisions about how it would organize its government and how it would relate to the world. For a variety of reasons, . . . neither the policies nor the constituencies of the New Deal were appropriate to the economic and political realities that faced Harry Truman. The conditions that had called for the New Deal having changed, the question facing postwar America was how to develop a new political formula for the organization and use of power.

Two possible courses seemed likely as the war came to an end. From the right end of the political spectrum, an anguished and bitter cry for a return to "normalcy" could be heard. Reflected in the Congress elected in 1946, conservative sentiment called for a return to business civilization; a holy, if inexpensive, crusade against communism; and a reassertion of once popular isolationist values. From the left a call was issued to carry the New Deal forward to its logical conclusion in some form of democratic socialism, American style (though, given the vocabulary of American politics, it could never be called that). Full employment, economic planning, national health insurance, and a commitment to peace organized through the United Nations—these would be the planks of a progressive program for America.

Whatever the differences between them, the right and left courses were both *political* options. Because neither was consensual, either would have required a popular mobilization and the building of new constituencies to support it. There was a sense of movement to both programs, one forward, the other back. Both implied struggle, dissent, controversy. Both were organized around an assertion of a particular vision and a sense of the means to achieve it. The key to understanding the formation of America's impasse, and the inability of both the Democrats and the Republicans to work their way out of it, lies in the fact that neither of these courses was chosen in 1946. Instead of making a political choice, America opted for an economic surrogate. A bipartisan coalition was formed to pursue economic expansion, at home through growth and overseas through empire. Once the rationale of the political system became the enhancement of growth, everything changed, including the role of political parties, the structure of political ideology, the nature of public policy, and the meaning of dissent. America embarked on a massive experiment. Politics would concern itself with the means—growth—and the ends, or purpose, of social life would take care of themselves.

Unlike political choice, economic growth offered a smooth and potentially harmonious future—instead of divisive, possibly ugly, and certainly disruptive struggles over redistributional issues. Rapid economic growth, it was felt, could expand the pie sufficiently so that it would not have to be cut in a different way. And expansion overseas could create an imperial dividend, a periodic bounty from empire that would augment the sugar in the pie in the first place. Between them, economic growth and the imperial dividend created a whole new approach to government, one that would not so much exercise political power to make choices as it would manage expansion and empire to avoid choice. Growth, in other words, was transpolitical. While liberals blame conservatives for America's impasse and conservatives say that the fault lies with liberals, the truth is that growth allowed policies that substituted economic performance for political ideology. America sought, not what would create the best, but what would work the best. United behind a growth strategy, America expanded enormously in the postwar period, witnessing, some say, the greatest economic miracle in the modern world. So overwhelming was this growth that it created its own brand of politics, a compromise over policy so pleasing and rewarding that it would continue with unstoppable force long after the growth came to a halt, thereby worsening America's economic performance with the same determination with which it had once enhanced it.

The political costs of economic growth were not calculated for some time, and many refuse to examine them even now. Yet in retrospect it seems clear what happened. In the late 1940s, advocates of growth were believers in liberal ideals like economic planning, social welfare, international idealism, and foreign aid. But once the quest for growth became an all-consuming passion, those liberal objectives became dependent on conservative instruments. Growth at home could not take place without business confidence, and so liberals set out to win business support with favorable policies. Overseas expansion, to be made palatable to a generally isolationist America, had to be rationalized in terms of national security, encouraging a dependence on the military. With liberal objectives tied so firmly to conservative means, America developed a postwar political formula filled with contradictory language. Social justice would be pursued with all the vigor of profit maximization, while America would export to the world both humanitarianism and military power. Liberalism, in short, was submerged into the quest for growth; when its head popped up again, it was no longer liberalism. Without growth, the Democratic party, as Carter's presidency demonstrated, was a political organization without a political vision, something clearly recognized by the voters in 1980.

But if liberalism was seduced by its devotion to growth, so was conservatism. In the late 1940s, there was a genuine conservative tradition in the United States. Its faith was in economic competition, its roots in the farmers and small businessmen of the Middle West, its vision isolationist and even pacifist, and its conception of trade protectionist. An expanding economy at home, pushed forward by increasingly concentrated corporations and the benefits of overseas trade, dominated by multinational corporations and protected by a flourishing defense industry located in the South and West, transformed American conservatism as thoroughly as it did New Deal liberalism. Ronald Reagan bears as much resemblance to Robert Taft as Jimmy Carter does to Franklin Roosevelt. In the 1980s, the Republican party . . . has become what the Democrats have rejected: the party of domestic economic growth and imperial expansion.

In their quest for respectability among business and the military, postwar liberals lost faith in their own objectives. Conservatives, whose links to business and some sectors of the military were strong, were incapable of becoming the majority party because they had given the world Herbert Hoover. For liberals, growth was a substitute for the respectability they lacked. For conservatives, growth became the key to the popularity they sought to gain. Just as liberals sublimated objectives like social justice into a quest for business and overseas expansion, conservatives would come to seek a balanced budget and stable prices through expanded profits and higher military spending. American liberalism lost its sense of purpose as it sought in expansion the resolution to its internal contradictions. With the arrival of the Reagan presidency, American conservatism promises to do exactly the same thing. . . .

America was fundamentally changed by World War II, in every conceivable way. Economically, the war had a wondrous impact upon the gross national product (GNP). In 1929, the GNP stood at $103.4 billion, which then fell to $55.8 billion by 1933. Six years of New Deal policies saw the figure rise to $90.8 billion in 1939, still below the peak of ten years earlier. During the war, however, economic activity grew by leaps and bounds. The GNP reached $100 billion by 1940, $129.9 in 1941, $158.3 in 1942, $192 in 1943, and $210 in 1944. At least this much can be said: war enabled production to take place once again.

But the need to turn out as many weapons as the economy was capable of generating was only a quantitative change, and there were important qualitative ones as well. Most noticeable was the growing role played by government. Public spending, $9 billion in 1940, increased tenfold to $98 billion in 1945. The government offered the staggering sum of $175 billion in prime contracts between June 1940 and September 1944. Over one-third of all manufacturing structures and equipment existing in the United States during this period was constructed through the $17 billion worth of new plants financed by government to speed the war effort. There could no longer be any doubt that government was capable of playing a positive role in economic stimulation.

In 1945, *Fortune* carried a Roper poll showing that only 41 percent of the American population thought that a postwar recession could be avoided. It was generally assumed in America that periods of bust would follow periods of boom the way that thunder follows lightning. Yet the conditions of wartime production augured a transformation in the cyclical nature of American capitalism. First, the sheer size of the mobilization involved, much greater than in World War I, ensured that prewar conditions would not return in the same form; the sharply reduced military budget for fiscal year (FY) 1947, for example, was still $13 billion *higher* than the last prewar budget of 1940. Similarly, the number of civilian workers on federal payrolls after the war, and the number of women and men in uniform, was much higher than a decade earlier. Second, vast savings by consumers, not spendable during the war, kept the economy afloat after the war had ended. Third, the Federal Reserve Board made a decision during the war to support the price of government securities at a predetermined rate, and this prevented tight-money advocates from constricting the economy in the late 1940s. Finally, the war had created an effective system of wage-and-price controls, enabling expansion to take place without rapidly rising prices. Policymakers were thus able to prove that full employment and stable prices could coexist, so long as a political authority with appropriate power existed to ensure it.

Yet another qualitative change in the American economy brought about by the war was the freedom given to the United States by its strength in the world economy. Most countries at most times worry that trading rivals will increase their share of the world's output and threaten the advantages of domestic manufacturers. For the United States in the postwar period, the problem was the exact opposite of this. The U.S. economy was so much richer than those of war-devastated Europe that the latter were unable to absorb American surplus production; domestic unemployment would result unless the United States worked to *improve* the relative economic standing of its rivals. Some sense of the American advantage in the world economy is given by the fact that almost half of the world's manufactured goods in 1947 were made in the United States. The dollar was far and away the world's strongest currency, especially since the collapse of the pound sterling. When the near U.S. monopoly on gold is considered—one estimate placed it as high as 72 percent of the world's supply in 1949—America seemed in a position to benefit from economic changes in the world, not to be held down by them as it was during the Great Depression.

Nor was any other country in the world powerful enough to challenge the United States militarily. Germany and Japan, having been defeated, became the objects of an American effort to increase their productivity while keeping them under American political protection. The so-called underdeveloped countries were as poor after the war as they had been before it, so there was no need to worry about them. Only from the Soviet Union could any possible challenge be forthcoming, and the Soviet Union had been an American ally during the war. In the late 1940s, and to the present day, there would be those who talked of a Soviet military threat to the United States, often with cataclysmic imagery. Certainly in the immediate postwar period these fears proved to be exaggerated. The Soviet Union had left its troops behind in Europe, but it had neither the weaponry nor the sophistication to challenge the United States at a time when policymakers allowed themselves to become haunted by a Soviet "threat."

Between them, domestic economic expansion, measured in the growth of the GNP, and the benefits to be obtained from unchallenged economic and military power combined to make the New Deal inappropriate to the situation of the late 1940s. New Deal measures had often been geared to doing—anything to get the economy out of its doldrums. But the postwar situation, with stimulation already in place, demanded something different. Two dominant points of view existed. There were a number of articulate economic activists who argued a fundamental restruc-turing of the economy in order to plan and direct the changes taking place. Domestic economic management, they claimed, must ensure full employment and the adequate use of all other resources, while America would join with the rest of the world in sponsoring global economic reforms to ensure greater prosperity. Opposed to these activists were businessmen and more orthodox economists, who held that, with the Depression over, the time had come to return to business as usual: a greater reliance on the private sector and international economic practices that increased American wealth, not the world's liquidity. In short, the fact that the economic situation of the late 1940s was different from that of the mid-1930s seemed to foreshadow a direc-tion distinct from the ad hoc character of New Deal emergency measures.

Such a direction could only come from the political system, yet the politics of the late 1940s were as stagnant as the economy was dynamic. Shortly before Amer-ica entered World War II, a political stalemate had emerged in the United States. The New Deal ran out of energy when its last major reform, a Wages and Hours Law, was passed in 1938. Conservative Democrats from the South and Republican isolation-ists from the West formed a coalition in Congress that was able to block Roosevelt from developing either a global foreign policy or a far-sighted domestic policy, yet the conservative bloc was still not strong enough to create an alternative government strategy of its own. National unity produced by war overshadowed this deadlock for five years, but it would emerge again when the war was over. And when the war did end, Americans discovered that the conditions of wartime production, the rise in influence of the military, and the creation of a new political mood all deepened the political stalemate by strengthening the veto power of the conservative bloc.

Relations between business and government—touchy and suspicious during the Great Depression—went through two major changes during World War II. First, business began a political offensive designed to regain a positive image and to absolve itself as much as possible from any blame for the Depression. This offensive has to be rated a success. The large number of business executives who came to Washington "without compensation" to direct the war effort extracted major political concessions for their economic experience. The National Resources Planing Board, an agency that some New Dealers hoped to use to guide the economy in the postwar period, was abolished. Jesse Jones, Roosevelt's secretary of commerce, led the campaign from within to restore business influence. No-strike pledges kept labor subservient. In the guise of defeating Germany, businessmen were also defeating the New Deal, and they were determined to preserve their victory once the war ended. The more liberal New Dealers were in dismay. "I don't like to overuse the word 'fascist,'" Chester Bowles, head of the Office of Price Administration, wrote to Vice-President

Henry Wallace in 1944, "but it does seem to me the only phrase that can be applied to the kind of thinking which I ran into among some groups in business."

The political offensive of business during the war was facilitated by a second change in its relationship with government: business had, under the exigencies of wartime planning, become more monopolistic. The American economy in the twentieth century has been divided into a competitive and a monopolistic sector, the former dependent on the market, the latter trying to control the market. With government assuming the risks of entrepreneurship through cost-plus contracting, the monopoly sector of the economy was strengthened during the war. Thirty-three corporations received over one-half of the total prime contracts, while ten alone received over 30 percent. Before the war there had been a significant element of antitrust sentiment in New Deal philosophy: Thurman Arnold, in charge of the antitrust division of the Justice Department, had tried to keep alive Louis Brandeis's faith in competition. This philosophy all but disappeared among liberals as the war brought concentration to a new peak and made competition seem somehow unpatriotic. With their power over markets more secure, monopoly-sector businessmen would be able to defeat, or at least to control, attempts to regulate them in the public interest. Indeed, a substantial portion of government intervention would become devoted to strengthening monopolization, not to curtailing it.

Besides a strengthened and revitalized business class, the war, not unexpectedly, had given rise to a powerful military apparatus, one closely connected to conservative Southern Democrats and Western Republicans. Before World War II, America had been an isolationist power, without a permanent standing army and without a substantial infrastructure in defense production. The creation of precisely such an infrastructure during the war raised the question of what would happen when peace returned. One does not need a conspiracy theory of history to suggest that military leaders and their supporters in the new defense industries would fight to preserve the privileges they had gained during the war. Spokesmen for the military sector were guilty of nothing more than the typically American pursuit of self-interest when they exaggerated military threats to the United States in order to enhance their economic and political power. The permanence of the new military sector, powerful in Congress due to the overrepresentation of the South, was a fact of life that made the political situation of the 1940s quite different from that of the 1930s.

Finally, war changed the nature of demagoguery in the United States. There has never been a time when America was without its advocates of simple-minded scapegoatism, but during the Depression the targets of the attack were often respectable elements, especially Wall Street. Even when anti-Semitic in nature, the demagoguery of the 1930s had a populistic tinge, enough to make established powers squirm. But if economic slowdowns unleash populistic themes, wars often give rise to reactionary ones. As early as the elections of 1944, the political coloration of the United States turned conservative. Right-wing appeals—anticommunism, racism, fear of modernity, antiurbanism—were gaining in strength day by day. Whoever could control the anger and frustration sparked by the war could ride to political power, and it became clear early on that business and the military were in a better position to channel this sentiment against the New Deal than the New Dealers were to use it to their own advantage. The objects of popular fury in the 1930s would become the beneficiaries of that fury in the 1940s.

As a result of these changes, the overwhelming political need to give direction to a set of economic transformations could not be met. Indeed, directions of all sorts seemed suspect. "A nation accustomed to the categorical yes or no, to war or peace and prosperity or depression," Eric Goldman wrote, "found itself in the nagging realm of the maybe. The liberals worried over the conservatives and the conservatives watched the liberals with an uneasiness akin to dread." The stalemate that had been foreshadowed in 1938 returned, and with a vengeance. Conservatives had become a major force in Congress, but liberals still held the executive. . . . [The deadlock was resolved by the emergence during the Truman years of a new politics of growth.] [R]apid economic growth could work to expand the federal budget, rewarding voters without offending vested interests. Economic growth would become the invisible glue that would hold [Truman's] strategy together. And since growth can only be obtained by offering concessions to businessmen in order to induce them to invest, [Truman's] popular electoral base could be held together only by following policies advantageous to big business. Domestic policy under the Democrats in the postwar years would become a search for the proper way to win business confidence.

The foreign policy consequences implicit in [Truman's] strategy were similarly unanticipated. Without a reform tradition to hold it together, the electoral coalition of the Democratic party could be unified around anticommunism. Furthermore, the creation of a *Pax Americana* rationalized through cold war policies would provide economic benefits in the form of an imperial dividend, just as a domestic growth strategy would expand the size of the pie. Finally, a move toward a global foreign policy and a domestic emphasis on anticommunism would, in Truman's words, "take the ball away from the right." For all these reasons, the Democrats were forced by the logic of a growth imperative, toward an anticommunist foreign policy, one that would provide immediate political rewards in the 1948 election. There were, however, long-term consequences. For one thing, the more Truman tried to steal the ball from the right, the stronger the right seemed to become. Moreover, just as a domestic growth strategy produced dependence on winning business confidence, an imperial foreign policy produced dependence on the military and its eventual industrial complex. Foreign policy under the Democrats in the postwar years would become a search for the proper way to win the confidence of the guardians of national security.

[It thus] followed [that] the pursuit of economic growth and the expansion of empire [were] the two directions that could solve the problems of the political stalemate. Growth, both in the economy and in the empire, would get around the logjam by widening the river. To pursue that growth, a new coalition came to power in American politics. This coalition advocated an overall expansion of the economy through macroeconomic policies made acceptable to the monopoly sector of the economy. From the surplus generated through growth, it offered domestic policies to the poor and the minorities that would, it was hoped, enable them to take part in the reshaping of the cities and countryside that would follow from growth priorities. Based upon the rapid expansion of the economy, it developed a foreign policy that combined a reorganization of the world under American economic hegemony with military power to ensure American influence. Finally, it offered to incorporate the world's poor into the growth machine through foreign aid and developmental assistance. The tasks established by the growth coalition were herculean, but anything seemed possible in an expanding economy. America had never before seen anything like this coalition, and it may never see anything like it again. The uniqueness of the growth coalition can be established by ascertaining what it was not.

While Truman kept alive the spirit of the New Deal in his Fair Deal rhetoric, the growth coalition that stirred during his presidency was *not* the same as the domestic coalition organized by Franklin Delano Roosevelt to support the New Deal. There was little room on ship for liberal politicians who kept alive an aggressive and articulate concern with income redistribution, economic planning, or international idealism. Radicals who had risen to power in the 1930s based upon their ability to mobilize discontent from below were replaced by "pragmatic" liberals who were sympathetic to monopoly power and anticommunism. Those liberal politicians who could not forget the New Deal but did join the growth coalition, like Chester Bowles of Connecticut or Wilson Wyatt of Kentucky, would always be somewhat out of place. The growth-oriented liberalism of the times was determined to exclude, in Arthur Schlesinger Jr.'s marvelous phrase, the "Dough-faced," those who were not hardheaded or realistic enough to understand that growth and empire, unlike dissent and reform, meant concessions to established sources of power.

But if the coalition lopped off the left end of opinion, it also isolated itself from the right. Mr. Republican, Senator Robert Taft of Ohio, was the *bête noire* of the new coalition, for his tight-money financial policies and his isolationism had no place in a world oriented to expansion. Growth policies presupposed the use of government at home to enlarge the economy and the use of government abroad to enhance the empire. The whole venture would be expensive (though its advocates claimed that it would pay for itself). It would mean a confrontation with traditional American values of localism and private virtue. Looking backward to Lockean liberalism and nativistic isolationism was as ideologically repugnant to the growth coalition as looking forward to social democracy and economic planning.

The rise of the growth coalition was facilitated—some would say mandated—by the economic transformations taking place in America. The three most important were economic concentration, growing state intervention, and expansion overseas. All three created a new economic basis that became the core turf of the growth coalition.

Robert Taft's Republicanism had been based on an alliance between competitive-sector businessmen operating close to the margin and small-scale farmers concentrated in the Midwest. Both forces were becoming anachronistic in the economic atmosphere of the late 1940s. Monopoly-sector businessmen, protected by their control over prices from labor costs and overseas competition, could afford to be more liberal toward domestic innovations like the welfare state and toward free trade. The growth of monopolization, linked to multinational expansion and to the debt-encouraging practices of Wall Street banks and investment houses, made the rise of the growth coalition possible.

But growth also changed the traditional basis of New Deal support. Roosevelt's electoral majorities had been formed by mobilizing sentiment among the dispossessed, from tenant farmers to the working class. Growth politics, however, implied organized interest groups, not mobilization from below. The crucial constituencies of growth politics were unions not workers, civil rights organizations not blacks. The growth coalition could be held together so long as liberal monopoly-sector businessmen were willing to engage in an informal alliance with similarly monopolistic unions, together expanding productivity so that both could benefit. In that way,

labor's almost instinctive protectionism could be modified to support free-trade policies, while the threat that labor posed by its reformism could be channeled instead
into cooperation with management. In other words, the social and economic basis of
the growth coalition was an East Coast–based, European-oriented, financial and
industrial elite located in large monopolistic corporations that had made its peace
with conservative, anticommunist labor leaders and Democratic party interest groups
that wanted urban growth and development.

The emergence of the growth coalition, then, was something new. Unlike conservative Republicanism, it favored state intervention at home and was opposed to
isolationism abroad. But unlike the New Deal, it was not a reformist, mobilizing
movement, and it sought free-trade policies toward the rest of the world. Sometimes
called the "vital center" and other times designated "cold war liberalism," the growth
coalition should properly be characterized by its dominant belief: the idea that
growth at home and expansion abroad could unify the interests of the dominant
sectors of the economy with an electoral base that would keep it in power so long
as growth continued. . . .

By 1950, the growth coalition had defeated any serious opposition to its left.
Henry Wallace and the Progressive party had been disgraced, and anticommunism
had established itself as a permanent feature in American political life. There was
still, however, a major problem on the right. The growth coalition was only half
formed; it required a Republican administration to complete it. . . .

[The] Eisenhower administration actually solidified the triumph of growth politics. After eight years of Republican rule, the old-fashioned Republican notions of
laissez-faire monetarism and overseas isolationism could barely be heard. (Indeed,
when the Republican right would make itself visible again, in 1964, it would bear
little relationship to Taftism; from this time forward, the "right" would advocate
more extreme cold war policies than the center and would base itself on a military
sector that was heavily dependent on government spending.) Eisenhower legitimated
growth by not abandoning it. His main domestic advisers . . . were hardly economic
activists, . . . but nor were they monetarists. The administration's specialists on defense and foreign policy . . . were holding down the military budget, but they surely
were not isolationists. With Eisenhower, ideas about growth did not rush forward
into the future, but neither did they slip backwards into the past.

During the 1950s, the political vocabulary of the United States underwent a
major transformation. When the New Deal was the decisive frame of reference, debate was divided into two camps called liberal and conservative. Liberals were
those who believed that the government should play a positive role in correcting
the abuses of capitalism by promoting a concern with equality and social justice.
Conservatives argued that business had made America great and that therefore as
few reforms as possible should be passed that would undermine its privileges.
While the terms liberal and conservative were retained in America, their meaning
shifted as growth priorities were accepted by both parties. From now on, a liberal
was one who believed that growth should happen rapidly and a conservative, one
who believed that growth should happen in a more tempered fashion. There were
other differences, of course. Liberals were willing to use government to bring about
more rapid growth, and they also argued that growth could create a fiscal dividend
out of which more welfare benefits could be financed. In addition, liberals combined
their notions of economic expansion at home with a call for imperial expansion

overseas; the creation of the national security state and an aggressive foreign policy were basically liberal inventions. Similarly, conservatives, though committed to growth, wished to see it occur through the private sector, with Washington acting like a rabid fan, cheering business on. Moreover, conservatives did not want growth to occur at such a fast pace that it would cause inflation; and, tied more closely to the protectionist and competitive sector of the economy, they were dubious about a zealous pursuit of overseas empire. But these were differences in emphasis, not in basic outlook. By the end of the Eisenhower period, words like liberal and conservative no longer meant what they did during the New Deal. A senator like Paul Douglas and a Republican like Nelson Rockefeller agreed on little else but spending huge sums to promote economic expansion, making them both "liberals." Arthur Burns had little in common with Everett Dirksen or Richard Russell, but they all urged caution in too rapid a commitment to expansion, making them all "conservatives."

Growth created its own particular politics. Liberal notions of growth were embodied in a constellation of forces: the executive branch of the Democratic party; Eastern Republicanism; unions, particularly in the monopoly sector; constituents of the New Deal voting coalition; the free-trade, monopolistic, financial wing of business; universities; and downtown redevelopment interests in the major cities. Conservative growth advocates settled in the Southern and congressional wing of the Democratic party, the Western wing of the Republican party, the military-industrial complex, the water–public works–Army Corps of Engineers network, agribusiness, protectionist and isolationist business concerns, and, ultimately, the aerospace, high technology industries of the 1960s. Neither wing of the growth network could govern by itself. Liberals, with a built-in electoral majority, needed to make their policies acceptable to business and the military in order to pass legislation. Conservatives, secure among the powerful, needed to liberalize their programs in order to win national elections. As each wing of the growth network lurched toward the center in search of what it did not have, a pattern of politics was created that would last for a generation. Here are the main features of what I will call *growth politics:*

1. Liberal advocates of growth would, in general, dominate the executive branch, while Congress would institutionalize the power of conservative ideas about growth. Thus, the passage of legislation in the postwar years often represented uneasy compromises between contrasting conceptions of growth. . . .
2. Despite a later cynicism about the political parties, there were real differences between them, but the differences were not ideological ones. Democrats, at least most of them, saw domestic and overseas growth as a means of solving problems, while Republicans saw problems with domestic and overseas growth. The debates between the parties were real, but they concerned how fast and at what cost growth should be achieved.
3. In spite of these differences in approach, the parties often became indistinguishable in practice. For in order to carry out their nations, liberals had to win the confidence of business and the military and therefore they made their notions more conservative, while conservatives, distrusted by the voters, expanded their ideas to make them more liberal.
4. Since growth was the agreed-upon goal, politics in America would no longer be divided along even minimal class lines, as it was becoming during the New Deal, and would no longer be encumbered by discussions of "issues." Debates

would concern means, not ends. Major questions of public policy were simply removed from debate. Growth, in short, presupposed the suppression of fundamental political choice. The purpose of campaigns and elections was to ratify technical decisions about how expeditiously growth was occurring, not to mandate radical departures in policy.

5. As a result of all the preceding, neither wing of the growth coalition would seek to mobilize discontent from below, to tap new sources of support among underrepresented groups, or to encourage whatever popular protest existed in society. Liberal growth advocates connected themselves to interests like unions, not to passions like the labor movement. Conservatives needed popular support to come to power, but discovered a preference for demagogic themes ("Had enough?" "law and order") as an alternative to building a mass base. There would be few new sources of political energy forthcoming. "Politics" would come to mean a discussion among interest groups, not an attempt to develop a vision of a better society.

6. Finally, each wing of the growth coalition would discover, over time, that it had more in common with the other than it did with the base out of which it had emerged. Liberal growth advocates found themselves to be more comfortable with the conservative wing of the growth coalition than they did with old-fashioned progressives and unreconstructed New Dealers, while conservative growth advocates could talk more easily to hard-headed economic activists than they could to extremists on the radical right. The two wings of the growth coalition deeply needed each other, and while they would engage in political combat in public, they would often arrange harmonious compromises in private.

The consolidation of this growth-oriented pattern of politics under Eisenhower was the most important consequence of the Republican interregnum of the 1950s. Not only did it imply a containment of the isolationist and laissez-faire right, it also curtailed the last stirrings of the New Deal left. . . .

By 1960, expectations of growth had become such an institutionalized feature of American politics that, the next time the liberal wing of the coalition came to power, it would not find itself hampered as it was under Truman. The transformation that had come over the American political system was apparent within a year after John F. Kennedy assumed office.

The Legacies of World War II

ALAN BRINKLEY

"The great majority of Americans," Archibald MacLeish said in 1943, "understand very well that this war is not a war only, but an end and a beginning—an end to things known and a beginning of things unknown. We have smelled the wind in the streets that changes weather. We know that whatever the world will be when the war ends, the world will be different."

Excerpt from *Liberalism and Its Discontents* by Alan Brinkley (Harvard University Press: 1998). Excerpt previously published in different forms in *The New York Times* and in *The War in American Culture*, edited by Erenberg & Hirsch (University of Chicago Press: 1995). Reprinted by permission of University of Chicago Press and the author.

Almost everyone who looked ahead to the postwar era realized, as MacLeish did, that the war had unleashed large forces that would produce a new world and a new American society. But Americans greeted the prospects for change in many different ways. MacLeish—a liberal, a New Dealer, and an administrator in the wartime government—welcomed change and believed it could be harnessed (through the efforts of an enlightened government) to the goal of creating a better and more just society. Others viewed the future with trepidation, many of them hoping to preserve the patterns of power and wealth that had shaped the world they had known before the war. The social and cultural legacy of World War II was the product of broad social forces that no individuals or institutions could ultimately control. But it was also the result of many visions of the postwar world among many groups of Americans—almost all of them certain that the war validated their often sharply different, and even conflicting, expectations.

In the prologue to *Six Armies in Normandy,* his classic portrait of the 1944 Allied invasion of France, the historian John Keegan captured one critical aspect of how the war affected the United States. He wrote of his own wartime experiences as a child in the English countryside when, a few months before D-Day, the Americans arrived. Almost overnight, he recalls, his "backwater" town filled with GIs. "How different they looked from our own jumble-sale champions, beautifully clothed in smooth khaki, as fine in cut and quality as a British officer's—an American private, we confided to each other at school, was paid as much as a British captain, major, colonel." The British army traveled about in "a sad collection of underpowered makeshifts." The Americans rode in "magnificent, gleaming . . . four-wheel-drive juggernauts." For a few months—before they vanished suddenly one night in early June—they dominated the countryside, dazzling girls, overwhelming roads, shops, and pubs, distributing largesse. "Thus" Keegan recalled, "I made my first encounter with the bottomless riches of the American economy."

Even as a child, Keegan had understood the role of abundance in American life and the role of World War II in producing it. The war ended the Depression and made the nation rich again. It created expectations of abundance that would survive for more than a generation. And it removed what had in the 1930s been deep doubts about the ability of the capitalist economy ever again to experience substantial growth. By 1944, as Keegan suggests, American abundance was already capturing the global imagination and firing the hopes of the American people themselves. The vast productive power of the United States supplied both its own armed forces and those of its allies with airplanes, ships, tanks, and ammunition. It fed, clothed, and housed the American people, who experienced only modest privations, and it helped feed, clothe, and house much of the rest of the world as well. Alone among the major nations, the United States faced the future in 1945 with an intact and thriving industrial economy poised to sustain a long period of prosperity and growth. Gross National Product in the war years rose from $91 billion to $166 billion; 15 million new jobs were created, and the most enduring problem of the Depression— massive unemployment—came to an end; industrial production doubled; personal incomes rose (depending on the location) by as much as 200 percent.

Abundance created a striking buoyancy in American life in the early 1940s that the war itself only partially counterbalanced. Suddenly, people had money to spend again and—despite the many shortages of consumer goods—at least some things to spend it on. The theater and movie industries did record business. Resort hotels, casinos, and race tracks were jammed with customers. Advertisers, and at times even the government, exhorted Americans to support the war effort to ensure a future of material comfort and consumer choice for themselves and their children. "Your people are giving their lives in useless sacrifice," the *Saturday Evening Post* wrote in a mock letter to the leaders of wartime Japan. "Ours are fighting for a glorious future of mass employment, mass production, and mass distribution and ownership." Even troops at the front seemed at times to justify their efforts with reference to the comforts of home more than to the character of the enemy or the ideals America claimed to be defending. "They are fighting for home," John Hersey once wrote from Guadalcanal (with at least a trace of dismay), because "Home is where the good things are— the generosity, the good pay, the comforts, the democracy, the pie."

One legacy of World War II, therefore, was the return of abundance, and with it the relegitimation of capitalism. Another was a rising popular expectation of economic security and material comfort—of what was already becoming known as "the American dream," a dream that rested on visions of increasing consumption. But abundance also helped strengthen other hopes for change. As Hersey's statement suggests, to some the "American dream" meant more than apple pie alone. Democracy, he said, was part of the mix—not as an alternative to visions of material comfort, but as both a precondition for and a result of them. Defining what democracy meant, mediating among the very different visions the word inspired among Americans, created some of the great struggles of both wartime and the postwar era.

One of the first such conflicts emerged over the political implications of abundance itself, and of the "democratic" initiatives it spawned. Archibald MacLeish and many other liberals eager to see the survival and expansion of the New Deal interpreted the return of economic growth as a mandate to pursue their emerging goal of "full employment" through purposeful government action. A broad coalition of Keynesian economists, union leaders, agricultural activists, consumer groups, and many others rallied in 1944 and 1945 behind what ultimately became the Employment Act of 1946, but which they at first called the "Full Employment" bill—a bill that, had it been passed in its original form, would have committed the government to using Keynesian tools to stimulate economic growth to levels that would ensure very low joblessness. Other liberals rallied around the related proposals that had emerged during the war from the National Resources Planning Board, the New Deal's only real planning agency, which called for, among other things, a major expansion of the welfare programs the New Deal had launched and (in the spirit of full employment) an expansion as well of public works planning to provide the stimuli they believed the post-war economy would often need.

Out of the confluence of abundance and democracy, in other words, had come a vision of expanded liberal state. Freed from the immediate pressures of the Great Depression, convinced by the wartime growth that the economy was not as irretrievably stagnant as they once had feared, liberals seized on abundance as the basis for an ambitious social and economic agenda that would, if successful, greatly expand the role of the state in ensuring prosperity and protecting the beleaguered.

But to many other Americans, and to Americans, and to the conservative Republicans and Democrats who already by 1943 were coming to dominate the United

States Congress, abundance had a very different impact—and the idea of postwar democracy took a very different form. To them the end of the Depression removed whatever justification there had been for the New Deal interventions into the economy and mandated a return to a less regulated market, a less profligate government, and a less expansive welfare state. One by one, in 1943 and 1944, Congress reduced or eliminated New Deal programs that economic growth seemed to have obviated: the Works Progress Administration, the Civilian Conservation Corps, the National Youth Administration, and many others. It abolished the National Resources Planning Board, in retribution for its ambitious and—to conservatives—alarming proposals. It began efforts, which would culminate in 1948, to weaken the Wagner Act. Abundance, they argued, was proof that there was no longer any need for the "socialism" of the New Deal, that it was time to return to what they considered true democracy—a regime of untrammeled economic freedom and minimal government.

Politics was only one of many realms in which the war—the abundance it produced and the hopes for democracy it inspired—provided conflicting lessons and divided legacies. Nowhere was that clearer than in the experiences of African Americans in the 1940s. Prosperity transformed the material circumstances of many black men and women; the war against fascism—and its democratic rationale—transformed their expectations. But the war also reinforced opposition to their hopes.

Two million African Americans left the rural South in the 1940s, more than the total number of migrants in the three decades before (decades that included what is still known as the Great Migration before and during World War I). They moved for many reasons, some of them unrelated to the war. The mechanization of agriculture (and of cotton picking in particular) eliminated the demand for the labor of many black farmers in the South. The sharecropping system, already weakened by the Depression and by New Deal farm subsidies that often made it more profitable for landowners to leave their property fallow than to let it out to tenants, all but disintegrated during the war. Many African Americans also moved because the war created economic opportunities in industrial cities. With millions of men leaving the workforce to join the military, traditional barriers that had kept blacks out of some factories collapsed, at least for a time. The number of blacks employed in manufacturing more than doubled during the war; and there were major increases in the number of African Americans employed as skilled craftsmen or enrolled in unions. There was a substantial movement of black women out of domestic work and into the factory and the shop.

The wartime migration also helped carry the question of race out of the countryside and into the city, out of the South and into the North. The growing concentration of black populations in urban areas made organization and collective action easier and more likely. It made African Americans more important politically. Now that many of them lived in the North, where they could vote more or less at will, they became an increasingly significant force in the Democratic party (to which virtually all African Americans had become committed during the 1930s, in response to the New Deal). Demographic changes, in short, laid the groundwork for the political mobilization of American blacks both during and after the war. There was growing membership and increasing activism in the Urban League, the NAACP, and other existing civil rights organizations. A new and more militant organization emerged: the Congress of Racial Equality—more outspoken, less accommodation-ist than most older ones. And already during World War II, in Washington, D.C., Detroit, and other cities, there were demonstrations against racial discrimination—picketing, sit-ins, occasionally violence—that anticipated the civil rights movement of a decade and more later.

Black Americans who attempted to explain these modest but significant politi-cal stirrings did so by pointing to the nature of the war itself. In North Carolina one African American told a visiting journalist: "No clear thinking Negro can afford to ignore our Hitlers here in America. As long as you have men like [Governor Eugene] Talmadge in Georgia [an outspoken white supremacist] we have to think of the home front whether we want to or not." Many black men and women talked openly of the "Double V," which stood for simultaneous victory over the Axis abroad and over racism at home. "If we could not believe in the realization of demo-cratic freedom for ourselves," one black journalist wrote, "certainly no one could ask us to die for the preservation of that ideal for others." To engage in the struggle for freedom in the world while ignoring the struggle for freedom at home was to make a mockery of both.

Some white Americans were beginning to make that connection too. *Fortune* magazine published an article in June 1942 entitled "The Negro's War," which sug-gested the slow shift in thinking among many whites about the nation's "racial ques-tion." The essay catalogued the long list of legitimate grievances African Americans were raising against their country, and it argued, in effect, that the war required America to do something about them. It cited with alarm Japanese propaganda about racial injustice in America, describing a recent race riot in Detroit as "a boon to the Japanese and . . . the German . . . propagandists." And it argued, in terms that clearly resonated with the larger sense of mission that the war had aroused (and that Henry Luce, *Fortune*'s publisher, had endorsed with notable enthusiasm), that

> . . . this is a war in which ideas . . . are sometimes substitutes for armies. The Negro's fate in the U.S. affects the fate of white American soldiers in the Philippines, in the Caribbean, in Africa; bears on the solidity of our alliance with 800 million colored people in China and India; influences the feelings of countless neighbors in South America. In this shrunken world of ours, a fracas in Detroit has an echo in Aden, and what a southern Congressman considers to be a small home-town affair can actually interfere with grand strategy.

This growing awareness of the nation's racial burdens forced many liberals, even if slowly and incompletely, to reconsider one of the staples of New Deal thought: that the principal goal of public life was to confront economic, not racial or cultural, issues. Perhaps, some liberals began now to think, the problems of the modern world were not purely economic. Perhaps class was not the only, or even the best, concept with which to analyze social problems. Perhaps race, ethnicity, relig-ion, and culture—the divisive, "irrational" issues that had so damaged the Demo-cratic party in the 1920s and from which white liberals had taken pains to distance themselves in the 1930s—were, in fact, essential to understanding America after all. "One of the greatest problems of democratic civilization," the great liberal theologian Reinhold Niebuhr wrote in 1944, "is how to integrate the life of its var-ious subordinate ethnic, religious and economic groups in the community in such a way that the richness and harmony of the whole community will be enhanced and not destroyed by them." Niebuhr dismissed the smug liberal confidence of the 1920s that had anticipated what he called a "frictionless harmony of ethnic groups" and the capacity of economic progess alone to achieve "their eventual assimilation in one racial unity." Instead, he called on "democratic society" to use "every strategem of education and every resource of religion" to fight the influence of racial bigotry— a bigotry that would not wither away simply as a result of material prosperity.

Early in 1944 an explosive event helped galvanize this growing but still murky sense of urgency: the publication of Gunnar Myrdal's *An American Dilemma.* Myrdal, an eminent Swedish sociologist whom the Carnegie Foundation had commissioned in the late 1930s to supervise a major examination of America's "race problem," described the "American dilemma" in part as an economic problem— the failure of American society to extend its riches to its black citizens. But it was also a moral dilemma—a problem in the hearts and minds of white Americans, a problem born of the impossible attempt to reconcile a commitment to freedom and democracy with the effort to deny one group of citizens a set of basic rights guaranteed to everyone else. In the shadow of Nazi tyranny, such a contradiction seemed to Myrdal—and to many readers of his book—especially glaring as he made clear in his powerful concluding chapter:

> The three great wars of this country have been fought for the ideals of liberty and equality to which the nation was pledged. . . . Now America is again in a life-and-death struggle for liberty and equality, and the American Negro is again watching for signs of what war and victory will mean in terms of opportunity and rights for him in his native land. To the white American, too, the Negro problem has taken on a significance greater than it has ever had since the Civil War. . . . The world conflict and America's exposed position as the defender of the democratic faith is thus accelerating an ideological process which was well under way.

An American Dilemma became one of those rare books that help define a moment in history, and its reputation grew rapidly over the next several years. That Myrdal was a European and a distinguished scholar; that he couched his findings in the presumably objective language of social science; that a respected, nonpartisan foundation had sponsored the project; that a large number of prominent academics had collaborated with Myrdal on it; that the book itself was nearly 1,500 pages long, with mountains of data and over 500 pages of footnotes, lending it an air of profound scholarly authority: all helped make its findings seem almost unassailable. It was a "study to end all studies," something close to a definitive analysis of the problem.

And yet it would be a mistake to exaggerate the impact of the war on the willingness of Americans to confront the nation's "race problem." For the war did not simply inspire those who believed in racial equality to reconsider the nation's customs and institutions. It also inspired those who did not defend white supremacy with renewed ardor. Among white Americans, and among white southerners in particular, there were many who considered the war not a challenge to but a confirmation of their commitment to preserving the old racial order. To them democracy meant their right to order their society as they pleased and to sustain the customs and institutions they had always known. This interpretation of democracy was visible, for example, in the Congress, where southern members led by the notorious John Rankin of Mississippi sought to obstruct the GI Bill of Rights until they could feel certain it would not threaten white supremacy. It was evident in the redoubled commitment of many white veterans when they returned home to the South to protect the world they knew. And because much of what they sought to protect was their idealized vision of white women, a vision much romanticized during the war, segregation assumed a specially heightened importance for many of them. In much of the country the World War II generation—the young men who returned from the war fired with determination to make a better world—produced dynamic young leaders impatient with old structures and injustices. In much of the South the new generation of leaders emerging from the war became especially militant defenders of the region's racial institutions.

World War II changed America's racial geography economically, spatially, and ideologically. It ensured that the system of segregation and oppression that had enjoyed a dismal stability for more than half a century would never be entirely stable again. But it ensured, too, that the defenders of that system would confront the new challenges to it with a continued and even strengthened commitment.

In much the same ambiguous, incomplete way the war challenged traditional notions of the role of women in America. Nearly six million women joined the paid workforce during World War II (raising the total number of working women by 60 percent). The new workers were much more likely to be married than earlier female workers had been. They were more likely to have young children. And they were more likely to work in jobs—including some heavy industrial jobs—that had previously been reserved for men (who were now in short supply). Hence the famous image of "Rosie the Riveter." Some women found the experience transforming. In the absence of fathers, brothers, husbands, and boyfriends, many women lived, worked, and traveled alone for the first time in their lives. Some joined unions. Others wore uniforms—as members of the WAACs and WAVEs and other female military organizations.

For many it was an experience of unprecedent freedom; and as a female aircraft worker later recalled, "It really opened up another viewpoint on life." The popular folklore of the time described "Rosie the Riveter" as someone pitching in to win the war but eager to return to home and family. In fact most working women came to the end of the war determined not to return to a purely domestic life. Some lost their jobs when peace arrived and the men came home, but most of those who did looked for work somewhere else. The number of females in the paid workforce never declined to its prewar levels, and it continued to grow throughout the 1950s and beyond.

And yet while the war (and the economic opportunities it opened up) was creating new expectations among many women, it was confirming more traditional expectations among many men. At the front, fighter pilots gave their planes female names and painted bathing beauties on their nosecones. Sailors pasted pin-ups inside their lockers, and infantrymen carried them (along with pictures of wives, mothers, and girlfriends) in their knapsacks. The most popular female icon was Betty Grable, whose picture found its way into the hands of over 5 million fighting men by the end of the war. She was a mildly erotic figure to be sure, but she was not a sex goddess; in her films, she generally played wholesome, innocent young women, the kind any guy would want to marry. And she became a model at the front for the modest, genteel girlfriend or wife many servicemen dreamed of finding on their return. In 1943, when she married the bandleader Harry James and had a child, her popularity actually grew—as if the image of domesticity had enhanced, rather than diminished, her appeal. Thousands of servicemen sent letters to her, suggesting how central her image had become to their own notion of the meaning of the war. . . . When John Hersey compiled his list of comfortable images that he claimed motivated GIs to fight ("generosity, good pay . . . pie"), he might well have added another vision of the kind of world men were hoping to return to: a world of healthy, heterosexual love, a world in which supportive, nurturing women were waiting to welcome their men back and make a home for them.

For the servicemen who remained in America during the war, and for soldiers and sailors in cities far from home in particular, the company of friendly, "wholesome" women was, the military believed, critical to maintaining morale. USOs recruited thousands of young women to serve as hostesses in their clubs—women who were expected to dress nicely, dance well, and chat happily with lonely men. Other women joined "dance brigades" and traveled by bus to military bases for social evenings with servicemen. They, too, were expected to be pretty, to dress attractively (and conservatively), and to interact comfortably with men they had never met before and would likely never see again. Neither the USO hostesses nor the members of the "dance brigades" were supposed to offer anything more than chaste companionship. The USO actually forbade women to have dates with soldiers after parties in the clubs, and the members of the "dance brigades" were expected to have no contact with servicemen except during the dances. The military sent chaperones to most social events and established clear "rules" for both servicemen and the women who sought to entertain them. Clearly, such regulations were sometimes violated. But while the military took elaborate measures to root out homosexuals and lesbians from their ranks (unceremoniously dismissing many of them with undesirable discharges), it quietly tolerated other relationships. "Healthy" heterosexuality was more important than chastity.

But there was a dark counter-image to this official view of women as wholesome nurturing companions. It was the image of brassy independent, and hence dangerous women who—in the fluid social atmosphere of the war years—were becoming more numerous, more visible, and more mobile. One result of that anxiety was a new war agency: the Social Protection Division (SPD) of the Office of Community War Services. Its job was, in essence, to protect men from women. Originally, that meant getting rid of the red-light districts that had sprung up around military bases around the country, districts that military leaders feared would expose servicemen to venereal diseases. But before long the SPD was engaged in a more general effort to round up "promiscuous" females (which often meant single women who seemed in any way "loose" or provocative). A battle against venereal disease had quickly escalated to become a larger attack on independent, sexually active women.

For the rest of the war the SPD engaged in something like a witch-hunt, searching out "suspicious" women, or women of "low character" in the vicinity of military bases; enlisting local police and even hotel detectives to spy on suspected women and arrest them if they were found alone anywhere with a serviceman; encouraging citizens to offer anonymous tips. The government was, in effect, waging war on promiscuous women. Servicemen, the SPD implicitly argued, were simply acting out natural urges; they were the victims. The women were the aggressors—"throwing themselves at the soldiers," one official noted, luring presumably helpless men into sin and possibly disease. In enforcing these new directives, the SPD gradually came not to worry very much about whether supposedly "loose" women were, in fact, infected with VD. Any "promiscuous" woman could *become* a carrier, even if she was not yet one. Men needed to be protected from them all. State and local governments were pressured to change their own laws, and in some places there were quite extraordinary measures to restrict the freedom of movement of single, unescorted women, of whom there were, of course, a great many during the war. Some women were summarily arrested and quarantined for weeks, even months, if found to be infected. Some women were detained for many days even without any evidence of infection if there was other evidence that they might be of "loose" morals.

There is an apparent contradiction in American social history in the first decade or so after the war. On one side was the new reality of women moving in unprecedented numbers into the paid workforce. On the other side was the growing power of a more traditional image of women as wives, mothers, and homemakers. But that postwar paradox is simply a continuation of the contrary experiences of women and men during the war itself: for many women, the exhilarating discovery of new freedoms and opportunities; for many men, a fear of independent women and a strengthened expectation of traditional family life.

☒ *F U R T H E R   R E A D I N G*

Acuna, Rodolfo. *Occupied America: A History of Chicanos* (1981).

Anderson, Karen Tucker. *Wartime Women: Sex Roles, Family Relations, and the Status of Women During World War II* (1981).

Berube, Allen. *Coming Out Under Fire: The History of Gay Men and Women in World War Two* (1990).

Blum, John Morton. *V Was for Victory: Politics and American Culture During World War II* (1976).

Buchanan, A. Russell. *The United States and World War II* (1964).

Campbell, D'Ann Mae. *Women at War with America: Private Lives in a Patriotic America* (1984).

Capeci, Dominic J. *The Harlem Riot of 1943* (1977).

Catton, Bruce. *The War Lords of Washington* (1948).

Costello, John. *Virtue Under Fire: How World War II Changed Our Social and Sexual Attitudes* (1985).

Dalfiume, Richard M. *Desegregation in the United States Armed Forces; Fighting on Two Fronts: 1939–1953* (1969).

Dallek, Robert. *Franklin D. Roosevelt and American Foreign Policy, 1933–1945* (1979).

Daniels, Roger. *Concentration Camps USA: Japanese Americans and World War II* (1971).

Divine, Robert A. *Roosevelt and World War II* (1969).

Erenberg, Lewis A., and Susan E. Hirsh. *The War in American Culture* (1996).

Evans, Peter B., Dietrich Rueschemeyer, and Theda Skocpol, eds. *Bringing the State Back In* (1985).

Funigiello, Philip J. *The Challenge to Urban Liberalism* (1978).

Graham, Otis L. Jr. *Toward a Planned Society: From Roosevelt to Nixon* (1976).

Harris, Mark Jonathan, Franklin D. Mitchell, and Stephen Schecter, eds. *Homefront: America During World War II* (1984).

Hartmann, Susan. *The Home Front and Beyond* (1982).

Hill, Robert A. ed. *The FBI's RACON: Racial Conditions in the United States During World War II* (1995).

Hobsbawm, Eric. *The Age of Extremes* (1994).

Honey, Maureen. *Creating Rosie the Riveter: Class, Gender, and Propaganda During World War II* (1984).

Hooks, Michael. *Forging the Military Industrial Complex* (1991).

Irons, Peter. *Justice at War* (1983).

Karl, Barry D. *The Uneasy State: The United States from 1915 to 1945* (1983).

Koppes, Clayton R., and Gregory D. Black. *Hollywood Goes to War* (1987).

Leigh, Michael. *Mobilizing Consent: Public Opinion and American Foreign Policy, 1937–1947* (1986).

Lichtenstein, Nelson. *Labor's War at Home: The CIO in World War II* (1982).

McNeill, William H. *America, Britain, and Russia* (1953).

May, Dean L. *From New Deal to New Economics: The American Liberal Response to the Recession of 1937* (1981).

Milkman, Ruth. *Gender at Work: The Dynamics of Job Segregation by Sex During World War II* (1988).

O'Brien Paul, and Lyn Hudson Parsons, eds. *The Home-Front War* (1995).

Okihiro, Gary Y. *Whispered Silences: Japanese Americans and World War* (1996).

O'Neill, William L. *A Democracy at War* (1993).

Perrett, Geoffrey. *Days of Sadness, Years of Triumph: The American People, 1939–1945* (1973).

Pfeffer, Paula E. *A. Philip Randolph* (1990).

Polenberg, Richard. *War and Society: The United States, 1941–1945* (1972).

Reed, Merle E. *Seedtime for the Modern Civil Rights Movement* (1991).

Roeder, George H. Jr. *The Censored War* (1993).

Samuel, Lawrence R. *Pledging Allegiance* (1997).

Sears, Steven W., ed. *World War II* (1991).

Sherry, Michael S. *In the Shadow of War* (1995).

Terkel, Studs. *"The Good War": An Oral History of World War II* (1984).

Tuttle, William M. *Daddy's Gone to War* (1993).

Winkler, Allan J. *Home Front U.S.A.* (1986).

Wyman, David S. *The Abandonment of the Jews: America and the Holocaust, 1941–1945* (1984).

From World War II to the Cold War: The Atomic Bombing of Japan

XXX

The United States' decision to drop atomic bombs on the Japanese cities of Hiroshima and Nagasaki on August 6 and 9, 1945, was a pivotal event in world history. Rooted in the twentieth-century revolution in physics, the bombing opened a radically new chapter in the application of science and engineering, one that would threaten not just to transform the world but to destroy it. It signaled, too, a revolution in the nature of warfare, a marriage of the traditional rivalries of nation-states with an awesome new technology of unprecedented destructiveness. It brought to an end the most destructive war in human history and foreshadowed a new Cold War that would shape international affairs for the next forty years.

Not surprisingly, the decision to unleash the bombs has provoked continuing historical debate. Was their use necessary, as President Harry S Truman argued at the time, to bring the war to a close and to save both American and Japanese lives? Or would the Japanese soon have been defeated anyway by the U.S. naval blockade and aerial bombardment? What would have been the impact on the Japanese of the planned declaration of war by the Soviet Union? To what degree was Truman's resort to the bombing influenced by growing conflict between the United States and the Soviet Union: did the administration hope to intimidate the Russians in Eastern Europe or finish the war in the Pacific before they could enter the fighting and thus demand a voice in the postwar settlement?

Debate has raged, too, over other possible reasons (beyond strategic objectives) for the United States' decision and has at the same time raised chilling moral questions. For example, to what extent was the decision influenced by racial prejudice and by the institutionalized wartime depiction of the Japanese as evil and inhuman? Before using the bomb, should the United States have demonstrated its terrible destructiveness—perhaps in Tokyo harbor, as some scientists suggested at the time— or at least have provided an explicit warning? Was the use of atomic bombs, weapons that in a blinding instant killed tens of thousands of men, women, and children, immoral? Was the bombing any more immoral than the reliance on weapons that produced the millions of other deaths during World War II, than the aerial assaults

on London and Dresden, or than the awful firebombing of Tokyo? What is one to say
of a weapon that not only kills but, through radiation and the resulting genetic damage, continues to kill long after the debris settles? Does the bomb's immorality lie in
more than the holocaust unleashed over Hiroshima and Nagasaki on those August
days of 1945; does it further rest on the potential of atomic warfare to wreak destruction on a scale that would make even those horrors seem small by comparison?

Still other questions haunt those who have debated the bombing of Hiroshima
and Nagasaki. For example, how does one assess the ultimate costs of the new age
of atomic warfare that followed the fateful event—costs measured not only by the
taxes necessary to sustain new nuclear technologies but by the resultant delays in
or denials of productive social investments? Have atomic weapons, by their very
destructiveness, made war so terrible as to be unthinkable, and the world hence
more peaceful? Or has the proliferation of atomic technology, especially in an international system no longer dominated by the bipolar struggle of the United States
and the U.S.S.R., made our world unimaginably dangerous?

₩ D O C U M E N T S

As the top-secret Manhattan Project neared completion, U.S. leaders debated the use of
the new weapon that the scientists and engineers were to produce. In Document 1, an
interim committee appointed by President Truman recommends the bomb's immediate
use. In Document 2, a group of scientists engaged in work on the bomb at the University
of Chicago urge a demonstration of the bomb's destructiveness on some uninhabited
target. Their proposal was rejected, however, by the government's own scientific
advisory committee, as Document 3 reveals. "Because of the urgency of this matter,"
J. Robert Oppenheimer, the director of the Manhattan Project laboratory at Los Alamos,
New Mexico, wrote in a covering memorandum, "the panel was not able to devote as
extended a collective deliberation to the problem as it undoubtedly warrants." In Document 4, Undersecretary of the Navy Ralph Bard, in a memorandum to Secretary of War
Henry Stimson, urges that the United States explore diplomatic alternatives to the bomb.
The initial successful test of the bomb on July 16, 1945, is described in Document 5
by General Leslie R. Groves, the commanding general of the Manhattan Project. As
an excerpt from the president's diary (Document 6) reveals, the bomb was much on
Truman's mind as he met with Soviet premier Joseph Stalin and British prime minister
Winston Churchill at Potsdam. The final selection, Document 7, is drawn from a report
by the U.S. Strategic Bombing Survey. It is based on captured Japanese documents and
interviews with Japanese military and political leaders conducted during the fall of 1945.

1. President Harry S Truman's Advisers
Discuss the Atomic Bomb, May 1945

Secretary [of War Henry L.] Stimson explained that the Interim Committee had
been appointed by him with the approval of the President, to make recommendations on temporary war-time controls, public announcement, legislation, and postwar organization. The Secretary gave high praise to the brilliant and effective
assistance rendered to the project by the scientists of the country and expressed

National Archives, Manhattan Engineer District Records, Harrison-Bundy Files, RG 77, "Notes of the
Interim Committee Meetings, May 31, 1945."

great appreciation to the four scientists present for their great contributions to the work and their willingness to advise on the many complex problems that the Interim Committee had to face. He expressed the hope that the scientists would feel completely free to express their views on any phase of the subject.

The Committee had been termed an "Interim Committee" because it was expected that when the project became more widely known a permanent organization established by Congressional action or by treaty arrangements would be necessary.

The Secretary explained that General Marshall shared responsibility with him for making recommendations to the President on this project with particular reference to its military aspects; therefore, it was considered highly desirable that General Marshall be present at this meeting to secure at first hand the views of the scientists.

The Secretary expressed the view, a view shared by [Army Chief of Staff] General [George C.] Marshall, that this project should not be considered simply in terms of military weapons, but as a new relationship of man to the universe. This discovery might be compared to the discoveries of the Copernican theory and of the laws of gravity, but far more important than these in its effect on the lives of men. While the advances in the field to date had been fostered by the needs of war, it was important to realize that the implications of the project went far beyond the needs of the present war. It must be controlled if possible to make it an assurance of future peace rather than a menace to civilization.

It was pointed out that one atomic bomb on [an] arsenal would not be much different from the effect caused by any Air Corps strike of present dimensions. However, Dr. [J. Robert] Oppenheimer [Director of the Manhattan Project's Los Alamos Research Laboratory] stated that the visual effect of an atomic bombing would be tremendous. It would be accompanied by a brilliant luminescence which would rise to a height of 10,000 to 20,000 feet. The neutron effect of the explosion would be dangerous to life for a radius of at least two-thirds of a mile.

After much discussion concerning various types of targets and the effects to be produced, *the Secretary expressed the conclusion, on which there was general agreement, that we could not give the Japanese any warning; that we could not concentrate on a civilian area; but that we should seek to make a profound psychological impression on as many of the inhabitants as possible. At the suggestion of Dr. [James B.] Conant [President of Harvard University and Chairman of the National Defense Research Committee] the Secretary agreed that the most desirable target would be a vital war plant employing a large number of workers and closely surrounded by workers' houses.*

2. Atomic Scientists Urge an Alternative Course, June 1945

The only reason to treat nuclear power differently from all the other developments in the field of physics is its staggering possibilities as a means of political pressure in peace and sudden destruction in war. All present plans for the organization of research, scientific and industrial development, and publication in the field of nucleonics are conditioned by the political and military climate in which one expects those

National Archives, Harrison-Bundy Files, RG 77, "Memorandum on 'Political and Social Problems' [associated with the use of the bomb], from Members of the Metallurgical Laboratory of the University of Chicago, [June 1945]."

plans to be carried out. Therefore, in making suggestions for the postwar organization of nucleonics, a discussion of political problems cannot be avoided. The scientists on this Project do not presume to speak authoritatively on problems of national and international policy. However, we found ourselves, by the force of events, the last five years in the position of a small group of citizens cognizant of a grave danger for the safety of this country as well as for the future of all the other nations, of which the rest of mankind is unaware. We therefore felt it our duty to urge that the political problems, arising from the mastering of nuclear power, be recognized in all their gravity, and that appropriate steps be taken for their study and the preparation of necessary decisions. We hope that the creation of the Committee by the Secretary of War [Henry L. Stimson] to deal with all aspects of nucleonics, indicates that these implications have been recognized by the government. We feel that our acquaintance with the scientific elements of the situation and prolonged preoccupation with its world-wide political implications, imposes on us the obligation to offer to the Committee some suggestions as to the possible solution of these grave problems.

The development of nuclear power not only constitutes an important addition to the technological and military power of the United States, but also creates grave political and economic problems for the future of this country.

Nuclear bombs cannot possibly remain a "secret weapon" at the exclusive disposal of this country, for more than a few years. The scientific facts on which their construction is based are well known to scientists of other countries. Unless an effective international control of nuclear explosives is instituted, a race of nuclear armaments is certain to ensue following the first revelation of our possession of nuclear weapons to the world. Within ten years other countries may have nuclear bombs, each of which, weighing less than a ton, could destroy an urban area of more than five square miles. In the war to which such an armaments race is likely to lead, the United States, with its agglomeration of population and industry in comparatively few metropolitan districts, will be at a disadvantage compared to the nations whose population and industry are scattered over large areas.

We believe that these considerations make the use of nuclear bombs for an early, unannounced attack against Japan inadvisable. If the United States would be the first to release this new means of indiscriminate destruction upon mankind, she would sacrifice public support throughout the world, precipitate the race of armaments, and prejudice the possibility of reaching an international agreement on the future control of such weapons.

Much more favorable conditions for the eventual achievement of such an agreement could be created if nuclear bombs were first revealed to the world by a demonstration in an appropriately selected uninhabited area.

If chances for the establishment of an effective international control of nuclear weapons will have to be considered slight at the present time, then not only the use of these weapons against Japan, but even their early demonstration may be contrary to the interests of this country. A postponement of such a demonstration will have in this case the advantage of delaying the beginning of the nuclear armaments race as long as possible. If, during the time gained, ample support could be made available for further development of the field in this country, the postponement would substantially increase the lead which we have established during the present war, and our position in an armaments race or in any later attempt at international agreement will thus be strengthened.

On the other hand, if no adequate public support for the development of nucleonics will be available without a demonstration, the postponement of the latter may be deemed inadvisable, because enough information might leak out to cause other nations to start the armaments race, in which we will then be at a disadvantage. At the same time, the distrust of other nations may be aroused by a confirmed development under cover of secrecy, making it more difficult eventually to reach an agreement with them.

If the government should decide in favor of any early demonstration of nuclear weapons it will then have the possibility to take into account the public opinion of this country and of the other nations before deciding whether these weapons should be used in the war against Japan. In this way, other nations may assume a share of responsibility for such a fateful decision.

To sum up, we urge that the use of nuclear bombs in this war be considered as a problem of long-range national policy rather than military expediency, and that this policy be directed primarily to the achievement of an agreement permitting an effective international control of the means of nuclear warfare.

3. U.S. Science Advisers Endorse Dropping the Bomb, June 1945

You have asked us to comment on the initial use of the new weapon. This use, in our opinion, should be such as to promote a satisfactory adjustment of our international relations. At the same time, we recognize our obligation to our nation to use the weapons to help save American lives in the Japanese war.

1. To accomplish these ends we recommend that before the weapons are used not only Britain, but also Russia, France, and China be advised that we have made considerable progress in our work on atomic weapons, that these may be ready to use during the present war, and that we would welcome suggestions as to how we can cooperate in making this development contribute to improve international relations.

2. The opinions of our scientific colleagues on the initial use of these weapons are not unanimous: they range from the proposal of a purely technical demonstration to that of the military application best designed to induce surrender. Those who advocate a purely technical demonstration would wish to outlaw the use of atomic weapons, and have feared that if we use the weapons now our position in future negotiations will be prejudiced. Others emphasize the opportunity of saving American lives by immediate military use, and believe that such use will improve the international prospects, in that they are more concerned with the prevention of war than with the elimination of this specific weapon. We find ourselves closer to these latter views; we can propose no technical demonstration likely to bring an end to the war; we see no acceptable alternative to direct military use.

National Archives, Manhattan Engineer District Records, Harrison-Bundy Files, RG 77, "Recommendations on the Immediate Use of Nuclear Weapons, June 16, 1945."

3. With regard to these general aspects of the use of atomic energy, it is clear that we, as scientific men, have no proprietary rights. It is true that we are among the few citizens who have had occasion to give thoughtful consideration to these problems during the past few years. We have, however, no claim to special competence in solving the political, social, and military problems which are presented by the advent of atomic power.

4. Undersecretary of the Navy Ralph Bard Urges Alternatives, June 1945

Memorandum on the Use of S-1 Bomb

Ever since I have been in touch with this program I have had a feeling that before the bomb is actually used against Japan that Japan should have some preliminary warning for say two or three days in advance of use. The position of the United States as a great humanitarian nation and the fair play attitude of our people generally is responsible in the main for this feeling.

During recent weeks I have also had the feeling very definitely that the Japanese government may be searching for some opportunity which they could use as a medium of surrender. Following the three-power conference emissaries from this country could contact representatives from Japan somewhere on the China Coast and make representations with regard to Russia's position and at the same time give them some information regarding the proposed use of atomic power, together with whatever assurances the President might care to make with regard to the Emperor of Japan and the treatment of the Japanese nation following unconditional surrender. It seems quite possible to me that this presents the opportunity which the Japanese are looking for.

I don't see that we have anything in particular to lose in following such a program. The stakes are so tremendous that it is my opinion very real consideration should be given to some plan of this kind. I do not believe under present circumstances existing that there is anyone in this country whose evaluation of the chances of the success of such a program is worth a great deal. The only way to find out is to try it out.

Ralph A. Bard

5. General Leslie Groves Reports on a Successful Test, July 1945

1. This is not a concise, formal military report but an attempt to recite what I would have told you if you had been here on my return from New Mexico.
2. At 0530, 16 July 1945, in a remote section of the Alamogordo Air Base, New Mexico, the first full scale test was made of the implosion type atomic fission

National Archives, Manhattan Engineer District Records, Harrison-Bundy Files, RG 77, "Interim Committee, International Control."

General Leslie R. Groves, Memorandum for the Secretary of War, July 18, 1945, *Foreign Relations of the United States: The Berlin Conference,* 1945 (Washington, D.C.: GPO, 1967), 1361–1363.

bomb. For the first time in history there was a nuclear explosion. And what an explosion! . . . The bomb was not dropped from an airplane but was exploded on a platform on top of a 100-foot-high steel tower.

3. The test was successful beyond the most optimistic expectations of anyone. Based on the data which it has been possible to work up to date, I estimate the energy generated to be in excess of the equivalent of 15,000 to 20,000 tons of TNT; and this is a conservative estimate. Data based on measurements which we have not yet been able to reconcile would make the energy release several times the conservative figure. There were tremendous blast effects. For a brief period there was a lighting effect within a radius of 20 miles equal to several suns in midday; a huge ball of fire was formed which lasted for several seconds. This ball mushroomed and rose to a height of over ten thousand feet before it dimmed. The light from the explosion was seen clearly at Albuquerque, Santa Fe, Silver City, El Paso, and other points generally to about 180 miles away. The sound was heard to the same distance in a few instances but generally to about 100 miles. Only a few windows were broken although one was some 125 miles away. A massive cloud was formed which surged and billowed upward with tremendous power, reaching the substratosphere at an elevation of 41,000 feet, 36,000 feet above the ground, in about five minutes, breaking without interruption through a temperature inversion at 17,000 feet which most of the scientists thought would stop it. Two supplementary explosions occurred in the cloud shortly after the main explosion. The cloud contained several thousand tons of dust picked up from the ground and a considerable amount of iron in the gaseous form. Our present thought is that this iron ignited when it mixed with the oxygen in the air to cause these supplementary explosions. Huge concentrations of highly radioactive materials resulted from the fission and were contained in this cloud.

4. A crater from which all vegetation had vanished, with a diameter of 1,200 feet and a slight slope toward the center, was formed. In the center was a shallow bowl 130 feet in diameter and 6 feet in depth. The material within the crater was deeply pulverized dirt. The material within the outer circle is greenish and can be distinctly seen from as much as 5 miles away. The steel from the tower was evaporated. 1,500 feet away there was a four-inch iron pipe 16 feet high set in concrete and strongly guyed. It disappeared completely.

5. One-half mile from the explosion there was a massive steel test cylinder weighing 220 tons. The base of the cylinder was solidly encased in concrete. Surrounding the cylinder was a strong steel tower 70 feet high, firmly anchored to concrete foundations. This tower is comparable to a steel building bay that would be found in typical 15 or 20 story skyscraper or in warehouse construction. Forty tons of steel were used to fabricate the tower which was 70 feet high, the height of a six story building. The cross bracing was much stronger than that normally used in ordinary steel construction. The absence of the solid walls of a building gave the blast a much less effective surface to push against. The blast tore the tower from its foundations, twisted it, ripped it apart and left it flat on the ground. The effects on the tower indicate that, at that distance, unshielded permanent steel and masonry buildings would have

been destroyed. I no longer consider the Pentagon a safe shelter from such a bomb. Enclosed are a sketch showing the tower before the explosion and a telephotograph showing what it looked like afterwards. None of us had expected it to be damaged.

6. The cloud traveled to a great height first in the form of a ball, then mushroomed, then changed into a long trailing chimney-shaped column, and finally was sent in several directions by the variable winds at the different elevations. It deposited its dust and radioactive materials over a wide area.

6. President Truman Discusses the Bomb at Potsdam, July 1945

[Potsdam]
July 17, [19]45

Just spent a couple of hours with Stalin. Joe Davies called on Maiski and made the date last night for noon today. Promptly a few minutes before twelve I looked up from the desk and there stood Stalin in the doorway. I got to my feet and advanced to meet him. He put out his hand and smiled. I did the same[,] we shook[,] I greeted Molotov and the interpreter, and we sat down. After the usual polite remarks we got down to business. I told Stalin that I am no diplomat but usually said yes & no to questions after hearing all the argument [sic]. It pleased him. I asked him if he had the agenda for the meeting. He said he had and that he had some more questions to present. I told him to fire away. He did and it is dynamite—but I have some dynamite too which I am not exploding now. He wants to fire [Generalissimo Francisco] Franco [the Spanish fascist dictator], to which I wouldn't object and divide up the Italian colonies, and other mandates, some no doubt that the British have. Then he got on the Chinese situation[,] told us what agreements had been reached and what was in abeyance. Most of the big points are settled. He'll be in the Jap War on August 15th. Fini Japs when that comes about. We had lunch[,] talked socially[,] put on a real show drinking toasts to everyone, then had pictures made in the back yard. I can deal with Stalin. He's honest—but smart as hell.

[Potsdam]
July 18, [19]45

At breakfast with nephew Harry, a sergeant in the Field Artillery [in which Truman had served as a Captain during World War I]. He is a good soldier and a nice boy. They took him off [the troopship] Queen Elizabeth at Glasco [Glasgow] and flew him here. Sending him home Friday. Went to lunch with P.M. [British Prime Minister Winston Churchill] at 1:30 walked around to British Hqrs [Headquarters]. Met at the gate by Mr. Churchill. Guard of honor drawn up. Fine body of men Scottish

---

Harry S Truman diary, July 17, 18, and 25, 1945, President's Secretary's Files, Papers of the President, Harry S Truman Library, Independence, Mo.

Guards Band played the Star Spangled Banner. Inspected Guard and went in for lunch. P.M. & I ate alone. Discussed Manhattan [Project] (it is a success). Decided to tell Stalin about it. Stalin had told P.M. of telegram from Jap Emperor asking for peace. Stalin also read his answer to me. It was satisfactory. Believe Japs will fold up before Russia comes in.

I am sure they will when Manhattan appears over their homeland. I shall inform Stalin about it at an opportune time. Stalin's luncheon was a most satisfactory meeting. I invited him to come to the U.S. Told him I'd send the Battleship Missouri for him if he'd come. He said he wanted to cooperate with U.S. in peace as we had cooperated in War but it would be harder. Said he was grossly misunderstood in the U.S. and I was misunderstood in Russia. I told him that we each could help to remedy that situation in our home countries and that I intended to try with all I had to do my part at home. He gave me a most cordial smile and said he would do as much in Russia.

We then went to the conference and it was my job to present the Ministers' proposed agenda. There were three proposals and I banged them through in short order, much to the surprise of Mr. Churchill. Stalin was very much pleased. Churchill was too after he had recovered. I'm not going to stay around this terrible place all summer just to listen to speeches. I'll go home to the Senate for that.

[Potsdam]
July 25, 1945

We met at 11 A.M. today. That is Stalin, Churchill and the U.S. President. But I had a most important session with Lord Mountbatten & General Marshall before that. We have discovered the most terrible bomb in the history of the world. It may be the fire destruction prophesied in the Euphrates Valley Era, after Noah and his fabulous Ark.

Anyway we "think" we have found the way to cause a disintegration of the atom. An experiment in the New Mexico desert was startling—to put it mildly. Thirteen pounds of the explosive caused the complete disintegration of a steel tower 60 feet high, created a crater 6 feet deep and 1,200 feet in diameter, knocked over a steel tower 1/2 mile away and knocked men down 10,000 yards away. The explosion was visible for more than 200 miles and audible for 40 miles and more.

This weapon is to be used against Japan between now and August 10th. I have told the Sec[retary]. of War, Mr. [Henry] Stimson to use so that military objectives and soldiers and sailors are the target and not women and children. Even if the Japs are savages, ruthless, merciless, and fanatic, we as the leader of the world for the common welfare cannot drop this terrible bomb on the old Capital [Kyoto] or the new [Tokyo].

He & I are in accord. The target will be a purely military one and we will issue a warning statement asking the Japs to surrender and save lives. I'm sure they will not do that, but we will have given them the chance. It is certainly a good thing for the world that Hitler's crowd or Stalin's did not discover this atomic bomb. It seems to me to be the most terrible thing ever discovered, but it can be made the most useful.

7. The U.S. Strategic Bombing Survey Concludes That the Bomb Was Unnecessary, 1946

1. Blockade of Japan's sea communications exploited the basic vulnerability of an island enemy which, with inherently second-power resources, was struggling to enlarge its capabilities by milking the raw materials of a rich conquered area. Acute dependence upon imports of such basic items as oil, iron ore, coal, bauxite, food, etc., caused Japan's shipping position even in the fall of 1941 to appear deficient to several members of the Jushin [an informal group of elder statesmen] whose opinions were declared to [then prime minister, General Hideki] Tojo before the Pearl Harbor attack. These fears were well-founded, at least for long-term fighting, since Japan began the war with 6,000,000 tons of merchant shipping, which were barely sufficient for estimated minimum requirements. Her capacity to build was quickly exceeded by losses. Eighty-eight percent of Japan's total merchant shipping available during the war was sunk. United States submarines sank 55 percent of the total lost. Our Navy and Army air forces made important contributions by sinking 40 percent of Japan's total shipping lost, by interdiction of sea routes, and by an aerial mining program carried out by B-29s in the last months of the war which sealed off the vital Inland Sea and disrupted every major home island port. The blockade prevented exploitation of conquered resources, kept Japan's economy off balance, created shortages of materials which in turn limited war production, and deprived her of oil in amounts sufficient to immobilize fleet and air units and to impair training. These effects were intimately associated with the political conditions culminating in the fall of Tojo and [former premier, General Kunikai] Koiso. The direct military and economic limitations imposed by shortages created virtually insoluble political as well as economic problems in attempting to achieve war production adequate for the defense of Japan. The special feeling of vulnerability to blockade, to which a dependent island people are ever subject, increased and dramatized, especially to the leaders, the hopelessness of their position and favored the growing conviction that the defeat was inevitable.

2. While the blockade was definitive in strangling Japan's war mobilization and production, it cannot be considered separately from the pressure of our concurrent military operations, with which it formed a shears that scissored Japan's military potential into an ineffectual remnant. In the early engagements that stemmed the Japanese advance and in the subsequent battle for bases, the application of our air power against vital forces which Japan committed piecemeal in defense of these perimeter positions enabled us largely to destroy her navy and reduce her air forces to impotence before the home islands could be brought under direct air attack. Throughout these operations we were employing air power effectively and potently in ways the Japanese leaders understood and feared, and had no adequate defense to withstand. Although a core of biter-end resistance lay in Japan's army and navy until the Imperial rescript was signed, it should be noted that Tojo's collapse and the introduction of peace-making factions into the succeeding Koiso government

"The Political Target Under Assault," *Japan's Struggle to End the War*, ed. (Washington, D.C.: GPO 1946), 9–13.

quickly followed the loss of Saipan in July 1944. Also, after the costly and vitiating defeats in the Palaus, Philippines, and at Iwo Jima, Koiso was in turn succeeded shortly after our Okinawa landings of 1 April 1945 by the [Admiral Baron Kantaro] Suzuki cabinet, which was formed with the specific mandate to terminate the war. In these campaigns, dictated by our need for air mastery and won by immediate air control, while Japan's loss of effective naval and land-based air forces was overwhelming, her military attrition was not complete, since our operations used up by no means all of her ground and Kamikaze forces. Japan's principal land armies were in fact never defeated, a consideration which also supported the military's continued last-ditch resistance to the surrender decision. It nevertheless appears that after the loss of the Marianas in July–August 1944, the military commands, though unconvinced of final victory, viewed defense against our subsequent operations as affording an opportunity for only a limited success, a tactical victory which might, so they hoped, have created a purchase from which to try for a negotiated peace under terms more favorable than unconditional surrender.

3. Fear of home island bombing was persuasive to the political leaders even before its direct effects could be felt. News of the B-29 and its intended capabilities reached Japan in 1943. B-29 raids on Kyushu [with Shikoku, Hokkaido, and Honshu, and Japanese home islands] and southern Honshu [the main home island] targets began from China bases on 15 June 1944. With the loss of Saipan in early July 1944, many leaders became wholly convinced of Japan's eventual defeat, one factor being that from Marianas bases the homeland would be brought under the kind of intensive, shattering air assault even then being administered to their German partner. The timing of the strategic bombing attack affected its role in the surrender decision. After the Marianas were lost but before the first attacks were flown in November 1944, Tojo had been unseated and peacemakers introduced into the Government as prominent elements. The war economy had already passed its peak, fleet and air forces had been critically weakened, confidence of the "intelligentsia" in the Government and the military had been deflated, and confidence of the people in eventual victory was weakening. By mid-1944 shortages of food and civilian supplies were reflected in reduced living standards. Therefore the actual physical destruction wrought by strategic bombing assumed the role of an accelerator, to assist and expedite forces already in motion. It added a tremendous quantitative weight to those forces. Since the means of resisting direct air attacks had already been largely destroyed, it represented the full exploitation of air control by an air weapon. These attacks became definitive in the surrender decision because they broadened the realization of defeat by bringing it home to the people and dramatized to the whole nation what the small peace party already knew. They proved day in and day out, and night after night that the United States did control the air and could exploit it. They lowered morale by demonstrating the disadvantages of total war directly, added a vital increment of both actual and clearly foreseeable future production loss by both precision and area attacks, and applied pressure on the surrender decision by eliminating the hope of successful final resistance.

4. When Japan was defeated without invasion, a recurrent question arose as to what effect the threat of a home-island invasion had had upon the surrender decision. It was contended that the threat of invasion, if not the actual operation, was a requirement to induce acceptance of the surrender terms. On this tangled issue the evidence

and hindsight are clear. The fact is, of course, that Japan did surrender without invasion, and with its principal armies intact. Testimony before the Survey shows that the expected "violation of the sacred homeland" raised few fears which expedited the decision to surrender beforehand. Government and Imperial household leaders felt some concern for the "destruction of the Japanese people," but the people were already being shattered by direct air attacks. Anticipated landings were even viewed by the military with hope that they would afford a means of inflicting casualties sufficiently high to improve their chances of a negotiated peace. Preparation of defenses against landings diverted certain resources from dispersal and cushioning moves which might have partially mitigated our air blows. But in Japan's then depleted state, the diversion was not significant. The responsible leaders in power read correctly the true situation and embraced surrender well before invasion was expected.

5. So long as Germany remained in the war that fact contributed to the core of Japanese resistance. Slight evidence exists that some hope was held for a long-promised German miracle weapon. A telegram received on 6 May in the German embassy at Tokyo revealed that Hitler was dead, the promised new weapon had failed to materialize, and that Germany would surrender within a matter of hours. [Lord Keeper of the Privy Seal, Marquis Koichi] Kido believed, presumably on Japanese Army representations, that the Army would not countenance peace moves so long as Germany continued to fight. It is not clear whether this was a face-saving position, designed to avoid a prior Japanese surrender. In any case on 9 May 1945, immediately after the Nazi capitulation, General [Korechika] Anami, the War Minister, asked the Cabinet for an Imperial conference to reconsider the war situation. The significant fact, however, is that Japan was pursuing peace before the Nazis collapsed, and the impoverishment and fragmentation of the German people had already afforded a portent of similar consequences for an intransigent Japan.

6. The Hiroshima and Nagasaki atomic bombs did not defeat Japan, nor by the testimony of the enemy leaders who ended the war did they persuade Japan to accept unconditional surrender. The Emperor [Hirohito], the Lord Privy Seal, the Prime Minister, the Foreign Minister [Shigenori Togo], and the Navy Minister [Admiral Mitsumara Yonai] had decided as early as May of 1945 that the war should be ended even if it meant acceptance of defeat on allied terms. The War Minister and the two chiefs of staff opposed unconditional surrender. The impact of the Hiroshima attack was to bring further urgency and lubrication to the machinery of achieving peace, primarily by contributing to a situation which permitted the Prime Minister to bring the Emperor overtly and directly into a position where his decision for immediate acceptance of the Potsdam Declaration could be used to override the remaining objectors. Thus, although the atomic bombs changed no votes of the Supreme War Direction Council concerning the Potsdam terms, they did foreshorten the war and expedite the peace.

Events and testimony which support these conclusions are blue-printed from the chronology established in the first sections of this report:

(a) The mission of the Suzuki government, appointed 7 April 1945, was to make peace. An appearance of negotiating for terms less onerous than unconditional surrender was maintained in order to contain the military and bureaucratic elements still determined on a final Bushido ["The Way of the Warrior," the pre-1868-Samurais' code of honor, which advocated fighting to the death] defense, and perhaps even more importantly to obtain freedom to create peace with a minimum of personal danger and internal obstruction. It seems clear however that in extremis the peace-makers would have peace, and peace on any terms. This was the gist of advice given to Hirohito by the Jushin in February, the declared conclusion of Kido in April, the underlying reason for Koiso's fall in April, the specific injunction of the Emperor to Suzuki on becoming premier which was known to all members of his cabinet.

(b) A series of conferences of the Supreme War Direction Council before Hirohito on the subject of continuing or terminating the war began on 8 June and continued through 14 August. At the 8 June meeting the war situation was reviewed. On 20 June the Emperor, supported by the Premier, Foreign Minister, and Navy Minister, declared for peace; the Army Minister and the two chiefs of staff did not concur. On 10 July the Emperor again urged haste in the moves to mediate through Russia, but Potsdam intervened. While the Government still awaited a Russian answer, the Hiroshima bomb was dropped on 6 August.

(c) Consideration of the Potsdam terms within the Supreme War Direction Council revealed the same three-to-three cleavage which first appeared at the Imperial conference on 20 June. On the morning of 9 August Premier Suzuki and Hirohito decided at once to accept the Potsdam terms; meetings and moves there-after were designed to legalize the decision and prepare the Imperial rescript. At the conclusive Imperial conference, on the night of 9–10 August, the Supreme War Direction Council still split three-to-three. It was necessary for the Emperor finally to repeat his desire for acceptance of the Potsdam terms.

(d) Indubitably the Hiroshima bomb and the rumor derived from interrogation of an American prison (B-29 pilot) who stated that an atom bomb attack on Tokyo was scheduled for 12 August introduced urgency in the minds of the Government and magnified the pressure behind its moves to end the war.

7. The sequence of events just recited also defines the effect of Russia's entry into the Pacific war on 8 August 1945. Coming 2 days after the Hiroshima bomb, the move neither defeated Japan nor materially hastened the acceptance of surrender nor changed the votes of the Supreme War Direction Council. Negotiation for Russia to intercede began the forepart of May 1945 in both Tokyo and Moscow. [Prince Fuminaro] Konoye, the intended emissary to the Soviets, stated to the Survey that while ostensibly he was to negotiate, he received direct and secret instructions from the Emperor to secure peace at any price, notwithstanding its severity. [Hisatsune] Sakomizu, the chief cabinet secretary, alleged that while awaiting the Russian answer on mediation, Suzuki and Togo decided that were it negative direct overtures would be made to the United States. Efforts toward peace through the Russians, fore-stalled by the imminent departure of Stalin and Molotov for Potsdam, were answered by the Red Army's advance into Manchuria. The Kwantung army [the Japanese army in China], already weakened by diversion of its units and logistics to bolster island defenses in the South and written off for the defense of Japan proper, faced inescapable defeat.

There is little point in attempting more precisely to impute Japan's uncondi-tional surrender to any one of the numerous causes which jointly and cumulatively were responsible for Japan's disaster. Concerning the absoluteness of her defeat there can be no doubt. The time lapse between military impotence and political ac-ceptance of the inevitable might have been shorter had the political structure of Japan permitted a more rapid and decisive determination of national policies. It seems clear, however, that air supremacy and its later exploitation over Japan proper was the major factor which determined the timing of Japan's surrender and obviated any need for invasion.

Based on a detailed investigation of all the facts and supported by the testimony of the surviving Japanese leaders involved, it is the Survey's opinion that certainly prior to 31 December 1945, and in all probability prior to 1 November 1945, Japan would have surrendered even if the atomic bombs had not been dropped, even if Russia had not entered the war, and even if no invasion had been planned or contemplated.

☒ E S S A Y S

In the two decades following World War II, most historians echoed the conclusions of Secretary of War Henry L. Stimson and other American leaders that the bomb was used to save lives and bring the war to a speedy conclusion. In the 1960s and early 1970s, however, many Cold War historians began to argue that the bomb's use was dictated less by military necessity than by a desire to intimidate the Russians and end the war in the Pacific before Soviet entry might complicate plans for the postwar occupation. Thus, the bombing of Hiroshima and Nagasaki marked not so much the end of World War II, but the beginning of the Cold War. Some historians attributed the bomb's use to the inexperience and insecurities of Harry Truman, who learned of the Manhattan Project only after he became president. Others, linking the droppings of the bomb to the wartime internment of Americans of Japanese ancestry, suggested that racism might have influenced the decision. Still others emphasized bureaucratic politics, secrecy, and the "technological fanaticism" that accompanied the growing use of weapons of mass destruction. According to Stanford University historian Barton J. Bernstein:

> By the early 1990s, most historians of the atomic bombing had come to conclude that the bomb was at least probably unnecessary, that the November 1945 invasion would probably (or definitely) have been unlikely even if the bomb had not been used, and that various alternative means, especially if pursued in some combination, would probably (or definitely) have ended the war without either the invasion or the bomb.

If most historians seemed to agree, the same could not be said of many other Americans, especially veterans organizations and conservatives in Congress and the press. Thus, the attempt by the Smithsonian Institution's National Air and Space Museum to mount a less than celebratory exhibition to coincide with the fiftieth anniversary of the bomb was met by a firestorm of criticism. The museum's curators and their allies in the historical profession were no match for the powerful cultural claims of the American "war story" or for the crude political power of congressional conservatives. Bowing to pressure, the secretary of the Smithsonian canceled the exhibition, and the museum's director was forced to resign.

In the first essay, historian Robert J. Maddox, a long-time critic of "revisionist" historians, defends the decision to drop the bomb. In the second essay, Gar Alperovitz, whose book *Atomic Diplomacy* (1965) was among the first to critically examine the bomb's use, reiterates the case against the decision.

The Biggest Decision: Why We Had
to Drop the Atomic Bomb

ROBERT JAMES MADDOX

On the morning of August 6, 1945, the American B-29 *Enola Gay* dropped an atomic bomb on the Japanese city of Hiroshima. Three days later another B-29, *Bock's Car,* released one over Nagasaki. Both caused enormous casualties and physical destruction. These two cataclysmic events have preyed upon the American conscience ever since. The furor over the Smithsonian Institution's *Enola Gay* exhibit and over the mushroom-cloud postage stamp last autumn are merely the most obvious examples. Harry S Truman and other officials claimed that the bombs caused Japan to surrender, thereby avoiding a bloody invasion. Critics have accused them of at best failing to explore alternatives, at worst of using the bombs primarily to make the Soviet Union "more manageable" rather than to defeat a Japan they knew already was on the verge of capitulation.

By any rational calculation Japan was a beaten nation by the summer of 1945. Conventional bombing had reduced many of its cities to rubble, blockade had strangled its importation of vitally needed materials, and its navy had sustained such heavy losses as to be powerless to interfere with the invasion everyone knew was coming. By late June advancing American forces had completed the conquest of Okinawa, which lay only 350 miles from the southernmost Japanese home island of Kyushu. They now stood poised for the final onslaught.

Rational calculations did not determine Japan's position. Although a peace faction within the government wished to end the war—provided certain conditions were met—militants were prepared to fight on regardless of consequences. They claimed to welcome an invasion of the home islands, promising to inflict such hideous casualties that the United States would retreat from its announced policy of unconditional surrender. The militarists held effective power over the government and were capable of defying the emperor, as they had in the past, on the ground that his civilian advisers were misleading him.

Okinawa provided a preview of what invasion of the home islands would entail. Since April 1 the Japanese had fought with a ferocity that mocked any notion that their will to resist was eroding. They had inflicted nearly 50,000 casualties on the invaders, many resulting from the first large-scale use of kamikazes. They also had dispatched the superbattleship *Yamato* on a suicide mission to Okinawa, where, after attacking American ships offshore, it was to plunge ashore to become a huge, doomed steel fortress. *Yamato* was sunk shortly after leaving port, but its mission symbolized Japan's willingness to sacrifice everything in an apparently hopeless cause.

The Japanese could be expected to defend their sacred homeland with even greater fervor, and kamikazes flying at short range promised to be even more devastating than at Okinawa. The Japanese had more than 2,000,000 troops in the home islands, were training millions of irregulars, and for some time had been

From "Why We Had to Drop the Atomic Bomb" by Robert James Maddox, from *American Heritage,* May/June 1995. Reprinted by permission of *American Heritage* magazine, a division of Forbes, Inc. © Forbes, Inc., 1995.

conserving aircraft that might have been used to protect Japanese cities against American bombers.

Reports from Tokyo indicated that Japan meant to fight the war to a finish. On June 8 an imperial conference adopted "The Fundamental Policy to Be Followed Henceforth in the Conduct of the War," which pledged to "prosecute the war to the bitter end in order to uphold the national polity, protect the imperial land, and accomplish the objectives for which we went to war." Truman had no reason to believe that the proclamation meant anything other than what it said.

Against this background, while fighting on Okinawa still continued, the President had his naval chief of staff, Adm. William D. Leahy, notify the Joint Chiefs of Staff (JCS) and the Secretaries of War and Navy that a meeting would be held at the White House on June 18. The night before the conference Truman wrote in his diary that "I have to decide Japanese strategy—shall we invade Japan proper or shall we bomb and blockade? That is my hardest decision to date. But I'll make it when I have all the facts."

Truman met with the chiefs at three-thirty in the afternoon. Present were Army Chief of Staff Gen. George C. Marshall, Army Air Force's Gen. Ira C. Eaker (sitting in for the Army Air Force's chief of staff, Henry H. Arnold, who was on an inspection tour of installations in the Pacific), Navy Chief of Staff Adm. Ernest J. King, Leahy (also a member of the JCS), Secretary of the Navy James Forrestal, Secretary of War Henry L. Stimson, and Assistant Secretary of War John J. McCloy. Truman opened the meeting, then asked Marshall for his views. Marshall was the dominant figure on the JCS. He was Truman's most trusted military adviser, as he had been President Franklin D. Roosevelt's.

Marshall reported that the chiefs, supported by the Pacific commanders Gen. Douglas MacArthur and Adm. Chester W. Nimitz, agreed that an invasion of Kyushu "appears to be the least costly worthwhile operation following Okinawa." Lodgment in Kyushu, he said, was necessary to make blockade and bombardment more effective and to serve as a staging area for the invasion of Japan's main island of Honshu. The chiefs recommended a target date of November 1 for the first phase, code-named Olympic, because delay would give the Japanese more time to prepare and because bad weather might postpone the invasion "and hence the end of the war" for up to six months. Marshall said that in his opinion, Olympic was "the only course to pursue." The chiefs also proposed that Operation Cornet be launched against Honshu on March 1, 1946.

Leahy's memorandum calling the meeting had asked for casualty projections which that invasion might be expected to produce. Marshall stated that campaigns in the Pacific had been so diverse "it is considered wrong" to make total estimates. All he would say was that casualties during the first thirty days on Kyushu should not exceed those sustained in taking Luzon in the Philippines—31,000 men killed, wounded, or missing in actin. "It is a grim fact," Marshall said, "that there is not an easy, bloodless way to victory in war." Leahy estimated a higher casualty rate similar to Okinawa, and King guessed somewhere in between.

King and Eaker, speaking for the Navy and the Army Air Forces respectively, endorsed Marshall's proposals. King said that he had become convinced that Kyushu was "the key to the success of any siege operations." He recommended that "we should do Kyushu now" and begin preparations for invading Honshu. Eaker "agreed completely" with Marshall. He said he had just received a message from Arnold also expressing "complete agreement." Air Force plans called for the use of forty groups of heavy bombers, which "could not be deployed without the use of airfields on Kyushu." Stimson and Forrestal concurred.

Truman summed up. He considered "the Kyushu plan all right from the military standpoint" and directed the chiefs to "go ahead with it." He said he "had hoped that there was a possibility of preventing an Okinawa from one end of Japan to the other," but "he was clear on the situation now" and was "quite sure" the chiefs should proceed with the plan. Just before the meeting adjourned, McCloy raised the possibility of avoiding an invasion by warning the Japanese that the United States would employ atomic weapons if there were no surrender. The ensuing discussion was inconclusive because the first test was a month away and no one could be sure the weapons would work.

In his memoirs Truman claimed that using atomic bombs prevented an invasion that would have cost 500,000 American lives. Other officials mentioned the same or even higher figures. Critics have assailed such statements as gross exaggerations designed to forestall scrutiny of Truman's real motives. They have given wide publicity to a report prepared by the Joint War Plans Committee (JWPC) for the chiefs' meeting with Truman. The committee estimated that the invasion of Kyushu, followed by that of Honshu, as the chiefs proposed, would cost approximately 40,000 dead, 150,000 wounded, and 3,500 missing in action for a total of 193,500 casualties.

That those responsible for a decision should exaggerate the consequences of alternatives is commonplace. Some who cite the JWPC report profess to see more sinister motives, insisting that such "low" casualty projections call into question the very idea that atomic bombs were used to avoid heavy losses. By discrediting that justification as a cover-up, they seek to bolster their contention that the bombs really were used to permit the employment of "atomic diplomacy" against the Soviet Union.

The notion that 193,500 anticipated casualties were too insignificant to have caused Truman to resort to atomic bombs might seem bizarre to anyone other than an academic, but let it pass. Those who have cited the JWPC report in countless op-ed pieces in newspapers and in magazine articles have created a myth by omitting key considerations: First, the report itself is studded with qualifications that casualties "are not subject to accurate estimate" and that the projection "is admittedly only an educated guess." Second, the figures never were conveyed to Truman. They were excised at high military echelons, which is why Marshall cited only estimates for the first thirty days on Kyushu. And indeed, subsequent Japanese troop buildups on Kyushu rendered the JWPC estimates totally irrelevant by the time the first atomic bomb was dropped.

Another myth that has attained wide attention is that at least several of Truman's top military advisers later informed him that using atomic bombs against Japan would be militarily unnecessary or immoral, or both. There is no persuasive evidence that any of them did so. None of the Joint Chiefs ever made such a claim, although one inventive author has tried to make it appear that Leahy did by braiding together several unrelated passages from the admiral's memoirs. Actually, two days after Hiroshima, Truman told aides that Leahy had "said up to the last that it wouldn't go off."

Neither MacArthur no Nimitz ever communicated to Truman any change of mind about the need for invasion or expressed reservations about using the bombs. When first informed about their imminent use only days before Hiroshima, MacArthur responded with a lecture on the future of atomic warfare and even after Hiroshima strongly recommended that the invasion go forward. Nimitz, from whose jurisdiction the atomic strikes would be launched, was notified in early 1945. "This sounds fine," he told the courier, "but this is only February. Can't we get one sooner?" Nimitz later would join Air Force generals Carl D. Spaatz, Nathan Twining, and Curtis LeMay in recommending that a third bomb be dropped on Tokyo.

Only Dwight D. Eisenhower later claimed to have remonstrated against the use of the bomb. In his *Crusade in Europe,* published in 1948, he wrote that when Secretary Stimson informed him during the Potsdam Conference of plans to use the bomb, he replied that he hoped "we would never have to use such a thing against any enemy," because he did not want the United States to be the first to use such a weapon. He added, "My views were merely personal and immediate reactions; they were not based on any analysis of the subject." . . .

The best that can be said about Eisenhower's memory is that it had become flawed by the passage of time. Stimson was in Potsdam and Eisenhower in Frankfurt on July 16, when word came of the successful test. Aside from a brief conversation at a flag-raising ceremony in Berlin on July 20, the only other time they met was at Ike's headquarters on July 27. By then orders already had been sent to the Pacific to use the bombs if Japan had not yet surrendered. Notes made by one of Stimson's aides indicate that there was a discussion of atomic bombs, but there is no mention of any protest on Eisenhower's part. Even if there had been, two factors must be kept in mind. Eisenhower had commanded Allied forces in Europe, and his opinion on how close Japan was to surrender would have carried no special weight. More important, Stimson left for home immediately after the meeting and could not have personally conveyed Ike's sentiments to the President, who did not return to Washington until after Hiroshima.

On July 8 the Combined Intelligence Committee submitted to the American and British Combined Chiefs of Staff a report entitled "Estimate of the Enemy Situation." The committee predicted that as Japan's position continued to deteriorate, it might "make a serious effort to use the U.S.S.R. [then a neutral] as a mediator in ending the war." Tokyo also would put out "intermittent peace feelers" to "weaken the determination of the United Nations to fight to the bitter end, or to create inter-allied dissension." While the Japanese people would be willing to make large concessions to end the war, "For a surrender to be acceptable to the Japanese army, it would be necessary for the military leaders to believe that it would not entail discrediting warrior tradition and that it would permit the ultimate resurgence of a military Japan."

Small wonder that American officials remained unimpressed when Japan proceeded to do exactly what the committee predicted. On July 12 Japanese Foreign Minister Shigenori Togo instructed Ambassador Naotaki Sato in Moscow to inform the Soviets that the emperor wished to send a personal envoy, Prince Fuminaro Konoye, in an attempt "to restore peace with all possible speed." Although he realized Konoye could not reach Moscow before the Soviet leader Joseph Stalin and Foreign Minister V.M. Molotov left to attend a Big Three meeting scheduled to begin in Potsdam on the fifteenth, Togo sought to have negotiations begin as soon as they returned.

American officials had long since been able to read Japanese diplomatic traffic through a process known as the MAGIC intercepts. Army intelligence (G-2) prepared for General Marshall its interpretation of Togo's message the next day. The report listed several possible constructions, the most probable being that the Japanese "governing clique" was making a coordinated effort to "stave off defeat" through Soviet intervention and an "appeal to war weariness in the United States." The report added that Undersecretary of State Joseph C. Grew, who had spent ten years in Japan as ambassador, "agrees with these conclusions."

Some have claimed that Togo's overture to the Soviet Union, together with attempts by some minor Japanese officials in Switzerland and other neutral countries to get peace talks started through the Office of Strategic Services (OSS), constituted clear evidence that the Japanese were near surrender. Their sole prerequisite was retention of their sacred emperor, whose unique cultural/religious status within the Japanese polity they would not compromise. If only the United States had extended assurances about the emperor, according to this view, much bloodshed and the atomic bombs would have been unnecessary.

A careful reading of the MAGIC intercepts of subsequent exchanges between Togo and Sato provides no evidence that retention of the emperor was the sole obstacle to peace. What they show instead is that the Japanese Foreign Office was trying to cut a deal through the Soviet Union that would have permitted Japan to retain its political system and its prewar empire intact. Even the most lenient American officials could not have countenanced such a settlement.

Togo on July 17 informed Sato that "we are not asking the Russians' mediation in *anything like unconditional surrender* [emphasis added]." During the following weeks Sato pleaded with his superiors to abandon hope of Soviet intercession and to approach the United States directly to find out what peace terms would be offered. "There is . . . no alternative but immediate unconditional surrender," he cabled on July 31, and he bluntly informed Togo that "your way of looking at things and the actual situation in the Eastern Area may be seen to be absolutely contradictory." The Foreign Ministry ignored his pleas and continued to seek Soviet help even after Hiroshima.

"Peace feelers" by Japanese officials abroad seemed no more promising from the American point of view. Although several of the consular personnel and military attachés engaged in these activities claimed important connections at home, none produced verification. Had the Japanese government sought only an assurance about the emperor, all it had to do was grant one of these men authority to begin talks through the OSS. Its failure to do so led American officials to assume that those involved were either well-meaning individuals acting alone or that they were being orchestrated by Tokyo. Grew characterized such "peace feelers" as "familiar weapons of psychological warfare" designed to "divide the Allies."

Some American officials, such as Stimson and Grew, nonetheless wanted to signal the Japanese that they might retain the emperorship in the form of a constitutional monarchy. Such an assurance might remove the last stumbling block to surrender, if not when it was issued, then later. Only an imperial rescript would bring about an orderly surrender, they argued, without which Japanese forces would fight to the last man regardless of what the government in Tokyo did. Besides, the emperor could serve as a stabilizing factor during the transition to peacetime.

There were many arguments against an American initiative. Some opposed retaining such an undemocratic institution on principle and because they feared it might later serve as a rallying point for future militarism. Should that happen, as one assistant Secretary of State put it, "those lives already spent will have been sacrificed in vain, and lives will be lost again in the future." Japanese hard-liners were certain to exploit an overture as evidence that losses sustained at Okinawa had weakened American resolve and to argue that continued resistance would bring further concessions. Stalin, who earlier had told an American envoy that he favored abolishing the emperorship because the ineffectual Hirohito might be succeeded by "an energetic and vigorous figure who could cause trouble," was just as certain to interpret it as a treacherous effort to end the war before the Soviets could share in the spoils.

There were domestic considerations as well. Roosevelt had announced the unconditional surrender policy in early 1943, and it since had become a slogan of the war. He also had advocated that peoples everywhere should have the right to choose their own form of government, and Truman had publicly pledged to carry out his predecessor's legacies. For him to have formally *guaranteed* continuance of the emperorship, as opposed to merely accepting it on American terms pending free elections, as he later did, would have constituted a blatant repudiation of his own promises.

Nor was that all. Regardless of the emperor's actual role in Japanese aggression, which is still debated, much wartime propaganda had encouraged Americans to regard Hirohito as no less a war criminal than Adolf Hitler or Benito Mussolini. Although Truman said on several occasions that he had no objection to retaining the emperor, he understandably refused to make the first move. The ultimatum he issued from Potsdam on July 26 did not refer specifically to the emperorship. All it said was that occupation forces would be removed after "a peaceful and responsible" government had been established according to the "freely expressed will of the Japanese people. When the Japanese rejected the ultimatum rather than at last inquire whether they might retain the emperor, Truman permitted the plans for using the bombs to go forward.

Reliance on MAGIC intercepts and the "peace feelers" to gauge how near Japan was to surrender is misleading in any case. The army, not the Foreign Office, controlled the situation. Intercepts of Japanese military communications, designated ULTRA, provided no reason to believe the army was even considering surrender. Japanese Imperial Headquarters had correctly guessed that the next operation after Okinawa would be Kyushu and was making every effort to bolster its defenses there.

General Marshall reported on July 24 that there were "approximately 500,000 troops in Kyushu" and that more were on the way. ULTRA identified new units arriving almost daily. MacArthur's G-2 reported on July 29 that "this threatening development, if not checked, may grow to a point where we attack on a ratio of one (1) to one (1) which is not the recipe for victory." By the time the first atomic bomb fell, ULTRA indicated that there were 560,000 troops in southern Kyushu (the actual figure was closer to 900,000), and projections for November 1 placed the number at 680,000. A report, for medical purposes, of July 31 estimated that total battle and nonbattle casualties might run as high as 394,859 *for the Kyushu operation alone.* This figure did not include those men expected to be killed outright, for obviously they would require no medical attention. Marshall regarded Japanese defenses as so formidable that even after Hiroshima he asked MacArthur to consider alternate landing sites and began contemplating the use of atomic bombs as tactical weapons to support the invasion.

The thirty-day casualty projection of 31,000 Marshall had given Truman at the June 18 strategy meeting had become meaningless. It had been based on the assumption that the Japanese had about 350,00 defenders in Kyushu and that naval and air interdiction would preclude significant reinforcement. But the Japanese buildup since that time meant that the defenders would have nearly twice the number of troops available by "X-day" than earlier assumed. The assertion that apprehensions about casualties are insufficient to explain Truman's use of the bombs, therefore, cannot be taken seriously. On the contrary, as Winston Churchill wrote after a conversation with him at Potsdam, Truman was tormented by "the terrible responsibilities that rested upon him in regard to the unlimited effusions of American blood."

Some historians have argued that while the first bomb *might* have been required to achieve Japanese surrender, dropping the second constituted a needless barbarism. The record shows otherwise. American officials believed more than one bomb would be necessary because they assumed Japanese hard-liners would minimize the first explosion or attempt to explain it away as some sort of natural catastrophe, precisely what they did. The Japanese minister of war, for instance, at first refused even to admit that the Hiroshima bomb was atomic. A few hours after Nagasaki he told the cabinet that "the Americans appeared to have one hundred atomic bombs . . . they could drop three per day. The next target might well be Tokyo."

Even after both bombs had fallen and Russia entered the war, Japanese militants insisted on such lenient peace terms that moderates knew there was no sense even transmitting them to the United States. Hirohito had to intervene personally on two occasions during the next few days to induce hard-liners to abandon their conditions and to accept the American stipulation that the emperor's authority "shall be subject to the Supreme Commander of the Allied Powers." That the militarists would have accepted such a settlement before the bombs is farfetched, to say the least.

Some writers have argued that the cumulative effects of battlefield defeats, conventional bombing, and naval blockade already had defeated Japan. Even without extending assurances about the emperor, all the United States had to do was wait. The most frequently cited basis for this contention is the *United States Strategic Bombing Survey,* published in 1946, which stated that Japan would have surrendered by November 1 "even if the atomic bombs had not been dropped, even if Russia had not entered the war, and even if no invasion had been planned or contemplated." Recent scholarship by the historian Robert P. Newman and others has demonstrated that the survey was "cooked" by those who prepared it to arrive at such a conclusion. No matter. This or any other document based on information available only after the war ended is irrelevant with regard to what Truman could have known at the time.

What often goes unremarked is that when the bombs were dropped, fighting was still going on in the Philippines, China, and elsewhere. Every day that the war continued thousands of prisoners of war had to live and die in abysmal conditions, and there were rumors that the Japanese intended to slaughter them if the home-land was invaded. Truman was Commander in Chief of the American armed forces, and he had a duty to the men under his command not shared by those sitting in moral judgment decades later. Available evidence points to the conclusion that he acted for the reason he said he did: to end a bloody war that would have become far bloodier had invasion proved necessary. One can only imagine what would have happened if tens of thousands of American boys had died or been wounded on Japanese soil and then it had become known that Truman had chosen not to use weapons that might have ended the war months sooner.

Hiroshima: Historians Reassess

GAR ALPEROVITZ

Earlier this year, the nation witnessed a massive explosion surrounding the Smith-sonian Institution's planned *Enola Gay* exhibit. As the 50th anniversary of the August 6, 1945, atomic bombing of Hiroshima approaches, Americans are about to receive another newspaper and television barrage.

Any serious attempt to understand the depth of feeling the story of the atomic bomb still arouses must confront two critical realities. First, there is a rapidly expanding gap between what the expert scholarly community now knows and what the public has been taught. Second, a steady narrowing of the questions in dispute on the most sophisticated studies has sharpened some of the only controversial issues in the historical debate.

Consider the following assessment:

> Careful scholarly treatment of the records and manuscripts opened over the past few years has greatly enhanced our understanding of why the Truman administration used atomic weapons against Japan. Experts continue to disagree on some issues, but critical questions have been answered. The consensus among scholars is that the bomb was not needed to avoid an invasion of Japan and to end the war within a relatively short time. It is clear that alternatives to the bomb existed and that Truman and his advisers knew it.

The author of that statement is not a revisionist; he is L. Samuel Walker, chief historian of the U.S. Nuclear Regulatory Commission. Nor is he alone in that opinion. Walker is summarizing the findings of modern specialists in his literature review in the Winter 1990 issue of *Diplomatic History*. Another expert review, by University of Illinois historian Robert Messer, concludes that recently discovered documents have been "devastating" to the traditional idea that using the bomb was the only way to avoid an invasion of Japan that might have cost many more lives.

Even allowing for continuing areas of dispute, these judgments are so far from the conventional wisdom that there is obviously something strange going on. One source of the divide between expert research and public understanding stems from a common feature of all serious scholarship: as in many areas of specialized re-search, perhaps a dozen truly knowledgeable experts are at the forefront of modern studies of the decision to use the atomic bomb. A second circle of generalists—historians concerned, for instance, with the Truman administration, with World War II in general, or even with the history of air power—depends heavily on the archival digging and analysis of the first circle. Beyond this second group are authors of general textbooks and articles and, still further out, journalists and other popular writers.

One can, of course, find many historians who still believe that the atomic bomb was needed to avoid an invasion. Among the inner circle of experts, however, conclusions that are at odds with this official rationale have long been commonplace. Indeed, as early as 1946 the U.S. Strategic Bombing Survey, in its report *Japan's Struggle to End the War,* concluded that "certainly prior to 31 December 1945, and in all probability prior to 1 November 1945, Japan would have surrendered even if the atomic bombs had not been dropped, even if Russia had not entered the war, and even if no invasion had been planned or contemplated."

Similarly, a top-secret April 1946 War Department study, *Use of Atomic Bomb on Japan,* declassified during the 1970s but brought to broad public attention only in 1989, found that "the Japanese leaders had decided to surrender and were merely looking for sufficient pretext to convince the die-hard Army Group that Japan had lost the war and must capitulate to the Allies." This official document judged that Russia's early-August entry into the war "would almost certainly have furnished this pretext, and would have been sufficient to convince all responsible leaders that surrender was unavoidable." The study concluded that even an initial November 1945 landing on the southern Japanese island of Kyushu would have been only a "remote" possibility and that the full invasion of Japan in the sprint of 1946 would not have occurred.

Military specialists who have examined Japanese decision-making have added to expert understanding that the bombing was unnecessary. For instance, political scientist Robert Pape's study, "Why Japan Surrendered," which appeared in the Fall 1993 issue of *International Security,* details Japan's military vulnerability, particularly its shortages of everything from ammunition and fuel to trained personnel: "Japan's military position was so poor that its leaders would likely have surrendered before invasion, and at roughly the same time in August 1945, even if the United States had not employed strategic bombing or the atomic bomb." In this situation, Pape stresses, "The Soviet invasion of Manchuria on August 9 raised Japan's military vulnerability to a very high level. The Soviet offensive ruptured Japanese lines immediately, and rapidly penetrated deep into the rear. Since the Kwantung Army was thought to be Japan's premier fighting force, this had a devastating effect on Japanese calculations of the prospects for home island defense." Pape adds, "If their best forces were so easily sliced to pieces, the unavoidable implication was that the less well-equipped and trained forces assembled for [the last decisive home island battle] had no chance of success against American forces that were even more capable than the Soviets."

Whether the use of the atomic bomb was in fact necessary is, of course, a different question from whether it was believed to be necessary at the time. Walker's summary of the expert literature is important because it underscores the availability of the alternatives to using the bomb, and because it documents that "Truman and his advisers knew" of the alternatives.

Several major strands of evidence have pushed many specialists in the direction of this startling conclusion. The United States had long since broken the enemy codes, and the president was informed of all important Japanese cable traffic. A critical message of July 12, 1945—just before Potsdam—showed that the Japanese emperor himself had decided to intervene to attempt to end the war. In his private journal, Truman bluntly characterized this message as the "telegram from [the] Jap Emperor asking for peace."

Other intercepted messages suggested that the main obstacle to peace was the continued Allied demand for unconditional surrender. Although the expert literature once mainly suggested that only one administration official—Undersecretary of State Joseph Grew—urged a change in the surrender formula to provide assurances for Japan's emperor, it is now clear that with the exception of Secretary of State James Byrnes, the entire top echelon of the U.S. government advocated such a change. By June 1945, in fact, Franklin Roosevelt's secretary of state, Edward Stettinius (who remained in office until July 3); the undersecretary of state; the secretary of war; the secretary of the navy; the president's chief of staff, Admiral William Leahy; and Army Chief of Staff General George Marshall—plus all the members of the Joint Chiefs of Staff (JCS)—had in one way or another urged a clarification of the surrender formula. So, too, had the British military and civilian Leadership, including Prime Minister Winston Churchill. Along with Grew, the Joint Chiefs in particular recommended that a statement be issued to coincide with the fall of Okinawa, on or around June 21.

At that time, war crimes trials were about to begin in Germany; the idea that the emperor might be hanged was a possibility Tokyo could not ignore. Because the Japanese regarded the emperor as a deity—more like Jesus or the Buddha than an ordinary human being—most top American officials deemed offering some assurances for the continuance of the dynasty an absolute necessity. The Joint Staff Planners, for instance, advised the Joint Chiefs in an April 25, 1945, report that "unless a definition of unconditional surrender can be given which is acceptable to the Japanese, there is no alternative to annihilation and no prospect that the threat of absolute defeat will bring about capitulation."

Secretary of War Henry Stimson took essentially the same position in a July 2 memorandum to Truman. Moreover, he offered his assessment that a surrender formula could be acceptable to the Japanese, and stated, "I think the Japanese nation has the mental intelligence and versatile capacity in such a crisis to recognize the folly of a fight to the finish and to accept the proffer of what will amount to an unconditional surrender."

As University of Southern Mississippi military historian John Ray Skates has noted in his book, *The Invasion of Japan: Alternative to the Bomb,* "[General] Marshall, who believed that retention [of the emperor] was a military necessity, asked that the members [of the Joint Chiefs of Staff] draft a memorandum to the president recommending that the Allies 'do nothing to indicate that the emperor might be removed from office upon unconditional surrender.'"

The other option that seemed likely to bring an end to the fighting concerned the Soviets. Joseph Stalin had promised to enter the war against Japan roughly three months after the May 8 defeat of Germany, which put the target date on or around August 8. Earlier in the war, the United States had sought Russia's help primarily to pin down Japanese armies in Manchuria and thus make a U.S. invasion of the home islands easier. By midsummer, however, Japan's position had deteriorated so much that top U.S. military planners believed the mere shock of a Red Army attack might be sufficient to bring about surrender and thus make an invasion unnecessary.

As early as February 1955, Harvard historian Ernest May, in an article in *Pacific Historical Review,* observed that the "Japanese diehards . . . had acknowledged since 1941 that Japan could not fight Russia as well as the United States and Britain." May also observed that because Moscow had been an outlet for various Japanese peace feelers, when the Soviet declaration of war finally occurred it "discouraged Japanese hopes of secretly negotiating terms of peace." Moreover, in the end, "the Emperor's appeal [to end the war] probably resulted, therefore, from the Russian action, but it could not, in any event, have been long in coming."

The importance to U.S. leaders of the "Russian shock option" for ending the war—which was widely discussed even in the 1945 press—disappeared from most scholarly studies during the Cold War. We now know, however, that as of April 29, 1945, the Joint Intelligence Committee (JIC), in a report titled *Unconditional Surrender of Japan,* informed the JCS that increasing "numbers of informed Japanese, both military and civilian, already realize the inevitability of absolute defeat." The JIC further advised that "the increasing effects of air-sea blockade, the progressive and cumulative devastation wrought by strategic bombing, and the collapse of Germany (with its implications regarding redeployment) should make this realization widespread within the year."

The JIC pointed out, however, that a Soviet decision to join with the United States and Great Britain would have enormous force and would dramatically alter the equation: "The entry of the USSF into the war would, together with the foregoing factors, convince most Japanese at once of the inevitability of complete defeat." [Emphasis added.]

By mid-June, Marshall advised Truman directly that "the impact of Russian entry [into the war] on the already hopeless Japanese may well be the decisive action levering them into capitulation at the time or shortly thereafter if we land in Japan." Again, Marshall's advice to Truman came almost a month before news of the emperor's personal intervention was received and four and a half months before even a preliminary Kyushu landing was to take place.

In July, the British general Sir Hastings Ismay, chief of staff to the minister of defence, summarized the conclusions of the latest U.S.-U.K. intelligence studies for Churchill in this way: "When Russia came into the war against Japan, the Japanese would probably wish to get out on almost any terms short of the dethronement of the Emperor."

On several occasions, Truman made abundantly clear that the main reason he went to Potsdam to meet Stalin was to make sure the Soviets would, in fact, enter the war. The atomic bomb had not yet been tested, and, as Truman later stated in his memoirs, "If the test [of the atomic bomb] should fail, then it would be even more important to us to bring about a surrender before we had to make a physical conquest of Japan."

Some of the most important modern documentary discoveries relate to this point. After Stalin confirmed that the Red Army would indeed enter the war, the president's "lost" Potsdam journal (found in 1978) shows him writing: "Fini Japs when that comes about." And the next day, in an exuberant letter to his wife, Truman wrote that with the Soviet declaration of war, "we'll end the war a year sooner now, and think of the kids who won't be killed!"

It is also obvious that if assurances for the emperor were put forward together with the Soviet attack, the likelihood of an early Japanese surrender would be even greater. The JIC recognized this in its April 29, 1945, report, observing that there first had to be a realization of the "inevitability of defeat," which the JIC judged a Soviet declaration of war would produce. Once "the Japanese people, as well as their leaders, were persuaded both that absolute defeat was inevitable and that unconditional surrender did not imply national annihilation, surrender might follow fairly quickly."

Reexamining the Record

Many more documentary finds support the view that top U.S. officials, including Truman, understood that use of the bomb was not required to end the war before an invasion. However, as Robert Messer observed in the August 1985 issue of *Bulletin of the Atomic Scientists,* the implications of Truman's diary and letters alone

> for the orthodox defense of the bomb's use are devastating: if Soviet entry alone would end the war before an invasion of Japan, the use of atomic bombs cannot be justified as the only alternative to that invasion. This does not mean, of course, that having the bomb was not useful. But it does mean that for Truman the end of the war seemed at hand; the issue was no longer when the war would end, but how and on whose terms. If he believed that the war would end with Soviet entry in mid-August, then he must have realized that if the bombs were not used before that date they might well not be used at all.

Minimally, the president's contemporaneous diary entries, together with his letter to his wife, raise fundamental questions about Truman's subsequent claims that the atomic bomb was used because it was the only way to avoid "a quarter million," "a half million," or "millions" of casualties.

Or consider the views of the late historian Herbert Feis, who was for decades the voice of orthodox opinion on the subject and a friend of Stimson's as well as an adviser to three World War II–era cabinet secretaries. It is rarely noted that Feis recognized—and emphasized—that by July 1945 there was a very good chance the war could have been ended without dropping the atomic bombs on Hiroshima and Nagasaki had the United States combined even the mere threat of

> Russian attack with assurances for the emperor. He wrote in his 1961 work *Japan Subdued: The Atomic Bomb and the End of the War in the Pacific:* "I think it may be concluded that . . . the fighting would have continued into July at least, unless . . . the American and Soviet governments together had let it be known that unless Japan laid down its arms at once, the Soviet Union was going to enter the war. That, along with a promise to spare the Emperor, might well have made an earlier bid for surrender effective."

Feis's only reservation was that Stalin might not have wanted to signal his willingness to join the war against Japan at this time, a rather odd idea that many documents now available show to be illusory. In addition, if a mere announcement of Soviet intentions might have forced a surrender, as the JIC pointed out, the reality of the attack would have been even more powerful.

Related to this question is the fact that so many World War II military leaders are on record as stating that the bomb was not needed. Dwight Eisenhower, for instance, reported in his 1963 *Mandate for Change* that he had the following reaction when Secretary of War Stimson informed him that the atomic bomb would be used:

> During his recitation of the relevant facts, I had been conscious of a feeling of depression and so I voiced to him my grave misgivings, first on the basis of my belief that Japan was already defeated and that dropping the bomb was completely unnecessary, and secondly because I thought that our country should avoid shocking world opinion by the use of a weapon whose employment was, I thought, no longer mandatory as a measure to save American lives.

Historian Stephen Ambrose notes in his biography of Eisenhower that he also clearly stated that he personally urged Truman not to use the atomic bomb. Eisenhower's opinion in other public statements in the early 1960s was identical: "Japan was, at that very moment, seeking some way to surrender with a minimum loss of 'face.' . . . It wasn't necessary to hit them with that awful thing."

Admiral William Leahy, President Truman's chief of staff and the top official who presided over meetings of both the JCS and the U.S.-U.K. Combined Chiefs of Staff, also minced few words in his 1950 memoirs *I Was There:* "The use of this barbarous weapon at Hiroshima and Nagasaki was of no material assistance in our war against Japan. . . . []n being the first to use it, we . . . adopted an ethical standard common to the barbarians of the Dark Ages. I was not taught to make war in that fashion, and wars cannot be won by destroying women and children."

The Army Air Forces commander, General Henry "Hap" Arnold, put it this way in his 1949 *Global Mission:* "It always appeared to us that atomic bomb or no atomic bomb the Japanese were already on the verge of collapse." Britain's General Ismay said in his memoirs that his initial reaction on hearing of the successful atomic test was one of "revulsion." He had previously observed: "for some time past it had been firmly in my mind that the Japanese were tottering."

The strong language used by high-level military figures often comes as a shock to those not familiar with the documents, memoirs, and diaries now available. Defenders of the decision sometimes suggest that such views represent only after-the-fact judgments or are the result of interservice rivalry. However, in view of the traditional unwillingness of uniformed military officers to criticize their civilian superiors—and also the extraordinary importance of the historic issue—it is difficult to explain so many statements, made with such force, on such grounds alone.

All of these assessments also bear on the question of the number of lives that might possibly have been lost if the atomic bomb had not been used. Over the last decade, scholars of very different political orientations, including Barton Bernstein, Rufus Miles Jr., and John Ray Skates, have all separately examined World War II U.S. military planning documents on this subject. These documents indicate that if an initial November 1945 landing on Kyushu had gone forward, estimates of the number of lives that would have been lost (and therefore possibly saved by use of the atomic bombs) were in the range of 20,000 to 26,000. In the unlikely event that a subsequent full-scale invasion had been mounted in 1946, the maximum estimate found in such documents was 46,000.

Even these numbers, however, confuse the central issue: If the war could have been ended by clarifying the terms of surrender and/or allowing the shock of the Russian attack to set in, then no lives would have been lost in an invasion. Fighting was minimal in August 1945 as both sides regrouped, and the most that can be said is that the atomic bombs might have saved the lives that would have been lost in the time required to arrange final surrender terms with Japan. That saving lives was not the highest priority, however, seems obvious from the choices made in July: If the United States really wished to end the war as quickly and as surely as possible—and to save as many lives as possible—then, as Marshall pointed out as early as June, the full force of the Russian shock plus assurances for the emperor's future could not be left out of the equation.

Moreover, if we accept Stimson's subsequent judgment that "history might find" that the decision to delay assurances for the emperor "had prolonged the war," then, as historian Martin Sherwin noted in the October 19, 1981, *Nation,* the atomic bomb may well have cost lives. Why? Lives were lost during the roughly two-month delay in clarifying the surrender terms. Many historians believe the delay was caused by the decision to wait for the atomic test at Alamogordo, New Mexico, on July 16, and then, the bombs' use on Japan in early August. Several thousand American soldiers and sailors died between Grew's initial May 28 proposal to clarify the "unconditional" terms and the final surrender on August 14.

The Path Not Taken

Some of the basic questions debated in the expert literature concern why alternatives for ending the war were not pursued. Little dispute remains about why the Soviet option was discarded, however. Once the bomb was proven to work, the president reversed course entirely and attempted to stall a Red Army attack. A week after the Alamogordo test, for instance, Churchill observed that "it is quite clear that the United States do not at the present time desire Russian participation in the war against Japan." Similarly, the diary of Navy secretary James Forrestal indicates that by July 28 Secretary of State Byrnes was "most anxious to get the Japanese affair over with before the Russians got in." And the private journal of Byrnes's personal assistant, Walter Brown, confirms that Byrnes was "hoping for time, believing [that] after [the] atomic bomb Japan will surrender and Russia will not get in so much on the kill, thereby being in a position to press claims against China." Meanwhile, every effort was made to speed up production and delivery of the weapon. These efforts were successful: Hiroshima was bombed on August 6, two days before Russia declared war on Japan. Nagasaki was bombed on the 9th.

A traditional argument as to why the surrender formula for Japan was not modified is that it was politically impossible for Truman to alter the "unconditional" language, that to do so would make him look soft on Japan. There is certainly evidence that some people felt this way, notably Roosevelt's ailing former secretary of state, Cordell Hull, and Assistant Secretaries of State Archibald MacLeish and Dean Acheson. There is some evidence (mainly from the period after the bombings) that Byrnes feared criticism if the rhetoric of unconditional surrender was abandoned. However, it does not appear that the president himself was much worried about such matters. Truman's views, as described in contemporaneous records, indicate that he generally seemed to favor altering the terms, and there is little evidence of concern about political opposition. Stimson's diary reports of July 24 and August 10, in particular, make it clear that neither Byrnes nor Truman were at all "obdurate" on the question. And, of course, a few days after the bombings the Japanese were given the assurances they sought: Japan would still have an emperor.

Moreover, many leading newspapers at the time were pressing for—rather than resisting—a clarification of terms. The *Washington Post,* for instance challenged the "unconditional surrender" formula head on in a June 11, 1945, editorial titled "Fatal Phrase": "President Truman, of course, has already stated that there is no thought of destroying the Japanese people, but such assurances, even from so high a source, are negated by that fatal phrase." The *Post* stressed that the two words

> remain a great stumbling block to any propaganda effort and the perpetual trump card of the Japanese die-hards for their game of national suicide. Let us amend them; let us give Japan conditions, harsh conditions certainly, and conditions that will render her diplomatically and militarily impotent for generations. But also let us somehow assure those Japanese who are ready to plead for peace that, even on our terms, life and peace will be better than war and annihilation.

Similarly, recent research has indicated that far from pushing the president to maintain a hard line, many leading Republicans urged him to modify the terms to get an early surrender, preferably before the Soviets entered the war. Former president Herbert Hoover, for instance, went to see Truman about the issue in late May, and on July 3, the *Washington Post* reported that "Senator [Wallace] White [Jr.] of Maine, minority leader, declared . . . that the Pacific war might end quickly if President Truman would state specifically just what unconditional surrender means for the Japanese."

The "Preferred" Options

Martin Sherwin has suggested that the atomic bomb was used because it was "preferred" to the other options. Although it is sometimes thought that sheer momentum carried the day, there is no doubt that it was, in fact, an active choice. When Truman and Byrnes cut the critical assurances to the emperor out of paragraph 12 of the draft Potsdam Proclamation, they did so against the recommendation of virtually the entire top American and British leadership. Truman and Byrnes had to reverse the thrust of a near-unanimous judgment that the terms should be clarified. Truman's journal also indicates that he understood that the proclamation in final form— without the key passage—was not likely to be accepted by Japan.

If the Soviet option for ending the war was shelved for political and diplomatic reasons—and if the political reasons for not modifying the surrender formula no longer look so solid—is there any other explanation for why the Japanese were not told their emperor would not be harmed, that he could stay on the throne in some innocuous position like that of the king of England? Some historians, of course, continue to hold that the bomb's use was militarily necessary—or perhaps inevitable because of the inherited technological, bureaucratic, and military momentum that built up during the war. Others suggest that because huge sums had been spent developing the weapon, political leaders found it impossible not to use it. Still others have probed the intricacies of decision-making through an analysis of bureaucratic dynamics.

Of greatest interest, perhaps, is another factor. The traditional argument has been that solely military considerations were involved in the decision to use the bomb; increasingly, however, the once controversial idea that diplomatic issues—especially the hope of strengthening the West against the Soviet Union—played a significant role in the decision has gained widespread scholarly acceptance. Although analysts still debate exactly how much weight to accord such factors, that they were involved is now well established for most experts.

Modern research findings, for instance, clearly demonstrate that from April 1945 on, top American officials calculated that using the atomic bomb would enormously bolster U.S. diplomacy vis-à-vis the Soviet Union in negotiations over postwar Europe and the Far East. The atomic bomb was not, in fact, initially brought to Truman's attention because of its relationship to the war against Japan, but because of its likely impact on diplomacy. In late April, in the midst of an explosive confrontation with Stalin over the Polish issue, Secretary of War Stimson urged discussion of the bomb because, as he told Truman, it had "such a bearing on our present foreign relations and . . . such an important effect upon all my thinking in this field."

Stimson, for his part, regarded the atomic bomb as what he called the "master card" of diplomacy toward Russia. However, he believed that sparring with the Soviet Union in the early spring, before the weapon was demonstrated, would be counterproductive. Before a mid-May meeting of a cabinet-level committee considering Far Eastern issues, Stimson observed that "the questions cut very deep and [were] powerfully connected with our success with S-1 [the atomic bomb]." Two days later, he noted in his diary that

> I tried to point out the difficulties which existed and I thought it premature to ask those questions; at least we were not yet in a position to answer them. . . . It may be necessary to have it out with Russian on her relations to Manchuria and Port Arthur and various other parts of North China, and also the relations of China to us. Over any such tangled weave of problems the [atomic bomb] secret would be dominant and yet we will not know until after that time probably . . . whether this is a weapon in our hands or not. We think it will be shortly afterwards, but it seems a terrible thing to gamble with such big stakes in diplomacy without having your master card in your hand.

Stimson's argument for delaying diplomatic fights with the Soviet Union was also described in another mid-May diary entry after a conversation with Assistant Secretary of War John McCloy:

> The time now and the method now to deal with Russia was to keep our mouths shut and let our actions speak for words. The Russians will understand them better than anything else. It is a case where we have got to regain the lead and perhaps do it in a pretty rough and realistic way. . . .This [is] a place where we really held all the cards. I called it a royal straight flush and we mustn't be a fool about the way we play it. They can't get along without our help and industries and we have coming into action a weapon which will be unique. Now the thing is not to get into unnecessary quarrels by talking too much and not to indicate any weakness by talking too much; let our actions speak for themselves.

Stimson's files indicate that Truman had come to similar conclusions roughly a month after taking office. Quite specifically—and against the advice of Churchill, who wanted an early meeting with Stalin before American troops were withdrawn from Europe—the president postponed his only diplomatic encounter with the Soviet leader because he first wanted to know for certain that the still-untested atomic bomb actually worked. Stimson's papers indicate the president's view was that he would have "more cards" later. In a 1949 interview, Truman recalled telling a close associate before the test, "If it explodes as I think it will I'll certainly have a hammer on those boys" (meaning, it seemed clear, the Russians as well as the Japanese).

Evidence in the Stimson diaries suggests that the broad strategy was probably secretly explained to Ambassador Averell Harriman and British foreign minister Anthony Eden at this time. Scientists in the field also got an inkling that there was a link between the Potsdam meeting with Stalin and the atomic test. J. Robert Oppenheimer, for instance, later testified before the U.S. Atomic Energy Commission that "I don't think there was any time where we worked harder at the speedup than in the period after the German surrender."

The timing was perfect. The first successful atomic test occurred on July 16, 1945, and Truman sat down for discussions with Stalin the very next day. Stimson's diary includes this entry after a full report of the test result was received:

> [Churchill] told me that he had noticed at the meeting of the [Big] Three yesterday that Truman was evidently much fortified by something that had happened and that he stood up to the Russians in a most emphatic and decisive manner, telling them as to certain demands that they absolutely could not have and that the United States was entirely against them. He said "Now I know what happened to Truman yesterday. I couldn't understand it. When he got to the meeting after having read this report he was a changed man. He told the Russians just where they got on and off and generally bossed the whole meeting."

The July 23, 1945, diary entry of Lord Alanbrooke, chairman of the U.K. Chiefs of Staff Committee, provides a description of both Churchill's own reaction and further indirect evidence of the atomic bomb's impact of American attitudes:

> [The prime minister] had absorbed all the minor American exaggerations and, as a result, was completely carried away. . . . We now had something in our hands which would redress the balance with the Russians. The secret of this explosive and the power to use it would completely alter the diplomatic equilibrium which was adrift since the defeat of Germany. Now we had a new value which redressed our position (pushing out his chin and scowling); now we could say, "If you insist on doing this or that, well . . . And then where are the Russians!"

Refusing to Face the Past

There is no longer much dispute that ending the war with Japan before the Soviet Union entered it played a role in the thinking of those responsible for using the atomic bomb. There is also evidence that impressing the Russians was a consideration. Scholarly discussion of this controversial point has been heated, and even carefully qualified judgments that such a motive is "strongly suggested" by the available documents have often been twisted and distorted into extreme claims. It is, nevertheless, impossible to ignore the considerable range of evidence that now points in this direction.

Particularly important has been research illuminating the role played by Byrnes. Although it was once believed that Stimson was the most important presidential adviser on atomic matters, historians increasingly understand that Byrnes had the president's ear. Indeed, in the judgment of many experts, he fairly dominated Truman during the first five or six months of Truman's presidency.

Byrnes, in fact, had been one of Truman's mentors when the young unknown from Missouri first came to the Senate. In selecting the highly influential former Supreme Court justice as secretary of state, Truman put him in direct line of succession to the presidency. By also choosing Byrnes as his personal representative on the high-level Interim Committee—which made recommendations concerning the new weapon—Truman arranged to secure primary counsel on both foreign policy and the atomic bomb from a single trusted adviser.

There is not much doubt about Byrnes's general view. In one of their very first meetings, Byrnes told Truman that "in his belief the atomic bomb might well put us in a position to dictate our own terms at the end of the war." Again, at the end of May, Byrnes met, at White House request, with atomic scientist Leo Szilard. In his 1949 *A Personal History of the Atomic Bomb,* Szilard recalled that

> Mr. Byrnes did not argue that it was necessary to use the bomb against the cities of Japan in order to win the war . . . Mr. Byrnes's . . . view [was] that our possessing and demonstrating the bomb would make Russia more manageable in Europe.

Stimson's friend Herbert Feis judged a quarter century ago that the desire to "impress" the Soviets almost certainly played a role in the decision to use the atomic bomb. On the basis of currently available information it is impossible to prove precisely to what extent Byrnes and the president were influenced by this consideration. Nevertheless, just as the discovery of new documents has led to greater recognition of the role of diplomatic factors in the decision, research on Byrnes's role—and the consistency of his attitude throughout this period—has clarified our understanding of this motive. Writing in the August 18, 1985, *New York Times,* Yale historian Gaddis Smith summarized this point: "It has been demonstrated that the decision to bomb Japan was centrally connected to Truman's confrontational approach to the Soviet Union."

Quite apart from the basic judgment as to the necessity of and reasons for the bomb's uses the issue of why the public is generally ignorant of so many of the basic facts discussed in the expert literature remains. For one thing, the modern press has been careless in its reporting. During this year's *Enola Gay* controversy at the Smithsonian, few reporters bothered to seriously consult specialist literature, or to present the range of specific issues in contention among the experts. Instead, historians who still remain unqualified defenders of the decision as dictated solely by military necessity were often cited as unquestioned authoritative sources. Many reporters repeated as fact the myth that "over a million" Americans would have perished or been wounded in an invasion Japan. Only a handful wrote that among the many historians who criticized the Smithsonian for its "cleansing" of history were conservatives and others who disagreed about the specific issue, but begged for an honest discussion of the questions involved.

Emotional issues were also at work. Time and again, the question of whether dropping the atomic bomb was militarily necessary has become entangled with the separate issue of anger at Japan's sneak attack and the brutality of its military. The Japanese people have an ugly history to confront, including not only Pearl Harbor but also the bombing of Shanghai, the rape of Nanking, the forced prostitution of Korean women, the horror of the Bataan death march, and systematic torture and murder of American and other prisoners of war. Even so, the question of Hiroshima persists.

Americans also have often allowed themselves to confuse discussion of research findings on Hiroshima with criticism of American servicemen. This is certainly unjustified (as the comments of military leaders like Eisenhower, Leahy, and Arnold suggest). The Americans serving in the Pacific in 1945 were prepared to risk their lives for their nation; by this most fundamental test, they can only be called heroes. This is neither the first nor the last time, however, that those in the field were not informed of what was going on at higher levels.

Finally, we Americans clearly do not like to see our nation as vulnerable to the same moral failings as others. To raise questions about Hiroshima is to raise doubts, it seems to some, about the moral integrity of the country and its leaders. It is also to raise the most profound questions about the legitimacy of nuclear weapons in general. America's continued unwillingness to confront the fundamental questions about Hiroshima may well be at the root of the quiet acceptance that has characterized so many other dangerous developments in the nuclear era that began in 1945.

✖ *F U R T H E R   R E A D I N G*

Allen, Thomas, and Norman Polmar. *Code-Name Downfall: The Secret Plan to Invade Japan—And Why Truman Dropped the Bomb* (1994).

Alperovitz, Gar. *Atomic Diplomacy: Hiroshima and Potsdam* (1965).

———, *The Decision to Use the Atomic Bomb and the Architecture of an American Myth* (1995).

Bernstein, Barton J., ed. *The Atomic Bomb: The Critical Issues* (1976). See also, Bernstein's many articles on the decision to use the bomb, especially "The Atomic Bombings Reconsidered," *Foreign Affairs* 176 (1995), 135–52.

Bird, Kai, and Lawrence Lifshultz, eds. *Hiroshima's Shadow* (1990).

Boyer, Paul. *By the Bomb's Early Light: American Thought and Culture at the Dawn of the Atomic Age* (1985).

Bulletin of Concerned Asian Scholars, (April–June, 1995).

Committee for the Compilation of Material on Damage Caused by the Atomic Bombs in Hiroshima and Nagasaki. *Hiroshima and Nagasaki: The Physical, Medical, and Social Effects of the Atomic Bombings,* trans. by Ishikawa Eisei and David L. Swain (1981).

Dower, John W. *War Without Mercy: Race and Power in the Pacific War* (1986).

Feis, Herbert. *The Atomic Bomb and the End of World War II* (1966).

Frank, Richard B. *Downfall: The End of the Imperial Japanese Empire* (1999).

Fussell, Paul. *Thank God for the Atom Bomb, and Other Essays* (1988).

Hachiya, Michihiko. *Hiroshima Diary: The Journal of a Japanese Physician, August 6–September 30, 1945* (1955).

Hamby, Alonzo. *Man of the People: A Life of Harry S. Truman* (1995).

Harwitt, Martin. *An Exhibit Denied: Lobbying the History of Enola Gay* (1997).

Herken, Gregg. *The Winning Weapon: The Atomic Bomb in the Cold War* (1981).

Hersey, John. *Hiroshima* (1946).

Hewlett, Richard G., and Oscar G. Anderson. *The New World, 1939–1946: A History of the United States Atomic Energy Commission* (1962).

Hogan, Michael J., ed. *Diplomatic History* (1995). A somewhat different version of this special issue was published as *Hiroshima in History and Memory* (1996).

Holloway, David. *Stalin and the Bomb: The Soviet Union and Atomic Energy, 1939–1956* (1994).

Ibuse, Masuji. *Black Rain* (1969).

Japan Broadcasting Corporation (NHK). *Unforgettable Fire: Pictures Drawn by Atomic Bomb Survivors* (1977).

Lifton, Robert Jay. *Death in Life: Survivors of Hiroshima* (1967).

Linenthal, Edward T., and Tom Englehardt, eds., *History Wars: The Enola Gay and Other Battles for the American Past* (1996).

Minear, Richard H. "Atomic Holocaust, Nazi Holocaust: Some Reflections," *Diplomatic History,* Spring, 1995.

——— ed. and trans. *Hiroshima: Three Witnesses* (1990).

Newman, Robert P. *Truman and the Hiroshima Cult* (August 1995).

Nitze, Paul H., with Ann M. Smith and Steven L. Rearden. *From Hiroshima to Glasnost: At the Center of Decision-Making—A Memoir* (1989).

Osada, Arata, comp. *Children of Hiroshima* (1980).

Rhodes, Richard. *The Making of the Atomic Bomb* (1986).

Selden, Kyoko, and Mark Selden, eds. *The Atomic Bomb: Voices from Hiroshima and Nagasaki* (1989).

Sherry, Martin. *The Rise of American Air Power: The Creation of Armageddon* (1987).

Sherwin, Martin J. *A World Destroyed: The Atomic Bomb and the Grand Alliance* (1975).

Sigal, Leon V. *Fighting to a Finish: The Politics of War Termination in the United States and Japan, 1945* (1988).

Skates, John Ray. *The Invasion of Japan: Alternative to the Bomb* (1994).

Walker, J. Samuel. *Prompt and Utter Destruction: President Truman and the Use of Atomic Bombs Against Japan* (1997).

CHAPTER
3

The Cold War Begins

⋙

Germany's final defeat in the spring of 1945 ended an era in which European nations had dominated world politics through their vast colonial empires and commercial networks. The United States and the Soviet Union would take the lead in the new era. The United States, which alone among the great powers had escaped the devastation of war on its own soil, was in 1945 unquestionably the most powerful nation in the world, and the prospect of a new American-led world—what magazine publisher Henry Luce had called an American century— seemed realistic. The U.S.S.R., although it had suffered enormous losses during the war, remained the most powerful military presence on the European continent, and propelled by its own history and ideology, soon challenged American leadership. The conflict between these two powerful nations, what came to be called the Cold War, not only would shape international relations for the next forty-five years but would deeply affect both nations' political, economic, and cultural life.

The Cold War would ultimately embrace much of the Third World (comprising Africa, Asia, Latin America, and the Middle East), where it often transformed local struggles into "hot" proxy wars between the superpowers. Yet the Cold War began in Europe, just as, forty-five years later, it would come to an end on that continent. It was here that the United States' vision of a postwar world of American-led liberal democracies ran up against the Soviet Union's fears for its own security and its determination to refashion much of Eastern Europe in its own image.

There is an enormous historical literature on the Cold War, filled with conflicting interpretations. Was conflict precipitated by an aggressive and expansionist U.S.S.R., as most early, "orthodox" interpretations of the Cold War insisted? Or, as later generations of "revisionist" historians have argued, was the United States, in its efforts to create a postwar world that reflected its own interests, also responsible? What were the sources of U.S. policy: domestic politics? A need to secure foreign markets? Strategic and geopolitical considerations? What role did misperception play in shaping U.S. and Soviet responses? To what extent did allies and clients successfully maneuver the great powers? Could the Cold War have been avoided, or its enormous costs in lost lives, distorted priorities, and political repression somehow minimized? Or will the disorder that is likely to accompany the dissolution of the Cold War make some now yearn for the lost stability of the "long peace"?

70

XXX *D O C U M E N T S*

One of the first issues to divide the United States and the Soviet Union was the future of postwar Poland. In Document 1, President Harry S Truman, who had only recently acceded to the presidency following the death of Franklin D. Roosevelt, agrees with hard-line advisers who argue that Soviet actions in Poland are part of a larger pattern of communist expansion that ought to be resisted. Russian fears that a truly independent Poland would threaten the security of Russian borders are voiced in Document 2 by Soviet leader Joseph Stalin, who insists that the United States is going back on assurances made by Roosevelt at the February 1945 Big Three meeting at Yalta in the Crimea.

By July 1946, conflict with the Soviet Union had grown to the point that Secretary of Commerce and former vice president Henry A. Wallace would appeal to Truman (Document 3) to reverse what he believed was the warlike drift of U.S. policy. Most of Truman's advisers took a very different view, however, which White House aide Clark M. Clifford and his assistant, George M. Elsey, summarize in the conclusion of Clifford's September 1946 report to the president, reprinted here as Document 4. The Soviets were reaching similar conclusions, as recorded in the September 1946 report of Soviet ambassador Nikolai Novikov, excerpts from which are printed as Document 5. Yet not until 1947 would Truman publicly embrace the new diplomacy of "containment" in calling for economic and military assistance to suppress a rebellion against the Greek government and announcing the Truman Doctrine (Document 6), a broad new policy of support for "free peoples" throughout the world. The implementation of such a policy quickly led American leaders such as Undersecretary of State Dean Acheson to appeal for economic aid to Europe (Document 7), in what would eventually become the Marshall Plan. The new diplomacy would also require a massive expansion of U.S. military programs, as the president's national security advisers would argue in NSC-68, an April 1950 report to the president, the conclusions of which are reproduced here as Document 8. In the final document, President Truman and his advisers discuss the U.S. response to North Korean's invasion of South Korea in June 1950. The Korean War, which followed the communist revolution in China, the Soviet Union's explosion of its first atomic bomb, and the sudden rise to notoriety of Senator Joseph McCarthy, became the linchpin of the Cold War, shaping in turn the politics, culture, and foreign policies of the United States for decades to come.

1. President Harry S Truman and His Advisers Debate U.S. Policy Toward the U.S.S.R., April 1945

The Secretary of State [Edward R. Stettinius Jr.] told the meeting that Mr. [V. M.] Molotov [Soviet Union's foreign minister] had arrived in good spirits yesterday and had had a good talk with the President [Harry S Truman] yesterday evening but that at the Foreign Ministers meeting later great difficulties had developed over the Polish question. The continuance of the meeting this morning had produced no improvement and a complete deadlock had been reached on the subject of the carrying out of the Yalta agreement on Poland. The Secretary said that the truth of the matter was the Lublin or Warsaw Government was not representative of the Polish people and that it was now clear that the Soviet Government intended to try to enforce

Charles E. Bohlen, Memorandum of meeting at the White House, April 23, 1945, *Foreign Relations of the U.S.: Diplomatic Papers, Vol. 5, 1945, Europe* (Washington, D.C.: GPO, 1967), 252–255.

upon the United States and British Governments this puppet government of Poland and obtain its acceptance as the legal government of Poland. He said that as they all recalled at Yalta an agreement had been reached regarding the formation of a new Polish Government representative of the people by means of the reorganization of the present provisional government in consultation with other Polish democratic leaders. He said it had been made plain to Mr. Molotov how seriously the United States Government regarded this matter and how much public confidence would be shaken by our failure to carry out the Crimean [Yalta] decision.

The President said that he had told Mr. Molotov last night that he intended fully to carry out all the agreements reached by President Roosevelt at the Crimea. He added that he felt our agreements with the Soviet Union so far had been a one way street and that could not continue; it was now or never. He intended to go on with the plans for San Francisco [the organizing meeting of the United Nations] and if the Russians did not wish to join us they could go to hell. The President then asked in rotation the officials present for their view.

[Secretary of War Henry L.] Stimson said that this whole difficulty with the Russians over Poland was new to him and he felt it was important to find out what the Russians were driving at. He said in the big military matters the Soviet Government had kept their word and that the military authorities of the United States had come to count on it. In fact he said that they had often been better than their promise. He said it was important to find out what motives they had in mind in regard to these border countries and that their ideas of independence and democracy in areas that they regarded as vital to the Soviet Union are different from ours. Mr. Stimson remarked that they had a good deal of trouble on minor military matters and it was necessary in these cases to teach them manners. In this case he said that without fully understanding how seriously the Russians took this Polish question we might be heading into very dangerous water. He remarked that 25 years ago virtually all of Poland had been Russian.

[Secretary of the Navy James V.] Forrestal said that he felt that this difficulty over Poland could not be treated as an isolated incident, that there had been many evidences of the Soviet desire to dominate adjacent countries and to disregard the wishes of her allies. He said he had felt that for some time the Russians had considered that we would not object if they took over all of Eastern Europe into their power. He said it was his profound conviction that if the Russians were to be rigid in their attitude we had better have a show down with them now than later.

Ambassador [to the Soviet Union W. Averell] Harriman said that in regard to Mr. Stimson's question as to the issues and the motives he felt that when [Soviet leader Josef] Stalin and Molotov had returned to Moscow after Yalta they had been informed by Bierut (the present head of the provisional government) concerning the situation in Poland and had realized that the provisional government was in a shaky condition and that the introduction of any genuine Polish leader such as Mikolajczyk would probably mean the elimination of the Soviet hand-picked group. He remarked that the real issue was whether we were to be a party to a program of Soviet domination of Poland. He said obviously we were faced with a possibility of a real break with the Russians but he felt that if properly handled it might be avoided. The President said that he had no intention of delivering an ultimatum to Mr. Molotov but merely to make clear the position of this Government.

Mr. Stimson observed that he would like to know how far the Russian reaction to a strong position on Poland would go. He said he thought that the Russians perhaps were being more realistic than we were in regard to their own security.

Admiral [William D.] Leahy [senior military adviser to the president] said that he had left Yalta with the impression that the Soviet Government had no intention of permitting a free government to operate in Poland and that he would have been surprised had the Soviet Government behaved any differently than it had. In his opinion the Yalta agreement was susceptible to two interpretations. He added that he felt that it was a serious matter to break with the Russians but that we should tell them that we stood for a free and independent Poland.

The Secretary of State then read the part of the Yalta decision relating to the formation of the new Government and the holding of free elections and said he felt that this was susceptible of only one interpretation.

General [George C.] Marshall [Army Chief of Staff] said he was not familiar with the Polish issue and its political aspects. He said from the military point of view the situation in Europe was secure but that they hoped for Soviet participation in the war against Japan at a time when it would be useful to us. The Russians had it within their power to delay their entry into the Far Eastern war until we had done all the dirty work. He said the difficulties with the Russians such as in the case of Crossword usually straightened out. He was inclined to agree with Mr. Stimson that possibility of a break with Russia was very serious.

Mr. Stimson observed that he agreed with General Marshall and that he felt that the Russians would not yield on the Polish question. He said we must understand that outside the United States with the exception of Great Britain there was no country that understood free elections; that the party in power always ran the election as he well knew from his experience in Nicaragua. [In 1927 Stimson served as President Coolidge's special emissary to Nicaragua.]

Admiral [Ernest J.] King [Chief of Naval Operations] inquired whether the issue was the invitation to the Lublin Government to San Francisco. The President informed him that that was a settled matter and not the issue. The issue was the execution of agreements entered into between this Government and the Soviet Union. He said he intended to tell Mr. Molotov that we expected Russia to carry out the Yalta decision as we were prepared to do for our part.

Ambassador Harriman then remarked that while it was true that the Soviet Union had kept its big agreements on military matters that those were decisions which it had already reached by itself but that on other miliary matters it was impossible to say they had lived up to their commitments. He said for example over a year ago they had agreed to start on preparations for collaboration in the Far Eastern war but that none of these had been carried out. He asked General Deane to express his opinion.

General [John R.] Deane [commander of the U.S. military mission in the Soviet Union] said that he felt that the Soviet Union would enter the Pacific war as soon as it was able irrespective of what happened in other fields. He felt that the Russians must do this because they could not afford too long a period of let down for their people who were tired, there was only a short season in which offensive action against Manchuria was possible, and that they would not dare attempt a Bulgarian gambit in the Far East. He said he was convinced after his experiences in Moscow that if we were afraid of the Russians we would get nowhere and he felt that we should be firm when we were right.

The President then thanked the military representation and said that he felt that he had their point of view well in mind and would ask the Secretary of State and his advisers to stay behind to work out the details of his forthcoming talk with Mr. Molotov.

The President then said that he was satisfied that from a military point of view there was no reason why we should fail to stand up to our understanding of the Crimean agreements and he requested the Secretary of State to prepare for him (1) a statement to be handed to Mr. Molotov for communication to Marshal Stalin, (2) a list of points he might mention orally to Mr. Molotov, and (3) a draft of a statement to the press. He said he would be prepared to receive the Secretary of State and his advisers just as soon as this could be done and afterwards he would see Mr. Molotov. The Secretary agreed and said he would have the drafts in the President's hands by 5:00 o'clock.

2. Russian Premier Joseph Stalin Defends Soviet Policy in Eastern Europe, April 1945

The Chairman of the Council of People's Commissars of the Soviet Union (Stalin) to President Truman

[Moscow,] 24 April 1945

I have received your joint with Prime Minister Churchill message of April 18, and have also received on April 24 the message transmitted to me through V. M. Molotov.

1. From these messages it is clear that you continue to consider the Provisional Polish Government not as a kernel for the future government of national unity, but just like one of the groups equal to any other group of Poles.

Such an understanding of the position of the Polish Government and such an attitude towards it is very difficult to reconcile with the decisions of the Crimea Conference on Poland. At the Crimea Conference all three of us, including also President Roosevelt, proceeded from the fact that the Provisional Polish Government, as the one now operating in Poland and enjoying the confidence and support of the majority of the Polish people, should be the kernel, i.e., the main part of the new reorganized government of nation unity. You, evidently, do not agree to such an understanding of the matter. Declining the Yugoslav example as a pattern for Poland, you thereby confirm the Provisional Polish Government cannot be considered as a basis and kernel for the future government of national unity.

2. It is also necessary to take into account the fact that Poland borders with the Soviet Union, what cannot be said of Great Britain and the United States.

The question on Poland has the same meaning for the security of the Soviet Union as the question on Belgium and Greece for the security of Great Britain.

Stalin to Truman, April 24, 1945, *Foreign Relations of the U.S.: Diplomatic Papers, Vol. 5, 1945, Europe* (Washington, D.C.: GPO, 1967), 263–264.

You, apparently, do not agree that the Soviet Union has a right to make efforts that there should exist in Poland a government friendly toward the Soviet Union, and that the Soviet government cannot agree to existence in Poland of a government hostile toward it. Besides everything else, this is demanded by the blood of the Soviet people abundantly shed on the field of Poland in the name of liberation of Poland. I do not know whether there has been established in Greece a really representative government, and whether the government in Belgium is really democratic. The Soviet Union was not consulted when these governments were being established there. The Soviet Government did not lay claim to interference in these affairs as it understands the whole importance of Belgium and Greece for the security of Great Britain.

It is not clear why, while the question on Poland is discussed it is not wanted to take into consideration the interests of the Soviet Union from the point of view of its security.

3. Such conditions must be recognized [as] unusual when two governments— those of the United States and Great Britain—beforehand settle with the Polish question in which the Soviet Union is first of all and most of all interested and put the government of the U.S.S.R. in an unbearable position trying to dictate to it their demands.

I have to state that such a situation cannot favor a harmonious solution of the question on Poland.

4. I am ready to fulfill your request and do everything possible to reach a harmonious solution, but you demand too much of me. In other words, you demand that I renounce the interests of security of the Soviet Union, but I cannot turn against my country.

In my opinion there is one way out of this situation: to adopt the Yugoslav example as a pattern for Poland. I believe this would allow [us] to come to a harmonious solution.

3. Secretary of Commerce Henry A. Wallace Urges a Conciliatory Approach, July 1946

My dear Mr. President:

I hope you will excuse this long letter. Personally I hate to write long letters, and I hate to receive them.

My only excuse is that this subject is a very important one—probably the most important in the world today. I checked with you about this last Thursday and you suggested after Cabinet meeting on Friday that you would like to have my views.

I have been increasingly disturbed about the trend of international affairs since the end of the war, and I am even more troubled by the apparently growing feeling among the American people that another war is coming and the only way that we can head it off is to arm ourselves to the teeth. Yet all of past history indicates that an armaments race does not lead to peace but to war. The months just ahead may well be the crucial period which will decide whether the civilized world will go

Wallace to Truman, July 1946, Truman Papers, Harry S Truman Library, Independence, Mo.

down in destruction after the five or ten years needed for several nations to arm themselves with atomic bombs. Therefore I want to give you my views on how the present trend toward conflict might be averted.

How do American actions since V-J Day appear to other nations? I mean by actions the concrete things like $13 billion for the War and Navy Departments, the Bikini tests of the atomic bomb and continued production of bombs, the plan to arm Latin America with our weapons, production of B-29s and planned production of B-36s, and the effort to secure air bases spread over half the globe from which the other half of the globe can be bombed. I cannot but feel that these actions must make it look to the rest of the world as if we were only paying lip service to peace at the conference table. These facts rather make it appear either (1) that we are preparing ourselves to win the war which we regard as inevitable or (2) that we are trying to build up a predominance of force to intimidate the rest of mankind. How would it look to us if Russia had the atomic bomb and we did not, if Russia had 10,000-mile bombers and air bases within a thousand miles of our coast lines and we did not? . . .

Other Problems of American-Russian Relationships

I believe that for the United States and Russia to live together in peace is the most important single problem facing the world today. Many people, in view of the relatively satisfactory outcome of the recent Paris Conference, feel that good progress is being made on the problem of working out relations between the Anglo-Saxon powers and Russia. This feeling seems to me to be resting on superficial appearances more productive of a temporary truce than of final peace. On the whole, as we look beneath the surface in late July of 1946, our actions and those of the western powers in general carry with them the ultimate danger of a third world war—this time an atomic world war. As the strongest single nation, and the nation whose leadership is followed by the entire world with the exception of Russia and a few weak neighboring countries in Eastern Europe, I believe that we have the opportunity to lead the world to peace.

4. White House Aide Clark M. Clifford Summarizes the Case for the Hard Line, September 1946

The primary objective of United States policy toward the Soviet Union is to convince Soviet leaders that it is in their interest to participate in a system of world cooperation, that there are no fundamental causes for war between our two nations, and that the security and prosperity of the Soviet Union, and that of the rest of the world as well, is being jeopardized by aggressive militaristic imperialism such as that in which the Soviet Union is now engaged.

However, these same leaders with whom we hope to achieve an understanding on the principles of international peace appear to believe that a war with the United

Excerpts from Clark M. Clifford, Memorandum for the President, September 24, 1946, Truman Papers, Harry S Truman Library, Independence, Mo.

States and the other leading capitalistic nations is inevitable. They are increasing their military power and the sphere of Soviet influence in preparation for the "inevitable" conflict, and they are trying to weaken and subvert their potential opponents by every means at their disposal. So long as these men adhere to these beliefs, it is highly dangerous to conclude that hope of international peace lies only in "accord," "mutual understanding," or "solidarity" with the Soviet Union.

Adoption of such a policy would impel the United States to make sacrifices for the sake of Soviet-U.S. relations, which would only have the effect of raising Soviet hopes and increasing Soviet demands, and to ignore alternative lines of policy, which might be much more compatible with our own national and international interests. . . .

As long as the Soviet Government maintains its present foreign policy, based upon the theory of an ultimate struggle between Communism and Capitalism, the United States must assume that the U.S.S.R. might fight at any time for the twofold purpose of expanding the territory under communist control and weakening its potential capitalist opponents. The Soviet Union was able to flow into the political vacuum of the Balkans, Eastern Europe, the Near East, Manchuria, and Korea because no other nation was both willing and able to prevent it. Soviet leaders were encouraged by easy success and they are now preparing to take over new areas in the same way. The Soviet Union, as Stalin euphemistically phrased it, is preparing "for any eventuality."

Unless the United States is willing to sacrifice its future security for the sake of "accord" with the U.S.S.R. now, this government must, as a first step toward world stabilization, seek to prevent additional Soviet aggression. The greater the area controlled by the Soviet Union, the greater the military requirements of this country will be. Our present military plans are based on the assumption that, for the next few years at least, Western Europe, the Middle East, China, and Japan will remain outside the Soviet sphere. If the Soviet Union acquires control of one or more of these areas, the military forces required to hold in check those of the U.S.S.R. and prevent still further acquisitions will be substantially enlarged. That will also be true if any of the naval and air bases in the Atlantic and Pacific, upon which our present plans rest, are given up. This government should be prepared, while scrupulously avoiding any act which would be an excuse for the Soviets to begin a war, to resist vigorously and successfully any efforts of the U.S.S.R. to expand into areas vital to American security.

The language of military power is the only language which disciples of power politics understand. The United States must use that language in order that Soviet leaders will realize that our government is determined to uphold the interests of its citizens and the rights of small nations. Compromise and concessions are considered, by the Soviets, to be evidences of weakness and they are encouraged by our "retreats" to make new and greater demands.

The main deterrent to Soviet attack on the United States, or to attack on areas of the world which are vital to our security, will be the military power of this country. It must be made apparent to the Soviet Government that our strength will be sufficient to repel any attack and sufficient to defeat the U.S.S.R. decisively if a war should start. The prospect of defeat is the only sure means of deterring the Soviet Union.

The Soviet Union's vulnerability is limited due to the vast area over which its key industries and natural resources are widely dispersed, but it is vulnerable to atomic weapons, biological warfare, and long-range air power. Therefore, in order to maintain our strength at a level which will be effective in restraining the Soviet Union, the United States must be prepared to wage atomic and biological warfare. A highly mechanized army, which can be moved either by sea or by air, capable of seizing and holding strategic areas, must be supported by powerful naval and air forces. A war with the U.S.S.R. would be "total" in a more horrible sense than any previous war and there must be constant research for both offensive and defensive weapons.

Whether it would actually be in this country's interest to employ atomic and biological weapons against the Soviet Union in the event of hostilities is a question which would require careful consideration in the light of the circumstances prevailing at the time. The decision would probably be influenced by a number of factors, such as the Soviet Union's capacity to employ similar weapons, which can not now be estimated. But the important point is that the United States must be prepared to wage atomic and biological warfare if necessary. The mere fact of preparedness may be the only powerful deterrent to Soviet aggressive action and in this sense the only sure guaranty of peace.

The United States, with a military potential composed primarily of highly effective technical weapons, should entertain no proposal for disarmament or limitation of armament as long as the possibility of Soviet aggression exists. Any discussion on the limitation of armaments should be pursued slowly and carefully with the knowledge constantly in mind that proposals on outlawing atomic warfare and long-range offensive weapons would greatly limit United States strength, while only moderately affecting the Soviet Union. The Soviet Union relies primarily on a large infantry and artillery force and the result of such arms limitation would be to deprive the United States of its most effective weapons without impairing the Soviet Union's ability to wage a quick war of aggression in Western Europe, the Middle East, or the Far East.

The Soviet Government's rigid controls on travellers, and its internal security measures, enable it to develop military weapons and build up military forces without our knowledge. The United States should not agree to arms limitations until adequate intelligence of events in the U.S.S.R. is available and, as long as this situation prevails, no effort should be spared to make our forces adequate and strong. Unification of the services and the adoption of universal military training would be strong aids in carrying out a forthright United States policy. In addition to increasing the efficiency of our armed forces, this program would have a salutary psychological effect upon Soviet ambitions. . . .

In addition to maintaining our own strength, the United States should support and assist all democratic countries which are in any way menaced or endangered by the U.S.S.R. Providing military support in case of attack is a last resort; a more effective barrier to communism is strong economic support. Trade agreements, loans, and technical missions strengthen our ties with friendly nations and are effective demonstrations that capitalism is at least the equal of communism. The United States can do much to ensure that economic opportunities, personal freedom, and social equality are made possible in countries outside the Soviet sphere by generous financial assistance. Our policy on reparations should be directed toward strengthening the areas we are endeavoring to keep outside the Soviet sphere. Our efforts to break down trade barriers, open up rivers and international waterways, and bring about economic unification of countries, now divided by occupation armies, are also directed toward the re-establishment of vigorous and healthy non-communist economies.

The Soviet Union recognizes the effectiveness of American economic assistance to small nations and denounces it bitterly by constant propaganda. The United States should realize that Soviet propaganda is dangerous (especially when American "imperialism" is emphasized) and should avoid any actions which give an appearance of truth to the Soviet charges. A determined effort should be made to expose the fallacies of such propaganda.

There are some trouble-spots which will require diligent and considered effort on the part of the United States if Soviet penetration and eventual domination is to be prevented. In the Far East, for example, this country should continue to strive for a unified and economically stable China, a reconstructed and democratic Japan, and a unified and independent Korea. We must ensure Philippine prosperity and we should assist in the peaceful solution, along noncommunistic lines, of the political problems of Southeast Asia and India. . . .

Our best chances of influencing Soviet leaders consist in making it unmistakably clear that action contrary to our conception of a decent world order will redound to the disadvantage of the Soviet regime whereas friendly and cooperative action will pay dividends. If this position can be maintained firmly enough and long enough, the logic of it must permeate eventually into the Soviet system. . . .

Within the United States, communist penetration should be exposed and eliminated whenever the national security is endangered. The armed forces, government agencies, and heavy industries are the principal targets for communistic infiltration at present.

Because the Soviet Union is a highly centralized state, whose leaders exercise rigid discipline and control of all governmental functions, its government acts with speed, consistency, and boldness. Democratic governments are usually loosely organized, with a high degree of autonomy in government departments and agencies. Government policies at times are confused, misunderstood, or disregarded by subordinate officials. The United States can not afford to be uncertain of its policies toward the Soviet Union. There must be such effective coordination within the government that our military and civil policies concerning the U.S.S.R., her satellites, and our Allies are consistent and forceful. Any uncertainty or discrepancy will be seized immediately by the Soviets and exploited at our cost.

Our policies must also be global in scope. By time-honored custom, we have regarded "European Policy," "Near Eastern Policy," "Indian Policy," and "Chinese Policy" as separate problems to be handled by experts in each field. But the areas involved, far removed from each other by our conventional standards, all border on the Soviet Union and our actions with respect to each must be considered in the light of overall Soviet objectives.

Only a well-informed public will support the stern policies which Soviet activities make imperative and which the United States Government must adopt. The American people should be fully informed about the difficulties in getting along with the Soviet Union, and the record of Soviet evasion, misrepresentation, aggression, and militarism should be made public.

In conclusion, as long as the Soviet Government adheres to its present policy, the United States should maintain military forces powerful enough to restrain the Soviet Union and to confine Soviet influence to its present area. All nations not now within the Soviet sphere should be given generous economic assistance and political support in their opposition to Soviet penetration. Economic aid may also be given to the Soviet Government and private trade with the U.S.S.R. permitted provided the results are beneficial to our interests and do not simply strengthen the Soviet program. We should continue to work for cultural and intellectual understanding between the United States and the Soviet Union but that does not mean that, under the guise of an exchange program, communist subversion and infiltration in the United States will be tolerated. In order to carry out an effective policy toward the Soviet Union, the United States Government should coordinate its own activities, inform and instruct the American people about the Soviet Union, and enlist their support based upon knowledge and confidence. These actions by the United States are necessary before we shall ever be able to achieve understanding and accord with the Soviet Government on any terms other than its own.

Even though Soviet leaders profess to believe that the conflict between Capitalism and Communism is irreconcilable and must eventually be resolved by the triumph of the latter, it is our hope that they will change their minds and work out with us a fair and equitable settlement when they realize that we are too strong to be beaten and too determined to be frightened.

5. Soviet Ambassador Nikolai Novikov Reports on the U.S. Drive for World Supremacy, September 1946

The foreign policy of the United States, which reflects the imperialist tendencies of American monopolistic capital, is characterized in the postwar period by a striving for world supremacy. This is the real meaning of the many statements by President Truman and other representatives of American ruling circles: that the United States has the right to lead the world. All the forces of American diplomacy—the army, the air force, the navy, industry, and science—are enlisted in the service of this foreign policy. For this purpose broad plans for expansion have been developed and are being implemented through diplomacy and the establishment of a system of naval and air bases stretching far beyond the boundaries of the United States, through the arms race, and through the creation of ever newer types of weapons. . . .

Europe has come out of the war with a completely dislocated economy, and the economic devastation that occurred in the course of the war cannot be overcome in a short time. All of the countries of Europe and Asia are experiencing a colossal need for consumer goods, industrial and transportation equipment, etc. Such a situation provides American monopolistic capital with prospects for enormous shipments

Nikolai Novikov, in *Origins of the Cold War: The Novikov, Kennan and Roberts "Long Telegram" of 1946,* ed. Kenneth M. Jensen; trans. Kenneth M. Jensen and John Glad (Washington, D.C.: United States Institute of Peace, 1991).

of goods and the importation of capital into these countries—a circumstance that would permit it to infiltrate their national economies.

Such a development would mean serious strengthening of the economic position of the United States in the whole world and would be a stage on the road to world domination by the United States.

On the other hand, we have seen a failure of calculations on the part of U.S. circles which assumed that the Soviet Union would be destroyed in the war or would come out of it so weakened that it would be forced to go begging to the United States for economic assistance. Had that happened, they would have been able to dictate conditions permitting the United States to carry out its expansion in Europe and Asian without hindrance from the U.S.S.R.

In actuality, despite all of the economic difficulties of the postwar period connected with the enormous losses inflicted by the war and the German fascist occupation, the Soviet Union continues to remain economically independent of the outside world and is rebuilding its national economy with its own forces.

At the same time the U.S.S.R.'s international position is currently stronger than it was in the prewar period. Thanks to the historical victories of Soviet weapons, the Soviet armed forces are located on the territory of Germany and other formerly hostile countries, thus guaranteeing that these countries will not be used again for an attack on the U.S.S.R. In formerly hostile countries, such as Bulgaria, Finland, Hungary, and Romania, democratic reconstruction has established regimes that have undertaken to strengthen and maintain friendly relations with the Soviet Union. In the Slavic countries that were liberated by the Red Army or with its assistance—Poland, Czechoslovakia, and Yugoslavia—democratic regimes have also been established that maintain relations with the Soviet Union on the basis of agreements on friendship and mutual assistance.

The enormous relative weight of the U.S.S.R. in international affairs in general and in the European countries in particular, the independence of its foreign policy, and the economic and political assistance that it provides to neighboring countries, both allies and former enemies, has led to the growth of the political influence of the Soviet Union in these countries and to the further strengthening of democratic tendencies in them.

Such a situation in Eastern and Southeastern Europe cannot help but be regarded by the American imperialists as an obstacle in the path of the expansionist policy of the United States.

The foreign policy of the United States is not determined at present by the circles in the Democratic party that (as was the case during Roosevelt's lifetime) strive to strengthen the cooperation of the three great powers that constituted the basis of the anti-Hitler coalition during the war. The ascendance to power of President Truman, a politically unstable person but with certain conservative tendencies, and the subsequent appointment of [James F.] Byrnes as Secretary of State meant a strengthening of the influence on U.S. foreign policy of the most reactionary circles of the Democratic party. The constantly increasing reactionary nature of the foreign policy course of the United States, which consequently approached the policy advocated by the Republican party, laid the groundwork for close cooperation in this field between the far right wing of the Democratic party and the Republican party. . . .

At the same time, there has been a decline in the influence on foreign policy of those who follow Roosevelt's course for cooperation among peace-loving countries. Such persons in the government, in Congress, and in the leadership of the Democratic party are being pushed farther and farther into the background. The contradictions in the field of foreign policy existing between the followers of [Henry] Wallace and [Claude] Pepper, on the one hand, and the adherents of the reactionary "bi-partisan" policy, on the other, were manifested with great clarity recently in the speech by Wallace that led to his resignation from the post of Secretary of Commerce. Wallace's resignation means the victory of the reactionary course that Byrnes is conducting in cooperation with [Senator Arthur] Vandenberg and [Senator Robert] Taft.

Obvious indications of the U.S. effort to establish world dominance are also to be found in the increases in military potential in peacetime and in the establishment of a large number of naval air bases both in the United States and beyond its borders.

In the summer of 1946, for the first time in the history of the country, Congress passed a law on the establishment of a peacetime army, not on a volunteer basis but on the basis of universal military service. The size of the army, which is supposed to amount to about one million persons as of July 1, 1947, was also increased significantly. The size of the navy at the conclusion of the war decreased quite insignificantly in comparison with wartime. At the present time, the American navy occupies first place in the world, leaving England's navy far behind, to say nothing of those of other countries.

Expenditures on the army and navy have risen colossally, amounting to 13 billion dollars according to the budget for 1946–47 (about 40 percent of the total budget of 36 billion dollars). This is more than ten times greater than corresponding expenditures in the budget for 1938, which did not amount to even one billion dollars.

Along with maintaining a large army, navy, and air force, the budget provides that these enormous amounts also will be spent on establishing a very extensive system of naval and air bases in the Atlantic and Pacific oceans. According to existing official plans, in the course of the next few years 228 bases, points of support, and radio stations are to be constructed in the Atlantic Ocean and 258 in the Pacific. . . .

The establishment of American bases on the islands that are often 10,000 to 12,000 kilometers from the territory of the United States and are on the other side of the Atlantic and Pacific oceans clearly indicates the offensive nature of the strategic concepts of the commands of the U.S. army and navy. This interpretation is also confirmed by the fact that the American navy is intensively studying the naval approaches to the boundaries of Europe. For this purpose, American naval vessels in the course of 1946 visited the ports of Norway, Denmark, Sweden, Turkey, and Greece. In addition, the American navy is constantly operating in the Mediterranean Sea.

All of these facts show clearly that a decisive role in the realization of plans for world dominance by the United States is played by its armed forces.

One of the stages in the achievement of dominance over the world by the United States is its understanding with England concerning the partial division of the world on the basis of mutual concessions. The basic lines of the secret agreement between the United States and England regarding the division of the world consist, as shown by facts, in their agreement on the inclusion of Japan and China in the sphere of influence of the United States in the Far East, while the United States, for its part, has agreed not to hinder England either in resolving the Indian problem or in strengthening its influence in Siam and Indonesia.

In connection with this division, the United States at the present time is in control of China and Japan without any interference from England. . . .

In recent years American capital has penetrated very intensively into the economy of the Near Eastern countries, in particular into the oil industry. At present there are American oil concessions in all of the Near Eastern countries that have oil deposits (Iraq, Bahrain, Kuwait, Egypt, and Saudi Arabia). American capital, which made its first appearance in the oil industry of the Near East only in 1927, now controls about 42 percent of all proven reserves in the Near East, excluding Iran. Of the total proven reserves of 26.8 billion barrels, over 11 billion barrels are owned by U.S. concessions. Striving to ensure further development of their concessions in different countries (which are often very large—Saudi Arabia, for example), the American oil companies plan to build a trans-Arabian pipeline to transport oil from the American concession in Saudi Arabia and in other countries on the southeastern shore of the Mediterranean Sea to ports in Palestine and Egypt.

In expanding in the Near East, American capital has English capital as its greatest and most stubborn competitor. The fierce competition between them is the chief factor preventing England and the United States from reaching an understanding on the division of spheres of influence in the Near East, a division that can occur only at the expense of direct British interests in this region. . . .

It must be kept in mind, however, that incidents such as the visit by the American battleship *Missouri* to the Black Sea straits, the visit of the American fleet to Greece, and the great interest that U.S. diplomacy displays in the problem of the straits have a double meaning. On the one hand, they indicate that the United States has decided to consolidate its position in the Mediterranean basin to support its interests in the countries of the Near East and that it has selected the navy as the tool for this policy. On the other hand, these incidents constitute a political and military demonstration against the Soviet Union. The strengthening of U.S. positions in the Near East and the establishment of conditions for basing the American navy at one or more points on the Mediterranean Sea (Trieste, Palestine, Greece, Turkey) will therefore signify the emergence of a new threat to the security of the southern regions of the Soviet Union.

Relations between the United States and England are determined by two basic circumstances. On the one hand, the United States regards England as its greatest potential competitor; on the other hand, England constitutes a possible ally for the United States. Division of certain regions of the globe into spheres of influence of the United States and England would create the opportunity, if not for preventing competition between them, which is impossible, then at least of reducing it. At the same time, such a division facilitates the achievement of economic and political cooperation between them. . . .

The current relations between England and the United States, despite the temporary attainment of agreements on very important questions, are plagued with great internal contradictions and cannot be lasting.

The economic assistance from the United States conceals within itself a danger for England in many respects. First of all, in accepting the [U.S.] loan, England finds herself in a certain financial dependence on the United States from which it will not be easy to free herself. Second, it should be kept in mind that the conditions created by the loan for the penetration by American capital of the British Empire can entail serious political consequences. The countries included in the British Empire or dependent on it may—under economic pressure from powerful American capital—reorient themselves toward the United States, following in this respect the example of Canada, which more and more is moving away from the influence of England and orienting itself toward the United States. The strengthening of American positions in the Far East could stimulate a similar process in Australia and New Zealand. In the Arabic countries of the Near East, which are striving to emancipate themselves from the British Empire, there are groups within the ruling circles that would not be averse to working out a deal with the United States. It is quite possible that the Near East will become a center of Anglo-American contradictions that will explode the agreements now reached between the United States and England.

The "hard-line" policy with regard to the U.S.S.R. announced by [Secretary of State James F.] Byrnes after the rapprochement of the reactionary Democrats with the Republicans is at present the main obstacle on the road to cooperation of the Great Powers. It consists mainly of the fact that in the postwar period the United States no longer follows a policy of strengthening cooperation among the Big Three (or Four) but rather has striven to undermine the unity of these countries. The objective has been to impose the will of other countries on the Soviet Union. This is precisely the tenor of the policy of certain countries, which is being carried out with the blessing of the United States, to undermine or completely abolish the principle of the veto in the Security Council of the United Nations. This would give the United States opportunities to form among the Great Powers narrow groupings and blocs directed primarily against the Soviet Union, and thus to split the United Nations. Rejection of the veto by the Great Powers would transform the United Nations into an Anglo-Saxon domain in which the United States would play the leading role.

The present policy of the American government with regard to the U.S.S.R. is also directed at limiting or dislodging the influence of the Soviet Union from neighboring countries. In implementing this policy in former enemy or Allied countries adjacent to the U.S.S.R., the United States attempts, at various international conferences or directly in these countries themselves, to support reactionary forces with the purpose of creating obstacles to the process of democratization of these countries. In so doing, it also attempts to secure positions for the penetration of American capital into their economies. . . .

One of the most important elements in the general policy of the United States, which is directed toward limiting the international role of the U.S.S.R. in the postwar world, is the policy with regard to Germany. In Germany, the United States is taking measures to strengthen reactionary forces for the purpose of opposing democratic reconstruction. Furthermore, it displays special insistence on accompanying this policy with completely inadequate measures for the demilitarization of Germany.

The American occupation policy does not have the objective of eliminating the remnants of German Fascism and rebuilding German political life on a democratic basis, so that Germany might cease to exist as an aggressive force. The United States is not taking measures to eliminate the monopolistic associations of German industrialists on which German Fascism depended in preparing aggression and waging war. Neither is any agrarian reform being conducted to eliminate large landholders, who were also a reliable support for the Hitlerites. Instead, the United States is considering the possibility of terminating the Allied occupation of German territory before the main tasks of the occupation—the demilitarization and democratization of Germany—have been implemented. This would create the prerequisites for the revival of an imperialist Germany, which the United States plans to use in a future war on its side. One cannot help seeing that such a policy has a clearly outlined anti-Soviet edge and constitutes a serious danger to the cause of peace.

The numerous and extremely hostile statements by American government, political, and military figures with regard to the Soviet Union and its foreign policy are very characteristic of the current relationship between the ruling circles of the United States and the U.S.S.R. These statements are echoed in an even more unrestrained tone by the overwhelming majority of the American press organs. Talk about a "third war," meaning a war against the Soviet Union, and even a direct call for this war—with the threat of using the atomic bomb—such is the content of the statements on relations with the Soviet Union by reactionaries at public meetings and in the press. At the present time, preaching war against the Soviet Union is not a monopoly of the far-right, yellow American press represented by the newspaper associations of Hearst and McCormick. This anti-Soviet campaign also has been joined by the "reputable" and "respectable" organs of the conservative press, such as the *New York Times* and *New York Herald Tribune.* Indicative in this respect are the numerous articles by Walter Lippmann in which he almost undisguisedly calls on the United States to launch a strike against the Soviet Union in the most vulnerable areas of the south and southeast of the U.S.S.R.

The basic goal of this anti-Soviet campaign of American "public opinion" is to exert political pressure on the Soviet Union and compel it to make concessions. Another, no less important goal of the campaign is the attempt to create an atmosphere of war psychosis among the masses, who are weary of war, thus making it easier for the U.S. government to carry out measures for the maintenance of high military potential. It was in this very atmosphere that the law on universal military service in peacetime was passed by Congress, that the huge military budget was adopted, and that plans are being worked out for the construction of an extensive system of naval and air bases.

Of course, all of these measures for maintaining a high military potential are not goals in themselves. They are only intended to prepare the conditions for winning world supremacy in a new war, the date for which, to be sure, cannot be determined now by anyone, but which is contemplated by the most bellicose circles of American imperialism.

Careful note should be taken of the fact that the preparation by the United States for a future war is being conducted with the prospect of war against the Soviet Union, which in the eyes of American imperialists is the main obstacle in the path of the United States to world domination. This is indicated by facts such as the tactical training of the American army for war with the Soviet Union as the future opponent, the siting of American strategic bases in regions from which it is possible to launch strikes on Soviet territory, intensified training and strengthening of Arctic regions as close approaches to the U.S.S.R., and attempts to prepare Germany and Japan to use those countries in a war against the U.S.S.R.

6. The Truman Doctrine, March 1947

Mr. President, Mr. Speaker, Members of the Congress of the United States:

The gravity of the situation which confronts the world today necessitates my appearance before a joint session of the Congress.

The foreign policy and the national security of this country are involved.

One aspect of the present situation, which I present to you at this time for your consideration and decision, concerns Greece and Turkey.

The United States has received from the Greek Government an urgent appeal for financial and economic assistance. Preliminary reports from the American Economic Mission now in Greece and reports from the American Ambassador in Greece corroborate the statement of the Greek Government that assistance is imperative if Greece is to survive as a free nation.

I do not believe that the American people and the Congress wish to turn a deaf ear to the appeal of the Greek Government.

Greece is not a rich country. Lack of sufficient natural resources has always forced the Greek people to work hard to make both ends meet. Since 1940, this industrious, peace loving country has suffered invasion, four years of cruel enemy occupation, and bitter internal strife.

When forces of liberation entered Greece they found that the retreating Germans had destroyed virtually all the railways, roads, port facilities, communications, and merchant marine. More than a thousand villages had been burned. Eighty-five percent of the children were tubercular. Livestock, poultry, and draft animals had almost disappeared. Inflation had wiped out practically all savings.

As a result of these tragic conditions, a militant minority, exploiting human want and misery, was able to create political chaos which, until now, has made economic recovery impossible. . . .

The very existence of the Greek state is today threatened by the terrorist activities of several thousand armed men, led by Communists, who defy the government's authority at a number of points, particularly along the northern boundaries. A Commission appointed by the United Nations Security Council is at present investigating disturbed conditions in northern Greece and alleged border violations along the frontier between Greece on the one hand and Albania, Bulgaria, and Yugoslavia on the other.

Meanwhile, the Greek Government is unable to cope with the situation. The Greek army is small and poorly equipped. It needs supplies and equipment if it is to restore authority to the government throughout Greek territory.

Greece must have assistance if it is to become a self-supporting and self-respecting democracy. . . .

No government is perfect. One of the chief virtues of a democracy, however, is that its defects are always visible and under democratic processes can be pointed out and corrected. The government of Greece is not perfect. Nevertheless it represents 85 percent of the members of the Greek Parliament who were chosen in an election last year. Foreign observers, including 692 Americans, considered this election to be a fair expression of the views of the Greek people.

Public Papers of the Presidents of the United States: Harry S Truman, 1945–53 (Washington, D.C.: GPO, 1963), 176–180.

The Greek Government has been operating in an atmosphere of chaos and extremism. It has made mistakes. The extension of aid by this country does not mean that the United States condones everything that the Greek Government has done or will do. We have condemned in the past, and we condemn now, extremist measures of the right or the left. We have in the past advised tolerance, and we advise tolerance now.

Greece's neighbor, Turkey, also deserves our attention.

The future of Turkey as an independent and economically sound state is clearly no less important to the freedom-loving peoples of the world than the future of Greece. The circumstances in which Turkey finds itself today are considerably different from those of Greece. Turkey has been spared the disasters that have beset Greece. And during the war, the United States and Great Britain furnished Turkey with material aid.

Nevertheless, Turkey now needs our support.

Since the war Turkey has sought additional financial assistance from Great Britain and the United States for the purpose of effecting that modernization necessary for the maintenance of its national integrity.

That integrity is essential to the preservation of order in the Middle East.

The British Government has informed us that, owing to its own difficulties, it can no longer extend financial or economic aid to Turkey.

As in the case of Greece, if Turkey is to have the assistance it needs, the United States must supply it. We are the only country able to provide that help.

I am fully aware of the broad implications involved if the United States extends assistance to Greece and Turkey, and I shall discuss these implications with you at this time.

One of the primary objectives of the foreign policy of the United States is the creation of conditions in which we and other nations will be able to work out a way of life free from coercion. This was a fundamental issue in the war with Germany and Japan. Our victory was won over countries which sought to impose their will, and their way of life, upon other nations.

To ensure the peaceful development of nations, free from coercion, the United States has taken a leading part in establishing the United Nations. The United Nations is designed to make possible lasting freedom and independence for all its members. We shall not realize our objectives, however, unless we are willing to help free peoples to maintain their free institutions and their national integrity against aggressive movements that seek to impose upon them totalitarian regimes. This is no more than a frank recognition that totalitarian regimes imposed upon free peoples, by direct or indirect aggression, undermine the foundations of international peace and hence the security of the United States.

The peoples of a number of countries of the world have recently had totalitarian regimes forced upon them against their will. The Government of the United States has made frequent protests against coercion and intimidation, in violation of the Yalta agreement, in Poland, Rumania, and Bulgaria. I must also state that in a number of other countries there have been similar developments.

At the present moment in world history nearly every nation must choose between alternative ways of life. The choice is too often not a free one.

One way of life is based upon the will of the majority, and is distinguished by free institutions, representative government, free elections, guarantees of individual liberty, freedom of speech and religion, and freedom from political oppression.

The second way of life is based upon the will of a minority forcibly imposed upon the majority. It relies upon terror and oppression, a controlled press and radio, fixed elections, and the suppression of personal freedoms.

I believe that it must be the policy of the United States to support free peoples who are resisting attempted subjugation by armed minorities or by outside pressures.

I believe that we must assist free peoples to work out their own destinies in their own way.

I believe that our help should be primarily through economic and financial aid which is essential to economic stability and orderly political processes.

The world is not static, and the *status quo* is not sacred. But we cannot allow changes in the *status quo* in violation of the Charter of the United Nations by such methods as coercion, or by such subterfuges as political infiltration. In helping free and independent nations to maintain their freedom, the United States will be giving effect to the principles of the Charter of the United Nations.

It is necessary only to glance at a map to realize that the survival and integrity of the Greek nation are of grave importance in a much wider situation. If Greece should fall under the control of an armed minority, the effect upon its neighbor, Turkey, would be immediate and serious. Confusion and disorder might well spread throughout the entire Middle East.

Moreover, the disappearance of Greece as an independent state would have a profound effect upon those countries in Europe whose peoples are struggling against great difficulties to maintain their freedoms and their independence while they repair the damages of war.

It would be an unspeakable tragedy if these countries, which have struggled so long against overwhelming odds, should lose that victory for which they sacrificed so much. Collapse of free institutions and loss of independence would be disastrous not only for them but for the world. Discouragement and possibly failure would quickly be the lot of neighboring peoples striving to maintain their freedom and independence.

Should we fail to aid Greece and Turkey in this fateful hour, the effect will be far reaching to the West as well as to the East. . . .

7. Undersecretary of State Dean Acheson Calls for Economic Aid to Europe, May 1947

Here are some of the basic facts of life with which we are primarily concerned today in the conduct of foreign relations:

The first is that most of the countries of Europe and Asia are today in a state of physical destruction or economic dislocation, or both. Planned, scientific destruction of the enemy's resources carried out by both sides during the war has left factories destroyed, fields impoverished and without fertilizer or machinery to get them back in shape, transportation systems wrecked, populations scattered and on the border-line of starvation, and long-established business and trading connections disrupted.

"Acheson's Delta Council Speech, May 8, 1947," *Department of State Bulletin* 16, no. 411 (May 18, 1947), 991–994.

Another grim fact of international life is that two of the greatest workshops of Europe and Asia—Germany and Japan—upon whose production Europe and Asia were to an important degree dependent before the war have hardly been able even to begin the process of reconstruction because of the lack of a peace settlement. As we have seen, recent efforts at Moscow to make progress towards a settlement for Germany and Austria have ended with little accomplishment. Meanwhile, political instability in some degree retards revival in nearly every country of Europe and Asia.

A third factor is that unforeseen disasters—what the lawyers call "acts of God"—have occurred to the crops of Europe. For two successive years unusually severe droughts have cut down food production. And during the past winter storms and floods and excessive cold unprecedented in recent years have swept northern Europe and England with enormous damage to agricultural and fuel production. These disasters have slowed down the already slow pace of reconstruction, have impeded recovery of exports, and have obliged many countries to draw down irreplaceable reserves of gold and foreign exchange, which had been earmarked for the importation of reconstruction materials, for the purchase of food and fuel for subsistence.

The accumulation of these grim developments has produced a disparity between production in the United States and production in the rest of the world that is staggering in its proportions. The United States has been spared physical destruction during the war. Moreover, we have been favored with unusually bountiful agricultural crops in recent years. Production in this country is today running at the annual rate of 210 billion dollars. . . .

Your Congress has authorized and your Government is carrying out a policy of relief and reconstruction today chiefly as a matter of national self-interest. For it is generally agreed that until the various countries of the world get on their feet and become self-supporting there can be no political or economic stability in the world and no lasting peace or prosperity for any of us. Without outside aid, the process of recovery in many countries would take so long as to give rise to hopelessness and despair. In these conditions freedom and democracy and the independence of nations could not long survive, for hopeless and hungry people often resort to desperate measures. The war will not be over until the people of the world can again feed and clothe themselves and face the future with some degree of confidence. . . .

Since world demand exceeds our ability to supply, we are going to have to concentrate our emergency assistance in areas where it will be most effective in building world political and economic stability, in promoting human freedom and democratic institutions, in fostering liberal trading policies, and in strengthening the authority of the United Nations.

This is merely common sense and sound practice. It is in keeping with the policy announced by President Truman in his special message to Congress on March 12 on aid to Greece and Turkey. Free peoples who are seeking to preserve their independence and democratic institutions and human freedoms against totalitarian pressures, either internal or external, will receive top priority for American reconstruction aid. This is no more than frank recognition, as President Truman said, "that totalitarian regimes imposed on free peoples, by direct or indirect aggression, undermine the foundations of international peace and hence the security of the United States."

8. The President's Advisers
Urge Military Expansion, April 1950

Within the past thirty-five years the world has experienced two global wars of tremendous violence. It has witnessed two revolutions—the Russian and the Chinese—of extreme scope and intensity. It has also seen the collapse of five empires—the Ottoman, the Austro-Hungarian, German, Italian, and Japanese—and the drastic decline of two major imperial systems, the British and the French. During the span of one generation, the international distribution of power has been fundamentally altered. For several centuries it had proved impossible for any one nation to gain such preponderant strength that a coalition of other nations could not in time face it with greater strength. The international scene was marked by recurring periods of violence and war, but a system of sovereign and independent states was maintained, over which no state was able to achieve hegemony.

Two complex sets of factors have now basically altered this historical distribution of power. First, the defeat of Germany and Japan and the decline of the British and French Empires have interacted with the development of the United States and the Soviet Union in such a way that power has increasingly gravitated to these two centers. Second, the Soviet Union, unlike previous aspirants to hegemony, is animated by a new fanatic faith, antithetical to our own, and seeks to impose its absolute authority over the rest of the world. Conflict has, therefore, become endemic and is waged, on the part of the Soviet Union, by violent or non-violent methods in accordance with the dictates of expediency. With the development of increasingly terrifying weapons of mass destruction, every individual faces the ever-present possibility of annihilation should the conflict enter the phase of total war.

On the one hand, the people of the world yearn for relief from the anxiety arising from the risk of atomic war. On the other hand, any substantial further extension of the area under the domination of the Kremlin would raise the possibility that no coalition adequate to confront the Kremlin with greater strength could be assembled. It is in this context that this Republic and its citizens in the ascendancy of their strength stand in their deepest peril.

The issues that face us are momentous, involving the fulfillment or destruction not only of this Republic but of civilization itself. They are issues which will not await our deliberations. With conscience and resolution this Government and the people it represents must now take new and fateful decisions. . . .

Our overall policy at the present time may be described as one designed to foster a world environment in which the American system can survive and flourish. It therefore rejects the concept of isolation and affirms the necessity of our positive participation in the world community.

This broad intention embraces two subsidiary policies. One is a policy which we would probably pursue even if there were no Soviet threat. It is a policy of attempting to develop a healthy international community. The other is the policy of "containing" the Soviet system. These two policies are closely interrelated and interact on one

Excerpts from "NSC-68: A Report to the National Security Council," April 14, 1950, from *The Naval War College Review* 27/6, May/June 1975, pp. 51–108. Reprinted by permission of the Naval War College Review.

another. Nevertheless, the distinction between them is basically valid and contributes to a clearer understanding of what we are trying to do.

The policy of striving to develop a healthy international community is the long-term constructive effort which we are engaged in. It was this policy which gave rise to our vigorous sponsorship of the United Nations. It is of course the principal reason for our long continuing endeavors to create and now develop the Inter-American system. It, as much as containment, underlay our efforts to rehabilitate Western Europe. Most of our international economic activities can likewise be explained in terms of this policy.

In a world of polarized power, the policies designed to develop a healthy international community are more than ever necessary to our own strength. . . .

A comprehensive and decisive program to win the peace and frustrate the Kremlin design should be so designed that it can be sustained for as long as necessary to achieve our national objectives. It would probably involve:

1. The development of an adequate political and economic framework for the achievement of our long-range objectives.
2. A substantial increase in expenditures for military purposes adequate to meet the requirements for the tasks listed in Section D-1.
3. A substantial increase in military assistance programs, designed to foster co-operative efforts, which will adequately and efficiently meet the requirements of our allies for the tasks referred to in Section D-1-*e*.
4. Some increase in economic assistance programs and recognition of the need to continue these programs until their purposes have been accomplished.
5. A concerted attack on the problem of the United States balance of payments, along the lines already approved by the President.
6. Development of programs designed to build and maintain confidence among other peoples in our strength and resolution, and to wage overt psychological warfare calculated to encourage mass defections from Soviet allegiance and to frustrate the Kremlin design in other ways.
7. Intensification of affirmative and timely measures and operations by covert means in the fields of economic warfare and political psychological warfare with a view to fomenting and supporting unrest and revolt in selected strategic satellite countries.
8. Development of internal security and civilian defense programs.
9. Improvement and intensification of intelligence activities.
10. Reduction of Federal expenditures for purposes other than defense and foreign assistance, if necessary by the deferment of certain desirable programs.
11. Increased taxes. . . .

Conclusions and Recommendations

The foregoing analysis indicates that the probable fission bomb capability and possible thermonuclear bomb capability of the Soviet Union have greatly intensified the Soviet threat to the security of the United States. This threat is of the same character as that described in NSC 20/4 (approved by the President on November 24, 1948) but is more immediate than had previously been estimated. In particular, the United States now faces the contingency that within the next four or five years the Soviet Union will possess the military capability of delivering a surprise atomic attack of such weight that the United States must have substantially increased general air, ground, and sea strength, atomic capabilities, and air and civilian defenses to deter war and to provide reasonable assurance, in the event of war, that it could survive the initial blow and go on to the eventual attainment of its objectives. In turn, this contingency requires the intensification of our efforts in the fields of intelligence and research and development. . . .

In the light of present and prospective Soviet atomic capabilities, the action which can be taken under present programs and plans, however, becomes dangerously inadequate, in both timing and scope, to accomplish the rapid progress toward the attainment of the United States' political, economic, and military objectives which is now imperative.

A continuation of present trends would result in a serious decline in the strength of the free world relative to the Soviet Union and its satellites. This unfavorable trend arises from the inadequacy of current programs and plans rather than from any error in our objectives and aims. These trends lead in the direction of isolation, not by deliberate decision but by lack of the necessary basis for a vigorous initiative in the conflict with the Soviet Union.

Our position as the center of power in the free world places a heavy responsibility upon the United States for leadership. We must organize and enlist the energies and resources of the free world in a positive program for peace which will frustrate the Kremlin design for world domination by creating a situation in the free world to which the Kremlin will be compelled to adjust. Without such a cooperative effort, led by the United States, we will have to make gradual withdrawals under pressure until we discovered one day that we have sacrificed positions of vital interest.

It is imperative that this trend be reversed by a much more rapid and concerted build-up of the actual strength of both the United States and the other nations of the free world. The analysis shows that this will be costly and will involve significant domestic financial and economic adjustments.

The execution of such a build-up, however, requires that the United States have an affirmative program beyond the solely defensive one of countering the threat posed by the Soviet Union. This program must light the path to peace and order among nations in a system based on freedom and justice, as contemplated in the Charter of the United Nations. Further, it must envisage the political and economic measures with which and the military shield behind which the free world can work to frustrate the Kremlin design by the strategy of the cold war; for every consideration of devotion to our fundamental values and to our national security demands that we achieve our objectives by the strategy of the cold war, building up our military strength in order that it may not have to be used. The only sure victory lies in the frustration of the Kremlin design by the steady development of the moral and material strength of the free world and its projection into the Soviet world in such a way as to bring about an internal change in the Soviet system. Such a positive program—harmonious with our fundamental national purpose and our objectives—is necessary if we are to regain and retain the initiative and to win and hold the necessary popular support and cooperation in the United States and the rest of the free world.

This program should include a plan for negotiation with the Soviet Union, developed and agreed with our allies and which is consonant with our objectives. The United States and its allies, particularly the United Kingdom and France, should always be ready to negotiate with the Soviet Union on terms consistent with our objectives. The present world situation, however, is one which militates against successful negotiations with the Kremlin—for the terms of agreements on important pending issues would reflect present realities and would therefore be unacceptable, if not disastrous, to the United States and the rest of the free world. After a decision and a start on building up the strength of the free world has been made, it might then be desirable for the United States to take an initiative in seeking negotiations in the hope that it might facilitate the process of accommodation by the Kremlin to the new situation. Failing that, the unwillingness of the Kremlin to accept equitable terms or its bad faith in observing them would assist in consolidating popular opinion in the free world in support of the measures necessary to sustain the build-up.

In summary, we must, by means of a rapid and sustained build-up of the political, economic, and military strength of the free world, and by means of an affirmative program intended to wrest the initiative from the Soviet Union, confront it with convincing evidence of the determination and ability of the free world to frustrate the Kremlin design of a world dominated by its will. Such evidence is the only means short of war which eventually may force the Kremlin to abandon its present course of action and to negotiate acceptable agreements on issues of major importance.

The whole success of the proposed program hangs ultimately on recognition by this Government, the American people, and all free peoples, that the cold war is in fact a real war in which the survival of the free world is at stake. Essential prerequisites to success are consultations with Congressional leaders designed to make the program the object of non-partisan legislative support, and a presentation to the public of a full explanation of the facts and implications of the present international situation. The prosecution of the program will require of us all the ingenuity, sacrifice, and unity demanded by the vital importance of the issue and the tenacity to persevere until our national objectives have been attained.

9. President Truman and His Advisers Determine the United States' Response to the Invasion of South Korea, June 26, 1950

GENERAL [HOYT S.] VANDENBERG reported that the First Yak [North Korean] plane had been shot down.

THE PRESIDENT remarked that he hoped that it was not the last.

GENERAL VANDENBERG read the text of the orders which had been issued to our Air Forces calling on them to take "aggressive action" against any planes interfering with their mission or operating in a manner unfriendly to the South Korean forces. He indicated, however, that they had been avoiding combat where the direct carrying-out of their mission was not involved.

U.S. Department of State, *Foreign Relations of the United States, 1950, Korea* (Washington, D.C.: GPO, 1976), VII, 179–183.

MR. [DEAN] ACHESON suggested that an all-out order be issued to the Navy and Air Force to waive all restrictions on their operations in Korea and to offer the fullest possible support to the South Korean forces, attacking tanks, guns, columns, etc., of the North Korean forces in order to give a chance to the South Koreans to reform.

THE PRESIDENT said he approved this.

MR. [FRANK] PACE inquired whether this meant action only south of the thirty-eighth parallel.

MR. ACHESON said this was correct. He was making no suggestion for any action across the line.

GENERAL VANDENBERG asked whether this meant also that they should not fly over the line.

MR. ACHESON said they should not.

THE PRESIDENT said this was correct; that no action should be taken north of the thirty-eighth parallel. He added "not yet." . . .

MR. ACHESON said that the second point he wished to bring up was that orders should be issued to the Seventh Fleet to prevent an attack on Formosa.

THE PRESIDENT said he agreed.

MR. ACHESON continued that at the same time the National Government of China should be told to desist from operations against the mainland and that the Seventh Fleet should be ordered to see that those operations would cease.

MR. ACHESON said his third point was an increase in the United States military forces in the Philippines and an acceleration of aid to the Philippines in order that we might have a firm base there.

THE PRESIDENT said he agreed.

MR. ACHESON said his fourth point was that aid to Indochina should be stepped up and that a strong military mission should be sent. . . .

THE PRESIDENT said that he had a letter from the Generalissimo [Jiang Jieshi] about one month (?) ago to the effect that the Generalissimo might step out of the situation if that would help. He said this was a private letter and he had kept it secret. He said that we might want to proceed along those lines in order to get Chinese forces helping us. He thought that the Generalissimo might step out if MacArthur were put in.

MR. ACHESON said that the Generalissimo was unpredictable and that it was possible that he might resist and "throw the ball game." He said that it might be well to do this later.

THE PRESIDENT said that was alright. He himself thought that it was the next step. . . .

MR. ACHESON added in regard to the Formosan situation that he thought it undesirable that we should get mixed up in the question of the Chinese administration of the Island.

THE PRESIDENT said that we were not going to give the Chinese "a nickel" for any purpose whatever. He said that all the money we had given them is now invested in United States real estate. . . .

MR. [JOHN D.] HICKERSON read the draft of the Security Council resolution recommending that UN members render such assistance as was needed to Korea to repel the attack.

THE PRESIDENT said that was right. He said we wanted everyone in on this, including Hong Kong.

GENERAL [OMAR] BRADLEY reported that British Air Marshall Tedder had come to see him, was generally in accord with our taking the firm position, and gave General Bradley a full report of the forces which the British have in that area.

MR. [DEAN] RUSK pointed out that it was possible the Russians would come to the Security Council meeting and cast a veto. In that case we would still take the position that we could act in support of the Charter.

THE PRESIDENT said that was right. He rather wished they would veto. He said we needed to lay a base for our action in Formosa. He said that he would work on the draft of his statement tonight and would talk to the Defense and State Departments in the morning regarding the final text.

MR. RUSK pointed out that it was Mr. [George F.] Kennan's estimate that Formosa would be the next likely spot for a Communist move.

SECRETARY [LOUIS A.] JOHNSON reported that SCAP's [Supreme Commander to the Allied Powers] guess was that the next move would be on Iran. He thought there should be a check on this.

GENERAL [J. LAWTON] COLLINS said that SCAP did not have as much global information as they have in Washington. He and Mr. Pace stated that they have asked for full reports all over the world in regard to any developments, particularly of Soviet preparations.

SECRETARY JOHNSON suggested to Mr. Acheson that it would be advisable to have some talks with the UK regarding possible action in Iran.

MR. ACHESON said he would talk with both the British and French. . . .

MR. ACHESON suggested that the President might wish to get in Senator [Tom] Connally and other members of the Senate and House and tell them what had been decided.

THE PRESIDENT said that he had a meeting scheduled for 10:00 tomorrow morning with the Big Four [congressional leaders] and that he would get in any others that the Secretary thought should be added. He suggested that Secretaries Acheson and Johnson should also be there. . . .

GENERAL COLLINS stated that the military situation in Korea was bad. It was impossible to say how much our air can do. The Korean Chief of Staff has no fight left in him.

MR. ACHESON stated that it was important for us to do something even if the effort were not successful.

MR. JOHNSON said that even if we lose Korea this action would save the situation. He said this action "suits me." He then asked whether any of the military representatives had any objection to the course of action which had been outlined. There was no objection.

GENERAL VANDENBERG, in response to a question that Mr. [Thomas] Finletter, said that he bet a tank would be knocked out before dark.

THE PRESIDENT said he had done everything he could for five years to prevent this kind of situation. Now the situation is here and we must do what we can to meet it. He had been wondering about the mobilization of the National Guard and asked General Bradley if that was necessary now. If it was he must go to Congress and ask for funds. He was merely putting the subject on the table for discussion. He repeated we must do everything we can for the Korean situation—"for the United Nations."

GENERAL BRADLEY said that if we commit our ground forces in Korea we cannot at the same time carry out our other commitments without mobilization. He wondered if it was better to wait now on the question of mobilization of the National Guard. He thought it would be preferable to wait a few days.

THE PRESIDENT said he wished the Joint Chiefs to think about this and to let him know in a few days' time. He said "I don't want to go to war."

GENERAL COLLINS stated that if we were going to commit ground forces in Korea we must mobilize.

MR. ACHESON suggested that we should hold mobilization in reserve. . . .

GENERAL COLLINS remarked that if we had had standing orders we could have stopped this. We must consider this problem for the future.

THE PRESIDENT said he agreed.

☒ *E S S A Y S*

In the first essay, Yale historian John Lewis Gaddis, the preeminent post-revisionist historian of the Cold War, argues that the Cold War was the product of what he calls Soviet unilateralism. Soviet behavior, Gaddis argues, "alarmed not just Americans but a good portion of the rest of the world as well." In a subsequent book, *Now We Know: Rethinking Cold War History* (1997), Gaddis returned to this theme, emphasizing not only Russian history and Soviet ideology, but also Stalin's personality, which Gaddis characterized as "authoritarian, paranoid, and narcissistic." In the second essay, diplomatic historian Thomas G. Paterson of the University of Connecticut emphasizes the broad, expansionist goals of U.S. foreign policy and what he argues was the persistent exaggeration of the Soviet threat by U.S. leaders. "The story of Truman's foreign policy," he concludes, "is basically an accounting of how the United States, because of its own expansionism and exaggeration of the Soviet threat, became a global power."

Soviet Unilateralism and the Origins of the Cold War

JOHN LEWIS GADDIS

Wartime lack of concern over the powerful position the Soviet Union would occupy in the postwar world had been predicated upon the assumption that the Russians would continue to act in concert with their American and British allies. So long as the Grand Alliance remained intact, Western statesmen could assure each other, Moscow's emergence as the dominant Eurasian power would pose no threat. But during the final months of the war, there began to appear unsettling indications of a determination on Stalin's part to secure postwar interests without reference to the corresponding interests of his wartime associates. It was these manifestations of unilateralism that first set off alarm bells in the West about Russian intentions; the resulting uneasiness in turn stimulated deeper and more profound anxieties.

"I am becoming increasingly concerned," Secretary of State [Cordell] Hull warned Ambassador W. Averell Harriman early in 1944, "over the . . . successive moves of the Soviet Government in the field of foreign relations." Hull went on to observe in this message, drafted by Soviet specialist Charles E. Bohlen, that whatever the legitimacy of Moscow's security interests in Eastern Europe—"and as you know we have carefully avoided and shall continue to avoid any disruption with the Soviet Government on the merits of such questions"—unilateral actions to secure those interests "cannot fail to do irreparable harm to the whole cause of international collaboration." The American people would not be disposed to participate in any postwar scheme of world organization which would be seen "as a cover for another great power to pursue a course of unilateral action in the international sphere based on superior force." It was "of the utmost importance that the principle of consultation and cooperation with the Soviet Union be kept alive at all costs, but some measures of cooperation in relation to world public opinion must be forthcoming from the Soviet Government."

This document reflects as well as any other the point from which American statesmen began to develop concerns about the postwar intentions of the Soviet Union. The United States had not challenged Moscow's determination to retain the boundaries it had secured as a result of Stalin's unsavory pact with Hitler in 1939, nor had it questioned the Russians' right to a postwar sphere of influence in what remained of Eastern Europe. It was prepared to grant similar concessions in East Asia in return for eventual U.S.S.R. participation in the war against Japan. But because the Roosevelt administration had justified American entry into the war as a defense of self-determination, and because it had committed the nation to participation in a postwar world collective security organization as a means of implementing that principle, it required from the Soviet Union a measure of discretion and restraint in consolidating these areas of control. Unilateral action seemed likely to endanger the balance of power, not by allowing the Russians to dominate areas beyond their borders—that domination was assumed—but rather by weakening the American capacity for countervailing action in the postwar world by provoking, first, public disillusionment and then, as a consequence, a revival of the isolationism the President and his advisers had fought so long and so hard to overcome.

The Russians, to put it mildly, were less than sensitive to these concerns. As their armies moved into Eastern Europe in 1944 they immediately set out to undermine potential sources of opposition, not just in the former enemy countries of Rumania, Bulgaria, and Hungary, but most conspicuously of all in Poland, which had been, after all, an ally. The callousness with which the Red Army allowed the Germans to decimate the anti-communist resistance in Warsaw late that summer shocked Western statesmen; meanwhile British and American representatives on Allied Control Commissions in the Balkans found themselves denied any significant influence in shaping occupation policies there as well. Moscow had interpreted Western restraint as a sign of weakness, Harrison reported in September: "Unless we take issue with the present policy there is every indication that the Soviet Union will become a world bully wherever their interests are involved. . . . No written agreements can be of any value unless they are carried out in a spirit of give and take and recognition of the interests of other people."

Franklin Roosevelt made valiant efforts at Yalta to make Stalin aware of the need to observe the proprieties in Eastern Europe, but these proved unsuccessful almost at once when the Soviet leader interpreted agreements made to hold free elections there as in fact license to impose still tighter control on Poland and Rumania. "Averell is right," Roosevelt complained three weeks before his death. "We can't do business with Stalin. He has broken every one of the promises he made at Yalta." FDR had not been prepared, on the basis of these difficulties, to write off all possibilities of postwar cooperation with the Russians. But Soviet unilateralism does appear to have convinced him, by the time of his death, that efforts to win Stalin's trust had not worked; and that future policy toward the Soviet Union would have to be based on a strict *quid pro quo* basis.

Harry S Truman emphatically agreed. Although the new Chief Executive had had no direct experience in the conduct of foreign affairs, he could have hardly believed more firmly in the importance of keeping one's word. "When I say I'm going to do something, I do it," he once wrote, "or [I] bust my insides trying to do it." It was characteristic of him that he did not believe in divorce because "when you make a contract you should keep it." Convinced that the Yalta agreements on free elections in Eastern Europe were in fact contracts, determined to demonstrate decisiveness in an awesome and unexpected position of responsibility, Truman resolved—probably more categorically than Roosevelt would have done—to hold the Russians to what they had agreed to. It was this determination that occasioned the new President's sharp rejoinder to Soviet Foreign Minister V. M. Molotov after less than two weeks in office: "Carry out your agreements and you won't get talked to like that." A month later he complained again that the Russians were not honoring their agreements: they were, he told Henry Wallace, "like people from across the tracks whose manners were very bad."

The experience of meeting Stalin personally at Potsdam seems to have modified the President's attitude somewhat. The Soviet autocrat evoked memories of the Kansas City political boss Tom Pendergast, a man with whom deals could be made because he had always kept his word. "I can deal with Stalin," Truman noted in his diary at Potsdam. "He is honest—but smart as hell." Disturbed by rumors of the dictator's ill health, the President worried about what would happen "if Joe suddenly passed out" because his potential successors lacked sincerity. For several years afterward, there persisted in Truman's mind the notion that difficulties with the Russians reflected Stalin's internal political problems—interference from a recalcitrant Politburo was the most frequent explanation—rather than any personal desire on the Soviet leader's part to violate his word.

But deals had to be honored if they were to work, and with the return of peace instances of Soviet unilateralism began to proliferate. Reasonably free elections took place in Hungary and Czechoslovakia, but only in those countries: Moscow's grip on Poland, Rumania, and Bulgaria remained as tight as ever. The Russians joined the French in resisting central economic administration of occupied Germany; they also arbitrarily transferred a substantial portion of that country's eastern territory to Poland. Attempts to reunify another divided nation, Korea, came to naught as the Russians refused to tolerate anything other than a satellite government there. The Soviet Union rejected participation in the World Bank and the International Monetary Fund, institutions American planners regarded as critical for postwar economic recovery. And Stalin was showing strong signs, as 1945 ended, of exploiting the presence of Soviet troops in northern Iran to carve out yet another sphere of influence there. He was "trying to find a basis for an understanding which would give him confidence that an agreement reached with the Russians would be lived up to," Truman told his advisers in December 1945. He had such confidence in dealing with the British, the Dutch, and the Chinese (though not the French), "but there is no evidence yet that the Russians intend to change their habits so far as honoring contracts is concerned."

The Chief Executive's initial inclination had been to regard these difficulties simply as failures of communication; with that explanation in mind, he had authorized Secretary of State [James F.] Byrnes to make one more effort to settle them at a hastily called meeting of foreign ministers in Moscow in December. By that time, though, public and Congressional impatience with Soviet unilateralism had considerably intensified. Sensitive to these pressures, irritated by Byrnes' eagerness to reach agreements without consulting him, Truman early in 1946 proclaimed to himself—if not directly to Byrnes, as he later claimed—his intention to stop "babying" the Soviets: "Unless Russia is faced with an iron fist and strong language another war is in the making. Only one language do they understand—'how many divisions have you?' I do not think we should play at compromise any longer."

There was, in fact, no compromise when the Russians failed to meet their agreed-upon deadline for removing their troops from Iran: instead the administration confronted Moscow publicly in the United Nations Security Council and forced a humiliating withdrawal. Truman drew the appropriate conclusions: "Told him to tell Stalin I held him to be a man to keep his word," he noted in his appointment book after a meeting with the newly designated ambassador to the Soviet Union, Walter Bedell Smith, on March 23. "Troops in Iran after March 2 upset that theory." By June, he was writing to the author Pearl Buck that "the United States has performed no unfriendly act nor made a single unfriendly gesture toward the great Russian nation. . . . How has Russia met our friendly overtures?" The following month, after *New York Times* correspondent Brooks Atkinson had published a series of articles highly critical of the Russians, Truman pointedly invited him to the White House. That same day he told his advisers that he was "tired of our being pushed around," that "here a little, there a little, they are chiseling from us," and that "now is [the] time to take [a] stand on Russia."

It was in this spirit that the President authorized the first comprehensive study of Soviet-American relations to be carried out within the government. Compiled under the direction of his Special Counsel, Clark M. Clifford, and written after consultations with the Departments of State, War, Navy, the Joint Chiefs of Staff, and the Director of Central Intelligence, the report acknowledged that agreements between nations were at times susceptible to differing interpretations. Nonetheless, it argued, there existed a persistent pattern on Moscow's part of either unilaterally implementing such agreements in such a way as to serve Soviet interest, or encouraging satellites to do so. "[T]here is no question," the report emphasized, "where the primary responsibility lies."

The implications could only be that the Soviet Union had no intention of cooperating with the West to maintain the existing balance of power; that it sought to expand its own influence as widely as possible without regard for the security requirements of its former allies; and that, when circumstances were right, it would be prepared to risk war to attain that objective. American policy could no longer be based upon the assumption of shared interests, therefore; priorities henceforth would have to be directed toward the accumulation of sufficient military strength to deter war if possible and to win it if necessary, while at the same time keeping open possibilities for dealing with the Russians should a change of heart in the Kremlin eventually occur. "[I]t is our hope," the report concluded, "that they will eventually change their minds and work out with us a fair and equitable settlement when they realize that we are too strong to be beaten and too determined to be frightened."

President Truman received the Clifford report on September 24, four days after he had fired Henry Wallace from the Cabinet for publicly advocating a more conciliatory policy toward the Soviet Union. There is no question that he agreed with its general conclusions: on the day before he dismissed Wallace he had complained in his diary about

> Reds, phonies, and . . . parlor pinks [who] can see no wrong in Russia's four and one half million armed forces, in Russia's loot of Poland, Austria, Hungary, Rumania, Manchuria. . . . But when we help our friends in China who fought on our side it is terrible. When Russia loots the industrial plant of those same friends it is all right. When Russia occupies Persia for oil that is heavenly.

But Truman chose not to use the Clifford report, as he might have, to justify increased military appropriations; instead he ordered all copies to be locked in the White House safe, where they remained for the duration of the administration. "There is too much loose talk about the Russian situation," he had written former Vice President John Nance Garner on the day after Wallace's dismissal. "We are not going to have any shooting trouble with them but they are tough bargainers and always ask for the whole earth, expecting maybe to get an acre."

The President's cautious reaction to the manifestations of Soviet unilateralism catalogued in the Clifford report reflected a desire to avoid hasty and ill-considered action, but certainly no continuing assumption of common interest. Repeated demonstrations of Moscow's callousness to the priorities and sensibilities of its former allies had by this time virtually drained the reservoir of good will toward the Russians that had built up during the war. American leaders had been inclined, for many months, to give the Kremlin the benefit of the doubt: to assume, despite accumulating evidence to the contrary, that difficulties with Moscow had arisen out of misunderstandings rather than fundamental conflicts of interest. But such charitableness could not continue indefinitely, as Winston Churchill pointed out in the summer of 1946: "The American eagle sits on his perch, a large strong bird with formidable beak and claws. . . . Mr. Gromyko [Soviet ambassador] is sent every day to prod him with a sharp sickle, now on his beak, now under his wing, now in his tail feathers. All the time the eagle keeps quite still, but it would be a great mistake to suppose that nothing is going on inside the breast of the eagle." . . .

Americans had not always found cooperation with authoritarian regimes to be impossible: the Russian-American relationship itself had been friendly throughout most of its early history, despite the vast cultural and political differences that separated the two countries. But toward the end of the 19th century a combination of circumstances—increasing repression within Russia, a keener American sensitivity to conditions inside other countries, growing rivalries between Washington and

St. Petersburg over spheres of influence in East Asia—had produced in the United States the suspicion that a connection existed between autocratic rule at home and aggressiveness in foreign affairs. Parallel concerns had accompanied the deterioration of relations with imperial Germany prior to World War I; certainly participation in that conflict, which Woodrow Wilson justified by stressing the linkage between autocracy and aggression, served powerfully to reinforce this idea. Determination to remain aloof from European involvements caused Americans to worry less about such matters during the 1920s and early 1930s—indeed, the economic distress of the latter decade even produced in some circles a grudging respect for dictatorships— but the experience of fighting Germany and Japan during World War II brought back repugnance for arbitrary rule with a vengeance. It would not take very many signs of aggressiveness on the part of totalitarian regimes in the postwar world— even totalitarian former allies—to convince Americans that the connection between domestic despotism and international expansionism still prevailed.

"If we fought Germany because of our belief that a police state and a democratic state could not exist in the same world," Rear Admiral Ellery W. Stone told Secretary of the Navy James Forrestal in July 1946, then "it must necessarily follow that we could not afford to lie down before Russia." The simple fact that the Soviet Union was a totalitarian state raised suspicions that its foreign policy would proceed from priorities incompatible with those of the democracies—priorities now elaborately enshrined in the procedures the United Nations had established for settling international disputes. Totalitarian states, Americans assumed, relied upon force or the threat of force to secure their interests; such nations could hardly be expected to share Washington's aspiration to see the rule of law ultimately govern relations between nations. "[I]t is not Communism but Totalitarianism which is the potential threat," publisher Arthur Hays Sulzberger pointed out. ". . . [O]nly people who have a Bill of Rights are not the potential enemies of other people." . . .

It was no accident, then, that when the President in the most famous speech of his career characterized the world as divided between two ways of life, one reflecting "the will of the majority," the other based "upon the will of a minority forcibly imposed upon the majority," it was the distinction between democracy and totalitarianism to which he referred. By so doing, he implicitly linked his own justification of American action to restore the balance of power in Europe to those advanced by Franklin Roosevelt in the Atlantic Charter and by Woodrow Wilson in the Fourteen Points: in each case the assumption was the ultimate incompatibility of autocratic and democratic institutions. The fact that this particular autocracy also embraced the ideology of communism was, for Truman, relatively insignificant.

That certainly was not the case for most Americans, though. Nothing—not even totalitarianism—did more to arouse suspicion about the Soviet Union's behavior than that country's long-standing and self-proclaimed intention to seek the overthrow of capitalist governments throughout the world. American hostility toward communism went back to the earliest days of the Bolshevik Revolution: to Russia's abandonment of the Allied cause in World War I; to the terror expropriations, and executions that soon followed; to the postwar Red Scare, with its suggestion that even the United States might not be immune from the bacillus of revolution. The Soviet Union's commitment to communism had been the primary justification for Washington's refusal to recognize that country until 1933; and even after that date

Moscow's claim to be the vanguard of world revolution had continued to plague relations with Washington. Stalin implicitly acknowledged the corrosive effects of ideology upon his dealings with the West in 1943 when, eager for an Anglo-American commitment to establish a Second Front, he abolished the Comintern, Lenin's designated instrument for bringing about the world proletarian revolution. But there could be no guarantee that such restraint would continue once Moscow's enemies had been defeated. As a Department of State memorandum put it in 1944, it was necessary to keep in mind the Soviet conviction that "there is an irreconcilable chasm between 'socialism' and 'capitalism' and that any temporary association in a common interest [is] an association of expediency for a specific purpose but with no underlying affinity of fundamental interest, civilization, or tradition."

"I expressed it as my view that it would not be difficult to work with Russia provided we were dealing with her only as a national entity," James Forrestal noted in his diary during the summer of 1945. "[T]he real problem was whether or not Russian policy called for a continuation of the Third International's objectives, namely, world revolution and the application of the political principles of the dialectical materialists for the entire world." Evidence that the Kremlin still harbored such ambitions arose from two sets of circumstances: the Russians' use of communist parties in Eastern Europe as instruments with which to create their sphere of influence there; and the increasing success of communist parties in Western Europe, the Eastern Mediterranean, and China. In retrospect, it is not at all clear that these phenomena were related: the popularity of communist parties outside the Soviet sphere grew primarily out of their effectiveness as resistance fighters against the Axis; in Eastern Europe the communists owed their prominence chiefly to Moscow's reliance on them to consolidate its control. Nor was it obvious that the Soviet Union's use of foreign communist parties to promote its interests necessarily proved an ideological motivation for its policies.

But these fine points were difficult to keep in mind as the end of the war brought increases in the militancy—and anti-American rhetoric—of all communist parties, not least that of the Soviet Union itself. When combined with the indisputable evidence of Moscow's unilateral expansionism, when considered against the record of how Nazi Germany had used "fifth columns" before the war, it is not surprising that concern about the ideological dimension of the Soviet challenge should have surfaced as well. "The tendency is increasingly marked," the British Embassy in Washington reported in August 1946, "to detect the Soviet mind or hand behind every move which seems to threaten or embarrass the United States or its friends, and to link events in one part of the world with those in another." The editors of *Newsweek* put it more bluntly: "U.S. officials in the best position to judge fear they have confirmation that the Soviet Government has made up its mind that capitalism must be destroyed if Communism is to live."

Both the "totalitarian" and the "ideological" explanations of Soviet behavior had in common the assumption that one was dealing with a compulsive internally driven process, unresponsive to gestures of restraint or goodwill from the outside. There had been yet a third interpretation of Moscow's unilateralism, popular during the war, that had seen it as growing out of a quite understandable preoccupation with security capable of being alleviated by patient Western efforts to win the Russians' trust. President Roosevelt himself had made this "insecurity" theory the basis of his policy toward the Soviet Union, and it had remained very much alive—though under increasing challenge—during the first months of the Truman administration. But theories require validation if they are to be sustained: however persuasive the "insecurity" model of Soviet behavior may be in retrospect, what struck most observers at the time was the utter imperviousness of Stalin's regime to the gestures of restraint and goodwill that emanated from the West during and immediately after the war. Moscow's perceived failure to reciprocate these initiatives made it more and more difficult to sustain an interpretation of Soviet actions based on "insecurity," as Henry Wallace found out when he attempted during the spring and summer of 1946, to revive it within the inner councils of the government. The "totalitarian" and "ideological" models were the obvious alternatives.

It is ironic that the individual most influential in discrediting "insecurity" as an explanation of Soviet unilateralism shared many of its basic assumptions. George F. Kennan had never been inclined to interpret Soviet behavior in either strictly totalitarian or ideological terms. As a keen student of Russian history and culture, he was fully aware of the lack of self-confidence that plagued the Stalinist government, and of the extent to which its unilateralism was defensively motivated. But he emphatically did not share the view of Wallace and others that these attitudes could be modified from the outside. It was in an effort to bring official Washington to see that point that Kennan crafted the February 1946 "long telegram," to this day the single most influential explanation of postwar Soviet behavior, and one which powerfully reinforced the growing tendency within the United States to interpret Moscow's actions in a sinister light.

The "long telegram" had the great influence that it did because it provided a way to fuse concerns about totalitarianism and communism in dealing with the Soviet Union. It portrayed that state as one in which an autocratic tradition had become incorporated within an ideological compulsion to treat the outside world as hostile. The conclusion was clear: no actions the United States or its Western allies could take would alleviate Stalin's suspicion; the best one could do was to look to one's own defenses—and to the strength and self- confidence of one's own society—and wait for the internal forces of change within the Soviet system to have their effect.

There is a definite psychological satisfaction, when confronted with a phenomenon one does not understand, in finding a simple but persuasive explanation. Whatever the actual intentions of its author, the "long telegram" performed that function within the government in 1946; a similar analysis would find a wider audience the following year in the form of the famous "X" article in *Foreign Affairs*. The "totalitarian-ideological" model of Soviet behavior provided a clear, plausible, and in many ways, gratifying explanation of the Russians' failure to cooperate with their former allies in building a lasting peace: it absolved the United States of responsibility for the breakdown of wartime cooperation; it made any future relaxation of tensions dependent upon changes of heart in Moscow, not Washington. Americans did not welcome the onset of the Cold War. But the rationale they worked out to account for its appearance at least had the advantage of allowing them to approach the coming contest with a reasonably clear conscience.

The Soviet Union's emergence as a potential adversary closed an obvious gap in Washington's thinking about the postwar world. A generalized sense of vulnerability, related both to historical experience and to technological change, had caused United States officials to regard preservation of a global balance of power as a vital interest even before specific challenges to that balance had manifested themselves. This situation of perceived vulnerability in the absence of apparent threat accounts for the failure of the United States to deploy forces and establish bases in the way one might have expected had the Russians been seen as the enemy from the beginning. But Soviet unilateralism, together with the conclusions about the roots of Soviet behavior that unilateralism provoked, had by 1947 created a credible source of danger, with the result that American strategy now took on a clearer and more purposeful aspect.

Central to it was the defense of Western Europe, a priority so basic that it was more often assumed than articulated. "[I]t is not a question of what men think now," the Joint Chiefs of Staff noted in the spring of 1947; "[it] is something that has been demonstrated by what we have had to do, though tardily, and therefore at greater risk and cost, in actual warfare in the past. . . . The entire area of Western Europe is in first place as an area of strategic importance to the United States." And yet, American planners had given remarkably little thought to the means by which that part of the world might be secured against Soviet expansionism. Their assumption— again mostly unstated—had been that Great Britain would provide the necessary counter presence, and that the United States could concern itself with other matters. It had done just that throughout 1946, concentrating on resisting Soviet pressures aimed at Iran and Turkey, consolidating its position in Japan and southern Korea, mediating the Chinese civil war, and attempting to resolve the diplomatic stalemate over Germany.

The British decision to withdraw military assistance from Greece and Turkey in February 1947 forced a reconsideration of these priorities, not because two countries were of critical importance in and of themselves, but because of the way in which London's action dramatized the failure of Western Europe as a whole to recover from the war. A major consequence of that conflict had been, in [British geopolitician Sir Halford] Mackinder's terminology, a severe weakening of the "rim-land" states surrounding the Soviet "heartland," leaving only the "world island"— effectively the United States—as a countervailing balance. But it was not until 1947 that Washington officials realized the full implications of that fact and set about taking corrective action.

At no point—despite references to the possibility of war in the 1946 Clifford report—did these officials seriously anticipate a Soviet military attack in Europe. Estimates of Moscow's intentions, whether from the Pentagon, the State Department, or the intelligence community, consistently discounted the possibility that the Russians might risk a direct military confrontation within the foreseeable future. Several considerations contributed to that judgment, not least of which was the damage the Soviet Union itself had suffered during the war and the still relatively primitive character of its air and naval forces. But these estimates also suggested that the Russians would not need to use force to gain their objectives, because of the ease with which war-weakened neighbors could be psychologically intimidated. "[I]f the countries of the world lose confidence in us," General George A. Lincoln of the War Department General Staff told the Senate Foreign Relations Committee early in April 1947, "they may in effect pass under the Iron Curtain without any pressure other than the subversive pressure being put on them."

American planners assumed a direct correlation between economic health, psychological self-confidence, and the capacity for defense. As a State-War-Navy Coordinating Committee report noted that same month: "[E]conomic weaknesses may give rise to instability and subsequently to political shifts which adversely affect the security of the U.S." This could happen through "boring from within" tactics or the threat of overwhelming external force, but in either event the outcome from the standpoint of American interests would be grim. "Without further prompt and substantial aid from the United States," Under Secretary William Clayton argued, "economic, social, and political disintegration will overwhelm Europe." . . .

But it was the psychological implications of an extension of Soviet influence over Europe that probably most concerned American leaders. Although the term "domino theory" would not come into currency for another decade, administration officials worried deeply about the "bandwagon" effect that might ensue if the perception became widespread that the momentum in world affairs was on the Russians' side. And despite the United States' own history of isolationism, despite its relative self-sufficiency, there was a very real fear of what might happen if the nation were left without friends in the world. In one sense, this fear grew out of the tradition of American exceptionalism: the United States had always viewed itself as both apart from and a model for the rest of the world; it could hardly have regarded with equanimity evidence that its example was no longer relevant. But, in another sense, it was precisely the unexceptional character of Americans in relation to the rest of the world that was at issue here: who was to say that, buoyed by success in Europe, the totalitarian instinct might not take hold in the United States as well? "There is a little bit of the totalitarian buried somewhere, way down deep, in each and every one of us," George Kennan reminded students at the National War College in the spring of 1947. "It is only the cheerful light of confidence and security which keeps this evil genius down. . . . If confidence and security were to disappear, don't think that he would not be waiting to take their place."

The strategy of containment brought together the new American interest in maintaining a global balance of power with the perceived Muscovite challenge to that equilibrium in a part of the world that could hardly have been more pivotal— Western Europe. It sought to deal with that danger primarily by economic rather than military means; its goal was not so much the creation of an American hegemony as it was a re-creation of independent centers of power capable of balancing each other as well as the Russians. This is hardly the place to evaluate the success of that strategy or to trace its subsequent mutations and incarnations: these subjects have received excessively lengthy treatment elsewhere. Suffice it to say that the strategy could not have evolved without the perception of vulnerability brought about by the war, and the all-too-successful—if inadvertent—efforts of the Russians to give that abstraction an alarming reality.

Soviet historians have argued with unsurprising consistency through the years that the United States over-reacted to the "threat" posed by the U.S.S.R. in the wake of World War II. During the late 1960s and early 1970s, a number of American students of the early Cold War expressed agreement with that conclusion, though not with the methods that had been used to arrive at it. In an interesting inversion of Kennan's theory regarding Russian behavior, these accounts portrayed official Washington as having in one way or another fabricated the myth of a hostile Soviet Union in order to justify its own internally motivated drive for international hegemony. The difficulty with this argument was the impossibility of verifying it, for without access to Soviet sources there could be no definite conclusions regarding its accuracy: one cannot credibly assess responsibility when one can confirm the motives of only one side. The intervening years have brought us no nearer to a resolution of that problem, but they have witnessed the emergence of several new lines of historical interpretation that appear to call into question the thesis of American "over-reaction."

One of these involves a reconsideration of Stalin's policy by a new generation of scholars equally conversant, not only with the very limited number of Soviet and Eastern European sources that are available, but with the overwhelming array of recently declassified American and British documents as well. The effect of this work is to confirm neither the "totalitarian" nor the "ideological" explanations of Stalin's actions that were popular during the early Cold War years, but rather to see that dictator as having followed an "imperial" model of expansion: a pattern of behavior motivated by insecurity and characterized by caution, to be sure, but one that was also incapable of defining the limits of security requirements and that sought, as a result, to fill power vacuums where this could be done without encountering resistance. The effect of this policy was twofold: to incorporate within the Soviet sphere what Vojtech Mastny has called "a cluster of sullen dependencies" that probably contributed to more than they subtracted from Moscow's nervousness; and to alarm, and ultimately alienate, the United States and its Western European allies, who saw Stalin's inability to define the full extent of his security requirements as likely to undermine their own.

It may well be, as William Taubman has argued, that the West gave up on the possibility of cooperation with the West. But Taubman points out that any such cooperation would have been on the Kremlin leader's terms and for his purposes; it would have been designed "to foster Soviet control of Eastern Europe whether directly (in the case of Poland, Rumania, and Bulgaria) or indirectly (in Hungary and Czechoslovakia); to expand Soviet influence in Western Europe, the Near East, and Asia; to position the U.S.S.R. for even greater gains when the next Western economic crisis struck; and to achieve all this while subsidized to the tune of at least six billion dollars in American credits." Western statesmen may perhaps be pardoned for not having shared this particular vision of the postwar world.

Nor are they condemned, in the new historiography, for having resorted to a strategy of containment; indeed Mastny goes so far as to suggest the West's responsibility for the coming of the Cold War lies more in the passive and dilatory character of its response than in its aggressiveness; "any Western policy likely to restrain [Stalin] would have had to follow a harder rather than a softer line; it would also have had a better chance to succeed if applied sooner rather than later." Containment no doubt reinforced Stalin's suspicion of the West, but it can hardly be said to have created it; without containment, according to this new line of interpretation, the fears Western statesmen held at the time regarding Soviet expansionism might well have become reality.

Historians are also beginning to study the involvement of third parties in the early Cold War; this work sheds new light on the question of who saw whom as a threat. What emerges from it so far is the extent to which states along the periphery of the U.S.S.R. tended to share Washington's concern about Soviet intentions, and indeed to welcome American intervention in their affairs as a counterweight. The Norwegian historian Geir Lundestad has pointed out that Washington's influence actually expanded more rapidly than did that of the Russians in the postwar world, but he argues that this happened because the United States was *encouraged* to assert its power in order to balance that of the Russians. Bruce Kuniholm has documented a similar pattern in the Near East: in 1946 the Iranian government was demanding not less but greater American interference in its internal affairs on the grounds, as the U.S. ambassador put it, that "[t]he only way they can think of to counteract one influence is to invite another." But the clearest case of all is the policy of Great Britain, which as Terry Anderson and Robert Hathaway have demonstrated, amounted almost to a conspiracy to involve the United States more actively in world affairs.

"If we cannot have a world community with the Russians as a constructive member," a British Foreign Office official stated early in 1946, "it seems clear that the next best hope for peace and stability is that the rest of the world, including the vital North American arsenal, should be united in defense of whatever degree of stability we can attain." This is as good a summary of London's early Cold War policy, under both the Churchill and Attlee governments, as one is apt to find. The British had come earlier than their American allies to the conclusion that cooperation with the Russians was not going to be possible; certainly they welcomed—and, at times, sought to reinforce—the increasing indications from Washington throughout 1946 and early 1947 that the Truman administration had come to share that view. Their analysis of the reasons for Soviet unilateralism roughly paralleled that of the Americans; nor were they inclined to find fault—apart from some wincing at the rhetorical excesses involved—with the strategies Washington proposed to deal with that problem. Indeed, if anything, London's attitude was that the Americans were not doing enough; it was this conviction that led Foreign Secretary Ernest Bevin late in 1947 to propose to the United States a formal and permanent peacetime military alliance with Western Europe.

It is, of course, easy to see self-serving motivations at work in the invitations the British government and its counterparts in Western Europe and the Near East extended to the United States to expand its influence in their parts of the world. It could be argued that had that desire for an American presence not existed, these "third party" assessments of Russian intentions might have been considerably less alarmist than they were. But that is missing the point, for it is also the case that had a credible Soviet threat not presented itself, these countries would not have been seeking the expansion of American power in the first place. "It has really become a matter of the defence of western civilisation," the British Foreign Office concluded early in 1948:

> [N]ot only is the Soviet government not prepared at the present state to co-operate in any real sense with any non-Communist . . . Government, but it is actively preparing to extend its hold over the remaining portion of continental Europe and, subsequently, over the Middle East and no doubt the bulk of the Far East as well. . . . [P]hysical control of the Eurasian land mass and eventual control of the whole World Island is what the Politburo is aiming at—no less a thing than that. The immensity of the aim should not betray us into believing in its impracticality. Indeed, unless positive and vigorous steps are shortly

taken by those other states who are in a position to take them . . . the Soviet Union will gain political and strategical advantages which will set the great Communist machine in action, leading either to the establishment of a World Dictatorship or (more probably) to the collapse of organised society over great stretches of the globe.

It is significant that this top-secret Foreign Office document, circulated only within the highest levels of the British government and declassified only after the passage of more than three decades, should have revealed an assessment of the Soviet threat more sweeping in character and apocalyptic in tone than anything in the record of private or public statements by major American officials at the time. The progression from Mackinder to [author of *The Decline of the West* Oswald] Spengler, it appears, was easier than one might think.

History, inescapably, involves viewing distant pasts through the prism of more recent ones. The incontestable fact that the United States overreacted more than once during the subsequent history of the Cold War to the perceived threat of Soviet and/or "communist" expansionism has, to an extent, blinded us to the equally demonstrable fact that in the immediate postwar years the behavior of the Russians alarmed not just Americans but a good portion of the rest of the world as well. How well-founded that alarm was—how accurately it reflected the realities that shaped Soviet policy—are issues upon which there are legitimate grounds for disagreement. But to deny that the alarm itself was sincere, or that Americans were not alone in perceiving it, is to distort the view through the prism more than is necessary. Fear, after all, can be genuine without being rational. And, as Sigmund Freud once pointed out, even paranoids can have real enemies.

An Exaggerated Threat and the Rise of American Globalism

THOMAS G. PATERSON

On April 12, 1945, Vice President Truman was presiding over the United States Senate. He was bored, his thoughts wandering to a poker game scheduled that evening with friends at the Statler Hotel. Shortly after gaveling the Senate to adjournment that afternoon, Truman dropped into the private office of Speaker of the House Sam Rayburn to discuss some legislation and to strike a few liquid blows for liberty. Soon Truman learned that the White House had called: he should come over immediately and quietly. He put down his bourbon and water, apologized to Rayburn for the hurried departure, and hailed his chauffeur. Once in the White House Truman was escorted to the second floor study of Eleanor Roosevelt. There sad faces signaled Truman for the first time that something momentous was about to happen. Mrs. Roosevelt placed her hand on Truman's shoulder and announced that President Franklin D. Roosevelt had died. "Is there anything I can do for you?" asked a stunned Truman. Eleanor Roosevelt shook her head and replied: "Is there anything we can do for you? For you are the one in trouble now."

Trouble indeed. As Truman confided to his diary that day, "the weight of the Government had fallen on my shoulders . . . . I knew the President had a great many meetings with Churchill and Stalin. I was not familiar with any of these things and it was really something to think about. . . ." In fact, Truman as Vice President had never been included in high-level foreign policy discussions; between the inauguration and the President's death, Truman had met only three times with Roosevelt. And foreign affairs had never been a primary interest of Truman's; he had not sat, for example, on the Foreign Relations Committee during his ten years as a senator. Shortly after becoming President, Truman admitted to the Secretary of State that he "was very hazy about the Yalta [Conference] matters," especially about Poland. Later he would lament that Roosevelt "never did talk to me confidentially about the war, or about foreign affairs or what he had in mind for the peace after the war." The weight of foreign policy had fallen on him, and he knew so little. "I was plenty scared." Apprehensive and insecure though he was, Truman was not content to sit in Roosevelt's shadow or brood about his inadequacies and new responsibilities. He would be "President in his own right," he told his first Cabinet meeting. And through trial and error he became so.

About three months after assuming office, a more self-assertive but still self-doubting Truman boarded a ship for Europe, there to meet at Potsdam, near Berlin, with two of recent history's most imposing figures, Winston Churchill and Josef Stalin. "I sure dread this trip, worse than anything I've had to face," he wrote his beloved wife Bess. On July 16, 1945, Truman visited Berlin, where he witnessed the heavy destruction of the city, like much of Europe, now reduced to rubble. "I was thankful," he wrote later, "that the United States had been spared the most unbelievable devastation of this war." At the Potsdam Conference Truman quickly took the measure of the eloquent Churchill and austere Stalin. "The boys say I gave them an earful, " he boasted. He told his wife that "I reared up on my hind legs and told 'em where to get off and they got off."

Truman's assertiveness at Potsdam on such issues as Poland and Germany stemmed not only from his forthright personality, but also from his learning that America's scientists had just successfully exploded an atomic bomb which could be used against Japan to end World War II. And more, it might serve as a diplomatic weapon to persuade others to behave according to American precepts. The news of the atomic test's success gave Truman "an entirely new feeling of confidence . . . ," Secretary of War Henry L. Stimson recorded in his diary. "Now I know what happened to Truman yesterday," commented Churchill. "When he got to the meeting after having read this report he was a changed man. He told the Russians just where they got off and generally bossed the whole meeting."

Truman soon became know for what he himself called his "tough method." He crowed about giving Russia's Commissar for Foreign Affairs, V. M. Molotov, a "straight "one-two" to the jaw" in their first meeting in the White House not long after Roosevelt's death. Yet Secretary Stimson worried about the negative effects of Truman's "brutal frankness," and Ambassador Harriman was skeptical that the President's slam-bang manner worked to America's advantage. Truman's brash, salty style suited his bent for the verbal brawl, but it ill-fit a world of diplomacy demanding quiet deliberation, thoughtful weighing of alternatives, patience, flexibility, and searching analysis of the motives and capabilities of others. If Truman "took 'em for a ride," as he bragged after Potsdam, the dangerous road upon which he raced led to the Cold War. "It isn't any use kicking a tough hound [like the Russians] around because a tough hound will kick back," retired Secretary Cordell Hull remarked after witnessing deteriorating Soviet-American relations.

The United States entered the postwar period, then, with a new, inexperienced, yet bold President who was aware of America's enviable power in a world hobbled by war-wrought devastation and who shared the popular notion of "Red Fascism." To study this man and the power at his command, the state of the world in which he acted, his reading of the Soviet threat, and his declaration of the containment doctrine to meet the perceived threat further helps us to understand the origins of the Cold War. Truman's lasting legacy is his tremendous activism in extending American influence on a global scale—his building of an American "empire" or "hegemony." We can disagree over whether this postwar empire was created reluctantly, defensively, by invitation, or deliberately, by self-interested design. But few will deny that the drive to contain Communism fostered an exceptional, worldwide American expansion that produced empire and ultimately, and ironically, insecurity, for the more the United States expanded and drove in foreign stakes, the more vulnerable it seemed to become—the more exposed it became to a host of challenges from Communists and non-Communists alike.

In the aftermath of a war that bequeathed staggering human tragedy, rubble, and social and political chaos, "something new had to be created," recalled Dean Acheson. America's task "was one of fashioning, trying to help fashion what would come after the destruction of the old world." . . .

. . . The question of how disintegration could be reversed preoccupied Truman officials. Thinking in the peace and prosperity idiom, they believed that a failure to act would jeopardize American interests, drag the United States into depression and war, spawn totalitarianism and aggression, and permit the rise of Communists and other leftists who were eager to exploit the disorder. The prospects were grim, the precedents for action few, the necessities certain, the consequences of inaction grave. This formidable task of reconstruction drew the United States and the Soviet Union into conflict, for each had its own model for rebuilding states and each sought to align nations with its foreign policy.

Political turmoil within nations also drew America and Russia into conflict, for each saw gains to be made and losses to be suffered in the outcome of the political battles. Old regime leaders vied with leftists and other dissidents in state after state. In Poland, the Communist Lublin Poles dueled the conservative London Poles; in Greece the National Liberation Front contested the authority of the British-backed conservative Athens government; in China Mao Zedong's forces continued the civil war against Jiang Jieshi's (Chiang Kai-shek's) Nationalist regime. In occupied Germany, Austria, and Korea, the victors created competitive zones and backed different political groups. Much seemed at stake: economic ties, strategic bases, military allies, intelligence posts, and votes in international organizations. When the United States and the Soviet Union meddled in these politically unstable settings in their quest for influence, they collided—often fiercely.

The collapse of old empires also wrenched world affairs and invited confrontation between America and Russia. Weakened by the war and unable to sustain colonial armies in the field, the imperialists were forced to give way to nationalists who had long worked for independence. The British withdrew form India (and Pakistan) in 1947, from Ceylon and Burma the next year. The Dutch left Indonesia in 1949. The French clung to Indochina, engaged in bloody war, but departed in 1954. The European imperialists also pulled out of parts of Africa and the Middle East. The United States itself in 1946 granted independence to the Philippines. Decolonization produced a shifting of power within the international system and the emergence of new states whose allegiances both the Americans and Russians avidly sought.

With postwar economies, societies, politics, and empires shattered, President Truman confronted an awesome set of problems that would have bedeviled any leader. He also had impressive responsibilities and opportunities, because the United States had escaped from World War II not only intact but richer and stronger. America's abundant farmlands were spared from the tracks of marching armies, its cities were never leveled by bombs, and its factories remained in place. During the war, America's gross national product skyrocketed and every economic indicator, such as steel production, recorded significant growth. In the postwar years, Americans possessed the power, said Truman, "either to make the world economy work or, simply by failing to take the proper action, to allow it to collapse." To create the American-oriented world the Truman Administration desired, and to isolate adversaries, the United States issued or withheld loans (giving one to Britain but not to Russia), launched major reconstruction programs like the Marshall Plan, and offered technical assistance through the Point Four Program. American dollars and votes also dominated the World Bank and International Monetary Fund, transforming them into instruments of American diplomacy.

The United States not only possessed the resources for reconstruction, but also the implements of destruction. The United States had the world's largest Navy, floating in two oceans, the most powerful Air Force, a shrinking yet still formidable Army, and a monopoly of the most frightening weapon of all, the atomic bomb. Not until after the Korean War did the United States stockpile many atomic bombs, but Secretary of State James F. Byrnes, like other American leaders, was known to say that he liked to use the atomic bomb for diplomatic leverage at conferences. Once, during a social occasion at the London Conference in the fall of 1945, Byrnes and Molotov bantered. The Soviet Commissar asked Byrnes if he had an atomic bomb in his "side pocket." Byrnes shot back that the weapon was actually in his "hip pocket." And, "if you don't cut out all this stalling and let us get down to work, I am going to pull an atomic bomb out of my hip pocket and let you have it." Although Molotov apparently laughed, he could not have been amused, for he suspected that the Americans counted on the bomb as an implied threat to gain Soviet diplomatic concessions—and, as the supreme weapon, to blast the Soviet Union into smithereens in a war. Henry L. Stimson, for one, disapproved of "atomic diplomacy," because, he explained to the President, if Americans continued to have "this weapon rather ostentatiously on our hip, their [the Russians'] suspicions and their distrust of our purposes and motives will increase."

Because of America's unusual postwar power, the Truman Administration could expand the United States sphere of influence beyond the Western Hemisphere and also intervene to protect American interests. But this begs a key question: Why did President Truman think it necessary to project American power abroad, to pursue an activist, global foreign policy unprecedented in United States history? The answer has several parts. First, Americans drew lessons from their experience in the 1930s. While indulging in their so-called "isolationism," they had watched economic depression spawn political extremism, which in turn, produced aggression and war. Never again, they vowed. No more appeasement with totalitarians, no more Munichs. "Red Fascism" became a popular phrase to express this American idea. The message seemed evident: To prevent a reincarnation of the 1930s, the United States would have to use its vast power to fight economic instability abroad. Americans felt compelled to project their power, second, because they feared, in the peace-and-prosperity thinking of the time, economic doom stemming from an economic sickness abroad that might spread to the United States, and from American dependency on overseas supplies of raw materials. To aid Europeans and other peoples would not only help them, but also sustain a high American standard of living and gain political friends, as in the case of Italy, where American foreign aid and advice influenced national elections and brought defeat to the left. The American fear of postwar shortages of petroleum also encouraged the Truman Administration to penetrate Middle Eastern oil in a major way. In Saudi Arabia, for example, Americans built and operated the strategically important Dhahran Airport and dominated that nation's oil resources.

Another reason why Truman projected American power so boldly derived from new strategic thinking. Because of the advent of the air age, travel across the world was shortened in time. Strategists spoke of the shrinkage of the globe. Places once deemed beyond American curiosity or interest now loomed important. Airplanes could travel great distances to deliver bombs. Powerful as it was, then, the United States also appeared vulnerable, especially to air attack. As General Carl A. Spaatz emphasized: "As top dog, America becomes target No. 1." He went on to argue that fast aircraft left no warning time for the United States. "The Pearl Harbor of a future war might well be Chicago, or Detroit, or even Washington." To prevent such an occurrence, American leaders worked to acquire overseas bases in both the Pacific and Atlantic, thereby denying a potential enemy an attack route to the Western Hemisphere. Forward bases would also permit the United States to conduct offensive operations more effectively. The American strategic frontier had to be pushed outward. Thus the United States took the former Japanese-controlled Pacific islands of the Carolines, Marshalls, and Marianas, maintained garrisons in Germany and Japan, and sent military missions to Iran, Turkey, Greece, Saudi Arabia, China, and to fourteen Latin American states. The Joint Chiefs of Staff and Department of State lists of desired foreign bases, and of sites where air transit rights were sought, included such far-flung spots as Algeria, India, French Indochina, New Zealand, Iceland, and the Azores. When asked where the American Navy would float, Navy Secretary James Forrestal replied: "Wherever there is a sea." Today we may take the presumption of a global American presence for granted, but in Truman's day it was new, even radical thinking, especially after the "isolationist" 1930s.

These several explanations for American globalism suggest that the United States would have been an expansionist power whether or not the obstructionist Soviets were lurking about. That is, America's own needs—ideological, political, economic, strategic—encouraged such a projection of power. As the influential National Security Council Paper No. 68 (NSC-68) noted in April 1950, the "overall policy" of the United States was "designed to foster a world environment in which the American system can survive and flourish." This policy "we would probably pursue even if there were no Soviet threat."

Americans, of course, did perceive a Soviet threat. Thus we turn to yet another explanation for the United States' dramatic extension of power early in the Cold War: to contain the Soviets. The Soviets unsettled Americans in so many ways. Their harsh Communist dogma and propagandistic slogans were not only monotonous; they also seemed threatening because of their call for world revolution and for the demise of capitalism. In the United Nations the Soviets cast vetoes and even on occasion walked out of the organization. At international conference their *"nyets"* stung American ears. When they negotiated, the Soviets annoyed their interlocuters by repeating the same point over and over again, delaying meetings, or abruptly shifting positions. Truman labeled them "pigheaded," and Dean Acheson thought them so coarse and insulting that he once allowed that they were not "housebroken."

The Soviet Union, moreover, had territorial ambitions, grabbing parts of Poland, Rumania, and Finland, and demanding parts of Turkey. In Eastern Europe, with their Red Army positioned to intimidate, the Soviets quickly manhandled the Poles and Rumanians. Communists in 1947 and 1948 seized power in Hungary and Czechoslovakia. Some Americans predicted that the Soviet military would roll across Western Europe. In general, Truman officials pictured the Soviet Union as an implacable foe to an open world, an opportunistic nation that would probe for weak spots, exploit economic misery, snuff out individual freedom, and thwart self-determination. Americans thought the worst, some claiming that a Soviet-inspired international conspiracy insured perennial hostility and a creeping aggression aimed at American interests. To Truman and his advisers, the Soviets stood as the world's bully, and the very existence of this menacing bear necessitated an activist American foreign policy and an exertion of American power as a "counterforce."

But Truman officials exaggerated the Soviet threat, imagining an adversary that never measured up to the galloping monster so often depicted by alarmist Americans. Even if the Soviets intended to dominate the world, or just Western Europe, they lacked the capabilities to do so. The Soviets had no foreign aid to dispense; outside Russia Communist parties were minorities; the Soviet economy was seriously crippled by the war; and the Soviet military suffered significant weaknesses. The Soviets lacked a modern navy, a strategic air force, the atomic bomb, and air defenses. Their wrecked economy could not support or supply an army in the field for very long, and their technology was antiquated. Their ground forces lacked motorized transportation, adequate equipment, and troop morale. A Soviet *blitzkrieg* invasion of Western Europe had little chance of success and would have proven suicidal for the Soviets, for even if they managed to gain temporary control of Western Europe by a military thrust, they could not strike the United States. So they would have to assume defensive positions and await crushing American attacks, probably including atomic bombings of Soviet Russia itself—plans for which existed.

Other evidence also suggests that a Soviet military threat to Western Europe was more myth than reality. The Soviet Union demobilized its forces after the war, dropping to about 2.9 million personnel in 1948. Many of its 175 divisions were under-strength, and large numbers of them were engaged in occupation duties, resisting challenges to Soviet authority in Eastern Europe. American intelligence sources reported as well that the Soviets could not count on troops of the occupied countries, which were quite unreliable, if not rebellious. At most, the Soviets had 700,000 to 800,000 troops available for an attack against the West. To resist such an attack, the West had about 800,000 troops, or approximate parity. For these reasons, top American leaders did not expect a Soviet onslaught against Western Europe. They and their intelligence sources emphasized Soviet military and economic weaknesses, not strengths, Soviet hesitancy, not boldness.

Why they did Americans so fear the Soviets? Why did the Central Intelligence Agency, the Joint Chiefs of Staff, and the President exaggerate the Soviet threat? The first explanation is that their intelligence estimates were just that—estimates. The American intelligence community was still in a state of infancy, hardly the well-developed system it would become in the 1950s and 1960s. So Americans lacked complete assurance that their figures on Soviet force deployment or armaments were accurate or close to the mark. When leaders do not know, they tend to assume the worst of an adversary's intentions and capabilities, or to think that the Soviets might miscalculate, sparking a war they did not want. In a chaotic world, the conception of a single, inexorably aggressive adversary also brought a comforting sense of knowing and consistency.

Truman officials also exaggerated the Soviet threat in order "to extricate the United States from commitments and restraints that were no longer considered desirable." For example, they loudly chastised the Soviets for violating the Yalta agreements; yet Truman and his advisers knew the Yalta provisions were at best vague and open to differing interpretations. But, more, they purposefully misrepresented the Yalta agreement on the vital question of the composition of the Polish government. In so doing, they hoped to decrease the high degree of Communist participation that the Yalta conferees had insured when they stated that the new Polish regime would be formed by reorganizing the provisional Lublin (Communist) government. Through charges of Soviet malfeasance Washington sought to justify its own retreat from Yalta, such as its abandonment of the $20 billion reparations figure for Germany (half of which was supposed to go to the Soviet Union).

Another reason for the exaggeration: Truman liked things in black and white, as his aide Clark Clifford noted. Nuances, ambiguities, and counterevidence were often discounted to satisfy the President's preference for the simpler answer or his pre-conceived notions of Soviet aggressiveness. In mid-1946, for example, the Joint Chiefs of Staff deleted from a report to Truman a section that stressed Soviet weaknesses. American leaders also exaggerated the Soviet threat because it was useful in galvanizing and unifying American public opinion for an abandonment of recent and still lingering "isolationism" and support for an expansive foreign policy. Kennan quoted a colleague as saying that "if it [Soviet threat] had never existed, we would have had to invent it, to create a sense of urgency we need to bring us to the point of decisive action." The military particularly overplayed the Soviet threat in order to persuade Congress to endorse larger defense budgets. This happened in 1948–49 with the creation of the North Atlantic Treaty Organization. NATO was established not to halt a Soviet military attack, because none was anticipated, but to give Europeans a psychological boost—a "will to resist." American officials believed that the European Recovery Program would falter unless there was a "sense of security" to buttress it. They nurtured apprehension, too, that some European nations might lean toward neutralism unless they were brought together under a security umbrella. NATO also seemed essential to help members resist internal subversion. The exaggerated, popular view that NATO was formed to deter a Soviet invasion of Western Europe by conventional forces stems in part, from Truman's faulty recollection in his published memoirs.

Still another explanation for why Americans exaggerated the Soviet threat is found in their attention since the Bolshevik Revolution of 1917 to the utopian Communist goal of world revolution, confusing goals with actual behavior. Thus Americans believed that the sinister Soviets and their Communist allies would exploit postwar economic, social, and political disorder, not through a direct military thrust, but rather through covert subversion. The recovery of Germany and Japan became necessary, then, to deny the Communists political opportunities to thwart American plans for the integration of these former enemies into an American system of trade and defense. And because economic instability troubled so much of Eurasia, Communist gains through subversion might deny the United States strategic raw materials.

Why dwell on this question of the American exaggeration of the Soviet threat? Because it over-simplified international realities by under-estimating local conditions that might thwart Soviet/Communist successes and by over-estimating the Soviet ability to act. Because it encouraged the Soviets to fear encirclement and to enlarge their military establishment, thereby contributing to a dangerous weapons race. Because it led to indiscriminate globalism. Because it put a damper on diplomacy; American officials were hesitant to negotiate with an opponent variously described as malevolent, deceitful, and inhuman. They especially did not warm to negotiations when some critics were ready to cry that diplomacy, which could produce compromises, was evidence in itself of softness toward Communism.

Exaggeration of the threat also led Americans to misinterpret events and in so doing to prompt the Soviets to make decisions contrary to American wishes. For example, the Soviet presence in Eastern Europe, once considered a simple question of the Soviets' building an iron curtain or bloc after the war, is now seen by historians in more complex terms. The Soviets did not seem to have a master plan for the region and followed different policies in different countries. Poland and Rumania were subjugated right away; Yugoslavia, on the other hand, was an independent Communist state led by Josip Tito, who broke dramatically with Stalin in 1948; Hungary conducted elections in the fall of 1945 (the Communists got only 17 percent of the vote) and did not suffer a Communist coup until 1947; in Czechoslovakia, free elections in May 1946 produced a non-Communist government that functioned until 1948; Finland, although under Soviet scrutiny, affirmed its independence. The Soviets did not have a firm grip on Eastern Europe before 1948—a prime reason why many American leaders believed the Soviets harbored weaknesses.

American policies were designed to roll the Soviets back. The United States reconstruction loan policy, encouragement of dissident groups, and appeal for free elections alarmed Moscow, contributing to a Soviet push to secure the area. The issue of free elections illustrates the point. Such a call was consistent with cherished American principle. But in the context of Eastern Europe and the Cold War, problems arose. First, Americans conspicuously followed a double standard which foreigners noted time and again; that is, if the principle of free elections really mattered, why not hold such elections in the United States' sphere of influence in Latin America, when an unsavory lot of dictators ruled? Second, free elections would have produced victories for anti-Soviet groups. Such results could only unsettle the Soviets and invite them to intervene to protect their interests in neighboring states—just as the United States had intervened in Cuba and Mexico in the twentieth century when hostile groups assumed power. In Hungary, for example, it was the non-Communist leader Ferenc Nagy who delayed elections in late 1946 because he knew the Communist Party would lose badly, thereby possibly triggering a repressive Soviet response. And, third, the United States had so little influence in Eastern Europe that it had no way of insuring free elections—no way of backing up its demands with power.

Walter Lippmann, among others, thought that the United States should tame its meddling in the region and make the best out of a bad arrangement of power. "I do believe," he said in 1947, "we shall have to recognize the principle of boundaries of spheres of influence which either side will not cross and have to proceed on the old principle that a good fence makes good neighbors." Kennan shared this view, as did one State Department official who argued that the United States was incapable of becoming a successful watchdog in Eastern Europe. American "barkings, growlings, snappings, and occasional bitings," Cloyce K. Huston prophesized, would only irritate the Soviets without reducing their power. Better still, argued some analysts, if the United States tempered its ventures into European affairs, then the Soviets, surely less alarmed, might tolerate more openness. But the United States did not stay out. Americans tried to project their power into a region where they had little chance of succeeding, but had substantial opportunity to irritate and alarm the always suspicious Soviets. In this way, it has been suggested, the United States itself helped pull down the iron curtain.

Another example of the exaggeration of the Soviet threat at work is found in the Truman Doctrine of 1947. Greece was beset by civil war, and the British could no longer fund a war against Communist-led insurgents who had a considerable non-Communist following. On March 12, Truman enunciated a universal doctrine: It "must be the policy of the United States to support free peoples who are resisting attempted subjugation by armed minorities or by outside pressures." Although he never mentioned the Soviet Union by name, his juxtaposition of words like "democratic" and "totalitarian" and his references to Eastern Europe made the menace to Greece appear to be the Soviets. But there was and is no evidence of Soviet involvement in the Greek civil war. In fact, the Soviets had urged both the Greek Communists and their allies the Yugoslavs to stop the fighting for fear that the conflict would draw the United States into the Mediterranean. And the Greek Communists were strong nationalists. The United States nonetheless intervened in a major way in Greek affairs, becoming responsible for right-wing repression and a military establishment that plagued Greek politics through much of its postwar history. As for Turkey, official Washington did not expect the Soviet Union to strike militarily against that bordering nation. The Soviets were too weak in 1947 to undertake such a major operation, and they were asking for joint control of the Dardanelles largely for defense, for security. Then why did the President, in the Truman Doctrine speech, suggest that Turkey was imminently threatened? American strategists worried that Russia's long-term objective was the subjugation of its neighbor. But they also wished to exploit an opportunity to enhance the American military position in the

Mediterranean region and in a state bordering the Soviet Union. The Greek crisis and the Truman Doctrine speech provided an appropriate environment to build up an American military presence in the Eastern Mediterranean for use against the Soviets should the unwanted war ever come.

Truman's alarmist language further fixed the mistaken idea in the American mind that the Soviets were unrelenting aggressors intent upon undermining peace, and that the United States, almost alone, had to meet them everywhere. Truman's exaggerations and his commitment to the containment doctrine did not go unchallenged. Secretary Marshall himself was startled by the President's muscular anti-Communist rhetoric, and he questioned the wisdom of overstating the case. The Soviet specialist Llewellyn Thompson urged "caution" in swinging too far toward "outright opposition to Russia. . . ." Walter Lippmann, in reacting to both Truman's speech and George F. Kennan's now famous "Mr. 'X'" article in the July 1947 issue of the journal *Foreign Affairs,* labeled containment a "strategic monstrosity," because it made no distinctions between important or vital and not-so-important or peripheral areas. Because American power was not omnipresent, Lippmann further argued, the "policy can be implemented only by recruiting, subsidizing and supporting a heterogeneous array of satellites, clients, dependents and puppets." He also criticized the containment doctrine for placing more emphasis on confrontation than on diplomacy.

Truman himself came to see that there were dangers in stating imprecise, universal doctrines. He became boxed by his own rhetoric. When Mao Zedong's forces claimed victory in 1949 over Jiang's regime, conservative Republicans, angry Democrats and various McCarthyites pilloried the President for letting China "fall." China lost itself, he retorted. But his critics pressed the point: if containment was to be applied everywhere, as the President had said in the Truman Doctrine, why not China? Truman appeared inconsistent, when, in fact, in the case of China, he was ultimately prudent in cutting American losses where the United States proved incapable of reaching its goals. Unable to disarm his detractors on this issue, Truman stood vulnerable in the early 1950s to political demagogues who fueled McCarthyism. The long-term consequences in this example have been grave. Democrats believed they could never lose "another China"—never permit Communists or Marxists, whether or not linked to Moscow, to assume power abroad. President John F. Kennedy later said, for example, that he could not withdraw from Vietnam because that might be perceived as "another China" and spark charges that he was soft on Communism. America, in fact, could not bring itself to open diplomatic relations with the People's Republic of China until 1979.

Jiang's collapse joined the Soviet explosion of an atomic bomb, the formation of the German Democratic Republic (East Germany), and the Sino-Soviet Friendship Treaty to arouse American feeling in late 1949 and early 1950 that the Soviet threat had dramatically escalated. Although Kennan told his State Department colleagues that such feeling was "largely of our own making" rather than an accurate accounting of Soviet actions, the composers of NSC-68 preferred to dwell on a more dangerous Soviet menace in extreme rhetoric not usually found in a secret report. But because the April 1950 document was aimed at President Truman, we can certainly understand why its language was hyperbolic. The fanatical and militant Soviets, concluded NSC-68, were seeking to impose "absolute authority over the rest of the world." America had to frustrate the global "design" of the "evil men" of the Kremlin, who were unrelentingly bent on "piecemeal aggression" against the "free world" through military force, infiltration, and intimidation. The report called for a huge American and allied military build-up and nuclear arms development.

NSC-68, most scholars agree, was a flawed, even amateurish document. It assumed a Communist monolith that did not exist, drew alarmist conclusions based upon vague and inaccurate information about Soviet capabilities, made grand, unsubstantiated claims about Soviet intentions, glossed over the presence of many non-democratic countries in the "free world," and recommended against negotiations with Moscow at the very time the Soviets were advancing toward a policy of "peaceful co-existence." One State Department expert on the Soviet Union, Charles E. Bohlen, although generally happy with the report's conclusions, faulted NSC-68 for assuming a Soviet plot for world conquest—for "oversimplifying the problem." No, he advised, the Soviets sought foremostly to maintain their regime and to extend it abroad "to the degree that is possible without serious risk to the internal regime." In short, there were limits to Soviet behavior. But few were listening to such cautionary voices. NSC-68 became American dogma, especially when the outbreak of the Korean War in June of 1950 sanctified it as a prophetic "we told you so."

The story of Truman's foreign policy is basically an accounting of how the United States, because of its own expansionism and exaggeration of the Soviet threat, became a global power. Truman projected American power after the Second World War to rehabilitate Western Europe, secure new allies, guarantee strategic and economic links, and block Communist or Soviet influence. He firmly implanted the image of the Soviets as relentless, worldwide transgressors with whom it is futile to negotiate. Through his exaggeration of the Soviet threat, Truman made it very likely that the United States would continue to practice global interventionism years after he left the White House.

⋙ F U R T H E R   R E A D I N G

Allison, Graham, and Gregory Treverton, eds. *Rethinking America's Security: Beyond the Cold War to New World Order* (1992).
Ambrose, Stephen. *Rise to Globalism: American Foreign Policy, 1938–1980s* (1976).
Anderson, Terry H. *The United States, Great Britain, and the Cold War, 1944–1947* (1981).
Andrew, Christopher, and Oleg Gordievsky. *KGB: The Inside Story of Its Foreign Operations from Lenin to Gorbachev* (1990).
Bisell, Richard M. Jr., with Jonathan E. Lewis and Frances T. Pudlow. *Reflections of a Cold Warrior: From Yalta to the Bay of Pigs* (1996).
Blum, Robert M. *Drawing the Line: The Origins of American Containment Policy in East Asia* (1982).
Boll, Michael. *Cold War in the Balkans* (1984).
Borovik, Genrikh. *The Philby Files: The Secret Life of Master Spy Kim Philby,* ed. Philip Knightley (1994).
Brands, H. W. *The Devil We Knew* (1993).
———. *Inside the Cold War: Loy Henderson and the Rise of the American Empire, 1918–1961* (1991).
Brinkley, Douglas. *Dean Acheson: The Cold War Years, 1952–1971* (1992).
Buhite, Russell D. *Decisions at Yalta: An Appraisal of Summit Diplomacy* (1986).
Callahan, David. *Dangerous Capabilities: Paul Nitze and the Cold War* (1990).
Clifford, Clark M., with Richard Holbrooke. *Counsel to the President: A Memoir* (1991).

Davis, Lynn Etheridge. *The Cold War Begins: Soviet-American Conflict over Eastern Europe* (1974).

Donovan, Robert J. *Conflict and Crisis: The Presidency of Harry S. Truman, 1945–1948* (1977).

———. *The Tumultuous Years: The Presidency of Harry S. Truman, 1949–1953* (1982).

Eckes, Alfred E. Jr. *A Search for Solvency: Bretton Woods and the International Monetary System, 1941–1971* (1975).

Fawcett, Louise. *Iran and the Cold War: The Azerbaijan Crisis of 1946* (1992).

Feis, Herbert. *From Trust to Terror* (1970).

Freeland, Richard. *The Truman Doctrine and the Origins of McCarthyism* (1973).

Gaddis, John Lewis. *The Long Peace: Inquiries into the History of the Cold War* (1987).

———. *Russia, the Soviet Union, and the United States* (1978).

———. *Strategies of Containment* (1982).

———. *The United States and the Origins of the Cold War, 1941–1947* (1972).

———. *We Now Know: Rethinking Cold War History* (1997).

Gardner, Lloyd C. *Architects of Illusion: Men and Ideas in American Foreign Policy, 1941–1949* (1970).

Gardner, Lloyd C., Arthur M. Schlesinger Jr., and Hans J. Morgenthau. *Origins of the Cold War* (1970).

Gormly, James L. *The Collapse of the Grand Alliance, 1945–1948* (1987).

Graebner, Norman, ed. *The National Security: Its Theory and Practice, 1945–1960* (1986).

Grose, Peter. *Gentleman Spy: The Life of Allen Dulles* (1994).

Hamby, Alonzo L. *Man of the People: A Life of Harry S. Truman* (1994).

Herring, George C. *Aid to Russia, 1941–46: Strategy, Diplomacy, the Origins of the Cold War* (1973).

Hersberg, James. *James B. Conant: Harvard to Hiroshima and the Making of the Nuclear Age* (1993).

Hogan, Michael J. *The Marshall Plan: America, Britain, and the Reconstruction of Western Europe, 1947–1952* (1987).

———. ed. *America in the World: The Historiography of American Foreign Relations Since 1941* (1995).

Hogan, Michael J., and Thomas G. Paterson, eds. *Explaining the History of American Foreign Relations* (1991).

Holloway, David. *Stalin and the Bomb* (1994).

Hoopes, Townsend, and Douglas Brinkley. *Driven Patriot: The Life and Times of James Forrestal* (1992).

Hunter, Allen, ed. *Re-Thinking the Cold War* (1998).

Iatrides, John O., and Linda Wrigley, eds. *Greece at the Crossroads: The Civil War and Its Legacy* (1995).

Isaacson, Walter, and Evan Thomas. *The Wise Men, Six Friends and the World They Made: Acheson, Bohlen, Harriman, Kennan, Lovett, McCloy* (1986).

Kofsky, Frank. *Harry S. Truman and the War Scare of 1948: A Successful Campaign to Deceive the Nation* (1993).

Kolko, Gabriel. *The Politics of War: The World and United States Foreign Policy, 1943–1945* (1968).

Kolko, Joyce, and Gabriel Kolko. *The Limits of Power: The World and United States Foreign Policy, 1945–1954* (1972).

Kovrig, Bennett. *Of Walls and Bridges: The United States and Eastern Europe* (1991).

Kuniholm, Bruce R. *The Origins of the Cold War in the Near East: Great Power Conflict and Diplomacy in Iran, Turkey, and Greece* (1980).

Leffler, Melvyn P. "The American Conception of National Security and the Beginnings of the Cold War, 1945–1948," *American Historical Review* 89 (1984), 346–381.

———. *A Preponderance of Power: National Security, the Truman Administration, and the Cold War* (1992).

Levering, Ralph. *The Cold War* (1988).

Maddox, Robert J. *From War to Cold War: The Education of Harry S. Truman* (1988).

————. *The New Left and the Origins of the Cold War* (1973).

Mastny, Vojtech. *Russia's Road to the Cold War: Diplomacy, Warfare, and the Politics of Communism, 1941–1945* (1979).

Mayers, David Allan. *Cracking the Monolith: U.S. Policy Against the Sino-Soviet Alliance, 1949–1955* (1986).

Messer, Robert L. *The End of an Alliance: James F. Byrnes, Roosevelt, Truman, and the Origins of the Cold War* (1982).

Miller, James E. *The United States and Italy, 1940–1950* (1986).

Milward, Alan. *The Reconstruction of Western Europe, 1945–51* (1984).

Paterson, Thomas G. *Meeting the Communist Threat: Truman to Reagan* (1988).

————. *On Every Front: The Making of the Cold War* (1979).

————. *The Origins of the Cold War* (1984).

————. *Soviet-American Confrontation* (1973).

Raack, R. C. *Stalin's Drive to the West, 1938–1945: The Origins of the Cold War* (1995).

Schaller, Michael. *The American Occupation of Japan: The Origins of the Cold War in Asia* (1985).

Smith, Gaddis. *Dean Acheson* (1972).

Taubman, William. *Stalin's American Policy: From Entente to Détente to Cold War* (1982).

Theoharis, Athan G. *The Yalta Myths* (1970).

Thomas, Hugh. *Armed Truce: The Beginnings of the Cold War, 1945–46* (1987).

Thompson, Kenneth W. *Cold War Theories* (1981).

Ulam, Adam. *The Rivals: America and Russia Since World War II* (1972).

Walker, Martin. *The Cold War: A History* (1994).

Wells, Samuel F. Jr. "Sounding the Tocsin: NSC-68 and the Soviet Threat," *International Security* 4 (1979), 116–158.

Williams, William A. *The Tragedy of American Foreign Policy* (1962).

Yergin, Daniel. *Shattered Peace: The Origins of the Cold War and the National Security State* (1977).

Zubok, Vladislav, and Constantine Pleshakov. *Inside the Kemlin's Cold War: From Stalin to Khrushchev* (1996).

C H A P T E R
4

Affluence

and Discontent

in the 1950s

XX

*For most Americans, the 1950s were a decade of unprecedented prosperity,
economic growth, high employment, and the rapid spread of homesteads in
suburbia. It was a decade marked not only by the mass production of consumer
goods and services but also by the increasingly important role of advertising and
mass communication in organizing consumption—in ensuring that what was
produced was in fact consumed. It was a decade in which young baby boomers
emerged as a market, a menace, and a cultural force. It was a decade, finally,
when all of the big ideological and political conflicts of the 1930s and 1940s
seemed played out, leaving a contented if bland consensus in their wake.*

*This vision was accurate to a point. Economic prosperity stood as a blessing
and an achievement for a nation that had just emerged from depression and war,
but significant controversies endured amid the tract houses, automobile ads, and
TV dinners. Some problems lurked just below the surface. Poverty had not been
driven from the land; it would be rediscovered in America's cities and rural
communities with a splash in the early 1960s. Other problems had been festering
for a long time. Race relations, for example, had reemerged in the 1940s as an
important national issue, and the movement against segregation in the South
and of African Americans from the South to the North made certain that civil
rights would remain on the national agenda. Some anxieties were the product of
the comforts of prosperity. Commentators—conservative, liberal, and those in between—lamented that comfort had made Americans soft, bereft of passion, and
perhaps unable to respond to the challenges that remained ahead. Youth in
particular, seeming both too wild and too placid, attracted their concern. Finally,
a hot war in Korea, the Cold War, and the fear that subversives could take it all
away—the American family, the comfort and freedom that Americans had fought
for—unsettled the apparent consensus. Amid the celebration of prosperity, many
Americans nursed an appreciation for the fragility and incompleteness of the good
times and their freedom.*

☒ D O C U M E N T S

The tendency in thinking about the history of twentieth-century America is to take a decade-by-decade approach, seeing each decade as having distinctive problems, characteristics, and themes. If that approach has its weaknesses for other decades, its shortcomings are legion for the 1950s. For each theme that might encapsulate the decade, there is a countertheme; and some developments, such as the expansion of mass culture, had their roots in a much earlier time. One thing is certain: the years following World War II opened a great number of new opportunities to many Americans, the prospect of which was both welcome and a bit frightening. The following documents illustrate some of the twitchiness in American culture as Americans made sense of their dangerous bounty. The years following the war brought the vaunted baby boom, but that vast group of youth seemed to threaten the culture. In Document 1, a writer for *Life* magazine remarks on the consumer muscle of teenagers in the 1950s. If that was the good news about youth (as makers of all sorts of goods discovered), Document 2, an article from *Newsweek,* offers some bad new about the dangers of juvenile delinquency. Commentators blamed mass culture—including movies, rock 'n' roll, and television—at least in part for declining moral values. Document 3, from *U.S. News and World Report,* describes some of the fears television in particular inspired about Americans' apparently increasing passivity. Like youth, sexuality became both a product to be celebrated and sold in the 1950s and a force to be feared. Although new organizations (and the famous "Kinsey Report") argued that gay and lesbian behavior was not outside the norm, homosexuals, like communists, became the target of investigators searching for subversives in governments, as Document 4 illustrates. Some worries inspired quick answers, as Document 5 suggests in its advice on how to respond to a nuclear attack.

1. *Life* Magazine Identifies
the New Teen-age Market, 1959

To some people the vision of a leggy adolescent happily squealing over the latest fancy present from Daddy is just another example of the way teen-agers are spoiled to death these days. But to a growing number of businessmen the picture spells out the profitable fact that the American teen-agers have emerged as a big-time consumer in the U.S. economy. They are multiplying in numbers. They spend more and have more spend on them. And they have minds of their own about what they want.

The time is past when a boy's chief possession was his bike and a girl's party wardrobe consisted of a fancy dress worn with a string of dime-store pearls. What Depression-bred parents may still think of as luxuries are looked on as necessities by their offspring. Today teen-agers surround themselves with a fantastic array of garish and often expensive baubles and amusements. They own 10 million phonographs, over a million TV sets, 13 million cameras. Nobody knows how much parents spend on them for actual necessities nor to what extent teen-agers act as hidden persuaders on their parents' other buying habits. Counting only what is spent to satisfy

Excerpts from "A Young $10 Billion Power: The US Teen-age Consumer Has Become a Major Factor in the Nation's Economy," *Life,* August 31, 1959, 78–84. Courtesy of *Life* Magazine. Reprinted with permission.

their special teen-age demands, the youngsters and their parents will shell out about $10 billion this year, a billion more than the total sales of GM.

Until recently businessmen have largely ignored the teen-age market. But now they are spending millions on advertising and razzle-dazzle promotional stunts. Their efforts so far seem only to have scratched the surface of a rich lode. In 1970, when the teen-age population expands from its present 18 million to 28 million, the market may be worth $20 billion. If parents have any idea of organized revolt, it is already too late. Teen-age spending is so important that such action would send quivers through the entire national economy. . . .

At 17 Suzie Slattery of Van Nuys, Calif., fits any businessman's dream of the ideal teen-age consumer. The daughter of a reasonably well-to-do TV announcer, Suzie costs her parents close to $4,000 a year, far more than average for the country but not much more than many of the upper middle income families of her town. In an expanding economy more and more teen-agers will be moving up into Suzie's bracket or be influenced as consumers by her example.

Last year $1,500 was spent on Suzie's clothes and $550 for her entertainment. Her annual food bill comes to $900. She pays $4 every two weeks at the beauty parlor. She has her own telephone and even has her own soda fountain in the house. On summer vacation days she loves to wander with her mother through fashionable department stores, picking out frocks or furnishings for her room or silver and expensive crockery for the hope chest she has already started.

As a high school graduation present, Suzie was given a holiday cruise to Hawaii and is now in the midst of a new clothes-buying spree for college. Her parents' constant indulgence has not spoiled Suzie. She takes for granted all the luxuries that surround her because she has had them all her life. But she also has a good mind and some serious interests. A top student in her school, she is entering Occidental College this fall and will major in political science. . . .

Some Fascinating Facts About a Booming Market

FOOD: Teen-agers eat 20% more than adults. They down 3½ billion quarts of milk every year, almost four times as much as is drunk by the infant population under 1. Teen-agers are a main prop of the ice cream industry, gobble 145 million gallons a year.

BEAUTY CARE: Teen-agers spent $20 million on lipstick last year, $25 million on deodorants (a fifth of total sold), $9 million on home permanents. Male teen-agers own 2 million electric razors.

ENTERTAINMENT: Teen-agers lay out more than $1.5 billion a year for entertainment. They spend about $75 million on single pop records. Although they create new musical idols, they are staunchly faithful to the old. Elvis Presley, still their favorite, has sold 25 million copies of single records in four years, an all-time high.

HOMEMAKERS: Major items like furniture and silver are moving into the teen-age market because of growing number of teen-age marriages. One third of all 18- and 19-year-old girls are already married. More than 600,000 teen-agers will be married this year. Teen-agers are now starting hope chests at 15.

CREDIT RISKS: Some 800,000 teen-agers work at full-time jobs and can buy major items on credit.

2. *Newsweek* Decries the Problem of Dangerous Teens, 1955

Call him "Tarzan." That's what he calls himself.

His real name is Frank Santana and he looks like a malnourished mouse, but he thinks he's quite a guy—especially when he's carrying a gun.

A slim, dark, adenoidal kid of 17, he was strutting down a street in the Bronx last week with a dozen members of his gang, the Navajos. They were in uniform. They wore blue jeans and leather jackets, trimmed in yellow and emblazoned with the insigne of the gang, a portrait of a Plains Indian. And they were looking for Golden Guineas. The Golden Guineas are a gang of teen-agers, too. The day before a group of them had caught "Tarzan" and given him a pushing around. The Navajos wanted revenge.

Model

William Blankenship Jr., 15, came up the street. He wasn't a Navajo or a Golden Guinea. He wasn't a member of any gang. He was a model student in high school, the son of a research chemist who spent his spare time working to prevent juvenile delinquency.

"Tarzan" gave his gun, a .32-caliber Italian automatic, to a lieutenant to hold. He grabbed Blankenship and accused him of being a Golden Guinea. The lieutenant, Ralph Falcon, 16, "Superman," waved the gun menacingly.

"Don't point that gun at me," cried Blankenship.

"Superman" put the gun in his belt.

"Don't chicken out," then screamed "Tarzan" at "Superman."

He grabbed the gun and fired, killing Blankenship.

The Navajos scattered.

The cops found "Tarzan" at his apartment. They found the gun in the bathroom water tank. They also found a pair of brass knuckles.

"Why did you shoot the kid?" the policemen asked.

"Tarzan" looked at his fists.

"I didn't want to bang up these knuckles," he said. "I'm a boxer, you know. So I used a gun." He added with an air of apology: "I'm not very good at street fighting, anyway."

Jungle

It took a crime as senseless as the murder of young Blankenship last week to make Americans aware of a chilling fact: In several of the nation's cities, and particularly in New York and Chicago, juvenile delinquency is actually becoming organized gangsterism. The old Prohibition mobs are gone. Yet some of the cities remain jungles. Where the Prohibition mobsters prowled, teen-age hoodlums, organized like armies, have taken over. They are not just "bad kids." They are criminals. And they don't hesitate to kill. The Prohibition mobsters killed for a purpose. The teen-agers often will kill simply for the sake of killing or because, like Frank Santana, they don't want to "chicken out." . . .

Juvenile delinquents come from every class of society, but the teen-age gang is a phenomenon of the slums. And it is a phenomenon also of the so-called minority groups. Sociologists say the gangs give the youngsters a sense of status and a feeling of "belonging." The trouble is, they can become vicious.

Escaped

"Gangs," says Cook County Sheriff Joseph D. Lohman, a professional criminologist and a onetime professor of sociology at the University of Chicago, "attract young-sters because they fill a need that is lacking in society. They provide an escape from the boredom and distasteful conditions that parents and schools impose. There is excitement in gang conflict and action. There are new and challenging experiences. The gang solves a boy's problems by offering what parents and society fail to pro-vide the restless, growing adolescent."

The gangs range in size from a dozen youngsters to 50 or 100 or even 250. All the members of each gang live in the same neighborhood; usually, they are from the same racial group. They give themselves names like the Navajos, the Golden Guineas, the Jolly Gents, the Baldies, the Redwings. And they call themselves social clubs or athletic clubs.

Trouble Makers

In New York, the police say, there are about 100 teen-age gangs. Of these, about 50 are listed by the cops as "active." This means they are trouble makers. They wage wars in the streets with other gangs and they commit crimes.

Like Frank Santana's Navajos, the gangs usually wear uniforms—in New York, blue jeans and leather jackets; in Chicago, pegged trousers and black Ike jackets. The Chicago teen-age hoods also affect ducktail haircuts.

The leaders are usually elected. And decisions usually are made by majority vote. The organization is rarely cohesive. Members come and go. They move out of the neighborhood; they go into the Army; they get married. Sometimes, gangs will disintegrate almost overnight. A few months later, a new gang will spring up, with many of the old members, but with a new name, a new insigne, and new leaders.

By and large, the gangs do not admit girls. Instead, they have girls' auxiliaries. In Chicago, for example, the Commanders have the Commandettes; the Hawks have the Squaws; the Mum-Checks have the Mum-Chicks. The girls also dress in uniform—in Chicago, blue jeans and jackets. Says one: "It's hard for girls to wear skirts when we sit on the corner with the guys. We'd get our skirts dirty."

Until last year, many of the Chicago gang girls wore their hair pony-tail style. Now they wear it bobbed.

Rumble

The girls often carry the weapons the boys use, since policemen hesitate to frisk a girl. And they are often the cause of gang wars—or rumbles, as the New York teen-agers call them. Members of two rival gangs will attend the same dance. A girl belonging to one gang will dance with a member of the other. The first gang's honor is hurt. So there will be a rumble. The hoods will fight out in the streets, sometimes with guns. And there will be casualties.

The gangs are as touchy as nations about their territories. When a gang from one neighborhood walks through another, that's considered an invasion and an act of war. . . .

Real guns are so easy to come by that few of the teen-age hoods bother with zip-guns now.

When boy and girl gang members start going steady, they exchange jackets or rings. In Chicago, the gang code demands that a boy seldom travel with his girl except in a car, called a "short." Frequently the boys steal the cars, in which case they are called "hot shorts."

At one suburban Chicago high school last winter, nearly 100 boys and girls crammed into fifteen shorts, most of them hot, and systemically raided and demolished a swanky North Shore dining place, causing damage that was estimated by police at nearly $250,000. "When they asked me to go along with them, I had to," a gang member explained. "If I didn't go along, they'd know I was chicken and I couldn't live around here any more."

One night last month, nearly 40 young toughs crashed a Delta Upsilon fraternity dance at the University of Chicago, hurled bottles, bricks, and clubs, stabbed a student in the back and beat up ten others. "They had it coming to them," a Mum-Check explained. "They always acted so superior. They thought they were better than us because they went to college. We felt it was about time to take care of them anyway."

Two weeks ago, after a rumor got around that one gang [member] was dating the girl friend of another gang's leader, the second gang grabbed baseball bats and raced through the city streets in two cars seeking revenge. They savagely slugged two boys, only to discover that neither boy was a member of the offending mob.

"Protection"

Steal-a-car clubs of six to eight teen-agers have become increasingly popular in Chicago. So has the practice of girl mobsters beating up other girls simply for laughs. The girl hoods also have adopted the practice of beating up motorists. One girl will play the part of a hitchhiker. When a car stops for her, the other girls will swarm out of hiding and start pummeling the driver.

In elementary and high schools in both New York and Chicago, the hoods frequently will force other students to pay them "protection money." Several youngsters who refused have been stabbed or slugged. Last year, one of the hoods was killed by three boys who got tired of paying him for "protection."

Says a thoughtful juvenile expert: "These street-corner group societies are organized on a system of values opposed to the values of their parents and society. We can't reach them through conventional means. The gangs are hostile to all organized help. They are systematically attacking society. It's not an individual problem but a group problem. Perhaps the viciousness of mankind in the past few decades has taken its ghastly toll on our youth."

What can be done about the teen-age gangs? Detroit helped to solve the problem by a get-tough policy. The police broke up the gangs. They established a curfew, and they enforce it.

What Answer?

Some jurists believe that police action is the only answer to the teen-age gangs. Others insist that beating up the teen-agers only makes them more antisocial. Officially, that is the attitude in New York. The city has established a Youth Board, which works with the gangs and attempts to direct them from antisocial to social ends.

This week, Henry Epstein, Deputy Mayor of New York, recommended to Mayor Robert F. Wagner that the work of the Youth Board be extended. And he recommended, also, that the city appropriate approximately $300,000 to private agencies working to prevent delinquency among youth.

3. *U.S. News and World Report* Assesses the Perils of Mass Culture and the Evils of Television, 1955

The biggest of the new forces in American life today is television. There has been nothing like it in the postwar decade, or in many decades before that—perhaps not since the invention of the printing press. Even radio, by contrast, was a placid experience.

The impact of TV on this country has been so massive that Americans are still wondering what hit them. Has the effect been good or bad? What permanent effects on the American way of life may be expected? These and other questions are considered in this survey.

Probably there are some people in the U.S. who have never seen a television program, but you would have to go into the hills to find them. Two out of three U.S. families now own their own sets, or are paying for them. In 32 million homes, TV dials are flicked on and off, from channel to channel, at least 100 million times between 8 A.M. and midnight.

Everywhere, children sit with eyes glued to screens—for three to four hours a day on the average. Their parents use up even more time mesmerized by this new marvel—or monster. They have spent 15 billion dollars to look since 1946.

Now, after nearly 10 years of TV, people are asking: "What hath TV wrought? What is this thing doing to us?"

Solid answers to this question are very hard to get. Pollsters, sociologists, doctors, teachers, the TV people themselves come up with more contradictions than conclusions whenever they start asking.

But almost everybody has an opinion and wants to air it.

What do these opinions add up to? People have strong views. Here are some widely held convictions, both against and for television:

That TV has kept people from going places and doing things, from reading, from thinking for themselves. Yet it is said also that TV has taken viewers vicariously into strange and fascinating spots and situations, brought distinguished and enchanting people into their living rooms, given them a new perspective.

That TV has interfered with schooling, kept children from learning to read and write, weakened their eyesight and softened their muscles. But there are those who hold that TV has made America's youngsters more "knowing" about life, more curious, given them a bigger vocabulary. Teaching by TV, educators say, is going to be a big thing in the future.

That TV arouses morbid emotions in children, glorifies violence, causes juvenile crime—that it starts domestic quarrels, tends to loosen morals and make people lazy and sodden. However, it keeps families together at home, provides a realm of cheap entertainment never before available, stimulates new lines of conversation.

That TV is giving the U.S. an almost primitive language, made up of grunts, whistles, standardized wisecracks and clichés—that it is turning the average American into a stereotype. Yet it is breaking down regional barriers and prejudices, ironing out accents, giving people in one part of the country a better understanding of people in other parts. That TV is making politics "a rich man's game," turning statesmanship into a circus, handing demagogues a new weapon. But it is giving Americans their first good look at the inside of their Government, letting them judge the people they elect by sight as well as by sound and fury.

That TV has distorted and debased Salesmanship, haunting people with singing "commercials" and slogans. However, because or in spite of TV, people are buying more and more things they never before thought they needed or wanted.

These are just some of the comments that people keep on making about TV. The experts say that it probably will be another generation before there is a firm basis of knowledge about television's impact on America.

Today's TV child, the boy or girl who was born with a TV set in his home, is too young to analyze his feelings. Older people, despite their frequent vehemence about TV, are still far from sure whether they have all Aladdin's lamp or hold a bear by the tail.

Goliath with Tubes

One thing you can be sure about. TV, a giant at 10, continues to grow like nobody's business. Here are some figures and comparisons: The 15 billion dollars that the U.S. people have invested in TV sets and repairs since the war is 15 per cent more than the country spent for new school and college buildings. About a billion more has gone into TV stations and equipment.

TV-viewing time is going *up,* not down, latest surveys show. This explodes the theory that people would taper off on television "once they got used to it."

"Pull" of popular TV programs is believed to be very effective. Pollsters report that three times as many people will leave a meal to answer questions at the door as will get up to abandon "Dragnet."

The number of families holding out against TV is declining to a small fraction. There still are 16 million families without sets, but most of these families either can't pay for sets or else live out of range of TV signals.

On an average evening, twice as many set owners will be watching TV as are engaged in any other form of entertainment or leisure activity, such as movie-going, card playing, or reading. Seven out of 10 American children watch TV between 6 and 8 o'clock most evenings.

Analysts are intrigued by the evidence that adults, not children, are the real television fans. The newest trend in viewing habits is a rise in the number of housewives who watch TV in the morning. One out of five with a set now watches a morning show with regularity.

What Is It?

Why do people want TV? A $67.50-per-week shoe repairman in San Francisco, puts it about as plainly as anyone can. "TV," he says, "is the only amusement I can afford." That was the reason he gave for paying four weeks' wages for his set.

The cobbler's comment explains TV's basic lure. It is free entertainment except for the cost of [the] set, and repairs and electricity. It becomes so absorbing that a broken set is a family catastrophe. People will pay to have the set fixed before they will pay the milk bill, if necessary.

What does TV do to people? What do people do with TV? The researchers are digging into these questions all the time. In general, they come to theories, rather than conclusions. There are three main theories:

THEORY "A": This is widely held by people whose professions bring them into close contact with juveniles—judges, district attorneys, police officers, ministers. It assumes that TV is bound to be affecting the American mind and character because it soaks up one to five hours a day or more that used to be spent in outdoor play, in games requiring reasoning and imagination, or in reading, talking, radio listening, or movie-going.

Even the more passive of these pursuits, the theory runs, required more exercise of brain than does TV watching. Then, too, many TV programs, the theorists say, are violent or in questionable taste.

Net effect, according to these people, is a wasting away or steady decline in certain basic skills among American youngsters. Children lose the ability to read, forfeit their physical dexterity, strength, and initiative.

Some see a definite connection between TV and juvenile delinquency. The Kefauver Subcommittee of the Senate Judiciary Committee has just explored this aspect. It stated:

"Members of the subcommittee share the concern of a large segment of the thinking public for the implications of the impact of this medium [television] . . . upon the ethical and cultural standards of the youth of America. It has been unable to gather proof of a direct casual relationship between the viewing of acts of crime and violence and the actual performance of criminal deeds. It has not, however, found irrefutable evidence that young people may not be negatively influenced in their present-day behavior by the saturated exposure they now receive to pictures and drama based on an underlying theme of lawlessness and crime which depict human violence."

THEORY "B": Mainly held by sociologists, communications economists, pollsters. This is that television is changing the American mind and character, although nobody knows for sure just how. The evidence is too fragmentary. The analysts are disturbed by some aspects of TV's effect on viewers. Some think TV is conditioning Americans to be "other directed," that is, getting the ideas from someone else. The early American, by contrast, is supposed to have been "inner directed," a man who thought things out for himself on the basis of his own reasoning.

A fancy name for this suspected effect of TV is "narcotic disfunction." This means that more and more men come home in the evening, drop into a chair in front of the TV set after supper and slip into a dream world of unreality.

However, the same researchers confess that TV can have a broadening influence, bringing to the masses a taste of the arts and sciences, a peek into government that they couldn't get any other way.

THEORY "C": This is what the TV people themselves like to think. It is that television is rapidly becoming "one more service" to the U.S. public, another medium such as newspapers, magazines, radio. Some people watch TV a lot, others very little. Most people want a set around, but some don't lean on it.

The TV people minimize the idea that TV is dominating American life. It is almost as if they were afraid their own baby is getting too big. What they usually say is that the people who allow their lives to be controlled by television were similarly dominated by radio and the movies—and that they are only a small minority.

The TV Habit

What do the theorists base their theories on? What have they found out about the place of the TV set in American life?

Many studies have been made of the "TV habit." Latest of these indicates that TV viewing reaches a peak just after a set enters a home, then falls off rather sharply. Next, viewing begins to rise again in the average home, building up, evidently, toward a new peak that is not yet measured.

The A. C. Nielsen Company, a market research organization that attaches mechanical recorders to sets in private homes, finds this: During the 12 months ended in April 1955, average use per day of TV sets was 4 hours and 50 minutes. That was up 4 per cent over the year before. . . .

Other studies indicate that women watch TV more than men do. Children, contrary to general impression, watch TV less than adults in the average home. Persons low in income, education, or job status as a rule spend more time in front of TV sets than those with more money and education.

What's on TV

What do people get on TV? What do they want? Three out of every four TV programs are entertainment shows. . . . In a typical week of the peak TV season, in January of last year, crime, comedy, variety, and Western shows accounted for 42.7 per cent of all TV program time on New York City screens. News accounted for 6.1 per cent of TV time—about the same share of time as was taken by quiz, stunt, and contest shows. Other informational types of TV shows, such as interviews, weather reports, travelogues, children's instructional programs, and cooking classes, got 16.2 per cent of the time.

Rating figures tend to show that people are getting just about what they want, in the opinion of the broadcasting industry. According to the "popularity" ratings of top shows, comedy and drama and straight entertainment are outpulling everything else.

What about information? The popularity cards seem to indicate the reaction is a stifled yawn. In a two-week period last June, when two comedy programs, the

"George Gobel Show" and "I Love Lucy," were at the top of the list, each reaching more than 13 million homes, the top-ranking informational programs were way down the line. The "March of Medicine," for example, was No. 62, reaching 6.57 million homes; "Meet the Press" was No. 150, getting to 1.14 million families.

Studies also have been made of how long various programs hold their audiences. Love and adventure performances, it develops, will keep about 85 per cent of the audience to the end. By contrast, the most gripping historical sketches hold only 65 per cent, and many hold less than one third of their starting viewers. Informational programs, again, rank near the bottom in "holding power."

Television critics, who write about TV programs in newspapers and magazines, are frequently harsh in their remarks about violence, sadism, bad taste on the screen. However, Dallas W. Smythe, a professor of communications economics at the University of Illinois, analyzed New York City programs for 1955 and concludes that programs which critics liked best seldom drew the biggest audiences.

The public is fickle. Top rating is hard to hold. The viewers tire rapidly of a particular show unless the producers manage to come up with fresh material, new appeals.

4. Congress Investigates Homosexuals as Subversives, 1950

On the Floor of the House of Representatives

Mr. Miller of Nebraska Mr. Chairman, I realize that I am discussing a very delicate subject. I cannot lay the bones bare like I could before medical colleagues. I would like to strip the fetid, stinking flesh off this skeleton of homosexuality and tell my colleagues of the House some of the facts of nature. I cannot expose all the putrid facts as it would offend the sensibilities of some of you. It will be necessary to skirt some of the edges, and I use certain Latin terms to describe some of these individuals. Make no mistake several thousand, according to police records, are now employed by the Federal Government.

I offer this amendment to the Vorys amendment in good faith. Recently the spotlight of publicity has been focused not only upon the State Department but upon the Department of Commerce because of homosexuals being employed in these and other departments of Government. Recently Mr. Peurifoy, of the State Department, said he had allowed 91 individuals in the State Department to resign because they were homosexuals. Now they are like birds of a feather, they flock together. Where did they go?

You must know what a homosexual is. It is amazing that in the Capital City of Washington we are plagued with such a large group of those individuals. Washington attracts many lovely folks. The sex crimes in the city are many.

In the Eightieth Congress I was the author of the sex pervert bill that passed this Congress and is now a law in the District of Columbia. It can confine some of these people in St. Elizabeth's Hospital for treatment. They are the sex perverts.

Congressional Record, 81st Cong., 2d sess., 1950, 96, pt. 4: 4527–4528.

Some of them are more to be pitied than condemned, because in many it is a pathological condition, very much like the kleptomaniac who must go out and steal, he has that urge; or like the pyromaniac, who goes to bed and wakes up in the middle of the night with an urge to go out and set a fire. He does that. Some of these homosexuals are in that class. Remember there were 91 of them dismissed in the State Department. That is a small percent of those employed in Government. We learned 2 years ago that there were around 4,000 homosexuals in the District. The Police Department the other day said there were between five and six thousand in Washington who are active and that 75 percent were in Government employment. There are places in Washington where they gather for the purpose of sex orgies, where they worship at the cesspool and flesh pots of iniquity. There is a restaurant downtown where you will find male prostitutes. They solicit business for other male customers. They are pimps and undesirable characters. . . .

So I offer this amendment, and when the time comes for voting upon it, I hope that no one will object. I sometimes wonder how many of these homosexuals have had a part in shaping our foreign policy. How many have been in sensitive positions and subject to blackmail. It is a known fact that homosexuality goes back to the Orientals, long before the time of Confucius; that the Russians are strong believers in homosexuality, and that those same people are able to get into the State Department and get somebody in their embrace, and once they are in their embrace, fearing blackmail, will make them go to any extent. Perhaps if all the facts were known these same homosexuals have been used by the Communists.

I realize that there is some physical danger to anyone exposing all of the details and nastiness of homosexuality, because some of these people are dangerous. They will go to any limit. Thee homosexuals have strong emotions. They are not to be trusted and when blackmail threatens they are a dangerous group.

The Army at one time gave these individuals a dishonorable discharge and later changed the type of discharge. They are not knowingly kept in Army service. They should not be employed in Government. I trust both sides of the aisle will support the amendment.

Mr. Dondero Was there any evidence or testimony before the gentleman's committee with respect to the number of people who were separated from the service in the Department of State who had later acquired positions in other departments of Government? I refer to those whose employment was considered a security risk. Was anything said before your committee on that subject?

Mr. Clevenger I will say to the gentleman, I brought that question up a year ago, as to whether the other departments would be alerted so that they might not hire these—we can name them now—these homosexuals. Until the Assistant Secretary of State, Mr. Peurifoy, made that word public over in the other body, we had insufficient information so far as the committee was concerned and could not tell you. In reply to my question we were informed they were not, and unofficially we were told, or at least I was told, that they have been employed in other sections of the Government, at least most of them were.

Mr. Dondero The reason I asked that question is that I made inquiry by letter to find out where these people went and whether they are now employed by our Government and I have not yet received a reply giving me any information on the subject.

Mr. Clevenger If the gentleman will look at the report he will find some information on that subject.

I am going to address myself now to conditions we have discovered in the Department of Commerce. When I asked the security officer if he would flag them, he said he would. I told him I was very much afraid he could not, because of an Executive order which was issued restricting the information being given on these people.

The air is full of stories. The press is full of stories. I am not passing on that.

In discussing the constitutionality of the so-called loyalty program, John Edgar Hoover, Director of the FBI, had occasion to cite a decision of the circuit court of appeals rendered on August 11, 1949, involving the Joint Anti-Fascist Committee. A portion of that decision is worthy of repetition here:

> Contrary to the contentions of the committee, nothing in the Hatch Act or the loyalty program deprives the committee or its members of any property rights. Freedom of speech and assembly is denied no one. Freedom of thought and belief is not impaired. Anyone is free to join the committee and give it his support and encouragement. Everyone has the constitutional right to do these things, but no one has a constitutional right to be a Government employee.

For emphasis permit me to repeat the last phrase, "but no one has a constitutional right to be a Government employee."

It seems to me that the crux of our entire security program lies in that phrase. It is indeed a privilege and certainly not a right to work for the Government and it is time we cleared the air on the misconceptions of a good many well-intentioned people who have been misled by the propaganda of the Communist and the fellow traveler into the belief that the burden of "proof of qualification" lies on the employer in this case, the Government, rather than on the employee. Nothing could be further from the truth. The Government has the right, nay the obligation, to set up standards for performance of duty not only for prospective employees but for those already on the rolls. This sacred obligation to the taxpayer implies the summary removal of any employee who does not measure up to these standards, the avails and crocodile tears of the fuzzy-minded to the contrary notwithstanding. It is tragically true that our present administration has been sadly lacking in the courage or capacity necessary to carry out these obligations but this does not excuse, or in no way alter or mitigate these obligations. . . .

I wish the American people would keep in mind the fact that a security risk does not have to be a member of the Communist Party or even of a Communist-front organization. It is not only conceivable but highly probable that many security risks are loyal Americans; however, there is something in their background that represents a potential possibility that they might succumb to conflicting emotions to the detriment of the national security. Perhaps they have relatives behind the iron curtain and thus would be subject to pressure. Perhaps they are addicted to an overindulgence in alcohol or maybe they are just plain garrulous. The most flagrant example is the homosexual who is subject to the most effective blackmail. It is an established fact that Russia makes a practice of keeping a list of sex perverts in enemy countries and the core of Hitler's espionage was based on the intimidation of these unfortunate people.

Despite this fact however, the Under Secretary of State recently testified that 91 sex perverts had been located and fired from the Department of State. For this the Department must be commended. But have they gone far enough? Newspaper accounts quote Senate testimony indicating there are 400 more in the State Department and 4,000 in Government. Where are they? Who hired them? Do we have a cell of these perverts hiding around Government? Why are they not ferreted out and dismissed? Does the Department of State have access to information in the files of the Washington Police Department? Are we to assume that the State Department has a monopoly on this problem? What are the other Departments of Government doing about this?

For years we had a public prejudice against mentioning in public such loathsome diseases as gonorrhea and cancer. In effecting cures for these maladies the medical people recognized the first step was in public education. These matters were brought before the public and frankly discussed and it was not until then that progress was really made. It is time to bring this homosexual problem into the open and recognize the problem for what it is.

The Commerce Department hearings are somewhat enlightening in regard to the entire security problem and I would suggest that interested Members read them in detail. . . .

Here we find that the Commerce Department has not located any homosexuals in their organization. Are we to believe that in the face of the testimony of the District of Columbia police that 75 percent of the 4,000 perverts in the District of Columbia are employed by the Government, that the Department of Commerce has none?

What is wrong with this loyalty program that dos not uncover these matters, and when it does, adopts an attitude of looking for proof of disloyalty in the form of overt acts rather than elements of security risk? Is it not possible for the Government to refuse employment on the grounds of lack of qualifications where risk is apparent? This is not necessarily an indictment or conviction; it is merely the exercise of caution for the common welfare.

5. Graphic Illustrations of How to Respond to a Nuclear Attack, 1950

Survival Secrets for Atomic Attacks

ALWAYS PUT FIRST THINGS FIRST

Try to Get Shielded

If you have time, get down in a basement or subway. Should you unexpectedly be caught out-of-doors, seek shelter alongside a building, or jump in any handy ditch or gutter.

Drop Flat on Ground or Floor

To keep from being tossed about and to lessen the chances of being struck by falling and flying objects, flatten out at the base of a wall, or at the bottom of a bank.

Bury Your Face in Your Arms

When you drop flat, hide your eyes in the crook of your elbow. That will protect your face from flash burns, prevent temporary blindness and keep flying objects out of your eyes.

NEVER LOSE YOUR HEAD

By 1950 the Federal Civil Defense Agency had reduced nuclear survival to a series of simple rules, including "jump in any handy ditch or gutter" and "never lose your head."

DIRECTION OF HEAT FLASH

If you are caught outdoors in a sudden attack, a hat will give you at least some protection from the 'heat flash'.

Fashion tips for the apocalypse. Men should wear wide-brimmed hats, women stockings and long-sleeved dresses. From Richard Gerstell's government-sponsored *How to Survive an Atomic Bomb* (1950).

Paul Boyer, *By the Bomb's Early Light: American Thought and Culture at the Dawn of the Atomic Age* (New York: Pantheon Books, 1985), 310–311.

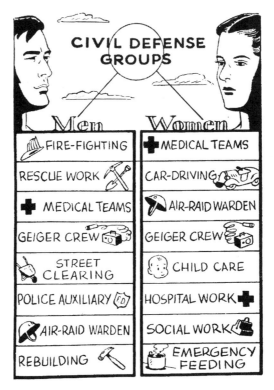

Here are some of the civil defense jobs open to men and women.

Even after the bomb fell, gender-role distinctions would be carefully preserved, in the view of 1950 civil-defense planners. (From Richard Gerstell, *How to Survive an Atomic Bomb.*)

Flee the city! An early 1950 real estate ad offers "good bomb immunity" in an upstate New York property (*Life*, February 27, 1950).

XX *E S S A Y S*

Historians have found reading the "texts" of mass culture—films, popular novels, magazines, and popular music—to be a fruitful way to unearth some of the cultural and political tensions of the 1950s. Historian Beth Bailey of the University of New Mexico describes how dating rituals changed in the 1950s and suggests what that tells us about the expectations of young men and women and their sometimes distraught parents. The late Roland Marchand, a prominent historian of advertising, examines a wide range of cultural artifacts and explores their connections to race relations, youth culture, and politics.

Rebels Without a Cause? Teenagers in the 1950s

BETH BAILEY

The United States emerged from the Second World War the most powerful and affluent nation in the world. This statement, bald but essentially accurate, is the given foundation for understanding matters foreign and domestic, the cold war and the age of abundance in America. Yet the sense of confidence and triumph suggested by that firm phrasing and by our images of soldiers embracing women as confetti swirled through downtown streets obscures another postwar reality. Underlying and sometimes overwhelming both bravado and complacency were voices of uncertainty. America at war's end was not naively optimistic.

The Great War had planted the seeds of the great depression. Americans wondered if hard times would return as the war boom ended. (They wouldn't.) The First World War had not ended all wars. Would war come again? (It would, both cold and hot.) And the fundamental question that plagued postwar America was, would American citizens have the strength and the character to meet the demands of this new world?

Postwar America appears in stereotype as the age of conformity—smug, materialistic, complacent, a soulless era peopled by organization men and their (house)wives. But this portrait of conformity exists only because Americans created it. Throughout the postwar era Americans indulged in feverish self-examination. Experts proclaimed crises, limned the American character, poked and prodded into the recesses of the American psyche. Writing in scholarly journals and for an attentive general public, theorists and social critics suggested that America's very success was destroying the values that had made success possible. Success, they claimed, was eroding the ethnic that had propelled America to military and industrial supremacy and had lifted American society (with significant exceptions seen clearly in hindsight) to undreamed-of heights of prosperity.

At issue was the meaning of the American dream. Did the American dream mean success through individual competition in a wide-open free marketplace? Or was the dream only of the abundance the American marketplace had made possible—the suburban American dream of two cars in every garage and a refrigerator-freezer in

"Rebels Without a Cause? Teenagers in the 1950s," by Beth Bailey, from *History Today* vol. 40 February 1990, pp. 25–31. Reprinted by permission of *History Today*.

every kitchen? One dream was of competition and the resulting rewards. The *making* of the self-made man—the process of entrepreneurial struggle—was the stuff of that dream. Fulfillment, in this vision, was not only through material comforts, but through the prominence, social standing, and influence in the public sphere one achieved in the struggle for success.

The new-style postwar American dream seemed to look to the private as the sphere of fulfillment, of self-definition and self-realization. Struggle was not desired, but stasis. The dream was of a private life—a family, secure, stable, and comfortable—that compensated for one's public (work) life. One vision highlighted risk; the other security. Many contemporary observers feared that the desire for security was overwhelming the "traditional" American ethic. In the dangerous postwar world, they asserted, the rejection of the public, of work and of risk would soon destroy America's prosperity and security.

The focus for much of the fear over what America was becoming was, not surprisingly, youth. Adult obsession with the new postwar generation took diverse forms—from the overheated rhetoric about the new epidemic of juvenile delinquency (too many rebels without causes) to astringent attacks on the conformity of contemporary youth. These critiques, though seemingly diametrically opposed, were based on the shared assumption that young people lacked the discipline and get-up-and-go that had made America great.

Perhaps nowhere in American culture do we find a richer statement of concern about American youth and the new America dream than in the debates that raged over "going steady," an old name for a new practice that was reportedly more popular among postwar teenagers than "bop, progressive jazz, hot rods, and curiosity (slight) about atomic energy." The crisis over the "national problem" of going steady is not merely emblematic—an amusing way into a serious question. "Going steady" seemed to many adults the very essence of the problem, a kind of leading indicator of the privatization of the American dream. Social scientists and social critics saw in the new security-first courtship patterns a paradigm for an emerging American character that, while prizing affluence, did not relish the risks and hard work that made it possible.

Certainly the change in courtship patterns was dramatic. And it was not hard to make a connection between the primary characteristics of teenagers' love lives and what they hoped to get out of American life in general. Before the Second World War, American youth had prized a promiscuous popularity, demonstrating competitive success through the number and variety of dates they commanded. Sociologist Willard Waller, in his 1937 study of American dating, gave this competitive system a name: "the campus rating complex." His study of Pennsylvania State University detailed a "dating and rating" system based on a model of public competition in which popularity was the currency. To be popular, men needed outward, material signs: an automobile, proper clothing, the right fraternity membership, money. Women's popularity depended on building and maintaining a reputation for popularity. They had to *be seen* with popular men in the "right" places, indignantly turn down requests for dates made at the "last minute," and cultivate the impression they were greatly in demand.

In *Mademoiselle*'s 1938 college issue, for example, a Smith college senior advised incoming freshmen to "cultivate an image of popularity" if they wanted dates.

"During your first term," she wrote, "get 'home talent' to ply you with letters, invitations, telegrams. College men will think, 'She must be attractive if she can rate all that attention.'" And at Northwestern University in the 1920s, competitive pressure was so intense that co-eds made a pact not to date on certain nights of the week. That way they could preserve some time to study, secure in the knowledge they were not losing ground in the competitive race for success by staying home.

In 1935, the Massachusetts *Collegian* (the Massachusetts State College student newspaper) ran an editorial against using the library for "datemaking." The editors proclaimed: "The library is the place for the improvement of the mind and not the social standing of the student." Social standing, not social life: on one word turns the meaning of the dating system. That "standing" probably wasn't even a conscious choice shows how completely these college students took for granted that dating was primarily concerned with competition and popularity. As one North Carolina teenager summed it up:

> Going steady with one date
> Is okay, if that's all you rate.

Rating, dating, popularity, competition: catchwords hammered home, reinforced from all sides until they seemed a natural vocabulary. You had to rate in order to date, to date in order to rate. By successfully maintaining this cycle, you became popular. To stay popular, you competed. There was no end; the competitive process defined dating. Competition was the key term in the formula—remove it and there was no rating, dating, or popularity.

In the 1930s and 1940s, this competition was enacted most visibly on the dance floor. There, success was a dizzying popularity that kept girls whirling from escort to escort, "cut in" on by a host of popular men. Advice columns, etiquette books, even student handbooks told girls to strive to be "once-arounders," to never be left with the same partner for more than one turn around the dance floor. On the dance floor, success and failure were easily measured. Wallflowers were dismissed out of hand. But getting stuck—not being "cut in" on—was taken quite seriously as a sign of social failure. Everyone noticed, and everyone judged.

This form of competitive courtship would change dramatically. By the early 1950s, "cutting in" had almost completely disappeared outside the deep south. In 1955, a student at Texas Christian University reported, "To cut in is almost an insult." A girl in Green Bay, Wisconsin, said that her parents were "astonished" when they discovered that she hadn't danced with anyone but her escort at a "formal." "The truth was," she admitted, "that I wasn't aware that we were supposed to."

This 180-degree reversal took place quickly—during the years of the Second World War—and was so complete by the early 1950s that people under eighteen could be totally unaware of the formerly powerful convention. It signaled not simply a change in dancing etiquette but a complete transformation of the dating system as well. Definitions of social success as promiscuous popularity based on strenuous competition had given way to new definitions, which located success in the security of a dependable escort.

By the 1950s, early marriage had become the goal for young adults. In 1959, 47 percent of all brides married before they turned nineteen, and up to 25 percent of students at many large state universities were married. The average age at marriage had risen to 26.7 for men and 23.3 for women during the lingering depression, but by 1951 the average age at marriage had fallen to 22.6 for men, 20.4 for women. And younger teens had developed their own version of early marriage.

As early as 1950, going steady had completely supplanted the dating-rating complex as the criterion for popularity among youth. A best-selling study of American teenagers, *Profile of Youth* (1949), reported that in most high schools the "mere fact" of going steady was a sign of popularity "as long as you don't get tied up with an impossible gook." The *Ladies' Home Journal* reported in 1949 that "every high school student . . . must be prepared to fit into a high-school pattern in which popularity, social acceptance and emotional security are often determined by the single question: does he or she go steady?" A 1959 poll found that 57 percent of American teens had gone or were going steady. And, according to *Cosmopolitan* in 1960, if you didn't go steady, you were "square."

The new protocol of going steady was every bit as strict as the old protocol of rating and dating. To go steady, the boy gave the girl some visible token, such as a class ring or letter sweater. In Portland, Oregon, steadies favored rings (costing from $17 to $20). In Birmingham, Michigan, the girl wore the boy's identity bracelet, but never his letter sweater. In rural Iowa, the couple wore matching corduroy "steady jackets," although any couple wearing matching clothing in California would be laughed at.

As long as they went steady, the boy had to call the girl a certain number of times a week and take her on a certain number of dates a week (both numbers were subject to local convention). Neither boy nor girl could date anyone else or pay too much attention to anyone of the opposite sex. While either could go out with friends of the same sex, each must always know where the other was and what he or she was doing. Going steady meant a guaranteed date for special events, and it implied greater sexual intimacy—either more "necking" or "going further."

In spite of the intense monogamy of these steady relationships, teenagers viewed them as temporary. A 1950 study of 565 seniors in an eastern suburban high school found that 80 percent had gone or were going steady. Out of that number, only eleven said they planned to marry their steady. In New Haven, Connecticut, high school girls wore "obit bracelets." Each time they broke up with a boy, they added a disc engraved with his name or initials to the chain. In Louisiana, a girl would embroider her sneakers with the name of her current steady. When they broke up, she would clip off his name and sew an X over the spot. An advice book from the mid-1950s advised girls to get a "Puppy Love Anklet." Wearing it on the right ankle meant that you were available, on the left that you were going steady. The author advised having "Going Steady" engraved on one side, "Ready, Willing 'n Waiting" on the other—just in case the boys could not remember the code. All these conventions, cheerfully reported in teenager columns in national magazines, show how much teenagers took it for granted that going steady was a temporary, if intense, arrangement.

Harmless as this system sounds today, especially compared to the rigors of rating and dating, the rush to go steady precipitated an intense generational battle. Clearly some adult opposition was over sex: going steady was widely accepted as a justification for greater physical intimacy. But more fundamentally, the battle over going steady came down to a confrontation between two generations over the meaning of the American dream. Security versus competition. Teenagers in the 1950s were trying to do the unthinkable—to eliminate competition from the popularity equation. Adults were appalled. To them, going steady, with its extreme rejection of competition in favor of temporary security, represented all the faults of the new generation.

Adults, uncomfortable with the "cult of happiness" that rejected competition for security, attacked the teenage desire for security with no holds barred. As one writer advised boys, "To be sure of anything is to cripple one's powers of growth." She continued, "To have your girl always assured at the end of a telephone line without having to work for her, to beat the other fellows to her is bound to lessen your powers of personal achievement." A male adviser, campaigning against going steady, argued: "Competition will be good for you. It sharpens your wits, teaches you how to get along well in spite of difficulties." And another, writing in *Esquire,* explained the going steady phenomenon this way: "She wants a mate; he being a modern youth doesn't relish competition."

As for girls, the argument went: "She's afraid of competition. She isn't sure she can compete for male attention in the open market: 'going steady' frees her from fear of further failures." The author of *Jackson's Guide to Dating* tells the story of "Judith Thompson," a not-especially-attractive girl with family problems, who has been going steady with "Jim" since she was fourteen. Lest we think that poor Judith deserves someone to care for her or see Jim as a small success in her life, the author stresses that going steady is one more failure for Judith. "Now that Judith is sixteen and old enough to earn money and help herself in other ways to recover from her unfortunate childhood, she has taken on the additionally crippling circumstance of a steady boyfriend. How pathetic. The love and attention of her steady boyfriend are a substitute for other more normal kinds of success." What should Judith be doing? "A good deal of the time she spends going steady with Jim could be used to make herself more attractive so that other boys would ask her for dates."

There is nothing subtle in these critiques of going steady. The value of competition is presumed as a clear standard against which to judge modern youth. But there is more here. There is a tinge of anger in these judgments, an anger that may well stem from the differing experiences of two generations of Americans. The competitive system that had emerged in the flush years of the 1920s was strained by events of the 1930s and 1940s. The elders had come of age during decades of depression and world war, times when the competitive struggle was, for many, inescapable. Much was at stake, the cost of failure all too clear. While youth in the period between the wars embraced a competitive dating system, even gloried in it, as adults they sought the security they had lacked in their youth.

Young people and their advocates made much of the lack of security of the postwar world, self-consciously pointing to the "general anxiety of the times" as a justification for both early marriage and going steady. But the lives of these young people were clearly more secure than those of their parents. That was the gift their parents tried to give them. Though the cold war raged it had little immediate impact on the emerging teenage culture (for those too young to fight in Korea, of course). Cushioned by unprecedented affluence, allowed more years of freedom within the protected youth culture of high school and ever-more-frequently college, young people did not have to struggle so hard, compete so ferociously as their parents had.

And by and large, both young people and their parents knew it and were genuinely not sure what that meant for America's future. What did it mean—that a general affluence, at least for a broad spectrum of America's burgeoning middle class, was possible without a dog-eat-dog ferocity? What did *that* mean for the American Dream of success? One answer was given in the runaway best seller of the decade, *The Man in the Gray Flannel Suit,* which despite the title was not so much about the deadening impact of conformity but about what Americans should and could dream in the postwar world.

The protagonist of the novel, Tom Rath (the not-so-subtle naming made more explicit by the appearance of the word "vengeful" in the sentence following Tom's introduction), has been through the Second World War, and the shadow of war hangs over his life. Tom wants to provide well for his family, and feels a nagging need to succeed. But when he is offered the chance at an old-style American dream—to be taken on as the protégé of his business-wise, driven boss, he says no. In a passage that cuts to the heart of postwar American culture, Tom tells his boss:

> I don't think I'm the kind of guy who should try to be a big executive. I'll say it frankly: I don't think I have the willingness to make the sacrifices. . . . I'm trying to be honest about this. I want the money. Nobody likes money better than I do. But I'm not the kind of guy who can work evenings and weekends and all the rest of it forever. . . . I've been through one war. Maybe another one's coming. If one is, I want to be able to look back and figure I spent the time between wars with my family, the way it should have been spent. Regardless of war, I want to get the most out of the years I've got left. Maybe that sounds silly. It's just that if I have to bury myself in a job every minute of my life, I don't see any point to it.

Tom's privatized dream—of comfort without sacrifice, of family and personal fulfillment—might seem the author's attempt to resolve the tensions of the novel (and of postwar American society). But the vision is more complex than simply affirmative. Tom's boss responds with sympathy and understanding, then suddenly loses control. "Somebody has to do the big jobs!" he says passionately. "This world was built by men like me! To really do a job, you have to live it, body and soul! You people who just give half your mind to your work are riding on our backs!" and Tom responds: "I know it."

The new American Dream had not yet triumphed. The ambivalence and even guilt implicit in Tom Rath's answer to his boss pervaded American culture in the 1950s—in the flood of social criticism and also in parents' critiques of teenage courtship rituals. The attacks on youth's desire for security are revealing, for it was in many ways the parents who embraced security—moving to the suburbs, focusing on the family. The strong ambivalence many felt about their lives appears in the critiques of youth. This same generation would find even more to criticize in the 1960s, as the "steadies" of the 1950s became the sexual revolutionaries of the 1960s. Many of the children of these parents came to recognize the tensions within the dream. The baby-boom generation accepted wholeheartedly the doctrine of self-fulfillment, but rejected the guilt and fear that had linked fulfillment and security. In the turbulence of the 1960s, young people were not rejecting the new American Dream of easy affluence and personal fulfillment, but only jettisoning the fears that had hung over a generation raised with depression and war. It turns out the 1950s family was not the new American Dream, but only its nurturing home.

Visions of Classlessness

ROLAND MARCHAND

The constraints and sacrifices of World War II did not prepare Americans to meet the realities of the postwar era with equanimity.* Expectations ran high, despite underlying anxieties about atomic perils and the possibility of a postwar depression. Wartime discourse resonated with acclamations of equality and promises of the coming of a better, technologically wondrous life for all. The common man, idealized in nostalgic imagery, would carve out a future of unobstructed independence. Centralized controls, bureaucratic complexities, diminished autonomy for the individual— these were largely dismissed as the temporary conditions of war. Postwar popular culture reflected these expectations, expressing complacent satisfaction in the realization of some and providing vicarious compensations for the intense disappointment of others.

World War II came closer than any other twentieth-century phenomenon to enacting the drama of the melting pot in the United States, as disparate groups and values seemed to fuse into a composite national culture. Four years of war brought unprecedented national consolidation. Vast wartime migrations—to the armed forces and to war industries and boomtowns—undermined regional loyalties and broadened provincial horizons. Class barriers, and even some of the outward identifying marks of class, seemed to disappear. The nation's dramatists of popular culture, its persuaders and performers, enlisted in the task of uniting the nation behind common assumptions.

The explicitly democratic themes of wartime popular culture promoted unity. Morale-builders stressed the idea of equal sacrifices and personalized the war through such democratic figures as G. I. Joe, Rosie the Riverter, Norman Rockwell's everyman figure in the "Freedom of Speech" poster, and Rockwell's Willie Gillis (the common man as G.I.). The war years also prolonged the modest redistribution of income from rich to poor that had begun during the 1930s. Although this process was to come to a standstill in the late 1940s, Americans emerged from the war confident of a snowballing trend toward economic democratization and a classless culture.

Meanwhile, in what Frank Fox has characterized as "World of Tomorrow" advertising, business interests painted stirring images of the technological future. Wartime research, when applied to consumer products, would bring new power and comfort to the common man in a "thermoplastic, aerodynamic, supersonic, electronic, gadgetonic" postwar world. Popular anticipation of a precise watershed moment—when the war would end and the "future" begin—took on a millennial cast. In style these wartime visions paralleled themes of the General Motors Futurama at the 1939 World's Fair. The message was one of man's technological dominion over nature, of machines as social solutions. Yet another wartime

---

"Visions of Classlessness, Quests for Dominion: American Popular Culture," by Roland Marchand, from *Reshaping America: Society and Institutions, 1945–1960,* ed. Robert H. Bremner and Gary W. Reichard (Ohio State University Press: 1982). Reprinted by permission of the Estate of Roland Marchand.

*I am indebted to the students in my fall 1979 undergraduate seminar, and to David Brody, Eckard Toy, and James Lapsley, for their criticism of ideas contained in an initial version of this essay.

message, infused in advertising and other forms of popular culture, promised that victory would restore a cherished version of the true American way of life, based on the small town, the corner drugstore, and the close-knit family—an image aptly described as "American Pastoral."

Instead, the postwar world brought bureaucratic complexity, cold war insecurity, and a shrunken sense of individual mastery. It produced a technology of atomic peril as well as material comfort. Inspired by the sweeping democratic promises of wartime ideology and a hunger for security and stability, Americans welcomed the notion of classless prosperity. Enticed by expectations of increased power and control, they reacted with dismay as they found themselves slipping into a condition of greater vulnerability and dependency. In response they embraced popular culture reveries that seemed to enhance their sense of personal dominion.

The postwar period saw the emergence of a popular culture more homogeneous than Americans had previously known, as the cold war reinforced the trend toward consolidation. This greater homogeneity also reflected changes in demography, increasingly centralized production of popular culture images and artifacts, and more effective dissemination of popular culture by the media.

One measure of increasing homogeneity was a decline in competition from ethnic cultures. By the time of World War II, unrestricted immigration had been cut off for a full generation. Between 1940 and 1960 the percentage of foreign-born declined from 8.8 percent to 5.4 percent, and the percentage of Americans with at least one parent of foreign birth fell from 17 percent to 13.5 percent. A decline in carriers of ethnic culture such as foreign-language newspapers, theaters, musical organizations, and social halls reflected these demographic changes. Commercial entertainment increasingly outrivaled the attractions of ethnic folk culture and filled the new increments of leisure time. Network radio expanded its nationalizing and homogenizing influence, and radio sets in use increased right up to the advent of an even more powerful agent of common popular culture—television. Between 1940 and 1950 the "big four" popular periodicals, *Life, Reader's Digest, Look,* and *Saturday Evening Post,* increased their combined total circulation by 105 percent. Although some groups did maintain "taste subcultures," more and more Americans read, heard, and saw the same popular fare.

Another measure of homogeneity was the decline of class and regional differences in clothing and recreation. During the late 1940s sales of traditional work clothes fell precipitously, with the production of men's casual pants and shirts rising almost as rapidly. More workers wore casual clothes on the job, and off work men of different classes seemed indistinguishable on the street. *Life* referred matter-of-factly in 1949 to blue jeans as part of a national teenage "uniform." By the 1950s these classless, vaguely "western" progeny of democratic G.I. dungarees had come to symbolize the triumph of denim as an equalizing casual wear for virtually all Americans. Steady increases in the length of paid vacations for workers had also begun to equalize the distribution of formal leisure time. The Bureau of Labor Statistics even argued that by 1950 the earlier, distinctively "working class" patterns of spare-time activities and expenditures had almost disappeared among urban workers.

Signs of a national culture abounded. In the early 1950s, as journalist Russell Lynes remarked, Sears, Roebuck ceased publication of regional catalogs on the grounds that tastes in furniture had become identical throughout the country. *Fortune* reported that tastes in food were "flattening" regionally. Merchandising consultants began to talk about a "standard middle-majority package," a laundry list of home furnishings and other consumer goods that should be marketable to all families. One suburb looked pretty much like another; what Louise Huxtable has characterized as "Pop Architecture" dominated the landscape everywhere. Local bowling palaces, motels, and auto showrooms quickly copied the flash, glitter, and eccentric shapes of Las Vegas's "architecture of the road." Even where franchised chains did not proliferate, the designers of shopping centers and the entrepreneurs of a thousand "miracle miles" created uniform visual imagery.

The leveling of styles was in many ways a leveling *down*—a fact that did not escape the champions of high culture. In their search for the culprits of cultural debasement, they excoriated first the threats to literacy, order, and good taste coming from the comic book industry, and then the affronts to high culture by the new monster, TV. No previous mass medium, not even radio, expanded its audience so explosively as television. Households with TV sets mounted from fewer than one million in 1949 to more than 46 million in 1960, at which point 90 percent of all American homes were consuming TV programming at an average rate of five hours per day. The convenience of TV and the national standards of performance it set were devastating to provincial commercial entertainment and much of ethnic culture.

The 1950s would later seem a golden age of diversity and cultural quality on TV. But, fixing their gaze on Hopalong Cassidy, Milton Berle, wrestling matches, and formula westerns, contemporary critics denounced the new medium as an attack on culture and literacy. With the advance of TV, homogenized franchise operations, and organizational bureaucracy, a major debate erupted among intellectuals over the prospects and perils of mass culture. Even political concerns seemed to fade before the social menace of mass culture. Did a debased mass culture involve passivity, conformity, and a stifling of creativity in the audience and a formulaic, manipulative, whatever-will-sell attitude by the producer? Then TV seemed to its critics to have unquestionably triumphed as *the* mass culture medium.

Actually, TV probably served more to nationalize and homogenize than either to uplift or degrade. Television advertising embedded slogans, brand names, and affective imagery into the national consciousness with a new intensity, creating symbols for a more uniform national language. Television also helped promote the "common language" functions of national sports spectatorship. Together with convenient air travel, TV made attractive the nationalizing of the professional sports leagues. Minor league baseball declined as did a multitude of more significant local institutions—ethnic clubs, local union meetings, local political clubs—contributing, in Martin Mayer's view, to individual feelings of anomie and powerlessness.

Manufacturers of TV sets fought this negative interpretation of the social impact of TV. Their ads nostalgically depicted warm family scenes in which the connective links of the old family circle were restored in the harmony of the family semicircle plus TV. However specious the implied claims that TV would keep the kids home and the generations together, TV did serve the momentarily unifying function of making children more frequent participants in (or cospectators of) their parents' entertainment.

A critical component of the popular culture that TV helped disseminate was "California Culture." Even before the war California had become the symbol of relaxed, prosperous outdoor living, linked to a "car culture." California led the nation in miles of highway and per capita ownership of cars. The supermarket and the "drive-in" flourished there. The Los Angeles area led the nation in new suburban developments, freeway construction, and experiments with outlying shopping complexes. Smog and traffic notwithstanding, the Los Angeles suburban landscape seemed the landscape of the future.

The media readily promoted California culture as mobile, changing, comparatively "democratic." It had a "life-style." The ambience of that life-style was just about everything that media advertisers liked to associate with their products—an image of the new, the enjoyable, the casual. California provided models of everything from sportswear to houses, and displayed an easy contempt for environmental limits. *The Gallup Poll* reported that it ranked number one among Americans as "best state" and "ideal place to live." Los Angeles scored first among cities for best-looking women and most-desired place to live. It ranked second in climate, beauty of setting, and gaiety of night life.

The imagery of California culture centered around the postwar fad in popular architecture—the California ranch house. A single-story, ground-hugging structure, it was adaptable to split-level form. Picture windows and other expanses of glass accentuated the idea of a free-flowing continuity of space and mood between indoors and outdoors. Population pressure and high costs had imposed limitations on the postwar suburban search for spaciousness. In response the ranch house nurtured illusions of open continuous space and freedom. This was particularly necessary as the sprawling ranch house (invariably pictured alone with no adjacent neighbors) was pared down to 1,200-square-foot tract dimensions.

Inside, the quest for openness was linked with architectural expressions of democracy and "togetherness" (a word coined by *McCall's* in a moment of nostalgia and marketing acumen). In a servantless setting the dining room often disappeared, and the door segregating the kitchen gave way to a counter or open vista that allowed the wife to maintain contact with family and guests. A new room appeared—an amalgam of rumpus room and den. Introduced as "the room without a name," it quickly gained status as the "family room"—a casual, nurturing, and democratic gathering place for all. Naturally, the new room was where the TV was lodged, to be followed in due course by TV trays and TV dinners.

By 1954 Russell Lynes pronounced the California ranch house "ubiquitous," a national symbol of the increasing unity of tastes of "the relatively poor and the relatively well-to-do," and "the standard new suburban dwelling in the suburbs of New York as of Boston, of Chicago as of . . . Los Angeles." Another commentator explained how the outdoor joys of the patio could be retained in midwestern ranch houses throughout spring and fall by the use of radiant heating coils in patio paving. Builders liked the construction efficiencies of the ranch style. Buyers saw in its casual informality, undecorated sense of impermanence, access to nature, and freedom from internal physical barriers an image of western openness and mobility.

The California ranch house seemed to epitomize the postwar dream of classlessness and dominion. Everybody, presumably, was moving to the suburbs. Everyone could belong to the modern, democratic version of the "landed gentry." Limitless energy would make possible heated patios, air-conditioners, and countless appliances. A prolonged do-it-yourself craze suggested that husband as well as wife could make the suburban home a fulfilling last refuge for the exercise of competence and control. Here the common American might evade international tensions and organizational complexities and thus regain a reassuring sense of individual dominion.

The dream of suburban comfort and microcosmic control was a striking instance of upper-middle-class myopia. "Everybody" was *not* moving to the suburbs, despite impressions conveyed by Sunday supplements, TV advertisements, and popular sociology. Most housing developments were priced out of the range of those below the median income. The migration that inundated the suburbs came primarily from those among the top 40 percent in family income, especially those of the professional and technological elites who made impressive gains in income after 1945. Moreover, the most highly publicized sociological studies of suburbia focused on areas that were even more affluent than average—thus exaggerating "typical" suburban prosperity. Since writers, academics, and advertising executives came from the very segment of society making the most rapid gains, they found it easy to believe everyone was riding the same wave of prosperity. The idea of a consummated classlessness struck them with the force of a revelation.

The celebration of this "classless prosperity" permeated the popular culture that other Americans of the era consumed. Russell Lynes helped popularize the new "obsolescence" of class with his essay "High-brow, Low-brow, Middle-brow" in 1949. *Life* magazine's version carried a striking two-page chart depicting the cultural tastes of Lynes's various "brows" in ten categories ranging from furniture to entertainment. Economic classes were obsolete, Lynes insisted; people now chose their pleasures and consumer goods strictly on the basis of individual taste. Sociologist William Whyte noted the "displacement of the old class criterion" by "the impulse to 'culture' and 'good taste.'" Values were "coming together," he concluded, and the suburbs had become the "second great melting pot."

"The distinction between economic levels in the ownership of tangibles is diminishing," the Bureau of Labor Statistics noted, thus "breaking down the barriers of community and class." Sportswriters celebrated the supposed democratization of golf: "Class lines are eliminated," they argued, "when the nation wears sports clothes." Producers of the big-money TV quiz shows nurtured popular enthusiasm for illusions of equality by creating such folk heroes as the "cop who knew Shakespeare." The sponsor of "The $64,000 Question" explained: "We're trying to show the country that the little people are really very intelligent. . . ." Winners were prototypes of the common man and woman, symbols of democratized intelligence. Advertisers now cast affluent suburban families not only as models of appropriate consumer styles but also as realistic portrayals of *average* Americans. In the 1920s and 1930s, Americans had known that they were seeing explicit models of high society "smartness" in many ads. Now they were encouraged to see the advertising models as mirrors of themselves.

Such images and perceptions of classlessness eventually found expression in the language itself. The 1961 *Webster's International Dictionary* acknowledged the existence of a new word not recognized in earlier editions: *life-style.* This new term, which gradually replaced the older phrase "way of life," conveyed nuances of classlessness. The phrase "way of life," had been fully compatible with a recognition of important economic class distinctions. Although people might be described as seeking to *choose* or *achieve* a certain "way of life," they could also easily be thought of as having inherited a particular way of life along with their class standing. But a "life-style" was less likely to seem class-determined or inherited. the word *style* suggested free choice, the uninhibited search for what looked and felt right. It might also connote a particular consumer-consciousness, a notion of choosing among various ensembles or "packages" of goods that represented a style consistency, i.e., that "went well together." Behind the rise of the word *life-style* lay the assumption that increases in real income, the equalizing qualities of new synthetic fabrics and suburban amenities, and the expansion of automobile and appliance ownership had created a totally middle-class society in which all significant differences were simply free expressions of personal tastes.

This vision reflected some real changes in American society. During the 1950s the average income of all families and individuals rose 26 percent in real dollars, and increased installment buying allowed many families to raise their living standard at an even greater rate. Still, as Richard Parker has pointed out, "among those who called themselves middle class, perhaps a majority have always lacked the money to be in fact what they believe they are." It was those of high income, as ever, who consumed the bulk of popular culture products and services—whether sports event admissions, frozen foods, cars, or hi-fi components. And the gains that *were* achieved by median and marginal sectors of the society did not represent gains in relative wealth or power. In fact, those below the top 40 percent remained stationary in their proportion of national income during the 1950s, and all but the wealthiest lost in relative power. Despite the National Advertising Council's puffery about "people's capitalism," corporate assets were more narrowly held in 1960 than in 1945.

Americans appreciated their new material comforts, but many no doubt sensed an erosion of independence and control as large organizations in media, government, and business overshadowed or preempted their spheres of competence and power. It fell to popular culture to exorcise these demons and provide compensating, vicarious adventures in potency and dominion.

Enter the Shmoo and Mike Hammer! Best described as a "snow-white ham with legs," the Shmoo appeared in cartoonist Al Capp's 1948 parable on the quandaries of prosperity. Lured musically into that consumer's paradise, the "Valley of the Shmoon," Capp's hero Li'l Abner recognized the Shmoo as utopia incarnate. The accommodating little creature, so eager to please that it would die of sheer happiness from one hungry look, provided for nearly all material needs. It laid eggs (in cartons) and gave milk (bottled). Broiled, it made the finest steak; roasted, it resembled pork; fried, it came out chicken. And Shmoos reproduced at a remarkable rate.

A national favorite, the Shmoo recapitulated wartime promises. It offered families in Capp's Dogpatch lifelong control over the necessities of life, just as Americans had been led to dream of a technological utopia. In another sense the Shmoo, endlessly and identically reproduced, conjured up intimations of conformity, of boring and emotionless satiety. So dull was this prospect that Capp eventually had his obliging and well-merchandised progeny commit "Shmooicide." Although the spirit of the Shmoo lived on in such tangible forms as the energy consumption binge, the national credit card, and the Playboy bunny, Capp found its appropriate cartoon replacement in the Kigmy, who loved to be kicked. Americans of the era, Capp implied, sought a target for the release of aggression as keenly as they yearned for the security of the Shmoo.

Mike Hammer's phenomenal success as a popular culture hero seemed to confirm that notion. First appearing in 1947 in Mickey Spillane's *I, the Jury,* detective Mike Hammer rewrote the history of American best-sellers with his escapades of vengeance. His self-righteous vigilantism breathed contempt for established institutions and authorities. He worried that prosperity would make Americans soft and weak. And he banished the specters of impotence and conformity by acting remorselessly and alone:

> . . . I killed more people tonight than I have fingers on my hands. I shot them in cold blood and enjoyed every minute of it. . . . They were Commies, Lee. They were red sons-of-bitches who should have died long ago. . . . I just walked into that room with a tommy gun and shot their guts out. They never thought that there were people like me in this country. They figured us all to be soft as horse manure. . . .

For Americans beginning to suffer from a vague closed-in feeling, a restless frustration stemming from Russian threats abroad and the restraints and manipulations of large organizations at home, Mike Hammer represented recovery of a lost dominion. In postwar popular culture the defense of traditional masculinity was difficult to separate from this search for renewed dominion. John Cawelti aptly describes Spillane's "love" scenes as stripteases, many of them unconsummated sexual provocations that led ultimately to "fulfillment in violence." Contempt for women, expressed in frequent violence and sadism by Mike Hammer and in manipulative detachment by such mutant successors as James Bond and the Hugh Hefner Playboy, may have expressed fears of feminine power that went beyond insecure resentments of fancied sexual teasing. Modern society seemed to place "feminine" restraints on man's dominion. In large organizations the executive as well as the worker had to "subdue his personality to another's . . . to act like a good old-fashioned wife." One response in the popular culture was to reassert a compensating image of masculinity that conceded nothing to feminine limitations. . . .

As if in reaction to the blurring of sexual stereotypes during the war, popular culture accentuated women's strictly "feminine" roles. With the home symbolizing the security and stability recently thwarted by war and depression, the paramount role was homemaker. Pert, streamlined housewives dominated the ads. Although married women were employed outside the home in greater numbers than ever before, the popular media romanticized domesticity and elevated it to the status of a national purpose.

Less "feminine" roles for women were disparaged. "Woman driver" jokes reached a peak, and advertisements helped reassert masculine roles. Whereas automobile advertisements in the late 1920s and early 1930s had portrayed nearly as many women as men behind the wheel, those of the mid-1950s depicted far more men than women drivers. The occasional strong, independent female movie roles of the late 1930s disappeared by the 1950s. The older film seductresses who had projected poise, self-assurance, and a sense of challenge were superseded, most strikingly, by Marilyn Monroe, queen of the sexual Shmoos. Her salient qualities were availability and vulnerability. In their contribution to popular psychology, *Modern Woman: The Lost Sex,* Ferdinand Lundberg and Marynia Farnham reinforced notions of the mutual exclusiveness of feminine and masculine qualities. Women's aspirations to masculine achievement lay at the base of modern confusions

and anxieties, they warned; only a return to total femininity could avert psychological disaster. In case children should fail to learn absolute gender distinctions from
other forms of socialization, Cliff May's *Western Ranch Houses* described how
dark wood paneling could be used to given the son's room a "strongly masculine
air" and the daughter's room would be designed with "built-in femininity."

The emphasis on traditional masculinity may have stemmed in part from the
fear that increasing leisure would tempt Americans to become soft—perhaps to
lose their competitive drive and their will to resist communism. Another part may
have arisen from the loss of a sense of achievement and mastery within the workplace and from indignities experienced in lives constrained by the actions of face-
less organizations. The increased collective power that had subdued nature with
vast highways and massive expenditures of electrical energy did not enhance the
power of individuals in their increasingly complex interactions with other people.
The traditional gender of the word *mastery* in American culture had been unequiv-
ocally male. Fears of powerlessness in the midst of mass society had unsurprisingly
triggered ritual efforts to reaffirm the masculine.

Americans of the postwar era also sought solace from anxieties and frustrations
by turning their search for dominion inward. Both religion and popular psychology
flourished in the postwar era, as did hybrids of the two.

Church membership advanced steadily during the late 1940s and early 1950s
until it reached the unprecedented level of 63 percent of all Americans. Works on
religion, from the Revised Standard Bible to Catherine Marshall's *A Man Called
Peter,* were nonfiction best-sellers. The religious novels of Lloyd Douglas and
Sholem Asch gained a comparable place in popular fiction. Billy Graham, using
every modern device from the card file to the television set, built upon his 1949
triumph in a Los Angeles evangelical crusade to gain a place among America's ten
most-admired men by the mid-1950s. Monsignor Fulton J. Sheen adapted his theatri-
cal style to the new media, and in 1953 was named television's man of the year.
Church construction advanced at record rates, and the appearance of drive-in churches
seemed to augur the assimilation of religion to a car culture that had already produced the drive-in restaurant and the drive-in movie.

In the atmosphere of a cold war against "atheistic" communism, religion tended
to merge with patriotism. In the mid-1950s Congress sought to formalize the union
by adding "under God" to the pledge of allegiance and establishing a prayer room
in the Capitol. The physical mobility of the 1940s also enhanced the church's role
as social anchor in the midst of social disruption, a place where new residents in a
community might make social contacts. Theologian Will Herberg concluded that
the three major faiths, Protestantism, Catholicism, and Judaism, had come to serve
as a new American "triple melting pot" for third-generation immigrants as ethnic
subcultures declined. But Herberg and other religious leaders also worried about
the quality of the new "religious awakening." What could one make of an enthusiasm
for faith in which 86 percent of all Americans declared the Bible to be the word of
God, yet 53 percent could not name a single one of the four Gospels? Perhaps the
answer lay in a 1957 Gallup poll in which 81 percent affirmed their expectation
that "religion can answer all or most of today's problems."

Postwar piety was paralleled by a surge of psychology. The prewar decades
had witnessed a considerable popularization of the concepts of psychology and

psychiatry, especially among the well-educated. World War II increased popular awareness of applied psychology and its contributions to personnel selection and "adjustment." Familiarity with psychological jargon—neurosis, inferiority complex, schizophrenia, maladjustment—was already widespread. But in the postwar years, psychology became a popular mania. Publishers responded to a thirst for self-analysis quizzes, how-to-do-it manuals, and psychological advice. A typical issue of *Reader's Digest* contained at least two articles of the "What's Your Personality?" and "Do You Think like a Man or a Woman?" variety.

Among books and films one could almost predict that if it was "serious," it was also psychological. Even the durable western tended to become a stage setting for the playing out of psychological dramas. Advertisers threw themselves headlong into motivation research and "depth interviews" in a search for those "deep-lying habits, feelings, aversions, inner compulsions, and complexes" that might inhibit the buying impulse. Artzybasheff included in his fanciful cartoon of "Improved Design for Modern Man" for *Life* in 1951 a hole in the side of the modern woman's head labeled "Aperture for easy access to brain compartment by psycho-analyst." When Lucy set up her "Psychiatric Help—5¢" booth in Charles Schulz's popular "Peanuts" comic strip, it simply marked with mild satire a logical conclusion to the trend toward universal dissemination of popular psychology.

The craze for the psychological explanation did not reflect unequivocal acceptance of psychological techniques. True, psychologists were much in demand to provide explanations of juvenile delinquency, rock 'n' roll music, marriage problems, personal aptitudes, and college panty raids. Even the Kinsey Reports on sexual practices were accepted as useful by a majority of Americans. But the frequency with which psychology and psychoanalysis served as topics for humor attested to deep ambivalence about psychology's "contributions." Although psychology promised a kind of control, an opportunity to reshape one's personality or gain a form of dominion by understanding and manipulating others, it also awakened fears that one might be the *object* rather than the *agent* of manipulation.

In *The Hidden Persuaders* (1957), Vance Packard found a large audience for his warnings about dangers embedded in motivation research and subliminal suggestion by advertisers. Americans might have been more alarmed if they had been fully aware of such new psychological "machines" and techniques as the "People Machine," Galvanic Skin Response, "Simulmatics," and "aroma mood music," to which some ad agencies were giving curious, if skeptical, attention. William Whyte, in *The Organization Man,* described the pressures toward conformity embodied in the proliferating personality tests given by business organizations. Whyte even appended a subversive chapter on "How to Cheat on Personality Tests" as his meager contribution to the preservation of personal dominion. Americans worried about "brain-washing," and 1950s science fiction movies were sometimes as concerned with loss of personal control, with invasion or infiltration by some alien force, as they were with the specter of atomic warfare. As the autonomy of the individual seemed to shrink, psychology, for all its fascination, still did not offer unequivocal assurance of gaining dominion over self.

Millions of Americans, however, hopefully sought such assurance from a fusion of psychology and religion. A major element in postwar popular culture was the "cult of reassurance," promoted most effectively by the Presbyterian minister Norman

Vincent Peale. An amalgam of psychology and religion, the cult gained its initial postwar impulse from Rabbi Joshua Liebman's prescriptions for the cure of inner tensions in *Peace of Mind* (1946). Liebman's book topped the best-seller list in 1947 and eventually sold a million copies. Peale advanced the movement's momentum with his best-selling *A Guide to Confident Living* (1949) and then with *The Power of Positive Thinking* (1952), which dominated the nonfiction best-seller charts from 1952 to 1955, soon surpassing two million copies.

Peale employed six psychiatrists and commanded radio and TV audiences in the millions. Although he had initially sought psychological knowledge for personal counseling, "Peale's deep attraction," as Donald Meyer writes, was to mass counseling. The message was simple: people's problems were individual. "Negative thinking," not technology, social forces, or institutional structures, was the cause of feelings of powerlessness and frustration. By using Peale's techniques, each follower could "become a more popular, esteemed, and well-liked individual," gaining new energy and peace of mind. Through psychological self-manipulation, each could gain control over circumstances rather than submitting to them. "Positive thinking" accepted and reinforced the notion of classlessness. It proved another popular culture prescription for the nagging sense of loss of dominion.

A popular culture of reassurance was not everybody's answer to powerlessness. It was true that certain consolidating tendencies—the influences of network television and the common language and repetitious visual landscapes of national advertising, pop architecture, and restaurant and motel chains—worked to reinforce the "adjustment" theme of applied psychology. And it was true also that the "packaging" craze in popular culture, from shopping centers to entertainment "worlds" like Disneyland, helped push forward the process of homogenization by offering convenience and relief from individual decision-making. In fact, the whole Disney empire, from the "disneyfication" of children's classics to TV's Mickey Mouse Club and the Davy Crockett craze, strikingly epitomized the trend toward uniformity. But consolidation in popular culture did not advance undisturbed. As regional, ethnic, and visible class divergences began to fade, new fissures appeared. Some pursued the quest for dominion not through adjustment and reassurance but rather through excitement, diversity, and vicarious rebellion.

The most obvious, and to contemporaries the most shocking, new breach in society was an apparently increasing division based on age. Juvenile delinquency had appeared to rise during World War II and afterward. The striking increase in disposable income and free time among teen-agers in the late 1940s stamped adolescence as a social phenomenon rather than simply a stage in individual development. "The brute fact of today," Dr. Robert Linder warned a Los Angeles audience in 1954, "is that our youth is no longer in rebellion but in a condition of downright active and hostile mutiny." In "a profound and terrifying change," youth now acted out its "inner turmoil."

Psychological analyses of juveniles, both delinquent and normal, abounded. The film industry, reacting to the loss of its mass audience to television, began to produce specialized films for minority audiences—one of which was teen-agers. Radio followed the same pattern. Advertisers soon recognized the existence of a massive teen-age market. Eugene Gilbert built a large marketing business by providing advertisers with inside information on teen-age consumers. His trick was spectacularly simple: employ teen-agers themselves to quiz other teen-agers about their wants and needs. Eventually *Life* confirmed the discovery of a teen-age market in an article entitled "A New $10 Billion Power: The U.S. Teen-age Consumer." *Life* personalized the story by featuring pictures of the loot accumulated by "the business-man's dream of the ideal teen-ager," Suzie Slattery from (where else?) California.

Attempts by the media to explore the rebellious aspects of the teen-age culture created new fissures in popular culture. In the movie *Rebel without a Cause* (1955), the plot and dialogue comprise a virtual textbook of popular psychology. The police lieutenant is an amateur psychologist; the hero's mother, a castrating female. The father's multiple complexes make him a complete buffoon. The hero's friend is a self-destructive neurotic, abandoned by his parents; and the heroine's father panics at her emerging sexuality and treats her with alternating rage and condescension. *Rebel without a Cause* was a "lesson" movie for parents: be careful and under-standing, or this (rebellion) could happen to you. But James Dean's portrayal of the teen-age hero, his most influential acting role, diverted attention to the style and mannerisms of the misunderstood "rebel." Youths made the movie theirs. Vicarious rebels adopted the James Dean image as an expression of contempt for the satiated and challengeless life of middle-aged suburban America.

The evolution of popular music revealed even more vividly the process of dis-ruption, the fraying of social nerves by age conflicts. Before the 1950s producers of popular music had largely ignored age differences, and the songs of adults and teen-agers were the same. As late as 1951 Gallup polls on favorite vocalists showed little variation among age groups. Far more significantly, the pollsters did not record responses for persons under 21. Yet teen-agers were already a major buying public for records, and the average age of purchasers continued to fall during the 1950s. With the rise of the 45 rpm record (cheap, unbreakable, easy to transport and change) and the transformation of radio in the early 1950s, the weight of teen-age preferences tipped the scales toward diversity in this form of popular culture.

Even earlier, fragmentation had begun to appear within the popular music industry. A boycott by radio stations in the early 1940s had broken the monopoly of the "big three" record companies. Radio disc jockeys gained new power, and technological advances meant that production of quality recordings was no longer confined to a handful of studios in New York, Chicago, and Los Angeles. Indepen-dent companies, the primary producers of "race" and "hillbilly" music, gained new opportunities. Still, the resulting tremors in the industry were relatively minor. From 1946 to 1953 the six dominant recording companies—Decca, Columbia, Victor, Capitol, MGM, and Mercury—recorded all but 5 of the 163 records that sold over a million copies.

Radio, in reaction to the abrupt abduction of its general audience by TV, cast about for minority tastes to satisfy. One market for subcultural programming was teen-agers. Specialized radio stations now gave them a medium of their own. Some argue that teen-age audiences created "rock 'n' roll." Others explain that TV, that powerful consolidating force in popular culture, was also, inadvertently, the cause of this vehicle of dissent and fragmentation. Both are largely correct; together these two forces set the stage for a popular culture explosion.

By 1953 certain ingredients of rock 'n' roll had been fermenting for several years. Migrations out of the South had increased national familiarity with "hillbilly" and black styles in music. In the late 1940s *Billboard* magazine, the arbiter of pop music, bolstered the respectability of both styles by rechristening the "hillbilly" category as "country and western" and race music" as "rhythm and blues." Elements of each style began to appear in pop hits. Meanwhile, with the postwar demise of the big bands, the individual singer gained prominence. Frank Sinatra epitomized the trend, winning the adulation of young "bobby-soxers" in the early 1940s and sustaining his popularity by projecting qualities of sincerity and involvement. Meanwhile, country singers Roy Acuff and then Hank Williams won huge followings with their sincere, emotional styles.

Against the backdrop of a pallid, taken-for-granted prosperity and cold war perils about which youth could do little, a thirst arose among the young for forms of popular culture that would permit expressions of highly personalized emotion. Frankie Laine ("Jezebel," "Your Cheatin' Heart," "I Believe") "sold Emotion . . . with a capital E" even more explicitly than did Sinatra. In 1951 Johnnie Ray stirred up a riotous teen-age response and set new standards for emotion and involvement in his popular hit "Cry." Ray, unlike Sinatra, was neither smooth nor controlled. He exposed an emotional vulnerability as he abandoned himself to the song's despair, "quivering, sobbing, crying and finally collapsing on the floor." Here were intimations not only of the impending rock 'n' roll performer as oracle of unconcealed emotion but also of the sensitive hero as victim.

It was in 1953 that Cleveland disc jockey Alan Freed, intrigued by his discovery that white adolescents were increasingly buying "rhythm and blues" records, initiated his "Moondog's Rock and Roll Party," playing records by black singers for a largely white teen-age radio audience. *Billboard* noted Freed's success. Record companies rushed to find white performers to "cover" (copy) up-tempo, heavy beat, rhythm and blues hits. Bill Haley and His Comets made the national pop charts with "Crazy Man Crazy" in 1953. The next year Haley's cover of "Shake, Rattle, and Roll" ranked in the top ten for twelve weeks, followed by an even longer run for "Rock around the Clock," the theme song from the popular film on juvenile delinquency *Blackboard Jungle.*

A mystique emerged that fused elements of Marlon Brando's role in *The Wild One,* James Dean's portrayal in *Rebel without a Cause,* J. D. Salinger's Holden Caulfield in *Catcher in the Rye,* the rebels of *Blackboard Jungle,* and the driving energy and aggressive sexuality of the new heroes of rock 'n' roll into a single image. The mystique emphasized a hunger for authenticity and sensitivity. In emotional expressiveness it ranged from moody insecurity to fierce independence with nuances of sexuality, pain, and violence. Raucous, exhibitionist rock 'n' roll singers disdained the "cool" of James Dean, but both expressed a contempt for hypocrisy and conventionality and used body language to convey emotion.

In 1956 the polarizing assault by rock 'n' roll on popular music (and on American culture generally) culminated. A black original, Little Richard's strident "Long Tall Sally," outsold Pat Boone's bland cover version. With his frantic movements and raucous shouts, Little Richard, in Charlie Gillett's words, was "coarse, uncultured, and uncontrolled, in every way hard for the musical establishment to take." The lines were being drawn largely on the basis of age, although the preference of many white teen-agers for "black" music added another dimension to the rift.

Critics of the new music and of the mixed-up, misunderstood hero decried the new mystique. The tough, self-pitying "sad-bad-boy" figures represented an "apotheosis of the immature." Rock 'n' roll used a jungle strain" to provoke a "wave of adolescent riot." How could a prosperous, middle-class nation find satisfaction in such moronic lyrics and "quivering adolescents"? *Time* compared rock 'n' roll concerts to Hitler's mass meetings, and other critics denounced the new music as nauseating and degenerate, an appeal to "vulgarism and animality." Could a consolidating popular culture even begin to bridge the gap suggested by such reactions?

Extreme views would remain irreconcilable. But 1955 elevated to stardom a versatile performer who brought the rock 'n' roll movement to a climax yet ultimately helped partially to reconcile rock with mainstream popular culture. Elvis Presley, the "hillbilly cat," as Greil Marcus writes, "deeply absorbed black music, and transformed it. . . ." The style of his early singles was "rockabilly"—"the only style of early rock 'n' roll that proved white boys could do it all—that they could be as strange, as exciting, as scary, and as free as the black men who were suddenly walking America's airwaves. . . ." Even as Elvis moved up to RCA and national fame in 1955 and 1956 with "Heartbreak Hotel" and "You Ain't Nuthin' But a Hound Dog," he continued to evoke sexuality, exhibitionism, and a defiance of restraint. Elvis projected emotional involvement; he encompassed the prized qualities of both toughness and vulnerability.

But Elvis not only fulfilled the image of frustrated, sensitive, rebellious hero for the new teen-age generation; he was also "hellbent on the mainstream." By the end of the 1950s, he had achieved hits with gospel songs and sentimental ballads. Eventually, one of his best-selling albums was "Blue Hawaii." His style encompassed schmaltz as well as rebellion, Las Vegas as well as Memphis. Along with Pat Boone, Bobby Darin, Bobby Rydell, Paul Anka, Ricky Nelson, and a host of new teen-age crooners, and with the added influence of Dick Clark's "American Bandstand" on TV, Elvis eased rock 'n' roll's way into the mainstream. The aura of challenge and threat in rock was overshadowed by the sentimentalities of teen-age love. By 1960 the popular music industry was fragmented. The venerable and consensus-based "Your Hit Parade" had expired after a period of senility, spurred on by rock 'n' roll. More concerned with the style of performance than with the song itself, the new rock audience was bored by interpretations of hit rock numbers by "Hit Parade" regulars. But, thus far, the fissure created in American popular culture by rock 'n' roll and generational stress had proved to be a crevice rather than a chasm.

Teen culture and rock 'n' roll, however, were not the only signs in the late 1950s of a possible countermarch in popular culture away from homogeneity toward segmentation. In reaction to the severe inroads of TV, movie-makers had sought specialized audiences that included intellectuals as well as teen-agers. Radio had fully adopted specialty programming. Gated, exclusive suburban developments gained in popularity. Portents of a difficult future for the great mass-circulation, general-audience magazines began to appear, as both *Life* and *Saturday Evening Post* lost advertising. Despite the "whitewardly mobile" messages of middle-class black magazines like *Ebony,* inklings could be found in the eventual movement of blacks to a more protective, conserving attitude toward the distinctive qualities of their own culture. On top of everything, enclaves of "beatniks" now flaunted a life-style even more irreconcilable with mainstream popular culture than that associated with rock 'n' roll.

One prospect for popular culture at the end of the 1950s was fragmentation, with increasing specialization in production and participation. But in one significant way, the consolidating process in American popular culture continued to move ahead. The history of modern popular culture is more characteristically an aspect of the history of business than an aspect of the histories of art, literature, music, or architecture. And the business interests that determined the available choices for *most* popular culture consumers had not been verging toward fragmentation or diversity. The "popular culture establishment"—in the form of CBS, NBC, and ABC, or General motors, Walt Disney Enterprises, MGM, and *Time-Life*, or the J. Walter Thompson, Young and Rubicam, and other great advertising agencies—certainly wielded a more extensive control over the range of products and images available to the public in 1960 than in 1945. These giants, like most of the small popular culture entrepreneurs, watched the sales figures, the Nielsen ratings, and the audience surveys and produced what would sell itself or sell the sponsor's goods. . . .

Beset by cold war fears and organizational complexities, Americans found solace in a popular culture that provided hopeful visions of an emerging classlessness and vicarious compensations for a hedged-in, manipulated feeling. Popular culture provided the fantasies, evasions, material artifacts, and vicarious experiences through which Americans tried to recapture a sense of dominion.

₩ F U R T H E R   R E A D I N G

Axelsson, Arne. *Restrained Response: American Novels of the Cold War and Korea, 1945–1962* (1990).
Bailey, Beth L. *From Front Porch to Back Seat: Courtship in Twentieth-Century America* (1988).
Barnouw, Eric. *Tube of Plenty: The Evolution of American Television* (1975).
Barson, Michael. *"Better Dead Than Red!"* (1992).
Biskind, Peter. *Seeing Is Believing: How Hollywood Taught Us to Stop Worrying and Love the Fifties* (1983).
Brandon, Barbara. *The Passion of Ayn Rand* (1986).
Byars, Jackie. *All That Hollywood Allows: Re-reading Gender in 1950s Melodrama* (1991).
Carmichael, Virginia. *Framing History: The Rosenberg Story and the Cold War* (1993).
Carter, Paul A. *Another Part of the Fifties* (1983).
Coontz, Stephanie. *The Way We Never Were: American Families and the Nostalgia Trap* (1992).
Davis, Kenneth C. *Two-Bit Culture: The Paperbacking of America* (1984).
Diamond, Sigmund. *Compromised Campus: The Collaboration of Universities with the Intelligence Community, 1945–1955* (1992).
Diggins, John Patrick. *The Proud Decades: America in War and Peace, 1941–1960* (1988).
Ehrenreich, Barbara. *The Hearts of Men: American Dreams and the Flight from Commitment* (1983).
Eisler, Benita. *Private Lives: Men and Women of the Fifties* (1986).
Englehardt, Tom. *The End of Victory Culture* (1995).
Fernlund, Kevin J., ed. *The Cold War American West, 1945–1989* (1998).
Foreman, Joel, ed. *The Other Fifties: Interrogating Midcentury American Icons* (1997).
Fox, Richard Wightman. *Reinhold Niebuhr: A Biography* (1986).
Galbraith, John K. *The Affluent Society* (1958).
———. *American Capitalism: The Concept of Countervailing Power* (1956).
Gans, Herbert. *The Levittowners* (1982).
———. *Popular Culture and High Culture* (1975).
Garber, Marjorie, and Rebecca L. Walkowitz, eds. *Secret Agents: The Rosenberg Case, McCarthyism, and Fifties America* (1995).

————. *A Cycle of Outrage: Juvenile Delinquency and the Mass Media in the 1950s* (1986).

Gilbert, James B. *Another Chance: Postwar America, 1945–1968,* rev. ed. (1986).

Hart, Jeffrey, *When the Going Was Good: American Life in the Fifties* (1982).

Harvey, Brett. *The Fifties: A Woman's Oral History* (1993).

Haut, Woody. *Pulp Culture: Hardboiled Fiction and the Cold War* (1995).

Hendra, Tony. *Going Too Far* (1988).

Henriksen, Margot A. *Dr. Strangelove's America: Society and Culture in the Atomic Age* (1997).

Hine, Thomas. *Populuxe* (1986).

Horowitz, Daniel, ed. *American Social Classes in the 1950s* (1995).

Inglis, Fred. *The Cruel Peace: Everyday Life and the Cold War* (1991).

Jackson, Kenneth T. *Crabgrass Frontier: The Suburbanization of America* (1985).

Jones, Landon Y. *Great Expectations: America and the Baby Boom Generation* (1980).

Lhamon, W. T. Jr. *Deliberate Speed: The Origins of a Cultural Style in the American 1950s* (1990).

Lipsitz, George. *Class and Culture in Cold War America* (1982).

Lowen, Rebecca S. *Creating the Cold War University: The Transformation of Stanford* (1997).

McNally, Dennis. *Desolate Angel: Jack Kerouac, the Beat Generation, and America* (1978).

Mark, David. *Democratic Vistas: Television in American Culture* (1984).

Marling, Karal Ann. *As Seen on TV: The Visual Culture of Everyday Life in the 1950s* (1994).

May, Elaine Tyler. *Homeward Bound: American Families in the Cold War Era* (1988).

May, Larry, ed. *Recasting America: Culture and Politics in the Age of Cold War America* (1989).

Meyerowitz, Joanne, ed. *Not June Cleaver: Women and Gender in Postwar America, 1945–1960* (1994).

Meyers, Donald B. *The Positive Thinkers* (1965).

Miller, Douglas T., and Marion Nowak. *The Fifties* (1977).

Miller, Herman Phillip. *Rich Man, Poor Man* (1964).

Mills, C. Wright. *White Collar: The American Middle Classes* (1951).

Nadel, Alan. *Containment Culture* (1995).

Nash, George H. *The Conservative Intellectual Movement in America Since 1945* (1976).

Neville, John F. *The Press, the Rosenbergs, and the Cold War* (1995).

Oakes, Guy. *The Imaginary War: Civil Defense and American Cold War Culture* (1994).

Packard, Vance. *The Hidden Persuaders* (1957).

Parker, Richard. *The Myth of the Middle Class* (1972).

Pells, Richard H. *The Liberal Mind in a Conservative Age: American Intellectuals in the 1940s and 1950s* (1985).

Pessen, Edward. *Losing Our Souls: The American Experience in the Cold War* (1993).

Rader, Benjamin. *In Its Own Image: How Television Has Transformed Sports* (1985).

Riesman, David. *The Lonely Crowd: A Study of the Changing American Character* (1950).

Rogin, Michael Paul. *Ronald Reagan, the Movie: And Other Episodes in Political Demonology* (1987).

Rose, Lisle A. *The Cold War Comes to Main Street: America in 1950* (1999).

Sayer, Nora. *Running Time: Films of the Cold War* (1982).

Schaub, Thomas Hill. *American Fiction in the Cold War* (1991).

Schrecker, Ellen W. *No Ivory Tower: McCarthyism and the Universities* (1986).

Siebers, Tobin. *Cold War Criticism and the Politics of Skepticism* (1993).

Silk, Mark. *Spiritual Politics* (1988).

Whitfield, Stephen J. *The Culture of the Cold War,* 2nd ed. (1996).

Whyte, William H. *The Organization Man* (1956).

John F. Kennedy,
the Cuban Revolution,
and the Cold War

XXX

To comprehend the nature of the United States' troubled relations with Cuba during the 1960s requires an understanding of at least three separate but interrelated topics: the history of U.S. relations with Latin America, especially the Caribbean; the response of the United States to social revolutions both in Latin America and throughout the Third World; and the United States' Cold War struggle with the Soviet Union. The history of relations between the United States and Cuba serves in turn to highlight patterns that were common to postwar U.S. policy throughout the Third World, including Southeast Asia and the Middle East.

Throughout the early twentieth century, the United States had exercised a dominant influence in Latin America and particularly in the Caribbean, featuring armed interventions in Cuba, Colombia (Panama), the Dominican Republic, Haiti, Nicaragua, and Mexico. The United States forswore such military actions in 1933 with Franklin D. Roosevelt's Good Neighbor Policy, but following World War II that policy was increasingly honored in the breach as the United States intervened directly or indirectly in Guatemala (under Eisenhower), Cuba (Kennedy), the Dominican Republic (Johnson), Chile (Nixon), Nicaragua (Reagan), Grenada (Reagan), Panama (Bush), and Haiti (Clinton). Seen from this perspective, Kennedy's "fixation" with Cuba was simply part of a deeply rooted historical pattern.

U.S. leaders were especially troubled by the growth of social revolutions throughout Latin America, revolutions that they feared would threaten the nation's economic interests—property, investments, and markets—as well as its strategic control of the region. Cuban revolutionary Fidel Castro, whose forces overthrew the dictatorship of Fulgencio Batista in 1959, posed a special threat as a result of his seizure of industries owned by U.S. investors and his rapid rise as a popular symbol of resistance to the United States.

It was the Cold War with the Soviet Union, however, that helped revive historic patterns of U.S. intervention and served to heighten and rationalize growing fears of social revolution. In Latin America as in Asia, the United States identified most revolutions with the foreign policies of the Soviet Union—in part because many Latin American revolutions were led by men and women who were socialists, if not communists; in part because the Soviet Union often supported such revolutions when it was in its interest to do so; but also because American leaders themselves seemed unable or unwilling to distinguish between indigenous social change and foreign subversion. Reflexive opposition to social revolutions thus became a cardinal theme of the Cold War era.

In 1954, for example, the United States engineered the overthrow of the democratically elected, reformist government of Guatemala. Established in 1944 following decades of dictatorship, the new Guatemalan government had introduced various reforms, including the nationalization of lands belonging to the powerful United Fruit Company. The protests of United Fruit, combined with (largely groundless) fears that Guatemala might become a beachhead of Soviet influence in the region, led the Eisenhower administration to launch a CIA-led coup that resulted in the overthrow of the Guatemalan government and the installation of a right-wing, pro-U.S. dictatorship. The success of the Guatemalan intervention served, in turn, as a model for the U.S. officials who planned the abortive 1961 Bay of Pigs landing in Cuba.

U.S.-Cuban relations were thus shaped by a long history of U.S. involvement in Cuban affairs, by strong opposition to the new economic programs of the Cuban revolution, and by a growing fear on the part of U.S. leaders that the victory of the Cuban revolutionaries would also become a Cold War victory for the Soviet Union. The process was dialectic: Castro was a dedicated revolutionary. Given the history of U.S.-Cuban relations, given also the extent of U.S. property and investments in the island, it was altogether likely that the revolution would evolve in ways antagonistic to American interests. U.S. opposition, and especially its failed attempt to overthrow the new Cuban government, strongly reinforced the direction and pace of that evolution, helping to propel Castro and the Cubans into an ever tighter embrace of the Soviet Union. This development, in turn, tempted the Soviets to introduce nuclear weapons into Cuba, thus setting the stage for the Cuban missile crisis.

✖ D O C U M E N T S

By October 1960, relations between the United States and the new Cuban government had already deteriorated. In Document 1, a 1960 speech before the United Nations, the new Cuban leader, Fidel Castro, traces the history of U.S. relations with his nation, defends the Cuban revolution, denounces U.S. efforts to overthrow his government, and praises the Soviet Union. Castro's speech, which is excerpted from the *United Nations Review,* follows the UN practice of paraphrasing the speaker's remarks, rather than reporting them directly. On March 13, 1961, Kennedy announced the Alliance for Progress (see Document 2), a boldly ambitious plan to stimulate economic development and democracy throughout Latin American while avoiding radical social revolutions of the Cuban variety. The alliance failed, partly because the Kennedy administration remained divided over the degree of support for social and economic reform versus military aid to right-wing (but pro-American) dictators, partly because Kennedy's successors weakened the program, and partly because many of Latin America's economic and political problems were simply beyond the ability of the United States to solve.

During the same month in which Kennedy introduced the Alliance for Progress, he and his advisers put the finishing touches on their plan for a CIA-backed invasion of Cuba by Cuban exiles. In the wake of its failure, Kennedy appointed a top-secret board of inquiry under General Maxwell Taylor. Document 3 is excerpted from the board's report, dated June 13, 1961. U.S. efforts to overthrow Castro included numerous plots to assassinate the Cuban leader. In 1975, following Watergate, a select committee of the U.S. Senate, chaired by Senator Frank Church of Idaho, opened an investigation of these and other covert activities by U.S. intelligence agencies.

During the summer of 1962, the Soviet Union began to ship nuclear missiles to Cuba. The discovery of these missiles in October 1962 precipitated the Cuban missile crisis. Document 4 is taken from the transcripts of two meetings on October 16, 1962, in which Kennedy and his top advisers first discussed possible responses to the crisis. Soviet premier Nikita Khrushchev's initial response to Kennedy's action, dated October 26, 1962, is reprinted as Document 5. Denouncing the blockade, Khrushchev offered to remove the missiles in return for a U.S. pledge not to invade Cuba, emotionally appealing to Kennedy to help avoid "the catastrophe of thermonuclear war." The announcement that the Soviet Union would withdraw the missiles from Cuba was widely interpreted as a victory for Kennedy and the United States. In Document 6, which records a series of meetings between Soviet official Anastas I. Mikoyan and Fidel Castro, Mikoyan seeks to placate the angry Cuban leader.

1. Fidel Castro Denounces
U.S. Policy Toward Cuba, 1960

The Prime Minister of Cuba recalled to the Assembly that many speakers who had preceded him on the rostrum had quite correctly referred to the problem of Cuba as one of the problems facing the world. As far as the world is concerned, he said, the problem of Cuba had come to a head in the last two years, and as such it was a new problem. Before that, the world had few reasons for knowing that his country existed; for many it was an offshoot—in reality, a colony—of the United States.

He traced the history of Cuba and referred to the law passed by the United States Congress at the time of the American military occupation of Cuba during the war with Spain, which, he claimed, said that the Constitution of Cuba—which was then being drafted—must have a rider under which the United States would be granted the right to intervene in Cuba's political affairs and to lease certain parts of the country for naval bases or for their coal deposits. In other words, the right to intervene and to lease naval bases was imposed by force by the legislative body of another country, since Cuban senators were clearly told that if they did not accept, the occupation forces would not be withdrawn.

The colonization of Cuba, he asserted, began with the acquisition of the best land by United States firms, concessions of Cuban natural resources and public services—concessions of all kinds. Cuba eventually had to fight to attain its independence, which was finally achieved after seven bloody years of tyranny "of those in our country who were nothing but the cat's-paws of those who dominated the country economically." The Batista Government of Cuba was appropriate for the United States monopolies, but not for the Cuban people.

United Nations Review (November 1960), 46–47.

How could any system inimical to the interests of the people stay in power unless by force? These were the governments that the guiding circles of United States policy preferred, he said, and that was why governments of force still ruled in Latin America. . . .

Mr. Castro traced some of the conditions which he said the successful revolution in Cuba had uncovered. Public services, he alleged, all belonged to United States monopolies and a major portion of the banking business, importing business, oil refineries, sugar production, the lion's share of arable land, and the most important industries in all fields in Cuba belonged to North American companies. The balance of payments from 1950 to 1960 was favorable to the United States by one billion dollars.

What the Revolutionary Government had wanted to do was to devote itself to the settling of its own problems at home; to carry out a program for the betterment of its people. But when the Revolutionary Government began to pass laws to overcome the advantages obtained by the monopolies, difficulties arose. Then "we began to be called communists; then we began to be painted red," he said.

The first unfriendly act perpetrated by the Government of the United States, he said, was to throw open its doors to a gang of murderers, bloodthirsty criminals who had murdered hundreds of defenceless peasants, who had never tired of torturing prisoners for many, many years, who had killed right and left. These hordes were received by the United States with open arms. Why this unfriendly act on the part of the Government of the United States toward Cuba? At the time Cuba could not understand, but now saw the reason clearly. The policy was part of an attitude of the United States.

He also criticized and blamed the United States Government for the fact that bombs were dropped on the sugar fields of Cuba before the harvest was in, and he accused the United States Government for allowing the planes which dropped the bombs to leave United States territory.

But, he said, aerial incursions finally stopped. Then came economic aggression. It was said that agrarian reform would cause chaos in agricultural production. That was not the case. Had it been so, the United States would not have had to carry on its economic aggression. They could have trusted in the Revolutionary Government's ruining the country. Fortunately that did not happen. Cuba needed new markets for its products. Therefore it signed a trade treaty with the Soviet Union to sell it a million tons of sugar and to purchase a certain amount of Russian products. Surely no one could say that was incorrect.

What could Cuba do? Go to the United Nations and denounce this economic aggression? The United Nations has power to deal with these matters; but it sought an investigation to be carried out by the Organization of American States. As a result, the United States was not condemned. No, the Soviet Union was condemned. All the Soviet Union had said was that if there was military aggression against Cuba, it would support the victims with rockets. Since when was the support of a weak country, conditioned on attack by a powerful country, regarded as interference? If there were no possibility that Cuba would be attacked, then there was no possibility that there would be Soviet support.

"We, the small countries," he added, "do not as yet feel too secure about the preservation of our rights. That is why, when we decide to be free, we know full well that we become free at our own risk."

The Cuban revolution, he continued, was changing. What was yesterday a land [of] misery, a land of illiterates, was gradually becoming one of the most enlightened, advanced, and developed lands of the continent. Developing this theme, he gave figures about the building of schools, housing, and industries, told of the success of plans for conservation of natural resources, medical plans, and other advances since the revolution.

In view of the tremendous reality of underdevelopment, the United States Government, at Bogotá, had come out with a plan for economic development, but he criticized it, saying that the governments of Latin America were being offered not the resources for economic development but resources for social development: houses for people who have no work, schools to which children could not go, and hospitals that would be unnecessary if there were enough food to eat. Cuba was not included in this proposed assistance, but they were not going to get angry about that because the Cubans were solving their own problems.

The Government of Cuba, he said, had always been ready to discuss its problems with the Government of the United States, but the latter had not been willing to do so. He quoted notes which had been addressed to the United States in January and February last, and a reply which said that the United States could not accept the conditions for negotiation laid down in those notes. The Government and the people of Cuba, he said, were much concerned "at the aggressive turn in American policy regarding Cuba" and denounced the efforts of the United States to promote "the organization of subversive movements against the Revolutionary Government of Cuba."

He also said the United States had taken over "in a military manner" Honduran territory—*Islas Cisnes* (Swan Islands)—in violation of treaties, set up a powerful broadcasting station for subversive groups, and was promoting subversion and the landing of armed forces in Cuba.

Turning to the subject of the United States leased naval base in Cuba, Mr. Castro said there was fear and concern in Cuba "of a country that has followed an aggressive and warlike policy possessing a base in the very heart of our island, that turns our island into the possible victim of any international conflict. It forces us to run the risk of any atomic conflict without us having even the slightest intervention in the problem." . . .

The case of Cuba, continued Mr. Castro, was the case of all the underdeveloped colonial countries and the problems he had described in relation to Cuba applied perfectly well to the whole of Latin America, where, he alleged, the economic resources were controlled by the North American monopolies. There is a United Nations report, he said, which explains how even private capital, instead of going to the countries which need it most for setting up basic industries, is preferably being channelled to the more industrialized countries. The development of Latin America, he added, would have to be achieved through public investment, planned and granted unconditionally without any political strings attached. In this, the problems of Latin America were like the problems of Africa and Asia.

"The world," he declared, "has been divided among the monopolistic interests, which do not wish to see the development of peoples but to exploit the natural resources of the countries and to exploit the people."

2. President John F. Kennedy Calls for an Alliance for Progress, 1961

One hundred and thirty-nine years ago this week the United States, stirred by the heroic struggles of its fellow Americans, urged the independence and recognition of the new Latin American Republics. It was then, at the dawn of freedom throughout this hemisphere, that [Simon] Bolívar spoke of his desire to see the Americas fashioned into the greatest region in the world, "greatest," he said, "not so much by virtue of her area and her wealth, as by her freedom and her glory."

Never, in the long history of our hemisphere, has this dream been nearer to fulfillment, and never has it been in greater danger.

The genius of our scientists has given us the tools to bring abundance to our land, strength to our industry, and knowledge to our people. For the first time we have the capacity to strike off the remaining bonds of poverty and ignorance—to free our people for the spiritual and intellectual fulfillment which has always been the goal of our civilization.

Yet at this very moment of maximum opportunity, we confront the same forces which have imperiled America throughout its history—the alien forces which once again seek to impose the despotisms of the Old World on the people of the New.

I have asked you to come here today so that I might discuss these challenges and these dangers.

Common Ties Uniting the Republics

We meet together as firm and ancient friends, united by history and experience and by our determination to advance the values of American civilization. For this new world of ours is not merely an accident of geography. Our continents are bound together by a common history—the endless exploration of new frontiers. Our nations are the product of a common struggle—the revolt from colonial rule. And our people share a common heritage—the quest for the dignity and the freedom of man.

The revolutions which gave us birth ignited, in the words of Thomas Paine, "a spark never to be extinguished." And across vast, turbulent continents these American ideals still stir man's struggle for national independence and individual freedom. But as we welcome the spread of the American Revolution to other lands, we must also remember that our own struggle—the revolution which began in Philadelphia in 1776 and in Caracas in 1811—is not yet finished. Our hemisphere's mission is not yet completed. *For our unfulfilled task is to demonstrate to the entire world that man's unsatisfied aspiration for economic progress and social justice can best be achieved by free men working within a framework of democratic institutions.* If we can do this in our own hemisphere, and for our own people, we may yet realize the prophecy of the great Mexican patriot, Benito Juarez, that "democracy is the destiny of future humanity."

Department of State Bulletin, XLIV, No. 1136 (April 3, 1961), pp. 471–474.

As a citizen of the United States let me be the first to admit that we North Americans have not always grasped the significance of this common mission, just as it is also true that many in your own countries have not fully understood the urgency of the need to lift people from poverty and ignorance and despair. But we must turn from these mistakes—from the failures and the misunderstandings of the past—to a future of peril but bright with hope.

Throughout Latin America—a continent rich in resources and in the spiritual and cultural achievements of its people—millions of men and women suffer the daily degradations of hunger and poverty. They lack decent shelter or protection from disease. Their children are deprived of the education or the jobs which are the gateway to a better life. And each day the problems grow more urgent. Population growth is outpacing economic growth, low living standards are even further endangered, and discontent—the discontent of a people who know that abundance and the tools of progress are at last within their reach—that discontent is growing. In the words of José Figueres, "once dormant peoples are struggling upward toward the sun, toward a better life."

If we are to meet a problem so staggering in its dimensions, our approach must itself be equally bold, an approach consistent with the majestic concept of Operation Pan America. Therefore I have called on all the people of the hemisphere to join in a new Alliance for Progress—*Alianza para Progreso*—a vast cooperative effort, unparalleled in magnitude and nobility of purpose, to satisfy the basic needs of the American people for homes, work and land, health and schools—*techo, trabajo y tierra, salud y escuela.* . . .

To achieve this goal political freedom must accompany material progress. Our Alliance for Progress is an alliance of free governments—and it must work to eliminate tyranny from a hemisphere in which it has no rightful place. Therefore let us express our special friendship to the people of Cuba and the Dominican Republic— and the hope they will soon rejoin the society of free men, uniting with us in our common effort.

This political freedom must be accompanied by social change. For unless necessary social reforms, including land and tax reform, are freely made, unless we broaden the opportunity of all our people, unless the great mass of Americans share in increasing prosperity, then our alliance, our revolution, our dream, and our freedom will fail. But we call for social change by free men—change in the spirit of Washington and Jefferson, of Bolívar and San Martín and Martí—not change which seeks to impose on men tyrannies which we cast out a century and a half ago. Our motto is what it has always been—progress yes, tyranny no—*progreso, sí, tiranía no!*

But our greatest challenge comes from within—the task of creating an American civilization where spiritual and cultural values are strengthened by an ever-broadening base of material advance, where, within the rich diversity of its own traditions, each nation is free to follow its own path toward progress.

The completion of our task will, of course, require the efforts of all the governments of our hemisphere. But the efforts of governments alone will never be enough. In the end the people must choose and the people must help themselves.

And so I say to the men and women of the Americas—to the *campesino* in the fields, to the *obrero* in the cities, to the *estudiante* in the schools—prepare your mind and heart for the task ahead, call forth your strength, and let each devote his energies to the betterment of all so that your children and our children in this hemisphere can find an ever richer and a freer life.

Let us once again transform the American Continent into a vast crucible of revolutionary ideas and efforts, a tribute to the power of the creative energies of free men and women, an example to all the world that liberty and progress walk hand in hand. Let us once again awaken our American revolution until it guides the struggles of people everywhere—not with an imperialism of force or fear but the rule of courage and freedom and hope for the future of man.

3. A Board of Inquiry Reports on the Bay of Pigs, 1961

1. Although the Cuban situation had been the subject of serious study in the Special Group [a senior oversight committee], Central Intelligence Agency [CIA], and other government agencies since 1958, this study takes as its point of departure the basic policy paper, "A Program of Covert Action Against the Castro Regime," approved by the President on 17 March 1960. This document, developed by the Central Intelligence Agency and indorsed by the Special Group, provided a program divided into four parts to bring about the replacement of the Castro regime by covert means:

   a. The creation of a responsible and unified Cuban opposition to the Castro regime located outside of Cuba.
   b. The development of means for mass communication to the Cuban people as a part of a powerful propaganda offensive.
   c. The creation and development of a covert intelligence and action organization within Cuba which would be responsive to the orders and directions of the exile opposition.
   d. The development of a paramilitary force outside of Cuba for future guerrilla action.

2. Since the primary purpose of this study is to examine the paramilitary actions growing out of this program and its successive modifications, the paragraph referring to the paramilitary aspects of the plan is quoted in its entirety:

   d. Preparations have already been made for the development of an adequate paramilitary force outside of Cuba, together with mechanisms for the necessary logistics support of covert military operations on the island. Initially a cadre of leaders will be recruited after careful screening and trained as paramilitary instructors. In a second phase a number of paramilitary cadres will be trained at secure locations outside of the United States so as to be available for immediate deployment into Cuba to organize, train, and lead resistance forces recruited there both before and after the establishment of one or more active centers of resistance. The creation of this capability will require a minimum of six months and probably closer to eight. In the meanwhile, a limited air capability for resupply and for infiltration and

Excerpts from *Operation Zapata: The "Ultrasensitive" Report and Testimony of the Board of Inquiry of the Bay of Pigs* (Frederick, Md.: 1981), 3–9, 11–15.

exfiltration already exists under CIA control and can be rather easily expanded if and when the situation requires. Within two months it is hoped to parallel this with a small air supply capability under deep cover as a commercial operation in another country.

3. It is apparent from the above excerpt that at the time of approval of this document the concept of paramilitary action was limited to the recruitment of a cadre of leaders and the training of a number of paramilitary cadres for subsequent use as guerrillas in Cuba.

4. The CIA began at once to implement the decisions contained in the policy paper on 17 March 1960. A target of 300 men was set for the recruitment of guerrillas to be trained covertly outside the United States. "Radio Swan" was installed on Swan Island and ready for broadcasting on 17 May 1960. Steps were taken to develop the FRD (*Frente Revolucionario Democrático*) as the Cuban front organization composed of a broad spectrum of Cuban political elements other than Communists and Batistianos. On August 18th, a progress report was given to the President and the Cabinet, at which time a budget of some $13 million was approved, as well as the use of Department of Defense personnel and equipment. However, it was specified at this time that no United States military personnel were to be used in a combat status.

5. Sometime in the summer of 1960 the paramilitary concept for the operation began to change. It appears that leaders in the CIA Task Force set up in January 1960 to direct the project were the first to entertain the thought of a Cuban strike force to land on the Cuban coast in supplementation of the guerrilla action contemplated under the March 17, 1960, paper. These CIA officers began to consider the formation of a small force of infantry (200–300 men) for contingency employment in conjunction with other paramilitary operations, and in June began to form a small Cuban tactical air force. Eventually it was decided to equip this force with B-26 aircraft which had been widely distributed to foreign countries including countries in Latin America.

6. There were ample reasons for this new trend of thought. The air drops into Cuba were not proving effective. There were increasingly heavy shipments of Communist arms to Cuba, accompanied by evidence of increasingly effective control of the civilian population by Castro. The Special Group became aware of these adverse factors which were discussed repeatedly in the Committee meetings during the fall of 1960. The minutes of the conferences indicate a declining confidence in the effectiveness of guerrilla efforts alone to overthrow Castro.

7. In this atmosphere the CIA began to implement the new concept, increasing the size of the Cuban force in training and reorienting the training toward preparation for its use as an assault force on the Cuban coast. On November 4th, CIA in Washington dispatched a cable to the project officer in Guatemala describing what was wanted. The cable directed a reduction of the guerrilla teams in training to 60 men and the introduction of conventional training for the remainder as an amphibious and airborne assault force. From that time on, the training emphasis was placed on the assault mission and there is no evidence that the members of the assault force received any further preparation for guerrilla-type operations. The men became deeply imbued with the importance of the

landing operation and its superiority over any form of guerrilla action to the point that it would have been difficult later to persuade them to return to a guerrilla-type mission. The final training of the Cubans was done by

[1½ lines deleted from transcript]

in Guatemala where 400–500 Cubans had been assembled. . . .

10. The Director of Central Intelligence [Allen Dulles] briefed the President [Eisenhower] on the new paramilitary concept on 29 November 1960 and received the indication that the President wished the project expedited. The concept was formally presented to the Special Group on December 8, 1960. At this meeting, [   ] in charge of the paramilitary section for the Cuba project, described the new concept as one consisting of an amphibious landing on the Cuban coast of 600–750 men equipped with weapons of extraordinarily heavy fire power. The landing would be preceded by preliminary air strikes launched from Nicaragua against military targets. Air strikes as well as supply flights would continue after the landing. The objective would be to seize, hold a limited area in Cuba, maintain a visible presence, and then to draw dissident elements to the landing force, which hopefully would trigger a general uprising. This amphibious landing would not entirely eliminate the previous concept for infiltrating guerrilla teams. It was expected that some 60–80 men would be infiltrated prior to the amphibious landing. . . .

16. On November 18, 1960, President-elect [John F.] Kennedy had first learned of the existence of a plan for the overthrow of Castro through a call on him at Palm Beach by Mr. [Allen] Dulles and Mr. [Richard] Bissell [Deputy Director of Central Intelligence for Plans]. He received his first briefing on the developing plan as President on January 28 at a meeting which included the Vice President [Lyndon B. Johnson], Secretary of State [Dean Rusk], Secretary of Defense [Robert McNamara], the Director of Central Intelligence [John McCone], the Chairman of the Joint Chiefs of Staff [General Maxwell Taylor], Assistant Secretary [of State Thomas] Mann, Assistant Secretary [of Defense Paul] Nitze, Mr. Tracy Barnes [Bissell's assistant], and Mr. McGeorge Bundy [the National Security Adviser].

After considerable discussion, the President authorized the following:

a. A continuation and accentuation of current activities of the CIA, including increased propaganda, increased political action, and increased sabotage. Continued overflights of Cuba were specifically authorized.

b. The Defense Department was to review CIA proposals for the active deployment of anti-Castro Cuban forces on Cuban territory and the results of this analysis were to be promptly reported to the CIA.

c. The State Department was to prepare a concrete proposal for action with other Latin American countries to isolate the Castro regime and to bring against it the judgment of the Organization of American States. It was expected that this proposal

[2½ lines deleted from transcript]

19. While the Joint Chiefs of Staff [JCS] supported the Trinidad Plan as one having "a fair chance of success" the plan encountered difficulties in other quarters. From its inception the plan had been developed under the ground rule that it must retain a covert character, that is, it should include no action which, if revealed, could not be plausibly denied by the United States and should look to the world as an operation exclusively conducted by Cubans. This ground rule meant, among other things, that no U.S. military forces or individuals could take part in combat operations. In due course it was extended to exclude pre-D-Day air strikes in support of the landing since such strikes could not have the appearance of being launched from Cuban soil before an airstrip had been seized by the landing force. This effort to treat as covert an operation which in reality could not be concealed or shielded from the presumption of U.S. involvement raised in due course many serious obstacles to the successful conduct of the operation which will be the subject of subsequent comment.

20. The President and his advisors were thoroughly aware of the difficulties of preserving the covert character of an operation as visible as a landing on a hostile shore and from the outset viewed the Trinidad Plan with caution. In particular, the State Department representatives opposed features of the plan because of the difficulty of concealing U.S. participation and also because of their fear of adverse reactions to the United States in Latin American countries and in the United Nations. They objected in particular to the conduct of any tactical air operations unless these aircraft were either actually or ostensibly based on Cuban soil.

21. On the other hand, working to overcome this reluctance to approve the Trinidad Plan was the need to decide quickly what to do with the Cuban Expeditionary Force. The President was informed that this force must leave Guatemala within a limited time and that, further, it could not be held together long in the United States if it were moved there. If the decision were taken to disband the force, that fact would soon become known and would be interpreted as a renunciation by the U.S. of the effort to free Cuba from Castro. Faced with two unattractive alternatives, the President and his advisors asked the CIA to come up with various proposals for the use of this force as alternatives to Trinidad.

22. These proposals were the subject of detailed consideration on March 11th when the President and the National Security Council met to consider the various plans then being entertained for Cuba. Mr. Bissell of CIA presented a paper entitled, "Proposed Operation Against Cuba" which summarized the action to date and presented four alternative courses of action. It concluded by recommending the Trinidad Plan which he described to be an operation in the form of an assault in force preceded by a diversionary landing as the action having the best chance of achieving the desired result. The assault in force was to consist of an amphibious/airborne assault with concurrent (but no prior) tactical air support, to seize a beachhead contiguous to terrain suitable for guerrilla operations. The provisional government would land as soon as the beachhead had been secured. If initial military operations were successful and especially if

there were evidence of spreading disaffection against the Castro regime, the provisional government could be recognized and a legal basis provided for U.S. logistic support.

23. The military plan contemplated the holding of a perimeter around a beachhead area. It was believed that initial attacks by the Castro militia, even if conducted in considerable force, could be successfully resisted. The scale of the operation, a display of professional competence, and determination on the part of the assault force would, it was hoped, demoralize the Castro militia, cause defections therefrom, impair the morale of the Castro regime, and induce widespread rebellion.

24. After full discussion of this plan the President indicated that he was willing to go ahead with the overall project, but that he could not endorse a plan so "spectacular" as Trinidad. He directed that the CIA planners come up with other alternative methods of employing the Cuban forces. An acceptable plan should provide for a "quiet" landing, preferably at night, without having the appearance of a World War II–type amphibious assault. The State Department requested that any beachhead seized should include an airfield capable of supporting B-26 operations, to which any tactical air operations could be attributed.

25. During the period 13–15 March the paramilitary staff of CIA worked intensively to devise a plan or plans having the desired characteristics, and presented a briefing to the JCS Working Group late in the morning of March 14. They produced for consideration three such alternatives as general concepts. They were based on three possible landing areas: (1) the Preston area on the north coast of Oriente Province; (2) the south coast of Las Villas between Trinidad and Cienfuegos; and (3) the eastern Zapata area near Cochinos Bay.

26. On March 14th these three alternatives were referred to the Joint Chiefs of Staff for their evaluation. The Joint Staff prepared this evaluation, the results of which the respective service action officers presented to their respective Chiefs prior to the JCS meeting on 15 March. At this meeting, following a briefing by the Joint Staff Working Group, the Joint Chiefs approved the evaluation and reported to the Secretary of Defense that of the three, the Zapata concept was considered the most feasible and the most likely to accomplish the objective. They added that none of the alternative concepts were considered as feasible and likely to accomplish the objective as the Trinidad Plan. . . .

28. On the same day as the Chiefs' action, March 15th, the President was briefed at the White House on the three alternative courses of action which the Chiefs had considered. After full discussion, the President again withheld approval of the plan and directed certain modifications to be considered. The CIA returned on the following day, March 16th and presented a modification for the landing at Zapata which Mr. Bissell considered on balance more advantageous than the Trinidad Plan, wherein there would be airdrops at first light instead of the previous day in the late afternoon, with the landing in the night and all the ships withdrawn from the objective area by dawn without completing the unloading at that time. The President authorized them to proceed with the plan, but still without giving it his formal approval.

4. President Kennedy and His Advisers Debate Options in the Missile Crisis, October 16, 1962

Meeting of 11:50 A.M.–12:57 P.M.

Lundahl [Art Lundahl, National Photographic Interpretation Center] This is a result of the photography taken Sunday, sir.

JFK Yeah.

Lundahl There's a medium-range ballistic missile launch site and two new military encampments on the southern edge of Sierra del Rosario in west central Cuba.

JFK Where would that be?

Lundahl Uh, west central, sir. That. . . .

JFK Yeah. . . .

Lundahl Well, on site on one of the encampments contains a total of at least fourteen canvas-covered missile trailers measuring 67 feet in length, 9 feet in width. The overall length of the trailers plus the tow-bars is approximately 80 feet. The other encampment contains vehicles and tents but with no missile trailers. . . .

JFK How far advanced is this? . . . How do you know this is a medium-range ballistic missile?

Lundahl The length, sir.

JFK The what? The length?

Lundahl The length of it. Yes.

JFK The length of the missile? Which part? I mean which . . .

Lundahl . . . the missile [word unintelligible] indicates which one is [words unintelligible]. . . .

JFK Is this ready to be fired?

Graybeal [Sidney Graybeal] No, sir.

JFK How long have we got. . . . We can't tell, I take it . . .

Graybeal No, sir.

JFK . . . how long before it can be fired?

Graybeal That depends on how ready the . . .

JFK But, what does it have to be fired from?

Graybeal It would have to be fired from a stable hard surface. This could be packed dirt; it could be concrete or, or asphalt. The surface has to be hard, then you put a flame deflect-, a deflector plate on there to direct the missile.

McNamara [Robert McNamara, secretary of defense] Would you care to comment on the position of nuclear warheads—this is in relation to the question from the president—explain when these can be fired?

Graybeal Sir, we've looked very hard. We can find nothing that would spell nuclear warhead in term *[sic]* of any isolated area or unique security in this particular area. The mating of the nuclear warhead to the missile from some of the other short range missiles there would take about, uh, a couple of hours to do this.

U.S. Department of State, *Foreign Relations of the United States, 1961–1963, Cuban Missile Crisis and Aftermath* (Washington, D.C.: GPO, 1996), XI, 31–45, 49–93.

McNamara: This is not defensed, I believe, at the moment?

Lundahl: Not yet, sir. . . .

Rusk [Dean Rusk, secretary of state] Don't you have to assume these are nuclear? . . .

McNamara There's no question about that. The question is one of readiness of the, to fire and—and this is highly critical in forming our plans—that the time between today and the time when the readiness to fire capability develops is a very important thing. To estimate that we need to know where these warheads are, and we have not yet found any probable storage of warheads and hence it seems extremely unlikely that they are now ready to fire or may be ready to fire within a matter of hours or even a day or two. . . .

JFK Secretary Rusk?

Rusk Yes. [Well?], Mr. President, this is a, of course, a [widely?] serious development. It's one that we, all of us, had not really believed the Soviets could, uh, carry this far. Uh, they, uh, seemed to be denying that they were going to establish bases of their own [in the same?] [words unintelligible] with a Soviet base, thus making it [essential to or essentially?] Cuban point of view. The Cubans couldn't [word unintelligible] with it anyhow, so. . . . Now, uhm, I do think we have to set in motion a chain of events that will eliminate this base. I don't think we [can?] sit still. The questioning becomes whether we do it by sudden, unannounced strike of some sort, or we, uh, build up the crisis to the point where the other side has to consider very seriously about giving in, or, or even the Cubans themselves, uh, take some, take some action on this. The thing that I'm, of course, very conscious of is that there is no such thing, I think, as unilateral action by the United States. It's so [eminently or heavily?] involved with 2 allies and confrontation in many places, that any action that we take, uh, will greatly increase the risks of direct action involving, uh, our other alliances and our other forces in other parts of the world. Uhm, so I think we, we have to think very hard about two major, uh, courses of action as alternatives. One is the quick strike. The point where we [make or think?], that is the, uh, overwhelming, overriding necessity to take all the risks that are involved doing that. I don't think this in itself would require an invasion of Cuba. I think that with or without such an invasion, in other words if we make it clear that, uh, what we're doing is eliminating this particular base or any other such base that is established. We ourselves are not moved to general war, we're simply doing what we said we would do if they took certain action. Uh, or we're going to decide that this is the time to eliminate the Cuban problem by actual eliminate the island.

The other would be, if we have a few days—from the military point of view, if we have the whole time—uh, then I would think that, uh, there would be another course of action, a combination of things that, uh, we might wish to consider. Uhm, first, uh, that we, uh, stimulate the OAS procedure immediately for prompt action to make quite clear that the entire hemisphere considers that the Rio Pact has been violated [and actually?] what acts should [we take or be taken?] in, under the terms of the Rio Pact. . . .

I think also that we ought to consider getting some word to Castro, perhaps through the Canadian ambassador in Havana or through, uh, his representative at the UN. Uh, I think perhaps the Canadian ambassador would be best, the better channel to get to Castro [apart?] privately and tell him that, uh, this is no longer support for Cuba, that Cuba is being victimized here, and that, uh, the Soviets are preparing Cuba for destruction or betrayal.

You saw the *[New York] Times* story yesterday morning that high Soviet officials were saying, "We'll trade Cuba for Berlin." This ought to be brought to Castro's attention. It ought to be said to Castro that, uh, uh, this kind of a base is intolerable and not acceptable. The time has now come when he must take the interests of the Cuban people, must now break clearly with the Soviet Union, prevent this missile base from becoming operational.

And I think there are certain military, uhm, uh, actions that we could, we might well want to take straight away. First, to, uh, to call up, uh, highly selective units [no more than?] 150,000. Unless we feel that it's better, more desirable to go to a general national emergency so that we have complete freedom of action. If we announce, at the time that we announce this development—and I think we do have to announce this development some time this week—uh, we announce that, uh, we are conducting a surveillance of Cuba, over Cuba, and we will enforce our right to do so. We reject the mission of secrecy in this hemisphere in any matters of this sort. We, we reinforce our forces in Guantanamo. We reinforce our forces in the southeastern part of the United States—whatever is necessary from the military point of view to be able to give, to deliver an overwhelming strike at any of these installations, including the SAM sites. And, uh, also, to take care of any, uh, MIGs or bombers that might make a pass at Miami or at the United States. Build up heavy forces, uh, if those are not already in position. . . .

I think also that we need a few days, uhm, to alert our other allies, for consultation with NATO. I'll assume that we can move on this line at the same time to interrupt all air traffic from free world countries going into Cuba, insist to the Mexicans, the Dutch, that they stop their planes from coming in. Tell the British, who, and anyone else who's involved at this point, that, uh, if they're interested in peace, that they've got to stop their ships from Cuban trade at this point. Uh, in other words, isolate Cuba completely without at this particular moment a, uh, a forceful blockade. . . .

But I think that, by large, there are, there are these two broad alternatives: one, the quick strike; the other, to alert our allies and Mr. Khrushchev that there is utterly serious crisis in the making here, and that, uh. . . . Mr. Khrushchev may not himself really understand that or believe that at this point. I think we'll be facing a situation that could well lead to general war. . . .

McNamara Mr. President, there are a number of unknowns in this situation I want to comment upon, and, in relation to them, I would like to outline very briefly some possible military alternatives and ask General Taylor to expand upon them.

But before commenting on either the unknowns or outlining some military alternatives, there are two propositions I would suggest that we ought to accept as, uh, foundations for our further thinking. My first is that if we are to conduct an air strike against these installations, or against any part of Cuba, we must agree now that we will schedule that prior to the time these missiles sites become operational. I'm not prepared to say when that will be, but I think it is extremely important that our talk and our discussion be founded on this premise: that any air strike will be planned to take place prior to the time they become operational. Because, if they become operational before the air strike, I do not believe we can state we can knock them out before they can be launched; and if they're launched there is almost certain to be, uh, chaos in part of the east coast or the area, uh, in a radius of six hundred to a thousand miles from Cuba.

Uh, secondly, I, I would submit the proposition that any air strike must be directed not solely against the missile sites, but against the missile sites plus the airfields plus the aircraft which may not be on the airfields but hidden by that time plus all potential nuclear storage sites. Now, this is a fairly extensive air strike. It is not just a strike against the missile sites; and there would be associated with it potential casualties of Cubans, not of U.S. citizens, but potential casualties of Cubans in, at least in the hundreds, more likely in the low thousands, say two or three thousand. It seems to me these two propositions, uh, should underlie our, our discussion.

Now, what kinds of military action are we capable of carrying out and what may be some of the consequences? Uh, we could carry out an air strike within a matter of days. We would be ready for the start of such an air strike within, within a matter of days. If it were absolutely essential, it could be done almost literally within a matter of hours. I believe the chiefs would prefer that it be deferred for a matter of days, but we are prepared for that quickly. The air strike could continue for a matter of days following the initial day, if necessary. Uh, presumably there would be some political discussions taking place either just before the air strike or both before and during. In any event, we would be prepared, following the air strike, for an air, invasion, both by air and by sea. . . . Associated with this air strike undoubtedly should be some degree of mobilization. Uh, I would think of the mobilization coming not before the air strike but either concurrently with or somewhat following, say possibly five days afterwards, depending upon the possible invasion requirements. The character of the mobilization would be such that it could be carried out in its first phase at least within the limits of the authority granted by Congress. There might have to be a second phase, and then it would require a declaration of a national emergency.

Now, this is very sketchily the military, uh, capabilities, and I think you may wish to hear General Taylor, uh, outline his choice. . . .

Taylor [General Maxwell Taylor, chairman of the Joint Chiefs of Staff] Uh, we're impressed, Mr. President, with the great importance of getting a, a strike with all the benefits of surprise, uh, which would mean *ideally* that we would have all the missiles that are in Cuba above ground where we can take them out. Uh, that, that desire runs counter to the strong point the secretary made if the other optimum would be to get every missile before it could, becomes operational. Uh, practically, I think the, our knowledge of the timing of the readiness is going to be so, so uh, difficult that we'll never have the, the exact permanent, uh, the perfect timing. . . . It's a little hard to say in terms of time how much I'm discussing. But we must do a good job the first time we go in there, uh, pushing a 100 percent just as far, as closely as we can with our, with our strike. . . .

I would also mention among the, the military actions we should take that once we have destroyed as many of these offensive weapons as possible, we should, should prevent any more coming in, which means a naval blockade. . . .

JFK What is the, uh, advant-. . . . Must be some major reason for the Russians to, uh, set this up as a. . . . Must be that they're not satisfied with their ICBMs. What'd be the reason that they would uh. . . .

Taylor What it'd give 'em is primary, it makes the launching base, uh, for short range missiles against the United States to supplement their rather [deceptive?] ICBM system, for example. There's one reason. . . .

Rusk Still, about why the Soviets are doing this, uh, Mr. McCone [John A. McCone, director of the Central Intelligence Agency] suggested some weeks ago that one thing Mr. Khrushchev may have in mind is that, uh, uh, he knows that we have a substantial nuclear superiority, but he also knows that we don't really live under fear of his nuclear weapons to the extent that, uh, he has to live under fear of ours. Also we have nuclear weapons nearby, in Turkey and places like that.

JFK How many weapons do we have in Turkey?

Taylor We have Jupiter missiles. . . .

McNamara? About fifteen, I believe it is. . .

Rusk Uhm, and that Mr. McCone expresses the view that Khrushchev may feel that it's important for us to learn about living under medium-range missiles, and he's doing that to sort of balance that, uh, that political, psychological [plank?]. I think also that, uh, Berlin is, uh, very much involved in this. Uhm, for the first time, I'm beginning really to wonder whether maybe Mr. Khrushchev is entirely rational about Berlin. We've [hardly?] talked about his obsession with it. And I think we have to, uh, keep our eye on that element. But, uh, they may be thinking that they can either bargain Berlin and Cuba against each other, or that they could provoke us into a kind of action in Cuba which would give an umbrella for them to take action with respect to Berlin. In other words like the Suez-Hungary combination. If they could provoke us into taking the first overt action, then the world would be confused and they would have, uh, what they would consider to be justification for making a move somewhere else. But, uh, I must say I don't really see the rationality of, uh, the Soviets' pushing it this far unless they grossly misunderstand the importance of Cuba to this country.

JFK Uh, eh, well, this, which . . . What you're really talking about are two or three different, uh, [tense?] operations. One is the strike just on this, these three bases. One, the second is the broader one that Secretary McNamara was talking about which is on the airfields and on the SAM sites and on anything else connected with, uh, missiles. Third is doing both of those things and also at the same time launching a blockade, which requires really the, uh, the, uh, third and which is a larger step. And the, as I take it, the fourth question is the, uh, degree of consultation.

RFK [Robert F. Kennedy] Mr. President.

JFK Yes.

RFK We have the fifth one, really, which is the invasion. I would say that, uh, you're dropping bombs all over Cuba if you do the second, uh, air, the airports, knocking out their planes, dropping it on all their missiles. You're covering most of Cuba. You're going to kill an awful lot of people, and, uh, we're going to take an awful lot of heat on it. . . .

JFK I don't believe it takes us, at least, uh. . . . How long did it take to get in a position where we can invade Cuba? Almost a month? Two months?

McNamara No, sir. . . .

JFK I think we ought to, what we ought to do is, is, uh, after this meeting this afternoon, we ought to meet tonight again at six, consider these various, uh, proposals. In the meanwhile, we'll go ahead with this maximum, whatever is needed from the flights, and, in addition, we will. . . I don't think we got much time on these missiles. They may be. . . . So it may be that we just have to, we can't wait two weeks while we're getting ready to, to roll. Maybe just have to just take *them out,* and continue our other preparations if we decide to do that. That may be where we end up. I think we ought to, beginning right now, be preparing to. . . . Because that's what we're going to do *anyway.* We're certainly going to do number one; we're going to take out these, uh, missiles. Uh, the questions will be whether, which, what I would describe as number two, which would be a general air strike. That we're not ready to say, but we should be in preparation for it. The third is the, is the, uh, the general invasion. At least were' going to do number one, so its seems to me that we don't have to wait very long. We, we ought to be making *those* preparations.

Bundy [McGeorge Bundy, assistant for national security affairs] You want to be clear, Mr. President, whether we have *definitely* decided *against* a political track. I, myself, think we ought. . .

Taylor? Well, we'll have . . .

Bundy. . . to work out a contingency on that.

Taylor? We, we'll develop both tracks.

Meeting of 6:30–7:55 P.M.

McNamara Mr. President, could I outline three courses of action we have considered and speak very briefly on each one? The first is what I would call the political course of action, in which we, uh, follow some of the possibilities that Secretary Rusk mentioned this morning by approaching Castro, by approaching Khrushchev, by discussing with our allies. An overt and open approach politically to the problem [attempting, or in order?] to solve it. This seemed to me likely to lead to no satisfactory result, and it almost stops subsequent military action. . . .

A second course of action we haven't discussed but lies in between the military course we began discussing a moment ago and the political course of action is a course of action that would involve declaration of open surveillance; a statement that we would immediately impose an, uh, a blockade against *offensive* weapons entering Cuba in the future; and an indication that with our open-surveillance reconnaissance which we would plan to maintain indefinitely for the future. . . .

But the third course of action is any one of these variants of military action directed against Cuba, starting with an air attack against the missiles. The Chiefs are strongly opposed to so limited an air attack. But even so limited an air attack is a very extensive air attack. It's not twenty sorties or fifty sorties or a hundred sorties, but probably several hundred sorties. Uh, we haven't worked out the details. It's very difficult to do so when we lack certain intelligence that we hope to have tomorrow or the next day. But it's a substantial air attack. . . . I don't believe we have considered the consequences of any of these actions satisfactorily, and because we haven't considered the consequences, I'm not sure we're taking all the action we ought to take now to minimize those. I, I don't know quite what kind of a world we live in after we've struck Cuba, and we, we've started it. . . .

Taylor And you'll miss some [missiles].

McNamara And you'll miss some. That's right. Now after we've launched sorties, what kind of a world do we live in? How, how do we stop at that point? I don't know the answer to this. I think tonight State and we ought to work on the consequences of any one of these courses of actions, consequences which I don't believe are entirely clear. . . .

JFK If the, uh, it doesn't increase very much their strategic, uh, strength, why is it, uh, can any Russian expert tell us why they. . . After all Khrushchev demonstrated a sense of caution [thousands?]. . .

Speaker? Well, there are several, several possible . . .

JFK . . . Berlin, he's been cautious, I mean, he hasn't been, uh . . .

Ball [George W. Ball, under secretary of state] Several possibilities, Mr. President. One of them is that he has given us word now that he's coming over in November to, to the UN. If, he may be proceeding on the assumption, and this lack of a sense of *apparent* urgency would seem to, to support this, that this *isn't* going to be discovered at the moment and that, uh, when he comes over this is something he can do, a ploy. That here is Cuba armed against the United States, or possibly use it to try to trade something in Berlin, saying he'll disarm Cuba, if, uh, if we'll yield some of our interests in Berlin and some arrangement for it. I mean, that this is a, it's a trading ploy.

Bundy I would think one thing that I would still cling to is that he's not likely to give Fidel Castro nuclear warheads. I don't believe that has happened or is likely to happen.

JFK Why does he put these in there though?

Bundy Soviet-controlled nuclear warheads [of the kind?] . . .

JFK That's right, but what is the advantage of that? It's just as if we suddenly began to put a major number of MRBMs [Medium-Range Ballistic Missiles] in Turkey. Now that'd be goddam dangerous, I would think.

Bundy Well, we *did,* Mr. President. . . .

JFK Yeah, but that was five years ago. . . .

Ball Yes, I think, I think you, you look at this possibility that this is an attempt to, to add to his strategic capabilities. A second consideration is that it is simply a trading ploy, that he, he wants this in so that he could, he could [words unintelligible]. . . .

Speaker? Isn't it puzzling, also, there are no evidence of any troops protecting the sites?

Taylor Well, there're troops there. At least there're tents. . . .

McNamara But they look like [words unintelligible]. It's as if you could walk over the fields into those vans.

JFK: Well, it's a goddam mystery to me. I don't know enough about the Soviet Union, but if anybody can tell me any other time since the Berlin blockade where the Russians have given us so clear provocation, I don't know when it's been, because they've been awfully cautious really. The Russians, I never. . . . Now, maybe our mistake was in not saying some time *before* this summer that if they do this we're [word unintelligible] to act. . . .

5. Soviet Premier Nikita Khrushchev Appeals to President Kennedy, October 26, 1962

[Moscow]

Dear Mr. President:

I have received your letter of October 25. From your letter, I got the feeling that you have some understanding of the situation which has developed and (some) sense of responsibility. I value this.

Now we have already publicly exchanged our evaluations of the events around Cuba and each of us has set forth his explanation and his understanding of these events. Consequently, I would judge that, apparently, a continuation of an exchange of opinions at such a distance, even in the form of secret letters, will hardly add anything to that which one side has already said to the other.

I think you will understand me correctly if you are really concerned about the welfare of the world. Everyone needs peace: both capitalists, if they have not lost their reason, and, still more, communists, people who know how to value not only their own lives, but, more than anything, the lives of the peoples. We, communists, are against all wars between states in general and have been defending the cause of peace since we came into the world. We have always regarded war as a calamity, and not as a game nor as a means of the attainment of definite goals, nor, all the more, as a goal in itself. Our goals are clear, and the means to attain them is labor. War is our enemy and a calamity for all the peoples.

It is thus that we, Soviet people, and, together with us, other peoples as well, understand the questions of war and peace. I can, in any case, firmly say this for the peoples of the socialist countries, as well as for all progressive people who want peace, happiness, and friendship among peoples.

I see, Mr. President, that you are too are not devoid of a sense of anxiety for the fate of the world, of understanding, and of what war entails. What would a war give you? You are threatening us with war. But you well know that the very least which you would receive in reply would be that you would experience the same consequences as those which you sent us. And that must be clear to us, people invested with authority, trust, and responsibility. We must not succumb to intoxication and petty passions, regardless of whether elections are impending in this or that country, or not impending. These are all transient things, but if indeed war should break out, then it would not be in our power to stop it, for such is the logic of war. I have participated in two wars and know that war ends when it has rolled through cities and villages, everywhere sowing death and destruction.

In the name of the Soviet Government and the Soviet people, I assure you that your conclusions regarding offensive weapons on Cuba are groundless. It is apparent from what you have written me that our conceptions are different on this score, or rather, we have different estimates of these or those military means. Indeed, in reality, the same forms of weapons can have different interpretations.

You are a military man and, I hope, will understand me. Let us take for example a simple cannon. What sort of means is this: offensive or defensive? A cannon is a defensive means if it is set up to defend boundaries or a fortified area. But if one concentrates artillery, and adds to it the necessary number of troops, then the same cannons do become an offensive means, because they prepare and clear the way for infantry to attack. The same happens with missile-nuclear weapons as well, with any type of this weapon. . . .

I believe that you have no basis to think this way. You can regard us with distrust, but, in any case, you can be calm in this regard, that we are of sound mind and understand perfectly well that if we attack you, you will respond the same way. But you too will receive the same that you hurl against us. And I think that you also understand this. My conversation with you in Vienna gives me the right to talk to you this way.

This indicates that we are normal people, that we correctly understand and correctly evaluate the situation. Consequently, how can we permit the incorrect actions which you ascribe to us? Only lunatics or suicides, who themselves want to perish and to destroy the whole world before they die, could do this. We, however, want to live and do not at all want to destroy your country. We want something quite different: to compete with your country on a peaceful basis. We quarrel with you, we have differences on ideological questions. But our view of the world consists in this, that ideological questions, as well as economic problems, should be solved not by military means, they must be solved on the basis of peaceful competition, i.e., as this is understood in capitalist society, on the basis of competition. We have proceeded and are proceeding from the fact that the peaceful coexistence of the two different social-political systems, now existing in the world, is necessary, that it is necessary to assure a stable peace. That is the sort of principle we hold. . . .

Let us normalize relations. We have received an appeal from the Acting Secretary General of the UN, U Thant, with his proposals. I have already answered him. His proposals come to this, that our side should not transport armaments of any kind to Cuba during a certain period of time, while negotiations are being conducted—and we are ready to enter such negotiations—and the other side should not undertake any sort of piratical actions against vessels engaged in navigation on the high seas. I consider these proposals reasonable. This would be a way out of the situation which has been created, which would give the peoples the possibility of breathing calmly. You have asked what happened, what evoked the delivery of weapons to Cuba? You have spoken about this to our Minister of Foreign Affairs. I will tell you frankly, Mr. President, what evoked it.

We were very grieved by the fact—I spoke about it in Vienna—that a landing took place, that an attack on Cuba was committed, as a result of which many Cubans perished. You yourself told me then that this had been a mistake. . . .

Why have we proceeded to assist Cuba with military and economic aid? The answer is: we have proceeded to do so only for reasons of humanitarianism. At one time, our people itself had a revolution, when Russia was still a backward country. We were attacked then. We were the target of attack by many countries. The USA participated in that adventure. . . .

You once said that the United States was not preparing an invasion. But you also declared that you sympathized with the Cuban counterrevolutionary emigrants, that you support them and would help them to realize their plans against the present government of Cuba. It is also not a secret to anyone that the threat of armed attack, aggression, has constantly hung, and continues to hang over Cuba. It was only this which impelled us to respond to the request of the Cuban government to furnish it aid for the strengthening of the defensive capacity of this country.

If assurances were given by the President and the government of the United States that the USA itself would not participate in an attack on Cuba and would restrain others from actions of this sort, if you would recall your fleet, this would immediately change everything. I am not speaking for Fidel Castro, but I think that he and the government of Cuba, evidently would declare demobilization and would appeal to the people to get down to peaceful labor. Then, too, the question of armaments would disappear, since, if there is no threat, then armaments are a burden for every people. Then, too, the question of the destruction, not only of the armaments which you call offensive, but of all other armaments as well, would look different. . . .

Let us therefore show statesmanlike wisdom. I propose: we, for our part, will declare that our ships, bound for Cuba, will not carry any kind of armaments. You would declare that the United States will not invade Cuba with its forces and will not support any sort of forces which might intend to carry out an invasion of Cuba. Then the necessity for the presence of our military specialists in Cuba would disappear.

Mr. President, I appeal to you to weigh well the aggressive, piratical actions, which you have declared the USA intends to carry out in international waters, would lead to. You yourself know that any sensible man simply cannot agree with this, cannot recognize your right to such actions.

If you did this as the first step towards the unleashing of war, well then, it is evident that nothing else is left to us but to accept this challenge of yours. If, however, you have not lost your self-control and sensibly conceive what this might lead to, then, Mr. President, we and you ought not now to pull on the ends of the rope in which you have tied the knot of war, because the more the two of us pull, the tighter that knot will be tied. And a moment may come when that knot will be tied so tight that even he who tied it will not have the strength to untie it, and then it will be necessary to cut that knot. And what that would mean is not for me to explain to you, because you yourself understand perfectly of what terrible forces our countries dispose.

Consequently, if there is no intention to tighten that knot and thereby to doom the world to the catastrophe of thermonuclear war, then let us not only relax the forces pulling on the ends of the rope, let us take measures to untie that knot. We are ready for this. . . .

These thoughts are dictated by a sincere desire to relieve the situation, to remove the threat of war.

Respectfully yours,

N. Khrushchev

6. Anastas I. Mikoyan and Fidel Castro
Review the Crisis, November 3–4, 1962

Mikoyan-Castro Meeting in Havana, November 3, 1962

[Castro:] The Soviet Union's concessions had a depressing effect. Psychologically, our people were unprepared for that. There was a feeling of deep disappointment, bitterness, pain. It was as if we had been deprived not of missiles but of the very symbol of solidarity. The announcement of the dismantling of the missile launchers and the return of the missiles to the Soviet Union was first taken by our people for a shameless lie. After all, the Cuban people knew nothing about the agreement— they didn't know that the missiles still belong to the Soviet side. They had no idea of the legal status of the weapon. They were used to a situation where the Soviet Union supplied us with arms that became our property.

"Why was that decision made unilaterally? Why are the missiles being taken away from us? Will all our arms be taken back?" These questions troubled all Cubans. In a matter of 48 hours, this feeling of bitterness and pain spread to the whole people. Events took place in rapid succession. On October 27, it was proposed to withdraw the weapon[s] from Cuba on condition that the bases in Turkey should be abolished. On October 28, there came orders for dismantling and permission for inspection.

It was unbelievable—everybody thought it was a lie.

Second, the message contained not a line about Cuba's advance consent. One might have thought that our consent is just a formal matter. But Cuba is something more than a small country with a small but courageous people. Our revolution is more important than the destiny of our country, the destiny of our people themselves. We must defend and preserve our revolution for the world. Our people felt that decisions taken without agreement with the Cuban government had caused moral damage to our revolution and told on its prestige in the eyes of Latin American peoples.

After the War of Independence, the Americans imposed the so-called Platt Amendment limiting the validity of the Cuban Constitution. That "amendment" denied our country the right to make its territory available for foreign military bases without the consent of the U.S. government. The Americans took advantage of it to grossly interfere in Cuban affairs. . . .

It seemed to many in those days that the Platt Amendment had come back to life. . . .

Besides, the situation is unchanged from the legal point of view, and so is the status quo after the present crisis.

1. The blockade established by the U.S. government is still there. The United States continues flouting freedom of the seas.
2. The Americans are trying to determine what weapons we may possess. They are organising control. The situation now shaping up is similar to the situation— past or present—in Morocco, Guinea, Ghana, Ceylon, and Yemen.
3. The United States continues violating Cuban airspace, expecting us to tolerate it. Besides, inspection has been authorised without asking us.

"Documents: Dialogue in Havana. The Caribbean Crisis," *International Affairs* (Moscow). No. 10 (1992), pp. 109–111, 114, 115, 116, 122, 123.

In the light of current events, we find it difficult to see the reasons for the withdrawal of the Soviet strategic weapon. The question arises: Was the matter considered and studied carefully enough? Or was it assumed from the start that the missiles would be pulled out, except that we didn't know? The information we had on the intentions and plans of the Soviet side was inadequate. When [the Cuban official] Che Guevara went to Moscow, the question of publishing the text of the agreement was raised. No clear answer was given. We had considered that the important thing was to have the missiles in Cuba. This is why we found it so hard to believe that they were being taken back to the Soviet Union.

Had there been a demand for the simultaneous abolition of the U.S. base at Guantánamo, our people would have appreciated the demand. . . .

[Mikoyan:] It so happened that we could not consult you before deciding. Imagine that a moment came when Cuba's—and possibly not only Cuba's—fate hung in the balance. The U.S. government had decided to commit aggression. It had massed warships with troops in the Caribbean and alerted a bomber force. Everything was ready for attack. Had we sent you our proposals, an answer might have come in a day or two—also because coding, decoding, and translation would have taken time. We had no time for that. We had to decide the same day. The following day Cuba might have been destroyed if not with atom bombs, then by means of bombers carrying rockets with conventional warheads. So massive an attack could have destroyed the launchers on Cuban territory and provided conditions for a naval landing. It was imperative to solve that complicated problem without delay. At about noon on Sunday, we met after receiving a coded message from Ambassador [to Cuba Aleksandr] Alexeyev. It said that there was information about stepped-up preparations for aggression. Information from other sources confirmed that a U.S. attack on Cuba might come in a matter of hours. We had to make a decision by ourselves on saving Cuba. . . .

We were compelled to decide. The loss of Cuba would have been irreplaceable for the whole international communist movement.

We don't necessarily have to keep missiles in Cuba to strike at the United States in case of need. We can do so from our territory. You know that we have a suitable weapon.

Our missiles in Cuba were detected too early. We had expected to be able to publish a declaration after the elections for the U.S. Congress, that is, by mid-November. . . .

Anastas Mikoyan's explanatory remarks were broken off by news of the death of his wife.

On reading the telegram, Cde. Mikoyan asked that it be interpreted for Cde. Fidel Castro.

Thereupon the conversation was broken off. Fidel Castro and [his adviser] Celia Sánchez, deeply perturbed, saw A. Mikoyan to the car.

Mikoyan-Castro Meeting in Havana, November 4, 1962

[Mikoyan:] I remember that after visiting Bulgaria [in May 1962], Nikita Khrushchev told you that all through his stay in that country he had been thinking of Cuba, fearing that the Americans might mount armed intervention with the aid of reactionary Latin American governments or commit outright aggression. They refuse to allow

Cuba to grow stronger, Nikita Khrushchev told us, and if Cuba were defeated, the whole world revolutionary movement would suffer a heavy blow. We must thwart the American imperialists' plans, he said. . . .

The only purpose of shipping Soviet troops and strategic arms to Cuba was to strengthen your defences. Ours was a containment plan, a plan intended to discourage the imperialists from playing with fire in regard to Cuba. Had we developed strategic arms in secrecy, with America knowing nothing about those arms' presence in Cuba, they would have served as a strong deterrent. That was the assumption we started from. Our military told us that Cuba's palm forests made it possible to dependably camouflage strategic missiles against detection from the air. . . .

In such a situation [U.S. invasion], we would have been unable to refrain from responding to aggression from the United States. That attack would have amounted to an attack on both you and us because we had Soviet troops and strategic missiles stationed in Cuba. A collision would inevitably have triggered a nuclear war. To be sure, we would have destroyed America and suffered severely for our part, but then our country is larger than America. Cuba would have been destroyed first. The imperialists would have done their utmost to destroy it.

We had 10 to 12 hours to go before the United States attacked Cuba. It was indispensable to use the art of diplomacy. Failure would have led to war. We had to use diplomatic means. . . .

As Kennedy agreed to Soviet troops being left in Cuba and as the Cubans kept powerful weapons and anti-aircraft missiles, we may consider that he made a concession for his part.

Kennedy's statement about nonaggression against Cuba by the United States and Latin American countries is another concession. If we take these reciprocal concessions and all other factors into account, we will see that we've won a big victory. Never before have the Americans made such statements. This is why we came to the conclusion that we were achieving the main goal, which is to preserve Cuba. There will be no attack on Cuba. Nor will there be any war. We are willing more favourable positions.

Of course, we should have sent our draft decision to Cuba, should have consulted you and secured your consent before publishing it. We would actually have done so in a normal situation. Fidel Castro wrote us in his letter [of October 26] that aggression within the next 24 hours was imminent. When we received the letter and discussed the situation, the start of aggression was only 10 to 12 hours away.

Let us compare the situation today with what it was before the crisis. At that time the Americans were planning armed intervention against Cuba. But now they have committed themselves not to attack Cuba. This is a great achievement. . . .

Frankly speaking, we had not all been thinking about the bases in Turkey. But when discussing the dangerous situation that had developed, we received information from the United States saying that, from what [Walter] Lippmann wrote in his column, the Russians might raise the question of abolishing the U.S. bases in Turkey. The possibility of our putting forward such a demand was discussed among Americans. The idea was debated in the United States. That was how that demand came to be advanced. Subsequently, however, we stopped insisting on it because the U.S. bases in that country are no problem for us. The Turkish bases are of little significance as we see it. They will be destroyed in case of war. Of course, they have some political significance but we don't pay them any particular attention although we plan to press for their elimination.

✖ E S S A Y S

In the first essay, diplomatic historian Thomas G. Paterson of the University of Connecticut places John F. Kennedy's policies toward Cuba in a broad perspective, linking U.S. attempts to overthrow the Castro government with the subsequent missile crisis. A prominent critic of U.S. Cold War policies, Paterson suggests that Kennedy was responsible for the failure of U.S. policy toward Cuba, a program that posed a real risk of nuclear war and left as its legacy a bitter hostility that continues even today to shape U.S.-Cuban relations. In the second essay, diplomatic historian Ernest R. May and political scientist Philip D. Zelikow, both of Harvard University, review the Cuban missile crisis. May and Zelikow draw on both the transcripts of deliberations within the White House (from their edited work The *Kennedy Tapes: Inside the White House During the Cuban Missile Crisis*) and on recently released Soviet documents.

Spinning Out of Control: Kennedy's War Against Cuba and the Missile Crisis

THOMAS G. PATERSON

"My God," muttered Richard Helms of the Central Intelligence Agency, "these Kennedys keep the pressure on about [Fidel] Castro." Another CIA officer heard it straight from John F. and Robert F. Kennedy: "Get off your ass about Cuba." Defense Secretary Robert McNamara remembered that "we were hysterical about Castro at the time of the Bay of Pigs and thereafter." When White House assistant Arthur Schlesinger Jr. returned from an early 1962 overseas trip, he told the president that people abroad thought that the administration was "obsessed with Cuba." President Kennedy himself acknowledged during the missile crisis that "most allies regard [Cuba] as a fixation of the United States."

This essay seeks, first, to explain the U.S. "fixation" with Cuba in the early 1960s, identifying the sources and negative consequences of the Kennedy administration's multitrack war against Cuba. Second, to demonstrate the considerable American responsibility for the onset of the dangerous missile crisis of fall 1962. Third, to explore Kennedy's handling of the crisis, questioning the thesis of deft, cautious management. And, last, to illustrate the persistence of the "fixation" by studying the aftermath of the missile crisis, when the revitalization of the U.S. war against Castro's government set Cuban-American relations on a collision course for decades.

"Spinning Out of Control: John F. Kennedy, the War Against Cuba, and the Missile Crisis" by Thomas G. Paterson, from *Major Problems in Foreign Relations,* Fifth Edition (Houghton Mifflin Company). Reprinted by permission of Thomas G. Paterson.

A knowledgeable and engaged President Kennedy spent as much or more time on Cuba as on any other foreign-policy problem. Cuba stood at the center of his administration's greatest failure, the Bay of Pigs, and its alleged greatest success, the missile crisis. Why did President Kennedy and his chief advisers indulge such an obessession with Cuba and direct so many U.S. resources to an unrelenting campaign to monitor, harass, isolate, and ultimately destroy Havana's radical regime? One answer springs from a candid remark by the president's brother, Robert F. Kennedy, who later wondered "if we did not pay a very great price for being more energetic than wise about a lot of things, especially Cuba." The Kennedys' famed eagerness for action became exaggerated in the case of Cuba. They always wanted to get moving on Cuba, and Castro dared them to try. The popular, intelligent, but erratic Cuban leader, who in January 1959 overthrew the U.S. ally Fulgencio Batista, hurled harsh words at Washington and defiantly challenged the Kennedy model of evolutionary, capitalist development so evident in the Alliance for Progress. As charismatic figures charting new frontiers, Kennedy and Castro often personalized the Cuban-American contest. To Kennedy's great annoyance, Castro could not be wheedled or beaten.

Kennedy's ardent war against *fidelismo* may also have stemmed from his feeling that Castro had double-crossed him. As a senator, Kennedy had initially joined many Americans in welcoming the Cuban Revolution as an advancement over the "oppressive" Batista dictatorship. Kennedy had urged a "patient attitude" toward the new government, which he did not see as Communist. Denying repeatedly that he was a Communist, Castro had in fact proclaimed his allegiance to democracy and private property. But in the process of legitimizing his revolution and resisting U.S. pressure, Castro turned more and more radical. Americans grew impatient with the regime's highly-charged anti-Yankeeism, postponement of elections, jailing of critics, and nationalization of property. The president rejected the idea that intense U.S. hostility toward the Cuban Revolution may have contributed to Castro's tightening political grip and flirtation with the Soviet Union. Nor did Kennedy and other Americans wish to acknowledge the measurable benefits of the revolution—improvements in education, medical care, and housing, and the elimination of the island's infamous corruption that once had been the American mafia's domain. Instead, Kennedy officials concluded that Cuba's was a "betrayed revolution."

Richard N. Goodwin, the young White House and State Department official, provided another explanation for the Kennedy "fixation" with Cuba. He remarked that "the entire history of the Cold War, its positions and assumptions, converged upon the 'problem of Cuba.'" The Cold War dominated international politics, and as Cuban-American relations steadily deteriorated, Cuban-Soviet relations gradually improved. Not only did Americans come to believe that a once-loyal ally had jilted them for the tawdry embrace of the Soviets; they also grew alarmed that Castro sneered at the Monroe Doctrine by inviting the Soviet military to the island. When Castro, in late 1961, declared himself a Marxist-Leninist, Americans who had long denounced him as a Communist felt vindicated. . . .

American politics also influenced the administration's Cuba policy. In the 1960 presidential campaign, Kennedy had seized the Cuban issue to counter Richard Nixon's charge that the inexperienced Democratic candidate would abandon Zinmen (Quemoy) and Mazu (Matsu) to Communism and prove no match for the hard-nosed

Khrushchev. "In 1952 the Republicans ran on a program of rolling back the Iron Curtain in Eastern Europe," Kennedy jabbed. "Today the Iron Curtain is 90 miles off the coast of the United States." He asked in private, "How would *we* have saved Cuba if we had [had] the power?" but he nonetheless valued the political payback from his attack. "What the hell," he informed his aides, "they never told us how they would have saved China." Apparently unaware that President Dwight D. Eisenhower had initiated a clandestine CIA program to train Cuban exiles for an invasion of the island, candidate Kennedy bluntly called for just such a project. After exploiting the Cuban issue, Kennedy, upon becoming president, could not easily have retreated.

Overarching all explanations for Kennedy's obsession with Cuba is a major phenomenon of the second half of the twentieth century: the steady erosion of the authority of imperial powers, which had built systems of dependent, client, and colonial governments. The strong currents of decolonization, anti-imperialism, revolutionary nationalism, and social revolution, sometimes in combination, undermined the instruments the imperial nations had used to maintain control and order. The Cuban Revolution exemplified this process of breaking up and breaking away. American leaders reacted so hostilely to this revolution not simply because Castro and his 26th of July Movement taunted them or because domestic politics and the Cold War swayed them, but also because Cuba, as symbol and reality, challenged U.S. hegemony in Latin America. The specter of "another Cuba" haunted President Kennedy, not just because it would hurt him politically, but because "the game would be up through a good deal of Latin America," as Under Secretary of State George Ball put it. The Monroe Doctrine and the U.S. claim to political, economic, and military leadership in the hemisphere seemed at stake. As Castro once remarked, "the United States *had* to fight his revolution."

The Eisenhower Administration bequeathed to its successor an unproductive tit-for-tat process of confrontation with Cuba and a legacy of failure. In November 1959, President Eisenhower decided to encourage anti-Castro groups within Cuba to "replace" the revolutionary regime and thus end an anti-Americanism that was "having serious adverse effects on the United States position in Latin America and corresponding advantages for international Communism." In March 1960 Eisenhower ordered the CIA to train Cuban exiles for an invasion of their homeland— this shortly after Cuba had signed a trade treaty with the Soviet Union. The CIA, as well, hatched assassination plots against Castro and staged hit-and-run attacks along the Cuban coast. As Cuba undertook land reform that struck at American interests and nationalized American-owned industries, the United States suspended Cuba's sugar quota and forbade American exports to the island, drastically cutting a once-flourishing commerce. On January 3, 1961, fearing an invasion and certain that the U.S. embassy was a "nest of spies" aligned with counterrevolutionaries who were burning cane fields and sabotaging buildings, Castro demanded that the embassy staff be greatly reduced. Washington promptly broke diplomatic relations with Havana.

Eisenhower failed to topple Castro, but U.S. pressure accelerated the radicalization of the revolution and helped open the door to the Soviets. Moscow bought sugar, supplied technicians, armed the militia, and offered generous trade terms. Although the revolution's radicalization was probably inevitable given Cuban conditions, it was not inexorable that Cuba would end up in the Soviet camp. Hostile U.S. policies helped to ensure that outcome.

To be sure, Kennedy inherited the Cuban problem from Eisenhower. But he did not simply continue his predecessor's anti-Castro policies. Kennedy greatly exaggerated the Cuban threat, attributing to Castro a capability to export revolution that the Cuban leader never had. Castro was "an affront to our pride" and a "mischief maker," the journalist Walter Lippmann wisely wrote, but he was not a "mortal threat" to the United States. Kennedy significantly increased the pressures against the upstart island. He inherited the Cuban problem—and he made it worse.

The questions of whether and under what conditions to approve an exile expedition dominated the president's discussion of Cuba in his first few months in office. Although Kennedy always reserved the authority to cancel the operation right up to the moment of departure, his choices pointed in one direction: Go. National security affairs adviser McGeorge Bundy later said that the president "really was looking for ways to make it work . . . and allowed himself to be persuaded it would work and the risks were acceptable."

The plan to invade Cuba at the Bay of Pigs began to unravel from the start. As the brigade's old, slow freighters plowed their way to the island, B-26 airplanes took to the skies from Nicaragua. On April 15, D-Day-minus-2, the brigade pilots destroyed several parked planes of Castro's meager air force. That same day, as part of a pre-invasion ploy, a lone, artificially damaged B-26 flew directly to Miami, where its pilot claimed that he had defected from the Cuban military and had just bombed his country's airfields. But the cover story soon cracked. Snooping journalists noticed that the nose cone of the B-26 was metal; Cuban planes had plastic noses. They observed too that the aircraft's guns had not been fired. The American hand was being exposed. The president, still insistent on hiding U.S. complicity, decided to cancel a second D-Day strike against the remnants of the Cuban air force.

Shortly after midnight on April 17, more than 1,400 commandoes motored in small boats to the beaches at Bahiá de Cochinos. The invaders immediately tangled with Castro's militia. Some commandoes never made it, because their boats broke apart on razor-sharp coral reefs. In the air, Castro's marauding airplanes shot down two brigade B-26s and sank ships carrying essential communications equipment and ammunition. Fighting ferociously, the brigade nonetheless failed to establish a beachhead. Would Washington try to salvage the mission? Kennedy turned down desperate CIA appeals to dispatch planes from the nearby U.S.S. *Essex,* but he did permit some jets to provide air cover for a new B-26 attack from Nicaragua. Manned this time by American CIA pilots, the B-26s arrived an hour after the jets had come and gone. Cuban aircraft downed the B-26s, killing four Americans. With Castro's boasting that the *mercenarios* had been foiled, the final toll proved grim: 114 of the exile brigade dead and 1,189 captured. One hundred-and-fifty Cuban defenders died.

Failures in intelligence, operations, decisionmaking, and judgment doomed the Bay of Pigs undertaking. Arrogant CIA architects knew too little about the landing site and assumed too much about Cuba. The agency's inspector general, for example, wrote in a post-invasion critique that the CIA "had no intelligence evidence that Cubans in significant numbers could or would join the invaders. . . ." The CIA also failed to assassinate Fidel Castro. As a CIA official admitted, the agency had intended "that Castro would be dead before the landing."

The most controversial operational question remains the canceled second D-Day air strike. Post-crisis critics have complained that the president lost his nerve and made a decision that condemned the expedition to disaster. Cuban air supremacy did prove important to Cuba's triumph. But was it decisive? A preemptive strike on D-Day against the Cuban air force would not have delivered victory to the invaders. After the first air attack, Castro had dispersed his planes; the brigade's B-26s would have encountered considerable difficulty in locating and destroying them. And, even if a D-Day assault had disabled all of Castro's planes, then what? The brigade's 1,400 warriors would have had to face Castro's army of 25,000 and the nation's 200,000 militia. The commandoes most likely would not have survived the overwhelming power of the Cuban military. . . .

Defeat did not chasten the Kennedys. On April 20, the president spoke out. "Let the record show," he boomed, "that our restraint is not inexhaustible." Indeed, the United States intended to defend the Monroe Doctrine and carry on a "relentless" struggle with Communism in "every corner of the globe." In familiar words, Kennedy declared that "the complacent, the self-indulgent, the soft societies are about to be swept away with the debris of history. Only the strong . . . can possibly survive." Attorney General Robert Kennedy remarked that the Bay of Pigs "insult needed to be redressed rather quickly."

Critical to understanding the frightening missile crisis of fall 1962 is the relationship between post–Bay of Pigs U.S. activities and the Soviet/Cuban decisions to place on the island nuclear-tipped missiles that could strike the United States, endangering the lives of 92 million people. In late April, after hearing from Cuban leaders that they expected a direct U.S. invasion and sought Soviet help to resist an attack, and after protesting the deployment of U.S. intermediate-range Jupiter missiles in Turkey, Nikita Khrushchev began to think about a missile deployment in Cuba; in late May, after dismissing the skepticism of some key advisers who judged his plan provocative to the United States and therefore highly explosive, he made the offer of missiles to Fidel Castro, who quickly accepted them; in early July, Raúl Castro initialed a draft agreement in Moscow; and in late August and early September, during a trip by Che Guevara to Moscow, the two nations put the treaty into final form. The plan called for the Soviets' installation on the island of forty-eight medium-range ballistic missiles (SS-4s with a range of 1,020 miles), thirty-two intermediate-range ballistic missiles (SS-5s with a range of 2,200 miles), 144 surface-to-air missiles (SAMs), theater-nuclear weapons (Lunas), forty-eight IL-28 light bombers (with a range of 600 miles), and 42,000 Soviet combat troops.

After the Bay of Pigs, the Kennedy administration launched a multitrack program of covert, economic, diplomatic, and propagandistic elements calculated to overthrow the Castro government. This multidimensional project prompted the Cuban/Soviet decisions of mid-1962. Secretary of Defense Robert McNamara said later: "If I had been in Moscow or Havana at that time [1961–1962], I would have believed the Americans were preparing for an invasion." Indeed, Havana had to fear a successful Bay of Pigs operation conducted by U.S. forces.

Encouraged by the White House, the CIA created a huge station in Miami called JMWAVE to recruit and organize Cuban exiles. In Washington, Robert Kennedy became a ramrod for action. At a November 4, 1961, White House meeting, the Attorney General insisted: "stir things up on the island with espionage, sabotage, general disorder. . . ." The president himself asked Colonel Edward Lansdale to direct Operation Mongoose—"to use our available assets . . . to help Cuba overthrow the Communist regime." Operation Mongoose and JMWAVE, although failing to unseat Castro, punished Cubans. CIA-handled saboteurs burned cane fields and blew up factories and oil storage tanks. In a December 1961 raid, for example, a seven-man team blasted a railroad bridge, derailed an approaching train, and torched a sugar warehouse. One group, Agrupación Montecristi, attacked a Cuban patrol boat off the northern coast of the island in May 1962. Directorio Revolucionario Estudiantil, another exile organization, used two boats to attack Cuba in August, hoping to hit a hotel where Castro was dining.

The CIA, meanwhile, devised new plots to kill Castro with poisonous cigars, pills, and needles. To no avail. Did the Kennedys know about these death schemes? In May 1961, Federal Bureau of Investigation Director J. Edgar Hoover informed Robert Kennedy that the CIA had hired mafia boss Sam Giancana to do some "dirty business" in Cuba. Kennedy noted on the margin of the Hoover memorandum that this information should be "followed up vigorously." A year later, the CIA briefed the attorney general about its use of mafia gangsters to assassinate Castro. If his brother Robert knew about these CIA assassination plots, the president surely did, for Robert was John's closest confidant. They kept little if anything from one another. President Kennedy apparently never directly ordered the assassination of Castro—at least no trail of documents leads to the White House. But, of course, nobody uttered the word "assassination" in the presence of the president or committed the word to paper, thereby honoring the principle of plausible deniability. Advisers instead simply mentioned the need to remove Castro. "And if killing him was one of the things that was to be done in this connection," assassination was attempted because "we felt we were acting within the guidelines," said the CIA's Richard Helms.

Intensified economic coercion joined these covert activities. The Kennedy administration, in February 1962, banned most imports of Cuban products. Washington also pressed its North Atlantic Treaty Organization allies to support the "economic isolation" of Cuba. The embargo hurt. Cuba had to pay higher freight costs, enlarge its foreign debt, and suffer innumerable factory shut-downs due to lack of spare parts once bought in the United States. Cuba's economic woes also stemmed from the flight of technicians and managers, a decline in tourism, high workers' absenteeism rates, the drying up of foreign capital investment, hastily conceived policies to diversify the economy, and suffocating government controls.

The Kennedy administration also engineered the ouster of Cuba from the Organization of American States in early 1962. The expulsion registered loudly in Havana, which interpreted it as "political preparation for an invasion." By spring 1962, moreover, fifteen Latin American states had answered Washington's call to break relations with Cuba. . . .

American military maneuvers heightened Cuban fears. One well publicized U.S. exercise, "Quick-Kick," staged during April and May, included 40,000 troops, seventy-nine ships, and 300 aircraft along the U.S. southeastern coast. An earlier exercise in April included an amphibious Marine landing on a small island near Puerto Rico. Havana protested these exercises as provocations, tests of U.S. war plans against Cuba. Some noisy American politicians, throughout 1962, called for the real thing: an invasion of Cuba. In summer 1962, moreover, the U.S. Army began a program to create Spanish-speaking units; the Cuban exiles who signed up had as their "primary" goal a "return to Cuba to battle against the Fidel Castro regime."

By the late spring and early summer of 1962, then, when Havana and Moscow discussed defensive measures that included missiles with warheads, Cuba felt besieged from several quarters. The Soviet Union had become its trading partner, and the Soviets, after the Bay of Pigs, had begun military shipments of small arms, howitzers, machine guns, armored personnel carriers, patrol boats, tanks, MiG jet fighters. Yet all this weaponry had not deterred the United States. And, given the failure of Kennedy's multitrack program to unseat Castro, "were we right or wrong to fear direct invasion" next, asked Fidel Castro. As he said in mid-1962, shortly after striking the missile-deployment agreement with the Soviets: "We must prepare ourselves for that direct invasion."

Had there been no exile expedition at the Bay of Pigs, no destructive covert activities, no assassination plots, no military maneuvers and plans, and no economic and diplomatic steps to harass, isolate, and destroy the Castro government in Havana, there would not have been a Cuban missile crisis. The origins of the October 1962 crisis derived largely from the concerted U.S. campaign to quash the Cuban Revolution. To stress only the global dimension (Soviet-American competition in the nuclear arms race) is to slight the local origins of the conflict. To slight these sources by suggesting from very incomplete declassified Soviet records that the "thought of deterring a U.S. invasion figured only incidentally" in Moscow's calculations, as argued by Ernest R. May and Philip D. Zelikow, editors of the tape recordings that Kennedy made during the crisis, is to overlook the substantial evidence of Soviet (and Cuban) preoccupation with the defense of Cuba and is to miss the central point that Premier Nikita Khrushchev would never have had the opportunity to install dangerous missiles in the Caribbean if the United States had not been attempting to overthrow the Cuban government. This interpretation does not dismiss the view that the emplacement of nuclear missiles in Cuba also served the Soviet strategic goal of catching up in the nuclear arms race. Rather, the interpretation in this essay emphasizes that both Cuba and the Soviet Union calculated that their interests would be served by putting nuclear-capable rockets on the island. Havana hoped to gain deterrent power to thwart an expected American invasion, and Moscow hoped to save a new socialist ally while enhancing the U.S.S.R.'s deterrent power in the Cold War. . . .

On October 14, an American U-2 plane photographed missile sites in Cuba, thus providing the first "hard" evidence, as distinct from the "soft" reports of exiles, that the island was becoming a nuclear base. "He can't do that to me!" snapped Kennedy when he saw the pictures on the 16th. He had warned the Soviets that the United States would not suffer "offensive" weapons in Cuba, although the warnings had come after the Cuban-Soviet agreement of early summer. Shortly before noon on October 16, the president convened his top advisers (a group eventually called the Executive Committee, or ExComm). His first questions focused on the firing readiness of the missiles and the probability that they carried nuclear warheads. The advisers gave tentative answers. All agreed that the missiles could become operational in a brief time. Discussion of military options (invasion? air strike?) dominated this first meeting. Kennedy's immediate preference became clear: "We're certainly going . . . to take out these . . . missiles." Kennedy showed little interest in negotiations. Perhaps his initial tilt toward military action derived from his knowledge of the significant U.S. military plans, maneuvers, and movement of forces and equipment undertaken after he signed NSAM-181, thus making it possible for the United States to respond with military effectiveness.

At a second meeting on the 16th, Secretary of State Dean Rusk argued against the surprise air strike that General Taylor had bluntly advocated. Rusk recommended instead "a direct message to Castro." At the close of Rusk's remarks, Kennedy immediately asked: "Can we get a little idea about what the military thing *is*?" Bundy then asked: "How gravely does this change the strategic balance?" McNamara, for one, thought "not at all," but Taylor disputed him. Kennedy himself seemed uncertain, but he did complain that the missile emplacement in Cuba "makes them look like they're co-equal with us." And, added Treasury Secretary C. Douglas Dillon, who obviously knew the president's competitive personality, the presence of the missiles made it appear that "we're scared of the Cubans." . . .

For the next several days, ExComm met frequently in tight secrecy and discussed four policy options: "talk them out," "squeeze them out," "shoot them out," or "buy them out." In exhausting sessions marked by frank disagreement and changing minds, the president's advisers weighed the advantages and disadvantages of invasion, bombing, quarantine, and diplomacy. The president gradually moved with a majority of ExComm toward a quarantine or blockade of Cuba: incoming ships would be stopped and inspected for military cargo. When queried if an air strike would knock out all of the known missiles, General Taylor said that "the best we can offer you is to destroy 90%. . . ." In other words, some missiles in Cuba would remain in place for firing against the United States. Robert Kennedy also worried that the Soviets might react unpredictably with military force, "which could be so serious as to lead to general nuclear war." In any case, the attorney general insisted, there would be no "Pearl Harbor type of attack" on his brother's record.

By October 22 the president had made two decisions. First, to quarantine Cuba to prevent further military shipments and to impress the Soviets with U.S. resolve to force the missiles out. If the Soviets balked, other, more drastic, measures would be undertaken. Second, Kennedy decided to inform the Soviets of U.S. policy through a television address rather than through diplomatic channels. Several advisers dubiously argued that a surprise public speech was necessary to rally world opinion behind U.S. policy and to prevent Khrushchev from issuing an ultimatum, but some ExComm participants recommended that negotiations be tried first. Former ambassador to the Soviet Union Charles Bohlen advised that Moscow would have to retaliate against the United States if its technicians died from American bombs. A stern letter to Khrushchev should be "tested" as a method to gain withdrawal of the missiles. "I don't see the urgency of military action," Bohlen told the president. And ambassador to the United Nations Adlai Stevenson appealed to an unreceptive Kennedy: "the existence of nuclear missile bases anywhere is negotiable before we start anything." Stevenson favored a trade: withdrawing the U.S. Jupiter missiles from Turkey and evacuating the Guantánamo naval base, turning it over to Cuba, in exchange for withdrawal of the Soviet missiles from Cuba. The president, according to the minutes of a October 20 ExComm meeting, "sharply rejected" Stevenson's proposal, especially on the issue of Guantánamo. Two days later, Kennedy once again scolded the ambassador, claiming that withdrawal from the naval base would indicate to Khrushchev "that we were in a state of panic." Going into the crisis, Kennedy refused to negotiate with either Khrushchev or Castro.

In his evening televised speech on October 22, Kennedy demanded that the Soviets dismantle the missiles in Cuba, and he announced the Caribbean quarantine as an "initial" step. Later that evening, in a telephone conversation, he told British prime minister Harold Macmillan that U.S. credibility was on the line; if he had not acted, America's resolve to defend Berlin might be questioned and Soviet success in deploying the missiles "would have unhinged us in all of Latin America." The missile crisis soon became an international war of nerves. More than sixty American ships began patrols to enforce the blockade. The Strategic Air Command went on nuclear alert, moving upward to Defense Condition (DEF-CON) 2 for the first time ever (the next level is deployment for combat). B-52 bombers, loaded with nuclear weapons, stood ready, while men and equipment moved to the southeastern United States to prepare for an invasion. The Soviets did not mobilize or redeploy their huge military, nor did they take measures to make their strategic forces less vulnerable. The Soviets also refrained from testing the quarantine: Their ships turned around and went home. But what next? On the 26th, Kennedy and some ExComm members, thinking that the Soviets were stalling, soured on the quarantine. Sentiment for military action strengthened.

On the afternoon of the 26th, an intelligence officer attached to the Soviet embassy, Aleksandr Feklisov (alias Fomin), met with ABC television correspondent John Scali and suggested a solution to the crisis: The Soviet Union would withdraw the missiles if the United States would promise not to invade Cuba. Scali scurried to Secretary of State Dean Rusk, who sent him back to Feklisov with the reply that American leaders were interested in discussing the proposal. As it turns out, and unbeknownst to American leaders, Feklisov was acting on his own and a report of his conversations with Scali did not reach the Soviet foreign secretary in Moscow until the late afternoon of October 27. Feklisov's independent intervention, in other words, did not influence the writing of the two critical letters that Khrushchev sent to Washington on the 26th and 27th, but ExComm thought the Feklisov initiative and Khrushchev's letters were linked, thus clearly signaling an earnest Soviet desire to settle.

Khrushchev's first letter, a rambling emotional private message that ruminated on the horrors of war, offered to withdraw the missiles if the United States pledged not to invade Cuba. The Soviet premier defended the initial installation of the missiles with the argument that the United States had been threatening the island. In the morning of October 27, another Khrushchev letter reached the president. Khrushchev now upped the stakes: He would trade the missiles in Cuba for the American missiles in Turkey. Kennedy felt boxed, because "we are now in the position of risking war in Cuba and in Berlin over missiles in Turkey which are of little military value." At first, Kennedy hesitated to accept a swap—because he did not want to appear to be giving up anything in the face of Soviet provocation; because he knew that the proud Turks would recoil from the appearance of being "traded off in order to appease an enemy"; and because acceptance of a missile trade would lend credence to charges that the United States all along had been applying a doubling standard. Kennedy told ExComm that Khrushchev's offer caused "embarrassment," for most people would think it "a very fair trade." Indeed, Moscow had played "a very good card."

In the afternoon of the 27th, more bad news rocked the White House. An American U-2 plane overflew the eastern part of the Soviet Union, probably because its equipment malfunctioned. "There is always some son of a bitch who doesn't get the word," the president remarked. Soviet fighters scrambled to intercept the U-2, and American fighter jets from Alaska, carrying Falcon missiles with nuclear warheads, took flight to protect the errant aircraft. Although the spy plane flew home without having sparked a dog fight, the incident carried the potential of sending the crisis to a more dangerous level.

Also on the 27th, a U-2 was shot down over Cuba and its pilot killed by a surface-to-air missile (SAM). The shoot-down constituted a serious escalation. A distressed McNamara, not knowing that the order to shoot was made independently by the Soviet air defense commander in Cuba without orders from Moscow, now thought "invasion had become almost inevitable." He urged that U.S. aircraft "go in and take out that SAM site." But Kennedy hesitated to retaliate, surely scared about taking a step toward a nuclear nightmare. The president decided to ignore Khrushchev's second letter and answer the first. The evening of the 27th, he also dispatched his brother Robert to deliver an ultimatum to Soviet Ambassador Anatoly Dobrynin: Start pulling out the missiles within forty-eight hours or "we would remove them." After Dobrynin asked about the Jupiters in Turkey, Robert Kennedy presented an important American concession: They would be dismantled if the problem in Cuba were resolved. As the president had said in an ExComm meeting, "we can't very well invade Cuba with all its toil . . . when we could have gotten them out by making a deal on the same missiles in Turkey." But, should the Soviets leak word of a "deal," Robert Kennedy told the Soviet ambassador, the United States would disavow the offer. Dobrynin, who judged President Kennedy a "hot-tempered gambler," cabled an account of the meeting to Moscow, pointing out that the "very upset" president's brother insisted that "time is of the essence" and that if another U.S. plane were shot at, the United States would return fire and set off "a chain reaction" toward "a real war."

On October 28, faced with an ultimatum and a concession, and fearful that the Cubans might precipitate a greater Soviet-American conflagration, Khrushchev retreated and accepted the American offer: the Soviet Union would dismantle its missiles under United Nations supervision and the United States would pledge not to invade Cuba. The crisis had ended—just when the nuclear giants seemed about to stumble over the brink. . . .

Many analysts give John F. Kennedy high marks for his handling of the Cuban missile crisis, applauding a stunning success, noble statesmanship, and model of crisis management. Secretary Rusk lauded Kennedy for having "ice water in his veins." The journalist Hugh Sidey has gushed over "the serene leader who guides the nation away from nuclear conflict." Arthur Schlesinger Jr. has effusively written that Kennedy's crisis leadership constituted a "combination of toughness and restraint, of will, nerve, and wisdom, so brilliantly controlled, so matchlessly calibrated." May and Zelikow celebrate Kennedy's "finest hours," sketching a "lucid" and "calm" president, who, in the end, steps back from the brink.

Kennedy's stewardship of policymaking during the crisis actually stands less as a supreme display of careful crisis management and more as a case of near misses, close calls, narrow squeaks, physical exhaustion, accidents, and guesses that together scared officials on both sides into a settlement, because, in the words of McGeorge Bundy, the crisis was "so near to spinning out of control." When McNamara recalled those weeks, he questioned the entire notion of crisis management because of "misinformation, miscalculation, misjudgment, and human fallibility." "We were in luck," Ambassador John Kenneth Galbraith ruminated, "but success in a lottery is no argument for lotteries."

During the hair-trigger days of the crisis, much went wrong, the level of danger constantly rose, and weary and irritable decisionmakers sensed that they were losing their grip. "A high risk of uncontrollable escalation" dogged the crisis, as McNamara recalled. So much came apart; so much could not be reined in. The two U-2 incidents—the shootdown over Cuba and the straying over Soviet territory—rank high on the list. Vice President Lyndon Johnson remarked at an ExComm meeting on October 27: "Imagine some crazy Russian captain" shooting down another American spy plane. Seeing American flares during a night reconnaissance flight, "he might just pull a trigger. Looks like we're playing Fourth of July over there or something. I'm scared of that." There was also the serious possibility that an exile group would attempt to assassinate Castro or raid the island. Operation Mongoose sabotage teams actually maneuvered inside Cuba during the crisis and could not be reached by their CIA handlers. What if this "half-assed operation," Robert Kennedy worried, ignited trouble? One of these teams actually did blow up a Cuban factory on November 8. . . .

ExComm members represented considerable intellectual talent and experience, but a mythology of grandeur, illusion of control, and embellishment of performance have obscured the history of the committee. ExComm debated alternatives under "intense strain," often in a "state of anxiety and emotional exhaustion," recalled Under Secretary Ball. McGeorge Bundy told Ball on October 24 that he (Bundy) was getting "groggy." Two advisers may have suffered such stress that they became less able to perform their responsibilities. An assistant to Adlai Stevenson recalled that he had had to become an ExComm "back-up" for the ambassador because, "while he could speak clearly, his memory wasn't very clear. . . ." Asked if failing health produced this condition, Vice Admiral Charles Wellborn answered that the "emotional state and nervous tension that was involved in it [missile crisis] had this effect." Stevenson was feeling "pretty frightened." So apparently was Dean Rusk. The president scratched on a notepad during an October 22 meeting: "Rusk rather quiet & somewhat fatigued." Robert Kennedy remembered that the secretary of state "had a virtually complete breakdown mentally and physically." Once, when Rusk's eyes swelled with tears, Dean Acheson barked at him: "Pull yourself together, . . . you're the only secretary of state we have." We cannot determine how stress affected the advice ExComm gave Kennedy, but at least we know that its members struggled against time, sleep, exhaustion, and themselves, and they did not always think clearheadedly at a time when the stakes were very high.

What about the president himself, gravely ill from Addison's disease and often in severe pain because of his ailing back? Dr. Max Jacobson, known as "Dr. Feelgood" by the Hollywood crowd that paid for his services, and a frequent visitor to the

White House, administered amphetamines and steroids to President Kennedy during the first days of the missile crisis. Medical doctors have reported that the effect of these unorthodox injections might have been supreme confidence and belligerence. One might speculate that JFK's inclination toward a bold military response at the start of the crisis was influenced by the doses of potent drugs he was taking. As the historian Michael Hunt has noted about ExComm meetings, moreover, the president at times "struggled to put a clear, complete sentence together." Indeed, "the proceedings degenerated at times into a babble that makes ExComm seem more like a kindergarten than a crisis-management team."

As for the Soviets, they too worried about their decisionmaking process and the crisis spinning out of control. Khrushchev, of course, had miscalculated from the outset. He somehow thought that the Americans would not discover the missiles until after all of them had become operational. He had no fallback plan once they were photographed. Because he had never informed his own embassy in Washington that missiles were being placed in Cuba, he had cut himself off from critical advice—counsel that would have alerted him to the certain vigorous U.S. response to the emplacement. "He was so confused," Dobrynin remarked after the crisis. Khrushchev's letter of October 26 to Kennedy betrayed desperation, if not disarray in the Kremlin: "You and I should not now pull on the ends of the rope in which you have tied a knot of war, because . . . [we might unleashing the] dread forces our two countries possess." As the shootdown of the U-2 over Cuba demonstrated, Khrushchev also had to wonder if *his* field officers got the word to be cautious.

Add to these worries the Soviet premier's troubles with Fidel Castro, who demanded a bold Soviet response to U.S. actions and who might provoke an incident with the United States that could escalate the crisis. Castro pressed the Soviets to use nuclear weapons to save Cuba should the United States attack. Soviet leaders urged Castro not to "initiate provocations" and to practice "self-restraint." Such "adventurists," remarked a Soviet decisionmaker about the Cubans. Khrushchev sternly told his advisers: "You see how far things can go. We've got to get those missiles out of there before a real fire starts."

President Kennedy helped to precipitate the missile crisis by harassing Cuba through his multitrack program. Then he reacted to the crisis by suspending diplomacy in favor of public confrontation. In the end, with the management of the crisis disintegrating, he frightened himself. In order to postpone doomsday, or at least to prevent a high-casualty invasion of Cuba, he moderated the American response and compromised. Khrushchev withdrew his mistake, while gaining what ExComm member Ambassador Llewellyn Thompson thought was the "important thing" all along for the Soviet leader: being able to say, "I saved Cuba. I stopped an invasion."

Although during the crisis such utterances as "Castro has to go," "cause something to crack" in Cuba, "I'd take Cuba away from Castro," and "dump" Castro punctuated ExComm meetings, the president said that restarting the task of removing Castro would have to wait until after achieving the immediate objective of dismantling the missile sites. After the missile imbroglio, the pre-crisis, "fixation" reasserted itself. For example, the State Department's Policy Planning Council on November 7 urged a "maximal U.S. strategy" to eliminate the Castro regime. The messy ending to the crisis—no formal accord was reached, no formal document signed—also left the Kennedy administration room to hedge on the no-invasion promise. Using the argument that the United States had agreed not to invade the island only if the missiles were withdrawn under United Nations inspection and that Castro had blocked such inspection, Kennedy refused to give an unqualified no-invasion pledge. On November 20, the president told a press conference that "if all offensive weapons systems are removed from Cuba and kept out of the hemisphere in the future, under adequate verification and safeguards, and if Cuba is not used for the export of aggressive Communist purposes, there will be peace in the Caribbean. . . . We will not, of course, abandon the political, economic, and other efforts of this hemisphere to halt subversion from Cuba nor our purpose and hope that the Cuban people shall some day be truly free. But these policies are very different from any intent to launch a military invasion of the island." Kennedy seemed to be adding a new condition—that Cuba must not stir up revolution in Latin America—and promising to continue efforts, short of military assault to overthrow the Castro government.

Kennedy's retreat to an ambiguous no-invasion promise reflected his administration's unrelenting determination to oust Castro. In early January 1963, the CIA director noted that "Cuba and the Communist China nuclear threat" were the two most prominent issues on Kennedy's foreign-policy agenda. Later that month, the president himself told the National Security Council that Cuba must become a U.S. hostage. "We must always be in a position to threaten Cuba as a possible riposte to Russian pressure against us in Berlin. We must always be ready to move immediately against Cuba" should the Soviets move against Berlin. "We can use Cuba to limit Soviet actions," he concluded. The administration set about once again to threaten Cuba, to "tighten the noose" around Cuba, although Kennedy grew impatient with exile attacks, because they did not deliver "any real blow at Castro."

In June 1963, the National Security Council approved a new sabotage program. The CIA quickly cranked up destructive plots and revitalized its assassination option by making contact with a traitorous Cuban official, Rolando Cubela. Code-named AM/LASH, he plotted with CIA operatives to kill Fidel Castro. In the fall of 1963, after Cuba probed for an accommodation with the United States, President Kennedy let preliminary steps be taken to open a Cuban-American dialogue through contacts at the United Nations. Yet, on the very day that Kennedy was assassinated, AM/LASH rendezvoused with CIA agents in Paris, where he received a ball-point pen rigged with a poisonous hypodermic needle. Like other assassination plots against Castro, this one failed.

After President Kennedy's death, the new Johnson administration decided to put the "marginal" and "tenuous" Cuban-American contacts "on ice." President Johnson also instructed his advisers to avoid "high risk actions" toward Cuba. Throughout the 1960s, as the United States became hostage to the war in Vietnam. Cuba receded as a top priority. Fidel Castro may have been correct when he remarked a decade after the missile crisis that Cuba "was saved by Vietnam. Who can say whether the immense American drive that went into Vietnam . . . would not have been turned against Cuba?" Except for a thaw in the mid to late-1970s, U.S.-Cuba relations remained frozen in hostility. Kennedy's "fixation" with Cuba fixed itself on U.S. Cuba policy for decades.

Aftermath

ERNEST R. MAY AND PHILIP D. ZELIKOW

Throughout the crisis, the Americans asked themselves repeatedly why the Soviets had decided to put missiles in Cuba despite Kennedy's explicit and repeated warnings. They differed in their guesses as to how the Soviets would react to U.S. statements and actions and why the Soviets did what they actually did. Why, for example, did most ships subject to Moscow's orders stop sailing for Cuba while some, particularly the *Gronzy,* kept going? Why did Soviet-manned SAM crews do nothing about U-2 flights from October 14 through October 26, then shoot one down on October 27? Why did Khrushchev change his terms for withdrawing the missiles? In the long private message received late on October 26, he seemed to say his only condition was a U.S. promise not to invade Cuba. In the message publicly broadcast on the morning of October 27 (U.S. time), he called in addition for removal of U.S. "offensive means" from Turkey. Why? And why, having publicly adopted this position, did Khrushchev back down on October 28?

Owing to the passage of time, the publication of memoirs by Khrushchev and others, and, most recently, a study by Aleksandr Fursenko and Timothy Naftali, based not only on newly opened archives but on Presidium and KGB files not yet accessible to other scholars, we have information on these questions well beyond that available to Kennedy and his circle. The two main findings are these. First, Kennedy and his advisers did not make any serious misjudgments about the Soviets. Most of what we know now confirms what was surmised by Kennedy's "demonologists," especially Thompson. Second, our best retrospective judgments about the Soviet side still entail guesswork; in all probability, no one will ever be able to answer with complete confidence *any* of the questions about the Soviets that bothered Kennedy and his advisers.

With these caveats, let us summarize what can now be said about each of the major puzzles, beginning with the question of why the Soviets put the missiles into Cuba and thus brought on the crisis. This actually separates, like a Russian doll, into several parts. Why did Khrushchev order in May 1962 that the Soviet Strategic Rocket Forces set up MRBM and IRBM launchers in Cuba, and why did he make such a secret of it? Had he announced his intentions or even told Kennedy privately that he planned to base IRBMs in Cuba, the crisis would have unfolded differently. Conceivably, there might have been no crisis at all. In the second meeting on October 16, Kennedy said, "Last month I should have said that we don't care." Looking back years later, Theodore Sorensen speculated that, if Kennedy had had foreknowledge, he might not have taken such a firm position: "I believe the President drew the line precisely where the Soviets were not and would not be; that is to say, if we had known that the Soviets were putting forty missiles in Cuba, we might under this hypothesis have drawn the line at one hundred, and said with great fanfare that we would absolutely not tolerate the presence of more than one hundred missiles in Cuba." It was the fact that Khrushchev lied to Kennedy and tried to surprise him that made the missile deployments such an excruciating test of Kennedy's mettle and the credibility of the United States. Why did Khrushchev not at least *consider* telling Kennedy what he had in mind?

Since the missiles were only en route to Cuba when Kennedy issued his September 4 warning, why did Khrushchev not at least pause to reconsider what he was doing? Since the Soviets understood the U-2's capabilities and knew that the United States conducted reconnaissance over Cuba, what made any of them think the secret could be kept? What did they plan to do if the secret were not to be kept? And, if the secret were kept, what did they plan to do, once the missiles were fully in place?

To explain the original Soviet decision, Kennedy and his advisers considered several hypotheses. Their favorite was that Khrushchev intended the missiles in Cuba as levers to loosen U.S. concessions regarding Berlin. A second hypothesis focused on the strategic balance. The Joint Chiefs of Staff, for example, presumed that Khrushchev had gambled as he did in order to get wider target coverage against the United States and offset the American lead in ICBMs. A third hypothesis was that Khrushchev had acted in order to protect Cuba from invasion. The only person in the Executive Committee who came close to asserting this view was Thompson, who argued, in the afternoon meeting of October 27, that the Jupiters in Turkey were of secondary interest to the Soviets. "The important thing for Khrushchev," he said, "is to be able to say: I saved Cuba. I stopped an invasion." (But Thompson was speaking then of how Khrushchev could save face; he was not necessarily saying that defense of Cuba had been uppermost among Khrushchev's original motives.) A fourth hypothesis presumed factional interplay in the Kremlin. Thus, whatever the motive or motives, they might not be Khrushchev's own. To account for the difference in content between Khrushchev's private letter and broadcast message, [McGeorge] Bundy [Special Assistant to the President] hazarded that the former was Khrushchev's, the latter that of "hard-nosed people overruling him."

Since 1962 no other hypotheses have been advanced to supplement the four voiced by Kennedy and his advisers. But they have had different fates. Berlin, oddly, dropped from sight. Hardly anyone writing retrospectively about the crisis, except the participants, stressed Berlin as a possible primary factor in Soviet decisions. The strategic-balance hypothesis proved more hardy. Two RAND analysts wrote a book not long after the crisis, developing at length the strategic-balance rationale for Khrushchev's actions. This argument has remained an important strain in writings about the crisis by historians and political scientists specializing in international relations or security studies. But the defense-of-Cuba hypothesis has proved the most robust and longest-lived, especially among historians. This view has derived its strength and longevity not only from the United States' demonstrated "arrogance of power" (in Senator Fulbright's phrase) before, during, and since the Vietnam War but also from documentary revelations concerning Operation Mongoose and pre-crisis invasion planning, as well as testimony from Khrushchev and other Russians.

What we now know indicates that Kennedy and his advisers understood the reasoning in the Kremlin better than have most scholars writing about the crisis in retrospect. While Khrushchev and his colleagues did indeed care a great deal about Cuba, the thought of deterring a U.S. invasion figures only incidentally in their discussions about the missile deployments. Calculations about the strategic nuclear balance were much more in evidence. Berlin was an omnipresent and dominating concern.

To summarize what we know about Soviet deliberations in 1962 is not, however, to state a final verdict on the motives guiding Soviet behavior before and during the crisis. The more we learn about Soviet decision-making in the Khrushchev era, the less confidence we can feel in any analyses that explain decisions in terms of a hierarchy of interest calculations. Eight points emerge from the accumulating evidence:

1. To interpret Soviet decisions is to interpret Khrushchev. He alone decided on policy. Other members of the Soviet elite who favored other policies could have their way only when Khrushchev was not around or not paying attention. No one could overrule him—yet.

2. Khrushchev made decisions largely on his own. Now and then, he would talk over a question with a fellow member of the Politburo or someone from the bureaucracy, but he did not systematically seek even advice, let alone policy analysis. He looked upon other members of the Politburo as potential enemies. He may have had some respect for military leaders; he treasured memories of working with generals on the Ukrainian front in World War II. But he probably heeded military men only with regard to narrowly military issues. Khrushchev never obtained advice and analysis such as Kennedy obtained from his Executive Committee, and, given the quality of the rest of the Soviet leadership, he could not have got it if he had tried.

3. Khrushchev acted more from instinct than from calculation. Whether Berlin or the strategic balance or concern about Cuba was uppermost in his mind at the time he ordered the missiles sent to Cuba, he himself could probably not have said. Having made a decision, however, he tended not to entertain second thoughts unless and until he had no choice. In both foreign and domestic affairs, he behaved like a roulette player who chooses a number and puts chips on the number until it produces a big payoff or the stack of chips has disappeared. Searching for the right adjective with which to characterize him, Fyodor Burlatsky and Georgi Shaknazarov, who had been aides to Khrushchev, agreed on the word *azartnyi,* which means, in Russian, "reckless" or "hotheaded."

4. Khrushchev's instincts in foreign affairs were disciplined by relatively little experience or knowledge. Sixty-eight in 1962, he had been a coal miner as a youth and then a party functionary for most of his life. He was party boss in Moscow at the time of Stalin's death, when, by outmaneuvering better-educated and less plebeian rivals, he became number one in the hierarchy. For practical purposes, he did not think at all about the world outside the Soviet Union until the mid-1950s, when it fell to him to test whether Stalin had been right in prophesying that the capitalist-imperialists would wring the necks of his successors. His first encounter with capitalist-imperialist leaders came when he met Eisenhower at the Geneva summit conference in 1955.

5. The framework into which Khrushchev fitted what he learned about the outside world was built around a rather simplistic version of Marxism-Leninism. Although he was intelligent, quick, shrewd, and capable of subtlety, his observations of the outside world were influenced by tenets he had absorbed and taught in his decades of party work. When he visited the United States in 1959, he was eager to meet Wall Streeters because he had grown up believing that they called the tunes

for U.S. political leaders. He seems to have assumed that U.S. decisions would usually be governed by crass interest. By the same token, although he knew of and had participated in the brutalities of Stalinism, he retained a romantic belief that Soviet-style socialism did ride the wave of the future and did promise eventual happiness for humankind. This viewpoint helps to account for his "secret speech" at the Twentieth Party Congress in 1956, exposing Stalin's crimes, as well as for his boastful prophecies that movements of national liberation would eventually bury the West.

6. Because of his narrow experience of the outside world, Khrushchev probably misread Kennedy. At Geneva in 1955, he had been a bit awed by Eisenhower. He changed his estimate a bit when he visited the United States in 1959 and saw an Eisenhower weakened by medical problems and on his way out of power. When he saw Kennedy in 1961 at Vienna, Khrushchev was more impressed than he had expected to be by the "young millionaire and . . . son of a millionaire," but whereas he had come away from Geneva crediting Eisenhower with toughness, he came away from Vienna crediting Kennedy with "flexibility." He would later praise Kennedy for being "realistic enough to see that now the might of the socialist world equaled that of the capitalist world."

7. Khrushchev's thinking about foreign affairs had been molded by the Suez-Hungary crisis of 1956. Before that crisis, the United States had treated the Soviet Union as on a par with Britain and France. During the crisis, the United States temporarily broke with the British and French, deploring their surprise attack on Egypt and demanding that they desist. Khrushchev joined in this demand. Blustering, he threatened the British that, if they did not pull out of Egypt, the Soviet Union might use its "modern destructive weapons." The British and French did withdraw, largely because of diplomatic and economic pressure from Washington, but Khrushchev credited his threats with having had decisive effect.

Because Britain thereafter abandoned its previous pretensions, and France did so until General Charles de Gaulle came to power in 1958, the Soviet Union became by default the other superpower, even at the moment of brutally crushing opposition in Hungary. Thereafter, it became Khrushchev's standard practice to make demands and talk loudly about Soviet rockets. Though he had had to back down more than once when he found the West united with regard to Berlin, and the Americans unflinching, Khrushchev still derived from the Suez experience the lesson that the way to succeed with foreign powers was to rattle rockets in their faces.

8. Khrushchev's decisions were influenced by Kremlin politics, but not in the way suggested by Bundy's reference to his "hard-nosed people." Although Khrushchev was in absolute control in Moscow, he knew that he might on almost any day find himself absolutely not in control. After Stalin's death, police head Lavrenti Beria and Premier Georgi Malenkov had formed, along with Khrushchev, a ruling triumvirate. Beria had been removed from power by gunfire, arranged for him by Khrushchev and Malenkov. As indication that Soviet politics were becoming more humane, Malenkov's removal involved mere demotion. Similar things happened to other Khrushchev opponents. Murder went out of fashion. But Khrushchev could never for a single day forget that he, too, might receive the Soviet equivalent of the black spot. In the spring of 1962, forced to admit the failure of his programs to increase croplands and farm output, he had to announce 20–30 percent increases

in the state-controlled prices of basic foods. This moved triggered protest that, in one city near the Black Sea, exploded into a revolt put down only through machine-gun fire and mass arrests. Possibly to defend against having the military old guard also regard itself as an injured party, Khrushchev allowed the Presidium to reverse his earlier massive reduction in resources for the military and heavy industry. Thus the period of Khrushchev's crucial decision to send missiles to Cuba was one in which he seriously needed some success to offset a string of losses.

A few years later, as he dictated his memoirs, Khrushchev remembered that during an official visit to Bulgaria, from May 14 to 20, 1962, "one thought kept hammering at my brain: what will happen if we lose Cuba?" We now know that Soviet-Cuban relations were deeper and much more complex than Americans realized. The Soviets had begun providing covert assistance to the Castro government in the spring of 1959, and secretly arranged the first sales of arms that autumn, well before the U.S. government had decided whether Castro would be a friend or foe. Some Americans and many Cubans suspected that the Castro regime harbored a secret radical agenda, that the security ministries were being brought under the control of pro-Soviet Communists in order to pursue this revolutionary agenda at home and abroad, and that this faction included Fidel Castro's brother, Raul, and Che Guevara, if not Fidel himself. Evidence from Soviet files shows that these suspicions were well founded.

From 1960 onward Castro repeatedly predicted horrific scenarios involving U.S. action against him, then took actions that made his prophecies self-fulfilling. In March 1960, blaming American agents for the catastrophic explosion of a ship carrying arms into Havana from Belgium (there is no evidence of any U.S. involvement in the event), he denounced Washington publicly and privately and tightened his relations with Moscow. In anticipation of nationalizing U.S. property and liquidating his domestic opponents, he sought further Soviet military, economic, and intelligence assistance to contend with the U.S. intervention that he asserted would surely follow. The Kremlin obliged with "a blank check to buy whatever he needed," including direct cash payments to Fidel. Though Washington did not know all this, Castro's March 1960 attacks did catalyze the Eisenhower administration's decision to begin preparing covert operations to overthrow the Cuban leader.

In June 1960 Castro nationalized U.S. oil refineries (which had refused to refine Soviet crude oil) and again told the Soviets that an invasion was imminent. At about the same time Khrushchev received an intelligence report from a Soviet spy at NATO that the "chiefs at the Pentagon" were hoping to launch a preventive strike against the Soviet Union (the report was untrue). Apparently this report was taken seriously, for in early July Khrushchev gave a speech stressing Soviet capabilities for nuclear attack on the United States. In his best Suez-crisis vein, Khrushchev threatened that Soviet rockets might fly if Washington chose to invade Cuba. The speech delighted the Cuban leader, who told the Soviets they had deterred an American attack. Castro then publicized his closer friendship with Moscow.

There was another invasion scare in October 1960, Fursenko and Naftali discovered, this time based on rumors that Cuban exiles were being trained by the CIA in Guatemala. (Such training was in fact taking place, but the force was still months from being ready.) The Soviet and Cuban governments, however, genuinely believing an attack to be imminent, mobilized troops and sounded loud public alarms. Moscow again threatened use of its nuclear missiles. When the invasion did not come, the Cubans again believed the Soviet threats had deterred it. In early November, in a private address heard by Cuban Communists and the Soviet KGB resident, Castro extolled Marxism, professed always to have been a Marxist, and said again and again: "Moscow is our brain and our great leader, and we must pay attention to its voice."

Both the Cubans and the Soviets were caught by surprise when the Cuban exiles actually invaded, in April 1961. Khrushchev again thundered support for Castro and warnings to Washington, adding this time the threat that the flames ignited in Cuba could touch off a chain reaction leading to conflict across the globe. Again the Soviets took some credit for deterring Kennedy from providing the military support that might have made the invasion succeed. And the Americans still failed to grasp that the Soviets and Cubans credited Soviet missiles for an apparent series of deterrent successes.

Increasingly, Khrushchev and the Soviet government linked their prestige with Castro's. They held out Cuba as the prime example of success in their newly announced global strategy of undermining capitalism through wars of national liberation in the less developed world. It offered the chief proof that the Soviet Union, not China, remained the vanguard of world revolution. Loss of Cuba, Khrushchev acknowledged, "would have been a terrible blow to Marxism-Leninism" and "would gravely diminish our stature throughout the world, but especially in Latin America."

In the fall of 1961 Castro asked for much larger arms shipments and especially for large numbers of the most modern antiaircraft missile, the SA-2. Khrushchev did not immediately act on this costly request. In the interval, Castro purged his government of perceived rivals, criticized the Soviets for not acting with sufficient revolutionary boldness, and began talking with China about possible economic assistance. Particularly alarming from the standpoint of Moscow was Castro's ousting of Anibal Escalante, the leader of the Cuban Communist Party, and of practically all Escalante's pro-Moscow cadres. Occurring in March 1962, the "Escalante affair" brought Soviet-Cuban relations to a point of near crisis.

In early April the Soviet government decided to meet Castro's demand for SA-2s. In addition to wanting to pacify Castro and keep him in their camp, Soviet officials were concerned once again with the possibility of a U.S. invasion. They had inklings of Operation Mongoose and of contingency planning by the U.S. military. Khrushchev's son-in-law, the editor of *Pravda*, claimed to have heard President Kennedy say that he viewed Cuba much as Khrushchev viewed Hungary. Though KGB sources in Washington downplayed chances of an invasion, Khrushchev and others in the Soviet government paid more attention to whispers of danger. Khrushchev later explained why. "I'm not saying we had any documentary proof that the Americans were preparing a second invasion," he wrote in his memoirs, "we didn't need documentary proof. We knew the class affiliation, the class blindness of the United States, and that was enough to make us expect the worst." Hence, on April 12 the Presidium approved the delivery of about 180 SA-2 missiles to Cuba and a battery of Soviet coastal-defense cruise missiles, along with trainers and a regiment of regular Soviet troops. A military mission was to survey additional needs. The United States knew nothing of this.

No new information about threats to Cuba seems to have arrived in Moscow between April 12, when the Presidium approved the SA-2s, and May 24, when the Presidium authorized sending to Cuba an entire Group of Soviet Forces, including the ballistic missiles. On May 18 Castro did ask the military mission for more coastal-defense missiles, and possibly for more Soviet troops (his own later testimony is vague on this point). But neither Castro nor any other Cuban nor any Soviet representative in Cuba mentioned nuclear weapons. Knowing that the presence of nuclear weapons in his country could both provoke and legitimize an American attack, Castro had stated repeatedly that Cuba had "no intention to offer any part of its territory to any state for the establishment of military bases."

Khrushchev, however, had begun to ponder this possibility not long after the decision on the SA-2s. Anastas Mikoyan, who had served with Khrushchev under Stalin, had the dacha just next to Khrushchev's in the Lenin Hills. He was probably the member of the Politburo whom Khrushchev came nearest to trusting, and in late April, in one of their one-on-one backyard chats, Khrushchev mentioned to Mikoyan that he was thinking of basing ballistic missiles in Cuba. Mikoyan's son, from whom we have the report of this conversation, says that his father reacted negatively. He had been to Cuba and had helped cement relations with Castro, and he predicted that Castro would reject the idea out of fear of the U.S. reaction. If Mikoyan did indeed try to discourage Khrushchev, he did not succeed. Khrushchev broached his idea to Defense Minister Rodion Malinovsky, who instantly became an enthusiastic supporter. Knowing not only that the Soviet Union was far behind the United States in ICBMs but that the existing ICBMs (SS-6s) were monstrous weapons of doubtful reliability and that successor models (SS-7s and SS-8s) were stalled in the two missile design bureaus, Malinovsky recognized in Khrushchev's proposal a way of shortening the time required to even the strategic balance. And Khrushchev was apparently enthusiastic. "Why not throw a hedgehog at Uncle Sam's pants?" he asked Malinovsky.

Certainly the Americans did not fully grasp how deeply, in the spring of 1962, Khrushchev and his colleagues felt that, in Malinovsky's words, "our inferior position was impossible to us." The United States touched the Soviets on the raw by completing the long-delayed deployment of 15 Jupiter IRBMs at 5 launch sites in Turkey. The first was set up in November 1961, the last in March 1962. The Soviets had known all about the planned deployment for years. Moscow had complained loudly about NATO's public decision, especially during 1958 and 1959, and probably knew that the missiles had finally been put in place. Although there is no evidence that Soviet planners attached any particular strategic significance to these obsolete systems or even to the nuclear-armed U.S. aircraft based in Turkey, which should have been more worrisome militarily, the deployment may have made it easier for Khrushchev and others to rationalize the decision concerning the missiles in Cuba. . . .

What happened after Khrushchev's initial talks with Mikoyan and Malinovsky remains murky. Apparently, Khrushchev put together a small group of top officials to consider the idea. Malinovsky's newly appointed deputy, also newly appointed as head of the Soviet Strategic Rocket Forces, Marshal Sergei S. Biryuzov, not only supported Malinovsky's view regarding the strategic advantages of missiles in Cuba but ventured the opinion that the missiles could be deployed without being discovered by the Americans. Mikoyan's son says that his father, who knew Cuban geography at first hand, regarded Biryuzov as "a fool" and was amazed that the marshal "thought there were places in the mountains where the Americans would not discover the missiles."

At the end of April the most trusted Soviet envoy in Havana, Alexander Alexeev (then the KGB resident), was recalled to Moscow, without knowing why. On May 7 Khrushchev told him that he would become the new ambassador to Cuba. On May 20, after returning from a weeklong trip to Bulgaria, Khrushchev summoned Alexeev and asked him how Castro would respond to a Soviet deployment of nuclear missiles to Cuba. A bit dumbfounded and intimidated, Alexeev, Moscow's premier expert on Fidel Castro, said he "could never suppose that Fidel Castro would agree to such a thing." Cuba was relying on its own defenses, built with Soviet aid. If the Soviet government "installed missiles, I thought this would provoke a rejection of the Cuban Revolution from the rest of the hemisphere."

Malinovsky immediately took issue with Alekseev, refusing to believe that "a socialist country could refuse our aid." Khrushchev said nothing, and then informed Alekseev that he and Marshal Biryuzov would be joining a delegation to Havana to explain matters to Castro. On May 21 Khrushchev formally presented his plan to the Defense Council, consisting of top civilian and military leaders (no uniformed military men were members of the Presidium), and received its unanimous approval. The initiative was then formally drafted by General Staff officers and presented by Malinovsky at a combined meeting of the Presidium and the Defense Council on May 24. Khrushchev offered his comments. After a pro forma discussion everyone agreed to the proposal. Five days later the delegation was in Havana.

Castro reluctantly agreed to the deployment. Though he was told over and over that the deployment was only for his own good, he and his colleagues always thought, and often said, that they were helping the Soviets change the global balance of military power in favor of socialism. Castro expected that the deployment would produce an intense crisis, but "we really trusted that they [the Soviets] were acting with knowledge of the entire situation."

Several other options were available to the Soviets. They could have signed a defense treaty with Cuba without deploying forces; deployed purely conventional forces, as already planned, forcing U.S. invaders to risk direct conflict with Soviet forces; deployed conventional forces armed with purely tactical nuclear weapons that could reach offshore targets but not the continental United States; or deployed nuclear-armed bombers, presenting a slower-moving and less nerve-racking challenge to the Americans. But apparently, none of these options had been analyzed except the flow of conventional arms authorized by the Presidium decision of April 12 and discussed by the subsequent military mission to Cuba. Certainly Khrushchev did not analyze them in any visible way. For the Soviet General Staff, Khrushchev's plan "was like a roll of thunder in a clear sky."

In addition to the deployments of arms and forces envisioned by the earlier decisions to aid Cuba (including the 140 air-defense missile launchers), Moscow followed up Castro's agreement with plans, approved in June, to deploy 40 land-based ballistic-missile launchers and 60 missiles in 5 missile regiments. These would be part of a full-size Group of Soviet Forces, more than 45,000 strong, with 4 motorized rifle regiments (and more than 250 armored fighting vehicles), a wing of the latest Soviet fighter aircraft (the MiG-21), about 80 nuclear-capable cruise missiles for coastal defense, and a regiment of more than 40 IL-28s.

After the fact the Americans speculated that the Soviets intended to develop Cuba into a full-scale strategic base. They were correct. The operation also included a plan to build a submarine base that would become the home port for an initial deployment of 11 submarines, including 7 carrying submarine-launched ballistic missiles (SLBMs) with 1-megaton-yield nuclear warheads. Basing Soviet missile submarines in the Caribbean would have transformed the strategic power of this previously weak and vulnerable arm of Moscow's nuclear forces.

In addition to the nuclear warheads for the ballistic missiles, low-yield nuclear weapons, each with an explosive power comparable to that of the atomic bombs used against Japan in 1945, would be provided for the coastal-defense cruise missiles. The Americans did not know that these cruise missiles were deployed with nuclear warheads. Nor did the Soviets plan to reveal this fact to them.

Khrushchev also checked his judgment, mainly with Biryuzov, on whether the deployment could be concealed, given that U.S. surveillance aircraft frequently overflew Cuba. After traveling to Cuba, Biryuzov and his delegation reported back that the terrain and camouflage efforts would indeed shield the missile sites from U.S. surveillance.

In July 1962 Raul Castro visited Moscow carrying one question for Khrushchev from Fidel: What would happen if the operation was discovered while in progress? Khrushchev answered that there was nothing to worry about; if there was trouble he would send out the Baltic fleet as a show of support. Castro later acknowledged that the Cubans "did not think that it was the Baltic fleet that would solve the problem. What we were thinking about was Soviet will and determination, about Soviet strength. And we got the statement of the top leader of the Soviet Union that there was nothing to worry about, that he would not allow it. So what was really protecting us was the global strategic might of the U.S.S.R., not the rockets here." Castro was presuming that Khrushchev had thought through how he would handle a nuclear confrontation if the missile deployment was discovered before it was complete. As Castro himself later realized, there is no evidence that Khrushchev ever seriously considered this question.

Khrushchev did have an image of what would happen if he succeeded in presenting the United States with a *fait accompli*. The Kennedy administration, he believed, would "swallow this bitter pill. . . . I knew that the United States could knock out some of our installations, but not all of them. If a quarter or even a tenth of our missiles survived—even if only one or two big ones were left—we could still hit New York, and there wouldn't be much of New York left." Viewing Kennedy as a young, inexperienced intellectual presiding over a dangerously bellicose military establishment, Khrushchev apparently thought that Kennedy would let him get away with trickery, and that he would end up with both the Soviet Union and Cuba better protected against the "chiefs in the Pentagon."

Khrushchev did not ask whether his ambassador in Washington or any other experts shared his estimate of the United States. Gromyko claimed later to have warned Khrushchev privately that "putting our missiles in Cuba would cause a political explosion in the United States," but that Khrushchev was unmoved by this advice. Commenting that Khrushchev "grossly misunderstood the psychology of his opponents," Ambassador Anatoly Dobrynin complained later: "Had he asked the embassy beforehand, we could have predicted the violent American reaction to his adventure once it became known. It is worth noting that Castro understood this. . . . But Khrushchev wanted to spring a surprise on Washington; it was he who got the surprise in the end when his secret plan was uncovered."

On May 12, in the midst of the key decisions about sending missiles to Cuba, Khrushchev spent about 14 hours with Kennedy's press aide, Pierre Salinger, then visiting Moscow. He barely mentioned Cuba. The central issue, Khrushchev said, was Berlin. Dobrynin, who took up his post at about this time, remembered that "Germany and Berlin overshadowed everything." Describing what he expected to be his position when negotiations on Berlin resumed, Khrushchev had written to Kennedy in 1961: "You have to understand, I have no ground to retreat further, there is a precipice behind."

The expression "precipice behind" vividly conveys the value Khrushchev now attached to success on Berlin. In another letter to Kennedy, Khrushchev protested that Washington's willingness to threaten a nuclear war to protect Berlin "can rest, excuse my harsh judgments, only on the megalomania, on an intention to act from the position of strength." In March 1962 he had promised Kennedy that "one way or another" he would force the Western troops out. In late April the negotiations in Geneva between Gromyko and Rusk had reached a stalemate over Berlin. Angering his West German allies, Kennedy had been willing to offer a *modus vivendi* that might allow the status quo to continue. But this had not been good enough for the Soviet government, which denounced the failure of the talks at the end of April.

Thus, in late April and early May 1962, when Khrushchev was in the final stages of his decision to send missiles to Cuba, Berlin clearly had a large place in his thinking. Having issued ultimatums in 1958 and again in 1961, demanding Western departure from Berlin by specified deadlines, and having let those deadlines pass with the promise of successful negotiations to the same end, he was being forced to acknowledge failure publicly. East Germans were demanding a tougher Soviet policy. The Americans, relying on their nuclear superiority, were pursuing a "policy of strength." In March 1962 Khrushchev told Dobrynin, just before the new ambassador left for Washington, that Berlin was the principal issue in U.S.-Soviet relations, said the U.S. was acting "particularly arrogant" about its nuclear deterrent, and concluded, "It's high time their long arms were cut shorter." He liked Kennedy and considered him a man of character, yet he also clearly believed "that putting pressure on Kennedy might bring us some success."

In Moscow, Ambassador Thompson, ignorant of Khrushchev's plans to send missiles to Cuba, was puzzled. No American knew Khrushchev better or had followed his positions more closely. Thompson could not understand why Khrushchev was increasing pressure on Berlin. "He must surely know our position is firm," and "it does not seem reasonable that he would wish further to commit his personal prestige which [is] already deeply engaged." And the pressure just kept increasing. The Soviets began telling Americans that, though they would wait until after the U.S. congressional elections, the Berlin issue would be forced to a conclusion in November.

By the beginning of September 1962 Khrushchev had arranged to unveil the existence of the missiles in Cuba and publicly sign a treaty with Castro in late November, after the congressional elections. He also planned, probably in a speech to the United Nations on the same trip, to renew his ultimatum for final resolution of the Berlin crisis, demanding the withdrawal of Western troops from their sectors. Khrushchev knew the United States would threaten war if he carried out his ultimatum. But by that time Khrushchev would have the missiles, poised in Cuba, to help him call America's bluff and finally carry his 4-year-old Berlin policy to a successful conclusion. . . .

Khrushchev's plans began to go awry at the end of August, when a U-2 overflight discovered the installation of some of the SA-2 air-defense missiles. President Kennedy then issued his September 4 warning to Khrushchev against placing "offensive weapons" in Cuba (an ambiguous term, but the Soviets knew what the Americans meant). The Americans, at least Bundy, speculated in the White House meetings that Khrushchev had not reacted to the warning because the decision to deploy the missiles had already been made. Bundy was half right.

The decision had been made, but the nuclear weapons themselves had still not been shipped. Khrushchev feared that the Americans might attack Cuba before the nuclear deterrent could be put in place. So, rather than abandon the deployment, he decided to add to it by rushing tactical nuclear weapons to Cuba that could immediately be used against invading ground forces. These rockets were called Lunas by the Soviets and FROGs in the West (for Free Rocket Over Ground). Khrushchev, vacationing at the Black Sea resort at Pitsunda, bullied the U.S. visitor, Stewart Udall, threatening that he could "swat your [America's] ass" if the United States chose to fight for Berlin. On the same day he received a visit from Mikoyan, bearing a report on how to get more nuclear weapons to Cuba. On September 7 Khrushchev approved the dispatch of 6 Luna rocket launchers with 12 nuclear-armed rockets, and 6 nuclear bombs for the IL-28s already being sent to Cuba. The Defense Ministry dissuaded Khrushchev from sending these weapons by airplane to Cuba. Instead they would be added to the shipment of MRBM warheads that would leave the Soviet Union on September 15. The ship left on schedule and arrived in Cuba on October 4. Khrushchev's other reaction to Kennedy's warning was the September 11 TASS statement that promised to defend Cuba while saying there was no need to send any missiles there. . . .

To provide defense against U-2 surveillance, Khrushchev had suggested in July that the SA-2 air-defense missiles go in first so they could shoot down U-2s and thwart detection of the missile installation. The vast plan for the shipments was reorganized accordingly, and the SA-2 missiles were in place and operational by late September. American fears of a U-2 shootdown had, after some discussion, deterred direct overflights of Cuba for more than a month, but they resumed in mid-October.

Soviet troops in Cuba had tracked the U-2 overflights of October 14, 15, and 17, but, strangely, they had orders not to fire at U.S. planes unless attacked. The missiles to shoot down the U-2s were in place, but were not allowed to fire at them. We have no evidence on why this was so. Perhaps in the aftermath of Kennedy's September warnings, the central authorities in Moscow did not want any clash and, for this or other reasons, had left in place standing orders not to fire, without covering the U-2 contingency. The Soviet forces in Cuba realized at the time of the overflights that the missile sites and IL-28s could well have been discovered. Fingers were pointed about adequate camouflage, though the construction of such complex sites for such large missiles was inherently hard to conceal. Yet, in a further mystery, there is no evidence that the commanders in Cuba ever dared to tell Moscow that the missile sites had been overflown and that the Americans probably knew about the missiles.

The Kremlin plunged into its own crisis deliberations on October 22, with news of the impending Kennedy speech. Unlike Kennedy, Khrushchev continued his usual foreign-policy process, consulting a small group of Presidium members aided by the defense and foreign ministers and the leading international expert from the Communist Party's Central Committee. When a formal decision was needed, Khrushchev convened the full Presidium. At this point the 36 MRBMs (for 24 launchers) were in Cuba, with their nuclear warheads. So were nearly 100 other nuclear warheads for the coastal-defense missiles, short-range rockets, and IL-28 bombers. Nuclear warheads to be carried on the IRBMs (for the 18 launch sites still under construction) were also in Cuba. The IRBMs themselves were still at sea.

Khrushchev worried that the Americans would attack Cuba. He considered turning the nuclear weapons over to the Cubans and letting them respond. But he assured his colleagues he would not let Castro use the MRBMs against the United States. Perhaps the Cubans could deter an invasion simply by threatening use of the short-range tactical nuclear weapons against an invading force. In such a case, of course, a U.S. air strike, by itself, would in effect be uncontested.

The Presidium first decided that Malinovsky should cable General Issa Pliyev, the commander of Soviet troops in Cuba, ordering him to bring his troops to combat readiness and to use all Cuban and Soviet forces, except the nuclear arms, to meet an attack. Then, changing its mind, it considered a message authorizing use of the tactical nuclear weapons but not the ballistic missiles. Malinovsky was uneasy about this instruction, worrying that the Americans might intercept it and use it as a pretext for striking with their own nuclear weapons. So the Kremlin sent the first draft, withholding final authorization for use of the nuclear weapons.

News of Kennedy's speech, announcing the quarantine, was greeted with relief when it arrived in the early morning of October 23. Reports also arrived from Soviet envoys. Dobrynin characterized the U.S. move as a general effort to reverse a decline in its world power, partly as a result of fears about Berlin. He warned that the Americans were preparing for a real test of strength, and then recommended that Moscow threaten a move against Berlin, starting with a ground blockade and "leaving out for the time being air routes so as not to give grounds for a quick confrontation." Yet Dobrynin added that Moscow should not be in a hurry actually to implement a blockade, "since an extreme aggravation of the situation, it goes without saying, would not be in our interests." Alexeev meanwhile reported from Havana that the Cubans had mobilized, would not fire on U.S. planes unless they fired first, would await the Soviet response, "and are placing their hopes on the wisdom of our decisions."

Relieved that the Americans had not attacked Cuba, and considering the U.S. imposition of a blockade a weaker response that left room for political maneuver, the Kremlin issued its flat, tough response on October 23. Khrushchev and his Presidium did decide to halt most of the 30 ships en route to Cuba, but they directed that the 4 carrying IRBMs and a fifth, loaded with nuclear warheads for these missiles, continue on course. They ordered that the 4 nuclear-armed submarines headed for Cuba also keep going. When Kuznetsov echoed Dobrynin's suggestion of countering the blockade with pressure against West Berlin, Khrushchev answered sharply that he could "do without such advice . . . we had no intention to add fuel to the conflict." Thus, General Curtis LeMay may have been right when he told Kennedy on October 19 that U.S. nuclear might would continue to safeguard Berlin. Nevertheless, some Soviet officials were ready to consider the option.

Tension increased on October 24. That morning brought Kennedy's brief, unyielding demand for strict Soviet observance of the OAS quarantine. It also brought Dobrynin's cable, reporting Robert Kennedy's saying flatly, "we intend to stop your ships." Replying defiantly to Kennedy, Khrushchev declared that Soviet captains would run the blockade. At the same time, however, the Presidium decision of the previous day was apparently reversed. As McCone reported on the morning of October 24, a fresh burst of signals had gone out to Soviet ships at sea in midmorning (Moscow time). The ships carrying the IRBMs now halted. A few ships with more innocent cargos, including the *Bucharest* and *Grozny,* became the ones sailing ahead to test the quarantine. (The ship carrying the nuclear warheads had already made it to a Cuban port.) It is possible but unlikely that this occurred without Khrushchev's knowledge, though he did not advise the Presidium of any change in orders and, indeed, spoke at its meeting on October 25 as if the ships carrying IRBMs were continuing on their way. Actual Soviet behavior justified Rusk's conclusion that, in the face of American firmness, Khrushchev "blinked." . . .

Khrushchev also criticized Kennedy's handling of the crisis, observing that Eisenhower would have handled it in a more mature way and remarking that Kennedy was younger than his eldest son. Khrushchev also said: "You cannot now take over Cuba." He admitted that ballistic missiles with nuclear warheads had been supplied to Cuba, but said the Cubans were volatile people and all the weapons were under the control of Soviet officers and would be used only if Cuba was attacked. If the United States really wanted to know what kind of weapons could defend Cuba, the Americans only had to attack, and they would find out very quickly. He said, according to Knox's report, that he was not interested in the destruction of the world, but if we all wanted to meet in hell, it was up to them. . . .

On the morning of October 25 the Soviet leadership had Kennedy's tough, terse reply to Khrushchev's message. Khrushchev reconvened the Presidium. He told them he did not want to trade "caustic remarks" any longer with Kennedy. Instead he wanted to turn around 4 ships that were still carrying IRBMs to Cuba and try to resolve the crisis. Conciliation had supplanted the previous day's defiance. Khrushchev announced to the Presidium his readiness to "dismantle the missiles to make Cuba into a zone of peace." He suggested sending a message including the words "Give us a pledge not to invade Cuba, and we will remove the missiles." He was also prepared to allow UN inspection of the missile sites. First, though, he wanted to be able to "look around" and be sure Kennedy really would not yield.

There is little evidence to explain why Khrushchev had changed his mind and decided to give in. Perhaps the tone of Kennedy's letter had underscored the certainty of a confrontation that Moscow could not hope to win without threatening nuclear retaliation, and Khrushchev was unwilling to make this threat. In any event, the Presidium approved his plan with the usual unanimous vote.

Later on October 25 the Soviets presumably received news that the *Bucharest* had been allowed to proceed toward Cuba. They may also have received news that the Americans had begun low-level reconnaissance flights over Cuba. On that day U Thant also issued his new appeal that Khrushchev keep his ships away from the quarantine line and that the United States avoid a direct confrontation. Khrushchev sent no messages to the U.S. government.

Khrushchev was stirred to action on October 26. That morning, according to Fursenko and Naftali, he received a series of intelligence reports of increased U.S. military readiness and preparations. Among these a KGB report from Washington stood out, saying that, according to a well-connected American journalist, a U.S. attack on Cuba was "prepared to the last detail" and "could begin at any moment." This report was based on conversations with Warren Rogers, a reporter for the *New York Herald Tribune,* who had simply expressed his own freewheeling, confident personal opinion. His status as the lead source on Khrushchev's desk that morning speaks volumes about the quality of Soviet intelligence and Soviet analysis.

Khrushchev presumably also received a report cabled on October 25 from Alexeev in Havana. Alexeev said that Castro had approved of the Soviet action to avoid a confrontation on the quarantine line. However, Castro now wanted to shoot down "one or two piratic American planes over Cuban territory" (that is, U.S. reconnaissance planes), and the Cuban leader did not take rumors of a possible U.S. invasion very seriously.

Khrushchev promptly made several moves. He sent instructions to accept U Thant's proposal for avoiding a confrontation at the quarantine line, thereby promising to keep Soviet ships away from this line. He also dictated the long letter to Kennedy suggesting a peaceful resolution of the crisis: if the United States would promise not to invade Cuba, "the necessity for the presence of our military specialists in Cuba would disappear." More a hint than a concrete proposal, this message was well within the guidelines approved by the Presidium the previous day, so Khrushchev did not seek that body's formal approval, but merely sent copies of the letter to the members. Khrushchev may also have suggested that a Soviet official in New York (probably KGB) urge U Thant to suggest a deal trading a noninvasion pledge for withdrawal of the missiles, though this cannot be confirmed. When the KGB resident in Washington, Feklisov, broached this idea to journalist John Scali that day, he was acting on his own initiative, perhaps prompted by his own worries about the ominous indicators that he had been reporting to Moscow. . . .

With his October 26 letter to Kennedy, Khrushchev had moved to defuse the threat of an imminent invasion, but he had still not conceded anything concrete. Moreover, by keeping the correspondence private, he had hidden his tentative move from Castro. Soviet military activity in Cuba continued without respite. By the next morning, October 27, Khrushchev came to a judgment, for reasons that are still obscure, that the Americans could be pushed harder. Perhaps he misjudged the signals being sent by the way they were enforcing the quarantine. In direct contrast to Castro, whose relaxed attitude about a U.S. invasion had switched to alarm on October 26, Khrushchev had switched from alarm on October 26 to a more relaxed attitude on October 27.

The Soviet commander in Cuba, General Issa Pliyev, reported to the Defense Ministry that the Cubans had concluded that a U.S. air strike would begin that night or at dawn on October 27 and that Castro had ordered air-defense units to fire at American aircraft if there was an attack. Pliyev said that he had dispersed nuclear warheads closer to their launchers. The Soviet leaders endorsed Pliyev's plans.

Nevertheless, when Khrushchev convened the Presidium he told them that the United States would not dare to attack Cuba. Five days had passed since Kennedy's speech, and nothing had happened. "To my mind they are not ready to do it now." Since, however, there was no guarantee against a U.S. attack, Khrushchev would make another, more concrete offer that both acknowledged the presence of missiles in Cuba and added the U.S. missiles in Turkey to the bargain. With that, he said, "we would win."

Just as there is little evidence to explain why Khrushchev reversed his assessment of U.S. intentions, there is little evidence to explain why he now chose to add the Turkish missiles as a bargaining point. The missiles in Turkey had not been an important topic in any of the previous Presidium discussions during the crisis. . . .

Khrushchev then further reduced the chance of success for his latest initiative by making his offer public. This move made U.S. acceptance extremely unlikely, especially given the implications for NATO of such a public trade. A public deal might save face for Khrushchev, but no face would be saved if the Americans rejected it—which almost any analyst would have predicted. The Turks publicly rejected the trade just as the Americans started to discuss it. Castro certainly expected the Americans to reject such a deal, and Alexeev reported to Moscow that Castro was comforted by that very prospect.

There is no evidence that Khrushchev or any member of the Presidium analyzed this point. Apparently the new proposal was broadcast over the radio in the interest of reducing transmission time, and "nobody foresaw that by making public the Turkish angle of the deal we created additional difficulties to the White House." Of course, Khrushchev's actions may not have been thoughtless. He could have offered a deal in order to stalemate the negotiations, not further them. The position was well designed for public consumption, if not for U.S. acceptance. Khrushchev may have hoped that the Americans would effectively back down by virtue of entering into prolonged and fruitless negotiations. But if this was Khrushchev's gambit, it was another example of recklessness, for the U.S reaction could well have been to abandon negotiations and turn to the use of military force. In fact, this was how most of President Kennedy's advisers did react.

Having dictated the message to President Kennedy, Khrushchev and his colleagues had second thoughts about Pliyev's dispersal of nuclear weapons. An order was quickly sent to Pliyev not to employ any nuclear weapons without express authorization from Moscow. Khrushchev also sent a message to Havana urging Alexeev to caution Castro against any rash actions.

Events during October 27 must have battered Khrushchev's complacency. A message from Castro, sent from Cuba on October 26, announced that a massive U.S. air strike and possibly also an invasion, was "almost inevitable" in the next 24 to 72 hours. In the event of invasion, Castro urged Khrushchev to consider "elimination of such a danger," plainly referring to use of Soviet nuclear weapons against the United States. "However difficult and horrifying this decision may be," Castro wrote, "there is, I believe, no other recourse."

The same day brought news about the incursion of the American U-2 into Siberian airspace. We have no evidence about how Khrushchev viewed that episode.

Then the Cubans shot at unarmed U.S. low-level reconnaissance aircraft. On October 26 Castro had given the order to fire on any aircraft entering Cuban airspace. Alexeev had reported this intention on October 25, but Moscow seems not to have noticed. Castro discussed his order with Soviet commanders on October 26; this fact may have been reported to Moscow too. On October 27 Khrushchev sent instructions to Alexeev to suggest that Castro rescind the order; but by then, of course, it was too late, even if Castro had wished to heed the advice.

When the U-2 came over it too was apparently, and falsely, perceived as posing a threat. Authority to fire had been delegated in the event of an American attack, and the local Soviet commanders (below Pliyev himself, who was temporarily unavailable) choose to interpret their instructions liberally in order to aid their excited Cuban comrades. Although a Soviet missile actually downed the plane, Khrushchev seems not to have fully grasped this fact until some time later.

Late in the afternoon of October 27 Khrushchev would have heard that the Americans had immediately rejected his public proposal with a press statement of their own. Alexeev reported telling Castro that "in the present circumstances it would not be fitting to aggravate the situation and initiate provocations." Castro understood, but "considering the rise in the army's martial spirit and the Americans' warning, our friends were compelled to take such a step."

Khrushchev was reportedly quite worried about the shootdown of the U-2. He was certainly a bit unnerved by Castro's urging to prepare for using nuclear weapons against the United States. A few days later, in another message to Castro, Khrushchev referred to this "very alarming" message in which "you proposed that we be the first to carry out a nuclear strike against the enemy's territory." Naturally, Khrushchev added, "you understand where that would lead us. It would not be a simple strike, but the start of a thermonuclear world war."

Kennedy's message to Khrushchev arrived late that evening, laying out the deal that would entail the verified withdrawal of Soviet "offensive weapons" in exchange for the noninvasion pledge. Khrushchev opened the Presidium session on the morning of October 28 with a very different assessment from the day before. He warned his colleagues that they were "face to face with the danger of war and of nuclear catastrophe, with the possible result of destroying the human race." He went on: "In order to save the world, we must retreat."

The new assessment was *not* apparently based on news of Robert Kennedy's October 27 conversation with Dobrynin. *After* Khrushchev made his declaration to the Politburo, word came in of the cable from Dobrynin reporting on the discussion in bleak, ominous terms. A summary of the cable was read to the Presidium. One of Khrushchev's staff recalled that the "entire tenor of the words by the President's brother, as they were relayed by Anatoly Dobrynin, prompted the conclusion that the time of reckoning had come." Khrushchev later told Castro that his warning of an imminent U.S. attack had been confirmed by other sources and that he had hurried to prevent it.

Khrushchev's resolve to yield was redoubled by Robert Kennedy's reported warning, and by his assurance that Jupiters would eventually be withdrawn from Turkey. Reportedly only Khrushchev, Gromyko, and Mikoyan had much to say at this Presidium session. "Others preferred to keep silent as if hinting to Khrushchev that since he had made his bed, he could sleep on it."

The tension was compounded by a report that at 5:00 P.M. Moscow time (9:00 A.M. in Washington), President Kennedy would be making another speech to the American people. In fact this was only going to be a rebroadcast of Kennedy's October 22 speech, but Khrushchev and his advisers feared an imminent announcement of U.S. military action. An urgent, conciliatory reply was prepared and hurriedly broadcast over the radio to be sure it reached Washington in time. Another message was rushed to Dobrynin in Washington, directing him to "quickly get in touch with R. Kennedy" and to pass on the following "urgent response: The thoughts which R. Kennedy expressed at the instruction of the President find understanding in Moscow. Today, an answer will be given by radio . . . and that response will be the most favorable. The main thing which disturbs the President, precisely the issue of the dismantling under international control of the rocket bases in Cuba, meets no objection and will be explained in detail." Pliyev received a cable chiding him for having been in such a "hurry" to shoot down the U-2. He was ordered to ground all Soviet jets in Cuba to avoid any further clashes with U.S. reconnaissance aircraft.

There was no time to consult with Castro. He learned of Khrushchev's decision over the radio, along with the rest of the world.

After the missile crisis was over, in January 1963, Khrushchev began walking away from his failed Berlin policy, by simply declaring victory. He began to argue that he had really won because in 1961 he had forced the West to accept the construction of the Berlin Wall and to live with a divided Berlin. This had not, of course, been his position in 1962.

Khrushchev still could not stop wondering whether the Americans would really have gone to nuclear war over Berlin. Surely they would not have made such a threat unless they were incredibly complacent about their nuclear superiority. His Cuban deployment would have punctured that complacency. It would have vividly demonstrated the vulnerability he wanted the Americans to feel, the vulnerability that should, would restrain them. After the Cuban venture failed, even after he had then also abandoned his 1962 plan of action on Berlin, Khrushchev still wanted to know: Had Washington been bluffing? In August 1963 Khrushchev asked Rusk point-blank: "Why should I believe that you Americans would fight a nuclear war over Berlin?" Rusk remembered, "That was quite a question . . . So I stared back at him and said, 'Mr. Chairman, you will have to take into account the possibility that we Americans are just goddamn fools.' We glared at each other, unblinking, and then he changed the subject and gave me three gold watches to take home to my children."

In November 1963 President Kennedy was murdered by a gunman who had long harbored grievances about Kennedy's hostility toward Castro's Cuba. In October 1964 Khrushchev was ousted from power by his Presidium colleagues. "You insisted that we deploy our missiles in Cuba," one of his Presidium accusers thundered. "This provoked the deepest crisis, carried the world to the brink of nuclear war, and even frightened terribly the organizer of this very danger." Khrushchev was blamed for the humiliating defeat.

⋙ *F U R T H E R   R E A D I N G*

Allison, Graham T. *Essence of Decision: Explaining the Cuban Missile Crisis* (1971).
Allison, Graham, and Gregory Treverton, eds. *Rethinking America's Security: Beyond the Cold War to New World Order* (1992).
Attwood, William. *The Twilight Struggle: Tales of the Cold War* (1987).
Ball, George. *The Past Has Another Pattern: Memoirs* (1982).
Barnet, Richard J. *Intervention and Revolution* (1972).

Bernstein, Barton J. "The Cuban Missile Crisis: Trading the Jupiters in Turkey?" *Political Science Quarterly* 95 (1980), 97–125.

———. "The Week We Almost Went to War," *Bulletin of the Atomic Scientists* 32 (1976), 12–21.

Beschloss, Michael R. *The Crisis Years: Kennedy and Khrushchev, 1960–1963* (1991).

Betts, Richard K., *Nuclear Blackmail and Nuclear Balance* (1987).

Bissell, Richard M. Jr., with Jonathan E. Lewis and Frances T. Pudlow. *Reflections of a Cold Warrior: From Yalta to the Bay of Pigs* (1996).

Blaisier, Cole. *The Hovering Giant: U.S. Responses to Revolutionary Change in Latin America* (1975).

Blight, James G., Bruce J. Allyn, and David A. Welch. *Cuba on the Brink: Castro, the Missile Crisis, and the Soviet Collapse* (1993).

Blight, James G., and David A. Welch. *On the Brink: Americans and Soviets Reexamine the Cuban Missile Crisis* (1989).

Brugioni, Dino A. *Eyeball to Eyeball: The Inside Story of the Cuban Missile Crisis* (1991).

Bundy, McGeorge. *Danger and Survival: Choices About the Bomb in the First Fifty Years* (1988).

Burner, David. *John F. Kennedy and a New Generation* (1988).

Chang, Laurence, and Peter Kornbluh, eds. *The Cuban Missile Crisis, 1962: A National Security Archive Documents Reader* (1992).

Cold War International History Project, *CWIHP Bulletin,* no. 5 (Spring 1995).

Divine, Robert A., ed., *The Cuban Missile Crisis* (1971).

Dobrynin, Anatoli. *In Confidence* (1995).

Dominguez, Jorge I. *Cuba: Order and Revolution* (1978).

Fursenko, Aleksandr, and Timothy Naftali. *"One Hell of a Gamble": Khrushchev, Castro, and Kennedy, 1958–1964* (1997).

Gaddis, John Lewis. *We Now Know: Rethinking Cold War History* (1997).

Garthoff, Raymond L. *Reflections on the Cuban Missile Crisis* (1987, 1989).

George, Alexander M., and Richard Smoke. *Deterrence in American Foreign Policy* (1964).

Goodwin, Richard N. *The American Condition* (1974).

Gribkov, Anatoli I., and William Y. Smith. *Operation ANADYR: U.S. and Soviet Generals Recount the Cuban Missile Crisis* (1994).

Gross, Peter. *Gentleman Spy: The Life of Allen Dulles* (1994).

Halperin, Maurice. *The Rise and Decline of Fidel Castro* (1972).

———. *The Taming of Fidel Castro* (1981).

Higgins, Trumbull. *The Perfect Failure* (1987).

Hillsman, Roger. *To Move a Nation: The Politics of Foreign Policy in the Administration of John F. Kennedy* (1967).

Johnson, Haynes B., et al., *The Bay of Pigs* (1964).

Kennedy, Robert F. *Thirteen Days: A Memoir of the Cuban Missile Crisis* (1969).

Kern, Montague, Patricia W. Levering, and Ralph B. Levering, *The Kennedy Crises: The Press, the Presidency, and the Foreign Policy* (1983).

Khrushchev Remembers: The Glasnost Tapes (1990).

LaFeber, Walter. *Inevitable Revolutions: The United States in Central America* (1983).

Larson, David A., ed. *The "Cuban Crisis" of 1962: Selected Documents, Chronology, and Bibliography,* 2nd ed. (1986).

Lebow, Richard Ned. *Between Peace and War* (1981).

Lebow, Richard Ned, and Janice Gross Stein. *We All Lost the Cold War* (1994).

Lechuga, Carlos. *In the Eye of the Storm: Castro, Khrushchev, Kennedy, and the Missile Crisis,* trans. Mary Todd (1995).

Lynn-Jones, Sean M., Steven E. Miller, and Stephen Van Evera, eds. *Nuclear Diplomacy and Crisis Management* (1990).

May, Ernest R., and Philip D. Zelikow, eds. *The Kennedy Tapes: Inside the White House During the Cuban Missile Crisis* (1997).

McCauliffe, Mary S., ed. *CIA Documents on the Cuban Missile Crisis* (1992).

McNamara, Robert. *Blundering into Disaster* (1986).

Nathan, James A., ed. *The Cuban Missile Crisis Revisited* (1992).

Nash, Philip. *The Other Missiles of October: Eisenhower, Kennedy, and the Jupiters, 1957–1963* (1997).

Operation ZAPATA: The "Ultrasensitive" Report and Testimony of the Board of Inquiry on the Bay of Pigs (1981).

Pachter, Henry M. *Collision Course: The Cuban Missile Crisis and Coexistence* (1963).

Paterson, Thomas G. *Contesting Castro: The United States and the Triumph of the Cuban Revolution* (1994).

Pope, Ronald R., ed., *Soviet Views on the Cuban Missile Crisis: Myth and Reality in Foreign Policy Analysis* (1982).

Powers, Thomas. *The Man Who Kept the Secrets* (1981).

Quirk, Robert E. *Fidel Castro* (1993).

Reeves, Richard. *President Kennedy: Profile of Power* (1993).

Roman, Peter J. *Eisenhower and the Missile Gap* (1995).

Rusk, Dean. *As I Saw It* (1990).

Sagan, Scott D. *The Limits of Safety: Organizations, Accidents, and Nuclear Weapons* (1993).

Seaborg, Glenn T., and Benjamin J. Loeb. *Kennedy, Khrushchev, and the Test Ban* (1981).

Smith, Gaddis. *The Last Years of the Monroe Doctrine, 1945–1993* (1994).

Sorensen, Theodore C. *Kennedy* (1965).

Szulc, Tad. *Fidel* (1986).

Thomspon, Kenneth W., ed., *The Kennedy Presidency* (1985).

Walton, Richard J. *The Cold War and Counterrevolution* (1972).

Welch, David A., ed. *Proceedings of the Hawk's Cay Conference on the Cuban Missile Crisis, March 5-8, 1987* (1987).

Welch, Richard E. Jr. *Response to Revolution: The United States and Cuba, 1959–1961* (1985).

White, Mark J. *The Cuban Missile Crisis* (1996).

Wills, Garry. *The Kennedy Imprisonment* (1983).

CHAPTER
6

Lyndon B. Johnson, the Great Society, and American Liberalism

The Great Society, as President Lyndon B. Johnson and others called the flood of social welfare legislation enacted between 1964 and 1968, marked a watershed in the evolution of the American welfare state. Like the New Deal of the 1930s, to which it has often been compared, it profoundly altered the scope and character of the federal government and profoundly affected the daily lives of millions of ordinary Americans.

During the Great Depression of the 1930s, the federal government had assumed some measure of new responsibilities toward the unemployed, the elderly, and the poor. The Social Security Act of 1935, with its provisions for unemployment insurance, old-age pensions, and support for dependent children, laid the foundation for the modern welfare state. More important, many Americans altered their basic assumptions about the proper role of government. By 1944 Roosevelt could speak confidently of an "economic bill of rights" that promised food, housing, jobs, and education for every American. Neither Roosevelt nor his immediate successors delivered on those promises, however, with the result that in the following two decades, little growth or innovation could be measured in the programs established during the New Deal.

All this changed in the mid-1960s when President Johnson, with the aid of an expanding U.S. economy and pliant Democratic majorities in Congress, won passage of a host of new laws on health, housing, education, and poverty. Although modest by comparison with the welfare state of most Western European countries, the new and expanded programs of the Great Society were nevertheless among the most important changes in American government in the postwar era. They touched the lives of ordinary Americans in myriad ways, from diminishing the fears with which older people faced the prospect of costly medical expenses to increasing the share of the gross national product assigned to this and other "entitlement" programs. By the early 1970s, the poverty rate had fallen to 11 percent, and even moderate conservatives like President Richard Nixon were considered broad income-support programs that were designed to reduce it even more. Nothing came of these efforts, however, and as the economy foundered in the mid-1970s, the rate of poverty leveled off and then began to rise, especially during the deep recession that accompanied the first two years of the Reagan administration.

During the 1980s, President Ronald Reagan and other conservatives launched major, if selective, attacks on welfare and other New Deal and Great Society programs. Some programs were eliminated, others sharply reduced. Many, especially broad-based entitlement programs such as Medicare and Social Security, proved highly resistant to change by either conservatives or liberals.

☒ D O C U M E N T S

Despite rapid economic growth and widespread prosperity in the 1950s, at the decade's end as many as 50 million Americans remained impoverished. Michael Harrington's 1962 book *The Other America,* from which Document 1 is taken, was part of a "rediscovery" of poverty during the early 1960s. In his first annual message to Congress on January 8, 1964 (Document 2), President Johnson called for sweeping reforms, including an "unconditional war on poverty." Conservatives, led by 1964 Republican presidential candidate Barry M. Goldwater, attacked Johnson's "Great Society" as an unwarranted expansion of federal power. In a 1964 campaign speech on behalf of Goldwater (Document 3), former actor and General Electric spokesman Ronald Reagan warned of the dangers of the "welfare state." Liberals, meanwhile, worried that Johnson, increasingly preoccupied with the growing war in Vietnam, would abandon domestic reform, the message of Jules Feiffer's 1965 cartoon (Document 4). By late 1966, however, the Johnson administration could boast of an unprecedented series of legislative victories, summarized in a report to the president by Lawrence O'Brien and Joseph Califano (Document 5). As Document 6 shows, the rate of poverty dramatically declined during the 1960s, although economists and other social scientists continued to argue about how much credit the administration deserved and how much was the product of the overall economic expansion.

1. Michael Harrington Describes the "Other America," 1962

There is a familiar America. It is celebrated in speeches and advertised on television and in the magazines. It has the highest mass standard of living the world has ever known.

In the 1950s this America worried about itself, yet even its anxieties were products of abundance. The title of a brilliant book was widely misinterpreted, and the familiar America began to call itself "the affluent society." There was introspection about Madison Avenue and tail fins; there was discussion of the emotional suffering taking place in the suburbs. In all this, there was an implicit assumption that the basic grinding economic problems had been solved in the United States. In

Excerpt from *The Other America* by Michael Harrington. Copyright © 1962, 1969, 1981 by Michael Harrington. Reprinted with the permission of Scribner, a Division of Simon & Schuster.

this theory the nation's problem were no longer a matter of basic human needs, of food, shelter, and clothing. Now they were seen as qualitative, a question of learning to live decently amid luxury.

While this discussion was carried on, there existed another America. In it dwelt somewhere between 40,000,000 and 50,000,000 citizens of this land. They were poor. They still are.

To be sure, the other America is not impoverished in the same sense as those poor nations where millions cling to hunger as a defense against starvation. This country has escaped such extremes. That does not change the fact that tens of millions of Americans are, at this very moment, maimed in body and spirit, existing at levels beneath those necessary for human decency. If these people are not starving, they are hungry, and sometimes fat with hunger, for that is what cheap foods do. They are without adequate housing and education and medical care.

The Government has documented what this means to the bodies of the poor. . . . But even more basic, this poverty twists and deforms the spirit. The American poor are pessimistic and defeated, and they are victimized by mental suffering to a degree unknown in Suburbia. . . .

The millions who are poor in the United States tend to become increasingly invisible. Here is a great mass of people, yet it takes an effort of the intellect and will even to see them.

I discovered this personally in a curious way. After I wrote my first article on poverty in America, I had all the statistics down on paper. I had proved to my satisfaction that there were around 50,000,000 poor in this country. Yet, I realized I did not believe my own figures. The poor existed in the Government reports; they were percentages and numbers in long, close columns, but they were not part of my experience. I could prove that the other America existed, but I had never been there.

My response was not accidental. It was typical of what is happening to an entire society, and it reflects profound social changes in this nation. The other America, the America of poverty, is hidden today in a way that it never was before. Its millions are socially invisible to the rest of us. No wonder that so many misinterpreted [John K.] Galbraith's title and assumed that "the affluent society" meant that everyone had a decent standard of life. The misinterpretation was true as far as the actual day-to-day lives of two-thirds of the nation were concerned. Thus, one must begin a description of the other America by understanding why we do not see it.

There are perennial reasons that make the other America an invisible land.

Poverty is often off the beaten track. It always has been. The ordinary tourist never left the main highway, and today he rides interstate turnpikes. He does not go into the valleys of Pennsylvania where the towns look like movie sets of Wales in the thirties. He does not see the company houses in rows, the rutted roads (the poor always have bad roads whether they live in the city, in towns, or on farms), and everything is black and dirty. And even if he were to pass through such a place by accident, the tourist would not meet the unemployed men in the bar or the women coming home from a runaway sweatshop.

Then, too, beauty and myths are perennial masks of poverty. The traveler comes to the Appalachians in the lovely season. He sees the hills, the streams, the foliage—but not the poor. Or perhaps he looks at a run-down mountain house and, remembering [French Enlightenment philosopher Jean-Jacques] Rousseau rather than seeing with his eyes, decides that "those people" are truly fortunate to be living the way they are and that they are lucky to be exempt from the strains and tensions of the middle class. The only problem is that "those people," the quaint inhabitants of those hills, are undereducated, underprivileged, lack medical care, and are in the process of being forced from the land into a life in the cities, where they are misfits.

These are normal and obvious causes of the invisibility of the poor. They operated a generation ago; they will be functioning a generation hence. It is more important to understand that the very development of American society is creating a new kind of blindness about poverty. The poor are increasingly slipping out of the very experience and consciousness of the nation.

If the middle class never did like ugliness and poverty, it was at least aware of them. "Across the tracks" was not a very long way to go. There were forays into the slums at Christmas time; there were charitable organizations that brought contact with the poor. Occasionally, almost everyone passed through the Negro ghetto or the blocks of tenements, if only to get downtown to work or to entertainment.

Now the American city has been transformed. The poor still inhabit the miserable housing in the central area, but they are increasingly isolated from contact with, or sight of, anybody else. Middle-class women coming in from Suburbia on a rare trip may catch the merest glimpse of the other America on the way to an evening at the theater, but their children are segregated in suburban schools. The business or professional man may drive along the fringes of slums in a car or bus, but it is not an important experience to him. The failures, the unskilled, the disabled, the aged, and the minorities are right there, across the tracks, where they have always been. But hardly anyone else is.

In short, the very development of the American city has removed poverty from the living, emotional experience of millions upon millions of middle-class Americans. Living out in the suburbs, it is easy to assume that ours is, indeed, an affluent society.

This new segregation of poverty is compounded by a well-meaning ignorance. A good many concerned and sympathetic Americans are aware that there is much discussion of urban renewal. Suddenly, driving through the city, they notice that a familiar slum has been torn down and that there are towering, modern buildings where once there had been tenements or hovels. There is a warm feeling of satisfaction, of pride in the ways things are working out: the poor, it is obvious, are being taken care of.

The irony in this . . . is that the truth is nearly the exact opposite to the impression. The total impact of the various housing programs in postwar America has been to squeeze more and more people into existing slums. More often than not, the modern apartment in a towering building rents at $40 a room or more. For, during the past decade and a half, there has been more subsidization of middle- and upper-income housing than there has been for the poor.

Clothes make the poor invisible too: America has the best-dressed poverty the world has even known. For a variety of reasons, the benefits of mass production have been spread much more evenly in this area than in many others. It is much easier in the United States to be decently dressed than it is to be decently housed, fed, or doctored. Even people with terribly depressed incomes can look prosperous.

This is an extremely important factor in defining our emotional and existential ignorance of poverty. In Detroit the existence of social classes became much more difficult to discern the day the companies put lockers in the plants. From that moment on, one did not see men in work clothes on the way to the factory, but citizens in slacks and white shirts. This process has been magnified with the poor throughout the country. There are tens of thousands of Americans in the big cities who are wearing shoes, perhaps even a stylishly cut suit or dress, and yet are hungry. It is not a matter of planning, though it almost seems as if the affluent society had given out costumes to the poor so that they would not offend the rest of society with the sight of rags.

Then, many of the poor are the wrong age to be seen. A good number of them (over 8,000,000) are sixty-five years of age or better; an even larger number are under eighteen. The aged members of the other America are often sick, and they cannot move. Another group of them live out their lives in loneliness and frustration: they sit in rented rooms, or else they stay close to a house in a neighborhood that has completely changed from the old days. Indeed, one of the worst aspects of poverty among the aged is that these people are out of sight and out of mind, and alone.

The young are somewhat more visible, yet they too stay close to their neighborhoods. Sometimes they advertise their poverty through a lurid tabloid story about a gang killing. But generally they do not disturb the quiet streets of the middle class.

And finally, the poor are politically invisible. It is one of the cruelest ironies of social life in advanced countries that the dispossessed at the bottom of society are unable to speak for themselves. The people of the other America do not, by far and large, belong to unions, to fraternal organizations, or to political parties. They are without lobbies of their own; they put forward no legislative program. As a group, they are atomized. They have no face; they have no voice. . . .

That the poor are invisible is one of the most important things about them. They are not simply neglected and forgotten as in the old rhetoric of reform; what is much worse, they are not seen.

2. President Lyndon B. Johnson Declares War on Poverty, 1964

Let this session of Congress be known as the session which did more for civil rights than the last hundred sessions combined; as the session which enacted the most far-reaching tax cut of our time; as the session which declared all-out war on human poverty and unemployment in these United States; as the session which finally recognized the health needs of all our older citizens; as the session which reformed our tangled transportation and transit policies; as the session which achieved the most effective, efficient foreign aid program ever; and as the session which helped to build more homes, more schools, more libraries, and more hospitals than any single session of Congress in the history of our Republic. . . .

This budget, and this year's legislative program, are designed to help each and every American citizen fulfill his basic hopes—his hopes for a fair chance to make good; his hopes for fair play from the law; his hopes for a full-time job on full-time

Public Papers of the Presidents of the United States: Lyndon B. Johnson, 1963–69, (Washington, D.C.: GPO, 1965), 704–707.

pay, his hopes for a decent home for his family in a decent community; his hopes for a good school for his children with good teachers; and his hopes for security when faced with sickness or unemployment or old age.

Unfortunately, many Americans live on the outskirts of hope—some because of their poverty, and some because of their color, and all too many because of both. Our task is to help replace their despair with opportunity.

This administration today, here and now, declares unconditional war on poverty in America. I urge this Congress and all Americans to join with me in that effort.

It will not be a short or easy struggle, no single weapon or strategy will suffice, but we shall not rest until that war is won. The richest Nation on earth can afford to win it. We cannot afford to lose it. One thousand dollars invested in salvaging an unemployable youth today can return $40,000 or more in his lifetime.

Poverty is a national problem, requiring improved national organization and support. But this attack, to be effective, must also be organized at the State and the local level and must be supported and directed by State and local efforts.

For the war against poverty will not be won here in Washington. It must be won in the field, in every private home, in every public office, from the courthouse to the White House.

The program I shall propose will emphasize this cooperative approach to help that one-fifth of all American families with incomes too small to even meet their basic needs.

Our chief weapons in a more pinpointed attack will be better schools, and better health, and better homes, and better training, and better job opportunities to help more Americans, especially young Americans, escape from squalor and misery and unemployment rolls where other citizens help to carry them.

Very often a lack of jobs and money is not the cause of poverty, but the symptom. The cause may lie deeper—in our failure to give our fellow citizens a fair chance to develop their own capacities, in a lack of education and training, in a lack of medical care and housing, in a lack of decent communities in which to live and bring up their children.

But whatever the cause, our joint Federal-local effort must pursue poverty, pursue it wherever it exists—in city slums and small towns, in sharecropper shacks or in migrant worker camps, on Indian Reservations, among whites as well as Negroes, among the young as well as the aged, in the boom towns and in the depressed areas.

Our aim is not only to relieve the symptom of poverty, but to cure it and, above all, to prevent it. No single piece of legislation, however, is going to suffice.

We will launch a special effort in the chronically distressed areas of Appalachia.

We must expand our small but our successful area redevelopment program.

We must enact youth employment legislation to put jobless, aimless, hopeless youngsters to work on useful projects.

We must distribute more food to the needy through a broader food stamp program.

We must create a National Service Corps to help the economically handicapped of our own country as the Peace Corps now helps those abroad.

We must modernize our unemployment insurance and establish a high-level commission on automation. If we have the brain power to invent these machines, we have the brain power to make certain that they are a boon and not a bane to humanity.

We must extend the coverage of our minimum wage laws to more than 2 million workers now lacking this basic protection of purchasing power.

We must, by including special school aid funds as part of our education program, improve the quality of teaching, training, our counseling in our hardest hit areas.

We must build more libraries in every area and more hospitals and nursing homes under the Hill-Burton Act, and train more nurses to staff them.

We must provide hospital insurance for our older citizens financed by every worker and his employer under Social Security, contributing no more than $1 a month during the employee's working career to protect him in his old age in a dignified manner without cost to the Treasury, against the devastating hardship of prolonged or repeated illness.

We must, as a part of a revised housing and urban renewal program, give more help to those displaced by slum clearance, provide more housing for our poor and our elderly, and seek as our ultimate goal in our free enterprise system a decent home for every American family.

We must help obtain more modern mass transit within our communities as well as low-cost transportation between them.

Above all, we must release $11 billion of tax reduction into the private spending stream to create new jobs and new markets in every area of this land.

3. President Ronald Reagan Warns of the Dangers of the Welfare State, 1964

It's time we asked ourselves if we still know the freedoms intended for us by the Founding Fathers. James Madison said, "We base all our experiments on the capacity of mankind for self-government." This idea that government was beholden to the people, that it had no other source of power except the sovereign people, is still the newest, most unique idea in all the long history of man's relation to man. For almost two centuries we have proved man's capacity for self-government, but today we are told we must choose between a left and right or, as others suggest, a third alternative, a kind of safe middle ground. I suggest to you there is no left or right, only an up or down. Up to the maximum of individual freedom consistent with law and order, or down to the ant heap of totalitarianism; and regardless of their humanitarian purpose those who would sacrifice freedom for security have, whether they know it or not, chosen this downward path. Plutarch warned, "The real destroyer of the liberties of the people is he who spreads among them bounties, donations, and benefits."

Today there is an increasing number who can't see a fat man standing beside a thin one without automatically coming to the conclusion the fat man got that way by taking advantage of the thin one. So they would seek the answer to all the problems of human need through government. Howard K. Smith of television fame has written, "The profit motive is outmoded. It may be replaced by the incentives of the welfare state." He says, "The distribution of goods must be effected by a planned economy."

Another articulate spokesman for the welfare state defines liberalism as meeting the material needs of the masses through the full power of centralized government. I for one find it disturbing when a representative refers to the free men and women of this country as the masses, but beyond this the full power of centralized government was the very thing the Founding Fathers sought to minimize. They knew you don't control things; you can't control the economy without controlling *people*. So we have come to a time for choosing. Either we accept the responsibility for our own destiny, or we abandon the American Revolution and confess that an intellectual belief in a far-distant capitol can plan our lives for us better than we can plan them ourselves.

Already the hour is late. Government has laid its hand on health, housing, farming, industry, commerce, education, and, to an ever-increasing degree, interferes with the people's right to know. Government tends to grow; government programs take on weight and momentum, as public servants say, always with the best of intentions, "What greater service we could render if only we had a little more money and a little more power." But the truth is that outside of its legitimate function, government does nothing as well or as economically as the private sector of the economy. . . .

Federal welfare spending is today ten times greater than it was in the dark depths of the Depression. Federal, state, and local welfare combined spend 45 billion dollars a year. Now the government has announced that 20 percent, some 9.3 million families, are poverty-stricken on the basis that they have less than a $3,000 a year income.

If this present welfare spending was prorated equally among these poverty-stricken families, we could give each family more than $4,500 a year. Actually, direct aid to the poor averages less than $600 per family. There must be some administrative overhead somewhere. Now, are we to believe that another billion dollar program added to the half a hundred programs and the 45 billion dollars, will, through some magic, end poverty? For three decades we have tried to solve unemployment by government planning, without success. The more the plans fail, the more the planners plan.

The latest is the Area Redevelopment Agency, and in two years less than one-half of one percent of the unemployed could attribute new jobs to this agency, and the cost to the taxpayer for each job found was $5,000. But beyond the great bureaucratic waste, what are we doing to the people we seek to help?

Recently a judge told me of an incidental in his court. A fairly young woman with six children, pregnant with her seventh, came to him for a divorce. Under his questioning it became apparent her husband did not share this desire. Then the whole story came out. Her husband was a laborer earning $250 a month. By divorcing him she could get an $80 raise. She was eligible for $350 a month from the Aid to Dependent Children Program. She had been talked into the divorce by two friends who had already done this very thing. But any time we question the schemes of the do-gooders, we are denounced as being opposed to their humanitarian goal. It seems impossible to legitimately debate their solutions with the assumption that all of us share the desire to help those less fortunate. They tell us we are always against, never for anything. Well, it isn't so much that liberals are ignorant. It's just that they know so much that isn't so.

4. A Liberal Cartoonist Worries That Johnson Has Abandoned the Great Society, 1965

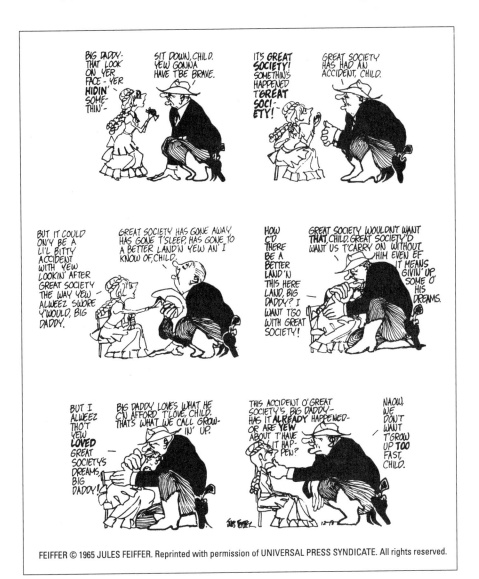

5. Two White House Aides Report the Achievements of the Great Society, 1966

Final Report to President Lyndon B. Johnson on the 89th Congress by Lawrence F. O'Brien and Joseph A. Califano Jr.

Here is our final summary of the 89th Congress.

A. Our Overall Assessment.   In a word, this was a fabulous and remarkable Congress. We say this not because of its unprecedented productivity—but because what was passed has deep meaning and significance for every man, woman, and child in this country—and for future generations. A particularly striking feature about the 89th was that its second session was as equally productive as the first.

Attached is a detailed appendix. It tells an impressive story of achievement.

In brief summary this is the record of the major legislation this Administration initiated and sponsored:

First session:	*87 measures*
	84 passed
Second session:	*113 measures*
	97 passed
Grand total:	*200 measures*
	181 passed
	19 did not
Batting average:	*.905*

B. The Major Accomplishments.   Of this list of 181 measures passed, we regard the following 60 as of landmark and historic significance:

The First Session

1. Medicare
2. Elementary and Secondary Education
3. Higher Education
4. Farm Bill
5. Department of Housing and Urban Development
6. Omnibus Housing Act (including rent supplements, and low and moderate income housing)
7. Social Security Increases
8. Voting Rights
9. Immigration Bill
10. Older Americans Act
11. Heart Disease, Cancer, and Stroke Research and Facilities
12. Law Enforcement Assistance Act
13. National Crime Commission
14. Drug Controls

Public Papers of the Presidents of the United States: Lyndon B. Johnson, 1963–69, vol. 2 (Washington, D.C.: GPO, 1967), 1193–1194.

15. Mental Health Research and Facilities
16. Health Professions Education
17. Medical Library Facilities
18. Vocational Rehabilitation
19. Inter-American Bank Fund Increases
20. Stepping Up the War Against Poverty
21. Arts and Humanities Foundation
22. Appalachia
23. Highway Beautification
24. Air Pollution (auto exhausts and research)
25. Water Pollution Control (water quality standards)
26. High Speed Ground Transportation
27. Extension and Strengthening of MDTA
28. Presidential Disability and Succession
29. Child Health Medical Assistance
30. Regional Development

The Second Session

1. The Department of Transportation
2. Truth in Packaging
3. Demonstration Cities
4. Funds for Rent Supplements
5. Funds for Teacher Corps
6. Asian Development Bank
7. Water Pollution (Clean Rivers)
8. Food for Peace
9. March Anti-inflation Package
10. Narcotics Rehabilitation
11. Child Safety
12. Viet-Nam Supplemental
13. Foreign Aid Extension
14. Traffic Safety
15. Highway Safety
16. Public Health Service Reorganization
17. Community Relations Service Reorganization
18. Water Pollution Control Administration Reorganization
19. Mine Safety
20. Allied Health Professions Training
21. International Education
22. Child Nutrition
23. Bail Reform
24. Civil Procedure Reforms
25. Tire Safety
26. Protection for Savers (increase in Federal Insurance for savings accounts)
27. The GI Bill
28. Minimum Wage Increase
29. Urban Mass Transit
30. Elementary and Higher Education Funds

6. Poverty in America, 1959–1997: A Graphic

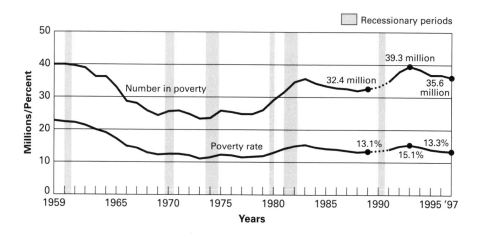

While the Great Society touched almost every issue affecting the lives of Americans, no part of its domestic legacy has produced more debate among historians and social scientists than its "war on poverty." This initiative echoes the deep divisions among Americans over the nature of poverty and government's appropriate response. Democratic liberals such as Sar A. Levitan and Robert Taggert have defended these efforts as part of "a dramatic acceleration of governmental efforts to insure the well-being of all citizens," in *The Promise of Greatness: The Social Programs of the Last Decade and Their Major Achievements* (1976). Theirs is the voice of Democratic liberalism, vigorously and unapologetically defending the vision and legacy of the Great Society. Radical critics have attacked the Great Society's many compromises and limitations, as well as the abandonment of reform by an administration increasingly preoccupied by the war in Vietnam. Conservatives, meanwhile, have attacked the Great Society as not only an unwarranted expansion of government, but as a failure in social policy. Thus, Charles Murray argued in *Losing Ground* (1984) that the Great Society not only failed to lift the poor from poverty, but actually encouraged growing welfare dependency. Although poverty in America was reduced by the long economic boom of the 1990s, the basic issues underlying the Great Society remain unresolved.

The essays that follow offer two very different but equally critical perspectives on the Great Society. In the first, political scientist Ira Katznelson of the New School for Social Research traces the failures of the Great Society not to the expansion of liberal programs in the 1960s, but to what he argues were the narrow limitations of postwar American liberalism from the 1940s onward. In the second essay, Gareth Davies reprises some of Charles Murray's themes, tracing what Davies describes as a shift from the "opportunity liberalism" of the early Great Society to what he calls the "entitlement liberalism" of the late Johnson and Nixon years.

Document 6, Census Bureau, March Current Population Survey.

Was the Great Society a Lost Opportunity?

IRA KATZNELSON

Some five weeks after the assassination of his predecessor, President Johnson received the report of the Task Force on Manpower Conservation. This committee of four included the secretary of labor, who chaired it, the secretary of health, education, and welfare, the secretary of defense, and the head of the Selective Service. The report focused on men rejected by the draft. It found "that one-third of the nation's youth would, on examination, be found unqualified for military service," and, second, "that poverty was the principal reason these young men failed to meet those physical and mental standards." In receiving the report, President Johnson announced (three days before he did so more widely in his first State of the Union address), "I shall shortly present to Congress a program designed to attack the roots of poverty in our cities and rural areas. . . . This war on poverty . . . will not be won overnight."

The principal drafter of the document was an assistant secretary of labor, Daniel Patrick Moynihan. At the end of the decade, when he was assistant to President Nixon for urban affairs, he wrote a stinging critique of the war he helped initiate. "The great failing of the Johnson Administration," he wrote, "was that an immense opportunity to institute more or less permanent social changes—a fixed full employment program, a measure of income maintenance—was lost while energies were expended in ways that very probably hastened the end of the brief period when such options were open, that is to say the three years from the assassination of Kennedy to the election of the Ninety-First Congress."

Was the Great Society a lost opportunity? Moynihan's appraisal was that of a disaffected liberal Democrat. Here, I wish to broaden this question in order to evaluate the character and legacy of the Great Society from the vantage point of its implications for the reform impulse and coalition that originated in the New Deal. I argue that the "opportunity" to achieve the social democratic potential of the New Deal was compromised not in the 1960s but in the 1940s. By social democracy I mean the attempts by labor and socialist movements in Western capitalist democracies to work through their electoral and representational political systems to achieve two principal goals: first, to effect interventions in markets that in the short run mitigate unequal distributional patterns, in the medium run promote more basic public controls over markets, and in the long run bring about a shift in social organization from capitalism to socialism; and, second, to secure the solidarity of their working-class base while reaching out for the allies they need to achieve majorities in elections and legislatures. The New Deal presented the possibility that such a strategic orientation, at least insofar as it concerned governmental activity to organize markets and mitigate market outcomes, might be feasible even in the United States, which had lacked such efforts. It is my central contention that key features of partisan politics and policy-making in the 1940s, a decade of war and reconversion, shaped the character of the Great Society's determinate limits (as well as its impressive achievements) more decisively than short-term causes. In turn, the Great Society significantly diminished subsequent prospects for a social democratic trajectory in American politics. The domestic policy choices made by the Johnson administration within the framework of the constraints inherited from the 1940s hastened major changes in the character of political debate, policy choice, and partisanship that haunt the Democratic party two decades later. . . .

The contraction of political space for the Left in American politics in the 1940s redefined the social forces undergirding social democratic possibilities in the Democratic party, and changed the locus of political debate from questions of social organization and class relations to issues of technical economics and interest group politics. These alterations to the political landscape defined the features the Democratic party took into the Eisenhower era; in so doing, they set the terms for the modest reform efforts of the Kennedy administration and the more assertive reformist attempt to utilize the state in the Johnson years. The Great Society, in turn, reinforced and exaggerated features of American politics that had only begun to appear in the 1940s: the reduction of labor to an interest group; the centrality of race; and an economist's definition of public policy and political choice. In this way, the Great Society's immense reform effort embodied Janus-like facings: it decisively broadened the social base of the Democratic party by incorporating blacks both within and outside of the South, yet it contracted the party's social base by contributing to the disaffections of an ever-narrowing labor movement; it substantially expanded the policy themes of American politics, but it did so in a way that simultaneously ruled out a politics of more vigorous intervention in the marketplace. The Great Society, in short, is best understood in terms of a larger dynamic of reform in the postwar era that undercut, more than it reinforced, the prospects for an American social democratic politics. The subsequent turn to the Right that culminated in the election of President Reagan on an explicit pro-market, anti-state platform with significant working-class support thus was facilitated by the way the Great Society embedded the trajectory of the 1940s.

Most explanations of the meaning of the Great Society, and the War on Poverty that nestled within it, begin, appropriately enough, with an assessment of its considerable ambition—the extraordinary range of its reformist efforts in social insurance and medical care, and the War on Poverty's unprecedented and rhetorically unconditional assault on poverty. Ironically, many accounts of the Great Society consider and choose between very short term and situational alternative explanations of the immediate causes of this program such as the electoral pressures of managing urban black and white ethnic political coalitions, the Kennedy administration's need to find an innovative domestic program, or the particular composition of policy-planning committees within the administration. I have no quarrel with these themes: they are not so much wrong as insufficient. . . .

I should like to . . . elongat[e] the time horizons of our consideration. This shift of just a few degrees can bring the Great Society as object of analysis into better focus.

I

"By the end of 1937," Richard Hofstadter has written, "it was clear that something had been added to the social base of reformism. The demands of a large and powerful labor movement, coupled with the interests of the unemployed, gave the later New

Deal a social-democratic tinge that had never been present before in American reform movements." To be sure, this proto-social democracy was a contested matter; just the same, it was part of the contest for the Democratic party. Even after a more conservative Congress was elected in 1938, the social democratic–labor wing of the party continued to define an important pole of political possibility.

It had many resources: the support of the president, at least in speech; the support of the labor movement and the rank and file (the labor vote for Roosevelt after 1936 was higher than corresponding electoral support in Europe for the social democrats); the votes of most farmers; concrete electoral cooperation between the labor movement and ethnic political machines; centers of bureaucratic strength within the state in such agencies as the National Resources Planning Board [NRPB] and the Department of Labor, committed to planning and vigorous interventions in the marketplace; and an intellectual climate in the knowledge community that considered a host of ideas drawn from the socialist movements, the planning profession, and the interventionist wing of Keynesian economics.

By the end of the 1940s, none of these features of a proto-social democracy held up.

In spite of the hopes and fears, of such analysts as C. Wright Mills, Daniel Bell, and Charles Lindblom, labor lost its radical edge and movement characteristics to become a congeries of trade unions out for the best possible deal. The NRPB was dissolved. The Department of Labor lost its capacity to intervene in manpower policy. The emergence of race onto the political agenda, and the failure of the CIO [Congress of Industrial Organizations] to unionize successfully in the postwar South, deeply divided the Democratic party, inhibited its legislative room for maneuver, and began to challenge the capacities of the Northern urban machines to appeal simultaneously to their white ethnic and growing black constituencies. And, perhaps most important, the range of debate among the policy-interested intelligentsia both changed and narrowed to a combination of pluralist political theory and the neo-classic synthesis in economics. Together, these developments sharply contracted the range and prospects of the progressive wing of the Democratic party.

At the beginning of this decade, the key political divide appeared to be between business and labor. Business threatened the social and economic order because of its potential for disinvestment, and labor, because of its capacity to disrupt capitalism at the point of production. The tensions between business and labor were intensified by uncertainties about whether prosperity and liberalism could go hand in hand in a democratic capitalist order. In this situation, labor as a political actor appeared to teeter between being an anticapitalist insurgent force and the most important presence in the left wing of the Democratic party in favor of significant planning and an intrusive version of Keynesianism.

That labor had the ability to lead a social democratic breakthrough in American politics that could build on the achievements of the New Deal and radicalize them was a commonplace of the early 1940s, one that appeared to be affirmed during World War II by such achievements as the organization by the CIO of Ford and Bethlehem Steel, the growth in the size of organized labor, the incorporation within labor's embrace of the previously unorganized female and black members of the labor force, and an extraordinary wave of strikes in the aftermath of the war. Further, during the New Deal, the labor movement broke with its traditional abjuration of partisan politics and integrated itself into the Democratic party through the instrumentality of the Non-Partisan League in 1936 and the Political Action Committee of the CIO in 1944, which, at the time, was widely thought to ensure a leftward tilt within the party.

Writing in 1944 as a committed social democrat, Daniel Bell warned that indicators of labor strength had an illusory quality. "The war has given labor its great numerical strength," he argued, "yet sapped it of its real strength" because of the price it exacted by way of integration into the dominant institutions and assumptions of the society. The quasi-corporatism of the war was a conservative version of statism, he insisted; after the war, he predicted, the leadership of the labor movement would be compelled to discipline its work force and limit its political horizons. He proved right. Inflation, not massive unemployment, emerged as the central and much more manageable threat of the reconversion period. It was "managed" in part by privately negotiated and relatively lucrative union contracts in basic industry. Meanwhile, a Keynesian program of government spending helped ensure that the bottom did not fall out of the demand side of the economy. An assault on the prerogatives of labor during the massive strike wave that followed the war culminated in the passage of the Taft-Hartley Act, which simultaneously produced a contraction of labor's ability to organize new workers and signified the acceptance by conservatives of the institution of collective bargaining within the limits of the act. Labor's inability to organize in the South, and the schisms between the non-Communist and Communist Left, further narrowed the scope of action of the labor movement. For these and other reasons, by the end of the 1940s labor's vision and potential contracted. This reorientation was remarkably successful; arguably, labor was the most potent of the host of interest groups active in American politics. At the same time, its most militant organizational tools had been lost to Taft-Hartley, and its position within the Democratic party was that of one of a number of important constituents. It seems telling that David Truman could write his magisterial text *The Governmental Process* at the end of the decade and subsume his treatment of labor within such chapters as those concerning the genesis of interest groups, interest groups and political parties, and the web of relationships in the administrative process.

This shift from labor as political opposition to labor as an interest group was paralleled by a remarkable transformation in the nature of public debate within what might be called, broadly, the policy community. At the beginning of the decade, these discussions were dominated by the discourse of political economy—the attempt "to understand economic events and arrangements in the framework of a comprehensive social theory, or at least as part of a social totality." Works as diverse as Joseph Schumpeter's *Capitalism, Socialism, and Democracy,* Karl Polanyi's *The Great Transformation,* and Friedrich Hayek's *The Road to Serfdom,* all of which were written and published in the first half of the decade, wrestled with the question of whether the tight ties between private property and market organization, on the one hand, and state ownership and bureaucratic management, on the other hand, were immutable; or, whether a "third way" could (or could not) be found to maximize the chances for prosperity *and* liberty in the postdepression, postwar world. At the end of the 1940s, by contrast, policy disputes were the province of economics, the attempt "to study the 'economic' in isolation from the 'social,' not by ignoring the latter but by taking it as a given." In political economy, however, the economy cannot be disentangled from society, history, and considerations of social organization and human nature.

Social organization and human nature were now to be taken for granted, either as givens or as exogenous variables. Even the radical impulses of Keynes were domesticated in a new synthesis of neoclassic economics and Keynesianism. Keynes had viewed his *General Theory* of 1936 as representing a radical rupture with the then current economic theory, particularly in its treatment of the pricing of capital assets and capitalist financial institutions (in that these elements produce a theory of instability, whereas, by contrast, the neoclassic tradition emphasizes market stability and tendencies toward equilibrium). Yet shortly after its publication, mainstream economists truncated Keynes and assimilated it into pre-Keynesian equilibrium analysis. Within the neoclassic synthesis that developed the capitalist economy was viewed as timeless. The synthesis did not allow for internal mechanisms of desta-bilization. The result, Hyman Minsky writes, was "the reduction of the Keynesian Revolution to a banality."

The neoclassic synthesis that became dominant within American economics by the end of the Truman years ruled out precisely those questions which had been basic to the policy debates of the early 1940s, and to the possibilities of a class-based social democratic politics within the Democratic party. Indeed, the shift to a domesticated Keynesianism as the given of policy debates went hand in hand with a labor movement content with enlarging its share of national wealth incrementally in negotiations with employers limited to wages, fringe benefits, and working conditions—private accords buttressed by government policies aimed at maintaining a level of aggregate demand consistent with a high demand for labor. Taken together, the collapse of the labor movement as a potentially social democratic force and the evaporation of the theoretical and academic bases for left-wing policy-making within American politics, demoralized the American Left, and put it in a position where it lacked a "third way" between an assertive, internationalist capitalism and the socialism of Soviet-type societies. Given this set of actually existing alternatives, Democrats on the Left joined the tight confines of the liberalism of the cold war. "By 1950," Daniel Bell judged, "American socialism as a political and social fact was simply a matter for history alone"; an American society based on class divisions had been supplanted by an interest-group society of voluntary associations. In short, in the 1940s, economics replaced political economies, and pluralism supplanted the politics of class.

To these two basic changes in the political landscape must be added a third: the introduction of what proved to be the solvent of race into the Democratic party coalition. The New Deal, in spite of a small number of token gestures, had had little to offer blacks in particular, and as such left the segregationist social organization of the South unchallenged. Within the Congress, the president's programs in the first and second New Deal passed with the support of all regional wings of the party.

During the 1920s, the Democratic party had widened its regional base beyond the South, and was transformed from a primarily rural to an urban-based electoral organization. Faced with the calamity of the depression, the white South subsumed its distinctive regional interests and supported the New Deal. At its convention of 1936, the party revoked its rule that required the approval of two-thirds of the delegates to designate the presidential nominee. This provision had been instituted to protect regional interests. Now, party leaders argued, it was no longer needed because the Democrats had become a genuinely national party. The tacit quid pro quo showed a high degree of tolerance for the racial civilization of the South by the party as a whole. This accommodation manifested itself in the absence of civil rights legislation, and the high degree of discretion left to the states in setting rules and benefit levels for most public assistance programs, including the Aid to Dependent Children provisions of the Social Security Act.

Writing in 1949, V. O. Key observed that "whatever phase of the Southern political process one seeks to understand," including the politics of cotton, free trade, agrarian poverty, and social relations, "sooner or later the trail of inquiry leads to the Negro." By that date, the partisan consistency support for the Democrats in the eleven former states of the Confederacy that had protected the system of white supremacy from national interference no longer could do so. With the voting realignments of the Roosevelt years, the South became only one element, and a minority one at that, in the coalitional structure of the Democratic party. With the massive migration of blacks to the North during World War II, their insertion into the urban-based politics of the North, and their integration into the mass production industries and the labor movement, questions of civil rights could no longer be contained as a regional matter. The character of the racial civilization of the South was placed on the national political agenda. With this, the solidarity of the Democratic party as an electoral vehicle and as a national force promoting the assertive use of the federal government to organize and reshape the market economy was compromised. The Dixiecrat rebellion of 1948 was only the most visible indicator of this change that had been manifest on a daily basis in the emergence of a blocking coalition of conservative Republicans and Southern Democrats in the Congress. In particular, any proposal that extended the planning capacity of the central state was seen, not without reason, as a direct challenge to the white supremacist arrangements of the South. For Republicans, an anti-statist position on such debates in the reconversion period as whether to decentralize or nationalize the Federal Employment Service or pass a Full Employment Act was primarily a stance against government intervention in the marketplace: for southerners, these votes were a hedge against the prospect of basic social reform.

The shifts from the politics of class to the politics of pluralism, from political economy to economics, and from the omission to the inclusion of race on the national political agenda proved mutually reinforcing. Taken together, these developments starkly reduced the prospects of strong social democratic–type intervention in the marketplace. Instead, they promoted a less intrusive set of public policies: less of a state capacity to directly plan and organize markets, and more of a state capacity to shape markets by fiscal policies focusing on spending levels and the promotion of adequate aggregate demand. This "fiscalization" of public policy went hand in hand with the strengthening of the Bureau of the Budget (and an enhanced role for economists within it), the creation of the Council of Economic Advisors, and the enhancement of what Peri Arnold calls the managerial presidency. By contrast, more assertive bureaucratic agencies such as the National Resources Planning Board and the Department of Labor either were eliminated entirely or were stripped of key interventionists functions. In turn, this new policy terrain reinforced the ascendancy of economics within the policy community, made it possible for the Democratic party to postpone the day of reckoning on civil rights, and confirmed the labor movement's truncated goals by facilitating the successful pursuit of Keynesian policies designed to underpin high wage settlements in the mass production industries.

With this interactive set of political, social-knowledge, and policy elements, what remained of the social democratic option for the Democratic party closed off. The Democratic party that remained competitive on the national scene during and immediately after the Eisenhower years conceded this in its discourse and practices. In the interregnum between the administrations of Truman and Kennedy the party's political formula did not alter, but it did undergo a developmental process. Each of the three main features of this formula that came to be defined in the late 1940s proved to have a powerful directionality. In the 1950s, labor narrowed its focus even more, race moved to the center of political life, and the hegemony of the neoclassical synthesis appeared complete.

This inheritance circumscribed and informed the character of the Great Society; in turn, the Johnson program reinforced, even exaggerated, each of its elements. The labor movement's confining self-definition was evinced by its concern only for the Great Society's extension of social insurance; by contrast, labor was almost totally disinterested in the War on Poverty. In spite of its early, and accurate, rhetoric to the effect that most poor people were white, these antipoverty efforts reinforced the emergence of race as a centerpiece of national politics just at the moment when class-based issues seemed settled. With regard to social knowledge, it was mainly economists working within the limits of their profession's consensus, rather than other kinds of policy professionals or more heterodox practitioners, who defined the contours and content of President Johnson's domestic initiatives.

II

Listen to Lyndon Johnson. In the midst of the presidential campaign of 1964, Johnson spoke to a business audience in Hartford, Connecticut. His theme was the current "period of prosperity that has never been equaled before in the annals of history of this country," and the challenge of communism to this achievement. "I am proud to say to you that we are standing up, we are resisting, and we are trying to halt the envelopment of freedom anywhere in the world." He quickly moved on to a characterization of the basis of this resistance: democratic government built on the base of "the free enterprise system." This successful economic order is one of a partnership between "capitalists," "managers," "workers," and "government." It is the partnership of these four elements, he held, that provides the basis for a democratic system of government capable of resisting the spread of communism. The speech concluded with a discussion, and a defense, of his budget policies and macroeconomic management.

The president's rhetoric is revealing of the self-satisfied context that informed the Great Society as a moment of political and social reform and of the Democratic party patrimony the Johnson administration brought to its domestic policies. Assertive yet reserved, reformist yet conservative, the Johnson program was the direct descendant of the substantive formula of the late Fair Deal that joined together the fiscal direction of markets by a neoclassic-Keynesian economic synthesis and a robust interest group politics at home to anti-Communist containment abroad. In the 1960s, the War on Poverty and the war in Vietnam were twin aspects of public policy rooted in precisely this coherent world view.

Within the constraints first established in the 1940s, the Johnson administration produced a broad and assertive domestic program in the grief-stricken aftermath of the murder of President Kennedy and the landslide victories of November 1964. Because of these constraints, the judgment of Pat Moynihan at the end of the 1960s rings half-true: if the Great Society was a missed opportunity for social democratic reform, the reasons are to be found mainly in the road not taken two decades earlier.

If a missed opportunity, the Great Society still marked one of this century's most vigorous moments of utilization of the state to shape markets and mitigate their distributional outcomes. President Johnson's Great Society, and the War on Poverty within it, built on initiatives begun in the Kennedy years that focused on juvenile delinquency. In 1964, the president soon proposed, and Congress approved, the most sweeping domestic legislative program since the New Deal. For a remarkable moment, the country's domestic politics focused sympathetically and constructively on the least advantaged, and the United States seemed prepared to override its historical reticence in finding a role for the state in mitigation of the distributive patterns of the market.

The War on Poverty was only one feature of what Johnson came to call his program for the Great Society, but this rubric alone captured a host of new programs for poor people: the Job Corps that focused on remedial programs for teenagers in residential settings to make them employable; the Neighborhood Youth Corps that provided training and work experience to adolescents who were in school or who had dropped out; the Manpower Development and Training Act that retrained unemployed workers; Head Start that provided preschool education; Upward Bound that helped talented high school students to prepare for college; the Teacher Corps, Title I of the Education and Secondary Education Act, and school lunch programs to improve schooling at the elementary and secondary levels; Foodstamps [sic] begun in the Kennedy administration, to supplement the budgets of the poor; Medicaid and neighborhood health centers to address the maldistribution of medical care in a fee-for-service system; Legal Services to partially equalize the availability of this service; Model Cities, a program to coordinate and concentrate urban development efforts in selected poverty areas; and, of course, Community Action. This most controversial feature of the War on Poverty was based on the provision in the Economic Opportunity Act of 1964 that stipulated "the maximum feasible participation of the residents of the areas and the members of groups served" in the design and decisions of community action agencies. The federal government contracted with these nongovernmental, community-based groups to administer federal antipoverty efforts and to develop local antipoverty programs in their areas. More broadly, the Great Society label encompassed fundamental civil rights legislation, Medicare for all Americans over the age of sixty-five, and enhancements to Social Security, among other programs.

The Great Society inaugurated a considerable shift in the construction of the federal budget. Military spending declined as a share of the whole, even during the Vietnam War; social welfare expenditures increased. Total public expenditures on social insurance and income transfer assistance programs doubled to $61 billion in the second half of the 1960s (rising from 4.6 percent to 6.1 percent of GNP). The most dramatic period of expansion spanned the fiscal years 1965–67, when the annual rate of increase, even after taking inflation into account, averaged about 15 percent; later, the pressures of Vietnam reduced the rate of growth in these programs to about 10 percent each year in real terms. These changes in the pattern of federal programs made a difference. Though it is difficult to separate out the effects of economic expansion and the effects of antipoverty programs on the reduction of poverty, the steep decline from the nearly one in five Americans who were poor by the official measure when the War on Poverty was declared to just over one in ten by 1973 at minimum represents a provocative correlation between governmental efforts and effects. Health care, hunger, unemployment, delinquency, manpower, training, community action, legal services, educational initiatives, and antidiscrimination legislation, moreover, defined an interrelated cluster of concerns that altered the boundary line between the state and the marketplace and that redefined the content of citizenship to include an enhanced social component.

In these ways, the Great Society revived some of the social democratic impulses of the New Deal and Fair Deal. The capacities of the state were mobilized to alter the abilities of its least-advantaged citizens to effectively participate and compete in labor markets and to mitigate the effects of market distributions. The aim, and the result, was a more equitable and less harsh society. . . .

Katz, like most sympathetic commentators who look back at least half wistfully at the Johnson domestic program in the age of Reagan, stresses the Great Society's willingness to utilize the state in unprecedented ways for social ends, but he downplays its other side: a non-ideological (self-consciously technical, trans-ideological) orientation to reform grounded in a very high degree of self-satisfaction with the country's economy and society. The Great Society was not an organic part of a larger vision or politics of the Left. It certainly lacked any of the anticapitalist or even critical content of its European social democratic counterparts. With the exception of Medicare, its politics did not promise any significant changes in the life conditions of the majority of Americans, or even the majority of supporters of the Democratic party. Substantively, it stopped well short of attempts to reorganize and modify the marketplace. It entirely left alone the organization of work, the patterns of investment, and the role of the business class. It did not call into question either the larger contours and rationality of the American political economy or the tools, a version of Keynesianism, that had been elaborated over the course of a quarter-century to manage the macroeconomic issues of growth, employment, and inflation. If at the heart of the Great Society was a *war* on poverty, this was a quite timid call to arms, with the enemy identified circumspectly.

The most compelling characteristic of the Great Society was that it was a program of mainstream economists and technicians who conceded from the start the framework of ideas and practices of the larger political economy. It sought to correct inequities and problems on the margin of a thriving system of production and consumption. If, for working people, as Arthur Stinchcombe observes, "Social Democracy is almost always compromise of basic principles for concrete advantages, while capitalist compromise is almost always an expedient to save the basic features of the system by bargaining away some concrete advantages," the Great Society entailed a constricted version of this trade-off.

Writing in an attempt to put "the Great Society in perspective," Brookings Institution scholar Henry Aaron observed that "none of the ideas embodied in the Great Society or the War on Poverty was really new. All had been foreshadowed in the New Deal or Fair Deal." This is partially, but not precisely, my point. For the ideas available in the period of the New Deal and Fair Deal were very capacious. They included national and regional economic planning and a highly interventionist Keynesianism as well as the public policies actually adopted or the policy discourse that came to prevail by the late 1940s. It is incontestable that the Great Society had ties of continuity with earlier periods of Democratic party reform: the key issue is how earlier outcomes of the contest within the Democratic party of competing reformist possibilities tacitly impressed assumptions and limits on the Johnson initiatives.

III

It is useful to contrast the New Deal and the Great Society. The New Deal was concerned, in the short and medium term, to restore the economy to a path of positive performance, and, in the medium and long term, to create a system of social insurance that would secure individuals against the vicissitudes of the labor market, and, in so doing, cushion the markets against themselves. At a time of great class-based turmoil, the New Deal, more than any previous American reform program, understood poverty as anchored in class relations as it aimed to put the working class back to work. And yet, its antipoverty measures were conceived as emergency efforts to deal with the temporary crisis of capitalism: they did not attempt a basic redistribution of wealth and income between the classes. Moreover, Roosevelt's program had nothing distinctive to offer to blacks except insofar as the New Deal promised renewed economic growth and prosperity for all.

The Great Society, by contrast, presumed such prosperity and a formula to secure it. Postwar economic development and growth in the United States, as elsewhere in the West in the 1960s, was robust and unprecedented. Economists grew confident they had reduced the business cycle to manageable proportions and to the dimensions of a technical problem. Broadly, supply and demand seemed to be in a high-employment equilibrium, and the societal relations of class appeared to be based more on harmony than on conflict. In this context, poverty was conceived of by the Great Society not as a matter of class relations even in the limited terms of the New Deal, but principally as a matter of race. The twin paths of civil rights legislation on public accommodations and voting rights and the War on Poverty were explicitly linked by President Johnson in his commencement address at Howard University in June 1965. There, he spoke of the special "burden that a dark skin can add to the search for a productive place in Society," of the fact that "unemployment strikes most swiftly and broadly at the Negro," of the need for a multicentered solution that goes beyond antidiscrimination legislation to questions of jobs, income, and housing.

Features of the Great Society could trace a direct lineage back to the New Deal; part of the Johnson program extended the social insurance provisions of the Social Security Act, especially as they concerned medical care for the elderly. But unlike the New Deal, the Great Society moved beyond the economy in general to the specificities of antipoverty policies, beyond social insurance to a host of non-insurance programs directed at the poor, and beyond class orientations to poverty to a confrontation with the intertwined questions of race and inequality.

In a penetrating essay that takes up the origins of the Great Society, Hugh Heclo notes the absence of an antipoverty legacy of the New Deal, as well as the lack of a popular ground swell in favor of such initiatives. Where, then, did the Great Society root itself? Following John Kingdon's work on agendas, Heclo argues that there was a fortuitous, and felicitous, conjuncture of three elements: the emergence of poverty, often connected to race relations, as a "problem" in the media and in public consciousness; the need of Presidents Kennedy and Johnson to find subjects for innovation; and, perhaps most important, the availability of a stream of policy proposals with a distinctive, and politically palatable, perspective on poverty by different kinds of policy experts.

This policy perspective that constituted the kit bag of ideas available to the Democratic presidents of the 1960s was principally that of economists who were concerned with human capital and incentives to opportunity, and of sociologists and social work professionals who had developed theories of blocked opportunity. Joined together, this package of orientations to policy had a coherent analysis and prescriptive perspective: its central intent was the integration of the poor into the growth economy and the social insurance state from which they had been excluded both for reasons of economic structure and individual behavior. Since the revitalization of the economy alone could not perform this feat of integration, the intervention of the state was required to incorporate all Americans into market mechanisms and into the public programs of collective insurance that went hand in hand with these labor markets.

Broadly speaking, this intervention took two new forms. The first (in what might be dubbed the Great Society of the economists) attempted to eliminate unemployment that was understood to be structural. From the start, economists had a high involvement in the formulation and implementation of the War on Poverty, and from the outset they impressed upon the programs a distinctive logic and theory of poverty, and thus of the kinds of interventions that were called for. . . .

The remedies of the economists could not be changes in programs of income transfers since the productivity characteristics of the poor would be left untouched. Thus, there was a need for policies targeted at the poor to improve their skills and behavioral traits, and thus their capacity to compete. These various programs, from the Job Corps to manpower training, would have to meet the rigorous tests of cost-benefit analysis. Thus, from the outset, the Office of Economic Opportunity convened an enormous amount of poverty research, and its economics-oriented staff was one of the first in Washington to adopt in the domestic arena the cost-effectiveness measures that Secretary of Defense [Robert] McNamara had brought with him from Ford.

The second form of intervention (what might be called the Great Society of the social policy experts), sought to change the institutionalized linkages between the poor and the state. It did so because it saw institutional barriers to the participation of poor people in the mainstream institutions of the economy and the polity, and because it believed that community activity of a grass-roots kind could effect behavioral changes in the poor as well. From this perspective, a host of behavioral pathologies afflicted the poor, including female-headed families, teenage pregnancy, very high dropout rates from secondary schooling, crime, ill-informed work habits, weak collective organization for self-help, and inattention to political matters. In addressing remedies, a number of different strands of thinking and action in social work, community organization, and social policy thinking intersected. . . .

What is striking, but scarcely noticed, is the close affinity between the War on Poverty of the economists and the War on Poverty of the social worker–social policy experts. Neither perspective understood poverty in terms of basic conflicts of interest; the central issue was not one of redistribution or of conflicting goals between the poor and the better-off. After all, the bounty of economic growth could suffice for everyone, and all Americans shared in a set of values, if only they could achieve them. Both groups of experts sought to enhance economic opportunity at the interface of structure and behavior. The basic structures of American Society were satisfactory; they needed adjustment, fine-tuning, enhanced access. The keys were manpower training, more grass-roots democracy, and a rigorous cost-benefit approach to the new programs.

The appeal of this rhetorical and policy construct for reform politicians at the national level in search of an innovative agenda is manifest. This was a program that displaced challenges to political authority to the local level and that did not threaten the central features of American capitalism, the distribution of goods and services, or prevailing ideological predispositions. It favored equality of opportunity rather than equality of results. It was not relief or the hated idea of the dole. Nor did it pose a challenge to the class compromise that underpinned the quasi-Keynesian growth of a big-government, social insurance state. It gave Democratic party leaders the chance to solidify their base in the black ghettos of the North and in the poorer areas of the rural South without disrupting their existing ties to white ethnic political machines or to the elite-dominated system of the Old South. Or, at the time, so it seemed.

The congressional Democratic party supported this program in overwhelming numbers across regional and ideological lines. But not without some uneasy moments. After the overwhelming passage of the Economic Opportunity Act of 1964 in the Senate, a group of Southern opponents appeared in the House led by Howard Smith, the chairman of the Rules Committee, who feared the creation of OEO would hasten racial integration. The administration protected the bill by conceding a veto to the governor of any state of any programs of community action not affiliated with institutions of higher education, and by allowing participation of private groups only if they had already displayed a "concern" for poverty, a clause meant to exclude such civil rights organizations as the NAACP. In the end, sixty of the one hundred Southern Democrats supported the bill, providing its margin of victory. At the same time, the fragility of Southern support was made clear; should race relations come to drive the issue of poverty, the cross-regional character of Democratic party support for Johnson's domestic agenda would cease. Later, the same would prove to be the case for politicians from white ethnic areas of the North and Midwest. But at the time of passage, the labor movement and big-city mayors like Richard Daley backed the president. And why not? The war on poverty he had inaugurated seemed to be on the periphery of their concerns.

The robustness of this program and the remarkable acquiescence of the Congress in it during the early part of Johnson's administration presented more than the appearance of assertive reform; the Great Society pushed its limits the possibilities inherent in the political formula of the late 1940s to utilize the state as a counterpoint to markets. But precisely because of this combination of vigor and limits, the cumulative result was a continuation of a negative spiral in the relationship between the social base and public policies of social democratic reform.

These central characteristics of the Great Society—its vigorous use of the state in a conservative way; the importance of policy intellectuals in the making and administering of the programs; the complementarity of the perspectives of economists, social policy experts, and politicians; its lack of challenge to prevailing patterns of authority, production, distribution, labor relations, or programs of social insurance; the relative inattention of the labor movement; and the partial overlap with issues of civil rights and race relations—were shaped decisively in the Democratic party, in the knowledge community, and in the labor movement of the 1940s. By the end of that decade, a host of decisions and developments had removed a wide range of interventionist, social democratic possibilities from the political agenda, possibilities that had remained live prospects within the range of ordinary politics at the end of the second New Deal. It was this reduction of political space, this closure of the agenda, and the deepening of distinctive patterns of politics and policy, that most shaped the character of the Great Society—what it was, and what it was not.

The reinforcement of the limited role of the labor movement, the identification of the party with blacks, rather than with cross-race, class-based policies, and the enhancement of the complacent orientation of the party's Keynesian economists who viewed the problems of employment, inflation, growth, and financial stability as merely technical rather than structural, left the Democrats very vulnerable to assaults from the Right in the 1970s. In the North, the party became dependent on a narrowly defined labor movement vulnerable to domestic disinvestment and stagflation, as well as on urban political organizations, the residues of the once robust political machines that had incorporated white ethnics into Democratic party politics and that had been bypassed by the War on Poverty's Community Action programs as mechanisms of mobilizing racial minorities in cities that were increasingly black and brown. The white South defected. Overall, the Democratic party electorate in presidential elections became more poor and less white. Locked into the limited analyses of neo-classic Keynesianism, the Democrats were unable to deal convincingly with the emergent economic instabilities, low growth, and inflation of the Ford and Carter years. Moreover, in the absence of either an engaged working-class social base in support of social democratic programs or realistic prospects for social democratic policies, the party embraced interest group pluralism as the only coherent strategy available. As a result, it found itself vulnerable to charges that it was nothing more than a holding company for special interests.

Thus, a central effect of the Great Society was its reinforcement of the tendencies of the 1940s, and with it, at the very moment of the most vigorous domestic reforms since the first term of Franklin Roosevelt, the exhaustion of the social democratic promise of the New Deal and the reinforcement of the centrifugal forces within the Democratic party. . . .

The "lost opportunity," lamented by Moynihan, for a more assertive social democratic program no longer existed in the early 1960s, as it had only two decades earlier. And yet, the Great Society did not lack for significance. It reminds us, as Katz asserts, that even within the limitations of American politics the current failures of the federal government are more matters of will than the absence of a potential institutional capacity. "In this recognition, there is at least some small cheer for dark days." At the same time, if the aspiration to renew the reform impulse is to have practical meaning, we must also come to understand how it was the Great Society reinforced just those aspects of the trajectory of the late 1940s which continue to present obstacles to the achievement of an American version of social democracy.

From Opportunity to Entitlement

GARETH DAVIES

Many liberals who had endorsed the self-help ethos of President Johnson's War on Poverty in 1964 came, by 1972, to embrace a very different approach, one that emphasized entitlement rather than opportunity. That their new orthodoxy represented the dominant strain was indicated by the liberal response to FAP [Family Assistance Plan]. Nevertheless, the concept of an unconditional entitlement to income was singular in a number of respects. First, it boldly confronted notions of reciprocal responsibility that had been long-accepted and retained widespread support, even among the poor. Second, such proposals as the Adequate Income Act of 1972 rested on the assumption that the causes of poverty were inseparable from its consequences: poverty was caused as well as defined by inadequate income. Such a judgment validated the redistributionist approach that had been rejected in 1964.

Finally, the new liberal orthodoxy embodied entirely different conceptions of dignity and dependency than had the Economic Opportunity Act. In 1964, liberals had shared the general tendency to equate dignity with self-sufficiency and to define dependency as its destructive opposite: long-term reliance on federal support. The evidence of Senator [George] McGovern's mail suggests that this remained the popular view. But by 1972, it had become more common for liberals to define dignity as freedom both from hardship and from the stigma hitherto attached to dependency. In turn, independence, far from connoting self-sufficiency in the conventional sense, meant freedom from want, however achieved. Dependency, in the old sense, was almost equated with independence in the new.

The importance of entitlement liberalism does not lie in its policy accomplishments. Insofar as the doctrine had policy consequences, they were the result of the reaction *against* a philosophy which never won much popular backing. The conservative reaction against the assumptions of the guaranteed income movement included a growing political interest in attaching work requirements to AFDC. This countertendency found substantive expression with Governor [Ronald] Reagan's "workfare" experiment in California and Senator Herman Talmadge's 1971 bid to improve the effectiveness of the Work Incentive Program.

During the 1970s, the traditional dichotomy between the deserving and undeserving poor, far from being erased (as entitlement liberals had hoped), was reinforced. Even as they consigned the Family Assistance Plan to defeat in October

1972, legislators simultaneously enacted the Supplemental Security Income program (SSI), guaranteeing an index-linked federal income to the aged, blind, and disabled. This was the first federal guarantee other than that for veterans, and it removed from state welfare rolls all of the categories covered by the Social Security Act (as amended), other than families with dependent children. By 1986, the federal government spent more on SSI than on AFDC, yet the program's enactment was—as Wilbur Cohen marveled—"[not] even controversial."

Four months prior to enacting SSI, Congress had approved a 20 percent increase in social security payments. In the view of Congressman Byrnes of Wisconsin, such an increase threatened the actuarial soundness of the program, yet in an election year the measure passed the Senate by 82 votes to 4, and the House by 302 to 35. Robert M. Ball, commissioner for Social Security, announced that "in truth we have a new social security program—a program that provides a new level of security to working people of all ages and to their families." [Political scientist] Martha Derthick observes that interest in poverty "lent momentum to welfare legislation generally, and because social security was the most popular and feasible form of such legislation, it won support when more controversial forms were stymied." Secretary Elliot Richardson, like his recent predecessors at HEW [Health, Education, and Welfare] tended to "support big increases in social security because that was the only place where big increases in social welfare spending could easily be had."

The principal beneficiaries of this turbulent period in social policy, therefore, were the elderly and the disabled. By contrast, those whom the entitlement liberals had endeavored to help, the "undeserving poor," were victims of a growing backlash. Three weeks after the death of FAP and one week after George McGovern's crushing defeat by President Nixon, Mitchell Ginsberg—former commissioner for welfare in New York City and an early disciple of entitlement—told the *Los Angeles Times* that "the hatred of welfare is unbelievable. There is a strong mood across the country to crack down, keep people off the rolls. Welfare reform is at a dead end. . . . We are now in the midst of a very sharp swing against doing something for the poor, for minorities." In recent years, Ginsberg had become increasingly insistent that the nation respect the rights of a newly assertive poor. . . . In effect, the failure of welfare reform allowed Ginsberg to rediscover the virtues of traditional liberalism, particularly the value of congruence with—and respect for—popular sentiment:

> It is clear that people like me who have been pushing for reform for years obviously haven't made too much progress. . . . We underestimated the depth of the opposition. We didn't pay enough attention to the concerns of people who were above the welfare line. The heart of the opposition to welfare comes from people just above it—blue-collar workers, trade unionists, though not labor leaders or high-level businessmen. It is the group below, the lower-middle-income worker. He's the guy who feels welfare is taking it away from him. We will have to pay attention to the ethnic groups who feel more threatened by "them."

In the aftermath of the failure of the entitlement revolution, Ginsberg's new two-part antipoverty plan attested to his rediscovery of opportunity liberalism. First, he proposed the expansion of health programs, better education, and further social security increases. Second, he recommended tax credits as a way of assisting the working poor (a proposal that bore fruit with the enactment of the Earned Income

Tax Credit). Above all, public policy had to embody a philosophy that Middle America found acceptable. "The alliance of welfare clients, social workers, and minorities won't do it," Ginsberg said. "They don't have enough influence. We have to move out to some other groups that we have too often disregarded."

Sobered by the lessons of the failed battle for welfare reform, growing numbers of liberals underwent the same process of education, relearning lessons about popular individualism that had only recently been self-evident. As the prospect for reform diminished in 1971, an aide suggested that Senator Jacob Javits might want to rethink proposals that he had sponsored the previous year:

> I see that you had one to completely eliminate any work requirements for women with school-age children. While at first glance this appears to be a liberal position, I believe that we should stop thinking of work requirements as punitive, and instead think of the potential therein for lifting an entire family unit out of the demoralizing poverty-welfare cycle.
>
> Part of the problem the working classes have with welfare is because liberals have created the impression that work is somehow punishment. They justifiably wonder why they are working (subject to "punishment") while the government seems to believe that it's unfair or unjust to require welfare recipients to work.

In conclusion, Javits's aide asked. "Why aren't we saying that we're giving the unfortunate an opportunity to be trained, to gain self-respect and a sense of achievement—a job?" Such rationales would indeed be deployed in support of welfare reform packages later in the decade, most notably President Carter's Program for Better Jobs and Income. More generally, the mid-1970s featured renewed liberal interest in proposals to guarantee a job to every American. Correspondingly, talk of an unconditional right to income largely disappeared from the language of liberalism.

If the entitlement revolution failed to reap substantive legislative reward, then neither did it have any discernible impact on attitudes to dependency, save perhaps to reinforce the traditional animus to which Ginsberg referred. During the next two decades, poverty among the elderly underwent a sharp decline, thanks to social security and SSI, but the same years saw an alarming increase in the number of poor children. Daniel Patrick Moynihan observes that, in a historic reversal of traditional patterns, "the rate of poverty among the very young in the United States has become nearly seven times as great as among the old." But despite the growth of poverty among youth, and the growing incidence of female-headed families, the number of children receiving AFDC actually declined after 1972, as did the real value of benefits to individual families. Between 1972 and 1987, welfare payments as a proportion of GNP fell from 0.60 percent to 0.36 percent. And between 1972 and 1984, the combined average value of AFDC and food stamp payments to a family of four declined, in real terms, by 20 percent.

In political terms, portentous—although more amorphous—legacies become apparent if one conceives of this abortive entitlement revolution as being part of a wider crisis of American liberalism. In this context, the costs of the Democratic Party's deviation from the New Deal tradition are readily apparent. Within eight years, the party of the "common man" underwent an astonishing transformation in ideology, such that by 1972 it could credibly be characterized by President Nixon and Vice President Spiro Agnew as the party of the "limousine liberals." . . .

For all its deviant qualities and unintended consequences, the entitlement revolution is susceptible to a rational explanation. Such an explanation must answer two related questions. First, why did policymakers on both the left and the right come to embrace the income maintenance response to poverty during the 1960s? And second, why did liberals do so to a degree that required them to endorse radically unpopular notions of unconditional entitlement? If the two questions are related, then the underlying dynamics are to some extent separable.

In intellectual terms, an important aspect of both problems is that the previously favored service strategy for combating deprivation simply became less plausible as the War on Poverty progressed. At the same time, its logical implausibility became politically problematic. The key factor in both instances was race. The Economic Opportunity Act of 1964 was founded on two vulnerable premises concerning the practicability of self-help. First, it tacitly assumed that the deserving poor could be raised to comfortable self-sufficiency were they furnished with appropriate skills and values (self-esteem, motivation, education, vocational skills). The War on Poverty thereby operated on the basis that the U.S. economic system was fundamentally beneficent. Second, the program was ostensibly colorblind; it proceeded from the claim that black and white poverty could be treated by the same individualistic methods.

The intellectual vulnerability of these claims was clear from the outset to many politicians, bureaucrats, and academics, but in terms of the political purpose of the War on Poverty in 1964, such vulnerability was not important. It gratified the crusading liberal impulse for such a war to be declared, but no immediate pressure for victory existed. More important, if some policymakers did worry about the peculiar nature of black poverty or the structural problems of the American economy, even they shared the overriding liberal conviction that any problem susceptible to definition had a solution. It was this hubristic conviction that underpinned the belief that liberal social engineers could exploit new knowledge to empower the individual and lessen his or her dependence on welfare.

By the summer of 1965, both of these fragile premises had suffered grievous blows, while the administration's political equation had also changed. In his Great Society address at Ann Arbor, President Johnson had seemed to envision a new "era of good feelings" based on the consensual pursuit of enlightened liberal goals. A year later, his commencement address at Howard University even sought to envelop an unprecedentedly ambitious civil rights agenda within that consensus. But the Watts riot both symbolized and accelerated a rising tide of militancy within black America, a tide that abruptly destroyed the luxury of autonomous activism that Johnson had hitherto enjoyed. From now until the end of his troubled presidency, Johnson would be responding to events that he was increasingly powerless to influence.

As racial tension increased, political pressures on the War on Poverty from both left and right mounted. Meanwhile, the intellectual basis for an unalloyed service strategy was greatly undermined. Within the administration, domestic policymakers devised new approaches to poverty that retained traditional objectives but incorporated a strong new income maintenance component; only when income were redistributed, it was now acknowledged, could opportunity be equalized. Outside the administration, vocal antipoverty activists and black militants were going much further, questioning the entire legitimacy of the Economic Opportunity Act's "blaming the victim" approach. In their response to the Moynihan Report, and with their contributions to the November 1965 planning conference "To Fulfill These Rights," such radicals developed a fundamentally new approach to tackling poverty: redistribute income and expect nothing in return.

With the War on Poverty now so strongly associated with the black struggle for equality, supporters of the Economic Opportunity Act felt inevitably reluctant to demand that the rights of the poor be contingent on their behavior. If through its social policy American society was atoning for 350 years of racial oppression (and President Johnson had implied such a connection at Howard University), how could it justly demand anything in return? Liberal guilt, uncertainty, and apprehension were to be shrewdly exploited in the years to come, as for example by the black-dominated National Welfare Rights Organization. Moreover, the success of George Wiley's campaign to organize welfare mothers in defense of their rights and in pursuit of a guaranteed income placed pressure on more traditional groups (such as the National Urban League) to move leftward.

The liberal constituency most obviously vulnerable to NWRO guaranteed income advocacy was the welfare bureaucracy. By the latter half of the Johnson presidency, both HEW and OEO administrators and social workers demonstrably anxious to appease demands to which they were in some measure already drawn by preference. Elected politicians, however, were more resistant to the income strategy in general, and seemingly impervious to the argument that long-term dependency was an acceptable response to able-bodied poverty. From the vantage point of the presidency, budgetary and economic strains, together with the growing conservatism of Congress and the nation, limited Johnson's ability to respond to the ever more insistent demands of the radicals. In so suddenly adverse an environment, what could he do other than pursue the gradualist approach that alone could command legislative approval and public consent? In this context, the instinctive sympathy Johnson felt for traditional and limited definitions of income entitlement was compounded by political necessity.

Liberal legislators, too, were initially cautious in embracing radical critiques of Great Society liberalism. During the first half of 1966, serious criticism of the president's domestic policies did begin to materialize, but attacks tended to focus on the size of Great Society programs rather than on their orientation. As the year wore on, however, ambitious liberal senators, such as Robert Kennedy and Abraham Ribicoff, progressively sharpened their critiques, beginning to demand basic redirection. An important source of such disengagement and restlessness was political opportunism. President Johnson's political authority and personal popularity were being dramatically weakened as the war in Vietnam intensified.

Vietnam's importance to the entitlement revolution is profound, albeit indirect. First, the bitterness and ill will it generated within liberal ranks inevitably impeded cooperation on domestic matters, and not simply because the war diverted funds from Great Society programs. Second, the language and style of protest represented by the growing antiwar movement came to be viewed by some dissenting politicians as embodying a New Politics through which the progressive spirit might yet emerge ascendant from the ashes of 1960s liberalism. By 1968, and much more strongly so thereafter, the NWRO was part of an extraordinarily eclectic and energetic coalition of discontents.

When Robert Kennedy observed in 1967 that the perspective of the New Left would soon constitute accepted orthodoxy, he was pondering a political landscape in which war, youth, dissent, and rioting had seemingly destroyed the basis for Democratic dominance. Equally, he contemplated dislocating events at home whose projection into the future might render transient the repressive spirit abroad in the land in 1966–1967. And even were that not the case, the strength of the New Politics within the Democratic Party was such that any serious bid for the presidential nomination must necessarily court the forces of dissent.

Only in 1970 did radical definitions of income entitlement gain important support among liberals. Not surprisingly, their principal exponents were politically ambitious Democrats with particular reason to display fealty to the New Politics coalition: Fred Harris, Eugene McCarthy, George McGovern. In a different political context, they might have responded to ghetto unrest and the failure of the War on Poverty by proposing to guarantee work to every American, an approach that would have boosted family income without offending the work-oriented values of the American public. Cost was one inhibiting factor, and legacies from the 1940s (when full employment liberalism had suffered a historically important defeat) may have constituted a second. Equally, however, retaining the link between economic security and employment would have offended the welfare rights lobby, which advocated a different form of entitlement: George Wiley had declared his goal to be a "guarantee[d] minimum income for every citizen without any exception, whether they work or not, whether they're able to work or not." Once George McGovern had won the Democratic nomination in 1972, thanks to the backing of a New Politics coalition which included the NWRO, he did indeed emphasize the employment route to economic security.

Yet by this time, the guaranteed income movement had deeper foundations than such unalloyed opportunism might imply. In addition to self-interest dictated by the strength of the New Politics coalition, there had occurred within liberal ranks a more general eroding of the traditional emphasis on mutual obligation. As the poor ceased to be conceived as citizens with responsibilities and instead were cast in the role of societal victims, obligations of citizenship that had been unquestioned in 1964 ceased to seem appropriate.

President Johnson, despite himself, had contributed to this process with the Howard University address. Subsequently, the 1966 report of his Advisory Council on Public Welfare boldly repudiated traditional expectations regarding the dependent poor. Its title, "Having the Power, We Have the Duty," may have been drawn from Lyndon Johnson's speech declaring war on poverty just two years before, but the "duties" that the phrase denoted were substantially enlarged. . . . And in 1968, the Kerner Commission's verdict on the previous summer's riots had apportioned rights and responsibilities in such a way that they appeared mutually exclusive rather than complementary.

The sheer breadth of support for the income strategy by this stage undoubtedly lent additional momentum to entitlement liberalism. Within the federal bureaucracy, among academics, in the business community, and within both political parties, the manifest failings of the War on Poverty had produced the conviction that income maintenance represented a more realistic response to deprivation. As has been seen, this conviction had first appeared within the Johnson administration as early as

1965, but as a means to the rehabilitative end rather than as an end in itself. Similarly, for Richard Nixon and [Congressman] Wilbur Mills, FAP would ultimately ease chronic dependency and protect the work ethic by extending support to the working poor. In this context, despite widespread support for some version of the income strategy during the Nixon years, entitlement liberalism as embodied by the Adequate Income Act of 1972 remains a singular phenomenon.

Having reached its zenith in opposition to President Nixon's welfare reform proposal, entitlement liberalism disappeared from view during the course of the 1970s and 1980s without having achieved any of its objectives. Such historians as Alonzo Hamby, contemplating the odyssey of American liberalism since Roosevelt, have associated President Johnson with the "politics of excess," arguing that it was with his leadership that the New Deal liberal tradition reached and overstretched its limits. In a similar vein, contemporary politicians and political commentators tend to characterize President Clinton's pledge to "end welfare as we know it" as a retreat from the big government activism of the New Deal and the Great Society.

Yet the case of welfare policy suggests that such interpretations are fundamentally flawed. In truth, both Franklin Roosevelt and Lyndon Johnson shared a sensitivity to their nation's dominant social philosophy and consistently resisted the counsel of those who found the traditional connection between work and economic security anachronistic. It was Johnson's liberal detractors and successors who abandoned a venerable tradition of liberal individualism, and they did so with politically costly results. With the "New Covenant" that he unveiled in 1988 and subsequently invoked again as president, Bill Clinton simply rediscovered a temporarily discarded old covenant whose principles had been central to the Economic Opportunity Act of 1964. The crusading optimism of the War on Poverty was conspicuously absent, and the question of how to restore the dependent poor to employment had yielded some different answers. Still, the question was the same and, to an as yet unacknowledged degree, the politics of welfare had come full circle.

₩ F U R T H E R   R E A D I N G S

Amenta, Edwin. *Bold Relief: Institutional Politics and the Origins of Modern American Social Policy* (1998).

Anderson. Martin. *Welfare: The Political Economy of Welfare Reform in the United States* (1978).

Andrew, John A., III. *Lyndon Johnson and the Great Society* (1999).

Auletta, Ken. *The Underclass* (1982).

Axinn, June, and Mark J. Stern. *Dependency and Poverty: Old Problems in a New World* (1988).

Bane, Mary Jo, and David T. Ellwood. *Welfare Realities: From Rhetoric to Reform* (1994).

Berkowitz, Edward, and Kim McQuaid. *Creating the Welfare State* (1980).

Bernstein, Irving. *Guns or Butter: The Presidency of Lyndon Johnson* (1996).

Block, Fred, et al. *The Mean Season: The Attack on the Welfare State* (1987).

Bornet, Vaughan. *The Presidency of Lyndon B. Johnson* (1983).

Burke, Vincent J., and Lee Burke. *Nixon's Good Deed: Welfare Reform* (1974).

Cammisa, Anne Marie. *From Rhetoric to Reform? Welfare Policy in American Politics* (1998).

Caro, Robert A. *The Years of Lyndon Johnson: Means of Ascent* (1990).

———. *The Years of Lyndon Johnson: The Path to Power* (1982).

Committee on Health Care for Homeless People (CHCHP). *Homelessness, Health, and Human Needs* (1988).

Conkin, Paul. *Big Daddy from the Pedernales: Lyndon Baines Johnson* (1986).

Dallek, Robert. *Lone Star Rising* (1991).

Danziger, Sheldon H., et al., eds. *Confronting Poverty: Prescriptions for Change* (1994).

Danziger, Sheldon H., and Daniel H. Weinberger, eds. *Fighting Poverty* (1986).

Davies, Gareth. *From Opportunity to Entitlement: The Transformation and Decline of Great Society Liberalism* (1996).

Divine, Robert A., ed. *The Johnson Years,* 3 vols. (1981, 1987, 1994).

Duncan, Greg. *Years of Poverty, Years of Plenty* (1984).

Edelman, Marian Wright. *Families in Peril: An Agenda for Social Change* (1987).

Ellwood, David T. *Poor Support: Poverty in the American Family* (1988).

Gans, Herbert J. *The War Against the Poor: The Underclass and Antipoverty Policy* (1995).

Gettleman, Marvin E., and David Mermelstein, eds. *The Great Society Reader: The Failure of American Liberalism* (1967).

Gilder, George. *Wealth and Poverty* (1981).

Ginzberg, Eli, and Robert M. Solow, eds. *The Great Society* (1974).

Ginzberg, Leon. *Conservative Social Welfare Policy* (1998).

Glasgow, Douglas G. *The Black Underclass: Poverty, Unemployment, and Entrapment of Ghetto Youth* (1980).

Handler, Joel F. *The Poverty of Welfare Reform* (1995).

Harrington, Michael. *The New American Poverty* (1984).

———. *The Other America* (1962).

Haveman, Robert H. *Poverty Policy and Poverty Research: The Great Society and the Social Sciences* (1987).

Heath. Jim F. *Decade of Disillusionment* (1976).

Jencks, Christopher. *Rethinking Social Policy: Race, Poverty, and the Underclass* (1992).

Jordan, Barbara C., and Elspeth D. Rostow, eds. *The Great Society: A Twenty Year Critique* (1986).

Kaplan, Marshall, and Peggy L. Cuciti, eds. *The Great Society and Its Legacy: Twenty Years of U.S. Social Policy* (1986).

Katz, Michael B. *Improving Poor People: The Welfare State, the "Underclass," and Urban Schools as History* (1995).

———. *The "Underclass" Debate: Views from History* (1993).

———. *The Undeserving Poor: From the War on Poverty to the War on Welfare* (1989).

Kearns, Doris. *Lyndon Johnson and the American Dream* (1976).

Kuttner, Robert. *The Economic Illusion: The False Choice Between Prosperity and Social Justice* (1984).

Levitan, Sar. *The Great Society's Poor Law: A New Approach to Poverty* (1969).

Levitan, Sar, and Isaac Shapiro. *Working But Poor: America's Contradiction* (1987).

Levitan, Sar, and Robert Taggert. *The Promise of Greatness* (1976).

Levy, Frank. *Dollars and Dreams: The Changing American Income Distribution* (1987).

Lieberman, Robert C. *Shifting the Color Line: Race and the American Welfare State* (1998).

McGeary, Michael G. H., and Laurence E. Lynn, eds. *Urban Change and Poverty* (1988).

Matusow, Allen. *The Unraveling of America: A History of Liberalism in the 1960s* (1984).

Meade, Lawrence M. *Beyond Entitlement: The Social Obligations of Citizenship* (1986).

Mishra, Ramesh, *The Welfare State in Crisis: Social Thought and Social Change* (1984).

Moon, J. Donald, ed. *Responsibility, Rights, and Welfare: The Theory of the Welfare State* (1988).

Moynihan, Daniel P. *Family and Nation* (1986).

———. *Maximum Feasible Misunderstanding* (1969).

Murray, Charles. *Losing Ground: American Social Policy, 1950–1980* (1984).

National Conference of Catholic Bishops. *Economic Justice for All* (1986).

Noble, Charles. *Welfare as We Knew It: A Political History of the American Welfare State* (1997).

Norris, Donald F., and Lyke Thompson, eds. *The Politics of Welfare Reform* (1995).
Patterson, James T. *America's Struggle Against Poverty* (1981).
Peterson, Paul, ed. *The New Urban Reality* (1985).
Piven, Frances Fox, and Richard A. Cloward. *The Breaking of the American Social Compact* (1997).
————. *The New Class War: Reagan's Attack on the Welfare State and Its Consequences* (1982).
————. *Regulating the Poor: The Functions of Public Welfare* 2nd ed. (1993).
Quadagno, Jill. *The Color of Welfare: How Racism Undermined the War on Poverty* (1994).
Rodgers, Harell R. Jr. *Poor Women, Poor Families: The Economic Plight of America's Female-Headed Households* (1986).
Ryan, William P. *Equality* (1982).
Schram, Sanford F. *Words of Welfare: The Poverty of Social Science and the Social Science of Poverty* (1995).
Schwarz, John E. *America's Hidden Success: A Reassessment of Twenty Years of Public Policy* (1983).
Skocpol, Theda. *Social Policy in the United States: Future Possibilities in Historical Perspective* (1995).
Sundquist, James L. *Politics and Policy: The Eisenhower, Kennedy, and Johnson Years* (1968).
Unger, Irwin. *The Best of Intentions: The Triumphs and Failures of the Great Society Under Kennedy, Johnson, and Nixon* (1996).
Warner, David C., ed. *Toward New Human Rights: The Social Policies of the Kennedy and Johnson Administrations* (1977).
Wier, Margaret. *Politics and Jobs* (1992).
————, ed. *The Social Divide: Political Parties and the Future of Activist Government* (1998).
Wilson, William Julius. *The Truly Disadvantaged: The Inner City, the Underclass, and Public Policy* (1987).
————. *When Work Disappears: The World of the New Urban Poor* (1996).
Zarefsky, David. *President Johnson's War on Poverty: Rhetoric and History* (1986).

C H A P T E R
7

Martin Luther King Jr.
and the Struggle
for African American Equality

XX

The drive for freedom and equality by African Americans was one of the most important developments in postwar America. The struggle played out not only in the courts and in the halls of Congress but in the streets, in churches, and at lunchroom counters throughout the nation. It was a struggle not just of individual leaders, however charismatic, but of ordinary men and women who found the courage and dignity to demand change. The changes they demanded, as the following documents and essays suggest, raise questions, many of them yet unresolved, that go to the heart of the American experience. For example, what do Americans mean when they profess to believe in equality? Do we believe in equality of condition or in equality of opportunity? How has race (or gender or class) limited the application of such beliefs? What actions are appropriate for government and other institutions to take in the pursuit of equality, and which are inappropriate?

XX *D O C U M E N T S*

World War II marked a watershed in the history of civil rights as many African Americans served in the armed forces, albeit in segregated units; as other blacks found work in defense plants; and as wartime rhetoric about freedom and democracy raised expectations of expanded civil rights. Most important, African Americans themselves displayed a new confidence and determination. The return of African American soldiers was nevertheless greeted by violence in parts of the South, as a *New York Times* report of July 27, 1946, reprinted as Document 1, reveals. At the core of the struggle for equality were issues of pride and self-esteem. In Document 2, an excerpt from *The Autobiography of Malcolm X,* the radical Muslin activist recalls the painful process of "conking" his hair to make it look like a white man's. In Document 3, Chief Justice Earl Warren delivers the Supreme Court's unanimous opinion in the historic case of

Brown v. Board of Education of Topeka, which declared separate educational facilities to be inherently unequal.

Beginning with the Montgomery bus boycott of 1955–1956, the history of the civil rights movement was increasingly shaped by courageous men and women who directly challenged the Jim Crow system of segregation and discrimination. In Document 4, an interview by reporter Howell Raines, Franklin McCain recalls the first sit-in of the 1960s. Only twenty-six years old when he helped lead the Montgomery boycott, Martin Luther King Jr. quickly became the movement's most charismatic leader. His address before the Lincoln Memorial during the March on Washington in August 1963 (Document 5) is one of the most famous speeches in American history. By the mid-1960s, however, King's leadership was increasingly challenged by younger, more radical activists such as Stokely Carmichael, a leader of the Student Nonviolent Coordinating Committee (SNCC), who in Document 6 defends the new call for "black power." Resistance to the civil rights movement occurred not just in the South, where beatings and even murder were not infrequent, but throughout the nation, including even federal law enforcement agencies such as the Federal Bureau of Investigation (FBI), which carried out an elaborate secret campaign to discredit King. Document 7 is excerpted from a 1976 investigation of the FBI by a U.S. Senate committee chaired by Democratic senator Frank Church of Idaho.

1. The *New York Times* Reports a Murder in Georgia, 1946

Monroe, Ga., July 26—Two young Negroes, one a veteran just returned from the war, and their wives were lined up last night near a secluded road and shot dead by an unmasked band of twenty white men.

The ghastly details of the multiple lynching were told today by Loy Harrison, a well-to-do white farmer who had just hired the Negroes to work on his farm. Harrison was bringing the Negroes to his farm when his car was waylaid by the mob eight miles from Monroe. Questioning of one of the Negroes by the mob indicated, Harrison said, that he was suspected of having stabbed his former employer, a white man. The Negroes, Roger Malcolm and George Dorsey, both 27, were removed from the car and led down a side road.

The women, who were sisters and who had just recently married Malcolm and Dorsey, began to scream. Then a mob member said that one of the women had recognized him.

"Get those damned women, too," the mob leader shouted.

Several of the men then came back and dragged the shrieking women from the automobile. A few moments later Mr. Harrison heard the shots—many of them and the mob dispersed.

The grotesquely sprawled bodies were found in a clump of bushes beside a little-used side road, the upper parts of the bodies scarcely recognizable from the mass of bullet holes.

Dorsey's mother, Monia Williams, said that her son had just been discharged after five years in the Army and that she had received his discharge button in the mail just this week.

The lynching was the first in the nation in nearly a year and was the first multiple lynching since two 14-year-old Negro boys were hanged by a Mississippi mob in October 1942. For Georgia it was the first lynching of more than one person since 1918 when ten Negroes were lynched in Brooks County.

2. Malcolm X Recalls Getting a "Conk," 1964

Shorty soon decided that my hair was finally long enough to be conked. He had promised to school me in how to beat the barbershops' three- and four-dollar price by making up congolene, and then conking ourselves.

I took the little list of ingredients he had printed out for me, and went to a grocery store, where I got a can of Red Devil lye, two eggs, and two medium-sized white potatoes. Then at the drugstore near the poolroom, I asked for a large jar of vaseline, a large bar of soap, a large-toothed comb and a fine-toothed comb, one of those rubber hoses with a metal sprayhead, a rubber apron, and a pair of gloves.

"Going to lay on that first conk?" the drugstore man asked me. I proudly told him, grinning, "Right!"

Shorty paid six dollars a week for a room in his cousin's shabby apartment. His cousin wasn't at home. "It's like the pad's mine, he spends so much time with his woman," Shorty said. "Now, you watch me—"

He peeled the potatoes and thin-sliced them into a quart-sized Mason fruit jar, then started stirring them with a wooden spoon as he gradually poured in a little over half the can of lye. "Never use a metal spoon; the lye will turn it black," he told me.

A jelly-like, starchy-looking glop resulted from the lye and potatoes, and Shorty broke in the two eggs, stirring real fast—his own conk and dark face bent down close. The congolene turned pale-yellowish. "Feel the jar," Shorty said. I cupped my hand against the outside, and snatched it away. "Damn right, it's hot, that's the lye," he said. "So you know it's going to burn when I comb it in—it burns *bad*. But the longer you can stand it, the straighter the hair."

He made me sit down, and he tied the string of the new rubber apron tightly around my neck, and combed up my bush of hair. Then, from the big vaseline jar, he took a handful and massaged it hard all through my hair and into the scalp. He also thickly vaselined my neck, ears, and forehead. "When I get to washing out your head, be sure to tell me anywhere you feel any little stinging," Shorty warned me, washing his hands, then pulling on the rubber gloves, and tying on his own rubber apron. "You always got to remember that any congolene left in burns a sore into your head."

The congolene just felt warm when Shorty started combing it in. But then my head caught fire.

I gritted my teeth and tried to pull the sides of the kitchen table together. The comb felt as if it was raking my skin off.

My eyes watered, my nose was running. I couldn't stand it any longer; I bolted to the washbasin. I was cursing Shorty with every name I could think of when he got the spray going and started soap-lathering my head.

He lathered and spray-rinsed, lathered and spray-rinsed, maybe ten or twelve times, each time gradually closing the hot-water faucet, until the rinse was cold, and that helped some.

"You feel any stinging spots?"

"No," I managed to say. My knees were trembling.

"Sit back down, then. I think we got it all out okay."

The flame came back as Shorty, with a thick towel, started drying my head, rubbing hard. *"Easy, man, easy!"* I kept shouting.

"The first time's always worst. You get used to it better before long. You took it real good, homeboy. You got a good conk."

When Shortly let me stand up and see in the mirror, my hair hung down in limp, damp strings. My scalp still flamed, but not as badly; I could bear it. He draped the towel around my shoulders, over my rubber apron, and began again vaselining my hair.

I could feel him combing, straight back, first the big comb, then the fine-toothed one.

Then, he was using a razor, very delicately, on the back of my neck. Then, finally, shaping the sideburns.

My first view in the mirror blotted out the hurting. I'd seen some pretty conks, but when it's the first time, on your *own* head, the transformation, after the lifetime of kinks, is staggering.

The mirror reflected Shorty behind me. We both were grinning and sweating. And on top of my head was this thick, smooth sheen of shining red hair—real red—as straight as any white man's.

3. *Brown* v. *Board of Education,* 1954

These cases come to us from the States of Kansas, South Carolina, Virginia, and Delaware. They are premised on different facts and different local conditions, but a common legal question justifies their consideration together in this consolidated opinion.

In each of the cases, minors of the Negro race, through their legal representatives, seek the aid of the courts in obtaining admission to the public schools of their community on a nonsegregated basis. In each instance, they had been denied admission to schools attended by white children under laws requiring or permitting segregation according to race. This segregation was alleged to deprive the plaintiffs of the equal protection of the laws under the Fourteenth Amendment. In each of the cases other than the Delaware case, a three-judge federal district court denied relief to the plaintiffs on the so-called "separate but equal" doctrine announced by this

Brown v. *Board of Education of Topeka et al.,* 324 U.S. 483 (1954).

Court in *Plessy* v. *Ferguson,* 163 U.S. 537. Under that doctrine, equality of treatment is accorded when the races are provided substantially equal facilities, even though these facilities be separate. . . .

The plaintiffs contend that segregated public schools are not "equal" and cannot be made "equal," and that hence they are deprived of the equal protection of the laws. . . .

In approaching this problem, we cannot turn the clock back to 1868 when the Amendment was adopted, or even to 1896 when *Plessy* v. *Ferguson* was written. We must consider public education in the light of its full development and its present place in American life throughout the Nation. Only in this way can it be determined if segregation in public schools deprives these plaintiffs of the equal protection of the laws.

Today, education is perhaps the most important function of state and local governments. Compulsory school attendance laws and the great expenditures for education both demonstrate our recognition of the importance of education to our democratic society. It is required in the performance of our most basic public responsibilities, even service in the armed forces. It is the very foundation of good citizenship. Today it is a principal instrument in awakening the child to cultural values, in preparing him for later professional training, and in helping him to adjust normally to his environment. In these days, it is doubtful that any child may reasonably be expected to succeed in life if he is denied the opportunity of an education. Such an opportunity, when the state has undertaken to provide it, is a right which must be made available to all on equal terms.

We come then to the question presented: Does segregation of children in public schools solely on the basis of race, even though the physical facilities and other "tangible" factors may be equal, deprive the children of the minority group of equal educational opportunities? We believe that it does.

In *Sweatt* v. *Painter, supra,* in finding that a segregated law school for Negroes could not provide them equal educational opportunities, this Court relied in large part on "those qualities which are incapable of objective measurement but which make for greatness in a law school." In *McLaurin* v. *Oklahoma State Regents, supra,* the Court, in requiring that a Negro admitted to a white graduate school be treated like all other students, again resorted to intangible considerations: ". . . his ability to study, to engage in discussions and exchange views with other students, and in general, to learn his profession." Such considerations apply with added force to children in grade and high schools. To separate them from others of similar age and qualifications solely because of their race generates a feeling of inferiority as to their status in the community that may affect their hearts and minds in a way unlikely ever to be undone. The effect of this separation on their educational opportunities was well stated by a finding in the Kansas case by a court which nevertheless felt compelled to rule against the Negro plaintiffs:

> Segregation of white and colored children in public schools has a detrimental effect upon the colored children. The impact is greater when it has the sanction of the law; for the policy of separating the races is usually interpreted as denoting the inferiority of the negro group. A sense of inferiority affects the motivation of a child to learn. Segregation with the sanction of law, therefore, has a tendency to [retard] the educational and mental development of negro children and to deprive them of some of the benefits they would receive in a racial[ly] integrated school system.

Whatever may have been the extent of psychological knowledge at the time of *Plessy* v. *Ferguson,* this finding is amply supported by modern authority. Any language in *Plessy* v. *Ferguson* contrary to this finding is rejected.

We conclude that in the field of public education the doctrine of "separate but equal" has no place. Separate education facilities are inherently unequal. Therefore, we hold that the plaintiffs and others similarly situated for whom the actions have been brought are, by reason of the segregation complained of, deprived of the equal protection of the laws guaranteed by the Fourteenth Amendment.

4. Franklin McCain Remembers
the First Sit-in, 1960

[Howell Raines] It was one of those group friendships that spring up among college freshmen. In the first semester at all-black North Carolina A&T College in Greensboro, he [Franklin McCain] and Ezell Blair Jr., David Richmond, and Joseph McNeil became inseparable. They would study together, eat together, and "as young freshmen often do in college dormitories late at night, when they finish studying or when they want to cop out from studying . . . resort to the old-fashion type bull session."

Through the fall, their talks continued. He remembers them as "elementary philosophers," young idealists talking about justice and injustice, hypocrisy, how imperfectly their society embodied its own ideals. Slowly their talks swung to a debate as old as philosophy itself: at what point does the moral man act against injustice? ". . . I think the thing that precipitated the sit-in, the idea of the sit-in, more than anything else, was that little bit of incentive and that little bit of courage that each of us instilled within each other."

[McCain] The planning process was on a Sunday night, I remember it quite well. I think it was Joseph who said, "It's time that we take some action now. We've been getting together, and we've been, up to this point, still like most people we've talked about for the past few weeks or so—that is, people who talk a lot but, in fact, make very little action." After selecting the technique, then we said, "Let's go down and just ask for service." It certainly wasn't titled a "sit-in" or "sit-down" at that time. "Let's just go down to Woolworth's tomorrow and ask for service, and the tactic is going to be simply this: we'll just stay there." We never anticipated being served, certainly, the first day anyway. "We'll stay until we get served." And I think Ezell said, "Well, you know that might be weeks, that might be months, that might be never." And I think it was the consensus of the group, we said, "Well, that's just the chance we'll have to take."

What's likely to happen? Now, I think that that was a question that all of us asked ourselves. . . . What's going to happen once we sit down? Of course, nobody had the answers. Even your wildest imagination couldn't lead you to believe what would, in fact, happen.

[Raines] Why Woolworth's?

[McCain] They advertise in public media, newspapers, radios, television, that sort of thing. They tell you to come in: "Yes, buy the toothpaste; yes, come in and buy the notebook paper. . . . No, we don't separate your money in this cash register; but, no, please don't step down to the hot dog stand. . . ." The whole system, of course, was unjust, but that just seemed like insult added to injury. That was just like pouring salt into an open wound. That's inviting you to do something. . . .

Once getting there . . . we did make purchases of schools supplies and took the patience and time to get receipts for our purchases, and Joseph and myself went over to the counter and asked to be served coffee and doughnuts. As anticipated, the reply was "I'm sorry, we don't serve you here." And of course we said, "We just beg to disagree with you. We've in fact already been served; you've served us already and that's just not quite true." The attendant or waitress was a little bit dumbfounded, just didn't know what to say under circumstances like that. And we said, "We wonder why you'd invite us in to serve us at one counter and deny service at another. If this is a private club or private concern, then we believe you ought to sell membership cards and sell only to persons who have a membership card. If we don't have a card, then we'd know pretty well that we shouldn't come in or even attempt to come in." That didn't go over too well, simply because I don't really think she understood what we were talking about, and for the second reason, she had no logical response to a statement like that. And the only thing that an individual in her case or position could do is, or course, call the manager. [Laughs] Well, at this time, I think we were joined by Dave Richmond and Ezell Blair at the counter with us, after that dialogue.

[Raines] Were you afraid at this point?

[McCain] Oh, hell yes, no question about that. [Laughs] At that point there was a policeman who had walked in off the street, who was pacing the aisle . . . behind us, where we were seated, with his club in his hand, just sort of knocking it in his hand, and just looking mean and red and a little bit upset and a little bit disgusted. And you had the feeling that he didn't know what the hell to do. You had the feeling that this is the first time that this big bad man with the gun and the club has been pushed in a corner, and he's got absolutely no defense, and the thing that's killing him more than anything else—he doesn't know what he can or what he cannot do. He's defenseless. Usually his defense is offense, and we've provoked him, yes, but we haven't provoked him outwardly enough for him to resort to violence. And I think this is just killing him; you can see it all over him.

People in the store were—we got mixed reactions from people in the store. A couple of old ladies . . . came up to pat us on the back sort of and say. "Ah, you should have done it ten years ago. It's a good thing I think you're doing."

[Raines] These were black ladies.

[McCain] No, these are white ladies.

[Raines] Really?

[McCain] Yes, and by the same token, we had some white ladies and white men come up and say to us, "Nasty, dirty niggers, you know you don't belong here at the lunch counter. There's a counter—" There was, in fact, a counter downstairs in the Woolworth store, a stand-up type counter where they sold hot dogs. . . .

[Raines] But at any rate, there were expressions of support from white people that day?

[*McCain*] Absolutely right. Absolutely. And I think probably that was certainly one incentive for additional courage on the part of us. And the other thing that helped us psychologically quite a lot was seeing the policeman pace the aisle and not be able to do anything. I think that this probably gave us more strength, more encouragement, than anything else on that particular day, on day one.

[*Raines*] Unexpected as it was, the well-wishing from the elderly white women was hardly more surprising than the scorn of a middle-aged black dishwasher behind the counter. She said, "That's why we can't get anyplace today, because of people like you, rabble-rousers, troublemakers. . . . this counter is reserved for white people, it always has been, and you are all aware of that. So why don't you go on out and stop making trouble?

He has since seen the woman at, of all places, a reunion commemorating the event in which she played so unsupportive a role.

[*McCain*] [She said] "Yes, I did say it and I said it because, first of all, I was afraid for what would happen to you as young black boys. Secondly, I was afraid of what would happen to me as an individual who had a job at the Woolworth store. I might have been fired and that's my livelihood. . . ."

It took me a long time to really understand that statement . . . but I know why she said it. She said it out of fear more than anything else. I've come to understand that, and my elders say to me that it's maturity that makes me understand why she said that some fifteen years ago.

[*Raines*] But, moved by neither praise nor scorn, he and the others waited for the waitress to return with the manager, a career Woolworth's employee named C. L. Harris.

[*McCain*] That was real amusin' as well [laughing] because by then we had the confidence, my goodness, of a Mack truck. And there was virtually nothing that could move us, there was virtually nothing probably at that point that could really frighten us off. . . . If it's possible to know what it means to have your soul cleansed—I felt pretty clean at that time. I probably felt better on that day than I've ever felt in my life. Seems like a lot of feelings of guilt or what-have-you suddenly left me, and I felt as though I had gained my manhood, so to speak, and not only gained it, but had developed quite a lot of respect for it. Not Franklin McCain only as an individual, but I felt as though the manhood of a number of other black persons had been restored and had gotten some respect from just that one day.

5. Martin Luther King Jr., "I Have a Dream," 1963

I am happy to join with you today in what will go down in history as the greatest demonstration for freedom in the history of our nation.

Fivescore years ago, a great American, in whose symbolic shadow we stand today, signed the Emancipation Proclamation. This momentous decree came as a great beacon light of hope to millions of Negro slaves who had been seared in the flames of withering injustice. It came as a joyous daybreak to end the long night of their captivity.

But one hundred years later, the Negro still is not free; one hundred years later, the life of the Negro is still sadly crippled by the manacles of segregation and the chains of discrimination; one hundred years later, the Negro lives on a lonely island of poverty in the midst of a vast ocean of material prosperity; one hundred years later, the Negro is still languished in the corners of American society and finds himself in exile in his own land.

So we've come here today to dramatize a shameful condition. In a sense we've come to our nation's capital to cash a check. When the architects of our republic wrote the magnificent words of the Constitution and the Declaration of Independence, they were signing a promissory note to which every American was to fall heir. This note was the promise that all men, yes, black men as well as white men, would be guaranteed the unalienable rights of life, liberty, and the pursuit of happiness.

It is obvious today that America has defaulted on this promissory note in so far as her citizens of color are concerned. Instead of honoring this sacred obligation, America has given the Negro people a bad check; a check which has come back marked "insufficient funds." We refuse to believe that there are insufficient funds in the great vaults of opportunity of this nation. And so we've come to cash this check, a check that will give us upon demand the riches of freedom and the security of justice.

We have also come to this hallowed spot to remind America of the fierce urgency of now. This is no time to engage in the luxury of cooling off or to take the tranquilizing drug of gradualism. Now is the time to make real the promises of democracy; now is the time to rise from the dark and desolate valley of segregation to the sunlit path of racial justice; now is the time to lift our nation from the quicksands of racial injustice to the solid rock of brotherhood; now is the time to make justice a reality for all God's children. It would be fatal for the nation to overlook the urgency of the moment. This sweltering summer of the Negro's legitimate discontent will not pass until there is an invigorating autumn of freedom and equality.

Nineteen sixty-three is not an end, but a beginning. And those who hope that the Negro needed to blow off steam and will now be content, will have a rude awakening if the nation returns to business as usual.

There will be neither rest nor tranquility in America until the Negro is granted his citizenship rights. The whirlwinds of revolt will continue to shake the foundations of our nation until the bright day of justice emerges.

But there is something that I must say to my people who stand on the warm threshold which leads into the palace of justice. In the process of gaining our rightful place we must not be guilty of wrongful deeds.

Let us not seek to satisfy our thirst for freedom by drinking from the cup of bitterness and hatred. We must forever conduct our struggle on the high plane of dignity and discipline. We must not allow our creative protest to degenerate into physical violence. Again and again we must rise to the majestic heights of meeting physical force with soul force.

The marvelous new militancy which has engulfed the Negro community must not lead us to a distrust of all white people, for many of our white brothers, as evidenced by their presence here today, have come to realize that their destiny is tied up with our destiny and they have come to realize that their freedom is inextricably bound to our freedom. This offense we share mounted to storm the battlements of injustice must be carried forth by a biracial army. We cannot walk alone.

And as we walk, we must make the pledge that we shall always march ahead. We cannot turn back. There are those who are asking the devotees of civil rights, "When will you be satisfied?" We can never be satisfied as long as the Negro is the victim of the unspeakable horrors of police brutality.

We can never be satisfied as long as our bodies, heavy with fatigue of travel, cannot gain lodging in the motels of the highways and the hotels of the cities. We cannot be satisfied as long as the Negro's basic mobility is from a smaller ghetto to a large one.

We can never be satisfied as long as our children are stripped of their selfhood and robbed of their dignity by signs stating "for whites only." We cannot be satisfied as long as a Negro in Mississippi cannot vote and a Negro in New York believes he has nothing for which to vote. No, we are not satisfied, and we will not be satisfied until justice rolls down like waters and righteousness like a mighty stream.

I am not unmindful that some of you have come here out of excessive trials and tribulation. Some of you have come fresh from narrow jail cells. Some of you have come from areas where your quest for freedom left you battered by the storms of persecution and staggered by the winds of police brutality. You have been the veterans of creative suffering. Continue to work with the faith that unearned suffering is redemptive.

Go back to Mississippi; go back to Alabama; go back to South Carolina; go back to Georgia; go back to Louisiana; go back to the slums and ghettos of the northern cities, knowing that somehow this situation can, and will be changed. Let us not wallow in the valley of despair.

So I say to you, my friends, that even though we must face the difficulties of today and tomorrow, I still have a dream. It is a dream deeply rooted in the American dream that one day this nation will rise up and live out the true meaning of its creed—we hold these truths to be self-evident, that all men are created equal.

I have a dream that one day on the red hills of Georgia, sons of former slaves and sons of former slave-owners will be able to sit down together at the table of brotherhood.

I have a dream that one day, even the state of Mississippi, a state sweltering with the heat of injustice, sweltering with the heat of oppression, will be transformed into an oasis of freedom and justice.

I have a dream my four little children will one day live in a nation where they will not be judged by the color of their skin but by [the] content of their character. I have a dream today!

I have a dream that one day, down in Alabama, with its vicious racists, with its governor having his lips dripping with the words of interposition and nullification, that one day, right there in Alabama, little black boys and black girls will be able to join hands with little white boys and white girls as sisters and brothers. I have a dream today!

I have a dream that one day every valley shall be exalted, every hill and mountain shall be made low, the rough places shall be made plain, and the crooked places shall be made straight and the glory of the Lord will be revealed and all flesh shall see it together.

This is our hope. This is the faith that I go back to the South with.

With this faith we will be able to hear out of the mountain of despair a stone of hope. With this faith we will be able to transform the jangling discords of our nation into a beautiful symphony of brotherhood.

With this faith we will be able to work together, to pray together, to struggle together, to go to jail together, to stand up for freedom together, knowing that we will be free one day. This will be the day when all of God's children will be able to sing with new meaning—"my country 'tis of thee; sweet land of liberty; of thee I sing; land where my fathers died, land of the pilgrim's pride; from every mountainside, let freedom ring"—and if America is to be a great nation, this must become true.

So let freedom ring from the prodigious hilltops of New Hampshire.

Let freedom ring from the mighty mountains of New York.

Let freedom ring from the heightening Alleghenies of Pennsylvania.

Let freedom ring from the snow-capped Rockies of Colorado.

Let freedom ring from the curvaceous slopes of California.

But not only that.

Let freedom ring from Stone Mountain of Georgia.

Let freedom ring from Lookout Mountain of Tennessee.

Let freedom ring from every hill and molehill of Mississippi, from every mountainside, let freedom ring.

And when we allow freedom to ring, when we let it ring from every village and hamlet, from every state and city, we will be able to speed up that day when all of God's children—black men and white men, Jews and Gentiles, Catholics and Protestants—will be able to join hands and to sing in the words of the old Negro spiritual, "Free at last, free at last; thank God Almighty, we are free at last."

6. Stokely Carmichael Explains "Black Power," 1967

One of the tragedies of the struggle against racism is that up to now there has been no national organization which could speak to the growing militancy of young black people in the urban ghetto. There has been only a civil rights movement, whose tone of voice was adapted to an audience of liberal whites. It served as a sort of buffer zone between them and angry young blacks. None of its so-called leaders could go into a rioting community and be listened to. In a sense, I blame ourselves— together with the mass media—for what has happened in Watts, Harlem, Chicago, Cleveland, Omaha. Each time the people in those cities saw Martin Luther King get slapped, they became angry; when the saw four little black girls bombed to death, they were angrier; and when nothing happened, they were steaming. We had nothing to offer that they could see, except to go out and be beaten again. We helped to build their frustration.

For too many years, black Americans marched and had their heads broken and got shot. They were saying to the country, "Look, you guys are supposed to be nice guys and we are only going to do what we are supposed to do—why do you beat us

"What We Want," by Stokely Carmichael explaining "Black Power" from *The New York Review of Books*. Vol. 7 (September 22, 1966), pp. 5–6, 8. Reprinted by permission of Kwame Ture (Stokely Carmichael).

up, why don't you give us what we ask, why don't you straighten yourselves out?" After years of this, we are at almost the same point—because we demonstrated from a position of weakness. We cannot be expected any longer to march and have our heads broken in order to say to whites: come on, you're nice guys. For you are not nice guys. We have found you out.

An organization which claims to speak for the needs of a community—as does the Student Nonviolent Coordinating Committee—must speak in the tone of that community, not as somebody else's buffer zone. This is the significance of black power as a slogan. For once, black people are going to use the words they want to use—not just the words whites want to hear. And they will do this no matter how often the press tries to stop the use of the slogan by equating it with racism or separatism.

An organization which claims to be working for the needs of a community—as SNCC does—must work to provide that community with a position of strength from which to make its voice heard. This is the significance of black power beyond the slogan.

Black power can be clearly defined for those who do not attach the fears of white America to their questions about it. We should begin with the basic fact that black Americans have two problems: they are poor and they are black. All other problems arise from this two-sided reality: lack of education, the so-called apathy of black men. Any program to end racism must address itself to that double reality.

Almost from its beginning, SNCC sought to address itself to both conditions with a program aimed at winning political power for impoverished Southern blacks. We had to begin with politics because black Americans are a propertyless people in a country where property is valued above all. We had to work for power, because this country does not function by morality, love, and nonviolence, but by power. Thus we determined to win political power, with the idea of moving on from there into activity that would have economic effects. With power, the masses could *make or participate in making* the decisions which govern their destinies, and thus create basic change in their day-to-day lives.

But if political power seemed to be the key to self-determination, it was also obvious that the key had been thrown down a deep well many years earlier. Disenfranchisement, maintained by racist terror, made it impossible to talk about organizing for political power in 1960. The right to vote had to be won, and SNCC workers devoted their energies to this from 1961 to 1965. They set up voter registration drives in the Deep South. They created pressure for the vote by holding mock elections in Mississippi in 1963 and by helping to establish the Mississippi Freedom Democratic Party (MFDP) in 1964. That struggle was eased, though not won, with the passage of the 1965 Voting Rights Act. SNCC workers could then address themselves to the question: "Who can we vote for, to have our needs met—how do we make our vote meaningful? . . ."

SNCC today is working in both North and South on programs of voter registration and independent political organizing. In some places, such as Alabama, Los Angeles, New York, Philadelphia, and New Jersey, independent organizing under the black panther symbol is in progress. The creation of a national "black panther party" must come about; it will take time to build, and it is much too early to predict its success. We have no infallible master plan and we make no claim to exclusive knowledge of how to end racism; different groups will work in their own different ways. SNCC cannot spell out the full logistics of self-determination but it can address itself to the problem by helping black communities define their needs, realize their strength, and go into action along a variety of lines which they must choose for themselves. Without knowing all the answers, it can address itself to the basic problem of poverty; to the fact that in Lowndes County, 86 white families own 90 percent of the land. What are black people in that county going to do for jobs, where are they going to get money? There must be reallocation of land, of money.

Ultimately, the economic foundations of this country must be shaken if black people are to control their lives. The colonies of the United States—and this includes the black ghettoes within its borders, north and south—must be liberated. For a century, this nation has been like an octopus of exploitation, its tentacles stretching from Mississippi and Harlem to South America, the Middle East, southern Africa, and Vietnam; the form of exploitation varies from area to area but the essential result has been the same—a powerful few have been maintained and enriched at the expense of the poor and voiceless colored masses. This pattern must be broken. As its grip loosens here and there around the world, the hopes of black Americans become more realistic. For racism to die, a totally different America must be born.

This is what the white society does not wish to face; this is why that society prefers to talk about integration. But integration speaks not at all to the problem of poverty, only the problem of blackness. Integration today means the man who "makes it," leaving his black brothers behind in the ghetto as fast as his sports car will take him. It has no relevance to the Harlem wino or to the cottonpicker making three dollars a day. As a lady I know in Alabama once said, "the food that Ralph Bunche eats doesn't fill my stomach."

Integration, moreover, speaks to the problem of blackness in a despicable way. As a goal, it has been based on complete acceptance of the fact that *in order to have* a decent house or education, blacks must move into a white neighborhood or send their children to a white school. This reinforces, among both black and white, the idea that "white" is automatically better and "black" is by definition inferior. This is why integration is a subterfuge for the maintenance of white supremacy. It allows the nation to focus on a handful of Southern children who get into white schools, at great price, and to ignore the 94 percent who are left behind in unimproved all-blacks schools. Such situations will not change until black people have power—to control their own schools boards, in this case. Then Negroes become equal in a way that means something, and integration ceases to be a one-way street. Then integration doesn't mean draining skills and energies from the ghetto into white neighborhoods; then it can mean white people moving from Beverly Hills into Watts, white people joining the Lowndes County Freedom Organization. Then integration becomes relevant. . . .

White America will not face the problem of color, the reality of it. The well-intended say: "We're all human, everybody is really decent, we must forget color." But color cannot be "forgotten" until its weight is recognized and dealt with. White America will not acknowledge that the ways in which this country sees itself are contradicted by being black—and always have been. Whereas most of the people who settled this country came here for freedom or for economic opportunity, blacks were brought here to be slaves. When the Lowndes County Freedom Organization chose the black panther as its symbol, it was christened by the press "the Black Panther Party"—but the Alabama Democratic Party, whose symbol is a rooster, has never been called the White Cock Party. No one ever talked about "white power" because power in this country *is* white. All this adds up to more than merely identifying a group phenomenon by some catchy name or adjective. The furor over that black panther reveals the problems that white America has with color and sex; the furor over "black power" reveals how deep racism runs and the great fear which is attached to it.

Whites will not see that I, for example, as a person oppressed because of my blackness, have common cause with other blacks who are oppressed because of blackness. This is not to say that there are no white people who see things as I do, but that it is black people I must speak to first. It must be the oppressed to whom SNCC addresses itself primarily, not to friends from the oppressing group.

From birth, black people are told a set of lies about themselves. We are told that we are lazy—yet I drive through the Delta area of Mississippi and watch black people picking cotton in the hot sun for fourteen hours. We are told, "If you work hard, you'll succeed"—but if that were true, black people would own this country. We are oppressed because we are black—not because we are ignorant, not because we are lazy, not because we're stupid (and got good rhythm), but because we're black.

I remember that when I was a boy, I used to go to see Tarzan movies on Saturday. White Tarzan used to beat up the black natives. I would sit there yelling, "Kill the beasts, kill the savages, kill 'em!" I was saying: Kill *me*. It was as if a Jewish boy watched Nazis taking Jews off to concentration camps and cheered them on. Today, I want the chief to beat hell out of Tarzan and send him back to Europe. But it takes time to become free of the lies and their shaming effect on black minds. It takes time to reject the most important lie; that black people inherently can't do the same things white people can do, unless white people help them.

The need for psychological equality is the reason why SNCC today believes that blacks must organize in the black community. Only black people can convey the revolutionary idea that black people are able to do things themselves. Only they can help create in the community an aroused and continuing black consciousness that will provide the basis for political strength. In the past, white allies have furthered white supremacy without the whites involved realizing it—or wanting it, I think. Black people must do things for themselves; they must get poverty money they will control and spend themselves, they must conduct tutorial programs themselves so that black children can identify with black people. This is one reason Africa has such importance: The reality of black men ruling their own nations gives blacks elsewhere a sense of possibility, of power, which they do not now have.

This does not mean we don't welcome help, or friends. But we want the right to decide whether anyone is, in fact, our friend. In the past, black Americans have been almost the only people whom everybody and his momma could jump up and call their friends. We have been tokens, symbols, objects—as I was in high school to many young whites, who liked having "a Negro friend." We want to decide who is our friend, and we will not accept someone who comes to us and says: "If you do X, Y, and Z, then I'll help you." We will not be told whom we should choose as allies. We will not be isolated from any group or nation except by our own choice. We cannot have the oppressors telling the oppressed how to rid themselves of the oppressor. . . .

Black people do not want to "take over" this country. They don't want to "get whitey"; they just want to get him off their backs, as the saying goes. It was for example the exploitation by Jewish landlords and merchants which first created black resentment toward Jews—not Judaism. The white man is irrelevant to blacks, except as an oppressive force. Blacks want to be in his place, yes, but not in order to terrorize and lynch and starve him. They want to be in his place because that is where a decent life can be had.

But our vision is not merely of a society in which all black men have enough to buy the good things of life. When we urge that black money go into black pockets, we mean the communal pocket. We want to see money go back into the community and used to benefit it. We want to see the cooperative concept applied in business and banking. We want to see black ghetto residents demand that an exploiting landlord or storekeeper sell them, at minimal cost, a building or a shop that they will own and improve cooperatively; they can back their demand with a rent strike, or a boycott, and a community so unified behind them that no one else will move into the building or buy at the store. The society we seek to build among black people, then, is not capitalist one. It is a society in which the spirit of community and humanistic love prevail. The word love is suspect; black expectations of what it might produce have been betrayed too often. But those were expectations of a response from the white community, which failed us. The love we seek to encourage is within the black community, the only American community where men call each other "brother" when they meet. We can build a community of love only where we have the ability and power to do so: among blacks.

As for white America, perhaps it can stop crying out against "black supremacy," "black nationalism," "racism in reverse," and begin facing reality. The reality is that this nation, from top to bottom, is racist; that racism is not primarily a problem of "human relations" but of an exploitation maintained—either actively or through silence—by the society as a whole. Camus and Sartre have asked, can a man condemn himself? Can whites, particularly liberal whites, condemn themselves? Can they stop blaming us, and blame their own system? Are they capable of the shame which might become a revolutionary emotion?

We have found that they usually cannot condemn themselves, and so we have done it. But the rebuilding of this society, if at all possible, is basically the responsibility of whites—not blacks. We won't fight to save the present society, in Vietnam or anywhere else. We are just going to work, in the way *we* see fit, and on our goals *we* define, not for civil rights but for all our human rights.

7. A Senate Committee Reports on the FBI's Campaign Against Martin Luther King Jr., 1976

From December 1963 until his death in 1968, Martin Luther King Jr. was the target of an intensive campaign by the Federal Bureau of Investigation to "neutralize" him as an effective civil rights leader. In the words of the man in charge of the FBI's "war" against Dr. King:

Senate Select Committee to Study Governmental Operations with Respect to Intelligence Activities, *Supplemental Detailed Staff Reports . . .,* vol. 3 (Washington, D.C.: GPO, 1976), 81–83, 133–137, 158–160.

No holds barred. We have used [similar] techniques against Soviet agents. [The same methods were] brought home against any organization against which we were targeted. We did not differentiate. This is a rough, tough business.

The FBI collected information about Dr. King's plans and activities through an extensive surveillance program, employing nearly every intelligence-gathering technique at the Bureau's disposal. Wiretaps, which were initially approved by Attorney General Robert F. Kennedy, were maintained on Dr. King's home telephone from October 1963 until mid-1965; the SCLC [Southern Christian Leadership Conference] headquarter's telephones were covered by wiretaps for an even longer period. Phones in the homes and offices of some of Dr. King's close advisers were also wiretapped. The FBI has acknowledged 16 occasions on which microphones were hidden in Dr. King's hotel and motel rooms in an "attempt" to obtain information about the "private activities of King and his advisers" for use to "completely discredit" them.

FBI informants in the civil rights movement and reports from field offices kept the Bureau's headquarters informed of developments in the civil rights field. The FBI's presence was so intrusive that one major figure in the civil rights movement testified that his colleagues referred to themselves as members of "the FBI's golden record club."

The FBI's formal program to discredit Dr. King with Government officials began with the distribution of a "monograph" which the FBI realized could "be regarded as a personal attack on Martin Luther King," and which was subsequently described by a Justice Department official as "a personal diatribe . . . a personal attack without evidentiary support."

Congressional leaders were warned "off the record" about alleged dangers posed by Reverend King. The FBI responded to Dr. King's receipt of the Nobel Peace Prize by attempting to undermine his reception by foreign heads of state and American ambassadors in the countries that he planned to visit. When Dr. King returned to the United States, steps were taken to reduce support for a huge banquet and a special "day" that were being planned in his honor.

The FBI's program to destroy Dr. King as the leader of the civil rights movement entailed attempts to discredit him with churches, universities, and the press. Steps were taken to attempt to convince the National Council of Churches, the Baptist World Alliance, and leading Protestant ministers to halt financial support of the Southern Christian Leadership Conference (SCLC), and to persuade them that "Negro leaders should completely isolate King and remove him from the role he is now occupying in civil rights activities." When the FBI learned that Dr. King intended to visit the Pope, an agent was dispatched to persuade Francis Cardinal Spellman to warn the Pope about "the likely embarrassment that may result to the Pope should he grant King an audience." The FBI sought to influence universities to withhold honorary degrees from Dr. King. Attempts were made to prevent the publication of articles favorable to Dr. King and to find "friendly" news sources that would print unfavorable articles. The FBI offered to play for reporters tape recordings allegedly made from microphone surveillance of Dr. King's hotel rooms.

The FBI mailed Dr. King a tape recording made from its microphone coverage. According to the Chief of the FBI's Domestic Intelligence Division, the tape was intended to precipitate a separation between Dr. King and his wife in the belief that the separation would reduce Dr. King's stature. The tape recording was accompanied by a note which Dr. King and his advisers interpreted as a threat to release the tape recording unless Dr. King committed suicide. The FBI also made preparations to promote someone "to assume the role of leadership of the Negro people when King has been completely discredited."

The campaign against Dr. King included attempts to destroy the Southern Christian Leadership Conference by cutting off its sources of funds. The FBI considered, and on some occasions executed, plans to cut off the support of some of the SCLC's major contributors, including religious organizations, a labor union, and donors of grants such as the Ford Foundation. One FBI field office recommended that the FBI send letters to the SCLC's donors over Dr. King's forged signature warning them that the SCLC was under investigation by the Internal Revenue Service. The IRS files on Dr. King and the SCLC were carefully scrutinized for financial irregularities. For over a year, the FBI unsuccessfully attempted to establish that Dr. King had a secret foreign bank account in which he was sequestering funds.

The FBI campaign to discredit and destroy Dr. King was marked by extreme personal vindictiveness. As early as 1962, Director Hoover penned on an FBI memorandum, "King is no good." At the August 1963 March on Washington, Dr. King told the country of his dream that "all the God's children, black men and white men, Jews and Gentiles, Protestants and Catholics, will be able to join hands and sing in the words of the old Negro spiritual, 'Free at last, free at last. Thank God, almighty, I'm free at last.'" The FBI's Domestic Intelligence Division described this "demagogic speech" as yet more evidence that Dr. King was "the most dangerous and effective Negro leader in the country." Shortly afterward, *Time* magazine chose Dr. King as the "Man of the Year," an honor which elicited Director Hoover's comment that "they had to dig deep in the garbage to come up with this one." Hoover wrote "astounding" across the memorandum informing him that Dr. King had been granted an audience with the Pope despite the FBI's efforts to prevent such a meeting. The depth of Director Hoover's bitterness toward Dr. King, a bitterness which he had effectively communicated to his subordinates in the FBI, was apparent from the FBI's attempts to sully Dr. King's reputation long after his death. Plans were made to "brief" congressional leaders in 1969 to prevent the passage of a "Martin Luther King Day." In 1970, Director Hoover told reporters that Dr. King was the "last one in the world who should ever have received" the Nobel Peace Prize.

✖ E S S A Y S

As the twentieth century drew to a close, historians continued to debate both the successes and the failures of the civil rights movement. The many laws, court decisions, and public policies that had sustained racial segregation since the nineteenth century were swept aside, but much of their legacy still remained deeply embedded in the nation's social structure. Although some mostly middle-class African Americans had profited from new economic opportunities created by the civil rights movement, the plight of many poor African Americans had actually deteriorated. The growing opposition to affirmative action and other minority programs, moreover, threatened to further slow the pace of change. This is the context for the two essays that follow. Vincent Gordon Harding, a friend of King and later director of the Martin Luther King Jr. Center for

Nonviolent Social Change in Atlanta, challenges the bland, unthreatening image of King that increasingly dominates public celebrations of his life. The second essay, excerpted from Thomas J. Sugrue's prizewinning study *The Origins of the Urban Crisis: Race and Inequality in Postwar Detroit* (1996), explores how a powerful combination of racial discrimination and deindustrialization defeated efforts to overcome the city's bitter history of segregation.

King as Disturber of the Peace

VINCENT GORDON HARDING

In the 1970s, as a fascinating variety of voices began to press the nation to decide where it stood concerning the memory and meaning of Martin Luther King Jr., and as we instinctively sought an easy way to deal with the unrelenting power of this disturber of all unjust peace, a black poet perhaps best reflected our ambivalence. Carl Wendell Hines wrote:

> Now that he is safely dead
> let us praise him
> build monuments to his glory
> sing hosannas to his name.
> Dead men make
> such convenient heroes; They
> cannot rise
> To challenge the images
> we would fashion from their lives.
> And besides,
> it is easier to build monuments
> than to make a better world.

Then as the voices of artists and family and millions of black people (and their votes, and their nonblack allies) began to build, the sad wisdom of Hines's words seemed to sharpen and to cut deeper at every moment. For it became increasingly clear that most of those who were leading the campaign for the national holiday had chosen, consciously or unconsciously, to allow King to become a convenient hero, to try to tailor him to the shape and mood of mainstream, liberal/moderate America.

Symbolic of the direction given the campaign has been the unremitting focus on the 1963 March on Washington, the never-ending repetition of the great speech and its dream metaphor, the sometimes innocent and sometimes manipulative boxing of King into the relatively safe categories of "civil rights leader," "great orator," harmless dreamer of black and white children on the hillside. And surely nothing could be more ironic or amnesiac than having Vice-President George Bush, the former head of the Central Intelligence Agency, the probable White House overseer of Contra actions, speaking words in King's honor. Or was it more ironic to watch the representatives of the Marine Corps, carrying fresh memories from the invasion of Grenada and from their training for Libya and for Nicaragua, playing "We Shall

Harding, Vincent. "Beyond Amnesia: Martin Luther King, Jr., and the Future of America," (pages 468–476) from the September 1987 issue of the *Journal of American History*. Reprinted by permission.

Overcome," while the bust of the prince of nonviolence was placed in the Capitol rotunda, without a word being spoken about nonviolence?

It appears as if the price for the first national holiday honoring a black man is the development of a massive case of national amnesia concerning who that black man really was. At both personal and collective levels, of course, it is often the case that amnesia is not ultimately harmful to the patient. However, in this case it is very dangerous, for the things we have chosen to forget about King (and about ourselves) constitute some of the most hopeful possibilities and resources for our magnificent and very needy nation. Indeed, I would suggest that we Americans have chosen amnesia rather than continue King's painful, uncharted, and often disruptive struggle toward a more perfect union. I would also suggest that those of us who are historians and citizens have a special responsibility to challenge the loss of memory, in ourselves and others, to allow our skills in probing the past to become resources for healing and for hope, not simply sources of pages in books or of steps in careers. In other words, if as Hines wrote, Martin King "cannot rise to challenge" those who would make him a harmless black icon, then *we* surely can—assuming that we are still alive.

Although there are many points at which our challenge to the comfortable images might be raised, I believe that the central encounters with King that begin to take us beyond the static March-on-Washington, "integrationist," "civil rights leader" image are located in Chicago and Mississippi in 1966. During the winter of that year King moved North. He was driven by the fires of Watts and the early hot summers of 1964 and 1965. Challenged and nurtured by the powerful commitment of Malcolm X to the black street forces, he was also compelled by his own deep compassion for the urban black community—whose peculiar problems were not fundamentally addressed by the civil rights laws so early won in the South. Under such urgent compulsion, King left his familiar southern base and stepped out on very unfamiliar turf. For Hamlin Avenue on Chicago's blighted West Side was a long way from the marvelous, costly victories of Selma, St. Augustine, and Birmingham, and Mayor Richard Daley was a consummate professional compared to the sheriffs, mayors, and police commissioners of the South. But King had made his choice, and it is one that we dare not forget.

By 1966 King had made an essentially religious commitment to the poor, and he was prepared to say:

> I choose to identify with the underprivileged. I choose to identify with the poor. I choose to give my life for the hungry. I choose to give my life for those who have been left out of the sunlight of opportunity. I choose to live for and with those who find themselves seeing life as a long and desolate corridor with no exit sign. This is the way I'm going. If it means suffering a little bit, I'm going that way. If it means sacrificing, I'm going that way. If it means dying for them, I'm going that way, because I heard a voice saying, "Do something for others."

We understand nothing about the King whose life ended in the midst of a struggle for garbage workers if we miss that earlier offering of himself to the struggle against poverty in America, to the continuing battle for the empowerment of the powerless— in this nation, in Vietnam, in South Africa, in Central America, and beyond.

In a sense, it was that commitment that took him from Chicago to Mississippi in the late spring of 1966, as he responded to the attempted assassination of James

Meredith, taking up with others that enigmatic hero's "march against fear." There on the highways of the Magnolia State we have a second crucial encounter with the forgotten King. He was an embattled leader, the King who was challenged, chastened, and inspired by the courageous, foolhardy Young Turks of the Student Nonviolent Coordinating Committee. He was attentive to those veterans of the struggle who raised the cry for "Black Power," who made public the long simmering challenge to King's leadership, who increasingly voiced their doubts about the primacy of nonviolence as a way of struggle, and who seemed prepared to read whites out of the movement. Perhaps the most important aspect of the Meredith March for King's development was the question the young people raised in many forms: "Dr. King, why do you want us to love white folk before we even love ourselves?" From then on the issues of black self-love, of black and white power, and of the need to develop a more militant form of nonviolence that could challenge and enlist the rising rage of urban black youth were never far from King's consciousness. Along with his deepening commitment to the poor, those were the subjects and questions that did much to shape the hero we have forgotten.

One of the reasons for our amnesia, of course, is that fact that the forgotten King is not easy to handle now. Indeed, he never was. In 1967, after spending two hectic weeks traveling with the impassioned black prophet, David Halberstam, a perceptive journalist, reported that

> King has decided to represent the ghettos; he will work in them and speak for them. But their voice is harsh and alienated. If King is to speak for them truly, then his voice must reflect theirs; it too must be alienated, and it is likely to be increasingly at odds with the rest of American society.

Halberstam was right, but only partly so. After the Selma marches of 1965, King's voice did sound harsher in its criticism of the mainstream American way of life and its dominant values—including the assumption that the United States had the right to police the world for "free enterprise." Not only did the white mainstream object to such uncompromising criticism from a "civil rights leader" who was supposed to know this place, but respectable black people were increasingly uncomfortable as well. For some of them were making use of the fragile doorways that the freedom movement had helped open. Others, after years of frustration, were finally being promoted into the positions of responsibility and higher earnings that their skills and experience should have earlier made available. Too often, King was considered a threat to them as well, especially as his commitment to the poor drove him to increasingly radical assessments of the systemic flaws in the American economic order, an order they had finally begun to enjoy.

But Halberstam, a man of words, saw only part of the picture. King did more than *speak* for the ghettos. He was committed to mobilizing and organizing them for self-liberating action. That was his deeper threat to the status quo, beyond words, beyond alienation. That was what King's friend Rabbi Abraham Heschel surely understood when he introduced King to an assembly of rabbis in these words: "Martin Luther King is a voice, a vision and a way. I call upon every Jew to harken to his voice, to share his vision, to follow in his way. The whole future of America will depend on the impact and influence of Dr. King."

Part of what we have forgotten, then, is King's vision, beyond the appealing dream of black and white children holding hands, beyond the necessary goal of "civil rights." From the outset, he held a vision for all America, often calling the black movement more than a quest for rights—a struggle "to redeem the soul of America." By the end of his life, no one who paid attention could mistake the depth and meaning of that vision. At the convention of the Southern Christian Leadership Conference (SCLC) in 1967, King announced, "We must go from this convention and say, 'America, you must be born again . . . your whole structure must be changed'" He insisted that "the problem of racism, the problem of economic exploitation, and the problem of war are all tied together." These, King said, were "the triple evils" that the freedom movement must address as it set itself to the challenge of "restructuring the whole of American society." This was the vision behind the call he issued in his final public speech in Memphis on April 3, 1968: "Let us move on in these powerful days, these days of challenge to make America what it ought to be. We have an opportunity to make America a better nation."

That final speech was delivered to a crowd of some two thousand persons, mostly black residents of Memphis who had come out in a soaking rain to hear King and to support the garbage workers' union in its struggle for justice. King's challenge to his last movement audience reminds us that he also carried a large and powerful vision concerning the role of black people and others of the "disinherited" in American society. His vision always included more than "rights" or "equal opportunity." On December 5, 1955, at the public meeting that launched the Montgomery bus boycott and Martin Luther King Jr. into the heart of twentieth century history, King had announced,

> We, the disinherited of this land, we who have been oppressed so long, are tired of going through the long night of captivity. And now we are reaching out for the daybreak of freedom and justice and equality.

As a result of that decision and that movement, King said,

> when the history books are written in the future somebody will have to say 'There lived a race of people, of black people, fleecy locks and black complexion, a people who had the moral courage to stand up for their rights, and thereby they injected a new meaning into the veins of history and of civilization.' And we're gonna do that. God grant that we will do it before it's too late.

From beginning to end, the grand vision, the magnificent obsession never left him, the audacious hope for America and its disinherited. Only in the light of that dual vision can we understand his voice, especially in its increasing alienation from the mainstream, in its urgent movement beyond the black and white civil rights establishment. In his last years, the vision led him to call repeatedly for "a reconstruction of the entire society, a revolution of values." Only as we recapture the wholeness of King's vision can we understand his conclusion in 1967 that "something is wrong with capitalism as it now stands in the United States." Only then can we grasp his word to his co-workers in SCLC: "We are not interested in being integrated into *this* value structure. Power must be relocated." The vision leads directly to the voice, calling for "a radical redistribution of economic and political power" as the only way to meet the real needs of the poor in America.

When our memories allow us to absorb King's vision of a transformed America and a transforming force of black people and their allies, then we understand his powerful critique of the American war in Vietnam. After he struggled with his conscience about how open to make his opposition, after he endured intense pressure to be quiet from Washington and from the civil rights establishment, King's social vision and his religious faith stood him in good stead. He spoke out in a stirring series of statements and actions and declared:

> Never again will I be silent on an issue that is destroying the soul of our nation and destroying thousands and thousands of little children in Vietnam. . . . the time has come for a real prophecy, and I'm willing to go that road.

Of course, King knew the costly way of prophets—as did the rabbi who called us "to follow in his way." We must assume that neither the black prophet nor his Jewish brother was speaking idle words, opening up frivolous ways. Rather those were visions, voices, and ways not meant to be forgotten.

Indeed, in a nation where the gap between rich and poor continues to expand with cruel regularity, where the numbers of black and Hispanic poor vie with each other for supremacy, where farmers and industrial workers are in profound crisis, where racism continues to proclaim its ruthless American presence, who can afford to forget King's compassionate and courageous movement toward justice? When the leaders of the country spew reams of lies to Congress and the people alike, in public and private statements, when the official keepers of the nation's best hopes seem locked in what King called "paranoid anti-communism," when we make cynical mercenaries out of jobless young people, sacrificing them to a rigid militarism that threatens the future of the world, do we dare repress the memory of a man who called us to struggle bravely toward "the daybreak of freedom and justice and equality"? Dare we forget a man who told us that "a nation that continues year after year to spend more money on military defense than on programs of social uplift is approaching spiritual death"?

Clearly, we serve our scholarship and our citizenship most faithfully when we move ourselves and others beyond amnesia toward encounters with the jagged leading edges of King's prophetic vision. When we do that we recognize that Martin King himself was unclear about many aspects of the "way" he had chosen. In his commitment to the poor, in his search for the redistribution of wealth and power in America, in his relentless stand against war, in his determination to help America "repent of her modern economic imperialism," he set out on a largely uncharted way. Still, several polestars pointed the way for him, and they may suggest creative directions for our personal and collective lives.

As King searched for a way for Americans to press the nation toward its best possibilities, toward its next birth of freedom and justice, he held fast to several basic assumptions. Perhaps it will help to remember them:

1. He seemed convinced that in the last part of the twentieth century, anyone who still held a vision of "a more perfect union" and worked toward that goal had to be prepared to move toward fundamental, structural changes in the mainstream values, economic and political structures, and traditional leadership of American society.

2. King believed that those who are committed to a real, renewed war against poverty in America must recognize the connections between our domestic economic and political problems and the unhealthy position that we occupy in

the military, economic, and political wards of the global community. In other words, what King called "the triple evils of racism, extreme materialism, and militarism" could be effectively fought only by addressing their reality and relationships in our life at home and abroad.

3. Unlike many participants in current discussions of poverty and "the underclass" in American society, King assumed that his ultimate commitment was to help find the ways by which the full energies and angers of the poor could be challenged, organized, and engaged in a revolutionary process that confronted the status quo and opened creative new possibilities for them and for the nation. . . .

4. By the last months of his life, as King reflected on the developments in the freedom movement since its energies had turned northward and since some of its participants had begun to offer more radical challenges to the policies of the federal government at home and abroad, he reached an inescapable conclusion. The next stages of the struggle for a just American order could no longer expect even the reluctant support from the national government that the movement had received since Montgomery. Now, he said, "We must formulate a program and we must fashion the new tactics which do not count on government good will, but instead serve to compel unwilling authorities to yield to the mandates of justice."

5. Defying most of the conventional wisdom of black and white America, King determined to hold fast to both of his fundamental, religiously based commitments: to the humanizing empowerment and transformation of the poor and of the nation and to the way of nonviolence and creative peace making. His attempt to create a Poor People's Campaign to challenge—and, if necessary, to disrupt—the federal government on its home ground was an expression of this wild and beautiful experiment in creating nonviolent revolution. Planning for a massive campaign of civic disobedience carried on by poor people of all races, aided by their un-poor allies, King announced, "We've got to make it known that until our problem is solved, America may have many, many days, but they will be full of trouble. There will be no rest, there will be no tranquility in this country until the nation comes to terms with [that problem]."

For those who seek a gentle, non-abrasive hero whose recorded speeches can be used as inspirational resources for rocking our memories to sleep, Martin Luther King Jr. is surely the wrong man. However, if there is even a chance that Rabbi Heschel was correct, that the untraditional King and his peace-disturbing vision, words, and deeds hold the key to the future of America, then another story unfolds, another search begins. We who are scholars and citizens then owe ourselves, our children, and our nation a far more serious exploration and comprehension of the man and the widespread movement with which he was identified.

Recently, the Afro-American liberation theologian Cornel West said of King, "As a proponent of nonviolent resistance, he holds out the only slim hope for social sanity in a violence-prone world." What if both the black theologian and the Jewish scholar-mystic are correct? What if the way that King was exploring is indeed vital to the future of our nation and our world? For scholars, citizens, or celebrants to forget the real man and his deepest implications would be not only faithless, but also suicidal. For in the light of the news that inundates us every day, where else do we go from here to make a better world?

The Continuing Racial Crisis

THOMAS J. SUGRUE

In late July 1967, one of the most brutal riots in American history swept through Detroit. On July 23, 1967, in the middle of a summer heat wave, the police decided to bust a "blind pig," an illegal after-hours saloon on Twelfth Street in the center of one of Detroit's largest black neighborhoods. Arrests for illegal drinking were common in Detroit, but usually the police dispersed the crowd and arrested a handful of owners and patrons, taking the names of the remainder. On the steamy July night, they decided to arrest all eighty-five people present and detained them—hot, drunk, and angry—outside the saloon until reinforcements could arrive.

By four in the morning, an hour after the bust, nearly two hundred people, attracted by the commotion behind the blind pig, had gathered to watch the proceedings. As the arrestees shouted allegations of police brutality, tempers rose. The crowd began to jeer and to throw bottles, beer cans, and rocks at the police. William Scott II, a son of one of the bar's owners, threw a bottle at a police officer and shouted "Get your god damn sticks and bottles and start hurtin' baby." By 8:00 A.M., a crowd of over three thousand had gathered on Twelfth Street. The riot raged out of control until it was suppressed by a combined force of nearly seventeen thousand law enforcement officers, National Guardsmen, and federal troops. After five days of violence, forty-three people were dead, thirty of them killed by law enforcement personnel. Altogether 7,231 men and women were arrested on riot-related charges. The property damage, still visible in vacant lots and abandoned buildings in Detroit, was extensive. Rioters looted and burned 2,509 buildings. $36 million in insured property was lost and undoubtedly millions more were lost by those without insurance, not to mention wages, income, and government costs.

Detroit was twice torn by cataclysmic violence in a period of less than twenty-five years. The extent of social and economic changes in the postwar period, however, made the context of Detroit's long hot summer of 1967 profoundly different from the violent summer of 1943. The vast majority of participants in the 1967 Detroit uprising were black (with the exception of armed officials who were overwhelmingly white); 1943 had involved black and white participants in roughly equal proportions. The changed racial demography of 1967 was hardly surprising, for over a third of Detroit residents were black in 1967, and few whites lived anywhere near the riot's epicenters on Linwood and Twelfth Street on the West Side and on Mack and Kercheval on the East Side. The riot of 1943 came at a time of increasing black and white competition for jobs and housing; by 1967, discrimination and deindustrialization had ensured that blacks had lost the competition. White resistance and white flight left a bitter legacy that galvanized black protest in the 1960s. Detroit's attempts to take advantage of the largesse of the Great Society offered too little, too late for Detroit's poor, but raised expectations nonetheless. Growing resentment, fueled by increasing militancy in the black community, especially among youth, who had suffered the brunt of economic displacement, fueled the fires of 1967.

For those who cared to listen, there were rumblings of discontent in the late 1950s and early 1960s. The problems of limited housing, racial animosity, and reduced economic opportunity for a segment of the black population in Detroit had led to embitterment. When sociologist John Leggett and his colleagues interviewed black Detroiters in 1957 and 1958, they found that many were seething with anger about their living and working conditions. When Leggett asked unemployed blacks to predict what would happen if there were another Great Depression, their answers were grimly prophetic. "There'd be widespread riots," answered one. "The young people won't take it," stated another. "They will steal. A lot of them steal now because they aren't working." A third also raised the issue of a youthful rebellion. "The younger generation won't take it; a lot of bad things would happen." "Oh Hot!" remarked another. "Everybody would get a ball bat and start swinging." Black youths, as Leggett's respondents knew, were increasingly alienated. They were most severely affected by the city's shrinking job market. Young people coming of age in Detroit in the mid- and late 1950s and 1960s faced a very different economic world from that of the previous generation. A black male in Detroit in 1945 or 1950 could realistically expect factory employment, even if his opportunities were seriously limited by discrimination. Blacks continued to suffer levels of unemployment disproportionate to those of Detroit residents in general, although labor force participation rates fluctuated with economic cycles. Still, even in the most flush of times, somewhere close to 10 percent of Detroit's black population was unemployed. Over the next three decades, with the exception of a cyclical boom in automobile employment in the mid- and late 1960s, few could rely on steady employment.

A survey of over three hundred young people in one of Detroit's most depressed inner-city neighborhoods in the early 1960s revealed the extent to which limited opportunities in Detroit's job market had narrowed the horizon of Detroit's young African Americans. Not a single respondent mentioned a career in "the broad middle range of occupations such as skilled trades, office, clerical, or technical occupations." The report noted that "replacing the whole middle range of occupations" in the "perceptual worlds" of the youth were a "whole range of deviant occupations— prostitution, numbers, malicing, corn whiskey, theft, etc." A growing number of young people turned to criminal activity, for "Under conditions where a gap in legitimate opportunity exists in the world, such deviant occupations grow up to fill the void. The motif is one of survival; it is not based on thrill seeking. What we call deviant occupations are in fact perceived to be common and in fact legitimate within the context of the culture in which these youths live." The situation changed little in the mid-1960s, even though the overall economy of Detroit improved. At the time of the 1967 riot, somewhere between 25 and 30 percent of young blacks (between ages eighteen and twenty-four) were out of work.

The combination of persistent discrimination in hiring, technological change, decentralized manufacturing, and urban economic decline had dramatic effects on the employment prospects of blacks in metropolitan Detroit. What was even more striking was the steady increase of adults who were wholly unattached to the urban labor market. Nearly one in five of all Detroit adults did not work at all or worked in the informal economy in 1950. The number grew steadily in the 1960s. The economic transformation of the city launched a process of deproletarianization, as growing numbers of African Americans, especially young men, joined the ranks of those who gave up on work. By 1980, nearly half of the adult male population had only tenuous connections to the city's formal labor market. The deproletarianization of the city's black population had far-reaching consequences: it shaped a pattern of poverty in the postwar city that was disturbingly new. Whereas in the past, most poor people had had some connection to the mainstream labor market, in the latter part of the twentieth century, the urban poor found themselves on the economic margins.

The deproletarianization of a growing number of Detroit's black workers was exacerbated by the persistent racial divide between blacks and whites in the metropolitan area. Detroit's blacks lacked the geographic mobility—common to other groups in other periods of American history—to adapt to the changing labor market. A visitor to Detroit in the 1960s would have found that despite the tremendous growth of Detroit's black population, the pattern of segregation in the metropolitan area remained intact. Throughout the postwar period whole neighborhoods lost their white populations as hundreds of thousands of white Detroiters fled to the burgeoning ring of suburbs that surrounded the city. Detroit's black population was mobile, but its movement was contained within sharply defined racial barriers.

Plant relocations, especially to rural areas and the South, severely limited the economic opportunities of Detroit's blacks. Detroit's waning industrial economy had less and less to offer them. But few black Detroiters in the 1960s had the option of following the exodus of employment; residential segregation and lack of resources kept most trapped in the city. In addition, the alternatives were hardly more appealing. Few considered moving to other major Rust Belt cities, whose economies, like Detroit's, were rapidly declining. And fewer had any desire to move to the small, overwhelmingly white Midwestern towns that attracted much of the nonmetropolitan industrialization of the postwar era. Small numbers headed west, and beginning in the 1970s, some began to return to the South. But opportunities in Detroit were, for many, still better than in Alabama's Black Belt, the Mississippi Delta, or the coal mines of West Virginia. Many remembered the promise of the 1940s and early 1950s and clung to the reasonable expectations that Detroit's economy would pick up again. Hope about the city's future was one option available to the unemployed and jobless. But more and more black Detroiters responded with anger to the city's economic and racial crisis.

Beginning in the late 1950s, African American civil rights activists in the city, after a period of retrenchment, engaged in a renewed militancy. As part of the nationwide civil rights movement, black Detroiters founded new, insurgent organizations like the Trade Union Leadership Council and began to refashion the agenda of established groups like the National Association for the Advancement of Colored People. In the early and mid-1960s, organized African American resistance to discrimination in work and housing accelerated. In 1963, nearly 250,000 blacks and whites, led by the Reverend Martin Luther King Jr., marched through Detroit. Inspired by the successes of the civil rights movement in the South, African American activists in Detroit led boycotts against local stores and businesses that discriminated against blacks. And interracial liberals took the struggle for open housing in a new direction, turning their sights on Detroit's middle- and upper-class suburbs, including Birmingham and Livonia, and lobbying hard for state and federal legislation that would prohibit discriminatory real estate practices. In all these ways, 1960s-era Detroit witnessed the emergence of a revitalized civil rights movement.

But many civil rights activists grew impatient with the glacial pace of change in Detroit. Black power organizations burgeoned in Detroit in the 1960s, offering an alternative to the mainstream civil rights activism of the postwar years. Detroit was home to the Reverend Albert Cleage, founder of the nationalist Shrine of the Black Madonna and an early and outspoken advocate of black power. At the same time, a younger generation of African Americans, who watched entry-level jobs vanish and who chafed at ongoing discrimination in Detroit's factories, grew more militant on the shop floor, eschewing the consensus politics and integrationism of the UAW for a new "revolutionary unionism." The black-led Revolutionary Union Movement (RUM) established footholds in Dodge and Chrysler plants, where whole departments remained devoid of African Americans, and where blacks remained underrepresented in local union offices.

The 1960s was a paradoxical time in Detroit. From the perspective of national politics, it seemed hopeful. The federal government enacted the most sweeping civil rights legislation since Reconstruction. At the same time, Detroit benefited tremendously from the expansion of federal urban spending during the Kennedy and Johnson administrations. In local politics, the balance of power also began to shift to the left, as Detroit's rapidly growing black populations gained electoral power. City politics remained stiffly polarized by the issues of race and housing, but as more blacks voted and were elected to office, they (and a small but vocal segment of white liberals) broke the stranglehold of the white neighborhood associations on local politics. Mayor Albert Cobo's successor, Louis Miriani, . . . recognized the power of blacks as a swing vote and tried, unsuccessfully, to accommodate both white neighborhood groups and blacks. His successor, Jerome Cavanagh, a little-known insurgent, won an upset victory in 1961 over Miriani. Cavanagh's election was almost accidental: he was supported by an unlikely alliance of African Americans and white neighborhood groups, both alienated (for different reasons) by Miriani's equivocal, middle-of-the-road position on race and housing.

Under Cavanagh, who astutely lobbied government officials for assistance, War on Poverty dollars flooded into Detroit. Detroit was second only to New York in the amount of federal dollars that it received in the 1960s. But officials channeled government assistance down familiar routes and established programs that did not fundamentally deviate from the limited agenda that social welfare, labor, and civil rights groups had set in the 1950s. By and large, War on Poverty programs embodied the conventional wisdom of mainstream economists and social welfare advocates, and focused on behavioral modification as the solution to poverty. The most far-reaching antipoverty programs targeted jobless youth. In 1962, Cavanagh established the Mayor's Committee on Community Action for Detroit Youth, and in 1963, the Michigan Employment Security Commissions established a special Detroit Metropolitan Youth Center. Both directed their energies largely toward black youth "deprived because of social, economic, cultural, or . . . personal conditions." Government, it was argued, should play a role in the transformation of youth culture. The problem with such initiatives, as Thomas F. Jackson has argued in his seminal article on antipoverty policy in the 1960s, was that they "failed to eliminate income poverty or reduce income inequality [or] to increase the aggregate supply of jobs in urban and other labor markets." The education, job training, and youth programs that were at the heart of the War on Poverty in Detroit were built on the same premises and suffered many of the same limitations as the previous generation of ad hoc programs. None responded adequately to deindustrialization and discrimination.

Simultaneous with the organized protest of civil rights groups were spontaneous outbursts of violent resistance on the streets of Detroit. A growing segment of the black population, especially young people who had little attachment to civil rights and reform organizations, began to vent their discontent at shopkeepers and police officers, the only two groups of whites who regularly appeared in largely black neighborhoods. Protests surrounding the shooting of a black youth by an East Side shopkeeper in 1964, a "mini-riot" on the Lower East Side in 1966, and the massive 1967 riot were the symptoms of growing discontent among Detroit's black poor in the 1960s. Detroit's rioters were disproportionately young black men, the group most affected by racial and economic dislocations, and the most impatient with the slow pace of civil rights reforms.

Further complicating the situation in the postwar era were hardening white racial prejudices. Whites grew increasingly bitter at the failure of their efforts to contain the city's expanding black population. The city was racked with housing protests throughout the mid-1960s, as mobile blacks continued to transgress the city's precarious racial boundaries. White neighborhood groups grew even more militant in their opposition to civil rights and open housing. In 1965, fresh off the Homeowners' Rights Ordinance campaign, white civic association advocate Thomas Poindexter revived the effort to abolish the Detroit Commission on Community Relations. The same year, twenty-five crosses burned throughout Detroit, including some in the Courville area, Lower West Side, and Wyoming Corridor, whose residents were involved in a last-ditch effort to stem racial transition. White Detroit groups pressured local politicians to oppose civil rights legislation. Their votes played a crucial role in the defeat of Michigan's Democratic governor, G. Mennen Williams, in 1966, and in the defeat of local referenda to raise taxes to pay for Detroit's increasingly African American public schools.

Most importantly, working- and lower middle-class whites continued to rally around racially conservative candidates. In 1968 and 1972, Detroit whites provided an impressive base for support for Alabama segregationist George C. Wallace as he forayed northward. The politician whose most famous declaration was "segregation now, segregation forever" found a receptive audience in one of the supposed bastions of liberal northern urban voters. Wallace's outspoken opposition to open housing, school integration, and the expansion of civil rights in the workplace resonated deeply with alienated white Detroiters. Wallace voters, to a far greater extent than supporters of other candidates, denounced racial integration and believed that the civil rights movement was moving too fast. Cheering crowds of thousands greeted Wallace when he appeared at Cobo Hall, the riverfront convention center. Like Wallace supporters elsewhere in the North, stalwart Democratic voters roared in applause when their candidate derided civil rights, "forced housing," welfare spending, urban crime, and big government. Wallace also tapped into the economic vulnerability of his blue-collar supporters. Pollsters found that Wallace voters were more pessimistic about the economy than the electorate at large. A UAW local in Flint, Michigan endorsed Wallace, and Ford workers at the company's shrinking River Rouge plant supported him in a straw poll. Wallace's troubled campaign faltered in Detroit in 1968. But emboldened by the depth of grassroots support that he found in the Rust

Belt, Wallace returned stronger than ever in 1972. He won the 1972 Michigan Democratic primary, sweeping every predominantly white ward in Detroit. Wallace found some of his most fervent support on Detroit's Northwest and Northeast sides, the final remaining bastions of homeowners' association activity in a city that was now over 45 percent African American. Following the lead of Wallace, Richard Nixon, and Spiro Agnew repudiated their party's moderate position on civil rights, wooed disaffected urban and southern white Democrats, and swept predominantly white precincts in Detroit in 1968 and 1972.

Racial cleavages also persisted in local politics. . . . They rallied in support of Detroit's overwhelmingly white police force, including its paramilitary STRESS (Stop Robberies, Enjoy Safe Streets) squad that was regularly accused of brutality toward black suspects. Anti-integration sentiment came to a head when white Detroiters rebelled against the *Milliken* v. *Bradley* court decision that called for interdistrict busing to eliminate metropolitan-wide educational segregation. The combination of the riot and growing black political power gave urgency to white resistance, but opposition to school integration and support of white conservative candidates for public office was the logical extension of the white racial politics that had divided Detroit in the 1940s and 1950s.

As the invisible boundaries within Detroit frayed, whites continued to flee from the city. . . . Fleeing whites brought the politics of local defensiveness with them to the suburbs, and found protection behind the visible and governmentally defended municipal boundaries of suburbia. By 1980, metropolitan Detroit had eighty-six municipalities, forty-five townships, and eighty-nine school districts. It was far more difficult for African Americans to cross suburban lines than it was for them to move into white urban neighborhoods. But when a few intrepid blacks tried to move into communities like Redford, Wayne, and Warren, they faced attacks and hostility like those that had plagued them in the city. Window breakings, arson, and threats largely prevented blacks from joining the ranks of working-class suburbanites. Whites also fiercely battled the Department of Housing and Urban Development's attempt to mandate the construction of integrated low-income housing in all-white suburbs.

More importantly, the grassroots racial politics that had dominated Detroit since the 1940s took deep root in suburbia. As the auto industry continued to reduce its Detroit labor force and shut down Detroit-area plants in the 1970s and 1980s, blue-collar suburbanites turned their anger against government-sponsored programs for African Americans, particularly affirmative action. Macomb County, the refuge for so many white East Side residents who fled black movement into their neighborhoods, became a bellwether for the troubled Democratic party in the 1970s and 1980s. Like whites still living in the city of Detroit, Macomb residents overwhelmingly supported Wallace in 1972. And in the 1980s, Macomb County became a bastion of "Reagan Democrats," angry antiliberal white voters who repudiated the party of Franklin D. Roosevelt for the Republican Party. Macomb was combed by pollsters and pundits alike who sought to explain why its Catholic, blue-collar workers had abandoned the New Deal for the New Rights.

The virulence of the white backlash of the 1970s and 1980s seems to lend support to the thesis of many recent commentators that the Democratic party made a grievous political error in the 1960s by ignoring the needs of white, working-class and middle-class voters in favor of the demands of the civil rights movement, black militants, the counterculture, and the "undeserving" poor. "The close identification of the Democratic party with the cause of racial justice," argues Allen Matusow, "did it special injury." Jonathan Rieder contends that the 1960s rebellion of the "silent majority" was in part a response to "certain structural limitations of liberal reform," especially "black demands" that "ran up against the limits of liberalism." Wallace's meteoric rise seems to sustain Thomas and Mary Edsall's argument that the Alabama independent "captured the central political dilemma of racial liberalism and the Democratic party: the inability of Democrats to provide a political home for those whites who felt they were paying—unwillingly—the largest 'costs' in the struggle to achieve an integrated society."

The Edsalls, Rieder, and Matusow, although they correctly emphasize the importance of white discontent as a national political force, err in their overemphasis on the role of the Great Society and the sixties rebellions in the rise of the "silent majority." To view the defection of whites from Democratic ranks simply as a reaction to the War on Poverty, civil rights, and black power movements ignores racial cleavages that shaped local politics in the north well before the tumult of the 1960s. Urban antiliberalism had deep roots in a simmering politics of race and neighborhood defensiveness that divided northern cities well before George Wallace began his first speaking tours in the Snowbelt, well before Lyndon Johnson signed the Civil Rights Act, well before the long, hot summers of Watts, Harlem, Chicago, Newark, and Detroit, and well before affirmative action and busing began to dominate the civil rights agenda. From the 1940s through the 1960s, Detroit whites fashioned a language of discontent directed against public officials, blacks, and liberal reformers who supported public housing and open housing. The rhetoric of George Wallace, Richard Nixon, Spiro Agnew, and Ronald Reagan was familiar to the whites who supported candidates such as Edward Jeffries, Albert Cobo, and Thomas Poindexter. The "silent majority" did not emerge de novo from the alleged failures of liberalism in the 1960s; it was not the unique product of the white rejection of the Great Society. Instead it was the culmination of more than two decades of simmering white discontent and extensive antiliberal political organization.

The most enduring legacy of the postwar racial struggles in Detroit has been the growing marginalization of the city in local, state, and national politics. Elected officials in Lansing and Washington, beholden to a vocal, well-organized, and defensive white suburban constituency, have reduced funding for urban education, antipoverty, and development programs. At the same time, Detroit—like its counterparts around the country—grapples with a declining tax base and increasingly expensive social, economic, and infrastructural problems.

F U R T H E R   R E A D I N G

Armor, David L. *Forced Justice: School Desegregation and the Law* (1995).

Ball, Howard, Dale Krane, and Thomas P. Lauth. *Comprised Compliance: Implementation of the 1965 Voting Rights Act* (1982).

Bartley, Numan V. *The Rise of Massive Resistance: Race and Politics in the South During the 1950s* (1969).

Bloom, Jack. *Class, Race, and the Civil Rights Movement* (1987).

Bowen, William G., and Derek Bok. *The Shape of the River* (1998).

Branch, Taylor. *Parting the Waters: America in the King Years, 1954–1963* (1988).

Brauer, Carl M. *John F. Kennedy and the Second Reconstruction* (1977).

Burk, Robert F. *The Eisenhower Administration and Black Civil Rights* (1984).

Burner, Eric. *And Gently Shall He Lead Them: Robert Moses and Civil Rights in Mississippi* (1994).

Burns, Stewart, ed. *Daybreak of Freedom: The Montgomery Bus Boycott* (1997).

Carson, Clayborne. *In Struggle: SNCC and the Black Awakening of the 1960s* (1981).

Cecelski, David S. *Along Freedom Road: Hyde County, North Carolina, and the Fate of Black Schools in the South* (1994).

Chafe, William H. *Civilities and Civil Rights: Greensboro, North Carolina, and the Black Struggle for Freedom* (1980).

Chalmers, David. *And the Crooked Places Made Straight: The Struggle for Social Changes in the 1960s* (1991).

Chappell, David. *Inside Agitators: White Southerners in the Civil Rights Movement* (1994).

Conley, Dalton. *Being Black, Living in the Red: Race, Wealth, and Social Policy in America* (1999).

Crawford, Vickie L., et al., eds. *Women in the Civil Rights Movement: Trailblazers and Torchbearers* (1990).

Dittmer, John. *Local People: The Struggle for Civil Rights in Mississippi* (1994).

Eagles, Charles W., and David L. Lewis, eds. *The Civil Rights Movement in America* (1986).

Eskew, Glen T. *But for Birmingham: The Local and National Movements in the Civil Rights Struggle* (1997).

Fairclough, Adam. *Race and Democracy: The Civil Rights Movement in Louisiana, 1915–1972)* (1995).

Farmer, James. *Lay Bare the Heart: An Autobiography of the Civil Rights Movement* (1985).

Findlay, James F. Jr. *Church People in the Struggle: The National Council of Churches and the Black Freedom Movement, 1950–1970* (1993).

Foreman, James. *The Making of Black Revolutionaries* (1985).

Formisano, Ron. *Boston Against Busing: Race, Class, and Ethnicity in the 1960s and 1970s* (1991).

Garrow, David J. *Bearing the Cross: Martin Luther King, Jr., and the Southern Christian Leadership Conference* (1987).

Glen, John M. *Highlander: No Ordinary School, 1932–1962* (1988).

Graham, Hugh Davis. *The Civil Rights Era: Origins and Development of National Policy, 1960–1972* (1990).

Greenberg, Jack. *Crusaders in the Courts: How a Dedicated Band of Lawyers Fought for the Civil Rights Movement* (1994).

Haley, Alex, comp. *The Autobiography of Malcolm X* (1965).

Hampton, Henry, and Steve Fayer. *Voices of Freedom: An Oral History of the Civil Rights Movement from the 1950s through the 1980s* (1990).

King, Martin L. Jr. *Where Do We Go from Here: Chaos or Community?* (1968).

———. *Why We Can't Wait* (1964).

King, Mary. *Freedom Song: A Personal Story of the 1960s Civil Rights Movement* (1987).

Kirp, David L., et al. *Our Town: Race, Housing, and the Soul of Suburbia* (1995).

Kluger, Richard. *Simple Justice* (1977).

Lawson, Steven F. *Running for Freedom: Civil Rights and Black Politics Since 1941* (1991).

Lawson, Steven F., and Charles Payne. *Debating the Civil Rights Movement, 1945–1968* (1998).

Lewis, David L. *King: A Biography* (1978).

Loevy, Robert D. *To End All Segregation: The Politics of the Passage of the Civil Rights Act of 1964* (1990).

Lukas, Anthony. *Common Ground* (1985).

McAdam, Doug. *Freedom Summer* (1988).

———. *Political Process and the Development of Black Insurgency, 1930–1970* (1982).

McMillen, Neil R. *The Citizens' Council: Organized Resistance to the Second Reconstruction, 1954–64* (1971).

Mann, Robert. *The Walls of Jericho: Lyndon Johnson, Hubert Humphrey, Richard Russell, and the Struggle for Civil Rights* (1996).

Marable, Manning. *Race, Reform, and Rebellion: The Second Reconstruction in Black America, 1945–1982* (1984).

Marsh, Charles. *God's Long Summer: Stories of Faith and Civil Rights* (1997).

Meier, August, and Elliot Rudwick. *CORE: A Study in the Civil Rights Movement, 1942–1968* (1972).

Morris, Aldon D. *The Origins of the Civil Rights Movement: Black Communities Organizing for Change* (1984).

Norrell, Robert. *Reaping the Whirlwind: The Civil Rights Movement in Tuskegee* (1985).

O'Reilly, Kenneth. *"Racial Matters": The FBI's Secret File on Black America, 1960–1972* (1989).

Payne, Charles M. *I've Got the Light of Freedom: The Organizing Tradition and the Mississippi Freedom Struggle* (1995).

Pickering, George. *Confronting the Color Line: The Broken Promise of the Civil Rights Movement in Chicago* (1986).

Raines, Howell, ed. *My Soul Is Rested: Movement Days in the Deep South Remembered* (1982).

Ralph, James Jr. *Northern Protest: Martin Luther King Jr., Chicago, and the Civil Rights Movement* (1993).

Sitkoff, Harvard. *The Struggle for Black Equality, 1954–1980* (1981).

Stern, Mark. *Calculating Visions: Kennedy, Johnson, and Civil Rights* (1992).

Sugrue, Thomas J. *The Origins of the Urban Crisis: Race and Inequality in Postwar Detroit* (1996).

Thernstrom, Abigail M. *Whose Votes Count? Affirmative Action and Minority Voting Rights* (1987).

Tushnet, Mark. *The NAACP's Legal Strategy Against Segregated Education, 1925–1950* (1987).

Tyson, Michael Eric. *The Making of Malcolm: The Myth and Meaning of Malcolm X* (1995).

Van Deburg, William L. *New Day in Babylon: The Black Power Movement and American Culture, 1965–1975* (1992).

Viorst, Milton. *Fire in the Streets: America in the 1960's* (1979).

Weisbrot, Robert. *Freedom Bound: A History of the American Civil Rights Movement* (1990).

Whitfield, Stephen J. *A Death in the Delta: The Story of Emmett Till* (1989).

Wilkins, Roy, and Tom Matthews. *The Autobiography of Roy Wilkins* (1982).

Wilkinson, J. Harvie, III. *From Brown to Bakke: The Supreme Court and School Integration: 1954–1978* (1979).

Williams, Juan. *Eyes on the Prize: America's Civil Rights Years, 1954–1965* (1965).

Wilson, William Julius. *The Truly Disadvantaged: The Inner City, the Underclass, and Public Policy* (1987).

Young, Andrew. *An Easy Burden: The Civil Rights Movement and the Transformation of America* (1996).

CHAPTER
8

Vietnam and the Crisis of American Empire

The Vietnam War was the most traumatic event in postwar American history. It cost the lives of more than fifty thousand Americans and of hundreds of thousands of Vietnamese and other Southeast Asians. It shattered the presidency of Lyndon Johnson, dealt the Democratic party a defeat from which it still has not recovered, and divided the American people more deeply than at any other time since the Civil War.

On one level, the war in Vietnam was the product of the Cold War and the projection of the ideas, interests, and strategies associated with that struggle onto a postcolonial world of nationalism and social revolution. It was also the logical outgrowth of America's postwar effort to maintain what Truman adviser Clark M. Clifford had once described as "our conception of a decent world order" or what Henry Luce had earlier called "an American century." The U.S. defeat in Vietnam, combined with the growing economic ascendancy of Japan and Western Europe, would mark a critical turning point in the postwar "American era."

Among the many questions that continue to preoccupy historians and other students of the Vietnam War, three in particular stand out: How (and why) did the United States come to tie its own fate to the creation and maintenance of an American-dominated, anticommunist regime in Southeast Asia? Given that commitment, how (and with what consequences) did the United States conduct the war? And finally, what are the lessons of Vietnam, especially in a world no longer dominated by the Cold War but in which the forces of nationalism and social revolution remain very powerful?

DOCUMENTS

As World War II drew to a close and Japanese control over Vietnam waned, the Vietminh, whose forces represented a powerful fusion of communism and nationalism, seized power throughout much of the country. With an eye toward winning U.S. support, they issued a Declaration of Independence (Document 1), which began with a familiar passage. The French effort to regain control of Vietnam and resulting First Indochina War (1946–1954) posed a dilemma for U.S. policymakers: should the United States accept the victory of a movement that, like that in China, was both communist and nationalist, or should it support the French colonial regime led by Boa Dai? In Document 2, State Department officials Raymond B. Fosdick and W. Walton Butterworth argue the two sides of the dilemma. The U.S. government, of course, followed the advice of the latter. Indeed, by 1954 the United States was underwriting an estimated 80 percent of the French war effort. Although President Eisenhower declined to commit U.S. armed forces in Vietnam, he expressed grave concerns about the consequences of a Vietminh victory at an April 27, 1954, press conference (Document 3), in which he compared the nations of Southeast Asia to a "row of dominoes."

The French defeat was sealed on July 21, 1954, by the Geneva Accords (Document 4), which temporarily divided Vietnam along the seventeenth parallel, established procedures for the nation's reunification, and sought to insulate it from further outside intervention. Despite the Geneva Accords, the United States soon replaced France as the dominant Western power in Vietnam. Its efforts to create and sustain a new, anti-communist government, however, drew the United States deeper and deeper into conflict with the National Liberation Front (NLF, or Vietcong) in the South and with the Democratic Republic of Vietnam (North Vietnam). At the center of the struggle were the many Vietnamese peasants whose poverty and alienation from the U.S.-backed government made them easy recruits for the NLF. In Document 5, excerpted from David Chanoff and Doan Van Toai's *Portrait of the Enemy* (1986), Nguyen Tan Thanh explains why he joined the Vietcong. In 1964, when American warships were fired upon in the Gulf of Tonkin off the North Vietnamese coast (where U.S. ships had been conducting electronic surveillance and providing cover for South Vietnamese attacks), President Lyndon Johnson seized the opportunity to push through Congress the Gulf of Tonkin Resolution (Document 6), which he would later use to justify the continuing U.S. war in Vietnam.

Although U.S. military advisers had been present in Vietnam since the 1950s, American combat troops did not arrive until early 1965. Not until July 28, 1965, did the Johnson administration decide to greatly expand the U.S. effort. Document 7 is composed of two memoranda, one by Secretary of Defense Robert S. McNamara urging escalation and one by Undersecretary of State George W. Ball arguing that the United States should seek a compromise solution. Johnson, of course, followed the advice of McNamara. Despite superior weapons and resources, U.S. military forces could never fully subdue their Vietnamese enemies. Still, in the war's early stages at least, its purpose seemed clear, even if its tactics did not, according to a Marine recruit who would later die in Vietnam (Document 8). A decade after the fall of Vietnam, Americans continued to debate the war's legacy. The Reagan administration in particular sought to overcome what it called the Vietnam syndrome and to prove that "America was back." Thomas J. Vallely, a Marine Corps veteran who later campaigned against the war, strongly criticizes this approach in Document 9.

1. The Vietnamese Declare Their Independence, 1945

"We hold truths that all men are created equal, that they are endowed by their Creator with certain unalienable Rights, among these are Life, Liberty and the pursuit of Happiness."

This immortal statement is extracted from the Declaration of Independence of the United States of America in 1776. Understood in the broader sense, this means: "All peoples on the earth are born equal; every person has the right to live to be happy and free."

Ho Chi Minh, *Selected Writings, 1920–1969* (Hanoi: Foreign Language Publishing House, 1973), 53-56.

The Declaration of Human and Civic Rights proclaimed by the French Revolution in 1791 likewise propounds: "Every man is born equal and enjoys free and equal rights."

These are undeniable truths.

Yet, during and throughout the last eighty years, the French imperialists, abusing the principles of "Freedom, equality and fraternity," have violated the integrity of our ancestral land and oppressed our countrymen. Their deeds run counter to the ideals of humanity and justice.

In the political field, they have denied us every freedom. They have enforced upon us inhuman laws. They have set up three different political regimes in Northern, Central, and Southern Viet Nam (Tonkin, Annam, and Cochinchina) in an attempt to disrupt our national, historical, and ethical unity.

They have built more prisons than schools. They have callously ill-treated our fellow-compatriots. They have drowned our revolutions in blood.

They have sought to stifle public opinion and pursued a policy of obscurantism on the largest scale; they have forced upon us alcohol and opium in order to weaken our race.

In the economic field, they have shamelessly exploited our people, driven them into the worst misery, and mercilessly plundered our country.

They have ruthlessly appropriated our rice fields, mines, forests, and raw materials. They have arrogated to themselves the privilege of issuing banknotes, and monopolized all our external commerce. They have imposed hundreds of unjustifiable taxes, and reduced our countrymen, especially the peasants and petty tradesmen, to extreme poverty.

They have prevented the development of native capital enterprises; they have exploited our workers in the most barbarous manner.

In the autumn of 1940, when the Japanese fascists, in order to fight the Allies, invaded Indochina and set up new bases of war, the French imperialists surrendered on bended knees and handed over our country to the invaders.

Subsequently, under the joint French and Japanese yoke, our people were literally bled white. The consequences were dire in the extreme. From Quang Tri up to the North, two millions of our countrymen died from starvation during the first months of this year.

On March 9th, 1945, the Japanese disarmed the French troops. Again the French either fled or surrendered unconditionally. Thus, in no way have they proved capable of "protecting" us; on the contrary, within five years they have twice sold our country to the Japanese.

Before March 9th, many a time did the Viet Minh League invite the French to join in the fight against the Japanese. Instead of accepting this offer, the French, on the contrary, let loose a wild reign of terror with rigour worse than ever before against Viet Minh's partisans. They even slaughtered a great number of our "*condamnés politiques*" imprisoned at Yen Bay and Cao Bang.

Despite all that, our countrymen went on maintaining, vis-à-vis the French, a humane and even indulgent attitude. After the events of March 9th, the Viet Minh League helped many French to cross the borders, rescued others from Japanese prisons, and, in general, protected the lives and properties of all the French in their territory.

In fact, since the autumn of 1940, our country ceased to be a French colony and became a Japanese possession.

After the Japanese surrender, our people, as a whole, rose up and proclaimed their sovereignty and founded the Democratic Republic of Viet Nam.

The truth is that we have wrung back our independence from Japanese hands and not from the French.

The French fled, the Japanese surrendered. Emperor Bao Dai abdicated, our people smashed the yoke which pressed hard upon us for nearly one hundred years, and finally made our Viet Nam an independent country. Our people at the same time overthrew the monarchical regime established tens of centuries ago, and founded the Republic.

For these reasons, we the members of the Provisional Government representing the entire people of Viet Nam, declare that we shall from now on have no more connections with imperialist France; we consider null and void all the treaties France has signed concerning Viet Nam, and we hereby cancel all the privileges that the French arrogated to themselves on our territory.

The Vietnamese people, animated by the same common resolve, are determined to fight to the death against all attempts at aggression by the French imperialists.

We are convinced that the Allies who have recognized the principles of equality of peoples at the Conferences of Teheran and San Francisco cannot but recognize the independence of Viet Nam.

A people which has so stubbornly opposed the French domination for more than 80 years, a people who, during these last years, so doggedly ranged itself and fought on the Allied side against Fascism, such a people has the right to be free, such a people must be independent.

For these reasons, we, the members of the Provisional Government of the Democratic Republic of Viet Nam, solemnly declare to the world:

"Viet Nam has the right to be free and independent and, in fact, has become free and independent. The people of Viet Nam decide to mobilise all their spiritual and material forces and to sacrifice their lives and property in order to safeguard their right of Liberty and Independence."

2. State Department Advisers Debate U.S. Support for the French in Vietnam, 1949

[November 4, 1949]

SECRET

MEMORANDUM FOR: Mr. [Philip C.] Jessup [Ambassador-at-Large]

In his memorandum of November 1 on Indochina, Mr. [Charles] Yost argues that "a further major advance of Communism will be considered as, and will in fact be, a defeat for the United States, whether or not we are directly involved." He therefore recommends, among other steps, support of the Bao Dai government (after the March 8 agreements are ratified), economic assistance to Bao Dai, etc.

Raymond B. Fosdick to Philip C. Jessup, November 4, 1949, National Archives 896.00/11-1849; and W. Walton Butterworth to Fosdick, November 17, 1949, National Archives, Lot Files, "French-Indochinese Relations, PSA, Box 5.

It seems to me this point of view fails to take into consideration the possible, and I think the probable, consequences of such a decision. In grasping one horn of the dilemma, it ignores the other. My belief is that the Bao Dai regime is doomed. The compromises which the French are so reluctantly making cannot possibly save it. The Indochinese are pressing toward complete nationalism and nothing is going to stop them. They see all too clearly that France is offering them a kind of semi-colonialism; and to think that they will be content to settle for less than Indonesia has gained from the Dutch or India from the British is to underestimate the power of the forces that are sweeping Asia today.

What kind of independence is France offering the Indochinese today in the March 8th agreements?

(1) The foreign policy of Indochina is to be under the final control of France.

(2) French military bases are to be established and the Indochinese Army in time of war is to be under French direction.

(3) France is to be in charge of the so-called General Services:

    (a) Control of immigration

    (b) Communications

    (c) Industrial development of Indochina

(4) Customs receipts are to be divided between France and Indochina in accordance with a formula to be agreed upon.

(5) Extraterritorial courts for French citizens are to be continued.

This shabby business is a mockery of all the professions we have made in the Indonesian case. It probably represents an improvement over the brutal colonialism of earlier years, but it is now too late in the history of the world to try to settle for the price of this cheap substitute. For the United States to support France in this attempt will cost us our standing and prestige in all of Southeast Asia. A lot of that prestige went down the drain with Chiang Kai-shek [President of the then-recently exiled Republic of China]; the rest of it will go down with the Bao Dai regime if we support it. Ambassador [to China, John] Stuart calls our relationship to this regime "shameful" and I am inclined to agree with him.

Ev[erett] Case argued yesterday that it is too late to do anything else except support Bao Dai. I disagree. It is never too late to change a mistaken policy, particularly when the policy involves the kind of damage that our adherence to the Generalissimo [Chiang Kai-shek] brought us. Why get our fingers burned twice?

Ho Chi Minh as an alternative is decidedly unpleasant, but as was pointed out at our meeting with FE yesterday, there may be unpredictable and unseen factors in this situation which in the end will be more favorable to us than now seems probable. The fundamental antipathy of the Indochinese to China is one of the factors. Faced with a dilemma like this the best possible course is to wait for the breaks. Certainly we should not play our cards in such a way that once again, as in China, we seem to be allied with reaction. Whether the French like it or not, independence is coming to Indochina. Why, therefore, do we tie ourselves to the tail of their battered kite?

RAYMOND B. FOSDICK
[Consultant to the State Department on *Far Eastern Affairs*]

[To:] Mr. [Raymond B.] Fosdick   November 17, 1949

[From:] Mr. [W. Walton] Butterworth [Assistant Secretary of State for Far Eastern Affairs]

Your November 4 Memorandum to Ambassador Jessup Regarding Indochina.

Mr. Jessup has referred to me your memorandum to him of November 4, 1949, regarding Indochina which I have read with much interest.

In general, the considerations which you raise have been very much in the foreground of our thinking. I do not believe, however, that we can necessarily conclude, as you apparently have, the Bao Dai regime is doomed. There is no doubt in my mind that Bao Dai's chances of establishing a viable non-Communist state are not brilliant, but I feel that under certain circumstances, which admittedly may never arise, he might be successful.

I think I can make our position clear by the following analogy: Because the odds are heavily against a horse entered in a given race, is no reason to withdraw that horse from the race although I agree that there is likewise no reason in these circumstances to back that horse heavily.

I agree that we should not support France in Indochina because such action will damage our standing and prestige in all of Southeast Asia, but I feel that without committing ourselves to another operation similar in some respects to that which took place in China, we must allow Bao Dai his opportunity to succeed and we must do nothing deliberately to eliminate his opportunity.

3. President Dwight D. Eisenhower Explains the Domino Theory, 1954

Q. Robert Richards, Copley Press Mr. President, would you mind commenting on the strategic importance of Indochina to the free world? I think there has been, across the country, some lack of understanding on just what it means to us.

The President You have, of course, both the specific and the general when you talk about such things.

First of all, you have the specific value of a locality in its production of materials that the world needs.

Then you have the possibility that many human beings pass under a dictatorship that is inimical to the free world.

Finally, you have broader considerations that might follow what you would call the "falling domino" principle. You have a row of dominoes set up, you knock over the first one, and what will happen to the last one is the certainty that it will go over very quickly. So you could have a beginning of a disintegration that would have the most profound influences.

Public Papers of the Presidents of the United States: Dwight D. Eisenhower, 1954 (Washington, D.C.: GPO, 1960), 382–383.

Now, with respect to the first one, two of the items from this particular area that the world uses are tin and tungsten. They are very important. There are others, of course, the rubber plantations and so on.

Then with respect to more people passing under this domination, Asia, after all, has already lost some 450 million of its peoples to the Communist dictatorship, and we simply can't afford greater losses.

But when we come to the possible sequence of events, the loss of Indochina, of Burma, of Thailand, of the Peninsula, and Indonesia following, now you begin to talk about areas that not only multiply the disadvantages that you would suffer through loss of materials, sources of materials, but now you are talking about millions and millions and millions of people.

Finally, the geographical position achieved thereby does many things. It turns the so-called island defensive chain of Japan, Formosa, of the Philippines and to the southward; it moves in to threaten Australia and New Zealand.

It takes away, in its economic aspects, that region that Japan must have as a trading area or Japan, in turn, will have only one place in the world to go—that is, toward the Communist areas in order to live.

So, the possible consequences of the loss are just incalculable to the free world.

4. Final Declaration of the Geneva Conference on Indochina, 1954

Final declaration, dated the 21st July, 1954, of the Geneva Conference on the problem of restoring peace in Indo-China, in which the representatives of Cambodia, the Democratic Republic of Viet-nam, France, Laos, the People's Republic of China, the State of Viet-nam, the Union of Soviet Socialist Republics, the United Kingdom, and the United States of America took part.

1. The Conference takes note of the Agreements ending hostilities in Cambodia, Laos, and Viet-nam and organizing international control and the supervision of the execution of the provisions of these agreements.

2. The Conference expresses satisfaction at the ending of hostilities in Cambodia, Laos, and Viet-nam; the Conference expresses its conviction that the execution of the provisions set out in the present Declaration and in the Agreements on the cessation of hostilities will permit Cambodia, Laos, [and] Viet-nam henceforth to play their part, in full independence and sovereignty, in the peaceful community of nations.

3. The Conference takes note of the declarations made by the Governments of Cambodia and of Laos of their intention to adopt measures permitting all citizens to take their place in the national community, in particular by participating in the next general elections, which, in conformity with the constitution of each of these countries, shall take place in the course of the year 1955, by secret ballot and in conditions of respect for fundamental freedoms.

Democratic Republic of Viet-Nam, *Documents Related to the Implementation of the Geneva Agreements Concerning Viet-Nam* (Hanoi, 1956), 181–183.

4. The Conference takes note of the clauses in the Agreement on the cessation of hostilities in Viet-nam prohibiting the introduction into Viet-nam of foreign troops and military personnel as well as of all kinds of arms and munitions. The Conference also takes note of the declarations made by the Governments of Cambodia and Laos of their resolution not to request foreign aid, whether in war material, in personnel, or in instructors except for the purpose of the effective defence of their territory and, in the case of Laos, to the extent defined by the Agreements on the cessation of hostilities in Laos.

5. The Conference takes note of the clauses in the Agreement on the cessation of hostilities in Viet-nam to the effect that no military base under the control of a foreign State may be established in the regrouping zones of the two parties, the latter having the obligation to see that the zones allotted to them shall not constitute part of any military alliance and shall not be utilized for the resumption of hostilities or in the service of an aggressive policy. The Conference also takes note of the declarations of the Governments of Cambodia and Laos to the effect that they will not join in any agreement with other States if this agreement includes the obligation to participate in a military alliance not in conformity with the principles of the Charter of the United Nations or, in the case of Laos, with the principles of the Agreement on the cessation of hostilities in Laos or, so long as their security is not threatened, the obligation to establish bases on Cambodian or Laotian territory for the military forces of foreign Powers.

6. The Conference recognizes that the essential purpose of the Agreement relating to Viet-nam is to settle military questions with a view to ending hostilities and that the military demarcation line is provisional and should not in any way be interpreted as constituting a political or territorial boundary. The Conference expresses its conviction that the execution of the provisions set out in the present Declaration and in the Agreement on the cessation of hostilities creates the necessary basis for the achievement in the near future of a political settlement in Viet-nam.

7. The Conference declares that, so far as Viet-nam is concerned, the settlement of political problems, effected on the basis of respect for the principles of independence, unity, and territorial integrity, shall permit the Vietnamese people to enjoy the fundamental freedoms, guaranteed by democratic institutions established as a result of free general elections by secret ballot. In order to ensure that sufficient progress in the restoration of peace has been made and that all the necessary conditions obtain for free expression of the national will, general elections shall be held in July 1956, under the supervision of an international commission composed of representatives of the Member States of the International Supervisory Commission, referred to in the Agreement on the cessation of hostilities. Consultations will be held on this subject between the competent representative authorities of the two zones from 20 July 1955 onwards.

8. The provisions of the Agreements on the cessation of hostilities intended to ensure the protection of individuals and of property must be most strictly applied and must, in particular, allow everyone in Viet-nam to decide freely in which zone he wishes to live.

9. The competent representative authorities of the Northern and Southern zones of Viet-nam, as well as the authorities of Laos and Cambodia, must not permit any individual or collective reprisals against persons who have collaborated in any way with one of the parties during the war, or against members of such persons' families.

10. The Conference takes note of the declaration of the Government of the French Republic to the effect that it is ready to withdraw its troops from the territory of Cambodia, Laos, and Viet-nam, at the request of the governments concerned and within periods which shall be fixed by agreement between the parties except in the cases where, by agreement between the two parties, a certain number of French troops shall remain at specified points and for a specified time.

11. The Conference takes note of the declaration of the French Government to the effect that for the settlement of all the problems connected with the re-establishment and consolidation of peace in Cambodia, Laos, and Viet-nam, the French Government will proceed from the principle of respect for the independence and sovereignty, unity, and territorial integrity of Cambodia, Laos, and Viet-nam.

12. In their relations with Cambodia, Laos, and Viet-nam, each member of the Geneva Conference undertakes to respect the sovereignty, the independence, the unity, and the territorial integrity of the above-mentioned States, and to refrain from any interference in their internal affairs.

13. The members of the Conference agree to consult one another on any question which may be referred to them by the International Supervisory Commission, in order to study such measures as may prove necessary to ensure that the Agreements on the cessation of hostilities in Cambodia, Laos, and Viet-nam are respected.

5. Nguyen Tan Thanh, a South Vietnamese Peasant, Explains Why He Joined the Vietcong (1961), 1986

I joined the VC [Vietcong] when I was thirty-five years old. I was married and had four children. I was leasing farmland—one hectare [about 2.5 acres]—that was very poor in quality, almost sterile. That was why the owner rented it out to us. Despite working hard all year round, we got only about 100 *gia* of rice out of it. Of this amount, 40 *gia* went to the landlord. We borrowed money to buy ducks and geese. We lived a very hard life. But I cultivated the land carefully, and in time it became fertile. When it did, the owner took it back; my livelihood was gone. I had to go back to my parents, to raise ducks for my father.

I was poor. I had lost my land and I didn't have enough money to take care of my children. In 1961 propaganda cadres of the Front [National Liberation Front] contacted me. These guys had joined the resistance against the French, and after Geneva they had stayed underground in the South. They came to all the poor farmers and made an analysis of the poor and rich classes. They said that the rich people had always served the French and had used the authority of the French to oppress the poor. The majority of the people were poor, not because they wasted their money but because they had been exploited by the landlords who had worked with the French. In the past, the ancestors of the poor had broken ground for tillage. Then powerful people had seized their land. Without any other means to live, the poor had become slaves of the landlords. The cadres told us that if the poor people don't stand up [to] the rich people, we would be dominated by them forever. The only way to ensure freedom and a sufficient life was to overthrow them.

When I heard the cadres, I thought that what they said was correct. In my village there were about forty-three hundred people. Of these, maybe ten were landlords. The richest owned five hundred hectares [1,236 acres], and the others had at least twenty hectares [49 acres] apiece. The rest of the people were tenants or honest poor farmers. I knew that the rich oppressed the poor. The poor had nothing to eat, and they also had no freedom. We had to get rid of the regime that allowed a few people to use their money and authority to oppress the others.

So I joined the Liberation Front. I followed the VC to fight for freedom and prosperity for the country. I felt that this was right.

6. The Gulf of Tonkin Resolution, 1964

Whereas naval units of the Communist regime in [North] Vietnam, in violation of the principles of the Charter of the United Nations and of international law, have deliberately and repeatedly attacked United States naval vessels lawfully present in international waters, and have thereby created a serious threat to international peace; and

Whereas these attacks are part of a deliberate and systematic campaign of aggression that the Communist regime in North Vietnam has been waging against its neighbors and the nations joined with them in the collective defense of their freedom; and

Whereas the United States is assisting the peoples of southeast Asia to protect their freedom and has no territorial, military, or political ambitions in that area, but desires only that these peoples should be left in peace to work out their own destinies in their own way: Now, therefore, be it

Resolved by the Senate and House of Representatives of the United States of America in Congress assembled, That the Congress approves and supports the determination of the President, as Commander in Chief, to take all necessary measures to repel any armed attack against the forces of the United States and to prevent further aggression.

Sec. 2. The United States regards as vital to its national interest and to world peace the maintenance of international peace and security in southeast Asia. Consonant with the Constitution of the United States and the Charter of the United Nations and in accordance with its obligations under the Southeast Asia Collective Defense Treaty, the United States is, therefore, prepared, as the President determines, to take all necessary steps, including the use of armed force, to assist any member or protocol state of the Southeast Asia Collective Defense Treaty requesting assistance in defense of its freedom.

Sec. 3. This resolution shall expire when the President shall determine that the peace and security of the area is reasonably assured by international conditions created by action of the United Nations or otherwise, except that it may be terminated earlier by concurrent resolution of the Congress.

Department of State Bulletin Vol. 51 No. 1313 (August 24, 1964), p. 268.

7. President Lyndon Johnson's Advisers Debate Expanding the War, 1965

Robert S. McNamara

[26 June 1965; revised 1 July 1965]

Introduction

Our objective is to create conditions for a favorable settlement by demonstrating to the VC [Viet Cong]/DRV [Democratic Republic of Vietnam—North Vietnam] that the odds are against their winning. Under present conditions, however, the chances of achieving this objective are small—and the VC are winning now—largely because the ratio of guerrilla to antiguerrilla forces is unfavorable to the government. With this in mind, we must choose among three courses of action with respect to South Vietnam: (1) Cut our losses and withdraw under the best conditions that can be arranged; (2) continue at about the present level, with U.S. forces limited to say, 75,000, holding on and playing for the breaks while recognizing that our position will probably grow weaker; or (3) expand substantially the U.S. military pressure against the Viet Cong in the South and the North Vietnamese in the North and at the same time launch a vigorous effort on the political side to get negotiations started. An outline of the third of these approaches follows.

I. Expanded Military Moves

The following military moves should be taken together with the political initiatives in Part II below.

A. Inside South Vietnam.   Increase U.S./SVN [South Vietnam] military strength in SVN enough to prove to the VC that they cannot win and thus to turn the tide of the war. . . .

B. Against North Vietnam.   While avoiding striking population and industrial targets not closely related to the DRV's supply of war material to the VC, we should announce to Hanoi and carry out actions to destroy such supplies and to interdict their flow into and out of North Vietnam. . . .

II. Expanded Political Moves

Together with the above military moves, we should take the following political initiatives in order (a) to open a dialogue with Hanoi, Peking, and the VC looking toward a settlement in Vietnam, (b) to keep the Soviet Union from deepening its military involvement and support of North Vietnam until the time when settlement can be

Robert S. McNamara, Memorandum for the President, June 26, 1965; revised July 1, 1965; George W. Ball to the President, memorandum, July 1, 1965; both in National Security File, National Security Council History, "Deployment of Major U.S. Forces to Vietnam, July 1965," Lyndon B. Johnson Library, Austin, Tex.

achieved, and (c) to cement the support for U.S. policy by the U.S. public, allies, and friends, and to keep international opposition at a manageable level. While our approaches may be rebuffed until the tide begins to turn, they nevertheless should be made. . . .

III. Evaluation of the Above Program

A. Domestic U.S. Reaction.   Even though casualties will increase and the war will continue for some time, the United States public will support this course of action because it is a combined military-political program designed and likely to bring about a favorable solution to the Vietnam problem.

B. Communist Reaction to the Expanded Programs.

1. Soviet. The Soviets can be expected to continue to contribute material and advisors to the North Vietnamese. Increased U.S. bombing of Vietnam, including targets in Hanoi and Haiphong, SAM [surface-to-air missile] sites, and airfields, and mining of North Vietnamese harbors, might oblige the Soviet Union to enter the contest more actively with volunteers and aircraft. This might result in minor encounters between U.S. and Soviet personnel.

2. China. So long as no U.S. or GVN [Government of Vietnam—South Vietnam] troops invade North Vietnam and so long as no U.S. or GVN aircraft attack Chinese territory, the Chinese probably will not send regular ground forces or aircraft into the war. However, the possibility of a more active Soviet involvement in North Vietnam might precipitate a Chinese introduction of land forces, probably dubbed volunteers, to preclude the Soviets' taking a pre-eminent position in North Vietnam.

3. North Vietnam. North Vietnam will not move towards the negotiating table until the tide begins to turn in the south. When that happens, they may seek to counter it by sending large numbers of men into South Vietnam.

4. Viet Cong. The VC, especially if they continue to take high losses, can be expected to depend increasingly upon the PAVN [People's Army of Vietnam, regular forces of North Vietnam] forces as the war moves into a more conventional phase; but they may find ways of continuing almost indefinitely their present intensive military, guerrilla, and terror activities, particularly if reinforced with some regular PAVN units. A key question on the military side is whether POL [petroleum-oil-lubricants], ammunition, and cadres can be cut off and if they are cut off whether this really renders the Viet Cong impotent. A key question on the political side is whether any arrangement acceptable to us would be acceptable to the VC.

C. Estimate of Success.

1. Militarily. The success of the above program from a military point of view turns on whether the increased effort stems the tide in the South; that in turn depends on two things—on whether the South Vietnamese hold their own in terms of numbers and fighting spirit, and on whether the U.S. forces can be effective in a quick-reaction reserve role, a role in which they have not been tested. The number of U.S. troops is too small to make a significant difference in the traditional 10-1 government-guerrilla formula, but it is not too small to make a significant difference in the kind of war which seems to be evolving in Vietnam—a "Third Stage" or conventional war in which it is easier to identify, locate, and attack the enemy. (South Vietnam has 141 battalions as compared with an estimated equivalent number of VC battalions. The 44 U.S./3d country battalions mentioned above are the equivalent of 100 South Vietnamese battalions.)

2. *Politically.* It is frequently alleged that such a large expansion of U.S. military personnel, their expanded military role (which would put them in close contact and offer some degree of control over South Vietnamese citizens), and the inevitable expansion of U.S. voice in the operation of the GVN economy and facilities, command, and government services will be unpopular; it is said that they could lead to the rejection of the government which supported this American presence, to an irresistible pressure for expulsion of the Americans, and to the greatly increased saleability of Communist propaganda. Whether these allegations are true, we do not know.

The political initiatives are likely to be successful in the early stages only to demonstrate U.S. good faith; they will pay off toward an actual settlement only after the tide begins to turn (unless we lower our sights substantially). The tide almost certainly cannot begin to turn in less than a few months, and may not for a year or more; the war is one of attrition and will be a long one. Since troops once committed as a practical matter cannot be removed, since U.S. casualties will rise, since we should take call-up actions to support the additional forces in Vietnam, the test of endurance may be as much in the United States as in Vietnam.

3. *Generally (CIA [Central Intelligence Agency] estimate).* Over the longer term we doubt if the Communists are likely to change their basic strategy in Vietnam (i.e., aggressive and steadily mounting insurgency) unless and until two conditions prevail: (1) they are forced to accept a situation in the war in the South which offers them no prospect of an early victory and no grounds for hope that they can simply outlast the U.S. and (2) North Vietnam itself is under continuing and increasingly damaging punitive attack. So long as the Communists think they scent the possibility of an early victory (which is probably now the case), we believe that they will persevere and accept extremely severe damage to the North. Conversely, if North Vietnam itself is not hurting, Hanoi's doctrinaire leaders will probably be ready to carry on the Southern struggle almost indefinitely. If, however, both of the conditions outlined above should be brought to pass, we believe Hanoi probably would, at least for a period of time, alter its basic strategy and course of action in South Vietnam.

Hanoi might do so in several ways. Going for a conference as a political way of gaining a respite from attack would be one. Alternatively it might reduce the level of insurgent activity in the hopes that this would force the U.S. to stop its punishment of the North but not prevent the U.S. and GVN from remaining subject to wearying harassment in the South. Or, Hanoi might order the VC to suspend operations in the hopes that in a period of temporary tranquility, domestic and international opinion would force the U.S. to disengage without destroying the VC apparatus or the roots of VC strength. Finally, Hanoi might decide that the U.S./GVN will to fight could still be broken and the tide of war turned back in favor of the VC by launching a massive PAVN assault on the South. This is a less likely option in the circumstances we have posited, but still a contingency for which the U.S. must be prepared.

George W. Ball

[1 July 1965]

1. A Losing War: The South Vietnamese are losing the war to the Viet Cong [formally, the National Liberation Front]. No one can assure you that we can beat the Viet Cong or even force them to the conference table on our terms no matter how many hundred thousand *white foreign* (U.S.) troops we deploy.

No one has demonstrated that a white ground force of whatever size can win a guerrilla war—which is at the same time a civil war between Asians—in jungle terrain in the midst of a population that refuses cooperation to the white forces (and the SVN [South Vietnam]) and thus provides a great intelligence advantage to the other side. Three recent incidents vividly illustrate this point:

(a) The sneak attack on the Danang Air Base which involved penetration of a defense perimeter guarded by 9,000 Marines. *This raid was possible only because of the cooperation of the local inhabitants.*

(b) The B-52 raid that failed to hit the Viet Cong *who had obviously been tipped off.*

(c) The search-and-destroy mission of the 173rd Airborne Brigade which spent three days looking for the Viet Cong, suffered 23 casualties, and never made contact with the enemy *who had obviously gotten advance word of their assignment.*

2. The Question to Decide: Should we limit our liabilities in South Viet-Nam and try to find a way out with minimal long-term cost?

The alternative—no matter what we may wish it to be—is almost certainly a protracted war involving an open-ended commitment of U.S. forces, mounting U.S. casualties, no assurance of a satisfactory solution, and a serious danger of escalation at the end of the road.

3. Need for a Decision Now: So long as our forces are restricted to advising and assisting the South Vietnamese, the struggle will remain a civil war between Asian peoples. Once we deploy substantial numbers of troops in combat it will become a war between the United States and a large part of the population of South Viet-Nam, organized and directed from North Viet-Nam and backed by the resources of both Moscow and Peiping [sic].

The decision you face now, therefore, is crucial. Once large numbers of U.S. troops are committed to direct combat they will begin to take heavy casualties in a war they are ill-equipped to fight in a non-cooperative if not downright hostile countryside.

Once we suffer large casualties we will have started a well-nigh irreversible process. Our involvement will be so great that we cannot—without national humiliation—stop short of achieving our complete objectives. *Of the two possibilities I think humiliation would be more likely than the achievement of our objectives—even after we had paid terrible costs.*

4. A Compromise Solution: Should we commit U.S. manpower and prestige to a terrain so unfavorable as to give a very large advantage to the enemy—or should we seek a compromise settlement which achieves less than our stated objectives and thus cut our losses while we still have the freedom of maneuver to do so?

5. Costs of Compromise Solution: The answer involves a judgment as to the costs to the United States of such a compromise settlement in terms of our relations with the countries in the area of South Viet-Nam, the credibility of our commitments, and our prestige around the world. In my judgment, if we act before we commit substantial U.S. forces to combat in South Viet-Nam we can, by accepting some short-term costs, avoid what may well be a long-term catastrophe. I believe we have tended greatly to exaggerate the costs involved in a compromise settlement. An appreciation of probable costs is contained in the attached memorandum.

6. With these considerations in mind, I strongly urge the following program:

A. *Military Program*

1. Complete all deployments already announced (15 battalions) but decide not to go beyond the total of 72,000 men represented by this figure.
2. Restrict the combat role of American forces to the June 9 announcement, making it clear to General Westmoreland that this announcement is to be strictly construed.
3. Continue bombing in the North but avoid the Hanoi-Haiphong area and any targets nearer to the Chinese border than those already struck.

B. *Political Program*

1. In any political approaches so far, we have been the prisoners of whatever South Vietnamese Government was momentarily in power. If we are ever to move toward a settlement it will probably be because the South Vietnamese Government pulls the rug out from under us and makes its own deal *or* because we go forward quietly without advance prearrangement with Saigon.
2. So far we have not given the other side a reason to believe that there is *any* flexibility in our negotiating approach. And the other side has been unwilling to accept what *in their terms* is complete capitulation.
3. Now is the time to start some serious diplomatic feelers, looking towards a solution based on some application of the self-determination principle.
4. I would recommend approaching Hanoi rather than any of the other probable parties (the National Liberation Front, Moscow, of Peiping). Hanoi is the only one that has given any signs of interest in discussion. Peiping has been rigidly opposed. Moscow has recommended that we negotiate with Hanoi. The National Liberation Front has been silent.
5. There are several channels to the North Vietnamese but I think the best one is through their representative in Paris, Mai Van Bo. Initial feelers with Bo should be directed toward a discussion both of the four points we have put forward and the four points put forward by Hanoi as a basis for negotiation. We can accept all but one of Hanoi's four points and hopefully we should be able to agree on some ground rules for serious negotiation—including no pre-conditions.
6. If the initial feelers lead to further secret exploratory talks we can inject the concept of self-determination that would permit the Viet Cong some hope of achieving some of their political objectives through local elections or some other device.
7. The contact on our side should be handled through a non-governmental cutout (possibly a reliable newspaperman who can be repudiated.)
8. If progress can be made at this level the basis can be laid for a multi-national conference. At some point obviously the government of South Viet-Nam will have to be brought on board but I would postpone this step until after a substantial feeling out of Hanoi.

9. Before moving to any formal conference we should be prepared to agree that once the conference is started (a) the United States will stand down its bombing of the North, (b) the South Vietnamese will initiate no offensive operations in the South, and (c) the DRV [Democratic Republic of Vietnam] will stop terrorism and other aggressive acts in the South.

10. Negotiations at the conference should aim at incorporating our understanding with Hanoi in the form of a multi-national agreement guaranteed by the United States, the Soviet Union, and possibly other parties, and providing for an international mechanism to supervise its execution.

8. Lieutenant Marion Lee Kempner, a Young Marine, Explains the War, 1966

Received October 20, 1966

Dear Mom, Dad, Shrub, Peach, and Early Bird: . . .

Dad, I would like to comment on your statement that this was the wrong war for us to be fighting. In the first place, of course, there has never been a right war for us to fight. War, as our German geniuses say, is politics of a different means, and as a play called *Command Decision* puts it, war is entered into when politics, reason, discussions, and civilization have failed. It is the return to the primeval ooze. Someone, I think Socrates, once said there are only two ways to treat a conquered enemy to make sure he never fights you again: either treat him so harshly as to render him incapable of ever rising again, or treat him so well that he never has any reason to go against you. The great error is to treat him half and half. Our punishment of the Indians is an example of the former, while the aid, help, and protection given to Germany and Japan are examples of the latter. The Versailles Treaty and the aftermath of the Civil War are the two times when we tried to do it half and half. This rule of thumb, valid as it may be, is difficult to apply in a guerrilla war situation, since all participants, both the good guys and the bad guys, are in the same place, and you can't treat them all good or all bad since that will reward or punish the wrong party—especially since we have not won this war yet. So the result is that we do it half and half. We reward those who are for us, neutral, or willing to give up their arms to us (Chu Hoy—Open Arms). It is these for whom we create CA projects like Phu Le 3 where, in the initial phases, he can find protection from VC if not the legal governmental predators, (but at least now he only has one to pay off to), medical and dietary aid, schools, and simply a chance. We punish others, sometimes, perhaps frequently, innocent others, by destroying their village, (which is almost never done, and wouldn't have been in No Name 1 except this Company has lost over 70 men dead and wounded in it or just outside of it), burning individual houses from which we get fire, or just make life so intolerable for them that they have to move. Now they can either go into our protected hamlet or they can go somewhere else, in which case they are probably VC or VC-influenced. Will it work? Wait and See.

As to the fair play bit, Dad, I am not sure what part of American history you're deriving it from. Sherman's march . . . makes a great deal of what we do here like an outdoor barbecue. The constant and consistent invasions of South American sovereign states had little to do with "traditions of decency," and the country which planned and perpetrated the fire bombing of Dusseldorf and Tokyo and the bombing of Nagasaki certainly can't claim any monopoly or tradition of "regard for mankind." We look out for our own interests, sometimes badly and occasionally well. As far as it being dreadful to have to participate here, it *is* dreadful being here; but as far as the participation, I personally have lost five to ten men in No Name, and was in fact, shot, myself, not 400 meters from it. This strategy may not be perfect, but it makes more sense than anything else I have heard lately, including atom bombing the place, trying to fight an orthodox war in a country which for the most part, is constructed to make that alternative a giant blood bath as Operation Prairie is proving, or kill all of them. . . . By the way, I don't know what the papers said, but the casualties to the 2/7 up at the DMZ were extremely heavy, with platoons of 10–15 men coming back, and all those who survived, to a man, having been hit by mortar fragments, all of which were infected. There was a real ass-kicking done up there, and although on paper we won, it was a hollow victory at best.

But what you're really worried about is what happens to the people if we aren't around to protect them. Although the cases are not exactly parallel, enough similarities exist to make Korea and Viet Nam comparable. Who in the world would have thought, 15 years ago, that the Koreans would have the second best army in the Far East, or that agricultural South Korea would become an industrial power as well? Villages like Phu Le 3 have Civil Defense troops, and sure, they are worthless at first, but they have improved before our eyes to the point where they stay and fight when attacked in their hamlet. Will they do so when we leave? Yes, if we give them long enough to develop and gain confidence. That may take years, but, Baby, we are still in Korea, and De Gaulle aside, we are still in Europe doing the same damn thing, more or less, and if you don't think Viet Nam is as important in the mid sixties as Korea was in the mid fifties or Europe in the late forties, then let me know, and I will write another manuscript on *that* subject. To be quite brutal about it, Pop, I would rather burn houses in No Name 1 than in Galveston. By destroying and killing with the one hand, and cultivating, encouraging, making more healthy and educated with the other, I am building a dike, and God help this country if we ever run out of people who are willing to sacrifice their fingers for such a cause!

I have not been able to secure the religious artifacts as yet. . . . I have received all packages sent parcel post and air mail at the same time. I have received no magazines lately, but did get a Christmas box from the Stirlings which was full of good things and kind thoughts and was very much appreciated. In the next package could you include *one* can of saddle soap, *one* bottle of tabasco sauce, and about 100 notebook pages of the type and size I have included herein? By the way, your thinking on the packages is great: just when I am running out of things like soap, shampoo, etc., I get a box of them. . . .

I guess this is all for a while, and although I may not write for a couple of days, it will take you a week to decipher this and to retype it, anyway.

Love,
Sandy

P.S. When is the baby due?

9. Wrong, Rambo! A Vietnam Veteran Looks Back, 1985

August 13, 1969. I was a 19-year-old member of India Company, 3d Battalion, 5th Marines. As we moved through a strip of Vietnam known to the Americans as the Arizona Territory, we walked into an L-shaped ambush sprung by the North Vietnamese Army.

The enemy's opening fire instantly killed our battalion commander and his radio operator. Pinned to the ground in a rice paddy, the rest of us faced a choice: lie low and wait to be picked off one at a time, or charge the enemy guns, and, with luck, some of us would shoot our way to safety.

Our wounded captain gave the order to charge. Somehow we outfought the enemy and turned them back. But not without a heavy price: Half of India Company lay dead or wounded.

The next day, those of us who survived rested in the tranquil refuge of China Beach, just 23 miles from where the battle had taken place, and began to write letters to the families of those who didn't. Searching for reasons to explain their sons' sacrifice, I sat on China Beach and questioned why America had come to Vietnam. I didn't have the answers. I decided then that those who had died in Vietnam had died for nothing.

After my tour in Vietnam was up, I came back to the States and fought to end the war. There had to be another way to be for freedom in the world than through tragedies like Vietnam. By ending the war, we could bring the survivors home from a place where they never should have been.

On the 14th of August, 1985, however, 16 years to the day since my first time there, I returned to China Beach. I came not as a Marine in combat gear, but as a civilian, a guest of the Vietnamese government, a member of the first group of American veterans to travel the land we fought upon with veterans of the Vietnamese army.

China Beach hadn't changed much. I thought again of those who had died. I thought of those who had come home wounded in body or spirit, many of them to die later in the States. I thought of how long it took our country to honor their service, finally on a black marble wall in Washington, on Veterans Day just three years ago tomorrow.

More than anything else, though, I no longer felt, as I had 16 years before, that my friends had died for nothing. For in their dying, we, as a nation, became wiser about ourselves, about the world and our role in it.

The members of India Company, and millions of other Americans, fought to change Vietnam. But, in the end, Vietnam changed little. What changed was America. Most Americans no longer accept the illusion that we can defy history, as we tried to in Vietnam. We should mourn the loss of American lives in Vietnam. We needn't mourn the loss of the illusions that brought us there.

Today, as a veteran, I am bothered that some would dishonor the memory of those who died in Vietnam by reviving America's shattered illusions. "Are you gonna let us win this time?" Rambo demands to know as impressionable kids watch in air-conditioned awe. As the Rambo illusion would have it, our gallant soldiers would've won in Vietnam if only they'd been turned loose by the bureaucratic wimps on the home front.

Wrong, Rambo, dead wrong. The bureaucrats didn't put us into a winnable war and then tie our hands. What they did was actually far worse. They put us into a war that was as unwinnable as it was immoral. They put us into a war that even they could not explain, and, so, young men died for old men's pride.

The fact is, the Vietnam War was probably settled long before we ever got there. Ho Chi Minh's forces gained dominance with their victory at Dien Bien Phu, a good decade before the first U.S. Marine landed. And our ally, what we knew for 20 years as South Vietnam, wasn't a real nation but a make-believe government with little popular support. An illusion.

The illusion of American invincibility should have been left behind in Vietnam. But, then there's Rambo, whose appeal, unfortunately, is not limited to youthful moviegoers alone. The Rambo mystique even invades Washington: While policy makers fall over themselves to flex American muscle in the world, macho journalists, from the safety of their typewriters, lob verbal grenades at tiny Third World countries.

The truth is, these veterans of tough-talk know as much about war as the gullible teen-agers flocking to suburban mall theaters for a glimpse of Rambo.

On China Beach this August, I wondered if we could have handled Vietnam differently. We tried to beat history—to stop the inevitable from happening, and we were wrong. We should learn from Vietnam that history can't be beaten.

But neither can history be ignored. We cannot allow the need to avoid another Vietnam let us selfishly retreat from the realistic problems of the world. America *does* have a role to play in the world, as a moral force, a beacon of hope, a model of democratic idealism. We cannot turn our backs to injustice, whatever its form, be it terrorism, tyranny, poverty, hunger, or torture.

We will come closer to knowing how we should engage the world if we understand what happened to us in Vietnam. We entered that war in defiance of history, we stayed there in defiance of morality. If we, as a nation, are to live up to our moral responsibilities and stand up for freedom around the globe, we had better be able to answer the questions I asked myself as a Marine at China Beach.

𝖂 *E S S A Y S*

In the first selection, political scientist and Southeast Asia specialist George McT. Kahin of Cornell University describes the critical sequence of events by which the United States supplanted the French and established its own client regime in South Vietnam. In the second essay, U.S. diplomatic historian George Herring of the University of Kentucky describes the final collapse of South Vietnam and discusses the war's legacy in both Southeast Asia and the United States.

The Cold War and American Intervention
in Vietnam

GEORGE McT. KAHIN

The middle months of 1954 marked a major turning point in the American relationship with Vietnam. It was during this period that the United States made the most fundamental decision of its thirty-year involvement—the critical prerequisite to the subsequent incremental steps that culminated in President [Lyndon] Johnson's famous escalation a decade later. Although this first major increase in American intervention was essentially political, it had important and clearly understood military implications. It was sustainable initially only by the threat of U.S. armed intervention and ultimately by its actual execution. So for the second time Washington attempted to establish an anticommunist government in Vietnam; but now it acted alone, no longer in association with France, and its effort was focused primarily on just the southern half of the country.

In this new departure the Eisenhower administration intervened directly in Vietnam, displacing France as the major external power. Rather than working through the French to support the Bao Dai regime, which claimed authority over all Vietnam, the United States took on the mission of establishing a separate noncommunist state in just the southern regroupment zone prescribed by the Geneva Agreements. The administration believed that, without the encumbrance of the old French colonial presence to undermine its nationalist legitimacy, a revamped Bao Dai regime, with Ngo Dinh Diem as its prime minister, could, if given sufficient American support, stand a good chance of competing effectively with the DRV [Democratic Republic of Vietnam, the government in the North led by Ho Chi Minh]. In addition, though their hopes on this score were apparently not so strong, senior U.S. officials thought it possible that this American-backed government would ultimately be able to absorb the North into a single anticommunist state. However unrealistic this second proposition, it was still the presidentially endorsed U.S. objective at least as late as 1958. In April of that year the National Security Council [NSC] reiterated its aim to "work toward the weakening of the Communists in the North and South Viet Nam in order to bring about the eventual peaceful reunification of a free and independent Viet Nam under anti-Communist leadership."

To understand this major shift in the United States' approach to Vietnam, one must assess the changed pattern of factors influencing American policy in the immediate post-Geneva period. The original, European-oriented calculations that had propelled the United States into its limited intervention in the early postwar years increasingly yielded place to considerations rooted primarily in the new ascendancy of communist power in China. Europe did still continue to exert an important influence on American Vietnam policy right through the Geneva Conference, however, because of the pivotal importance of the projected European Defense Community [EDC] to Washington's Soviet containment strategy. But when the French Parliament defeated EDC soon after the close of the conference,

From *Intervention: How America Became Involved in Vietnam* by George McT. Kahin. Copyright © 1986 by George McT. Kahin. Reprinted by permission of the Estate of George McT. Kahin.

European objectives ceased to have a significant effect on American policy toward Vietnam.

Although the French rejection of EDC only temporarily delayed German rearmament, it entailed the loss of most of France's once-formidable leverage with the United States, which had derived from Washington's uncertainty regarding French domestic politics and the extent to which France could be counted on to cooperate with American economic and military objectives in Europe. The potential of communism in France had by now dramatically ebbed, and the balance of her internal politics no longer threatened her continued presence in an American-led military alignment aimed at containing Soviet power in Europe. Indeed, the large noncommunist majority in the Chamber of Deputies saw such an alignment as clearly in their country's self-interest. The shoe was now on the other foot, for, as France began to face mounting militant nationalist pressures in her North African colonies during the fall of 1954, she badly needed American backing to maintain her ascendancy there.

Other factors important to the previous American preoccupation with Vietnam were, however, still operative: the enduring myth that communism was global and monolithic; the conviction that China was expansionist; and American domestic political pressures centering on the "loss of China" syndrome, whereby all administrations feared being accused of losing additional territory to communist control. But it was, of course, against the Democrats—not [President Dwight D.] Eisenhower's Republicans—that the charge of China's "loss" had been leveled. Moreover, in contrast to the American involvement in China's civil war, the congressional and public perception was thus far of primarily French, not American, responsibility for developments in Vietnam, and France stood out clearly as a lightning rod to divert attacks from the administration's record there. At this stage, fear of domestic criticism, although a factor, was not fundamental to the administration's new decision for a major American involvement. It would only become an important consideration after the Eisenhower administration had publicly committed itself to sustaining a separate state free of communist control in the southern half of Vietnam.

What, then, explains the decision to intervene directly in Vietnam? To the three above-mentioned continuing determinants two new major factors had now been added. First was [Secretary of State] John Foster Dulles's retrospective analysis—subscribed to by Eisenhower—of the American failure in China, and the lessons he derived from this for policy toward Southeast Asia; and second was the inspiration he and Eisenhower drew from a set of analogies between conditions and the potential for American actions in Vietnam, and recent American and British experiences in other parts of the world.

Dulles approached the conflicts between Southeast Asian peoples and the colonial powers with certain strongly held views. Like his predecessor, Dean Acheson [Secretary of State for President Harry S Truman], he had little faith in the self-governing capacity of Southeast Asians who gained their independence from colonial powers through revolution. He was convinced that, without the involvement and guidance of the democratic West, nationalist movements in these countries would probably be drawn into communist-controlled political channels—and this, he believed, was likely even after they had attained full independence. With respect to the peoples of Indochina and Indonesia in particular, he felt that until they attained a greater degree of political maturity, the West had an ongoing obligation to help ensure that communists did not take over; and if the Western colonial powers withdrew, the United States had a responsibility to assume this burden.

From Chiang Kai-shek's defeat in China, Dulles drew a lesson that he regarded as applicable to Southeast Asian countries threatened by communist power. One of the main reasons he saw for the failure of American China policy was that "The territorial integrity of China became a shibboleth. We finally got a territorially integrated China—for whose benefit? The Communists." In other words, while certainly aware of the faults of the Kuomintang [Chiang Kai-shek's political party, which ruled the Republic of China] regime, Dulles saw its defeat by the Chinese communists as largely attributable to American acquiescence in Chiang's short-sighted attempt to win control over the whole of China concurrently. A more effective strategy would have been to accept temporarily a loss of the country's territorial integrity, yielding part of it to communist power, while concentrating Kuomintang and American resources in order to husband as much of the mainland as possible free of Mao's control [Mao Tse-tung led the Chinese Communist party]. Chiang's residual mainland territory would have provided a base for mounting a rollback of communist control.

Some nine months before the beginning of the Geneva Conference on Indochina, this lesson was being applied to the situation in Indonesia. In late 1953 President Eisenhower counseled Hugh S. Cumming, his administration's first ambassador to Indonesia, that "as against a unified Indonesia which would fall to the Communists and a break up of that country into smaller segments he would prefer the latter." Dulles was more explicit, stating to the ambassador, "As between a territorially united Indonesia which is leaning and progressing towards communism and a break up of that country into racial and geographical units, I would prefer the latter as furnishing a fulcrum from which the United States could work later to help them eliminate communism in one place or another, and then in the end, if they so wish arrive back again at a united Indonesia."

If Eisenhower and Dulles considered this lesson from China to have such validity for Indonesia, it must have seemed even more applicable to the situation in Vietnam. In any case, their approach to Vietnam both during and after the Geneva Conference was consistent with, and undoubtedly to a significant extent shaped by, their perception of the causes of the "failure" in China.

But why did Eisenhower and Dulles believe that the United States had the capacity to implement in Vietnam what they considered to be the logical propositions derived from their retrospective analysis of the "failure" in China? That question cannot be answered without reference to the administration's evaluation of earlier American experiences in Greece, Iran, Guatemala, and especially the Philippines, together with what was regarded as an equally relevant British experience in Malaya. Its assessment of recent developments in these countries tended to reinforce an already self-assured and assertive postwar American "can-do" hubris, inclining policymakers to believe that the success of the United States in meeting challenges from communists or other socioeconomic radicals in these other places demonstrated abilities that could be applied in Vietnam. These combined to encourage the Eisenhower administration to intervene directly in Vietnam in the belief that it could work its own political will there to achieve a solution more consistent with American interests than that provided by the Geneva Conference.

A minority of American officials perceived that conditions in Vietnam were in fact fundamentally different from these other situations. But senior policymakers continued to draw inspiration and self-assurance from these precedents until well after the Eisenhower administration had embarked on a much deeper political intervention and commitment of American prestige in Vietnam. The simplistic analogies, sometimes referred to as "models," provided by these experiences continued to inform U.S. policy throughout [President John F.] Kennedy's administration and during the first part of Johnson's.

In Greece, where the United States had taken over from the British in late 1947, Washington believed that the critical factor in turning the tide against a peasant-backed, communist-led insurrection had been the injection of a large amount of American money, weaponry, and a military mission incorporating some five hundred advisers. American officials thought that this intervention, which had relied heavily on forced relocation of peasants, had been decisive in shoring up a faltering anti-communist government and forcing the insurgents to abandon their struggle and fade away into the hills within two years. The belief that this American experience in Greece was pertinent to Vietnam outlasted the Eisenhower administration. It was revived repeatedly under Kennedy and Johnson, especially by Walt Rostow, but also, though less insistently, by William P. Bundy, assistant secretary of state for Far Eastern affairs under Johnson, who had been in Greece during the American campaign there and as late as 1967 was still talking about the possibility of "a Greek solution" in Vietnam.

In Iran in 1953—just a year before the Eisenhower administration's major decision on Vietnam—a covert U.S. program mounted primarily by the CIA [Central Intelligence Agency] had brought down a radical, albeit noncommunist, government led by Mohammed Mossadegh that had been bent on ending foreign domination of the country's oil production, and then returned the recently ousted shah to power. The administration also took great satisfaction in the outcome of its largely covert intervention during the spring of 1954 in Guatemala. This had successfully ousted a noncommunist but radical president who had been willing to accept the support of communists as well as other political groups and been regarded as a threat to American economic interests.

Britain's experience in Malaya was at least as important as the Greek precedent. By 1953 the British were finally beginning to gain the upper hand in their effort to subdue an insurgency of some Malayan Chinese that had broken out five years previously. They attributed their success primarily to an extensive program of forced resettlement of rural Chinese, on whom their enemy was or might be reliant for food and intelligence. After 1959, when a communist-led insurgency finally re-emerged in South Vietnam, Washington saw the presumed Malayan analogy as especially relevant, and commenced to emphasize a policy of population resettlement in rural areas. The Kennedy administration was equally insistent on seeing a Malayan analogy and even more attracted to a resettlement strategy, a predilection that continued under Johnson and Nixon.

But the most influential of all these precedents was the recent example of the Philippines. During 1953–54 American officials helped secure the position of secretary of defense in the Philippines for their own candidate, Ramon Magsaysay, and they worked successfully to ensure his election as president. While he held these positions, they cooperated effectively with him to suppress a potent communist-led, agrarian-based insurgency, the Hukbalahap. The administration believed it could achieve similar results through its own chosen political instrument six hundred miles to the east in Vietnam. And if the CIA's Colonel Edward Lansdale had been so effective in helping to organize this effort in the Philippines, why should he not be equally successful in Vietnam? In January 1964 Assistant Secretary for East Asian Affairs Roger Hilsman was still looking for "a Vietnamese Magsaysay," and well into that year Secretary of Defense McNamara and Secretary of State Rusk, along with several other senior officials, were still seeing pertinent precedents in the Philippine and Malayan experiences.

The truth was that in character and context the Vietnam insurgency was only superficially akin, at best, to those in the Philippines, Malaya, and Greece. Nevertheless, the defeats of these earlier communist-led insurgencies, in combination with the heady American "successes" in Guatemala and Iran, encouraged the Eisenhower administration in its conviction that it had the capacity to work its will in determining Vietnam's political future.

Shaped primarily by Dulles, but with full support from the president, the administration's new Vietnam policy from the outset involved repudiating the two key political features of the Geneva Agreements: the stipulation that the line separating the two military zones "should not in any way be interpreted as constituting a political or territorial boundary," and the reunification elections, which had been an even more central condition for the armistice. The new policy also entailed two major positive steps by the United States. First, a mutual defense pact between it and several allies in effect treated the seventeenth parallel as a political boundary and provided in advance a measure of protection to the southern regroupment zone against attack by forces based in the North or against "internal subversion." Second, the United States displaced France's political and military presence in this area, taking over as paymaster to the Vietnamese civil servants and soldiers who had collaborated with the French and providing American training and advisers to the previously French-offered Vietnamese auxiliary component of the French expeditionary force. Still headed by Bao Dai as "chief of state," the "State of Vietnam" retained its name but was now restricted to the territory south of the seventeenth parallel. Into this area the United States pumped a massive amount of financial support, dwarfing what France had managed to provide.

These twin American efforts at an end run around some of Geneva's central provisions did not emerge fresh and full-blown after the conference. In the months preceding and during it, American policymakers had laid much of the groundwork for the two interdependent policies of building up a separate southern-Vietnamese state and protecting it from external assault and internal political opposition.

The still-unconsummated process of organizing United Action, initiated by the United States during the conference, now merged into an American-sponsored regional defense organization which was finally embodied in the Manila Pact of September 8, 1954 (ratified by the U.S. Congress February 19, 1955). In effect, the threat of an American-led anticommunist military intervention that had provided France with such useful leverage in Geneva was now spelled out with greater precision and institutionalized into a loosely structured alliance. Popularly known as SEATO (Southeast Asia Treaty Organization), it included the United States, Britain,

France, Australia, and New Zealand, together with the only three Asian states Washington could induce to join—the Philippines, Thailand, and Pakistan (the last-named expecting that membership would give it leverage against India). Initially, the French were sufficiently scrupulous about Geneva's provisions for the neutralization of Indochina to resist Dulles's attempt to include Cambodia, Laos, and especially South Vietnam (where the stipulation against adherence to any military alliance was explicit) as members of SEATO. But through the device of adding a protocol to the treaty projecting an "umbrella of protection" over these three areas, Dulles was able to circumvent the impediment. The protocol stipulated that the treaty's provisions extended to Cambodia, Laos, and "the free territory under the jurisdiction of the State of Vietnam," even though they were not signatories of the treaty. Prince Sihanouk [the Cambodian ruler] promptly repudiated Cambodia's inclusion, and with its neutralization in 1962 Laos was officially removed from jurisdiction of the protocol. Predictably, however, this protection was accepted by the French and Bao Dai for the temporary military regroupment zone south of the seventeenth parallel provided for at the Geneva Conference, now referred to as "the free territory of Vietnam." This was made explicit in a joint Eisenhower-Diem communiqué on May 11, 1957, after U.S. officials were satisfied the Ngo Dinh Diem's authority had been sufficiently established in this half of the country.

SEATO's members saw its main objective as being "to deter massive military aggression," the United States stipulating that its own involvement would be limited to cases where the aggressor was communist. Though all its signatories saw the alliance as a deterrent against a possible attack by China, the United States, France, and at least some other members regarded it as providing a similar deterrent against the possibility of an assault by Hanoi into the regroupment zone of French forces south of the seventeenth parallel.

SEATO's apparently broad international base disguised a decided lack of enthusiasm on the part of some of its participants, and it was never effective as a vehicle for collective action. The formula did, however, provide subsequent American administrations with the basis for inducing Americans to believe that U.S. military involvement in Indochina had international sanction. Much more important, it provided what the executive branch came to assert was congressional authority for direct military intervention there. Indeed, SEATO's significance ultimately lay more in what came to be construed as a congressional licensing of unilateral U.S. anticommunist military intervention in Southeast Asia than in its role as a collective defense organization. This was not what the Senate had had in mind when it approved the treaty, but what happened in practice.

Nevertheless, during the decade prior to the August 1964 Tonkin Gulf Resolution, SEATO provided the major rationale for a U.S. military role in Indochina. And when, within two years, the 1964 resolution had become discredited because of a crystallization of congressional suspicion as to the circumstances surrounding its passage, SEATO once more provided the president with what was asserted to be "the legal basis" for that involvement.

For two decades SEATO was referred to as an American "commitment." Having signed the treaty, the United States was indeed committed to it. But that treaty itself did not—as successive administrations encouraged the public to believe—commit the United States to defend South Vietnam. In fact, no such pledge was made either by the members of SEATO collectively or by the United States unilaterally. The *ex post facto* presidential interpretation of SEATO that alleged it did so departed widely from the mandate actually agreed to by the U.S. Senate and did violence to its intent. Yet this interpretation gradually became the accepted conventional public perception. It was strongly enough established in the Kennedy administration to be used as justification for escalating involvement beyond the largely political and economic dimension pursued by Eisenhower to the level of direct U.S. military intervention. . . . By granting protection in advance to Vietnam's southern regroupment zone against any attack by communist forces in the North, SEATO endowed the seventeenth parallel with the political character the Geneva Conference had prohibited and laid a foundation for recognizing a separate statehood for this southern area. This was, indeed, the administration's intention, and, five days before the conference concluded, Dulles informed an executive session of the Senate Foreign Relations Committee, "In fact the military regrouping [zones] will be apt to gradually become a live *de facto* political division. . . .

With SEATO providing the context for establishing an American-protected state in the southern half of Vietnam, the Eisenhower administration concurrently moved ahead with the second prong of its new Vietnam policy. This was the much more straightforward effort to endow that area with the attributes of governmental power, substituting a dependence on the United States for a previous dependence on France, and ensuring a leadership congenial to and shaped by the administration. This new American political venture retained the same name as its French-sponsored predecessor—the "State of Vietnam"—and Bao Dai stayed on as chief of state for some fifteen months after Geneva, thereby providing a transitional bridge. In this politically precarious period, while the French and Vietminh military forces regrouped and Paris incrementally transferred the fundamental attributes of government to the State of Vietnam, an American presence gradually replaced that of France. During this process Bao Dai, still comfortably ensconced on the French Riviera, progressively, albeit reluctantly, yielded more and more power to Ngo Dinh Diem, the Catholic leader and U.S. protégé whom he had appointed as prime minister in June 1954. . . .

By the beginning of May 1955, there was no longer any qualification in Washington's commitment to Diem. The remaining obstacle to the consolidation of a separate anticommunist southern state was the Geneva Conference's clear-cut stipulation that national reunification elections be held in mid-1956 and that consultations to prepare for them be conducted in mid-1955. Certainly some American officials acknowledged that the elections constituted a "binding commitment," and they, along with the French and British, were fearful that repudiating them would destroy the most important positive feature of the Geneva Conference—the military armistice. As the NSC reported, the French believed that "failure to hold elections would provoke a resumption of hostilities by the Vietminh in which France would be directly and involuntarily involved due to the probable presence at least of large numbers of the French Expeditionary Corps through 1955 and the first half of 1956." And American officials feared that, if a refusal to hold elections led to an end of the armistice and a renewal of Vietminh military activity, Britain and France might not support forceful U.S. action to counter it. At the SEATO meeting in February 1955, both allies made clear that this would indeed be the case.

A State Department intelligence report of September 15 expected that along with Canada and India of the International Control Commission, Britain and France would "continue to press for action in sufficient conformity with the agreements so that the Communists will have no excuse for breaking the cease-fire." It warned:

> If Diem is emboldened to reject or continue postponement of the elections stipulated in the Geneva Agreements, the DRV can be expected to seek its goal of unification (and control) through other means. Subject to calculation of what is feasible without stimulating U.S. military involvement the DRV would probably be prepared to use any methods necessary and would use pressures as strong as permitted by prevailing conditions in overall bloc relations with the non-communist world. . . . Should the DRV conclude that elections are unlikely in fact, it is probable that the communists will greatly increase their subversive as well as political pressures against the South. The DRV, however, would probably seek to avoid direct U.S. military intervention and would probably, therefore, choose a maximum guerrilla and subversive effort rather than direct aggression to obtain its objective of control over a unified Vietnam.

As late as the Kennedy administration it was acknowledged internally that, if Diem's government did not consider itself bound by the Geneva Agreements' provision for elections, then the legal basis of a demand for Vietminh compliance with features of the accords advantageous to the U.S. and Diem, "such as respect for [the] demarcation line and ceasefire," could be called into question. In short, one party to an agreement could not ignore a central provision it found unpalatable and expect the other party to adhere to provisions *it* disliked.

It was understood, then, that there were serious risks in supporting Diem's opposition to national elections, but the potential risks if they were held were regarded as even greater, for American intelligence sources were unanimous that Diem would lose any national election. Extensive studies by American intelligence bodies subsequent to the Geneva Conference all reinforced the conclusion that national elections could only lead to the DRV's victory. A report prepared by the State Department's Division of Research on February 1, 1955, considered that "Almost any type of election that could conceivably be held in Vietnam in 1956 would, on the basis of present trends, give the Communists a very significant if not decisive advantage." It went on to point out that the establishment of "conditions of electoral freedom . . . might operate to favor the Communists more than their opponents." Even in the South, it judged, "maximum conditions of freedom and the maximum degree of international supervision might well operate to Communist advantage and allow considerable Communist strength in the South to manifest itself at the polls." This analysis concluded that "It would appear on balance, therefore, seriously questionable whether the South should make a major issue of free political conditions in the period preceding and during whatever type of elections might finally be decided for Vietnam."

The Eisenhower administration could not afford to risk elections, and it encouraged Diem in his own, understandable disposition to avoid them. That the administration was aware of the implications of this decision is clear from a State Department assessment of September 1955: "Only if Diem were to feel sufficiently assured of direct U.S. support against Communist reprisals, and if the U.S. were prepared to accept the consequences of such a development including some degree of alienation of its Western allies and Asian neutrals, would Diem be likely to persist in a position directly opposed to eventual holding of elections."

The administration was prepared to give him those assurances and accept these consequences. The NSC Planning Board had concluded shortly before that, if denial of victory to Hanoi through prevention of all-Vietnam elections resulted in a renewal of hostilities, the United States had to be prepared to oppose the Vietminh "with U.S. armed forces if necessary, and feasible—consulting Congress in advance if the emergency permits—preferably in concert with the Manila Pact allies of the U.S., but if necessary alone." The United States then developed contingency plans for the immediate deployment of air and naval power in Vietnam in the event of "overt aggression by Vietminh forces." This would be followed by the "early movement of mobile U.S. [ground] forces for the purpose of conducting joint operations for tasks beyond the capabilities of South Vietnamese forces."

Sure of U.S. backing, Diem now assumed a bold and confident posture in opposition to the national elections that were so central to the Geneva Agreements (and indeed he now repudiated all of its political provisions that did not suit his interests). He and his American supporters insisted that, since the Bao Dai–Diem government had not itself agreed to the accords, it was not bound by them. Furthermore, they advanced the equally specious argument that the accords had stipulated "fundamental freedoms and democratic institutions" as prerequisites to any election (rather than as their anticipated consequences, as Article 14a actually posited) and that since these conditions did not yet exist it would be impossible for any meaningful voting to take place—even if by secret ballot under the aegis of the International Control Commission, as the agreements provided.

Initially American officials thought that, while avoiding the elections scheduled for mid-1956, Diem should at least make the gesture of participating in the preliminary consultations with representatives of the DRV on the plans for the conduct and supervision of the elections, which had been scheduled for mid-1955. On the basis of such consultation, it was argued, Diem's position that conditions for free elections and international supervision could not be met would appear more plausible. An unwillingness even to discuss the conditions for voting put him on weak ground for alleging in advance that it would not be fair. Moreover, the National Security Council concluded, "The over-all United States position in the world would be harmed by U.S. identification with a policy which appeared to be directed towards avoidance of elections," and "world opinion, and for that matter domestic U.S. opinion, would have difficulty in understanding why the U.S. should oppose in Vietnam the democratic procedures which the U.S. had advocated for Korea, Austria, and Germany." Senior American officials, however, were not disposed to pressure Diem to participate even in such preliminary consultations, and by the time the meetings were scheduled, official U.S. policy had swung behind him in his refusal to do so.

The Hanoi government had clearly not anticipated Diem's ability to repudiate this key provision of the Geneva Agreements. Along with most of the Geneva participants, it had assumed that until mid-1956 France would still be exercising sufficient authority in the South to ensure holding both the consultations and the subsequent elections. By mid-1955, however, most French troops had been sent to North Africa and the French economic and political presence had become overshadowed by that of the United States; during the three-month period before the 1956 elections were to be held, the French High Command for Vietnam was dissolved and the last French combat units were withdrawn. As was later acknowledged by Secretary of Defense Robert McNamara in a memorandum to President Johnson, "Only the U.S. presence after 1954 held the south together . . . and enabled Diem to refuse to go through with the 1954 provision calling for nationwide free elections in 1956."

During 1955 and 1956 Ho and Prime Minister Pham Van Dong sent repeated requests to Diem for consultations on holding elections. But these were ignored, as were Hanoi's numerous appeals to Britain and the Soviet Union, co-chairmen of the Geneva Conference, who, Hanoi understood, shared an ongoing responsibility for seeing that the agreements were implemented. Neither Britain nor the Soviet Union and China—both of which were bent upon pursuing policies of détente with the United States—showed much interest in seeing that the political provisions of Geneva were carried out. Moscow tried to pass the buck to Paris, saying France was primarily responsible for seeing them implemented. But with the withdrawal of her troops from Vietnam, France now had little political leverage there, and she was too dependent on American economic support and political backing of her interests elsewhere in the world, particularly North Africa, to challenge the repudiation of the elections.

The Soviet Union's demeanor led the State Department to conclude that it was "disinclined to risk broad policy objectives elsewhere in the world for the sake of rigid support for DRV demands." The State Department believed that Hanoi's dependence upon China and the Soviet Union for military supplies and economic support was sufficient to ensure that without their backing it would be reluctant to attack South Vietnam militarily, since this would involve "a substantial risk of U.S. (or broader Western) counteraction." Now less than two years after Geneva, Washington saw little prospect that Moscow or Peking would be inclined to provide such support. Consequently, the department concluded that Hanoi recognized its "inability to achieve a military victory against Western arms through an 'adventurist' attack unsupported by the Bloc."

Moscow's unwillingness to shoulder responsibility for implementing Geneva's political provisions was evident in talks held in April–May 1956 between representatives of Britain and the Soviet Union in their capacity as ongoing co-chairmen of the conference. Soviet Foreign Minister Andrei Gromyko "did not press for either the holding of elections or the reconvening of the Geneva Conference to discuss elections within a stated period" and agreed with his British counterpart on simply "maintaining the cease-fire, and essentially the [political] status-quo for the time being." The Soviet Union demonstrated the full extent of its disengagement in January 1957, when the Eisenhower administration was attempting to line up international support in its abortive effort to secure Saigon's representation in the United Nations. It was then that Khrushchev went so far as to propose that, along with North and South Korea, Diem's State of South Vietnam and the DRV be represented in the United Nations as "two separate states," a proposal with which the Peking government concurred, even though acknowledging that it was unacceptable to Hanoi. Since the data stipulated for the national reunification elections had by then passed, this proposition appears to have signaled implicit acceptance by Moscow and Peking of Vietnam's ongoing partition. Understandably, Ho Chi Minh, "in evident surprise, violently dissented."

By the beginning of 1957, then, China and the Soviet Union, as well as France and Britain, appeared content to let Vietnam remain divided, thereby increasing the Eisenhower administration's confidence that it could build a viable separate state in the southern half of the country without its additional transgressions against the Geneva Agreements being seriously challenged.

If the two communist powers, the world at large, or the American public harbored any doubts as to the Eisenhower administration's commitment to its mission of building a new Vietnamese state, these were undoubtedly dispelled in May 1957, when the administration invited the man it had chosen to head this state, Ngo Dinh Diem, on a two-week state visit to the United States. Not only was he accorded the signal honor of addressing a joint session of the American Congress, but Eisenhower had him flown in the presidential plane to Washington and personally met him at the airport—an honor bestowed on only one other foreign leader in the first four years of Eisenhower's presidency.

The decisive change in American policy that unfolded during the years immediately following the Geneva Conference was by no means inevitable; certainly it was not something the Eisenhower administration unwittingly backed into. It was a positive, calculated step into a direct and much deeper involvement than the earlier attempts to work through France. Moreover, this step was taken at a time when the United States had a clear option to avoid any direct commitment. Indeed, the Geneva Agreements offered the United States a broad avenue leading away from even the limited and indirect intervention it had pursued during the previous decade. The capitulation recognized at Geneva was, after all, generally viewed as French, not American, entailing responsibilities that were basically French. Instead of seizing on this clear option, the administration had moved assertively into a much more fundamental phase of intervention, and in doing so staked American honor and prestige on a policy that, once undertaken, was difficult to reverse.

The Meaning of Vietnam

GEORGE C. HERRING

The "peace" agreements of January 1973 merely established a framework for continuing the war without direct American participation. North Vietnam still sought unification of the country on its terms; South Vietnam struggled to survive as an independent nation, and some U.S. officials, including President Nixon, continued to support its aspirations. The cease-fire thus existed only on paper.

This last phase of the war was of remarkably short duration. Dependent on the United States from its birth, the Saigon government had great difficulty functioning on its own. Because of the Watergate scandals and American war-weariness, moreover, Nixon was not able to live up to his secret commitments to Thieu, and indeed in August 1974 he was forced to resign. Congress drastically cut back aid to South Vietnam, further eroding the Saigon government's faltering will to resist. When North Vietnam and the National Liberation Front (NLF) mounted a major offensive in the spring of 1975, South Vietnam collapsed with stunning rapidity, dramatically ending the thirty-year war and leaving the United States, on the eve of its third century, frustrated and bewildered. . . .

The fall of South Vietnam just fifty-five days after the onset of the North Vietnamese offensive was symptomatic of the malaise that had afflicted the nation since its birth. Originally created by the French, the Saigon regime could never overcome its origins as a puppet government. Political fragmentation, the lack of able and farsighted leaders, and a tired and corrupt elite which could not adjust to the revolution that swept Vietnam after 1945 afforded a perilously weak basis for nationhood. Given these harsh realities, the American effort to create a bastion of anticommunism south of the seventeenth parallel was probably doomed from the start. The United States could not effect the needed changes in South Vietnamese society without jeopardizing the order it sought, and there was no long-range hope of stability without revolutionary change. The Americans could provide money and weapons, but they could not furnish the ingredients necessary for political stability and military success. Despairing of the capacity of the South Vietnamese to save themselves, the United States had assumed the burden in 1965, only to toss it back in the laps of its clients when the American people tired of the war. The dependency of the early years persisted long after the United States had shifted to Vietnamization, however. To the very end and despite overwhelming evidence to the contrary, Thieu and his cohorts clung desperately to the belief that the United States would return and rescue them.

As comforting as it had been for Americans to find the causes of failure primarily in South Vietnam's weakness and Washington's errors, these alone do not explain the outcome of the war. The North Vietnamese and NLF were not superpeople, as they were often portrayed in antiwar propaganda. They made colossal blunders. They paid an enormous price for their success. Still, in waging this war they had distinct advantages. From the outset of the revolution, the Communists drew into the fold the best of the traditional Vietnamese ruling class and the most able and dedicated political activists, and they were thus blessed with superior leadership, from Ho Chi Minh at the top down to the village level. Skillful organizers, they tapped the well-springs of Vietnamese nationalism and the urge for social reform to effectively mobilize the people and resources of Vietnam "in a total and concentrated effort to seize power." Sold out by their allies at Geneva in 1954, they exploited the Sino-Soviet split in the Second Indochina War to secure maximum aid and retain maximum freedom of action. Drawing on Chinese models of revolutionary war, they improvised through trial and error a comprehensive, integrated strategy that blended military, diplomatic, and political methods to achieve the goal of liberating and unifying their country. They skillfully employed the concept of protracted war, perceiving that the Americans, like the French, could become impatient and that if they bled long enough might tire of the war. Above all, as William Duiker has written, they "mobilized the inchoate frustration and anger of the mass of the population and fashioned it into a fierce and relentless weapon of revolutionary war." . . .

With the North Vietnamese/NLF victory, the "dominoes" in Indochina quickly toppled. Cambodia, in fact, fell before South Vietnam, ending a peculiarly brutal war and initiating a period of enormous cruelty. Between 1970 and 1972, the United States had spent over $400 million in support of Lon Nol's government and army, and heavy bombing continued until Congress legislated its end in August 1973. In six months of 1973, the bombing exceeded 250,000 tons, more than was dropped on Japan in all of World War II. Lon Nol's government and army were ineffectual even by South Vietnamese standards, however, and with extensive support from North Vietnam and China, the Khmer Rouge pressed on toward Phnom Penh, using human-wave assaults in some areas. The government collapsed in mid-April, and the Khmer Rouge took over the capital on April 17. Thousands of lives were lost in the war, and over two million people were left as refugees. The country as a whole faced starvation for the first time in its history. Upon taking over, the Khmer Rouge imposed the harshest form of totalitarianism and began the forced relocation of much of the population.

The end in Laos was less convulsive. The Laotian "settlement" of 1962 had been a dead letter from the start. A flimsy coalition government nominally upheld a precarious neutrality, while outsiders waged war up and down the land. The North Vietnamese used Laotian territory for their infiltration route into South Vietnam and supported the insurgent Pathet Lao with supplies and as many as 20,000 "volunteers." While backing the "neutralist" government, the United States from 1962 to 1972 waged a "secret war" against North Vietnamese positions in Laos. When the bombing of North Vietnam was stopped at the end of 1968, Laos became the primary target. By 1973 the United States had dropped more than two million tons of bombs there, leaving many areas resembling a desert. At the same time, the CIA sponsored an army of Hmong tribesmen, led by General Vang Pao, which waged guerrilla warfare against the Ho Chi Minh Trail in Laos at a huge cost: more than 17,000 soldiers and 50,000 civilians had been killed by 1975. The U.S. withdrawal from South Vietnam left the government without any chance of survival. An agreement of February 1973 created a coalition government in which the Pathet Lao held the upper hand. With the fall of Cambodia and South Vietnam, the Pathet Lao took over, making no effort to hide its subservience to Vietnam. In one of the great human tragedies of the Indochina wars, America's loyal allies, the Hmong, were the victims of Pathet Lao genocide. Roughly 100,000, including the legendary Vang Pao, escaped. Another 100,000 were killed in a systematic campaign of extermination that employed bombing, artillery, and possibly chemical-biological weapons. Thousands more suffered in what the Pathet Lao euphemistically called "seminar camps."

The impact on world politics of America's failure in Vietnam was considerably less than U.S. policymakers had predicted. From Thailand to the Philippines, there was obvious nervousness, even demands for the removal of U.S. bases. Outside of Indochina, however, the dominoes did not fall. On the contrary, in the years after the end of the war, the non-Communist nations of Southeast Asia prospered and attained an unprecedented level of stability. The Soviet Union continued to build up its military arsenal in the 1970s, and spurred by American failure, it intervened in civil wars in Angola, Zaire, and Ethiopia. As with the United States, however, the Soviets' reach soon exceeded their grasp, luring them into their own quagmire in Afghanistan, a "bleeding wound" that reformist Soviet premier Mikhail Gorbachev bound up in the late 1980s only at great cost.

One of the most significant and ironic effects of the end of the Vietnam War was heightened tensions among the various Communist nations of East Asia. The brutal Pol Pot regime launched a grisly effort to rebuild Cambodia from the "Year

Zero," killing millions of its own people in the process. More important from the Vietnamese standpoint, Cambodia established close ties with China. In response to Khmer Rouge cross-border raids and to preserve a "friendly" government next door, Vietnam invaded Cambodia in 1978, drove out Pol Pot, established a puppet regime. China retaliated by invading Vietnam, provoking a short and inconclusive war. The United States, which had gone to war in Vietnam in 1965 to contain China, found itself in the ironic position in the mid-1980s of indirectly supporting China's efforts to contain Vietnam and sending "humanitarian" aid to an unlikely assortment of Cambodian bedfellows, including the notorious Pol Pot. . . .

In Vietnam itself, the principal legacy of the war has been continued human suffering. The ultimate losers, of course, were the South Vietnamese. The bloodbath predicted by some Americans did not occur, but many of those South Vietnamese who remained in Vietnam endured poverty, oppression, forced labor, and the horror of "reeducation" camps. More than 1.5 million so-called boat people fled the country after 1975. Some perished in flight; others languished in squalid refugee camps scattered throughout Southeast Asia. Around one million eventually resettled in the United States. Most of them had to give up all their personal possessions merely to escape, and many left family behind. The popular stereotype of the Vietnamese-Americans was one of assimilation and overachievement, the "model minority." In reality, many remained unassimilated and lived near or below the poverty line, depending on minimum-wage jobs or welfare. The new immigrants also endured alienation, encountered prejudice from Americans for whom they were a living reminder of defeat, and suffered from the popular image of the successful Asian, which implied that the unsuccessful had only themselves to blame.

Even for the ostensible winners, victory was a bittersweet prize. The Hanoi regime achieved its goal of hegemony in Indochina, but only temporarily and at a cost it could not afford. In time it became bogged down in its own "Vietnam" in Cambodia, for a decade waging a costly and generally ineffectual counterinsurgency against stubborn Cambodian guerrillas. The Vietnamese happily accepted in 1991 a United Nations–sponsored agreement that provided for their withdrawal from Cambodia and the holding of elections to form a coalition government.

Hanoi's long-standing goal of unifying Vietnam was achieved in name only. Historic differences between north and south were exacerbated during three decades of war, and even the most heavy-handed methods could not force the freewheeling and resilient south into a made-in-Hanoi mold. Just as it resisted American influence in the 1960s, southern Vietnam continued to resist outside influence, making the task of consolidation quite difficult. There were even signs that, in the classic tradition of the East, the ways of the conquered had rubbed off on the conqueror. The corruption and Western consumer culture that epitomized Saigon during the American war carried over to postwar Ho Chi Minh City, where the black market continued to flourish and bribery was necessary to accomplish anything. More significant, Saigon's mores afflicted the northern officials sent south to enforce revolutionary purity and even filtered north to Hanoi.

For all Vietnamese, the most pressing and enduring legacy of the war has been economic deprivation. Thirty years of conflict left the country in a shambles, and continued high military expenditures and the regime's ill-conceived postwar efforts to force industrialization and collectivize agriculture made things worse. The economic growth rate lagged at around 2 percent, and per capita income averaged around $100. Responding to necessity and emulating Gorbachev's perestroika, a more pragmatic regime dominated by southerners launched in the mid-1980s a program of *doi moi,* or renovation, hoping to stimulate growth by freeing up the economy, providing some capitalist incentives, and actively seeking foreign investment. Declaring 1990 the "Year of the Tourist," Hanoi even sought to promote economic development through tourism. Vietnamese leaders still claimed to be pursuing socialism, but they talked increasingly like capitalists, proclaiming the goal of a "prosperous country in which people are rich."

Doi moi brought modest gains. Agriculture flourished under the new system, and in a short time Vietnam became the world's third largest exporter of rice. The parallel or unofficial economy also prospered, especially in the cities, where there were signs of an incipient economic boom. Foreign investment jumped, making up for the termination of Soviet aid, and the growth rate increased to around 7 percent. There were significant increases in the production of consumer goods and foreign trade.

Horrendous problems remained. Despite the "tiny economic miracle" of the 1990s, Vietnam was still one of the world's poorest countries. The infrastructure was in horrible shape, and the economy suffered from ineffective management and lack of capital and technology. Intent on insulating itself from the changes sweeping Eastern Europe and the Soviet Union in the late 1980s, the regime did not join economic changes with political freedoms, thus raising major questions about the long-term effects of renovation. Per capita income was still estimated at no more than $200. The modest growth rate of the early 1990s was threatened by a population explosion, a rising gap between rich and poor, shortages of skilled labor, inadequate public services, the government's inability to collect taxes, and a corruption reportedly as pervasive as that in South Vietnam at the end of the war. Old-line socialists worried that economic growth might come at the expense of social justice. . . .

For America's allies, the war had consequences that exceeded the size of their contribution. In Australia, participation in Vietnam led to sharp internal divisions and conflict, and failure to recognize the contribution of those who served left a legacy of bitterness among veterans. In New Zealand, despite the small size of the commitment, the war aroused widespread opposition and eventually provoked a major foreign policy debate that raised searching questions about the nation's role in the world and especially its relations with the United States. For South Korea, participation in Vietnam produced major economic benefits, helping to stimulate its rise as a major economic power. Since the end of the war, the government has remained silent about its role. Only with the emergence of democracy in recent years has Vietnam become a subject for open discussion. Long alienated veterans who have borne their anger in silence now speak openly of the "blood money" earned at the price of those lives who "fuelled the modernization of the country."

Although the United States emerged physically unscathed, the Vietnam War was among the most debilitating in its history. The price tag has been estimated at $167 billion, a raw statistic that does not begin to measure the full economic cost. The war triggered an inflation that helped to undermine America's position in the world economy. It also had a high political cost, along with Watergate, increasing popular suspicion of government, leaders, and institutions. It discredited and crippled the military, at least for a time, and temporarily estranged the United States from much of the rest of the world.

Much like the effect of World War I on the Europeans, Vietnam's greatest impact was in the realm of the spirit. As no other event in the nation's history, it challenged American's traditional beliefs about themselves, the notion that in their relations with other people they have generally acted with benevolence, the idea that nothing is beyond reach. It was a fundamental part of a much larger crisis of the spirit that began in the 1960s, raising searching questions about America's history and values, marking a sort of end of American innocence.

The fall of Saigon had a profound impact. Some Americans expressed hope that the nation could finally put aside a painful episode from its past and get on with the business of the future. Among a people accustomed to celebrating peace with ticker-tape parades, however, the end of the war left a deep residue of frustration, anger, and disillusionment. Americans generally agreed that the war had been a "dark moment" in their nation's history. Some comforted themselves with the notion that the United States should never have become involved in Vietnam in the first place, but for others, particularly those who had lost loved ones, this was not enough. "Now it's all gone down the drain and it hurts. What did he die for?" asked a Pennsylvanian whose son had been killed in Vietnam. Many Americans expressed anger that the civilians did not permit the military to win the war. Others regarded the failure to win as a betrayal of American ideals and a sign of national weakness that boded poorly for the future. "It was the saddest day of my life when it sank in that we had lost the war," a Virginian lamented. The fall of Vietnam came at the very time the nation was preparing to celebrate the bicentennial of its birth, and the irony was painfully obvious. "The high hopes and wishful idealism with which the American nation had been born had not been destroyed," *Newsweek* observed, "but they had been chastened by the failure of America to work its will in Indochina."

In the immediate aftermath of the war, the nation experienced a self-conscious, collective amnesia. The angry debate over who lost Vietnam, so feared by Kennedy, Johnson, and Nixon, consisted of nothing more than a few sharp exchanges between the White House and Capitol Hill over responsibility for the April 1975 debacle. Perhaps because both parties were so deeply implicated in the war, Vietnam did not become a partisan political issue; because the memories were so painful, no one cared to dredge them up. On the contrary, many public figures called for restraint. Vietnam was all but ignored by the media. It was scarcely mentioned in the presidential campaign of 1976. "Today it is almost as though the war had never happened," the columnist Joseph C. Harsch noted in late 1975. "Americans have somehow blocked it out of their consciousness. They don't talk about it. They don't talk about its consequences."

Those 2.7 million men and women who served in Vietnam were the primary victims of the nation's desire to forget. Younger on the average by seven years than their World War II counterparts, having endured a war far more complex and confusing, Vietnam veterans by the miracles of the jet age were whisked home virtually overnight to a nation hostile to the war and indifferent to their plight. Some were made to feel the guilt for the nation's moral transgressions; others, responsibility for its failure. Most simply met silence. Forced to turn inward, many veterans grew profoundly distrustful of the government that had sent them to war and deeply resentful of the nation's seeming ingratitude for their sacrifices. The great majority adjusted, although often with difficulty, but many veterans experienced problems with drugs and alcohol, joblessness, and broken homes. Many also suffered from post-traumatic stress disorder, the modern term for what had earlier been called shell shock or battle fatigue. The popular image of the Vietnam veteran in the immediate postwar years was that of a drug-crazed, gun-toting, and violence-prone individual unable to adjust to civilized society. When America in 1981 gave a lavish welcome home to a group of hostages returned from a long and much-publicized captivity in Iran, Vietnam veterans poured out their bottled-up rage. They themselves constructed a memorial in Washington to honor the memory of the more than 58,000 comrades who did not return.

Within a short time after the end of the war, Vietnam's place in the national consciousness changed dramatically. The amnesia of the immediate postwar years proved no more than a passing phenomenon, and by the mid-1980s the war was being discussed to a degree and in ways that would have once seemed impossible. Vietnam produced a large and in some cases distinguished literature, much of it the work of veterans. Hollywood had all but ignored the war while it was going on, but in its aftermath filmmakers took up the subject with a vengeance, producing works ranging from the haunting *Deer Hunter,* to the surreal and spectacular *Apocalypse Now,* to Oliver Stone's antiwar epics, to a series of trashy films in which American superheroes returned to Vietnam to take care of unfinished business. No television leading man was worth his salt unless he had served in Vietnam. The Vietnam veteran, sometimes branded a war criminal in the 1960s, became a popular culture hero in the 1980s, the sturdy and self-sufficient warrior who had prevailed despite being let down by his government and nation. Millions of Americans each year went to the stark but moving V-shaped memorial on Washington's Mall, making it the most visited site in the nation's capital. Denounced by critics as a "black wall of shame" when it was under construction, the memorial evoked a profound emotional experience for many visitors and became a means of healing, a place for recognition of the costs of war. In 1993, a memorial was added to honor the 265,000 women who served in the military during the Vietnam War. In courthouses and communities across the nation, memorials were constructed to honor those who had served. . . .

Nowhere was the impact of Vietnam greater than on the nation's foreign policy. The war shattered the consensus that had existed since the late 1940s, leaving Americans confused and deeply divided on the goals to be pursued and the methods used. Even before the war had ended, the traumatic experience of Vietnam, combined with the apparent improvement of relations with the Soviet Union and China and a growing preoccupation with domestic problems, produced a drastic reordering of national priorities. From the late 1940s to the 1960s, foreign policy had consistently headed the ranking of national concerns, but by the mid-1970s it placed well down on the list. The public was "almost oblivious to foreign problems and foreign issues," opinion analyst Burns Roper remarked in late 1975.

The Vietnam experience also provoked strong opposition to military intervention abroad, even in defense of America's oldest and staunchest allies. Polls taken shortly before the fall of Saigon indicated that only 36 percent of the American people felt the United States should make and keep commitments to other nations, and only 34 percent expressed a willingness to send troops should the Russians attempt to take over West Berlin. A majority of Americans endorsed military intervention only in defense of Canada. "Vietnam has left a rancid aftertaste that clings to almost every mention of direct military intervention," the columnist David Broder observed.

The indifference and tendency toward withdrawal so manifest immediately after the war also declined sharply in the next decade. Bitter memories of Vietnam combined with the frustration of the Iranian hostage crisis to produce a growing assertiveness, a highly nationalistic impulse to defend perceived interests, even a yearning to restore the United States to its old position in the world. The breakdown of détente, the steady growth of Soviet military power, and the use of that power in the Horn of Africa and Afghanistan produced a profound nervousness about American security. The defense budget soared to mammoth proportions in the early 1980s, and support for military intervention in defense to traditional allies increased. Under the leadership of President Ronald Reagan, the nation embarked on a new global offensive against the Soviet Union and its clients.

The new nationalism was still tempered by lingering memories of Vietnam. Many Americans remained deeply skeptical of 1960s-style globalism and dubious of such internationalist mechanisms as foreign aid or even the United Nations. Fifteen years after the end of the war, a whopping majority still believed that intervention in Vietnam had been a mistake, producing strong opposition to military intervention abroad. Thus in the aftermath of Vietnam, the public mood consisted of a strange amalgam of nostalgia and realism, assertiveness and caution.

In the very different climate of the 1980s, the debate over Vietnam that had not taken place at the war's end assumed a central place in the larger and at times quite vocal debate over U.S. foreign policy. The basic issue remained the morality and wisdom of intervention in Vietnam. Concerned that in a new and even more dangerous Cold War a resurgent militance might lead to further disastrous embroilment, liberals urgently warned of the perils of another Vietnam. Fearful, on the other hand, that the so-called Vietnam syndrome had sapped America's will to defend legitimate interests and stand firmly against the evil of communism, some conservatives, including most notably President Reagan, spoke out anew on what they had always believed was a fundamental reality: that, as Reagan repeatedly proclaimed, Vietnam was "in truth a noble war," a selfless attempt on the part of the United States to save a free nation from outside aggression. Other conservatives conceded that the United States might have erred in getting involved in Vietnam in the first place, but they went on to insist that an important interest had been established that had to be defended for the sake of U.S. credibility throughout the world.

The second great issue on which Americans also sharply disagreed concerned the reasons for U.S. failure in Vietnam. Unwilling to concede that success had been beyond reach, many of the leading participants in the war concluded that America's failure had been essentially instrumental, a result of the improper use of available tools. General Westmoreland, Admiral Sharp, and others blamed the "ill-considered" policy of "graduated response" imposed on the military by civilian leaders, arguing that had the United States employed its military power quickly, decisively, and without limit, the war could have been won. Some conservatives indeed concluded that timid civilian leaders had prevented the military from winning the war, a view that worked its way into the popular culture. "Sir, do we get to win *this* time?" the movie hero Rambo asked upon accepting the assignment to return to Vietnam and fight the second round single-handedly.

Others viewed the fundamental mistake as the choice of tools rather than the way they were used, and they blamed an unimaginative military as much as civilians. Instead of trying to fight World War II and Korea over in Vietnam, they argued, the military should have adapted to the unconventional war in which it found itself and shaped an appropriate counterinsurgency strategy. Still other commentators, including some military theorists, agreed that military leaders were as responsible for the strategic failure as civilians, arguing that instead of mounting costly and counterproductive search-and-destroy operations against guerrillas in South Vietnam, the United States should have used its own forces against North Vietnamese regulars along the seventeenth parallel to isolate the north from the south.

The lessons drawn were as divergent as the arguments advanced. Those who felt that the United States lost because it did not act decisively concluded that if the nation became involved in war again, it must employ its military power quickly and without limit to win before public support began to erode. Those who felt that the basic problem was the formulation rather than the execution of strategy insisted that military and civilian leaders must examine more carefully the nature of the war they were in and formulate more precisely the ways in which American power could best be used to attain clearly defined objectives.

Such lessons depended on the belief systems of those who pronounced them, of course, and those who had opposed the war reached quite different conclusions. To some former doves, the fundamental lesson was never to get involved in a land war in Asia; to others, it was to avoid intervention in international trouble spots unless the nation's vital interests were clearly at stake. Some commentators warned that policymakers must be wary of the sort of simplistic reasoning that produced the domino theory and the Munich analogy. Others pointed to the weakness of South Vietnam and admonished that even a superpower could not save allies who were unable or unwilling to save themselves. For still others, the key lessons were that American power had distinct limits and that to be effective, American foreign policy had to be true to the nation's historic ideals.

Throughout the 1980s, the ghost of Vietnam hovered over an increasingly divisive debate on the proper U.S. response to revolutions in Central America. Shortly after taking office in 1981, Reagan committed U.S. prestige to defending the government of El Salvador against a leftist-led insurgency, in part in the expectation that success there might exorcise the Vietnam syndrome. When the quick victory did not materialize, the administration expanded U.S. military aid to El Salvador, created a huge military base in Honduras, and launched a not-so-covert war to overthrow the Sandinista government of Nicaragua. The administration insisted that the United States must support non-Communist forces to avert in Central America the bloodshed and misery that followed the end of the war in Vietnam. At the same time, the military and the Defense Department made it clear that they would not go to war under the conditions that had prevailed in Vietnam. On the other side, dovish critics ominously and repeatedly warned that U.S. intervention in Central America would lead straight into a quagmire like Vietnam.

The issues were squarely joined in the Persian Gulf War of 1991, which seemed, at times, to be as much about Vietnam as about Saddam Hussein's conquest of

Kuwait. Those who opposed going to war to liberate Kuwait warned that "Iraq was Arabic for Vietnam" and predicted a Vietnam-like quagmire in the desert. President George Bush, however, expressed from the outset his determination that the war in the Persian Gulf "would not be another Vietnam," and he and his military advisers, many of whom had fought in Vietnam, conducted the Gulf War largely on the basis of its perceived lessons. The President made it clear that American troops would not be forced to fight with "one hand tied behind their back," as had allegedly been the case in Vietnam, and the military employed maximum force as rapidly as possible to ensure a speedy victory. Media coverage was rigidly censored to prevent, as many claimed had happened in Vietnam, its stimulating antiwar sentiment. When the United States and its allies swiftly and decisively defeated Iraq, Bush in a euphoric victory statement exulted: "By God, we've kicked the Vietnam syndrome once and for all!"

The President's eulogy turned out to be premature. To be sure, success in the Gulf War helped restore the nation's confidence in its military institutions and weakened inhibitions against military intervention abroad. It did not, however, expunge deeply encrusted and still painful memories of an earlier and very different war. The President's own actions made this quite clear. In refusing to drive on to Baghdad and seek total victory over Iraq, Bush himself heeded fears of the political entanglements and military quagmire that might result from involvement in an alien and hostile area.

In the aftermath of the Gulf War, the ghosts of Vietnam still lingered. Emotional debates in 1993 and 1994 over possible military intervention in the brutal ethnic conflict in the former Yugoslavia called forth old and still bitter memories. A journalist surveying opinion in the American heartland in May 1993 found "an abiding fear that the Balkans are another Vietnam, a deep-seated angst that tends to outweigh concern that another holocaust is in the making." A number of senators, including Vietnam veterans like John McCain (a Republican from Arizona) and Hank Brown (a Republican from Colorado), expressed similar concerns, and President Bill Clinton's top advisers feared that intervention in Bosnia might be political death for him as Vietnam had been for Lyndon Johnson. In part because of perceived lessons of Vietnam, the United States kept a discreet distance from the Bosnian conflict.

Americans expressed little opposition when President Bush sent U.S. troops on a mission of mercy to war-torn Somalia in late 1992, but when those troops in the fall of 1993 became caught in the crossfire of Somalian politics and eighteen Americans were killed, the specter of Vietnam again rose like a storm cloud over the nation. Warnings about the dangers of incrementalism resonated of Vietnam. Calling Somalia a "true child of Vietnam," liberal *New York Times* columnist Anna Quindlen warned that once again, as in Vietnam, the United States had underestimated local nationalism and that once again, American soldiers were caught in an alien political culture expecting appreciation for their good works and getting shot at instead. Conservative Cal Thomas agreed with Quindlen's conclusion, if not her premises, arguing that Vietnam's lessons "included the realization that the United States cannot be the policeman of the world." The fear that Somalia might become another Vietnam forced an American pullout from that troubled nation, making it abundantly clear that the ghosts George Bush claimed to have buried still haunted the nation.

The ongoing debate over U.S. involvement in Vietnam raises as many questions as it answers. Many of the so-called lessons are based on historical givens that can never be proved. Whether the more decisive use of military power could have brought a satisfactory conclusion to the war without causing even more disastrous consequences remains at best unprovable. Whether the adoption of a more vigorous and imaginative counterinsurgency program at an earlier stage could have wrested control of the countryside from the NLF can never be known, and the ability of the United States to implement such a program in an alien political culture is at best highly questionable. That the United States exaggerated the importance of Vietnam, as liberals have suggested, seems clear. But their argument begs the question of how one determines the significance of a given area and the even more difficult question of assessing the ultimate costs of intervention at an early stage.

Each historical situation is unique, moreover, and to extract lessons from one and apply them indiscriminately to another, very different event is at best misleading. The Central American crisis of the 1980s resolved itself in a way that confounded the dire predictions, drawn from Vietnam, offered by each side in the U.S. political debate. America's military success in the Persian Gulf War reflected more the unique conditions of that conflict than the successful application of lessons drawn from Vietnam. The one valid lesson that might be drawn, therefore, is to view all historical lessons with a healthy dose of skepticism.

In light of their perceived victory in the Cold War, Americans may increasingly be tempted to view the Vietnam War as an anomaly. The collapse of the once-feared Soviet Union and its empire and the demise of communism left the government of Vietnam as an apparent anachronism, one of a handful of regimes clinging to a discredited doctrine. In this context, Americans may come to regard the Vietnam War as little more than a tactical setback in what turned out to be a strategic victory, a lost battle in a war eventually won.

In the new post–Cold War world order, Vietnam may even come to seem irrelevant. The crises of the new era bear little resemblance to those of the Cold War. The conflicts that provoke debates over possible intervention are primarily ethnic and tribal. For the United States, no vital interests appear to be at stake, and there is little or no profit to be gained from involvement. The main arguments advanced for intervention are to stop the human suffering, feed the hungry, or bring order out of chaos.

⋈ *F U R T H E R   R E A D I N G*

Anderson, David L. *Facing My Lai: Moving Beyond the Massacre* (1998).
———. *Trapped by Success: The Eisenhower Administration and Vietnam, 1953–1961* (1991).
———, ed. *Shadow on the White House: Presidents and the Vietnam War, 1945–1975* (1993).
Appy, Christian G. *Working-Class War: American Combat Soldiers and Vietnam* (1993).
Baritz, Loren. *Backfire: A History of How American Culture Led Us into Vietnam and Made Us Fight the Way We Did* (1985).
Beattie, Keith. *The Scar That Binds: American Culture and the Vietnam War* (1998).
Berman, Larry. *Lyndon Johnson's War: The Road to Stalemate in Vietnam* (1989).
———. *Planning a Tragedy* (1982).
Billings-Yun, Melanie. *Decision Against War: Eisenhower and Dien Bien Phu, 1954* (1988).

Braestrup, Peter. *Big Story: How the American Press and Television Reported and Interpreted the Crisis of Tet, 1968, in Vietnam and Washington* (1983).

————, ed. *Vietnam as History* (1984).

Brands, H. W. *The Wages of Globalism: Lyndon Johnson and the Limits of American Power* (1995).

Bundy, William. *A Tangled Web: The Making of Foreign Policy in the Nixon Presidency* (1998).

Buzzanco, Robert. *Masters of War: Military Dissent and Politics in the Vietnam Era* (1996).

Caputo, Philip. *A Rumor of War* (1977).

Cincinnatus. *Self-Destruction: The Deterioration and Decay of the U.S. Army During the Vietnam Era* (1981).

Clodfelter, Mark. *The Limits of Air Power: The American Bombing of North Vietnam* (1989).

Cohen, Warren I., And Nancy Bernkopf Tucker, eds. *Lyndon Johnson Confronts the World: American Foreign Policy, 1963–1968* (1994).

Dunn, Peter M. *The First Vietnam War* (1985).

Ehrhart, W. D. *Ordinary Lives: Platoon 1005 and the Vietnam War* (1999).

Emerson, Gloria. *Winners and Losers: Battles, Retreats, Gains, Losses, and Ruins from the Vietnam War* (1978).

Fall, Bernard B. *Street Without Joy* (1961).

FitzGerald, Frances. *Fire in the Lake: The Vietnamese and the Americans in Vietnam* (1972).

Gardner, Lloyd C. *Approaching Vietnam: From World War II Through Dienbienphu* (1988).

————. *Pay Any Price: Lyndon Johnson and the Wars for Vietnam* (1995).

Gelb, Leslie H., with Richard K. Betts. *The Irony of Vietnam: The System Worked* (1979).

Halberstam, David. *The Best and the Brightest* (1972).

Hallin, David C. *The "Uncensored War"* (1986).

Heineman, Kenneth. *Campus Wars: The Peace Movement at American State Universities in the Vietnam Era* (1993).

Hendin, Herbert, and Ann P. Hass. *Wounds of War: The Psychological Aftermath of Combat in Vietnam* (1985).

Hendrickson, Paul. *The Living and the Dead: Robert McNamara and Five Lives of a Lost War* (1996).

Herr, Michael. *Dispatches* (1977).

Herring, George C. *America's Longest War: The United States and Vietnam, 1950–1975*, 3rd ed. (1995).

————. *LBJ and Vietnam: A Different Kind of War* (1994).

Hess, Gary. *The United States Emergence as a Southeast Asian Power* (1987).

Hoopes, Townsend. *The Limits of Intervention* (1969, 1973).

Hunt, Michael H. *Lyndon Johnson's War: America's Cold War Crusade in Vietnam* (1996).

Isaacs, Arnold R. *Without Honor: Defeat in Vietnam and Cambodia* (1983).

Kaplan, Lawrence, Denise Artaud, and Mark R. Rubin, eds. *Dienbienphu and the Crisis in Franco-American Relations, 1954–1955* (1990).

Karnow, Stanley. *Vietnam: A History* (1983).

Kimball, Jeffrey P. *Nixon's Vietnam War* (1988).

————, ed. *To Reason Why: The Debate About the Causes of U.S. Involvement in the Vietnam War* (1990).

Kolko, Gabriel. *Anatomy of a War* (1985).

Krepinevich, Andrew F. Jr. *The Army and Vietnam* (1986).

Lake, Andrew, ed. *The Vietnam Legacy* (1976).

Levy, David W. *The Debate over Vietnam* (1991).

Lewy, Guenter. *America in Vietnam* (1978).

Moss, George Donelson. *Vietnam: An American Ordeal* (1989).

Newman, John M. *JFK and Vietnam: Deception, Intrigue, and the Struggle for Power* (1992).

Oberdorfer, Don. *Tet!* (1971).

Olson, James S., and Randy Roberts. *Where the Domino Fell: America and Vietnam, 1945–1990* (1991).

Palmer, Bruce Jr. *The 25 Year War* (1984).
Pike, Douglas. *PAVN: People's Army of Vietnam* (1986).
———. *Vietnam and the Soviet Union* (1987).
Podhoretz, Norman. *Why We Were in Vietnam* (1982).
Rust, William J. *Kennedy in Vietnam* (1985).
Schandler, Herbert Y. *Lyndon Johnson and Vietnam: The Unmaking of a President* (1977).
Schulzinger, Robert. *A Time for War: The United States and Vietnam, 1941–1975* (1997).
Shawcross, William. *Sideshow: Kissinger, Nixon, and the Destruction of Cambodia* (1979).
Sheehan, Neil. *A Bright Shining Lie: John Paul Vann and America in Vietnam* (1988).
Short, Anthony. *The Origins of the Vietnam War* (1989).
Small, Melvin. *Covering Dissent: The Media and the Anti–Vietnam War Movement* (1994).
Smith, R. B. *An International History of the Vietnam War,* 2 vols. (1983, 1985).
Snepp, Frank. *Decent Interval: An Insider's Account of Indecent Saigon's End* (1977).
Spector, Ronald. *The United States Army in Vietnam, Advice and Support: The Early Years* (1983).
Stanton, Shelby L. *The Rise and Fall of an American Army* (1985).
Summers, Harry F. Jr. *On Strategy* (1982).
Thompson, James C. *Rolling Thunder* (1980).
Turley, William S. *The Second Indochina War: A Short Political and Military History, 1954–1975* (1986).
VanDeMark, Brian. *Into the Quagmire: Lyndon Johnson and the Escalation of the Vietnam War* (1991).
Van Tieng Dung. *Our Great Spring Victory* (1980).
Vo Nguyen Giap and Van Tieng Dung. *How We Won the War* (1980).
Young, Marilyn B. *The Vietnam Wars: 1945–1990* (1991).
Yuen Foong Khong. *Analogies at War—Korea, Munich, Dien Bien Phu—The Vietnam Decisions of 1965* (1992).

CHAPTER
9

The New Left and
the Politics of the 1960s

✕✕✕

As the 1950s drew to a close and the chill of the McCarthy years faded and even Eisenhower's towering popularity waned, a new critical spirit quickened through-out much of America. It sprang from diverse sources: from the struggle against segregation that would soon become the modern civil rights movement; from a growing awareness that despite wide prosperity, millions of Americans remained trapped in poverty; from escalating fears of nuclear war and increasing opposition to the Cold War; from a dawning realization of the social and environmental costs of the postwar system; and from the rising self-consciousness of the new postwar "baby boom" generation. It was this spirit of disquietude to which John F. Kennedy appealed in his promise to "get America moving again" along a "new frontier." And it was this same spirit that informed the early history of Students for a Democratic Society (SDS) and the New Left.

SDS represented a self-consciously new radicalism that, shunning the Marxist clichés of the thirties, called for "participatory democracy" and a reconstruction of American society that would replace "power rooted in possession, privilege, or cir-cumstance [with] power and uniqueness rooted in love, reflectiveness, reason, and creativity." The new radicalism quickly divided into two powerful streams: one conventionally political, the other mainly cultural. SDS, which represented the first of these streams, would itself soon become radicalized and bitterly divided. The new cultural radicalism, meanwhile, swept up many young Americans in a tide of generational self-expression that featured bold new styles of music, dress, and behavior. After 1965, the New Left was increasingly defined by its opposition to the war in Vietnam, which brought thousands of new recruits into its ranks but which also contributed to its radicalization, repression, and eventual downfall.

Historians—many of whom were themselves deeply influenced by the new radicalism of the 1960s—have only begun to unpack the movement's meanings and significance. Not surprisingly, they have disagreed vigorously among themselves: some, echoing criticisms by the Old Left, fault the movement's lack of coherent ideology and disciplined organization; others, sympathetic to the movement's ori-gins, decry its disintegration into sectarian radicalism; still others, disillusioned or unsympathetic to begin with, view it as at best shallow and ephemeral, at worst hypocritical and destructive. The debate over the New Left, part of a larger debate over the meaning of the 1960s in American life, became one of the most contested battlegrounds in the "culture wars" of the 1980s and 1990s. It remains so even today, as Americans enter a new and very different century.

☒ D O C U M E N T S

The Port Huron Statement, excerpts from which are reprinted as Document 1, was written by student activist Tom Hayden and others and adopted at the annual convention of SDS in 1962. It reflects the early history of the New Left in its lack of doctrinaire ideology as well as in its spirit of hope and optimism. SDS was nevertheless dedicated throughout its early history to a more or less traditional politics of organization and struggle. The Sharon Statement, written as a founding document of the Young Americans for Freedom (Document 2), indicates the dissatisfaction of young conservatives with the 1950s status quo. Polite dissent took a radical turn by the late 1960s. Among the most radical splinter factions were the Weathermen, who took their name from Bob Dylan's "Subterranean Homesick Blues." The Weathermen's 1969 call for revolution is reprinted from *New Left Notes* (June 18, 1969) as Document 3.

By the late 1960s, disillusionment had set in: SDS was deeply divided; the war in Vietnam ground on; and the New Left had helped unseat Lyndon Johnson, only to get Richard Nixon as his successor. Many of the generation's new radicals sought to restore their own lives—and perhaps in their own small way, to work for the reform of the larger society—by fleeing to the rural countryside. Among them was Raymond Mungo. An excerpt, from his book *Total Loss Farm* (1970) is reprinted as Document 4.

Decades later, the meaning of the 1960s continues to be an issue of intense debate. In Document 5, former radicals Peter Collier and David Horowitz recall a New Left of "self-aggrandising romance with corrupt Third Worldism; . . . casual indulgence of Soviet totalitarianism; . . . [and] hypocritical and self-dramatising anti-Americanism." In Document 6, former SDS leader Tom Hayden offers a catalog of the decade's positive accomplishments.

1. The Port Huron Statement, 1963

We are people of this generation, bred in at least modest comfort, housed now in universities, looking uncomfortably to the world we inherit.

When we were kids the United States was the wealthiest and strongest country in the world: the only one with the atom bomb, the least scarred by modern war, an initiator of the United Nations that we thought would distribute Western influence throughout the world. Freedom and equality for each individual, government of, by, and for the people—these American values we found good, principles by which we could live as men. Many of us began maturing in complacency.

As we grew, however, our comfort was penetrated by events too troubling to dismiss. First, the permeating and victimizing fact of human degradation, symbolized by the Southern struggle against racial bigotry, compelled most of us from silence to activism. Second, the enclosing fact of the Cold War, symbolized by the presence of the Bomb, brought awareness that we ourselves, and our friends, and

Excerpts from The Port Huron Statement, 1963, State Historical Society of Wisconsin.

millions of abstract "others" we knew more directly because of our common peril, might die at any time. We might deliberately ignore, or avoid, or fail to feel all other human problems, but not these two, for these were too immediate and crushing in their impact, too challenging in the demand that we as individuals take the responsibility for encounter and resolution.

While these and other problems either directly oppressed us or rankled our consciences and became our own subjective concerns, we began to see complicated and disturbing paradoxes in our surrounding America. The declaration "all men are created equal . . ." rang hollow before the facts of Negro life in the South and the big cities of the North. The proclaimed peaceful intentions of the United States contradicted its economic and military investments in the Cold War status quo.

We witnessed, and continue to witness, other paradoxes. With nuclear energy whole cities can easily be powered, yet the dominant nation-states seem more likely to unleash destruction greater than that incurred in all wars of human history. Although our own technology is destroying old and creating new forms of social organization, men still tolerate meaningless work and idleness. While two-thirds of mankind suffers undernourishment, our own upper classes revel amidst superfluous abundance. Although world population is expected to double in forty years, the nations still tolerate anarchy as a major principle of international conduct and uncontrolled exploitation governs the sapping of the earth's physical resources. Although mankind desperately needs revolutionary leadership, America rests in national stalemate, its goals ambiguous and tradition-bound instead of informed and clear, its democratic system apathetic and manipulated rather than "of, by, and for the people."

Not only did tarnish appear on our image of American virtue, not only did disillusion occur when the hypocrisy of American ideals was discovered, but we began to sense that what we had originally seen as the American Golden Age was actually the decline of an era. The worldwide outbreak of revolution against colonialism and imperialism, the entrenchment of totalitarian states, the menace of war, overpopulation, international disorder, supertechnology—these trends were testing the tenacity of our own commitment to democracy and freedom and our abilities to visualize their application to a world in upheaval.

Our work is guided by the sense that we may be the last generation in the experiment with living. But we are a minority—the vast majority of our people regard the temporary equilibriums of our society and world as eternally functional parts. In this is perhaps the outstanding paradox: we ourselves are imbued with urgency, yet the message of our society is that there is no viable alternative to the present. Beneath the reassuring tones of the politicians, beneath the common opinion that America will "muddle through," beneath the stagnation of those who have closed their minds to the future, is the pervading feeling that there simply are no alternatives, that our times have witnessed the exhaustion not only of Utopias, but of any new departures as well. Feeling the press of complexity upon the emptiness of life, people are fearful of the thought that at any moment things might thrust out of control. They fear change itself, since change might smash whatever invisible framework seems to hold back chaos for them now. For most Americans, all crusades are suspect, threatening. The fact that each individual sees apathy in his fellows perpetuates the common reluctance to organize for change. The dominant institutions are complex enough to blunt the minds of their potential critics, and entrenched enough to swiftly dissipate or entirely repel the energies of protest and reform, thus limiting human expectancies. Then, too, we are a materially improved society, and by our improvements we seem to have weakened the case for further change.

Some would have us believe that Americans feel contentment amidst prosperity—but might it not better be called a glaze above deeply felt anxieties about their role in the new world? And if these anxieties produce a developed indifference to human affairs, do they not as well produce a yearning to believe there *is* an alternative to the present, that something *can* be done to change circumstances in the school, the workplaces, the bureaucracies, the government? It is to this latter yearning, at once the spark and engine of change, that we direct our present appeal. The search for truly democratic alternatives to the present, and a commitment to social experimentation with them, is a worthy and fulfilling human enterprise, one which moves us and, we hope, others today. On such a basis do we offer this document of our convictions and analysis: as an effort in understanding and changing the conditions of humanity in the late twentieth century, an effort rooted in the ancient, still unfulfilled conception of man attaining determining influence over his circumstances of life. . . .

Making values explicit—an initial task in establishing alternatives—is an activity that has been devalued and corrupted. The conventional moral terms of the age, the politician moralities—"free world," "people's democracies"—reflect realities poorly, if at all, and seem to function more as ruling myths than as descriptive principles. But neither has our experience in the universities brought us moral enlightenment. Our professors and administrators sacrifice controversy to public relations; their curriculums change more slowly than the living events of the world; their skills and silence are purchased by investors in the arms race; passion is called unscholastic. The questions we might want raised—what is really important? can we live in a different and better way? if we wanted to change society, how would we do it?—are not thought to be questions of a "fruitful, empirical nature," and thus are brushed aside. . . .

Theoretic chaos has replaced the idealistic thinking of old—and, unable to reconstitute theoretic order, men have condemned idealism itself. Doubt has replaced hopefulness—and men act out a defeatism that is labelled realistic. The decline of utopia and hope is in fact one of the defining features of social life today. The reasons are various: the dreams of the older left were perverted by Stalinism and never recreated; the congressional stalemate makes men narrow their view of the possible; the specialization of human activity leaves little room for sweeping thought; the horrors of the twentieth century, symbolized in the gas-ovens and concentration camps and atom bombs, have blasted hopefulness. To be idealistic is to be considered apocalyptic, deluded. To have no serious aspirations, on the contrary, is to be "tough-minded."

In suggesting social goals and values, therefore, we are aware of entering a sphere of some disrepute. Perhaps matured by the past, we have no sure formulas, no closed theories—but that does not mean values are beyond discussion and tentative determination. A first task of any social movement is to convince people that the search for orienting theories and the creation of human values is complex but worthwhile. We are aware that to avoid platitudes we must analyze the concrete conditions of social order. But to direct such an analysis we must use the guideposts of basic principles. Our own social values involve conceptions of human beings, human relationships, and social systems.

We regard *men* as infinitely precious and possessed of unfulfilled capacities for reason, freedom, and love. In affirming these principles we are aware of countering perhaps the dominant conceptions of man in the twentieth century: that he is a thing to be manipulated, and that he is inherently incapable of directing his own affairs. We oppose the depersonalization that reduces human beings to the status of things—if anything, the brutalities of the twentieth century teach that means and ends are intimately related, the vague appeals to "posterity" cannot justify the mutilations of the present. We oppose, too, the doctrine of human incompetence because it rests essentially on the modern fact that men have been "competently" manipulated into competence—we see little reason why men cannot meet with increasing skill the complexities and responsibilities of their situation, if society is organized not for minority, but for majority, participation in decision-making.

Men have unrealized potential for self-cultivation, self-direction, self-understanding, and creativity. It is this potential that we regard as crucial and to which we appeal, not to the human potentiality for violence, unreason, and submission to authority. The goal of man and society should be human independence: a concern not with image or popularity but with finding a meaning in life that is personally authentic; a quality of mind not compulsively driven by a sense of powerlessness, nor one which unthinkingly adopts status values, nor one which represses all threats to its habits, but one which has full, spontaneous access to present and past experiences, one which easily unites the fragmented parts of personal history, one which openly faces problems which are troubling and unresolved; one with an intuitive awareness of possibilities, an active sense of curiosity, an ability and willingness to learn.

This kind of independence does not mean egoistic individualism—the object is not to have one's way so much as it is to have a way that is one's own. Nor do we deify man—we merely have faith in his potential.

Human relationships should involve fraternity and honesty. Human interdependence is contemporary fact; human brotherhood must be willed however, as a condition of future survival and as the most appropriate form of social relations. Personal links between man and man are needed, especially to go beyond the partial and fragmentary bonds of function that bind men only as worker to worker, employer to employee, teacher to student, American to Russian.

Loneliness, estrangement, isolation describe the vast distance between man and man today. These dominant tendencies cannot be overcome by better personnel management, nor by improved gadgets, but only when a love of man overcomes the idolatrous worship of things by man.

As the individualism we affirm is not egoism, the selflessness we affirm is not self-elimination. On the contrary, we believe in generosity of a kind that imprints one's unique individual qualities in the relation to other men, and to all human activity. Further, to dislike isolation is not to favor the abolition of privacy; the latter differs from isolation in that it occurs or is abolished according to individual will. Finally, we would replace power and personal uniqueness rooted in possession, privilege, or circumstance by power and uniqueness rooted in love, reflectiveness, reason, and creativity.

As a *social system* we seek the establishment of a democracy of individual participation, governed by two central aims: that the individual share in those social decisions determining the quality and direction of his life; that society be organized to encourage independence in men and provide the media for their common participation.

In a participatory democracy, the political life would be based in several root principles:

• that decision-making of basic social consequence be carried on by public groupings;

• that politics be seen positively, as the art of collectively creating an acceptable pattern of social relations;

• that politics has the function of bringing people out of isolation and into community, thus being a necessary, though not sufficient, means of finding meaning in personal life;

• that the political order should serve to clarify problems in a way instrumental to their solution; it should provide outlets for the expression of personal grievance and aspiration; opposing views should be organized so as to illuminate choices and facilitate the attainment of goals; channels should be commonly available to relate men to knowledge and to power so that private problems—from bad recreation facilities to personal alienation—are formulated as general issues.

The economic sphere would have as its basis the principles:

• that work should involve incentives worthier than money or survival. It should be educative, not stultifying; creative, not mechanical; self-directed, not manipulated, encouraging independence, a respect for others, a sense of dignity, and a willingness to accept social responsibility, since it is this experience that has crucial influence on habits, perceptions, and individual ethics;

• that the economic experience is so personally decisive that the individual must share in its full determination;

• that the economy itself is of such social importance that its major resources and means of production should be open to democratic participation and subject to democratic social regulation.

Like the political and economic ones, major social institutions—cultural, education, rehabilitative, and others—should be generally organized with the well-being and dignity of man as the essential measure of success.

In social change or interchange, we find violence to be abhorrent because it requires generally the transformation of the target, be it a human being or a community of people, into a depersonalized object of hate. It is imperative that the means of violence be abolished and the institutions—local, national, international—that encourage nonviolence as a condition of conflict be developed.

These are our central values, in skeletal form. It remains vital to understand their denial or attainment in the context of the modern world.

2. The Sharon Statement, 1960

Adopted in conference at Sharon, Connecticut, on 11 September 1960.

In this time of moral and political crises, it is the responsibility of the youth of America to affirm certain eternal truths.

We, as young conservatives, believe:

"The Sharon Statement," from Young Americans for Freedom. Reprinted by permission.

That foremost among the transcendent values is the individual's use of his God-given free will, whence derives his right to be free from the restrictions of arbitrary force;

That liberty is indivisible, and that political freedom cannot long exist without economic freedom;

That the purpose of government is to protect those freedoms through the preservation of internal order, the provision of national defense, and the administration of justice;

That when government ventures beyond these rightful functions, it accumulates power, which tends to diminish order and liberty;

That the Constitution of the United States is the best arrangement yet devised for empowering government to fulfill its proper role, while restraining it from the concentration and abuse of power;

That the genius of the Constitution—the division of powers—is summed up in the clause that reserves primacy to the several states, or to the people, in those spheres not specifically delegated to the Federal government;

That the market economy, allocating resources by the free play of supply and demand, is the single economic system compatible with the requirements of personal freedom and constitutional government, and that it is at the same time the most productive supplier of human needs;

That when government interferes with the work of the market economy, it tends to reduce the moral and physical strength of the nation; that when it takes from one man to bestow on another, it diminishes the incentive of the first, the integrity of the second, and the moral autonomy of both;

That we will be free only so long as the national sovereignty of the United States is secure; that history shows periods of freedom are rare, and can exist only when free citizens concertedly defend their rights against all enemies;

That the forces of international Communism are, at present, the greatest single threat to these liberties;

That the United States should stress victory over, rather than coexistence with, this menace; and

That American foreign policy must be judged by this criterion: does it serve the just interests of the United States?

3. The Weathermen's Call for Revolution: "You Don't Need a Weatherman to Know Which Way the Wind Blows," 1969

People ask, what is the nature of the revolution that we talk about? Who will it be made by, and for, and what are its goals and strategy?

The overriding consideration in answering these questions is that the main struggle going on in the world today is between U.S. imperialism and the national

From *New Left Notes,* June 18, 1969. Reprinted with permission from *Weatherman* by Harold Jacobs. © Ramparts Press, 1970, pp. 51–53.

liberation struggles against it. This is essential in defining political matters in the whole world: because it is by far the most powerful, every other empire and petty dictator is in the long run dependent on U.S. imperialism, which has unified, allied with, and defended all of the reactionary forces of the whole world. Thus, in considering every other force or phenomenon, from Soviet imperialism or Israeli imperialism to "workers struggle" in France or Czechoslovakia, we determine who are our friends and who are our enemies according to whether they help U.S. imperialism or fight to defeat it.

So the very first question people in this country must ask in considering the question of revolution is where they stand in relation to the United States as an oppressor nation, and where they stand in relation to the masses of people throughout the world whom U.S. imperialism is oppressing.

The primary task of revolutionary struggle is to solve this principal contradiction on the side of the people of the world. It is the oppressed peoples of the world who have created the wealth of this empire and it is to them that it belongs; the goal of the revolutionary struggle must be the control and use of this wealth in the interests of the oppressed peoples of the world.

It is in this context that we must examine the revolutionary struggles in the United States. We are within the heartland of a world-wide monster, a country so rich from its world-wide plunder that even the crumbs doled out to the enslaved masses within its borders provide for material existence very much above the conditions of the masses of people of the world. The U.S. empire, as a world-wide system, channels wealth, based upon the labor and resources of the rest of the world, into the United States. The relative affluence existing in the United States is directly dependent upon the labor and natural resources of the Vietnamese, the Angolans, the Bolivians, and the rest of the peoples of the Third World. All of the United Airlines Astrojets, all of the Holiday Inns, all of Hertz's automobiles, your television set, car, and wardrobe already belong, to a large degree to the people of the rest of the world.

Therefore, any conception of "socialist revolution" simply in terms of the working people of the United States, failing to recognize the full scope of interests of the most oppressed peoples of the world, is a conception of a fight for a particular privileged interest, and is a very dangerous ideology. While the control and use of the wealth of the Empire for the people of the whole world is also in the interests of the vast majority of the people in this country, if the goal is not clear from the start we will further the preservation of class society, oppression, war, genocide, and the complete emiseration of everyone, including the people of the U.S.

The goal is the destruction of U.S. imperialism and the achievement of a classless world: world communism. Winning state power in the U.S. will occur as a result of the military forces of the U.S. overextending themselves around the world and being defeated piecemeal; struggle within the U.S. will be a vital part of this process, but when the revolution triumphs in the U.S. it will have been made by the people of the whole world. For socialism to be defined in national terms within so extreme and historical an oppressor nation as this is only imperialist national chauvinism on the part of the "movement."

4. Raymond Mungo Searches for a New Age at Total Loss Farm, 1970

Friday: Portsmouth, N.H.

The farm in Vermont had fooled us, just as we hoped it would when we moved there in early '68; it had tricked even battle-scarred former youth militants into seeing the world as bright clusters of Day-Glo orange and red forest, rolling open meadows, sparkling brooks and streams. I had lived in industrial, eastern New England all my life, though, as well as worse places like New York and Washington, D.C., so I might have known better. But Vermont had blurred my memory, and when we finally left the farm for Portsmouth, I was all Thoreau and Frost, October up North, ain't life grand, all fresh and eager to begin rowing up the Concord and Merrimack rivers in the vanished footsteps of old Henry D. himself. Verandah Porche, queen of the Bay State Poets for Peace, packed the failing '59 VW and we went tearing down the mountain, kicking up good earth from the dirt road and barely slowing down for the 18th-century graveyard and all manner of wild animals now madly racing for shelter against the sharp winds of autumn in these hills. The frost was on the pumpkin, it was our second autumn together, and warm vibrations made the yellow farmhouse fairly glow in the dying daylight as we pointed east, over the Connecticut River, heading for our rendezvous with what *he* called "the placid current of our dreams." Knockout October day in 1969 in Vermont. All the trees had dropped acid.

The idea had come to me in a dream. It was one of those nights after Steve brought the Sunshine (wotta drug) when I'd wake up and sit bolt upright, alarmed at a sudden capacity, or *power,* I had acquired, to *see far.* I could see eternity in the vast darkness outside my window and inside my head, and I remembered feeling that way when but an infant. In my dream I was floating silently downstream in a birchbark canoe, speechless me watching vistas of bright New England autumn open up with each bend, slipping unnoticed between crimson mountains, blessing the warm sun by day and sleeping on beds of fresh leaves under a canary harvest moon by night. I was on the road to no special place, but no interstate highway with Savarinettes and Sunoco for this kid; in my dream, I was on a natural highway through the planet, the everlovin' me-sustainin' planet that never lets you down. Said Henry: "I have not yet put my foot through it."

It was the farm that had allowed me the luxury of this vision, for the farm had given me the insulation from America which the peace movement promised but cruelly denied. When we lived in Boston, Chicago, San Francisco, Washington (you name it, we lived there; some of us still live there), we dreamed of a New Age born of violent insurrection. We danced on the graves of war dead in Vietnam, every corpse was ammunition for Our Side; we set up a countergovernment down there in Washington, had marches, rallies, and meetings; tried to fight fire with fire. Then Johnson resigned, yes, and the universities began to fall, the best and oldest ones first, and by God every 13-year-old in the suburbs was smoking dope and our numbers multiplying into the millions. But I woke up in the spring of 1968 and said, "This is not what I had in mind," because the movement had become my enemy; the movement was not flowers and doves and spontaneity, but another vicious system, the seed of a heartless bureaucracy, a minority Party vying for power rather than peace. It was then that we put away the schedule for the revolution, gathered together our dear ones and all our resources, and set off to Vermont in search of the New Age.

The New Age we were looking for proved to be very old indeed, and I've often wondered aloud at my luck for being 23 years old in a time and place in which only the past offers hope and inspiration; the future offers only artifice and blight. I travel now in a society of friends who heat their houses with hand-cut wood and eliminate in outhouses, who cut pine shingles with draw-knives and haul maple sugar sap on sleds, who weed potatoes with their university-trained hands, pushing long hair out of their way and thus marking their foreheads with beautiful penitent dust. We till the soil to atone for our fathers' destruction of it. We smell. We live far from the marketplaces in America by our own volition, and the powerful men left behind are happy to have us out of their way. They do not yet realize that their heirs will refuse to inhabit their hollow cities, will find them poisonous and lethal, will run back to the Stone Age if necessary for survival and peace.

Yet this canoe trip had to be made because there was adventure out there. We expected to find the Concord and Merrimack rivers polluted but still beautiful, and to witness firsthand the startling juxtaposition of old New England, land and water and mountains, and new America, factories and highways and dams; and to thus educate ourselves further in the works of God and man. We pushed on relentlessly, top speed 50 mph, in our eggshell Volkswagen (Hitler's manifestly correct conception of the common man's car), 100 miles to the sea. The week following, the week we'd spend in our canoe, was the very week when our countrymen would celebrate Columbus Day (anniversary of the European discovery of Americans), the New York Mets in the World (American) Series, and the National Moratorium to demand an "early end to the war." Since we mourn the ruthless extinction of the natives, have outgrown baseball, and long ago commenced our own total Moratorium on constructive participation in this society, our presence and support was irrelevant to all of these national pastimes. . . .

We *are* saving the world, of course, as the world for us extends to the boundaries of Total Loss Farm and the limits of our own experience; and Total Loss Farm is everywhere now, perhaps under your own rhubarb patch if you looked at it a little closer, and our experience all that anyone could hope to know of life. We were born and raised by parents who loved us at least until they lost us to a certain high-pitched whistle in the wind which they had gotten too old to hear; we work at maintaining ourselves, though our shared labor is seldom very taxing, for it takes little enough work to make plants grow, most of it is out of our hands, and our relationship to the work one of direct gratification and reward, as children insist on; we have children of our own, though they are fully peers by the time they've learned to eat and eliminate without physical help, and soon become more our masters than our students; and we die, sometimes in sulphurous flames, dramatic and shocking, other times silent and mysterious like the gone children wandering Europe with scenes of the parents engulfed in atrocity scrawled across their minds, but never to be spoken: " I come from Auschwitz, or Hué, or Boston, my father was shot for believing in God and hangs limp forever in front of our home as a reminder to the others; my mother was sold to the grim green soldiers for their sport, and my brother to be used as a woman; I escaped the country of the somnambulent and blind on the back of a wolf who prowled the ruins and took pity on me; I have come here to begin again."

Our parents must wonder where we are, this story is, as much as anything else, an attempt to fill them in, but it grows harder and harder to speak. Fortunately, it grows simultaneously less necessary. I have clothes on my back, though they are old, and a roof over my head and food for my belly. In this, I am luckier than many. I am surrounded by people who would give their own lives in defense of mine, for they know we will make it together or not at all. I wish to be reconciled with all of my enemies, and to live on the planet and glory in peaches to a ripe old age. I am willing to help you as much as I'm able, as a single person can help another, not as a movement or government can help a mass. I may ask for some help from you as well. If you come to my house with love in your heart and there's room for one more—for there isn't always—you may know I will feed you and house you for the night, if you need it. You may see me walking from town to town with my thumb outstretched to the highway, seeking a lift: don't pass me by.

You have seen me everywhere. I am not asking for the vote. I do not seek to be represented. I do not seek to tear down your buildings or march on your castle or sit at your desk. I am interested neither in destroying what you have put up nor in gaining control of your empire. I demand nothing, and nothing is my inheritance. I live in the world, in the woods, with my friends, where not many people come by and the planet is entire and friendly; we like to be left alone except by those who can help. You can help by giving the planet, and peace, a chance. I ask only that you treat yourself right, give yourself the best of everything; and in so doing, you will be acting for me as well. If you can't stop, at least wave as you go by. Slow down, perhaps stop working: you'll find the time for everything you really want to do.

Who am I? In the world of the farm, I am Grampaw, who still finds himself able to deliver of such bombastic lectures as this, thinks he has lived through such madness and chaos, such orgasm and ecstasy, that he has some lessons to give, sleeps with the dogs. I am a fool. I am also Pan, who does in Captain Hook with a sweep of his wooden sword: saying: I am youth! I am joy! I am freedom!

5. Two Disillusioned Ex-Radicals Bid Good-bye to the Sixties, 1985

When we tell our old radical friends that we voted for Ronald Reagan last November, the response is usually one of annoyed incredulity. After making sure that we are not putting them on, our old friends make nervous jokes about Jerry Falwell and Phyllis Schlafly, about gods that have failed, about ageing yuppies ascending to consumer heaven in their BMWs. We remind them of an old adage: "Anyone under 40 who isn't a socialist has no heart—anyone over 40 who is a socialist has no brain."

"Lefties for Reagan" by Peter Collier and David Horowitz. Copyright © 1985 by Peter Collier and David Horowitz. Originally published in *The Washington Post Magazine*. Reprinted by permission of Georges Borchardt, Inc., for the authors.

Inevitably the talk becomes bitter. One old comrade, after a tirade in which she had denounced us as reactionaries and crypto-fascists, finally sputtered, "And the worst thing is that you've turned your back on the *Sixties!*" That was exactly right: casting our ballots for Ronald Reagan was indeed a way of finally saying goodbye to all that—to the self-aggrandising romance with corrupt Third Worldism; to the casual indulgence of Soviet totalitarianism; to the hypocritical and self-dramatising anti-Americanism which is the New Left's bequest to mainstream politics.

The instruments of popular culture may perhaps be forgiven for continuing to portray the '60s as a time of infectious idealism, but those of us who were active then have no excuse for abetting this banality. If in some ways it was the best of times, it was also the worst of times, an era of bloodthirsty fantasies as well as spiritual ones. We ourselves experienced both aspects, starting as civil-rights and anti-war activists and ending as co-editors of the New Left magazine *Ramparts*. The magazine post allowed us to write about the rough beast slouching through America and also to urge it on through non-editorial activities we thought of as clandestine until we later read about them in the FBI and CIA files we both accumulated.

Like other radicals in those early days, we were against electoral politics, regarding voting as one of those charades used by the ruling class to legitimate its power. We were even more against Reagan, then governor of California, having been roughed up by his troopers during the People's Park demonstrations in Berkeley and tear-gassed by his National Guard helicopters during the University of California's Third World Liberation Front Strike.

But neither elections nor elected officials seemed particularly important compared with the auguries of Revolution the Left saw everywhere by the end of the decade—in the way the nefarious Richard Nixon was widening the war in Indo-China; in the unprovoked attacks by paramilitary police against the Black Panther Party; in the formation of the "Weather Underground," a group willing to pick up the gun or the bomb. It was a time when the apocalypse struggling to be born seemed to need only the slightest assist from the radical midwife.

When we were in the voting booth this past November (in different precincts but of the same mind) we both thought back to the day in 1969 when Tom Hayden came by the office and, after getting a *Ramparts* donation to buy gas masks and other combat issue for Black Panther "guerrillas," announced portentously:

"Fascism is here, and we're all going to be in jail by the end of the year."

We agreed wholeheartedly with this apocalyptic vision and in fact had just written in an editorial:

They system cannot be revitalized. It must be overthrown. As humanly as possible, but by any means necessary.

Every thought and perception in those days was filtered through the dark and distorting glass of the Viet Nam war.

The Left was hooked on Viet Nam. It was an addictive drug whose rush was a potent mix of melodrama, self-importance, and moral rectitude. Viet Nam was a universal solvent—the explanation for every evil we saw and the justification for every excess we committed. Trashing the windows of merchants on the main streets of America seemed warranted by the notion that these petty-bourgeois shopkeepers were cogs in the system of capitalist exploitation that was obliterating Viet Nam. Fantasising the death of local cops seemed warranted by the role they played as an occupying army in America's black ghettos, those mini–Viet Nams we yearned to see explode in domestic wars of liberation. Viet Nam caused us to acquire a new appreciation for foreign tyrants like Kim Il Sung of North Korea. Viet Nam also caused us to support the domestic extortionism and violence of groups like the Black Panthers, and to dismiss derisively Martin Luther King Jr. as an "Uncle Tom." (The Left has conveniently forgotten this fact now that it finds it expedient to invoke King's name and reputation to further its domestic politics.)

How naive the New Left was can be debated, but by the end of the '60s we were not political novices. We knew that bad news from South-east Asia—the reports of bogged-down campaigns and the weekly body counts announced by Walter Cronkite—was good for the radical agenda. The more repressive our government in dealing with dissent at home, the more recruits for our cause and the sooner the appearance of the revolutionary Armageddon.

Our assumption that Viet Nam would be the political and moral fulcrum by which we would tip this country toward revolution foresaw every possibility except one: that the United States would pull out. Never had we thought that the U.S., the arch-imperial power, would of its own volition withdraw from Indo-China. This development violated a primary article of our hand-me-down Marxism: that political action through normal channels could not alter the course of the war. The system we had wanted to overthrow worked tardily and only at great cost, but it worked.

When American troops finally came home, some of us took the occasion to begin a long and painful re-examination of our political assumptions and beliefs. Others did not. For the diehards, there was a post–Viet Nam syndrome in its own way as debilitating as that suffered by people who had fought there—a sense of emptiness rather than exhilaration, a paradoxical desire to hold on to and breathe life back into the experience that had been their high for so many years.

As the post–Viet Nam decade progressed, the diehards on the left ignored conclusions about the viability of democratic traditions that might have been drawn from America's exit from Viet Nam and from the Watergate crisis that followed it, a time when the man whose ambitions they had feared most was removed from office by the Constitution rather than by a coup. The only "lessons" of Viet Nam the Left seemed interested in were those that emphasized the danger of American power abroad and the need to diminish it, a view that was injected into the Democratic party with the triumph of the McGovernite wing. The problem with this use of Viet Nam as a moral text for American policy, however, was that the pages following the fall of Saigon had been whited out.

No lesson, for instance, was seen in Hanoi's ruthless conquest of the South, the establishment of a police state in Saigon, and the political oblivion of the National Liberation Front, whose struggle we on the Left had so passionately supported. It was not that credible information was lacking. Jean Lacouture wrote in 1976:

> Never before have we had such proof of so many detained after a war. Not in Moscow in 1917. Not in Madrid in 1939, not in Paris and Rome in 1944, nor in Havana in 1959. . . .

But this eminent French journalist, who had been regarded as something of an oracle when he was reporting America's derelictions during the war, was dismissed as a "sellout."

In 1977, when some former anti-war activists signed an "Appeal to the Conscience of Viet Nam" because of the more than 200,000 prisoners languishing in "Re-education Centres" and the new round of self-immolations by Buddhist monks, they were chastised by activist David Dellinger, Institute for Policy Studies fellow Richard Barnet, and other keepers of the flame in a *New York Times* advertisement that said in part:

> The present government of Viet Nam should be hailed for its moderation and for its extraordinary effort to achieve reconciliation among all of its people.

When tens of thousands of unreconciled "Boat People" began to flee the repression of their Communist rulers, Joan Baez and others who spoke out in their behalf were attacked for breaking ranks with Hanoi.

Something might also have been learned from the fate of wretched Cambodia. But Leftists seemed so addicted to finding an American cause at the root of every problem that they couldn't recognise indigenous evils. As the Khmer Rouge were about to take over, Noam Chomsky wrote that their advent heralded a Cambodian liberation, "a new era of economic development and social justice." The new era turned out to be the killing fields that took the lives of two million Cambodians.

Finally, Viet Nam emerged as an imperialist power, taking control of Laos, invading Cambodia, and threatening Thailand. But in a recent editorial, *The Nation* explains that the Vietnamese invaded Cambodia "to stop the killing and restore some semblance of civilised government to the devastated country." This bloody occupation is actually a "rescue mission," and should not "obscure the responsibility of the United States for the disasters in Indo-China," disasters that are being caused by playing the "China card" and refusing to normalise relations with Viet Nam. These acts on the part of the United States "make Vietnamese withdrawal from Cambodia unlikely"; only the White House can "remove the pressures on Viet Nam from all sides [that] would bring peace to a ravaged land." Such reasoning recalls the wonderful line from the Costa-Gavras film Z:

> Always blame the Americans. Even when you're wrong, you're right.

Another unacknowledged lesson from Indo-China involves the way in which Viet Nam has become a satellite of the Soviet Union (paying for foreign aid by sending labour brigades to its benefactor).

This development doesn't mesh well with the Left's ongoing romantic vision of Hanoi. It also threatens the Left's obstinate refusal to admit that during the mid-1970s—a time when American democracy was trying to heal itself from the twin traumas of the war and Watergate—the U.S.S.R. was demonstrating that totalitarianism abhors a vacuum by moving into Africa, Central America, South-east Asia, and elsewhere. Instead of evaluating the Soviets because of the change in what we used to call "the objective conditions," the Left rationalises Soviet aggressions as the spasms of a petrified bureaucracy whose policies are annoying mainly because they distract attention from U.S. malfeasance around the world.

If they were capable of looking intently at the Soviet Union, Leftists and Liberals alike would have to concur with Susan Sontag's contention (which many of them jeered at when she announced it) that Communism is simply left-wing fascism.

One of the reasons the Left has been so cautious in its reassessments of the Soviets is the fiction that the U.S.S.R. is on the side of "history."

This assumption is echoed in Fred Halliday's euphoric claim, in a recent issue of *New Left Review,* that Soviet support was crucial to 14 Third-World revolutions during the era of *détente* (including such triumphs of human progress as Iran and South Yemen), and in Andrew Kopkind's fatuous observation that "the Soviet Union has almost always sided with the revolutionists, the liberations, the insurgents." In Ethiopia?

Propped up by 200,000 Cuban legionnaires, the Marxist government of Mengistu Haile Mariam has as its main accomplishment a "Red Campaign of Terror" (its official designation) that killed thousands of people. Where were those who cheer the Soviets' work on behalf of the socialist *Zeitgeist* when this episode took place? Or this past fall when the Marxist liberator squandered more than $40 million on a party celebrating the 10th anniversary of his murderous rule while his people starved? Where were they to point out the moral when capitalist America rushed in 250 million metric tons of grain to help allay the Ethiopian starvation while the Soviets were managing to contribute only ten million metric tons? Where are they now that Mengistu withholds emergency food supplies from the starving provinces of Eritrea and Tigre because the people there are in rebellion against his tyranny?

Reagan is often upbraided for having described the Soviet Union as "an evil empire." Those opposed to this term seem to be offended aesthetically rather than politically. Just how wide of the mark is the President? Oppressing an array of nationalities whose populations far outnumber its own, Russia is the last of the old European empires, keeping in subjugation not only formerly independent states such as Estonia, Latvia, and Lithuania (Hitler's gift to Stalin), but also the nations of Eastern Europe. Every country "liberated" into the Soviet bloc has been transformed into a national prison, where the borders are guarded to keep the inmates in rather than the foreigners out. . . .

Soviet strategy is based on a brutal rejoinder to Mao's poetic notion (which we old New Leftists used to enjoy citing) about guerrillas being like fish swimming in a sea of popular support. The Soviet solution is to boil the sea and ultimately drain it, leaving the fish exposed and gasping on barren land. . . .

Perhaps the leading feature of the Left today is the moral selectivity that French social critic Jean-François Revel has identified as "the syndrome of the cross-eyed Left."

Leftists can describe Viet Nam's conquest and colonialisation of Cambodia as a "rescue mission," while reviling Ronald Reagan for applying the same term to the Grenada operation, although better than 90% of the island's population told independent pollsters they were grateful for the arrival of U.S. troops. . . .

The Left's memory can be as selective as its morality. When it comes to past commitments that have failed, the Leftist mentality is utterly unable to produce a coherent balance sheet, let alone a profit-and-loss statement. The attitude toward Soviet penetration of the Americas is a good example. Current enthusiasm for the Sandinista régime in Nicaragua should recall to those of us old enough to remember a previous enthusiasm for Cuba 25 years ago. Many of us began our "New Leftism" with the "Fair Play for Cuba" demonstrations. We raised our voices and chanted,

"Cuba Si! Yanqui No!" We embraced Fidel Castro not only because of the flamboyant personal style of the *barbudos* of his 26th of July Movement but also because Castro assured the world that his revolution belonged to neither Communists nor capitalists, that it was neither red nor black, but Cuban olive-green.

We attributed Castro's expanding links with Moscow to the U.S.-sponsored invasion of the Bay of Pigs, and then to the "secret war" waged against Cuba by U.S. intelligence and paramilitary organisations. But while Castro's apologists in the United States may find it expedient to maintain these fictions, Carlos Franqui and other old Fidelistas now in exile have made it clear that Castro embraced the Soviets even before the U.S. hostility became decisive, and that he steered his country into an alliance with the Soviets with considerable enthusiasm. Before the Bay of Pigs he put a Soviet general in charge of Cuban forces. Before the Bay of Pigs he destroyed Cuba's democratic trade-union movement, although its elected leadership was drawn from his own 26th of July Movement. He did so because he knew that the Stalinists of Cuba's Communist Party would be dependable cheerleaders and efficient policemen of his emerging dictatorship.

One symbolic event along the way that many of us missed was Castro's imprisonment of his old comrade Huber Matos, liberator of Matanzas Province, and one of the four key military leaders of the revolution. Matos's crime: criticising the growing influence of Cuban Communists (thereby jeopardising Castro's plans to use them as his palace guard). Matos's sentence: 20 years in a 4-by-11 concrete box. Given such a precedent, how can we fail to support Eden Pastora for taking up arms against early signs of similar totalitarianism in Nicaragua?

What has come of Cuba's revolution to break the chains of American imperialism? Soviets administer the still one-crop Cuban economy; Soviets train the Cuban army; and Soviet subsidies, fully one-quarter of Cuba's gross national product, prevent the Cuban treasury from going broke. Before the revolution, there were more than 35 independent newspapers and radio stations in Havana. Now, there is only the official voice of *Granma,* the Cuban *Pravda,* and a handful of other outlets spouting the same party line. Today in Cuba is a more abject and deformed colony of the Soviet empire than it ever was of America. The arch-rebel of our youth, Fidel Castro, has become a party hack who cheerfully endorsed the rape of Czechoslovakia in 1968 and endorses the ongoing plunder of Afghanistan today, an ageing pimp who sells his young men to the Russians for use in their military adventures in return for $10 billion a year.

In Leftist circles, of course, such arguments are anathema, and no historical precedent, however daunting, can prevent outbreaks of radical chic.

Epidemics of radical chic cannot be prevented by referring to historical precedents. That perennial delinquent Abbie Hoffman will lead his Potemkin-village tours of Managua. The Hollywood stars will dish up Nicaraguan president Daniel Ortega as an exotic hors-d'oeuvre on the Beverly Hills cocktail circuit. In the self-righteous moral glow accompanying such gatherings, it will be forgotten that, through the offices of the U.S. government, more economic and military aid was provided the Sandinistas in the first 18 months following their takeover than was given to Somoza in the previous 20 years, and that this aid was cut off primarily because of the clear signs that political pluralism in Nicaragua was being terminated.

Adherents of today's version of radical chic may never take seriously the words of Sandinista directorate member Bayardo Arce when he says that elections are a "hindrance" to the goal of "a dictatorship of the proletariat" and necessary only "as an expedient to deprive our enemies of an argument." They will ignore former Sandinista hero and now Contra leader Eden Pastora, who sees the Junta as traitors who have sold out the revolutionary dream. ("Now that we are occupied by foreign forces from Cuba and Russia, now that we are governed by a dictatorial government of nine men, now more than ever the Sandinista struggle is justified.") They will ignore opposition leader Arturo Cruz, an early supporter of the Sandinista revolution and previously critical of the Contras, when the worsening situation makes him change his mind and ask the Reagan administration to support them in a statement that should have the same weight as Andrei Sakharov's plea to the West to match the Soviet arms build-up.

American Leftists propose solutions for the people of Central America that they wouldn't dare propose for themselves. These armchair revolutionaries project their self-hatred and their contempt for the privileges of democracy—which allow them to live well and to think badly—on to people who would be only too grateful for the luxuries they disdain. Dismissing "bourgeois" rights as a decadent frill that the peoples of the Third World can't afford, Leftists spreadeagle the Central Americans between the dictators of the Right and the dictators of the Left. The latter, of course, are their chosen instruments for bringing social justice and economic well-being, although no Leftist revolution has yet provided impressive returns on either of these qualities and most have made the lives of their people considerably more wretched than they were before.

Voting is symbolic behaviour, a way of evaluating what one's country has been as well as what it might become. We do not accept Reagan's policies chapter and verse (especially in domestic policy, which we haven't discussed here), but we agree with his vision of the world as a place increasingly inhospitable to democracy and increasingly dangerous for America.

One of the few saving graces of age is a deeper perspective on the passions of youth. Looking back on the Left's revolutionary enthusiasms of the last 25 years, we have painfully learned what should have been obvious all along: that we live in an imperfect world that is bettered only with great difficulty and easily made worse—much worse. This is a conservative assessment, but on the basis of half a lifetime's experience, it seems about right.

6. Tom Hayden Recalls a Time of Greatness and Wonder, 1988

Looking back from life's mid-passage, what did the generation of the sixties achieve? What does it mean today?

By the most measurable standards, we accomplished more than we expected, more than most generations ever accomplish. Consider the most obvious:

• Students led the civil rights movement, which destroyed a century-old segregation system and which politically enfranchised twenty million blacks.

• Students were the backbone of the antiwar movement, which forced our government to abandon its policies in Vietnam and the nation to reconsider the Cold War.

•   Because of student criticism, most universities retreated from their traditional paternalism toward an acceptance of active student participation in decision making.

•   Movement activists were the key factor in making Lyndon Johnson withdraw from the presidency in 1968 and in transforming the political rules that permitted reformers to prevail in the Democratic party, which then endorsed "participatory democracy" in its 1972 platform.

•   The same movement was conceded the eighteen-year-old vote by the 1970s.

•   These movements were direct catalysts for the reemergence of the women's movement, the birth of environmentalism, and other diverse causes. In short, we opened up closed systems. From Georgia and Mississippi to the South as a whole, from Newark and Chicago to the cities of the North, from the 1965 Vietnam teach-ins to the 1973 War Powers Act, from the Democratic convention of 1968 to that of 1972, there was a steady evolution from patterns of exclusion toward greater citizen participation in basic decisions.

More generally, the New Left fostered a vision that gradually took hold throughout much of society. At the center of that vision was a moral view of human beings, "ordinary people" in the process of history, a view which held that systems should be designed for human beings and not the other way around. The dignity of the individual in this perspective could only be realized through active citizenship. That in turn required a society of citizens, or a democracy of participation, where individuals had a direct voice in the making of decisions about their own lives. We were expressing a rising dissatisfaction with all institutions, even liberal and expressly humane ones, that absorbed power into their hierarchies. Instead of "taking power," we imagined creating the new power out of the raw material of apathy. At the same time, new measurements of excellence, such as the quality of life and personal relationships, were to take on greater significance than external status symbols and material monuments, in both our lives and the existence of our country.

These perceptions and values are an ongoing legacy of our generation. They do not always prevail in our culture or politics today, nor are they always recognized as arising from the sixties. Yet their enduring and widening impact can be seen in a variety of ways. Enlightened business and labor viewpoints now concur that humane treatment of the worker, including participation in decision making, is not only an ethical good, but a plus for productivity as well. . . .

These findings were also reflected in an extraordinary work of social science, *Habits of the Heart,* published by a UC Berkeley team of researchers in 1985. One of their purposes was to review and revive the nineteenth-century French writer, Alexis de Toqueville [sic], whose observations in *Democracy in America* in some ways foreshadowed the theme of participatory democracy. De Toqueville [sic] celebrated the town meetings and voluntary associations that constituted the rich political core of early nineteenth-century American society and warned of the dangers of rampant individualism, under which participation could atrophy and be replaced by imperial forms of rule. The authors of *Habits of the Heart,* responding to the resurgent individualism of the religious right of the eighties, cited local chapters of the Campaign for Economic Democracy among the many representative efforts at restoring an emphasis on democracy at the community level, noting that "the morally concerned social movement, informed by republican and biblical sentiments, has stood us in good stead in the past and may still do so again."

These conclusions and many others like them represent nothing less than the maturing of the awkward formulation of *The Port Huron Statement* into the cultural vocabulary of the mainstream of American life.

The logical question then is why the New Left did not succeed in building an organized and permanent leftist presence on the American political spectrum? Why did we produce so few political leaders? Why did we, who were so able to shake existing institutions, leave so little behind? Part of me inclines to the view of the New Left's better administrative leaders, like Paul Booth and Richie Rothstein, that our profound distrust of leadership and structure doomed us to failure on the level of political organization.

But the American political system is inhospitable to third parties, isolating them before gradually absorbing their ideas and activists into the two-party system. The most that could have been organized out of the New Left might have been an "adult" SDS, a kind of American Civil Liberties Union for social justice. Of course, without the Kennedy assassinations the history of our generation would have been different, and I believe most of the New Left would have found itself politically involved as part of a new governing coalition by the end of the sixties, just as Millie Jeffrey's generation became linked with the politics of the New Deal. But it was not to be. Instead, in Jack Newfield's summary phrase, we became "might have beens."

In the end, most of the sixties generation was not narrowly political. Most were not interested in attaining office but in changing life-styles. They were not so interested in being opinion makers as in changing the climate of opinion. Most felt personally ambiguous or distrustful of ambition and power and lacked the qualities that carried others into political careers. They were more likely to become professors (Todd Gitlin, Bill Ayers, Dick Flacks, John Froines, Bob Ross), labor leaders (Karen Nussbaum, Richie Rothstein, Paul Booth), social service advocates (Vivian Rothstein, Mary Varela, Casey Hayden), lawyers (Dan Siegel, Anne Weills, Bernardine Dohrn and six other former members of the Weather Underground), filmmakers (Bruce Gilbert, Paula Weinstein, Mark Rosenberg, Thom Mount), or therapists and counselors (Connie Brown, Andrea Cousins), than politicians. But if few of us went from protest marching to political office, the changes that the sixties generation made in public attitudes nevertheless became a factor that all politicians had to take seriously, including Ronald Reagan, who spent most of his presidency trying to reverse the legacy of the sixties.

There are such strong feelings of nostalgia on the one hand and loss on the other among so many who went through those times because the sixties were about more than practical reforms. It was a decade not focused simply on specific goals, like the organization of American workers in the thirties or the issue agendas of the Populist and Socialist parties at the century's beginning. The goal of the sixties was a larger transformation. Perhaps the only parallels might have been during the times of the American Revolution and Civil War, when individuals became caught up in remaking America itself. The goal of the sixties was, in a sense, the completion of the vision of the early revolutionaries and the abolitionists, for Tom Paine and Frederick Douglass wanted even more than the Bill of Rights or Emancipation Proclamation. True democrats, they wanted the fulfillment of the American promise through a different quality of relations between people, between government and governed, a participatory democracy within a genuinely human community. The sixties movements were inspired toward that loftier goal and were blocked in the quest by the intervention of fate.

Like the American revolutionary period, the awakening of the early sixties was a unique ingathering of young people—many of them potential leaders—to proclaim and then try to carry out a total redemptive vision. This visionary quest is what bound each of us together in a community, from Gandhian Freedom Riders to disillusioned Marxists. The gods of our parents had failed or become idols. Then a new spiritual force came in 1960, to move in the world. We felt ourselves to be the prophets of that force. When we first used the term *revolution,* it was not about overthrowing power but about overcoming hypocrisy, through a faithfulness to a democratic and spiritual heritage. Then came rejection and both physical and spiritual martyrdom, and later a discovery that we ourselves were not pure. We faltered, lost our way, became disoriented above all by death upon death. What began on a soaring spirit suddenly was over, perhaps to be finished permanently. We who claimed to be masters of our future discovered that we were not.

The sacrifices were many, and there were no distinguished service medals. I found it revealing that there is nowhere a factual summary of all the suffering that people went through—shootings, beatings, firings, expulsions, arrests, not to mention psychological pain—to achieve quite elementary goals in the sixties decade. It is as if the sacrifices were not worthy of record, but should be suppressed and forgotten. With the help of Eric Dey, a UCLA graduate student, I developed a minimal estimate of our untabulated sacrifices:

• During the southern civil rights movement (1960–68), at least 28 activists were killed, and 31,000 people were arrested. There is no calculating the numbers who were beaten, fired, or expelled from schools.

• In the black civil disorders of 1965–70, 188 people were killed, at least 7,612 were injured, and another 52,920 were arrested.

• In the campus and antiwar protests of 1965–71, for which data are woefully unrecorded, at least 14 were killed, thousands were injured or expelled from colleges, and at least 26,358 were arrested.

• It therefore would be safe to estimate that in a society priding itself on its openness, 100,000 arrests of protesters occurred in the decade of the sixties. They were prophets without honor in their time.

For all these reasons, the sixties leave a sense of troubling incompleteness and shortcoming alongside that of proud achievement. But if the time has remained difficult to capture, it is also possible that the sixties are not over. The decade itself was perhaps only the beginning of a time of vast change that is not yet fulfilled. Our generation, after all, has only lived into its middle years. Why conclude that life's most powerful moments already are behind us? If the sixties are not over, it is up to the sixties generation to continue trying to heal our wounds, find our truth, and apply our ideals with a new maturity to our nation's future.

Since 1980, however, the official mood of the nation has been contrary to a spirit of reconciliation. Rather, the tone has been one of escape from bitter realities toward an immortalizing vision of nostalgia proposed by President Reagan. There has been a strong pressure to wipe out the "Vietnam syndrome," which allegedly left us prostrate before our enemies. Thanks to greater military spending, we are told that America is "back," is "standing tall," that the "naysayers" have been vanquished. I find this stance to be an armed reminder of the most rigid view of my parents' generation when they wanted to impose the lessons of their experience on their children and grandchildren. But my personal experience gives me faith that this official obsession with restoring a mythic past will give way to wiser consciousness in the era ahead. . . .

𝕏 E S S A Y S

As the last two documents illustrate, the 1960s remain contested terrain on which many of the decade's old battles continue to be fought. Indeed, much of the historical work on the new radicalism of the 1960s has been written by men and women who themselves participated in the era's remarkable events. In the first essay, historians Maurice Isserman of Hamilton College and Michael Kazin of Georgetown University, themselves former New Left activists, offer a sympathetic but balanced account of the movement's failures and successes. The second essay, by writer Rick Perlstein, surveys new books on the sixties by a younger generation of historians who remember the sixties dimly, if at all, and who seem much less constrained by the decade's memories (and loyalties).

The Contradictory Legacy of the Sixties

MAURICE ISSERMAN AND MICHAEL KAZIN

As easy it was to tell black from white
It was all that easy to tell wrong from right
And our choices were few and the thought never hit
That the one road we travelled would ever shatter and split.

—"Bob Dylan's Dream,"

from *The Freewheelin' Bob Dylan*

I

So wrote Bob Dylan, not yet twenty-two years old, in what was in 1963 a prophetic—or at least prematurely nostalgic—elegy for the illusions of youthful commitment. Shatter and split the new radicalism certainly did, in the space of only a decade and in a way that left many of its adherents embittered and its historical reputation in tatters. After Ronald Reagan's two victories at the polls, the sixties, viewed at the time as the beginning of a new era of reform, seem instead a short interregnum amid the larger rightward shift in American politics that began during Franklin Roosevelt's troubled second term and continued through the 1980s. What difference, if any, did the decade of cultural and political upheaval encapsulated by the rise and fall of the New Left make?

Though the origins of the New Left can be traced back at least to the mid-1950s, radicalism only began to reemerge as a significant undercurrent on American campuses in 1960 when a heretofore obscure group called the Student League for Industrial Democracy (SLID) renamed itself Students for a Democratic Society (SDS). Under the leadership of two recent University of Michigan graduates, Al Haber and Tom Hayden, SDS became a small but increasingly influential network of campus activists. At its official founding convention, held in Port Huron, Michigan, in 1962, SDS adopted a manifesto declaring that the ideas and organizational forms familiar to earlier generations of Marxian radicals were outmoded. The "Port Huron Statement" dedicated SDS to the achievement of "participatory democracy" inside its own movement and within the larger society. Initially engaged on a wide variety of fronts, from civil rights to nuclear disarmament to university reform, by the mid-1960s, many SDS founders had left the campuses to concentrate on community organizing in the slums of northern cities. Ironically, just as SDS leaders began to forsake the campus, the Berkeley Free Speech Movement in the fall of 1964 and the Vietnam teach-in movement in the spring of 1965 signaled the growing responsiveness of college students to radical ideas.

The steady escalation of the war in Vietnam from the spring of 1965 up to the Spring of 1968 spurred the growth of both a broadly based antiwar movement and of the campus New Left, and led the latter to adopt increasingly militant rhetoric and tactics. By the fall of 1967 the New Left had moved "from dissent to resistance." Teach-ins and silent vigils gave way to the seizure of campus buildings and disruptive street demonstrations. Under new and younger leadership SDS continued to grow, and eventually some of its original leaders, like Tom Hayden and Rennie Davis, were attracted back to antiwar organizing from the slums of Newark and Chicago.

In the aftermath of the bloody confrontations at the Chicago Democratic convention in the summer of 1968, and the indictment of Hayden, Davis, and six others for "conspiracy," most New Leftists abandoned whatever hopes they still cherished of reforming the existing political system. Declaring themselves allies and disciples of third-world Communist revolutionaries like Mao Zedong and Che Guevara, SDS leaders now conceived their principal role as one of "bringing the war home" to the "imperialist mother country." In 1969, SDS collapsed as small, self-proclaimed revolutionary vanguards squabbled over control of the organization, but the ranks of student radicals continued to increase through the 1969–70 school year. Polls showed that as many as three quarters of a million students identified themselves as adherents of the New Left. The national student strike that SDSers had long dreamed of but had never been able to pull off became a reality in the spring of 1970. Spontaneously organized in response to the invasion of Cambodia and the killing of four students at Kent State University, it effectively paralyzed the nation's university system.

The American writer John Dos Passos, describing the revolutionary exaltation and illusion of 1919 in his novel, *Three Soldiers,* declared: "Any spring is a time of overturn, but then Lenin was alive, the Seattle general strike had seemed the beginning of the flood instead of the beginning of the ebb." It soon became apparent to despairing New Leftists that the spring of 1970 marked a similar "beginning of the ebb." Former SDS president Carl Oglesby was one among many who took to the hills (literally, in his case) at the start of the new decade. As Oglesby would say in a bittersweet reflection years later: "There were a lot of good, righteous people showing up in places like Vermont and New Hampshire in those days. Lots of parties, great reefer, good acid. Lovely friends . . . I remember it with great fondness. It was almost the best part of the struggle. The best part of the struggle was the surrender."

When the sixties were over, it seemed to many former activists that they had accomplished nothing. The "participatory democracy" the New Left sought in its early years remained a utopian dream; the "revolutionary youth movement" it built in its waning years had collapsed; the tiny "new communist parties" that one-time New Leftists tried to organize in the 1970s only illustrated once again the wisdom of Marx's comments in *The Eighteenth Brumaire* on the way history repeatedly turns tragedy into farce.

Yet in surveying the ruins of these successive political failures, it is striking that while "nothing" was accomplished by the New Left in its short life, everything was different afterward. If the years that followed the 1960s did not live up to the hopeful vision of the future sketched out in the Port Huron Statement, still they did not mark a return to the previous status quo. America certainly became a more politically and culturally contentious society because of what happened in the 1960s—and in some respects it also became a more just, open, and egalitarian one. On the coldest, darkest, and most reactionary days of the Reagan ascendancy, there was more radical belief and activity to be seen in the United States than was present anytime in the 1950s. As an organizational presence the New Left had vanished, but as a force in American political culture its impact continued to be felt.

The New Left was shaped by and came to embody a profound dislocation in American culture, and, in the end, it had more impact on the ideas that Americans had about themselves and their society than on structures of power that governed their lives. Young radicals articulated a critique of "everyday life" in the United States, which was, in time, taken up by millions of people who had little notion of where those ideas originated. In the course of the sixties and seventies, many Americans came to recognize and reject the prevalence of racial and sexual discrimination, to ask new questions about the legitimacy of established institutions and authority, and to oppose military adventures abroad. To understand the New Left's role in this transition, historians need both to explore the organizational dynamics of radical groups like SDS and to analyze the ways in which American culture shaped the young radicals who emerged to challenge the received wisdom of their society.

II

. . . "Politics," as conventionally defined, was only of secondary importance in the rise of the new radicalism of the 1960s. The emergence and celebration of generationally defined life-styles preceded the appearance of the New Left and, for most Americans throughout the 1960s, continued to overshadow the fate of organizations, candidates, and causes. As contemporary observers and historians have since agreed, the phenomenon of the "baby boom" determined the contours of the sixties' dizzying pace of change. Between 1945 and 1946, the birth rate in the United States leaped 20 percent. Thereafter, it continued to climb, peaking in 1957 when over four million babies were born in a single year. The impact of this unexpected development, which reversed a century-long decline in the birth rate, had effects everywhere—from the spread of suburbia to the transformation of the university system. At each stage of its life, the baby-boom generation has proven to be a voracious consumer of material goods, from diapers and cribs to microwave ovens and video cassette recorders. It has also shown an enormous capacity to absorb new forms of entertainment, new images, and new ideas about politics and society.

Starting with the Davy Crockett fad of the early 1950s, cultural entrepreneurs seeking to tap the disposable income controlled by the nation's young perfected their pitch and inadvertently helped shape a distinctive generational consciousness. Hollywood soon learned to gear its offerings to the tastes of the new generation. While ostensibly condemning juvenile delinquency, such movies as *The Wild One* and *Rebel without a Cause* in effect established actors like Marlon Brando and James Dean as icons of youthful rebellion. Elvis Presley's fusion of country music and rhythm and blues combined with the frank sensuality of his stage presence signaled the arrival of a new musical era; major record producers were quick to take note and seek imitators. To a far greater extent than their parents, baby boomers grew up surrounded by and at home in a world of mass culture and mass consumption. And it was precisely because they were so deeply imbued with the promise and assumptions of that world—believing the advertisers who told them that a time of unending affluence and total freedom of choice was at hand—that they were willing, at least for a few years, to forego the quest for economic security and its material tokens that obsessed the older generation. The purveyors of mass culture were thus unintentionally acting as the gravediggers of a depression-inspired and cold war-reinforced conservative cultural consensus.

As a college education became the norm rather than a privilege, millions of young people found themselves in a new socially determined developmental stage that extended adolescence into the middle twenties or even later. By the early 1960s, "youth communities" had sprung up on the outskirts of college campuses, often in the cheap housing available on the edge of black ghettos. There, surrounded by their peers, largely freed from adult supervision and spared for the time being the responsibilities of career, family, and mortgage, young people began to experiment with new manners, mores, stimulants, sexual behavior, and, in due time, forms of political expression. . . .

At precisely the moment when the first wave of the baby boom reached the college campuses, the southern civil rights movement exploded into newspaper headlines and the nation's consciousness through the use of an innovative strategy of mass, nonviolent civil disobedience. The 1960 southern sit-in movement, which attracted fifty thousand participants in the space of a few months, was sparked by four black college freshmen in Greensboro, North Carolina, who decided on their own to challenge the segregation of a Woolworth's lunch counter. Rennie Davis, a founder of SDS who was a sophomore at Oberlin College in 1960, recalled: "Here were four students from Greensboro who were suddenly all over *Life* magazine. There was a feeling that they were us and we were them, and a recognition that they were expressing something we were feeling as well and they'd won the attention of the country."

For sympathetic college students, the civil rights movement blended the appeal of "making history" with the potential for testing one's own sense of personal "authenticity" through an existential (and for those who joined the freedom rides or the voter registration campaigns in the South, quite genuine) brush with danger. In her book *Personal Politics,* historian Sara Evans described the compelling example set by the young black volunteers of the Student Non-Violent Coordinating Committee: "Eating, sleeping, working side by side day after day, SNCC activists created a way of life more than a set of ideas." . . .

The superheated ideological atmosphere of 1950s cold war America played an important role in shaping the political outlook of college students at the start of the new decade. They had grown up in a political culture that stressed the division of the world into absolute good and absolute evil, freedom versus totalitarianism. The cold war was justified in much the same terms that had been used in the recent victorious struggle against the Axis powers. Yet, beneath the surface agreement among conservatives and liberals on the need to contain the Soviet threat, certain ambiguities still lurked. For many Americans, the cold war summoned up an uncritical identification with the emerging national security state. But some others, loyal to the liberatory and antiracist beliefs that had fueled the war against fascism, tendered their support for the "free world" on a more conditional basis. . . .

Norman Mailer in his 1957 essay "The White Negro" had already begun to refer to American society as "totalitarian"; in the decade that followed, a lot of loose talk would be heard on the Left comparing Nazi Germany and the United States. But one need not have subscribed to such misleading analogies to be drawn to the moral imagery and lessons provided by the Nuremburg trials. In fact, if resisters to evil could be found even under the extreme conditions of Nazi oppression, could less be expected of those who enjoyed the protections of liberal democracy? Joan Libby, a Mount Holyoke College student and antiwar activist in the mid-1960s, became an organizer for the National Moratorium Committee in 1969. Her parents disapproved of her antiwar activities, and she found herself relying on the Nuremburg analogy in her arguments with them:

> Both my parents were Jewish, and one of the things I had had to learn about, of course, was the Holocaust, and one of the lessons in that always is that you shouldn't stand by and think somebody else is going to do it. That's a serious lesson, I think, for susceptible young people like myself—a powerful one. It becomes sort of an imperative. There's always a double-edged sword when you bring people up with the notion that you should take [moral] positions on things. You never know where they'll come out.

In 1961, John F. Kennedy had sounded the call for a selfless dedication to the (vaguely defined) national cause, significantly posed in terms of individual choice: "Ask not what your country can do for you, ask what you can do for your country." The same spirit of self-sacrificing idealism that led many students to volunteer for the Peace Corps led others to the civil rights movement. Many young white volunteers felt that their civil rights activism was sanctioned from on high (although SNCC's black field workers never shared that particular illusion, knowing how unresponsive the Justice Department was to their requests for protection against racist attacks). A succession of emotional and political blows followed, with the cumulative effect of redirecting the spirit of idealism away from the official agenda being set in Washington: there was fear of nuclear annihilation during the Cuban missile crisis in October 1962, indignation over the brutal treatment of civil rights demonstrators in Birmingham in the spring of 1963, shock at Kennedy's assassination that fall, distrust the following summer as a result of the Democratic convention's "compromise" that prevented the seating of Fannie Lou Hamer and other black delegates from the Mississippi Freedom Democratic Party, and dismay over the escalation of the war in Vietnam in the spring of 1965.

In the early-to-mid 1960s, an essential prop of the old order gave way in the minds of tens of thousands of young people. In more jaded times, like those which followed the Vietnam War and the Watergate scandal, disbelief in the official pronouncements of American foreign-policy makers would lead primarily to cynicism and apathy; but, in the 1960s, when the fervor of cold war liberalism was still a potent force, such disillusionment was often the prelude to an intensely moralistic conversion to political activism.

Bob Dylan's rapid rise to fame was emblematic of the newly emerging cultural and political sensibility. Dylan's first album, a combination of folk and blues interpretations and his own ironic ballads, was released in February 1962. It sold an unremarkable five thousand copies in its first year. But Dylan's second album, released in May of 1963, found a broad new audience. *The Freewheelin' Bob Dylan,* which featured protest songs like "Blowin' in the Wind," "Masters of War," and "A Hard Rain's A Gonna Fall," sold 200,000 copies by July 1963. The following month, Peter, Paul, and Mary released a single of Dylan's "Blowin' in the Wind" that sold over 300,000 copies in less than two weeks, making it the first protest song ever to grace the hit parade.

Where were Dylan's new fans coming from, and what message did they seek in his music? "Blowin' in the Wind" was simultaneously a song about coming-of-age ("How many roads must a man walk down / Before you call him a man?") and about moral choice ("Yes, 'n' how many times can a man turn his head / Pretending he just doesn't see?"), as well as a promise that those who understood its message would soon help redeem the nation ("The answer, my friend, is blowin' in the wind / The answer is blowin' in the wind"). Young Americans in the 1960s were not the first generation to feel that they were more sensitive to hypocrisy and injustice than their elders. But due to the structural and ideological framework that had emerged in postwar America, they were primed for an opening to the Left in the early 1960s. The demographic bulge, the delayed entry into the adult world, the encouragement of generational consciousness by advertisers, the cultural identification with outsiders and marginal groups, the inspirational example of the civil rights movement, and the paradoxical influence of cold war liberalism were the raw materials from which a mass New Left would be fashioned over the next few years.

III

The chief organizational beneficiary of these trends would be SDS. As the war and the protests it inspired escalated in the mid-1960s, SDS grew rapidly. This occurred despite the fact that, after organizing the first antiwar march on Washington in April 1965, its leaders disdained sponsorship of any more such events because they did not address the root issue of an imperialist foreign policy—"stopping the seventh Vietnam from now," as one slogan put it. But the policies SDS leaders chose to embrace or reject had little to do with the organization's growth. As Steve Max, an early leader of the group, recalled in a recent interview: "The progression in SDS was to be more and more movement and less and less organization. It was a situation of a movement looking for a place to happen."

There were national headlines in the spring of 1965 when SDS's antiwar march attracted some twenty thousand participants. By the end of that school year, the SDS National Office (NO) was receiving a flood of letters from individuals and groups eager to affiliate, from places like Dodge City Community College in Kansas not previously known as loci of radical activity. It was no longer necessary for SDS to organize chapters: they organized themselves. Many recruits were members of preexisting local groups who sought access to the resources and prestige that only a national organization could provide. . . .

The NO set up a system of campus "travelers" and regional offices, but these did little more than service existing chapters, distribute literature, and make an occasional statement to the media. New members were seldom "converted" to SDS ideology. If the SDS "old guard" had had its way, the organization would have functioned chiefly as a recruiting pool for future community organizers. Instead, reflecting the loosely formulated set of ideas, concerns, and political priorities that new members brought with them into the national organization, SDS chapters increasingly focused their efforts on resisting the war in Vietnam. Students did not become activists because they joined SDS; they joined SDS because they were already activists.

The SDS annual national conventions were important mainly as places where SDSers from around the country could make contacts and share experiences. Labored efforts to chart a coordinated national strategy (like an abortive "Ten Days to Shake the Empire" plan in 1968) were almost universally ignored by local chapters. To the extent that people in SDS chapters learned to speak a common language and pursue a common political agenda, they did so through a process of osmosis rather than central direction.

Just at the moment when it began to develop a significant national presence, SDS lost the ability to set its own agenda. Starting in 1965, SDS's concerns and the pace of its development were largely reactions to decisions being made in the White House and the Pentagon. The escalation of the Vietnam War thus simultaneously strengthened and weakened SDS. In the matter of a few months, it transformed the group from a small network of activists, most of whom knew one another, into a national movement with hundreds of chapters—and an organizational infrastructure that never managed to make the transition. And while the war galvanized protesters, it also bred frustration and extremism in their ranks. Vietnam was a particularly volatile issue around which to build a mass movement. No partial victories or breathing spaces could be won: the movement would either force the government to end the war, or it would fail. As a result the peace movement, with the New Left at its core, constantly swung back and forth between near-millennial expectations and dark and angry despair.

As the political climate changed after 1965, so did the New Left's cultural style. The new members who flooded into SDS (dubbed the "prairie power" contingent because so many of them came from places other than the usual urban centers of radical strength) were less likely to share a theoretical sophistication or intellectual ambitions of the group's founding generation. The new breed tended to be unschooled in and impatient with radical doctrine, intensely moralistic, suspicious of "elitism" and "bureaucracy," and immersed in the new cultural currents running through college towns.

In January 1966, three members of the newly organized SDS chapter at the University of Oklahoma were among those arrested in a marijuana raid on a private party in Norman. Newspapers throughout the country picked up the story, linking SDS with pot-smoking. The Norman police chief unabashedly revealed to local reporters that his suspicions of the students had been aroused by their politics as much as their alleged drug use: "Several of these people have been active in the Society [SDS]. . . . One of them had a receipt showing he had just joined the SDS." High bail was set for all the defendants, and two of them were locked up incommunicado in a state mental hospital for observation because of their long hair.

Jeff Shero, an SDS campus traveler and leading exponent of "prairie power" within the organization, visited Norman soon after the bust. He reported back to the NO that the police had assembled prescription drugs and antiwar literature for sensationalized photographs. Local newspapers reported that a book on "homosexuality" was found in the raided apartment. They neglected to mention the name of the book's author—Sigmund Freud. Shero was both indignant and amused at the crudity of the official antics, but he concluded that the affair had not done SDS any real political harm. "The chapter probably isn't irreparably damaged," he wrote to the NO. "Chapter people were mixed as to the effect of the raid, some actually thought it would be beneficial."

Steve Max and a few other "old guard" leaders of SDS had a different reaction. Speaking in a tone that reflected the assumptions of his earlier involvement with the Communist youth movement, Max regarded it a matter of "Socialist discipline" that "unless the organization votes to carry on a Legalize marijuana through a civil disobedience campaign, then our members ought not place themselves and the organization in a position where they can be put out of commission so easily." He wanted the Norman chapter suspended until it had, through some unspecified procedure, reformed itself. In a subsequent letter, he reiterated, "If we don't start to draw the line someplace we are going to wind up with a federation of dope rings instead of a national political organization."

But sentiment in the hinterland seemed to run in a completely opposite direction. One member from Ohio reported to the NO that news of the Norman arrests "strikes home in the Ohio area since a number of people including three friends have been arrested on charges involving pot." Although he realized that SDS might have good reasons to avoid involvement in a campaign to legalize pot-smoking, "nevertheless, I think this area is another expression of the lack of individual freedom in the society for an individual desiring to control his own life without interference."

The Norman SDS chapter was not suspended. Moreover, within a few years, SDS would not simply regard the use of drugs as a question of individual choice but would endorse it as yet another emblem of the revolutionary disaffection of the young. "Our whole life is a defiance of Amerika," the newspaper of the Weatherman SDS faction exulted in 1969. "It's moving in the streets, digging sounds, smoking dope . . . fighting pigs." By the late sixties, marijuana and LSD were circulating freely at national SDS conventions.

Underlying the ability and willingness of so many young radicals, along with others of their generation, to experiment with new "life-styles" (including drugs) was the economic prosperity of the postwar era. New Leftists took affluence for granted and despised its corrupting influence, unlike the Socialists and Communists of the 1930s who denounced capitalism for its inability to provide the minimum decencies of life to the poor. . . .

Earlier generations of radicals had derided capitalism as an anarchic, irrational system; the new radicals scorned the system because it was *too* rational, based on a soul-destroying set of technological and bureaucratic imperatives that stifled individual expression. From university reform, where the slogan was "I am a human being, do not fold, spindle, or mutilate," to draft resistance, where the buttons read "Not with my life, you don't," the New Left championed a form of radical individualism that was authentically American in derivation and flavor—ironically, all too "American" for the organizational well-being of the movement. For this deeply rooted individualism prepared the way for the development of a movement cult of "confrontation."

In the Communist, Socialist, and Trotskyist movements of the 1930s, young radicals had prided themselves on their analytic abilities, their skill in debate, their command of the intricacies of Marxist theory. In contrast, a kind of emotional and moral plain-speaking was the preferred rhetorical style among SDS leaders. Authenticity, usually described as "commitment," was the political and personal value New Leftists were most eager to display, a quality that could best be established by the willingness to "put your body on the line." Overcoming any lingering squeamishness about breaking the law (and plate-glass windows) was the ultimate "gut-check" that alone could establish whether you were "part of the problem or part of the solution."

The political deficiencies of this personal stance were not lost on some SDSers, though they found themselves powerless to correct the situation. As early as 1965, Lee Webb, former SDS national secretary, complained in an international document that "SDS influences its membership to become more militant rather than more radical. . . . Calls to fight the draft, stop a troop train, burn a draft card, avoid all forms of liberalism, have become . . . the substitute for intellectual analysis and understanding." Late sixties SDS rhetoric, composed of equal parts Maoist jargon and black street rap, communicated little but the angry alienation of its practitioners. Nevertheless, it had a very potent appeal to the already-converted or would-be recruits in defining the cultural terrain of the movement—if you spoke the language, you were already a revolutionary. "Brothers," a high school student wrote to the NO in the late 1960s, "I sympathize with the movement and its goals. But information on what's going on is hard to come by in rural, conservative western Pennsylvania. Dig?"

By the late 1960s, SDS had grown to as many as a hundred thousand loosely affiliated members, while tens of thousands more could be counted as supporters of the movement. But off-campus, the New Left's activities, and the increasingly outrageous and opaque language in which they were justified, found few supporters. Ronald Reagan spoke for many Americans when he declared in the midst of the People's Park disorders in Berkeley in 1969 (which left one spectator dead from police buckshot), "If it's a blood bath they want, let it be now." The ferocity with which authorities sought to crack down on campus protest only exacerbated the appeal of extreme rhetoric and doctrines within SDS. In the summer of 1969 the organization splintered, with one small faction led by the Progressive Labor Party

(PLP) heading for the factories, and another small faction led by Weatherman heading for the "underground." Neither the PLP nor Weatherman enlisted more than a tiny fraction of SDS members under their banners, but Weatherman's cultural style—which included a fervent if erratic promotion of drugs, sex, and rock and roll—gave it a measure of influence on campuses that the dour dogmatists in the PLP were never able to match. In the early 1970s underground newspapers gave extensive coverage to Weatherman's bombings and "communiqués"; posters in college dorms invited Bernardine Dohrn and other Weatherman fugitives to seek shelter.

IV

The demise of SDS did not retard the flowering of cultural radicalism. From campus towns to the "youth ghettos" of big cities and even to American military bases in Vietnam, a diffuse set of "countercultural" ideas, symbols, and behaviors circulated. "Liberation" was easy to achieve, since it was defined as the practice of a communal, playful, and sensual life-style. While they often ignored or explicitly rejected the politics advocated by "power-tripping" radicals, those immersed in the countercul-ture embraced beliefs the earlier New Left had first popularized. Alternative, partici-patory communities based on decentralized, small-scale technology and an ethic of loving mutuality had all been prefigured by the Port Huron Statement, the civil rights movement, and SDS's community-organizing projects. Garbed in apolitical dress, this vision continued to attract believers (many of them from working-class back-grounds) who never would have considered attending an SDS meeting. In the mid-1970s, pollster Daniel Yankelovich called attention to the ways in which new attitudes toward authority, sexual morality, and self-fulfillment had spread from elite college campuses to much of the younger population: "Indeed," he wrote, "we are amazed by the rapidity with which this process is now taking place."

As the sixties ended, some radical leaders withdrew from the increasingly fractious realm of left-wing politics to join rural communes or mystical cults, or to embrace various "new age" therapies. The well-publicized voyage of Jerry Rubin from yippie revolutionary to yuppie networker is the best known, if not most repre-sentative, example of this process. Paul Potter, a former SDS president, was less self-serving and more reflective when he recorded his own painful withdrawal from the movement in his 1971 book *A Name for Ourselves.* Potter reaffirmed his belief in the values and concerns that had initially led him to the New Left, but rejected organized politics as a means of achieving a better world:

> I am less involved in changing America. . . . This does not mean that I am less angry or upset or horrified by this country than before. If anything, I am more profoundly and intuitively aware, day to day, of what an ugly society this is and how desperately it needs change. But my information comes less and less from the papers—more and more from my own experience with it. . . .

The emergence of a new feminist movement had the paradoxical effect of draw-ing many New Left women into more active political participation while hastening the political withdrawal of many men. In the late 1960s and early 1970s few male leaders of the New Left escaped being taken to task for sexism by women in the movement. What more decisive step could men take to indicate repentance for past misdeeds than to abdicate any further claim to leadership? With the movement foundering, the "politically correct" decision often served to rationalize personal inclinations. Coinciding with the decline of the antiwar movement, a widespread and decentralized network of women's "consciousness raising" groups, health clinics, bookstores, newspapers, publishing houses, and similar enterprises emerged, giving new meaning to the original New Left call for a "beloved community."

V

"The sixties are over," literary critic Morris Dickstein wrote in 1977, "but they remain the watershed of our recent cultural history; they continue to affect the ambiance of our lives in innumerable ways." The passage of more than a decade and Ronald Reagan's two terms in office have not lessened the truth of that observation. In the late 1980s, the conservative victors found it politically convenient to lump together the vestiges of New Deal–Great Society liberalism with the memory of the New Left to justify reversing both the social legislation and the "moral permissiveness" associated with the sixties. They were quite successful in cutting back or abolishing domestic programs that had no wealthy or powerful constituency. But as the New Right's plaintive refrain "Let Reagan be Reagan" indicated, conservatives did not have everything their own way in the 1980s. The right was forced to govern within a cultural environment that, in significant ways, limited what it could accomplish. Conservatives had to repackage many of their ideas and policies to appeal to a public that had caught a "democratic distemper" and was unwilling to defer automatically to its new governors. . . .

Right-wing movements also sought to exploit the mood of morally committed idealism that sixties radicals had done so much to create; in some instances, they proved more successful than their left-wing counterparts. The impulse to expose and attack illegitimate authority was turned against legislators who tried to "solve problems by throwing money at them," against a Democratic president who could neither free American hostages nor punish their captors, and against liberal judges perceived as protecting muggers, drug-pushers, or pornographers. At the same time, a vigorous libertarian spirit, itself a legacy of the sixties, acted as a countervailing force, preventing the New Right from imposing its version of morality on law and society. America's political culture in the 1980s thus contained enough contradictory impulses to baffle the pundits who assumed that Reagan's electoral victories represented a fundamental rightward shift.

American politics in the past decade has actually been characterized by the existence of a deep divide between two camps: one, a broad but disorganized Left, has attempted to defend and develop ideas, issues, and "life-styles" that emerged in the sixties; the other, an equally diverse but far better organized Right, has built its own influence around popular revulsion from those same images and practices. New Leftists thus succeeded in transforming American politics—though not according to the sanguine script laid out at Port Huron. The continued influence of the movements of the 1960s has been most pronounced in five aspects of contemporary American society: intellectual life, perceptions of race and of gender, foreign policy, and the language of politics itself. . . .

Significantly, many former radicals made careers in the "information industry," as academics, journalists, and media specialists. Conservative social scientists have done much viewing-with-alarm of this phenomenon. They blame a left-wing "new class" for undermining the public's faith in both domestic institutions and U.S. foreign policy. Opinion surveys of the "media elite" conducted by Robert Lichter and Stanley Rothman in the late 1970s found that print and electronic journalists and filmmakers overwhelmingly endorsed "strong affirmative action for blacks," as well as women's right to abortions; a near-majority agreed that the "U.S. exploits the Third World and causes poverty." Writing in *Partisan Review* in 1986, sociologist Paul Hollander condemned the Left's alleged "domination of the public political discourse" on campus, complaining that while its adherents may work "within the system," they are "without any sense of allegiance towards it." Prominent neoconservatives like Norman Podhoretz, Midge Decter, and Hilton Kramer sound similar alarms about the radical fifth columnists they believe have debauched American culture.

While these attacks on the "new class" suffer from hyperbole, they do gesture at a truth about contemporary thought. Radicals probably played a larger role in the universities and the media in the 1980s than at any previous time in American history. In the fields of history and literature, the most innovative scholars have been those who sympathetically illuminate the lives and thought of subaltern groups and "deconstruct" the works and reputations of famous writers and other authorities. Different schools of Marxism, feminism, and radical linguistic theory infuse this work, which, in the spirit of the New Left, questions not just established ideas (for that is the perpetual task of good scholarship) but the methods used to create them and the consequences that flow from their application in society. Far from having cloistered themselves, as some left-wing critics have charged, radical scholars have shown considerable concern for making their views available to a nonacademic audience. Radical perspectives, albeit somewhat diluted ones, find their way into a surprising number of mainstream venues, from National Public Radio programming to the op-ed pages of the *New York Times* and the *Wall Street Journal,* to the Smithsonian's National Museum of American History, to historical sites like Harpers Ferry and Colonial Williamsburg (where blacksmiths in period dress pepper their narratives with insights culled from recent literature about slavery and abolitionism by such radical scholars as John Blassingame, Eugene Genovese, and Eric Foner). . . .

Since the 1960s, the politics of race has been a major battleground between Left and Right. On the one hand, "new class" individuals and institutions exhibit a heightened level of racial sensitivity. The study of the history and culture of minority groups is a staple of public education, at least in urban areas. Black history was the subject of the most popular television event of the 1970s ("Roots"), while a black family served as the model of domesticity on the most popular situation comedy of the 1980s ("The Cosby Show"), and Oprah Winfrey, black hostess of the most popular daytime television talk show, portrayed her own career as the product of struggles by Sojourner Truth, Harriet Tubman, and Fannie Lou Hamer.

Millions of middle-class whites have joined with blacks in establishing a firm line demarcating acceptable from unacceptable public conduct and expression regarding race. Together they have succeeded in delegitimating beliefs that were the norm among white Americans only a generation earlier. Since the mid-1970s, any nationally prominent public figure who has castigated blacks as a people, even with humorous intent, has quickly lost reputation, employment, or both. Consider the firings of agriculture secretary Earl Butz in 1975 for telling a racist joke; of base-ball executive Al Campanis in 1987 for questioning, on a television show commemo-rating the anniversary of Jackie Robinson's major league debut, whether blacks had "the necessities" to make good managers; and of network football commentator Jimmy "the Greek" Snyder for claiming that blacks were bred by slaveholders to be faster and stronger than whites and for wanting to reserve front-office jobs for the latter. A record of hostility to the civil rights movement, even in the absence of evidence of personal racial prejudice, can also destroy careers. Judge Robert Bork's nomination to the Supreme Court was fatally damaged by the revelation that he had described the public accommodations section of the 1964 Civil Rights Act as embodying "a principle of unsurpassed ugliness," while Arizona governor Evan Meacham inspired a powerful impeachment movement when he refused to recognize Martin Luther King's birthday as a state holiday. The black leader, who, in his life-time, was harassed by the FBI, mistrusted by the presidents he dealt with, and openly despised by millions of whites, is today a national icon.

But the new consensus on racial equality is far from universal. The Boston bus-ing riots of the mid-1970s, the 1986 assault on three blacks who had the misfortune of having their car break down in the white Howard Beach neighborhood of New York City, and other events have revealed a bitter fraction of white working-class America that lashes out against those regarded as threats to its homes, jobs, and personal safety. Moreover, in the 1980s, students on major college campuses like Dartmouth, Penn State, and the University of Massachusetts (Amherst) engaged in racial slurs and, on a few occasions, even violence, demonstrating that segregation (albeit of an informal, interpersonal kind) still plagued these overwhelmingly white institutions. By opposing affirmative action (in the name of "equal opportunity") and welfare programs, conservative politicians have both contributed to and benefited from such conflicts.

Meanwhile, many middle-class whites share the perception that a black "under-class" has become fatally trapped within a nexus of family dissolution, drug abuse, and crime, past all reasonable hope of salvation. Radicals and liberals won an important victory when they transformed the public language and imagery of race. But at a time when racial inequality has become primarily a question of access to wealth and secure employment, they have, for the most part, fallen into a puzzled, if not indifferent, silence about issues more complicated than Jimmy the Greek's notions of slavery.

Attitudes about women and women's issues have undergone a similar change, taking a large cultural step forward while suffering a political step back, or at least sideward, in the struggle for equality of the sexes. The central ideological tenet of the new feminist movement was the idea that "the personal is political." The most intimate and seemingly mundane details of private life—housework and childcare, among many others—were seen as fundamentally linked to social power. In the late 1960s and early 1970s, feminists struck an enormously rich vein of anger and insight about personal issues that American radical movements had never system-atically addressed before.

The mass media, initially inclined to dismiss the new feminists with the trivializ-ing designation "bra-burners," by the mid-1970s made a dramatic about-face in their treatment of many of the movement's concerns. Notions like "equal pay for equal work" were easily assimilated into public discourse; today most young middle-class women routinely expect to have access to the same careers and to receive the same compensation as men. What is surprising, in retrospect, is how quickly other, more highly charged, issues—rape, abortion, family violence, incest—began to attract respectful coverage in the daily press and on television. Talk shows routinely broadcast heated discussions about sexuality, day care, and birth control. . . .

Feminists have succeeded in establishing a new "common sense" about gender roles among the urban middle class—and beyond. By the mid-1980s, according to a synthesis of opinion polls, a majority of Americans agreed with positions that, at the end of the 1960s, were the province of radical feminists. They supported federally subsidized day-care centers, sex education for the young, and the idea that men and women should share housework and child rearing equally. Women from constituencies that the New Left had tended to write off—the white working class, the Catholic church, the suburbs—came to embrace feminist ideas and proposals in the course of the 1970s even though many still feel constrained to preface their new beliefs with the disclaimer, "I'm no women's libber, but . . ." It was as if American society had been waiting for decades, with mounting nervousness and impatience, for some group to have the courage to come along and state the obvious about the problems between the sexes.

But, here too, not everyone was converted. The New Right accepted the challenge of "personal politics" and responded by organizing its own network of women activists. Phyllis Schlafly's Eagle Forum, the right-to-life movement, and similar groups proved quite adept at stirring, articulating, and channeling fears about the destruction of the male-headed "traditional family." In tandem with rising conservative politicians, they were able to block passage of the Equal Rights Amendment (despite the support the ERA consistently received in national polls). As a result, organized feminism stalled and began to be described, even by some Democrats, as merely another "special interest." . . .

The politics of the two major parties also reflect the impact of sixties radicalism. The most direct influence appears within the Democratic party. In many areas, local Democratic activists began to move left during the 1968 presidential campaign and, in time, found their forces strengthened by an infusion of former New Leftists. By the 1980s, left Democrats represented a variety of "single-issue" movements—black, Chicano, feminist, environmentalist, peace, gay and lesbian, and elderly—as much as they did the party apparatus itself. Such organizations as the National Organization for Women, the Sierra Club, and SANE saw their memberships swell in the early 1980s and developed increasingly professional and intermittently powerful lobbies in Washington. Liberal and radical Democratic activists helped transform Jesse Jackson into a serious candidate for president, promoted Geraldine Ferraro's vice-presidential nomination in 1984, and set the anti-interventionist tenor of the party's foreign policy debates. To the dismay of many party officials in the South, and those elsewhere nostalgic for the days of Jim Farley and Richard Daley, "New Politics"-style Democrats increasingly supply the financial backing, political energy, and moral élan that keeps the party organization afloat.

Yet what gives life to one side also provides opportunity for the other. Since the 1960s, conservative Republicans have lured away traditional Democratic voters by portraying the GOP as the only safe haven for the white ethnic working class against the onslaught of the civil rights movement and the political and social insurgencies it spawned. After taking a Watergate-induced pause in the mid-1970s, this backlash intensified, as millions of white northern voters joined southerners in rejecting the presidential candidates of their own party whom they perceived as apostles of weakness abroad and captives of single-issue "special interests" at home. Meanwhile, the New Right was using the specter of a hedonistic, God-denying counterculture to raise funds and recruit activists. Thus both parties, each in its own way, still lived off energy generated in the 1960s.

Notions of "personal politics" took on a new meaning in the late 1980s as a series of prominent political figures fell victim to revelations about private moral transgressions. Circumstantial evidence of adultery derailed front-runner Gary Hart's 1988 presidential campaign, while the Supreme Court nomination of the conservative jurist Douglas Ginsburg collapsed amid reports that he had occasionally used marijuana. A libertarian impulse favoring open discussion of previously taboo subjects meshed with a lurid soap-opera-and-supermarket-tabloid-fed curiosity about the misdeeds of the highly placed. The unlucky offenders were punished not so much for having strayed from standards of behavior that relatively few American adults under the age of forty-five had themselves upheld, as for their lack of "authenticity": Hart's self-portrait of himself as a dedicated family man and Ginsburg's "law-and-order" stance were revealed as shams. . . .

Populism, of course, has long been a staple of American political discourse. Ignatius Donnelly, Huey Long, and Saul Alinsky were winning votes or building movements out of such material long before young radicals moved to urban slums in the early 1960s. The unique contribution of the new radicals was to broaden the scope of the populist critique, challenging the legitimacy of cultural as well as political and economic power structures.

In ways both trivial and serious, the example, language, and actions of sixties radicals offered millions of Americans a way to express the discontent generated by the triple debacle of Vietnam, Watergate, and seventies stagflation. Often it was the New Left's style rather than its politics that wound up being recycled in the 1970s and 1980s. Some otherwise law abiding "right-to-life" demonstrators risked arrest blockading abortion clinics while singing, in paraphrase of John Lennon, "All we are saying / is give life a chance." Campus conservatives distributed leaflets accusing Gulf Oil of "corporate murder" because the firm does business with the pro-Soviet government of Angola. New Leftists succeeded in exposing the bankrupt policies of the liberal state in the 1960s. But that very success activated right-wing critics of liberalism who championed a "counterculture" of their own, based on biblical injunctions, the patriarchal family, and the economic homilies of nineteenth-century capitalism.

The contradictory legacy of the sixties thus provides evidence of both the failures and successes of the new radicalism—"failures" that were sometimes unavoidable, and sometimes self-inflicted, and "successes" that usually were recognized and were often the opposite of what was intended. Richard Hofstadter wrote in *The Age of Reform* that while it may be "feasible and desirable to formulate ideal programs of reform, it is asking too much to expect that history will move . . . in a straight line to realize them." Despite the best efforts of the Reagan administration and the New Right, the 1980s did not represent a return to the "normalcy" of the

1950s. Young radicals never became serious contenders for state power, but the issues they raised and the language in which those issues were dramatized became the normal fare of American politics.

Whether scorned as pro-Communistic and nihilistic or smothered in bland nostalgia, the New Left's reputation in the late 1980s was not all that its founders might have hoped for. But the message of the young radicals had certainly been received.

Who Owns the Sixties?

RICK PERLSTEIN

On August 13, 1994, some quarter-million pilgrims journeyed to upstate New York to experience Woodstock II. They were searching for the spirit of the Sixties. What they found was a messy debate over whether that staggeringly commercialized event was a proper tribute to the decade, or its proper burial.

For many Sixties faithful, the commemoration was plainly a sacrilege, and it fell to Maurice Isserman, a historian at Hamilton College, to explain why the original Woodstock was superior. "Partially by design, partially by accident," he wrote in the *Philadelphia Inquirer,* the 1969 Woodstock "evoked and jumbled together many of the most cherished myths enshrined in the national self-image: self-reliance, agrarian simplicity, and providential mission"—this "despite the entrepreneurial ambitions of its promoters, its slick promotion, and the miracles of sound technology and stagecraft which made it possible."

Another historian, however, begged to differ. "Most of the big figures at Woodstock in 1969 were hucksters," insisted Thomas Sugrue of the University of Pennsylvania, quoted in a *Washington Post* story the same day. "They were trying to make a buck and trying to make a name." And what of those who cherish memories of Woodstock as the apotheosis of the good, the true, and the libidinal? "It was just a rock concert," said the professor, "and it was memorable for two reasons: because there were gate crashers, and because the weather was bad."

Isserman, now forty-nine, had been a reveler at Max Yasgur's farm and a member of Students for a Democratic Society. Sugrue, who is thirty-three, says his most powerful Sixties memory is of watching National Guard tanks roll down the riot-torn streets of his Detroit neighborhood; he was five years old at the time. Isserman and Sugrue are both historians of the Sixties, and they are contending over the interpretation of a decade that remains among the most powerful historical reference points in American politics. That grand theme of the 1960s—the generation gap—has come to Sixties scholarship, and it has come to stay.

Few historians are more aware of this gap, or have done more to widen it, than David Farber, who, at thirty-nine, is the elder statesman of the post-Sixties Sixties interpreters. His first book, *Chicago '68* (Chicago, 1988), presented that year's tempestuous Democratic National Convention from three different sympathetically presented perspectives: the protesters who came to Chicago to disrupt the convention, the cops who beat them, and the Daley administration officials who presided

---

"Who Owns the Sixties?" by Rick Perlstein, from *Lingua Franca* (May/June 1996). Reprinted by permission from *Lingua Franca: The Review of Academic Life,* published in New York. www.linguafranca.com.

over the whole mess. "I don't know if my book was the very first of its kind," says Farber in the faculty cafeteria at Barnard College, where he is assistant professor of history. "But it was certainly among the first studies to treat the Sixties as an era, an era that is *over.*"

When Farber's book was published, a review in the *Village Voice* by baby-boomer novelist Carol Anshaw brooked no such revisionism. Next to sidebars of dewy Sixties reminiscences by *Voice* staffers ("I was plotting the overthrow of my high school," began one), Anshaw argued that "perhaps [Farber] wasn't the person to write this book." His study didn't convince, she harrumphed, because he "had no experience of a decade that was primarily experiential."

At the Barnard cafeteria, Farber recalls snatches of this seven-year-old review verbatim: "She said that the book was 'dangerous' for 'giving the establishment its due.'" He pauses, and continues: "I think the Sixties generation of activists saw themselves as acting *in* history. 'The Whole World Is Watching'—they were literally chanting it in the streets. And that's the irony that's heated up this debate so much. Because in the end, well, maybe they weren't the historical agents of change quite as much as they hoped."

For Farber, this irony has powerful consequences for his generation of scholars. The task of writing about the Sixties, Farber argued in a 1994 polemic in *The Chronicle of Higher Education,* "has been complicated . . . by generational politics within the academy, as older scholars who participated in the Sixties defend inter-pretations that stem from their own experiences." His conclusion: "People in the academy are kidding themselves if they believe that a young scholar is not bucking the already long odds of finding and keeping a decent job if he or she challenges certain myths of the Sixties."

Not surprisingly, many of the tenured radicals beg to differ. Todd Gitlin, professor of journalism . . . and a former president of SDS, admires Farber's scholarly work. But he finds Farber's assault on his elders in the *Chronicle* to be "reeking of resent-ment," and rooted in a mythologization of its own: "It's conventional for young people today," says Gitlin, "to say that the Sixties people, whoever they were, had all the fun, and none of the AIDS, and were cushioned by endless prosperity."

Whatever the merit of Farber's charges, there's little doubt that younger scholars are challenging "myths of the Sixties" from any number of—often contradictory—angles. Some argue that the New Left was far broader-based than previously sup-posed. Others suggest that its base, and its impact, was extremely narrow. Still others believe that the real story of the Sixties was the rise of a grassroots, antiestablishment movement called . . . the New Right.

Dustups over "the Sixties" are as old as the Sixties themselves. In 1960, the radical sociologist C. Wright Mills boasted in his "Letter to the New Left" that, after decades of left-wing doldrums, radicalized students were finally turning the political tide against an entrenched liberalism. A book published the same year by M. Stanton Evans concurred, sort of. In *Revolt on Campus,* Evans argued that students' frustra-tions "with the conformity of liberalism" promised that the Sixties would be the decade of student conservatism.

By the early Seventies, though, a consensus about the decade had begun to form in the scholarly literature: A salutary upsurge of democratic promise at the beginning of the Sixties was subverted by the dark seeds contained within it. That unsparing thesis was codified most influentially by Rice historian Allen J. Matusow in his magisterial 1983 work, *The Unraveling of America: A History of Liberalism in the 1960s* (HarperPerennial). Matusow laid the decline of America's grand liberal tradition at the feet of student radicalism's excesses; and he exerted a quiet influence on the writing of movement veterans such as Todd Gitlin, James Miller, and Maurice Isserman. In 1987, this trio's works appeared in rapid succession: Gitlin marched through the signal events of the decade in his encyclopedia *The Sixties: Years of Hope, Days of Rage* (Bantam); Miller proffered a rich collective biography of SDS's early leadership in *"Democracy Is in the Streets": From Port Huron to the Siege of Chicago* (Simon & Schuster); and Isserman chronicled the political roots of the New Left in *If I Had a Hammer: The Death of the Old Left and the Birth of the New Left* (Basic). All three books related the story of the Sixties in terms of the inspiring rise and tragic fall of the student protest movement. They were sympathetic to student radicalism but sober-minded about its consequences. And, with their rich detail and acute analyses, they set a standard for the writing of Sixties history that has yet to be equaled.

The insider accounts of the Sixties kept on coming; more than a score appeared in 1987–1988 alone. And, for the most part, they followed the Gitlin-Miller-Isserman narrative arc, which has become known among historians as the "declension hypothesis." It goes something like this: As the Fifties grayly droned on, springs of contrarian sentiment began bubbling into the best minds of a generation raised in unprecedented prosperity but well versed in the existential subversions of the Beats and *Mad* magazine. At the beginning of the Sixties, students went south to fight for civil rights with the Student Nonviolent Coordinating Committee, and came back to elite universities with the audacious goal of changing the world. They created new kinds of political organizations, foremost among them SDS, which were driven by a vague ideal called "participatory democracy." The new politics was to be scrupulously non-hierarchical and pragmatic, promising a humane alternative to both sectarian radicalism and technocratic liberalism.

Meanwhile, in a haze of marijuana smoke, the counterculture tested the limits of personal freedom. At first, the hippies maintained an arm's-length relationship with the politicos. But as the Vietnam War escalated, the line between activists and Aquarian began to blur—to the detriment of each. Writers sympathetic to the counterculture believe it self-destructed under the pressures of politicization; New Leftists see their movement folding under a crush of countercultural hedonism. Both agree that the Movement ended five years before the Vietnam War did, in a blaze of numbskull adventurism and Maoist masquerade. ("The future of our movement," went one particularly unfortunate slogan, "is the future of crime in the streets.") When it was all over, the Sixties left behind as its bittersweet legacy an America both more free and more divided than ever before.

That's a story, say the Young Turks, that's by turns misguided, distorted, irrelevant, or just plain wrong. Take the case of SDS. In the accounting of Gitlin, Isserman, and Miller, the radicals who built Students for a Democratic Society were, like their historians, secular, well-off denizens of elite universities like Harvard and Michigan, often Jewish, and typically refugees from either suburban ticky-tacky torpor or Old Communist Left families. Doug Rossinow, a Johns Hopkins Ph.D. who's finishing up a study of the SDS chapter in Austin, Texas, uncovers a different story. Rossinow is twenty-nine, and his attraction to his subject has little to do with any residual memories: "I never heard about SDS until I was in college. I got interested in this topic because I came across some reference to it in books, and there didn't seem to be a lot of scholarship."

When Rossinow set out to study the New Left, he chose to use a methodology born of the Sixties: he would write political history from the bottom up, from the experience of the rank and file rather than the leadership. Ironically, from Kirkpatrick Sale's *SDS* (1973) to Wini Breines's *Community and Organization in the New Left, 1962–1968* (1982) to James Miller's 1987 *"Democracy Is in the Streets,"* historians had typically written the history of student radicalism as the story of its leaders. But notes Rossinow, "When you look at SDS from the grass roots, you find surprising things." For example: In Texas at least, the most important inspiration for SDS's put-your-body-on-the-line brand of radicalism was not C. Wright Mills or Eldridge Cleaver, but the action-oriented Christianity imbibed at the local YMCA. With this point in mind, Rossinow presents the antiwar movement as one in a long line of Protestant reform movements stretching back to the American Revolution.

Rossinow's revisionist efforts are complemented by those of Ken Heineman, author of *Campus Wars: The Peace Movement at American State Universities in the Vietnam Era* (NYU, 1995). Heineman, who comes from a blue-collar family and calls himself a "reluctant Republican," finds working-class folk conspicuously absent from the existing historiography (excepting the figure of Joe Sixpack, the Movement's archetypal proletarian spoiler). Yet kids from blue-collar backgrounds formed a large portion of the antiwar activists at the nonelite schools he studied: SUNY-Buffalo, Michigan State, Penn State.

And Kent State. Heineman challenges the conventional wisdom on the Ohio National Guard's 1970 massacre there. Conventionally, it was Kent State that brought the Sixties to the blue-collar belt. The university, remarks Todd Gitlin in *The Sixties,* "was a heartland school, far from elite, the very type of campus where Richard Nixon's 'silent majority' was supposed to be training." If such naked repression could be visited on such sleepy backwaters (four dead in *Ohio,* of all places), then few partisans of the Movement, and certainly none in its vanguard, could be safe from state terror.

The only problem with this interpretation, Heineman points out, is that Kent State *was* the movement's vanguard. Kent Staters protested for the right to organize on campus a full year before the Free Speech Movement at Berkeley supposedly gave birth to white student activism. The Ohio school's first antiwar group was founded a year ahead of Berkeley's. And Kent State students were even among the founders of SDS's ultravanguardist terrorist spin-off, the Weathermen.

Kent State also raises another pointed question: Did Sixties radicalism really implode at the end of the decade? Or might it, in fact, have expanded its reach in the Seventies? According to the declension narrative, Kent State and other end-of-the-decade disasters sounded the death knell for a broad-based popular movement to change American society (after the shootings, wrote James Miller, "the New Left collapsed, plummeting into cultural oblivion as if it had been some kind of political Hula-Hoop"). In a 1994 article in *American Quarterly,* Doug Rossinow challenges this downbeat assessment: "It is difficult to see how one can view the post-1968 Left as a complete disaster unless one is unsympathetic or unaware of the women's liberation movement, which first emerged in 1967–1968." America *changed* in the Sixties, Rossinow insists. Most palpably, it changed in its gender arrangements—a shift in which New Left and the counterculture played an important but limited role.

This argument about the broader, less visible influence of Sixties radicalism was made most pointedly by Sara Evans in her 1979 book, *Personal Politics: The Roots of Women's Liberation in the Civil Rights Movement & the New Left* (Vintage). Alice Echols, the author of *Daring to Be Bad: Radical Feminism in America, 1967–1975* (Minnesota, 1989), concurs. "For Gitlin and Miller et al., the tragedy of the late Sixties was the fracturing of the Movement. And the New Left pretty much *does* go up in flames. Even so, I think the only way that women could have their own movements, and black people and gay people"—whose struggles likewise produced real changes in the structure of American society—"was, unfortunately, *outside* the larger movement."

Alice Echols's guarded optimism, about the Sixties legacy is shared by many former activists. But what veteran would applaud the message of another camp of scholars, led by U. Penn's Thomas Sugrue, who argue that the Promethean adventures of the New Left and the counterculture aren't all that relevant to understanding the Sixties in the first place? "There's more to the Sixties than social movements," says Sugrue, "a lot more. Let's think about the Black Panthers as an example, or SDS. They had very small memberships. They were made a big deal of in the media in the 1960s. But if you think about the long-term consequences of those groups in building political organizations, their power isn't as great as it appears. To talk about black power, let's look at the election of blacks to local offices after the Voting Rights Act passed. It's not as glamorous a story as Huey Newton walking up the steps of the California state capitol with a rifle. But in many ways it's a far more important story for its enduring effect on American politics.

"Sixties historiography is still so limited," he adds, "and Sixties veterans still have the corner on the market." Sugrue's not just talking about the likes of Todd Gitlin and Maurice Isserman, but also about a group of influential writers that includes Allen Matusow, Clinton pollster Stanley Greenberg *(Middle Class Dreams: The Politics and Power of the New American Majority)*, and Thomas and Mary Edsall *(Chain Reaction: The Impact of Race, Rights, and Taxes on American Politics)*. Call them the liberals-mugged-by-radicalism school: They see a Democratic Party that scared away its mass base when it veered from its early Sixties blend of Keynesian economics, labor-management cooperation, and racial integration toward a McGovernik capitulation to radicalism. Says Sugrue: "My argument"—supported by his research on housing riots in Detroit since the Forties—"is that white working-class and middle-class members of the Democratic coalition were *always* very tenuously allied to the liberal tradition."

One of the most powerful insights of new Sixties scholarship, then, may be that Reagan Democrats were a long time in the making. It was the nomination of Barry Goldwater, in 1964, after all, that first turned the Republican Party toward a right-wing populism cemented by "anti-Sixties" themes of law and order, patriotism, and "family values." This is the story told by Mary Brennan, a thirty-five-year old historian at Southwest Texas State University, in her book *Turning Right in the Sixties: The Conservative Capture of the GOP* (North Carolina, 1995), one of many new projects that takes chronicling the rise of the new conservatism as a central task of Sixties history. Attention to social movements on the left, says Brennan, misses a scorching irony of the decade: The real masters of grassroots organizing were on the right. "Right-wingers succeeded by exploiting hitherto untapped sources of discontent," she notes. "Moreover, building a political movement from the bottom up allowed conservatives to . . . avoid the [Republican Party's] liberal-controlled national organization."

Brennan could, of course, have written pretty much the same thing about SDS and the Democrats. That irony has not been lost on sociologists of political movements. Rebecca Klatch, the UC-San Diego–based author of *Women of the New Right* (Temple, 1987), is just now finishing up a comparative study of activists in SDS and in Young Americans for Freedom, the conservative group formed in 1960 on William F. Buckley Jr.'s Sharon, Connecticut, estate. Klatch finds striking parallels, including the groups' common sense of generational mission and their shared revulsion (voiced in almost identical language) for the liberal managerial state. She has even uncovered a long-forgotten solidarity movement between the libertarian right and left, which had its own organ, the journal *Left and Right.*

Maybe M. Stanton Evans's quixotic prediction that the Sixties would be the decade of student conservatism wasn't so quixotic after all. Cadres of Young Americans for Freedom activists, Pat Buchanan among them, formed the shock troops for the right-wing capture of the GOP (and later the nation). Nine years after the publication of his book on the rise of SDS, it's a story that James Miller regrets having missed. "In terms of the political history of this country, the New Left just isn't an important story," he says. Focus on it, says Miller, and you "evade the extraordinary success of the forces that first supported Goldwater, then Reagan as governor of California, and then Wallace. I can't help but see that absence in the historiography as integral to the mythologization of the Sixties."

The mythologization of the Sixties: that, according to David Farber, is exactly what is still wrong with Sixties scholarship today. Is his charge fair? Certainly many of the Sixties insiders have written books that are fragrant with self-criticism. But are other New Leftists manning the barricades again, this time to fight a rearguard battle against revisionism?

Richard Ellis, a political scientist at Oregon's Willamette University, thinks so. He's completed several chapters of a study called *The Illiberalism of Egalitarianism* (forthcoming from UP Kansas). It's a carefully argued work that provides a theoretical buttress for James Miller's and Todd Gitlin's insights into the fall of SDS. Like Miller and Gitlin, Ellis believes that the group devolved into dogmatic factionalism because its commitment to internal democracy and moral purity frustrated its attempts to work democratic reform in the larger society. When he submitted a version of this argument to the *Journal of American History* in 1994, he says, "the three readers I could identify were former members of SDS. It's as if you were writing on the Reagan administration and the journal sent your paper to Jeane Kirkpatrick, Ed Meese, and Casper Weinberger!" (One vet's reader's report: I don't think the author is asking the right questions and I disagree with her/his answers. I do not think her/his thesis is borne out by what I know. . . . I think it is a fundamental misreading of the New Left." The reviewer left it at that, without going on to explain what the right questions might be). . . .

Peter Braunstein, a graduate student at NYU who's writing a history of the counterculture as his dissertation, calls this phenomenon "possessive memory," and has delivered a theoretical paper on the subject at several Sixties conferences. Participating in a sweeping social movement, he reasons, creates a sense of self-regeneration so powerful that it can become a constitutive part of the activist's later identity. Possessive memory, he writes, "leaves the person and his memories in a lover's embrace: The person is in possession of his memories, and no one else can touch them; at the same time, his memories are in possession of him."

Pity the poor young historian who tries to pry them loose. "You interview people who defined themselves by their orientation to the drug culture," Braunstein observes, "and you take out a copy of the *East Village Other* and say, 'Here you say that LSD is the solution to all the world's problems. What was going through your head back then?' They'll say that drugs were merely fourteenth on the list of motivating factors for the counterculture." Braunstein marvels at this kind of revisionism. Then again, perhaps it's not surprising that historians of psychedelia encounter a memory lapse or two along the way.

Whatever difficulties are posed by studying the counterculture, the subject looms larger in current scholarship than it once did. And much of the new work is dedicated to demystification. Never mind the glamour of Hendrix or Joplin. From the perspective of the Woodstock II generation, the Sixties counterculture doesn't look that radical at all. Tom Frank, editor of the cultural criticism journal *The Baffler* and a University of Chicago Ph.D., makes the now-familiar point that the Sixties' rebel mystique was better suited to retailing than to revolution. In a forthcoming book on Sixties advertising to be published by Chicago, he writes: "When business leaders cast their gaze onto the youth culture bubbling around them, they saw both a reflection of their own struggle against the stifling bureaucratic methods of the past and an affirmation of a new dynamic consumerism that must replace the old."

David Farber, for his part, seconds Frank's argument. He likes to explain Sixties libertinism by quoting Ernest Dichter, a prominent corporate consultant in the 1950s. "One of the basic problems of prosperity," Dichter wrote, "is to demonstrate that the hedonistic approach to life is a moral and not an immoral one." This was the story corporate America was telling on the eve of the Sixties, says Farber, and it shouldn't be surprising that impressionable young Americans took businessmen at their word, with consequences Wall Street could neither have anticipated nor countenanced.

One might ask, then: Is a Sixties bell-bottom merely a Fifties tail fin rendered in cloth? It's a question that's bound to rankle Sixties veterans, of both the reconstructed and unreconstructed varieties. After all, was there ever a society more self-conscious about its own historical identity, its role as an *agent* of history, than America in the Sixties? In January 1960, Arthur Schlesinger Jr. wrote in *Esquire* that "from the vantage point of the Sixties, the Fifties . . . will seem simply a listless interlude, quickly forgotten, in which the American people collected itself for greater exertions and higher splendors in the future." At the decade's close, a Berkeley DJ used to sign off his newscast in the same spirit: "If you don't like the news, make some of your own."

At their boldest, the Sixties revisionists say farewell to this brand of Sixties exceptionalism. They argue that, *pace* Schlesinger and that Berkeley DJ, the Sixties may not have been all that special in the first place; that "the Sixties" can't survive distanced scholarly treatment of the Sixties. SDS, for all its searing drama, was not something new in the world—but just another religiously inflected reform movement like the teetotalers. Liberalism began its decline not in the Sixties but in the Forties. The counterculture was not a blot on the American creed but its apotheosis.

And, some add, only those who weren't part of the action have the perspective to see it all so clearly. "I teach a course on the Sixties now," says Thomas Sugrue. "But in fifty years there won't be courses on the history of America in the Sixties. When I look at the land of *Leave It to Beaver,* and then look at the Sixties, I see a bunch of commonalities. The Sixties memoir writers and historians see radical discontinuities. And that's because we're of different generations."

⋈ *F U R T H E R   R E A D I N G*

Anderson, Terry H. *The Movement and the Sixties* (1996).

Andrew, John A., III. *The Other Side of the Sixties: Young Americans for Freedom and the Rise of Conservative Politics* (1997).

Balogh, Brian, ed. *Integrating the Sixties* (1996).

Bloom, Alexander, and Wini Breines, eds. *"Takin' It to the Streets": A Sixties Reader* (1995).

Breines, Wini. *Community and Organization in the New Left, 1962–1968: The Great Refusal,* new ed. (1989).

Brennan, Mary C. *Turning Right in the Sixties* (1995).

Burner, David. *Making Peace with the 60s* (1998).

Chalmers, David Mark. *And the Crooked Places Made Straight: The Struggle for Social Change in the 1960's* (1996).

Chepesiuk, Ron. *Sixties Radicals, Then and Now* (1995).

Collier, Peter, and David Horowitz. *Destructive Generation: Second Thoughts About the Sixties* (1996).

Conlin, Joseph. *The Troubles: A Jaundiced Glance Back at the Movements of the Sixties* (1982).

Davis, James Kirkpatrick. *Assault on the Left: The FBI and the Sixties Antiwar Movement* (1997).

Ellis, Richard J. *The Dark Side of the Left* (1998).

Evans, Sara. *Personal Politics: The Origins of Women's Liberation in the Civil Rights Movement and the New Left* (1979).

Farber, David. *The Age of Great Dreams: America in the 1960s* (1994).

———. *Chicago '68* (1988).

———, ed. *The Sixties: From Memory to History* (1994).

Farrell, James J. *The Spirit of the Sixties: Making Postwar Radicalism* (1997).

Flacks, Richard. *Making History: The American Left and the American Mind* (1988).

Frank, Thomas. *The Conquest of the Cool: Business Culture, Counterculture, and the Rise of Hip Consumerism* (1997).

Fraser, Ronald, et al. *1968: A Student Generation in Revolt* (1988).

Gitlin, Todd. *The Sixties: Years of Hope, Days of Rage* (1987).

———. *The Whole World Is Watching* (1980).

Goldstein, Richard. *Reporting the Counterculture* (1989).

Hayden, Tom. *Reunion* (1988).

Heineman, Kenneth J. *Campus Wars: The Peace Movement at American State Universities in the Vietnam Era* (1994).

Isserman, Maurice. *If I Had a Hammer . . . The Death of the Old Left and the Birth of the New Left* (1987).

Jacobs, Ron. *The Way the Wind Blew: A History of the Weather Underground* (1997).

Kaiser, Charles. *1968 in America: Music, Politics, Chaos, Counterculture, and the Shaping of a Generation* (1997).

Katsiaficas, George. *The Imagination of the New Left: A Global Analysis of 1968* (1987).

Levitt, Cyril. *Children of Privilege: Student Revolt in the Sixties* (1984).

Lyons, Paul. *New Left, New Right, and the Legacy of the Sixties* (1996).

MacEdo, Stephen, ed. *Reassessing the Sixties: Debating the Political and Cultural Legacy* (1996).

Marwick, Arthur. *The Sixties: Cultural Revolution in Britain, France, Italy and the United States, 1958–c. 1974* (1998).

Matusow, Allen J. *The Unraveling of America: A History of Liberalism in the 1960s* (1984).

Mendel-Reyes, Meta. *Reclaiming Democracy: The Sixties in Politics and Memory* (1995).

Michener, James A. *Kent State: What Happened and Why* (1982).

Miles, Michael W. *The Radical Probe: The Logic of Student Rebellion* (1971).

Miller, James. *Democracy Is in the Streets* (1987).

Peck, Abe. *Uncovering the Sixties* (1985).

Polsgrove, Carol. *It Wasn't Pretty, Folks, But Didn't We Have Fun? Esquire in the Sixties* (1995).

Reich, Charles. *The Greening of America* (1970).

Rorabaugh, W. J. *Berkeley at War: The 1960s* (1990).

Rossinow, Douglas C. *Politics of Authenticity: Liberalism, Christianity, and the New Left in America* (1998).

Rossman, Michael. *The Wedding Within the War* (1973).

Roszak, Theodore. *The Making of a Counter-Culture* (1969).

Sale, Kirkpatrick. *SDS* (1973).

Steigerwald, David. *The Sixties and the End of Modern America* (1995).

Stevens, Jay. *Storming Heaven: LSD and the American Dream* (1998).

Tischler, Barbara L., ed. *Sights on the Sixties* (1992).

Unger, Irwin, and Debi Unger, eds. *The Times Were a Changin': The Sixties Reader* (1998).

Whalen, Jack, and Richard Flacks. *Beyond the Barricades: The Sixties Generation Grows Up* (1989).

Whitmer, Peter O. *Aquarius Revisited: Seven Who Created the Sixties Counterculture That Changed America* (1991).

Wolfe. Tom. *The Electric Kool-Aid Acid Test* (1969).

Wyatt, David. *Out of the Sixties: Storytelling and Vietnam Generation* (1993).

From the Feminine Mystique
to the New Feminism

✕✕

The publication in 1963 of Betty Friedan's The Feminine Mystique *opened a new chapter in American women's fight for equality, a struggle that in ensuing decades would transform American social relations. Like most revolutions, it was the product of a long historical gestation. Its roots lay in the broad social changes wrought by industrialization, urbanization, and the rise of a new economy based on mass consumption; the emergence of a more democratic and companionate family life; and the self-conscious strivings of nineteenth- and early-twentieth-century women for suffrage and sexual equality. The movement's immediate antecedents included the massive entry of women into the work force during World War II, a change only temporarily reversed during the late 1940s. But the postwar years also were marked by the insistence of virtually all of the country's cultural authorities that women ought to seek fulfillment exclusively as wives and mothers. It was the tension between this powerful "feminine mystique" and the as yet largely unarticulated aspirations of women for freedom and equality that Betty Friedan would record in her influential book.*

Through The Feminine Mystique, *women began to discover a common sense of frustration and even despair. Friedan, however, spoke for and to a largely middle-class audience of liberal women, some of whom would join her in 1966 in creating the National Organization for Women (NOW). Other, more radical voices were nurtured by the decade's civil rights movement and New Left. Out of the crucible of these movements, women (mostly young women) would forge the social agenda of the new feminism, an agenda that included not only the political and economic opportunities stressed by NOW but also a more radical challenge to definitions of gender roles in American society.*

The transformation sought by the new feminists would encounter strong opposition: the resistance of men and of male-dominated institutions, the sharp limits to change imposed by class and race, and the mobilization of social conservatives by the New Right during the 1980s. Feminists themselves remained divided over the means and ends of their movement. Women's fight for equality nevertheless continues to shape the landscape of American society. Like the civil rights movement, to which it has often been compared, it is an unfinished revolution whose final chapters will be written by Americans in the new millennium.

Document 1 includes excerpts from the opening chapter of Betty Friedan's *The Feminine Mystique* (1963). An analysis of the lives of college-educated, middle-class women in the 1950s, the book became a classic of the new feminism. The next year, Friedan was among the founders of the National Organization for Women (NOW), whose statement of purpose is reproduced as Document 2. NOW did not pay much attention to poor women. Document 3, an excerpt from the 1970 collection *Sisterhood Is Powerful*, addresses the connection between women's plight and broader economic conditions. Document 4, the Redstockings Manifesto, illustrates a radical turn among some feminists. Document 5, a *Redbook* article, demonstrates how feminist ideas had begun to penetrate the popular media by 1973. Phyllis Schlafly's best-selling book *The Power of the Positive Woman* argues against the mistakes of the feminist movement and its threat to both women and the traditional family. An excerpt from this book appears as Document 6.

1. Betty Friedan on the Problem That Has No Name, 1963

The problem lay buried, unspoken, for many years in the minds of American women. It was a strange stirring, a sense of dissatisfaction, a yearning that women suffered in the middle of the twentieth century in the United States. Each suburban wife struggled with it alone. As she made the beds, shopped for groceries, matched slipcover material, ate peanut butter sandwiches with her children, chauffeured Cub Scouts and Brownies, lay beside her husband at night—she was afraid to ask even of herself the silent question—"Is this all?"

For over fifteen years there was no word of this yearning in the millions of words written about women, for women, in all the columns, books, and articles by experts telling women their role was to seek fulfillment as wives and mothers. Over and over women heard in voices of tradition and of Freudian sophistication that they could desire no greater destiny than to glory in their own femininity. Experts told them how to catch a man and keep him, how to breastfeed children and handle their toilet training, how to cope with sibling rivalry and adolescent rebellion; how to buy a dishwasher, bake bread, cook gourmet snails, and build a swimming pool with their own hands; how to dress, look, and act more feminine and make marriage more exciting; how to keep their husbands from dying young and their sons from growing into delinquents. They were taught to pity the neurotic, unfeminine, unhappy women who wanted to be poets or physicists or presidents. They learned that truly feminine women do not want careers, higher education, political rights—the independence and the opportunities that the old-fashioned feminists fought for. Some women, in their forties and fifties, still remembered painfully giving up those dreams, but most of the younger women no longer even thought about them. A thousand expert voices applauded their femininity, their adjustment, their new maturity. All they had to do was devote their lives from earliest girlhood to finding a husband and bearing children.

By the end of the nineteen-fifties, the average marriage age of women in America dropped to 20, and was still dropping, into the teens. Fourteen million girls were engaged by 17. The proportion of women attending college in comparison with men dropped from 47 per cent in 1920 to 35 per cent in 1958. A century earlier, women had fought for higher education; now girls went to college to get a husband. By the mid-fifties, 60 per cent dropped out of college to marry, or because they were afraid too much education would be a marriage bar. Colleges built dormitories for "married students," but the students were almost always the husbands. A new degree was instituted for the wives—"Ph.T." (Putting Husband Through).

Then American girls began getting married in high school. And the women's magazines, deploring the unhappy statistics about these young marriages, urged that courses on marriage, and marriage counselors, be installed in the high schools. Girls started going steady at twelve and thirteen, in junior high. Manufacturers put out brassieres with false bosoms of foam rubber for little girls of ten. And an advertisement for a child's dress, sizes 3–6x, in the *New York Times* in the fall of 1960, said: "She Too Can Join the Man-Trap Set."

By the end of the fifties, the United States birthrate was overtaking India's. The birth-control movement, renamed Planned Parenthood, was asked to find a method whereby women who had been advised that a third or fourth baby would be born dead or defective might have it anyhow. Statisticians were especially astounded at the fantastic increase in the number of babies among college women. Where once they had two children, now they had four, five, six. Women who had once wanted careers were now making careers out of having babies. So rejoiced *Life* magazine in a 1956 paean to the movement of American women back to the home. . . .

Interior decorators were designing kitchens with mosaic murals and original paintings, for kitchens were once again the center of women's lives. Home sewing became a million-dollar industry. Many women no longer left their homes, except to shop, chauffeur their children, or attend a social engagement with their husbands. Girls were growing up in America without ever having jobs outside the home. In the late fifties, a sociological phenomenon was suddenly remarked: a third of American women now worked, but most were no longer young and very few were pursuing careers. They were married women who held part-time jobs, selling or secretarial, to put their husbands through school, their sons through college, or to help pay the mortgage. Or they were widows supporting families. Fewer and fewer women were entering professional work. The shortages in the nursing, social work, and teaching professions caused crises in almost every American city. Concerned over the Soviet Union's lead in the space race, scientists noted that America's greatest source of unused brainpower was women. But girls would not study physics: it was "unfeminine." A girl refused a science fellowship at Johns Hopkins to take a job in a real-estate office. All she wanted, she said, was what every other American girl wanted, to get married, have four children, and live in a nice house in a nice suburb.

The suburban housewife—she was the dream image of the young American women and the envy, it was said, of women all over the world. The American housewife—freed by science and labor-saving appliances from the drudgery, the dangers of childbirth, and the illnesses of her grandmother. She was healthy, beautiful, educated, concerned only about her husband, her children, her home. She had found true feminine fulfillment. As a housewife and mother, she was respected as a full and equal partner to man in his world. She was free to choose automobiles, clothes, appliances, supermarkets; she had everything that women ever dreamed of.

In the fifteen years after World War II, this mystique of feminine fulfillment became the cherished and self-perpetuating core of contemporary American culture. Millions of women lived their lives in the image of those pretty pictures of the American suburban housewife, kissing their husbands goodbye in front of the picture window, depositing their stationwagonsful of children at school, and smiling as they ran the new electric waxer over the spotless kitchen floor. They baked their own bread, sewed their own and their children's clothes, kept their new washing machines and dryers running all day. They changed the sheets on the beds twice a week instead of once, took the rug-hooking class in adult education, and pitied their poor frustrated mothers, who had dreamed of having a career. Their only dream was to be perfect wives and mothers; their highest ambition to have five children and a beautiful house, their only fight to get and keep their husbands. They had no thought for the unfeminine problems of the world outside the home; they wanted the men to make the major decisions. They gloried in their role as women, and wrote proudly on the census blank: "Occupation: housewife." . . .

If a woman had a problem in the 1950s and 1960s, she knew that something must be wrong with her marriage, or with herself. Other women were satisfied with their lives, she thought. What kind of a woman was she if she did not feel this mysterious fulfillment waxing the kitchen floor? She was so ashamed to admit her dissatisfaction that she never knew how many other women shared it. If she tried to tell her husband, he didn't understand what she was talking about. She did not really understand it herself. For over fifteen years women in America found it harder to talk about this problem than about sex. Even the psychoanalysts had no name for it. When a woman went to a psychiatrist for help, as many women did, she would say, "I'm so ashamed," or "I must be hopelessly neurotic." "I don't know what's wrong with women today," a suburban psychiatrist said uneasily. "I only know something is wrong because most of my patients happen to be women. And their problem isn't sexual." Most women with this problem did not go to see a psychoanalyst, however. "There's nothing wrong really," they kept telling themselves. "There isn't any problem."

But on an April morning in 1959, I heard a mother of four, having coffee with four other mothers in a suburban development fifteen miles from New York, say in a tone of quiet desperation, "the problem." And the others knew, without words, that she was not talking about a problem with her husband, or her children, or her home. Suddenly they realized they all shared the same problem, the problem that has no name. They began, hesitantly, to talk about it. Later, after they had picked up their children at nursery school and taken them home to nap, two of the women cried, in sheer relief, just to know they were not alone.

2. NOW Statement of Purpose, 1966

We, men and women who hereby constitute ourselves as the National Organization for Women, believe that the time has come for a new movement toward true equality for all women in America, and toward a fully equal partnership of the sexes, as part of the world-wide revolution of human rights now taking place within and beyond our national borders.

The purpose of NOW is to take action to bring women into full participation in the mainstream of American society now, exercising all the privileges and responsibilities thereof in truly equal partnership with men.

We believe the time has come to move beyond the abstract argument, discussion, and symposia over the status and special nature of women which has raged in America in recent years; the time has come to confront, with concrete action, the conditions that now prevent women from enjoying the equality of opportunity and freedom of choice which is their right as individual Americans, and as human beings.

NOW is dedicated to the proposition that women first and foremost are human beings, who, like all other people in our society, must have the chance to develop their fullest human potential. We believe that women can achieve such equality only by accepting to the full the challenges and responsibilities they share with all other people in our society, as part of the decision-making mainstream of American political, economic, and social life.

We organize to initiate or support action, nationally or in any part of this nation, by individuals or organizations, to break through the silken curtain of prejudice and discrimination against women in government, industry, the professions, the churches, the political parties, the judiciary, the labor unions, in education, science, medicine, law, religion, and every other field of importance in American society. . . .

There is no civil rights movement to speak for women, as there has been for Negroes and other victims of discrimination. The National Organization for Women must therefore begin to speak.

WE BELIEVE that the power of American law, and the protection guaranteed by the U.S. Constitution to the civil rights of all individuals, must be effectively applied and enforced to isolate and remove patterns of sex discrimination, to ensure equality of opportunity in employment and education, and equality of civil and political rights and responsibilities on behalf of women, as well as for Negroes and other deprived groups.

We realize that women's problems are linked to many broader questions of social justice; their solution will require concerted action by many groups. Therefore, convinced that human rights for all are indivisible, we expect to give active support to the common cause of equal rights for all those who suffer discrimination and deprivation, and we call upon other organizations committed to such goals to support our efforts toward equality for women.

WE DO NOT ACCEPT the token appointment of a few women to high-level positions in government and industry as a substitute for a serious continuing effort to recruit and advance women according to their individual abilities. To this end, we urge American government and industry to mobilize the same resources of ingenuity and command with which they have solved problems of far greater difficulty than those now impeding the progress of women.

WE BELIEVE that this nation has a capacity at least as great as other nations, to innovate new social institutions which will enable women to enjoy true equality of opportunity and responsibility in society, without conflict with their responsibilities as mothers and homemakers. In such innovations, America does not lead the Western world, but lags by decades behind many European countries. We do not accept the traditional assumption that a woman has to choose between marriage and motherhood, on the one hand, and serious participation in industry or the professions on the other. We question the present expectation that all normal women will retire from job or profession for ten or fifteen years, to devote their full time to raising children, only to reenter the job market at a relatively minor level. This in itself is a deterrent to the aspirations of women, to their acceptance into management or professional training courses, and to the very possibility of equality of opportunity or real choice, for all but a few women. Above all, we reject the assumption that these problems are the unique responsibility of each individual woman, rather than a base social dilemma which society must solve. True equality of opportunity and freedom of choice for women requires such practical and possible innovations as a nationwide network of child-care centers, which will make it unnecessary for women to retire completely from society until their children are grown, and national programs to provide retraining for women who have chosen to care for their own children full time.

WE BELIEVE that it is as essential for every girl to be educated to her full potential of human ability as it is for every boy—with the knowledge that such education is the key to effective participation in today's economy and that, for a girl as for a boy, education can only be serious where there is expectation that it will be used in society. We believe that American educators are capable of devising means of imparting such expectations to girl students. Moreover, we consider the decline in the proportion of women receiving higher and professional education to be evidence of discrimination. This discrimination may take the form of quotas against the admission of women to colleges and professional schools; lack of encouragement by parents, counselors, and educators; denial of loans or fellowships; or the traditional or arbitrary procedures in graduate and professional training geared in terms of men, which inadvertently discriminate against women. We believe that the same serious attention must be given to high school dropouts who are girls as to boys.

WE REJECT the current assumptions that a man must carry the sole burden of supporting himself, his wife, and family, and that a woman is automatically entitled to lifelong support by a man upon her marriage, or that marriage, home, and family are primarily woman's world and responsibility—hers, to dominate, his to support. We believe that a true partnership between the sexes demands a different concept of marriage, an equitable sharing of the responsibilities of home and children and of the economic burdens of their support. We believe that proper recognition should be given to the economic and social value of homemaking and child care. To these ends, we will seek to open a reexamination of laws and mores governing marriage and divorce, for we believe that the current state of "half-equality" between the sexes discriminates against both men and women, and is the cause of much unnecessary hostility between the sexes.

WE BELIEVE that women must now exercise their political rights and responsibilities as American citizens. They must refuse to be segregated on the basis of sex into separate-and-not-equal ladies' auxiliaries in the political parties, and they must demand representation according to their numbers in the regularly constituted party committees—at local, state, and national levels—and in the informal power structure, participating fully in the selection of candidates and political decision-making, and running for office themselves.

IN THE INTERESTS OF THE HUMAN DIGNITY OF WOMEN, we will protest and endeavor to change the false image of women now prevalent in the mass media, and in the texts, ceremonies, laws, and practices of our major social institutions. Such images perpetuate contempt for women by society and by women for themselves. We are similarly opposed to all policies and practices—in church, state, college, factory, or office—which, in the guise of protectiveness, not only deny opportunities but also foster in women self-denigration, dependence, and evasion of responsibility, undermine their confidence in their own abilities, and foster contempt for women.

NOW WILL HOLD ITSELF INDEPENDENT OF ANY POLITICAL PARTY in order to mobilize the political power of all women and men intent on our goals. We will strive to ensure that no party, candidate, President senator, governor, congressman, or any public official who betrays or ignores the principle of full equality between the sexes is elected or appointed to office. If it is necessary to mobilize the votes of men and women who believe in our cause, in order to win for women the final right to be fully free and equal human beings, we so commit ourselves.

WE BELIEVE THAT women will do most to create a new image of women by *acting* now, and by speaking out in behalf of their own equality, freedom, and human dignity—not in pleas for special privilege, nor in enmity toward men, who are also victims of the current half-equality between the sexes—but in an active, self-respecting partnership with men. By so doing, women will develop confidence in their own ability to determine actively, in partnership with men, the conditions of their life, their choices, their future, and their society.

3. Feminists Analyze the Welfare System, 1970

Welfare is one of our society's attempts to preserve the traditional role of woman as childbearer, socializer, and homemaker. Early in the twentieth century there was growing concern for the victims of "laissez-faire" capitalism. Laws were passed dealing with workmen's compensation, regulation of work conditions, and limitations on child labor. Prominent among the "victims" were female heads of families. Since the system only provided for women as secondary wage earners, they and their children suffered from extreme poverty. In addition to economic discrimination,

Excerpts from "Women and the Welfare System" by Carol Glassman, from *Sisterhood Is Powerful,* by Robin Morgan (Vintage Books: 1970). Reprinted by permssion of Carol Glassman.

these women suffered from the lack of community facilities to share the burdens of socializing children. Thus faced with the failure of the system to allow women to support their families through employment, the legislature chose as a solution the creation of a "substitute man." This man was the Social Security Act of 1935.

The act provided for federal participation in a nationwide program of direct economic assistance to the elderly, to the blind, and to dependent children. The law defined a dependent child as "under sixteen without parental support because of death, disability, or continued absence of a parent, and living in his own home with certain near relatives." The liberal rhetoric of the day claimed that if the state took over the burden of financial support, the woman would be freed to perform her "natural" and needed tasks of child care and housekeeping.

For its recipients, the welfare system carried with it most of the hazards of "housewife and mother," and few of the rewards. Domination by a husband was replaced with control over every aspect of a woman's life by the welfare agency. Strangers could knock at any hour to pass judgment on her performance as mother, housekeeper, and cook—as well as her fidelity to the welfare board. The welfare board, like a jealous husband, doesn't want to see any men around who might threaten its place as provider and authority. An ex-client describes this attitude when she says, "The welfare never tried to find out what you wanted to do. All they was trying to find out was, did you have another man . . . and that bugged me! I used to ask them, 'just because you was on the welfare didn't mean you didn't have to have friends, or couldn't have associates.'"

More powerful and efficient than any husband, the welfare board keeps a running file on all its wives. Case records include such things as evaluations of a welfare woman's housekeeping, her ability to budget her small income and pay her bills, and her "moral standards." Likewise, she is often scorned for activities that take her outside her home.

While the extent of man-hunting by the welfare board varies, one finds evidence of it in many case records. One narrative states that the case worker noticed a man's razor and brush while using the john. He then proceeded to question the woman, check the closets for men's clothing, talk to neighbors, etc. Another record contained letters written by the client to a male friend. The man's mother had turned them over to the case worker, telling her to have the client leave her son alone. The case worker then reports that she lectured the client on her behavior, adding that the client was rumored to be a prostitute. For most welfare women there has been no pattern according to the sex or race of the case worker to indicate what they should expect. The "bad" case workers have been both men and women, black and white.

Another client tells how she was treated on the first visit of her case worker: "She came in. She looked around, she looked in my closets. She went in so far as to look in my closet, and she said, 'Why are you going on welfare with such beautiful furniture.' She even suggested, 'Why don't you have a man keep you?'" Thus the welfare "husband" who provides support and authority does not allow another male to provide sex and companionship.

Throughout the welfare department one finds the combined view that poverty is due to individual *fault* and that *something is wrong with women who don't have men.* Over and over one hears said, "If they didn't have problems they wouldn't be on welfare." (Poverty, a discriminatory job market, inadequate community facilities are, of course, not the problem.) The official version of the attitude toward welfare women is presented in a check-off form used in New Jersey as part of the regular three-month check done on welfare women. (All other categories of assistance—Old Age, Blind, Disability—are checked on once a year.) The form (on which the case worker must check the description that suits the client) contains such captions as: "Disorganized due to mother's inability to function"; "Repeatedly without money, food—due to inability to plan, immaturity, compulsive, or unwise spending"; "Threat of eviction or cut off of utilities—reason: indifference or inexperience re: financial obligations"; "Exploitation resulting from illiteracy, physical or mental condition, or behavior problem of parent." Always the problem lies in the woman herself and not in the society.

For most women, welfare is synonymous with a loss of control over their lives. From her first encounters she is given the message, "You do what we say!" Vague, but widespread rumors about how welfare can have your kids taken away, or have your check cut off, go unquestioned. As most women come to welfare after a series of marital difficulties or after a losing struggle to support themselves and their kids through employment, they feel defeated and easily cowed. Led to believe that the welfare board has the right to delve into every aspect of their lives, few women will challenge the specific actions of a case worker. . . .

. . . A woman married for thirteen years talks of her reaction to first going on welfare:

> Men would approach you and proposition you. The sales people would look at you, always trying to sell you something, coming by with some gimmick. The landlord was exploiting on you, they was always putting their foot in your door. Doctors treated you differently 'cause you were on the welfare. All these things I started to notice. I had a really good pediatrician that I had taken all my children (seven) to when I had my husband. As soon as he found out I was on welfare, he told me he didn't take people on welfare. He knew me good; it made me feel just awful. I started to notice then that things were different when you were on welfare.

A woman who separates from her husband has full responsibility for the socialization of their children. This situation often puts her on welfare. Her husband is responsible for some support, but the System allows him to live on a much higher standard without restrictions on with whom and how he lives, without a ceiling on his income, and without someone telling him how to spend his money. He also has no other responsibilities for the care of the children. When the woman applies for welfare, his income is evaluated to determine his "capacity to support." According to the evaluation charts, a single man can earn $310 per month before he has a capacity to give his family any money. Yet on a welfare budget this amount supports a woman and three children. As a man's income goes up, the amount he can keep after support goes up. The woman's income stays static. While the Domestic Relations Courts are less lenient (especially to poor black men), a man brought in on a nonsupport complaint still has only to meet his payments and keep his address active. He has no other restrictions or responsibilities.

Old notions about "illegitimacy" and the immorality of mothers of "out of wedlock" children are prevalent throughout the welfare system. On the abovementioned check-off form a caption reads, "O.W. children: 1st pregnancy; 1st child; repeated pregnancies and/or children. Conditions that foster illegitimacy." Under a proposed solution it reads, "Improving environmental conditions seriously contributing to illegitimacy." Unwed mothers are required to bring paternity suits against the fathers of the children. At a pre-court interview with the welfare board's legal staff the woman is asked degrading and guilt-inducing questions—Where did you meet the man? When did you first have intercourse? How often? Where? Did you continue after you became pregnant? Did he suggest any "medicines" or "treatments" to promote abortion? Did he suggest a doctor? Did you ever pose as man and wife to friends? What are his favorite pool halls and taverns? Did he offer marriage? Many women tell of being threatened in court with jail or with the loss of their children for having O.W. kids. Juveniles are particularly vulnerable. One hears stories of young girls who are forced in court to swear not to have intercourse again. Another example is a sixteen-year-old daughter of a welfare woman who became pregnant by her boyfriend, who was a few years older. Although they planned to marry, they wanted to wait until they could save enough money to set up an apartment and get a solid start. When the baby was born the boy contributed to her support regularly. Yet in court they were told if they didn't marry she would be sent away as a juvenile delinquent and he would be jailed for contributing to the delinquency of a minor. They married.

It is the woman who is ultimately held responsible for pregnancy. While not being allowed to have control over her body, she is nevertheless held responsible for its products. Recently, birth-control information has become more accessible, but still scarce. Abortions are illegal. Married women can't have their tubes tied without their husband's consent.

The welfare system insists that when a man and woman live together they do so as a "family." Regardless of whether they are married or whether he is the father of any of her children, if they live together he must play the role of "family bread-winner" (with some supplementation from the welfare depending on his income). A welfare woman can only live with a man if she is willing to allow him to support her and her children and thereby be "husband" and man of the house. She cannot choose a relationship with a man who is not the father of her children, in which he has no rights or responsibilities toward the children. She cannot live with him just to meet her needs for sex and companionship.

But while preventing new or "non-family" forms of living together, the system is also an enormous deterrent to the traditional forms. It is usually beyond the means and desire of a poor or working-class man to take on the responsibility of a woman with children who are not his. The example of Mrs. Y is illustrative. Divorced with two children, her ex-husband had remarried and was now the father of several other children. Although he was under court order to support his first family, he could barely manage his second on his lowpaying job. Thus Mrs. Y was on welfare. She met Mr. Z, a night watchman and janitor, and married. They bought furniture on credit and tried to make a go of it. Her welfare check was drastically cut. For over a year they were underbudgeted because the case worker never bothered about, or didn't know how to take into account, Mr. Z's expenses. But even with the correction he was under enormous economic pressure which he could only see as due to the two children who weren't his. The marriage lasted another year till finally he left the house. Mrs. Y's welfare grant went back up. Had Mr. Z stayed and been ill or out of work, the welfare would not have met his needs or expenses, because he was not the father of any of the children.

From its inception, welfare has been both an economic band-aid and a fortifier of traditional family roles. The 1961 amendments which instituted the Aid to Families of Dependent Children with Unemployed or Underemployed Parents (AFDC-UP) was a further step in this same direction. AFDC-UP provided welfare assistance to two-parent families whose male member was unemployed or underemployed. Having already recognized in 1935 that the economy did not provide for female breadwinners, the 1961 amendments recognized that the same conditions existed for many groups of men. The welfare system was thus expanded to include another group of economic victims and to keep them living in families. Welfare becomes an artificial economic base for the family.

"I think it's the System, really! I think it's a big racket in one sense for them to keep people on welfare rather than give them jobs. Because it keeps somebody happy! I don't know who! I can't figure it out!" An answer to this question posed by an ex–welfare woman lies in an understanding of the capitalistic exploitation of the economic underclass of woman. As stated elsewhere, most women work at only part-time or seasonal jobs to supplement their husbands' incomes. In seasonal factories, as office temporaries, as holiday or rush-hour sales help, or as domestic help, employers are able to use this "surplus labor" of women, getting rid of it when no longer needed, and not paying a living wage. The welfare system as "husband" also allows his wives this role. The toy industries of New Jersey are typical examples of this system. Hiring large numbers of women on a seasonal basis, paying the minimum wage, these factories draw a large number of welfare and other poor women. Since the wages are so low that even single women have trouble living on them, so low that wages often are lower than a full welfare grant, the women remain on welfare. In essence, the welfare system subsidizes them to work for a non–living wage, much to the profit of management. Clearly, it's the industry which is on welfare!

The welfare system has also been used to depress wages in these industries. Until recently, the "extra" money a welfare woman could get from working was static. She would not benefit from a wage increase as the welfare would just deduct it from her grant. Likewise the women who work without reporting it are not going to take part in a movement for higher wage[s] or better conditions, for fear of getting caught. . . .

Most woman see their being on welfare as the fault of their personal histories and not as a socially determined result. Even black women, who often see welfare as generally connected to racism and poverty, still place great emphasis on the effects of their personal experiences—a bad marriage, the wrong man, leaving school, etc. One woman, who had tried to support her two daughters on her own, tells how long strenuous hours of work and severe problems with babysitters led to illness for one daughter, until finally she decided to stop working and apply for welfare. Still she views it as her own failure, not as a problem of an economy that doesn't provide a living "family" wage for its female workers, or have adequate provisions for child care and socialization by other than the biological mother. . . .

White welfare women, as compared to their black sisters, are much more in retreat from the world due to the absence of the male. Coming mostly from working-class or lower-middle-class backgrounds, they compensate for their exclusion from production and their seeming failure as wives with a heavy investment in the raising of their children. They view welfare as a disgrace and their own lives as failures and thus seek self-expression through their children. Many live on welfare for years without telling their families or friends. In one case a divorced woman would not even tell her teen-age children. Fear of, or actual experiences of abuse, ridicule, or exploitation cause them to internalize this negative view of themselves and retreat further into their shells. Therefore, they have little or no contact with each other and provide no mutual assistance. Unlike many black women, they are usually unwilling to fight for their rights and are more easily cowed. As one white welfare woman describes it, welfare was the last resort. "There was nothing else I could do. There really wasn't. I felt ashamed. Not guilty, but ashamed. Till this day I've told very few people that I'm on welfare . . . just ashamed."

Coming from a society with some history of fatherless families, black welfare women are less imbued with the value of the "little woman" and are more at home in somewhat aggressive and independent roles than the whites. While most black welfare women have attempted marriages, they are less likely to see their failure as an end to their own roles as sexual and reproductive adults. They find "purpose" in the raising of their children, but rarely retreat and live through them. Black welfare women have taken steps toward cooperative action, aided by the more social and communal nature of their communities. Thus, while the white women remain very isolated, the blacks move more freely through the local social centers, and this makes them more able to develop a life independent of their home and family. . . .

For many women, the welfare is a terrible economic and social trap. Those with small or numerous children are constantly tied to the house and kids with no means of getting out or relaxing. Working gets them nowhere and often complicates their financial state with less time to do economical shopping, cooking, sewing, etc. The burdens of work, kids, babysitters, and welfare are enormous. Depression, helplessness, and a downward spiral are not unknown to welfare women. Many feel trapped.

> Staying home always bored me. I never liked to stay home. I liked to work. Staying home definitely had an effect on me because I had to get into the same category as other welfare mothers who just sat home and did nothing but watch television, etc. But I didn't like that, I always liked to be doing something. . . . I got into it for a while, started to drink more. I had given up. I felt that there was no way out of this kind of a welfare situation.

Older women advise the young girl to go out into the world and be independent. "I think it's better for a young girl to go out and work than to be stuck on welfare. Once you get on welfare you kinda lose sight of the world, you get into your own little world. She would get more out of life by going to work and being independent." However, the reality is not so simple. The welfare woman who made the above statement has only one child, yet has lived in poverty, working almost full-time *and* receiving a full welfare grant. The lack of independence she felt on welfare led her to an active role in organizing other welfare women.

Many women have gained independence and strength from the lessons of their personal experiences as well as the "toughening" process of being on welfare. Having had to fight many battles, having borne many hardships on their own, and having lived for long periods without a man, they will never go back to dependent and subservient relationships. "I would like in a husband a man I could meet halfway. I wouldn't want him to do some things I've seen men do for women. I would like him to treat me as a woman, not as a little puppet. Then I don't want one to be mean to me. And I certainly don't want one that's too dominating, telling me everything to do, where I can go, what I can wear, what I should eat! This I can't stand." They search, often consciously, for a greater equality and mutual independence in their relationships and a more active and productive role in the society. "Up until two years ago I would have told my daughter her only goal in life would be to be a housewife and a mother. Not today, oh no, heavens no. First have pride in yourself and be somebody. Then worry about marriage after you've accomplished something and once you know who you are." It is particularly from this group of women that the welfare-rights movement has grown.

The welfare-rights movement began in the early Sixties with small groups of women getting together to help each other deal with the welfare system. In many cities these groups were connected to SDS organizing projects or OEO community action ventures or groups like CORE. As an outgrowth of work done by the Poverty Rights Action Center, in 1967 the National Welfare Rights Organization was established. It does not see itself as a women's movement, rather, it is a movement that happens to have as its constituency mostly women. Because of this view, welfare-rights movements rarely describe or analyze the welfare problem as a women's problem but rather as part of the national problems of poverty and racial oppression. While pushing nationally for a guaranteed annual income and an end to repressive controls over clients' lives, they do not concern themselves with the role of women in the economy or the status of the family. The organization, which is 99 percent women, has as its head a male executive director. Yet all its national officers are women. Local leadership is female. In cities and towns across the country women meet, work, and fight together against an oppressive system. Thus the welfare-rights movement is fertile ground for developing and spreading an analysis of the welfare system that sees it as part of the larger problem of women's oppression.

The experience of involvement in the welfare-rights movement has for many women brought out an independence and militancy long supressed. As a welfare-rights activist put it: "I'm the same person I always was but the welfare rights brought it out." The personal experiences of these women have taught them that they can't get by on an identity of wife and mother. They have had to come out of their homes and take an active part in the world around them. The experience is telling. They want a better deal but they don't want to go back home. As the movement for women's liberation spreads out from the middle class and into other sectors of the society, the welfare-rights women are its potential base among the female poor.

4. Redstockings Manifesto, 1970

I After centuries of individual and preliminary political struggle, women are uniting to achieve their final liberation from male supremacy. Redstockings is dedicated to building this unity and winning our freedom.

II Women are an oppressed class. Our oppression is total, affecting every facet of our lives. We are exploited as sex objects, breeders, domestic servants, and cheap labor. We are considered inferior beings, whose only purpose is to enhance men's lives. Our humanity is denied. Our prescribed behavior is enforced by the threat of physical violence.

Because we have lived so intimately with our oppressors in isolation from each other, we have been kept from seeing our personal suffering as a political condition. This creates the illusion that a woman's relationship with her man is a matter of interplay between two unique personalities, and can be worked out individually. In reality, every such relationship is a *class* relationship, and the conflicts between individual men and women are *political* conflicts that can only be solved collectively.

III   We identify the agents of our oppression as men. Male supremacy is the oldest, most basic form of domination. All other forms of exploitation and oppression (racism, capitalism, imperialism, etc.) are extensions of male supremacy: men dominate women, a few men dominate the rest. All power structures throughout history have been male-dominated and male-oriented. Men have controlled all political, economic, and cultural institutions and backed up this control with physical force. They have used their power to keep women in an inferior position. *All men* received economic, sexual, and psychological benefits from male supremacy. *All men* have oppressed women.

IV   Attempts have been made to shift the burden of responsibility from men to institutions or to women themselves. We condemn these arguments as evasions. Institutions alone do not oppress; they are merely tools of the oppressor. To blame institutions implies that men and women are equally victimized, obscures the fact that men benefit from the subordination of women, and gives men the excuse that they are forced to be oppressors. On the contrary, any man is free to renounce his superior position provided that he is willing to be treated like a woman by other men.

We also reject the idea that women consent to or are to blame for their own oppression. Women's submission is not the result of brainwashing, stupidity, or mental illness but of continual, daily pressure from men. We do not need to change ourselves, but to change men.

The most slanderous evasion of all is that women can oppress men. The basis for this illusion is the isolation of individual relationships from their political context and the tendency of men to see any legitimate challenge to their privileges as persecution.

V   We regard our personal experience, and our feelings about that experience, as the basis for any analysis of our common situation. We cannot rely on existing ideologies as they are all products of male supremacist culture. We question every generalization and accept none that are not confirmed by our experience.

Our chief task at present is to develop female class consciousness through sharing experience and publicly exposing the sexist foundation of all our institutions. Consciousness-raising is not "therapy," which implies the existence of individual solutions and falsely assumes that the male-female relationship is purely personal, but the only method by which we can ensure that our program for liberation is based on the concrete realities of our lives.

The first requirement for raising class consciousness is honesty, in private and in public, with ourselves and other women.

VI We identify with all women. We define our best interest as that of the poorest, most brutally exploited woman.

We repudiate all economic, racial, educational, or status privileges that divide us from other women. We are determined to recognize and eliminate any prejudices we may hold against other women.

We are committed to achieving internal democracy. We will do whatever is necessary to ensure that every woman in our movement has an equal chance to participate, assume responsibility, and develop her political potential.

VII We call on all our sisters to unite with us in struggle.

We call on all men to give up their male privileges and support women's liberation in the interest of our humanity and their own.

In fighting for our liberation we will always take the side of women against their oppressors. We will not ask what is "revolutionary" or "reformist," only what is good for women.

The time for individual skirmishes has passed. This time we are going all the way.

5. A *Redbook* Magazine Reader Discovers Consciousness-Raising, 1973

I have participated in a consciousness-raising group for some time now, exploring what it means to me to be a woman, discovering how I can transform the traditional female role into one that fits my own feelings and capabilities.

Consciousness-raising is basically a sensitizing process. Its purpose is to make a woman aware that as a woman she has been denied many opportunities for choice in her life. Through discussing her life on a personal level with others in her group, the reasoning goes, she will come to realize the extent to which the realities of her situation—including what has been expected of her and denied her, how she has been conditioned by parents, teachers, and other people to fit the "feminine" mold, and how she feels about herself—are shared by other women. Such new perspectives help prepare women to recognize and cope with discrimination and to take advantage of new opportunities arising for women today.

One of the first things consciousness-raising helped my group see is how unfair the institution of marriage is to women. Traditionally dependent upon her husband for financial support, a wife generally has been expected to fit in the community her husband chooses, be supportive of his career, wait on him and accommodate to his desires, fulfill housekeeping and childcare functions capably and do her best to "love, honor, and obey"—cheerfully.

Many women have accepted this secondary role and taken for granted the fact that their husbands have had more mobility and freedom of choice. In fact, few married women realize that marriage can restrict their legal rights—that in many states, for instance, a wife is not free to conduct such activities as taking out a loan, filing a suit, starting a business or disposing of personal property independently of her husband, legally marriage is not a partnership of equals.

Many women, including myself, believe that this inequality will not be overcome merely by the passage of fairer marriage and divorce legislation. We feel that married women must work for shared responsibility and privilege that may involve a difficult reassessment of marriage. In my case this has meant sharing child care, housework, and financial support of our family with my husband, a flexible arrangement that has taken into account our individual goals and interests and allowed us both to grow.

One function of the consciousness-raising group is to provide the support a woman needs to insist upon equality in her personal relationships and to work for more control over her own life, to give her the insight and strength to change aspects of her life—or of her marriage—that make her unhappy. Sometimes just knowing that other women share her feelings or face similar problems is enough. Or a group can suggest solutions to specific problems.

For example, when a 26-year old woman in my group was offered a job by a former boss, she was torn between her feelings of responsibility for her two-year old daughter and her desire to continue the work she'd enjoyed before her child was born—a conflict others of us also had faced. She realized that full-time work would make her feel she was missing the joys of watching her daughter grow; yet full-time motherhood left her lethargic and bored, she sometimes found it hard to summon the energy to do her housework. And she had been surprised, she told us, at her eagerness to take the job when it was offered.

Our group helped by listening as she voiced her qualms, by suggesting possibilities for child care and a part-time trial period on the job, and by supporting her right to choose what she wanted to do. Eventually she decided to take the job—working only three days a week—and before long she found that her daughter enjoyed her play group, her husband no longer came home to her complaints of boredom, and even the housework seemed easier. "Without the support of the group, taking a job again might have been an empty dream, a fantasy to turn over in my mind while I watched the soap operas," she said later.

If you are interested in joining a consciousness-raising group, there are many ways to go about it. You can check first with neighbors, friends, and acquaintances to find out if they know of any such group in your community. You can contact women's organizations in the area to see if they are helping to set up such groups— in many cities consciousness-raising groups are co-ordinated through women's centers and the YWCA. And you can watch the newspapers for items about or announcements of local group meetings. Also there are Women's Liberation groups at many colleges.

Some women I know who haven't found a group functioning in their community have started their own by encouraging interest on the part of friends, neighbors and acquaintances. If you are employed or do volunteer work in parents' or community projects you can talk with co-workers, and you can post a sign on a bulletin board where other women will see it, asking for those interested to contact you.

My group and most of the groups I know about follow certain basic guidelines. The best size for a group, for example, seems to be from seven to ten women—large enough for a variety of viewpoints, yet small enough for intimacy to develop—but anywhere from five to 15 members seems manageable. Usually meetings are held weekly at members' houses. The atmosphere of the meetings should be casual, with no interruptions from husband or children, so that each woman feels comfortable and able to speak frankly.

In general, groups follow similar patterns in their meetings. The first session is usually devoted to getting acquainted and overcoming the initial nervousness of those who don't know what to expect or who have misconceptions about the Women's Movement. Sometimes the women give their reasons for being drawn to the Movement and discuss what they hope it can accomplish.

The personalities and backgrounds of some women may make them better able to express themselves; a group should try to be aware of this and to insist that the more silent women participate. And it is important to stick to a weekly topic and not let the meeting deteriorate into chitchat or gossip.

Weekly topics are designed to trigger feelings the group can explore together and are best chosen the week before so that they can be mulled over during the week. Although it's natural for a group to stick at first to such subjects as how housekeeping can be less of a burden, most groups eventually get around to covering topics and answering questions like the following: Your parents and their relationship to each other and to you. Your feelings about marriage, having children, pregnancy and motherhood. Your relationship with other women, your relationships with men—are there recurring patterns? Do you ever feel invisible? How do you feel about growing old? Have you ever felt that men have pressured you into sexual relationships? Have you ever lied about orgasm? What would you like most to do in life and what has stopped you? Do you have difficulty expressing anger or asserting yourself? As a child were you encouraged in certain activities and discouraged from others? How were you educated? Do you see housework as a duty only you should perform or do you see it as a favor to your family?

Discussion proceeds in a circle with each woman speaking on the topic as it relates to her own life. While one woman is speaking others may question her, but she should finish before another woman begins.

In my group there were strained silences and halting testimony during the first few meetings, before members learned to trust one another and were able to overcome their nervousness. It takes a while to find the courage to expose problems that have been considered private; yet once women open up to one another, they often find that others share, or at least sympathize with, these problems. A friend of mine told me that members of her group found it easier to reveal themselves after they made a protective decision not to repeat to people outside the group personal information given at meetings. Several of my friends found that when they shared ideas from our group discussions with their husbands, they were better able to help them understand women's objections to some male attitudes and how these attitudes needed to be changed.

My experience in a consciousness-raising group has been tremendously exciting, and so have the experiences of my friends. Most of us went through periods of elation, anger, and frustration before achieving a new-found sense of power over our lives. We also felt a sense of closeness as we discovered how much we as women have in common and learned to work together. Once we realized how the stereotyped woman's role can limit individual growth, many of us reacted with anger, or with what one woman called "justifiable rage." But these feelings of anger are not the goal of consciousness-raising; they're part of the process. They motivate women to change, to develop their abilities, and to use these abilities with confidence in themselves.

Attempting to replace a traditional role with a new, self-determined one is a constant challenge to women like us who are working to liberate ourselves. But it is likely that the co-operation, sisterhood, individual initiative, and internal democracy that we develop through consciousness-raising will strongly influence the people and the institutions around us.

6. Phyllis Schlafly Proclaims the Power of the Positive Woman, 1977

The first requirement for the acquisition of power by the Positive Woman is to understand the differences between men and women. Your outlook on life, your faith, your behavior, your potential for fulfillment, all are determined by the parameters of your original premise. The Positive Woman starts with the assumption that the world is her oyster. She rejoices in the creative capability within her body and the power potential of her mind and spirit. She understands that men and women are different, and that those very differences provide the key to her success as a person and fulfillment as a woman.

The women's liberationist, on the other hand, is imprisoned by her own negative view of herself and of her place in the world around her. This view of women was most succinctly expressed in an advertisement designed by the principal woman's liberationist organization, the National Organization for Women (NOW), and run in many magazines and newspapers and as spot announcements on many television stations. The advertisement showed a darling curlyheaded girl with the caption: "This healthy, normal baby has a handicap. She was born female."

This is the self-articulated dog-in-the-manger, chip-on-the-shoulder, fundamental dogma of the women's liberation movement. Someone—it is not clear who, perhaps God, perhaps the "Establishment," perhaps a conspiracy of male chauvinist pigs—dealt women a full blow by making them female. It becomes necessary, therefore, for women to agitate and demonstrate and hurl demands on society in order to wrest from an oppressive male-dominated social structure the status that has been wrongfully denied to women through the centuries.

By its very nature, therefore, the women's liberation movement precipitates a series of conflict situations—in the legislatures, in the courts, in the schools, in industry—with man targeted as the enemy. Confrontation replaces cooperation as the watchword of all relationships. Women and men become adversaries instead of partners.

The second dogma of the women's liberationists is that, of all the injustices perpetrated upon women through the centuries, the most oppressive is the cruel fact that women have babies and men do not. Within the confines of the women's liberationist ideology, therefore, the abolition of this overriding inequality of

Excerpt from *The Power of the Positive Woman* by Phyllis Schlafly (1977). Reprinted by permission of the author.

women becomes the primary goal. This goal must be achieved at any and all costs—to the woman herself, to the baby, to the family, and to society. Women must be made equal to men in their ability *not* to become pregnant and *not* to be expected to care for babies they may bring into the world.

This is why women's liberationists are compulsively involved in the drive to make abortion and child-care centers for all women, regardless of religion or income, both socially acceptable and government-financed. Former Congresswoman Bella Abzug has defined the goal: "to enforce the constitutional right of females to terminate pregnancies that they do not wish to continue."

If man is targeted as the enemy, and the ultimate goal of women's liberation is independence from men and the avoidance of pregnancy and its consequences, then lesbianism is logically the highest form in the ritual of women's liberation. Many, such as Kate Millett, come to this conclusion, although many others do not.

The Positive Woman will never travel that dead-end road. It is self-evident to the Positive Woman that the female body with its baby-producing organs was not designed by a conspiracy of men but by the Divine Architect of the human race. Those who think it is unfair that women have babies, whereas men cannot, will have to take up their complaint with God because no other power is capable of changing that fundamental fact. On some college campuses, I have been assured that other methods of reproduction will be developed. But most of us must deal with the real world rather than with the imagination of dreamers. . . .

The third basic dogma of the women's liberation movement is that there is no difference between male and female except the sex organs, and that all those physical, cognitive, and emotional differences you *think* are there, are merely the result of centuries of restraints imposed by a male-dominated society and sex-stereotyped schooling. The role imposed on women is, by definition, inferior, according to the women's liberationists.

The Positive Woman knows that, while there are some physical competitions in which women are better (and can command more money) than men, including those that put a premium on grace and beauty, such as figure skating, the superior physical strength of males over females in competitions of strength, speed, and short-term endurance is beyond rational dispute.

In the Olympic Games, women not only cannot win any medals in competition with men, the gulf between them is so great that they cannot even qualify for the contests with men. No amount of training from infancy can enable women to throw the discus as far as men, or to match men in push-ups or in lifting weights. In track and field events, individual male records surpass those of women by 10 to 20 percent. . . .

The Positive Woman remembers the essential validity of the old prayer: "Lord, give me the strength to change what I can change, the serenity to accept what I cannot change, and the wisdom to discern the difference." The women's liberationists are expending their time and energies erecting a make-believe world in which they hypothesize that *if* schooling were gender-free, and *if* the same money were spent on male and female sports programs, and *if* women were permitted to compete on equal terms, *then* they would prove themselves to be physically equal. Meanwhile, the Positive Woman has put the ineradicable physical differences into her mental computer, programmed her plan of action, and is already on the way to personal achievement. . . .

Despite the claims of the women's liberation movement, there are countless physical differences between men and women. The female body is 50 to 60 percent water, the male 60 to 70 percent water, which explains why males can dilute alcohol better than women and delay its effect. The average woman is about 25 percent fatty tissue, while the male is 15 percent, making women more buoyant in water and able to swim with less effort. Males have a tendency to color blindness. Only 5 percent of persons who get gout are female. Boys are born bigger. Women live longer in most countries of the world, not only in the United States where we have a hard-driving competitive pace. Women excel in manual dexterity, verbal skills, and memory recall. . . .

Does the physical advantage of men doom women to a life of servility and subservience? The Positive Woman knows that she has a complementary advantage which is at least as great—and, in the hands of a skillful woman, far greater. The Divine Architect who gave men a superior strength to lift weights also gave women a different kind of superior strength.

The women's liberationists and their dupes who try to tell each other that the sexual drive of men and women is really the same, and that it is only societal restraints that inhibit women from an equal desire, an equal enjoyment, and an equal freedom from the consequences, are doomed to frustration forever. It just isn't so, and pretending cannot make it so. The differences are not a woman's weakness but her strength.

Dr. Robert Collins, who has had ten years' experience in listening to and advising young women at a large eastern university, put his finger on the reason why casual "sexual activity" is such a cheat on women:

> A basic flaw in this new morality is the assumption that males and females are the same sexually. The simplicity of the male anatomy and its operation suggest that to a man, sex can be an activity apart from his whole being, a drive related to the organs themselves.
>
> In a woman, the complex internal organization, correlated with her other hormonal systems, indicates her sexuality must involve her total self. On the other hand, the man is orgasm-oriented with a drive that ignores most other aspects of the relationship. The woman is almost totally different. She is engulfed in romanticism and tries to find and express her total feelings for her partner.
>
> A study at a midwestern school shows that 80 percent of the women who had intercourse hoped to marry their partner. Only 12 percent of the men expected the same.
>
> Women say that soft, warm promises and tender touches are delightful, but that the act itself usually leads to a "Is that all there is to it?" reaction. . . .
>
> [A typical reaction is]: "It sure wasn't worth it. It was no fun at the time. I've been worried ever since. . . ."
>
> The new morality is a fad. It ignores history, it denies the physical and mental composition of human beings, it is intolerant, exploitative, and is oriented toward intercourse, not love.

The new generation can brag all it wants about the new liberation of the new morality, but it is still the woman who is hurt the most. The new morality isn't just a "fad"—it is a cheat and a thief. It robs the woman of her virtue, her youth, her beauty, and her love—for nothing, just nothing. It has produced a generation of young women searching for their identity, bored with sexual freedom, and despondent from the loneliness of living a life without commitment. They have abandoned the old commandments, but they can't find any new rules that work. . . .

The differences between men and women are also emotional and psychological. Without woman's innate maternal instinct, the human race would have died out centuries ago. There is nothing so helpless in all earthly life as the newborn infant. It will die within hours if not cared for. Even in the most primitive, uneducated societies, women have always cared for their newborn babies. They didn't need any schooling to teach them how. They didn't need any welfare workers to tell them it is their social obligation. Even in societies to whom such concepts as "ought," "social responsibility," and "compassion for the helpless" were unknown, mothers cared for their new babies.

Why? Because caring for a baby serves the natural maternal need of a woman. Although not nearly so total as the baby's need, the woman's need is nonetheless real.

The overriding psychological need of a woman is to love something alive. A baby fulfills this need in the lives of most women. If a baby is not available to fill that need, women search for a baby-substitute. This is the reason why women have traditionally gone into teaching and nursing careers. They are doing what comes naturally to the female psyche. The schoolchild or the patient of any age provides an outlet for a woman to express her natural maternal need. . . .

This is not to say that every woman must have a baby in order to be fulfilled. But it is to say that fulfillment for most women involves expressing their natural maternal urge by loving and caring for someone.

The women's liberation movement complains that traditional stereotyped roles assume that women are "passive" and that men are "aggressive." The anomaly is that a woman's most fundamental emotional need is not passive at all, but active. A woman naturally seeks to love affirmatively and to show that love in an active way by caring for the object of her affections.

The Positive Woman finds somebody on whom she can lavish her maternal love so that it doesn't well up inside her and cause psychological frustrations. Surely no woman is so isolated by geography or insulated by spirit that she cannot find someone worthy of her maternal love. All persons, men and women, gain by sharing something of themselves with their fellow humans, but women profit most of all because it is part of their very nature.

One of the strangest quirks of women's liberationists is their complaint that societal restraints prevent men from crying in public or showing their emotions, but permit women to do so, and that therefore we should "liberate" men to enable them, too, to cry in public. The public display of fear, sorrow, anger, and irritation reveals a lack of self-discipline that should be avoided by the Positive Woman just as much as by the Positive Man. Maternal love, however, is not a weakness but a manifestation of strength and service, and it should be nurtured by the Positive Woman.

Most women's organizations, recognizing the preference of most women to avoid hard-driving competition, handle the matter of succession of officers by the device of a nominating committee. This eliminates the unpleasantness and the tension of a competitive confrontation every year or two. Many women's organizations customarily use a prayer attributed to Mary, Queen of Scots, which is an excellent analysis by a woman of women's faults:

> Keep us, O God, from pettiness; let us be large in thought, in word, in deed. Let us be done with fault-finding and leave off self-seeking. . . . Grant that we may realize it is the little things that create differences, that in the big things of life we are at one.

Another silliness of the women's liberationists is their frenetic desire to force all women to accept the title *Ms* in place of *Miss* or *Mrs.* If Gloria Steinem and Betty Friedan want to call themselves *Ms* in order to conceal their marital status, their wishes should be respected.

But that doesn't satisfy the women's liberationists. They want all women to be compelled to use *Ms* whether they like it or not. The women's liberation movement has been waging a persistent campaign to browbeat the media into using *Ms* as the standard title for all women. The women's liberationists have already succeeding in getting the Department of Health, Education, and Welfare to forbid schools and colleges from identifying women students as *Miss* or *Mrs.*

All polls show that the majority of women do not care to be called *Ms.* A Roper poll indicated that 81 percent of the women questioned said they prefer *Miss* or *Mrs.* to *Ms.* Most married women feel they worked hard for the *r* in their names, and they don't care to be gratuitously deprived of it. Most single women don't care to have their name changed to an unfamiliar title that at best conveys overtones of feminist ideology and is polemical in meaning, and at worst connotes misery instead of joy. Thus, Kate Smith, a very Positive Woman, proudly proclaimed on television that she is "Miss Kate Smith, not Ms." Like other Positive Women, she has been succeeding while negative women have been complaining.

Finally, women are different from men in dealing with the fundamentals of life itself. Men are philosophers, women are practical, and 'twas ever thus. Men may philosophize about how life began and where we are heading; women are concerned about feeding the kids today. No woman would ever, as Karl Marx did, spend years reading political philosophy in the British Museum while her child starved to death. Women don't take naturally to a search for the intangible and the abstract. The Positive Woman knows who she is and where she is going, and she will reach her goal because the longest journey starts with a very practical first step. . . .

The Five Principles

When the women's liberationists enter the political arena to promote legislation and litigation in pursuit of their goals, their specific demands are based on five principles.

1. They demand that a "gender-free" rule be applied to every federal and state law, bureaucratic regulation, educational institution, and expenditure of public funds. Based on their dogma that there is no real difference between men and women (except in sex organs), they demand that males and females have identical treatment always. Thus, if fathers are not expected to stay home and care for their infant children, then neither should mothers be expected to do so; and, therefore, it becomes the duty of the government to provide kiddy-care centers to relive mothers of that unfair and unequal burden.

The women's lib dogma demands that the courts treat sex as a "suspect" classification—just as race is now treated—so that no difference of treatment or separation between the sexes will ever be permitted, no matter how reasonable or how much it is desired by reasonable people.

XXX *E S S A Y S*

Feminists often pointed with pride to how their movement was one without leaders, central organization, or a fixed ideology. By some lights, it was not a movement at all, in that the issues it addressed and set of alliances were so diverse. These essays highlight some of the internal dynamics of feminism. In the first, Martha Davis discusses the difficulties feminists working on poor women's issues encountered in making common cause with antipoverty activists. Although both dealt with "women's issues" and poverty, they rarely worked together. In the second essay, historian Alice Echols analyzes some of the internal tensions of feminist politics in the 1960s and 1970s.

Welfare Rights and Women's Rights in the 1960s

MARTHA F. DAVIS

The year 1966 is often cited as the start of the "second wave" of the organized women's movement, marked by the formation of the National Organization for Women (NOW). However, 1966 also marked the formal inception of another, less enduring group of women activists, the National Welfare Rights Organization (NWRO), linked to a separate but related social movement focused on welfare rights. From 1966 to 1975, NWRO coordinated welfare mothers' activism to shore up public assistance for the poor and to establish a federally guaranteed annual income. At its height in 1968, NWRO claimed twenty thousand members nationwide and dozens of local chapters from California to New York.

The connection between the women's movement and the welfare rights movement has often been minimized or even denied. There was, however, a complicated relationship between these two movements, notable for the repeated and only partially successful efforts of the groups to establish closer ties around issues of common concern. Feminists' interest in collaborating with welfare rights activists was a natural outgrowth of their recognition that poverty was a "women's issue." . . .

[Yet], the welfare rights movement did not immediately identify itself as a women's movement or its issues as women's issues. Led by male lawyers and relying upon the support of professionals such as social workers, NWRO's initial orientation was informed by the politics of class and, to a lesser extent, race. Only as new leadership emerged from within and the larger women's movement gained strength did NWRO embrace a gendered critique of the welfare system. Legal strategies that initially defined the organizing principles of the movement ignored gender issues. Nor was this surprising, since the federal judiciary did not extend heightened scrutiny under the equal protection clause to sex-based classifications until the early 1970s. Although NWRO maintained loose ties to the civil rights and labor movements as well as the women's movement, its leadership, concerned that closer relationships with these larger, more powerful groups would alienate NWRO's constituency and dilute its message, stayed at arm's length.

Martha F. Davis, "Welfare Rights and Women's Rights in the 1960s," in *Journal of Policy History,* Vol. 8.1 (1996), pp. 144–165. Copyright 1996 by The Pennsylvania State University. Reproduced by permission of The Pennsylvania State University Press.

In the end, efforts to establish a close collaboration between NOW and NWRO foundered on the divides of class, race, and, since NWRO was initially led by men, gender. Only when NWRO's leadership was given our to welfare mothers themselves, shortly before NWRO's demise in 1975, did an alliance along gender lines begin to overcome the profound economic and racial differences that separated the women's movement from the welfare rights movement. But coming as it did in the mid-1970s, when the backlash to the War on Poverty was already well under way and broad support for the welfare rights movement had waned, this new alliance was too late to influence significantly the welfare programs it critiqued. Instead, welfare remained a program uninformed by the second wave of feminism. . . . However, the women's movement was significantly influenced by its on-again, off-again alliances with low-income women. A powerful analytical framework that views poverty as inextricably linked to the common barriers faced by women in society, such as violence, wage discrimination, and disproportionate family responsibilities, and at the same time recognizes the unique challenges facing poor women and the need for social supports to redress these burdens, grew out of the trial-and-error approach that NOW and NWRO muddled through in the 1960s.

The Origins of the National Welfare Rights Organization

Beginning in 1963 women around the country receiving Aid to Families with Dependent Children (AFDC) met, often at the neighborhood centers established by the federal Community Action Program (CAP), to talk about their experiences as welfare mothers. AFDC was a joint federal-state welfare program created in 1935 to provide cash benefits to single-parent families with children—almost exclusively female-headed families. CAP, a Great Society innovation, was designed to provide financial support for community-based antipoverty efforts by funding existing programs and stimulating new ones. Under one of the most controversial provisions of the law establishing the program, each CAP-funded effort was to be "developed, conducted, and administered with maximum feasible participation of residents in the areas and members of the groups served."

Gradually, these CAP-sponsored discussion groups evolved into vehicles for AFDC recipients to enter the political arena and to express their discontent. Organizations were often led by mothers on welfare. In Minnesota, for example, recipients founded the AFDC League to present legislative ideas on welfare to elected representatives. In Massachusetts, welfare recipients organized Mothers for Adequate Welfare. Similar groups were active in California, New York, and Ohio. By 1965, many local groups were firmly established and, with the support of neighborhood centers, beginning to use their muscle to confront local welfare administrations.

Although social workers and other professionals were often employed by CAP-funded programs, most early welfare rights organizations had no access to lawyers. A proposed legal component of CAP had been rejected initially. But through skillful lobbying by Edgar Cahn and Jean Camper Cahn, two young, politically connected lawyers who urged that legal services would give voice to a "civilian perspective" on the War on Poverty, federally funded legal services were incorporated into the program in 1965. The following year, three hundred legal service organizations received grants totaling $42 million. These new legal services lawyers changed the face of poverty law. Indeed, many of the young lawyers at legal offices set up by community action agencies hoped to pursue strategic litigation that would address structural causes of poverty. According to Edward Sparer, a leading poverty lawyer, "Central to the new legal aid lawyer's role is the task of helping to articulate and promote the hopes, the dreams and the real possibility for the impoverished to make the social changes that *they* feel are needed through whatever lawful methods are available.

The civil rights movement, and particularly the central role of legal rights in that movement, directly influenced and stimulated the organizing efforts of welfare recipients. As an initial matter, the notion of legal rights to equal treatment had already proved to be a potent organizing tool in the civil rights movement. This organizing concept was very familiar to both welfare recipients and movement leaders. Indeed, many of the principal organizers of the welfare rights movement, including George Wiley, executive director of the NWRO, had cut their teeth in the civil rights movement.

An African American raised in a white middle-class community in Rhode Island, Wiley was an unlikely leader for a poor people's movement. Far from being revolutionary, he was the first black member of a fraternity at Rhode Island State College, which he attended on a scholarship. Wiley completed a doctorate in chemistry at Cornell in 1957 and joined the faculty of Syracuse University in 1960. There he met and married Wretha Whittle, a graduate student from Texas, and began to take a serious interest in the civil rights movement.

In his initial foray into political organizing, Wiley helped establish the Syracuse chapter of the Congress for Racial Equality (CORE), an interracial civil rights organization founded in 1942, and then led the chapter in a series of demonstrations over school segregation and employment discrimination. Wiley's campaigns caught the attention of James Farmer, national director of CORE, and in 1964 Farmer offered Wiley a job as associate national director of the organization. Wiley accepted, arranged a sabbatical from his faculty post, and moved his family to New York City, where CORE was headquartered.

Despite his personal popularity, Wiley did not move toward black separatism as quickly as many others in CORE. His wife and several of his key aides were white and advocated an integrationist model. Moving in the same direction as Martin Luther King Jr. at the time, Wiley believed that CORE should shift its emphasis from racial to economic issues to lead an integrated movement of poor people. But CORE and other civil rights groups were beginning to advocate racial separatism and militancy—and the exclusion of whites from the organization's staff. The Brooklyn chapter of CORE even announced that it would abandon its civil rights advocacy to set up "a new world of [its] own," an agricultural community restricted to black members. Under the circumstances, there was no longer any room for someone like Wiley at CORE. He left in the winter of 1966, shut out in a power struggle that involved not only his political views but individual egos as well.

Hoping to start a new movement of welfare recipients and increase pressure for a federal guaranteed minimum income, Wiley gave up tenure, moved his family to Washington, D.C., and in May 1966 opened the Poverty/Rights Action Center, an organization dedicated to establishing a national welfare rights movement. In short order, Wiley began to capitalize on the existing welfare groups that had grown up around the CAP centers. In his first major action, he turned a local recipients' march from Cleveland to Columbus, Ohio, into a national media event. With two hundred marchers in Ohio and simultaneous demonstrations in fifteen states, the

June 1966 march was a launching pad for many local welfare organizations, including the City-Wide Coordinating Committee of Welfare Groups in New York City. On 6 August 1966, at the South Side YMCA in Chicago, Illinois, Wiley assembled 136 recipients from 100 welfare organizations, civil rights activists, social workers, and organizers in twenty-four cities to discuss the formation of a national welfare movement. Most of them were women, and the great majority of the welfare recipients were mothers receiving AFDC.

It was a propitious time to organize the poor. The neighborhood-based resources available through the War on Poverty, particularly community action centers and neighborhood legal services offices, provided a new opportunity to reach poor people at a time when the nation appeared poised to reconsider and possibly expand the scope of the welfare state. Spurred by the heightened activism of the time and the promise of new rights that would raise their benefits and increase their dignity, many women on welfare were prepared to take the risks if it would improve their family's lot.

The "special grants campaign" illustrates the way in which Wiley and other organizers used legal rights to organize welfare recipients and build the national movement. Most states in 1966 made available itemized grants to provide for [a] recipient's special needs, such as a winter coat, silverware, a broom, and other household necessities. Subject to their social workers' largesse when it came to doling out such things, few welfare recipients were aware that these special grants existed. NWRO-affiliates around the country drew up long lists of the available grants and distributed these lists to their members. The special-grants demands were then delivered to the local welfare administrations. Welfare rights organizations used these special-grants campaigns to help members navigate the welfare bureaucracy and, significantly, get additional grant money for their constituents.

At the August 1966 Chicago meeting the fledgling welfare rights organization identified four basic goals of a national welfare rights movement: (1) adequate income, (2) dignity, (3) justice, and (4) democratic participation. These goals reflected George Wiley's vision of an organization for all poor people; neither race nor gender was mentioned. But although written in gender-neutral terms, NWRO's goals also addressed the specific experiences of its primary constituents—poor women on AFDC. These included: midnight raids on their homes by welfare case-workers searching for male companions, capricious rejections of applications for benefits, and threats or intimidation directed toward welfare mothers.

Although not a product of theory or even self-conscious reflection, in practice many of the NWRO's goals targeted concerns unique to women. For example, the organization's "immediate goals" sought to stop "illegal practices by welfare departments, such as . . . discriminating against families with illegitimate children . . . [and] forcing mothers with young children to take jobs." Other "pressing goals" included "providing child care for welfare mothers who are able to and wish to work." "Longer-range goals" included "getting rid of 'man-in-the-house' and 'suitable home' regulations and laws, except as they apply to the *whole* public." Under "man-in-the-house" rules, if an AFDC mother was believed to be cohabiting or to have a boyfriend, her entire family could be thrown off the rolls on the assumption that her "boyfriend" should be providing support to the family. "Suitable home" regulations denied welfare benefits to households with out-of-wedlock children based on the mother's presumed immorality. Although not explicitly framed or conceived of in the language that the emerging women's rights movement simultaneously began to use, the NWRO was clearly focused on the central concerns of women on welfare: privacy, household necessities, and, in the guise of child-care issues, the tension between women's role in the home and in the workplace.

The National Organization for Women

In October 1966, two months after the NWRO's initial meeting, NOW held its first organizing conference in Washington, D.C. NOW had originated in June 1966, when professional women representing State Commissions on Women met in Washington, D.C., for their third annual conference. At the time, it was well known that the federal Equal Employment Opportunity Commission (EEOC) was failing to implement the ban on sex discrimination in the workplace contained in Title VII of the Civil Rights Act of 1964. But when the local women leaders attending the conference attempted to present a resolution demanding that the EEOC step up enforcement of the provision, conference organizers blocked the measure. Two dozen angry women who had supported the resolution left the meeting agreeing that it was time to form their own, independent lobbying group. Like the NWRO, NOW was indebted to the civil rights movement: NOW's founders wanted to create an organization that could do for women what the National Association for the Advancement of Colored People (NAACP) had done for civil rights. Betty Friedan, author of *The Feminine Mystique* (1963), who was at the conference gathering material for her second book, suggested that the new organization be called the National Organization for Women.

From the start, the issue of women's poverty was given a prominent place on NOW's agenda. As early as its first conference in 1966, when the nascent group adopted a set of fundamental goals for the new women's movement, NOW stated:

> We start with a concern for the plight of women who now live in poverty. The most serious victims of sex discrimination in this country are women at the bottom, including those who, unsupported, head a great percentage of the families in poverty; those women who work at low-paying, marginal jobs, or who cannot find work, and the seriously increasing numbers of high school dropouts who are girls. No adequate attention is being given to those women by any of the existing poverty programs.

Indeed, "[a]iding women in poverty and expanding opportunity" was listed as one of NOW's five targets for immediate action.

However, despite this rhetoric, many of NOW's early members—middle-class and elite community leaders—lacked the personal experience of poverty and brought little depth of understanding to the issue. For example, when NOW's Task Force on Women in Poverty was first established in late 1966, some NOW board members believed that women's disproportionate poverty could be best addressed by simply eliminating overt sex discrimination. They suggested that the Task Force's activities should be limited to urging that all federal antipoverty programs be administered without discrimination on the basis of sex.

In 1967, at its second national conference, NOW members passed a Bill of Rights that endorsed both a woman's right to have an abortion and the passage of the Equal Rights Amendment (ERA). Further, the Bill of Rights demanded "the right of women in poverty to secure job training, housing and family allowances on equal terms with men, without prejudice to a parent's right to remain at home caring for his or her children," and, echoing the NWRO's goals, a "revision of welfare legislation and poverty programs which deny women dignity, privacy, and self-respect." At the same time, members called on NOW to sponsor a conference on "Women in Poverty."

As more conservative members of NOW left the organization in protest over its positions on both abortion and the ERA, NOW's membership expanded to include more women influenced by the "women's liberation" movement. In contrast to NOW's earliest members, feminist activists from the "women's liberation" branch of the emerging women's movement, informed by New Left ideas and experience with the Students for a Democratic Society (SDS) and other leftist student groups, were younger, less well off, and generally more radical in their view of structural economic barriers facing women. With this influx, the organization moved to the political left. From 1967 on, NOW's tactics became more confrontational, including pickets, sit-ins, and demonstrations, reflecting the orientation of the organization's growing grassroots base. For example, in 1968 NOW's National Board joined in sponsoring the Poor People's Campaign on the Washington mall, and sponsored a national day of fasting to Free Women from Poverty." But despite the commitment of NOW's leadership and a small group of activists, the issue of women's poverty had not yet ignited the passions of the general NOW membership.

1967–1970: Arm's Length Collaboration   Throughout the late 1960s, NOW leaders frequently spoke out on women's poverty, including statements on the AFDC Work Incentive Program (WIN), participation in the 1968 Mothers Day March led by Coretta Scott King, and congressional testimony on economic issues facing poor and older women. But during this period, NOW consistently looked to NWRO, the only national low-income women's group, for leadership on issues involving poor women. This relatively passive stance frustrated the small core of NOW activists who believed that NOW should recruit more low-income members and seize the initiative in addressing women's poverty. This, however, was not simply a dispute about tactics. It reflected a broad, philosophical divide within NOW. For instance, because of their fight for equality with men in the workplace—Betty Friedan had long advocated meaningful work outside the home as the solution to "the problem that has no name"—many NOW members were ambivalent about NWRO's opposition to mandatory job-training programs and its position that women should have a right to stay home with their children. The felt that NOW could not straddle both sides of the work issue, yet confronting the differences between NOW's and NWRO's perspectives on the importance of women's work outside the home might well have accentuated them, thus undermining the effectiveness of both groups. Instead of resolving the dispute, NOW leaders glossed over it and limited themselves to general endorsements of NWRO's positions.

Similarly, NWRO had its doubt about closer ties to NOW. NWRO was generally reluctant to dilute its positions on welfare by collaborating with more broadly focused groups. Like many new organizations seeking to establish an identity, it was concerned that working in coalitions would result in more established, stable groups eclipsing NWRO's fundamental concerns. NWRO historian Guida West observed that "NWROs . . . tended to expect that the organized, middle-class women should be able and willing to provide financial support and 'services,' a role which most middle-class women rejected." In short, though the groups were generally mutually supportive, close collaboration between the NWRO and NOW would not come easily.

Crisis in NWRO   NWRO's efforts to find common ground with the women's rights movement were further frustrated when, beginning in 1968, changes in the welfare system undermined NWRO's organizing efforts and left its leaders preoccupied with internal organizational issues. The special-grants campaign orchestrated by NWRO was so successful in raising recipients' grant levels that in 1968 states and local welfare districts nationwide moved to eliminate special grants, replacing them with a nonitemized flat grant. With the demise of the special-grants system, which had formed the basis for much of NWRO's local organizing efforts, the welfare rights movement shifted its focus to the courts and the legislatures. Relying on both statutory and constitutional claims, but without raising arguments that drew on women's rights theories, litigation during this period successfully challenged the very foundation of the existing welfare system. State policies such as "man-in-the-house" rules, residency requirements, and denial of due process in cutting off benefits were eradicated in the short space of two years. Following these early court victories, NWRO initiated efforts to monitor their implementation.

In one of its last major mobilizations, NWRO took enforcement into its own hands in Nevada, where in December 1970 the state had announced a campaign against "welfare cheaters." Benefits had been denied to three thousand mothers and children and the benefits of many more were summarily reduced. Responding to pleas from local welfare rights organizers, NWRO organized "Operation Nevada." According to Sylvia Law, a lawyer who participated in the effort, "by the second week in February [1971], dozens of welfare leaders from around the country, some 40 lawyers, more than 70 law students, and organizers from the NWRO staff began to work in Nevada for periods ranging from a few days to a few weeks." Their hope was to provide a "model of resistance" in Nevada to deter the consideration of anti-welfare measures in other states.

The lawyers and organizers who descended on Nevada located people whose benefits had been terminated and were afraid to come forward, held seminars on recipients' rights, staged demonstrations, and represented individuals in fair hearings. They also initiated a federal lawsuit seeking to vacate all of the terminations and reductions on the ground that notice and hearing had not been provided, in violation of constitutional due process requirements.

The effort in Nevada was an unequivocal success, culminating in a court order reinstating the benefits previously denied. According to the court, "the [state] Administrator and his staff ran roughshod over the constitutional rights of eligible and ineligible recipients alike." Yet NWRO's lawyers remained uncertain about the prospects for defeating similar efforts in other states; litigation alone would not be enough to secure the rights of welfare recipients, and similar grassroots mobilizations would have to be repeated again and again across the country. . . .

With the demise of special grants, NWRO's membership dropped off; NWRO could no longer promise increased grants as a perk of membership. Unable to sustain a high level of grassroots activity, NWRO devoted the remainder of its energy, and its shrinking budget, to opposing President Nixon's welfare-reform proposal, the Family Assistance Plan (FAP). Many of the fundamental elements of the FAP, announced in late 1969, were attractive to NWRO leaders. Among other things, the scheme to replace AFDC with a federal minimum income would stabilize welfare support and relieve states of some of the fiscal burden of the rising welfare rolls. But the plan set the minimum assistance level at $1,600 for a family of four. The proposed minimum meant that only the handful of states paying less that $1,600 per year would raise grants for families on welfare. Most states would have been forced to continue supplementing the federal payment to meet recipients' minimal needs—a system resembling AFDC. In addition, NWRO objected to the FAP requirement that "employable" recipients take jobs at less than minimum wage.

After some debate and an initial false step in supporting the plan, NWRO finally rejected Nixon's proposal and instead initiated a campaign for a guaranteed income of $6,500 a year. One popular NWRO poster showed a picture of Nixon's three dogs posed in front of the White House with the caption: "This family of three has a yearly budget of $2,700. Their master, who lives in that white mansion, believes that a family of three *people* can live on $1,300 a year ($1,600 for a family of four) . . . for food, clothing, housing . . . everything!" NWRO's campaign even made some headway in Congress. In 1970, Senator Eugene McCarthy introduced the NWRO-drafted Adequate Income Act of 1970, establishing a guaranteed annual income of $6,500 per year for a family of four; thirty-two members of the House of Representatives also joined in the call for a guaranteed income of $6,500. Leaders of NWRO, including welfare recipients Johnnie Tillmon and Beulah Sanders, testified before Congress.

The debate over a guaranteed income was, however, short-lived. Opposed by both liberals and conservatives, although on very different grounds, by 1971 the FAP was effectively dead as a legislative package. Nixon formally abandoned the bill in 1972, leaving NWRO's legislative priorities, as well as its organizing efforts, in disarray. . . .

Different Perspectives   At the national level, NOW and NWRO leaders generally worked independently, often unable to find common ground. For example, acting on NOW's 1970 resolution to establish a liaison with NWRO, NOW President Karen DeCrow invited NWRO Executive Director George Wiley to speak at NOW's national board meeting. According to one NOW member who attended, Wiley "started out by saying that NWRO's primary goal was to place the black male back where he belonged—at the head of the family, not economic independence for women." NOW members realized that "he just didn't have his consciousness raised," concluding that a close relationship with NWRO would be difficult.

Conversely, NWRO activists were frustrated by NOW's blindered focus on the ERA as the route for addressing women's poverty. While NWRO leaders openly supported the ERA, it ranked low on their list of priorities for the welfare rights movement. NOW activists were well aware of this tension between the groups. Indeed, the March 1971 newsletter for NOW's Women in Poverty Task Force instructed NOW members to approach poor women as potential NOW members by focusing on "issues of immediate concern to women living beneath the poverty level." . . .

Other conflicts between NOW and NWRO were equally fundamental. Poor women tended to support protective labor legislation based on gender because of their concern about exploitation in largely unregulated, low-level jobs; NOW members opposed such legislation because it rested on assumptions about women's special vulnerability. NWRO opposed mandatory job programs for welfare recipients, arguing from past experience that the jobs resulting from such programs were not designed to move people out of poverty; their position was that poor women should be able to choose to stay home with their children. In contrast, NOW's instinct was to support work programs and to fight to make them equally available to women; such programs would contribute to NOW's general goal of severing women's ties to the home and opening all occupations to women.

The class and race differences that underlay these different perspectives are particularly clear from the results of two surveys. The first surveyed the backgrounds of NOW members attending the 1974 national conference in Houston: ten percent of the respondents reported a household income of below the poverty line; 90 percent of the respondents were white, with 5 percent black and 3 percent Latina. In contrast, the NWRO was composed exclusively of poor women, with about 90 percent of its members African American.

The following year, NOW initiated another survey, this time focusing on substantive issues. Respondents rated "employment and economic security" as their highest priority, followed by "layoffs in the economic crisis," advertising, health care, food, and housing. While these responses seem to suggest that NOW members accepted a broad definition of feminist goals complementing the priorities of the NWRO, the choices of strategy imply otherwise. The same respondents were asked to rank strategies for dealing with each priority area. The largest percentage, 62 percent, chose "compliance with present anti–sex discrimination and equal pay laws" as the primary strategy to be used in achieving employment and economic security; only 9 percent chose "support of a guaranteed annual income." In contrast to NWRO's broader economic focus and emphasis on economic security for those excluded from the workplace, NOW members remained fixed on formal, legal equality for those already in the workplace as the proper instrument for addressing women's poverty.

1972–1975 During the early 1970s, NOW's Women in Poverty Task Force and individual NOW leaders, such as NOW officer Aileen Hernandez, committed considerable resources to the issue of women and poverty. Still, some observers felt that NOW's efforts to mobilize grassroots lobbying and letter writing in support of its poverty positions were not particularly successful. Despite activism and demonstrated commitment at the highest levels of the organization, the perception remained that the general membership was, by and large, not prepared to make the leap from opposing sexism in the workplace and in antipoverty programs to looking at the larger economic issues contributing to women's disproportionate poverty and recommending pragmatic solutions, particularly if that required redistributing income.

This impression was reinforced by the media, which selectively reported on NOW's activities. At the 1973 NOW Convention, for example, NOW members voted to declare 1973 an "Action Year on Poverty." At the same conference, NOW debated its positions on prostitution, lesbianism, and rape. Only the later issues were covered by many members of the press. According to one report, "There was an uproar when some of the television news cameramen present turned on their lights and filmed only the debate on these three issues. . . .

In 1972 NWRO members were in the midst of waging an internal struggle to define their movement as a women's movement and to frame welfare rights as a women's issue. After its initial successes, the movement's legal campaign suffered a series of devastating setbacks when, in *Dandridge* v. *Williams, Jefferson* v. *Hackney,* and several other cases, the Supreme Court rejected their central claim that the constitution guaranteed minimum subsistence support of the needy.

A new approach to the issues was clearly warranted. Despite a membership made up almost entirely of women, including leaders of local NWRO affiliates, the national NWRO had been run almost exclusively by men since its inception, with welfare mothers acting as members of the executive board and in other representative capacities. George Wiley, NWRO executive director and founder of the organization, had long promised that the NWRO would be handed over to the welfare-mother activists when they were ready, but he seemed inclined to put off that day indefinitely.

Responding to membership pressure, in 1972 Wiley arranged for the appointment of Johnnie Tillmon, longtime Executive Board member and a welfare mother from Los Angeles, as associate director. This was not enough. In 1973 the membership revolted. Led by Tillmon, the NWRO Executive Committee demanded that Wiley develop a plan to place welfare mothers in the leadership of the organization.

Much like the emergence of black separatism, which led to Wiley's departure from CORE, women's demands that they be given the leadership of NWRO marked the end of Wiley's tenure as the organization's director. Wiley resigned and the NWRO Executive Committee appointed Johnnie Tillmon as NWRO's new executive director. Still, Wiley was not yet satisfied that welfare mothers could lead the organization. Before departing, he approached associate director Faith Evans and asked him to take over the organization. Evans refused, asserting that the Executive Committee's decision to appoint Tillmon should stand. According to Guida West, Evans "decried the fact that Wiley, like many other black leaders, had so little faith in poor women running their own organizations."

When Wiley left NWRO, the organization had a debt of $150,000. Further, because Wiley had not prepared to give up the reins of the organization, no one had been trained to take over his fund-raising and administrative duties. From January 1973 to March 1975, NWRO struggled to survive. Despite its new profile as an organization run by and for poor women, Faith Evans remained a key figure at NWRO and was chiefly responsible for reducing its debt to $28,000. In the end, however, there was no money to continue. In March 1975, NWRO filed for bankruptcy and closed its offices.

While NWRO's last two years were marked by financial and administrative stress, the leadership of poor women did make a difference in the organization's orientation. . . .

The first issue of *Ms.* magazine in 1973 reprinted a conversation with Johnnie Tillmon that became a classic statement of why welfare should be a women's issue. "I'm a woman. I'm a black woman. I'm a poor woman. I'm a fat woman. I'm a middle-aged woman. And I'm on welfare," the article began.

The truth is that AFDC is like a super-sexist marriage. You trade in *a* man for *the* man. But you can't divorce him if he treats you bad. He can divorce you, of course, cut you off anytime he wants. But in that case, *he* keeps the kids, not you. . . . In ordinary marriage, sex is supposed to be for your husband. On AFDC, you're not supposed to have any sex at all. . . . *The* man, the welfare system, controls your money. He tells you what to buy, where to buy it, and how much things cost. If things—rent, for instance—really cost more than he says they do, it's just too bad for you.

From this essay came the feminist shibboleth, "Every woman is only one man away from welfare."

Before NWRO's demise, NOW reinitiated its efforts to establish formal relations with NWRO. In March 1973, NOW president Wilma Heide wrote to NWRO board chairwoman Beulah Sanders to explore a liaison arrangement during NOW's Action Year Against Poverty. Further, in August 1974, NOW joined NWRO's Johnnie Tillmon in pressuring the U.S. Department of Labor to remove repressive requirements from the WIN welfare-to-work program. Perhaps if NWRO survived as an explicitly feminist organization, a new and productive alliance might finally have been established between the two groups. . . .

In sum, claims that NOW and other women's rights groups failed to address issues relevant to poor women through the 1960s and early 1970s present only half of the story. Rather than indifference, the division between low-income women's groups and other women's rights groups reflected the inherent, developmental structure of the women's movement. As Mayer N. Zald has observed, the movement "consists of a number of single-issue organizations as well as multi-issue organizations, [permitting] activists [to] work in areas which interest them, moving between organizations to avoid burn-out." It is this diversity and flexibility, illustrated by the coexistence of NOW, NWRO, and newer women's rights organizations, that have permitted the feminist movement to maintain high levels of mobilization, activity, and effectiveness for nearly three decades.

However, this structure does have consequences. Its success depends upon the ability of one group of activists, generally those most affected by a particular issue, to take a leadership role in formulating policy goals and mobilizing resources. Other feminist groups then act in a supportive capacity. But for women on welfare with few resources, little time to devote to organizing, and little credibility in the public policy arena, such an organizing model may be both impractical and ineffective. Instead, a stronger partnership between welfare rights groups and other feminists may be necessary in order to provide resources and lend weight to welfare rights activism, and ultimately to influence policy.

Whether such a partnership is possible remains an open question. From 1966 to 1975, NWRO and NOW worked more or less at arm's length, both because of NWRO's initial reluctance to collaborate and because of NOW's inability to mobilize its middle-class and elite membership around issues that either did not concern them or, even worse, that actually undermined fundamental principles such as the ERA. As a result, federal and state welfare policies during that period were seldom challenged on feminist grounds.

A closer working relationship between welfare rights activists and women's rights activists would have required both groups to confront and reconcile their differences around the issues of work, motherhood, and child care, perhaps developing a nuanced view that accounted for class and race differences, and even ceding some of their principles (at least for the time being) in order to move beyond the impasse that inhibited true collaboration. Given the heightened debate of poverty in the 1960s, such an exercise could well have influenced the structure of welfare policy and laid the groundwork for developing a strong national feminist movement ready to mobilize around welfare and women's poverty. Instead, the second wave of feminism has yet to influence significantly poverty policy. . . .

Women's Liberation and Sixties Radicalism

ALICE ECHOLS

On 7 September 1968 the sixties came to the Miss America Pageant when one hundred women's liberationists descended upon Atlantic City to protest the pageant's promotion of physical attractiveness and charm as the primary measures of women's worth. Carrying signs that declared, "Miss America Is a Big Falsie," "Miss America Sells It," and "Up Against the Wall, Miss America," they formed a picket line on the boardwalk, sang anti–Miss America songs in three-part harmony, and performed guerrilla theater. The activists crowned a live sheep Miss America and paraded it on the boardwalk to parody the way the contestants, and by extension, all women, "are appraised and judged like animals at a county fair." They tried to convince women in the crowd that the tyranny of beauty was but one of the many ways that women's bodies were colonized. By announcing beforehand that they would not speak to male reporters (or to any man for that matter), they challenged the sexual division of labor that consigned women reporters to the "soft" stories and male reporters to the "hard" news stories. Newspaper editors who wanted to cover the protest were thus forced to pull their female reporters from the society pages to do so.

The protesters set up a "Freedom Trash Can" and filled it with various "instruments of torture"—high-heeled shoes, bras, girdles, hair curlers, false eyelashes, typing books, and representative copies of *Cosmopolitan, Playboy,* and *Ladies' Home Journal.* They had wanted to burn the contents of the Freedom Trash Can but were prevented from doing so by a city ordinance that prohibited bonfires on the boardwalk. However, word had been leaked to the press that the protest would include a symbolic bra-burning, and, as a consequence, reporters were everywhere. Although they burned no bras that day on the boardwalk, the image of the bra-burning, militant feminist remains part of our popular mythology about the women's liberation movement.

The activists also managed to make their presence felt inside the auditorium during that night's live broadcast of the pageant. Pageant officials must have known that they were in for a long night when early in the evening one protester sprayed Toni Home Permanent Spray (one of the pageant's sponsors) at the mayor's booth. She was charged with disorderly conduct and "emanating a noxious odor," an irony that women's liberationists understandably savored. The more spectacular action

"Nothing Distant About It" by Alice Echols, from *The Sixties: From Memory to History,* edited by Dave Farber. Copyright © 1994 by the University of North Carolina Press. Used by permission of the publisher.

occurred later that night. As the outgoing Miss America read her farewell speech, four women unfurled a banner that read, "Women's Liberation," and all sixteen protesters shouted "Freedom for Women," and "No More Miss America" before security guards could eject them. The television audience heard the commotion and could see it register on Miss America's face as she stumbled through the remainder of her speech. But the program's producer prevented the cameramen from covering the cause of Miss America's consternation. The TV audience did not remain in the dark for long, because Monday's newspapers described the protest in some detail. As the first major demonstration of the fledgling women's liberation movement, it had been designed to make a big splash, and after Monday morning no one could doubt that it had.

In its wit, passion, and irreverence, not to mention its expansive formulation of politics (to include the politics of beauty, no less!), the Miss America protest resembled other sixties demonstrations. Just as women's liberationists used a sheep to make a statement about conventional femininity, so had the Yippies a week earlier lampooned the political process by nominating a pig, Pegasus, for the presidency at the Democratic National Convention. Although Atlantic City witnessed none of the violence that had occurred in Chicago, the protest generated plenty of hostility among the six hundred or so onlookers who gathered on the boardwalk. Judging from their response, this new thing, "women's liberation," was about as popular as the antiwar movement. The protesters were jeered, harassed, and called "commies" and "man-haters." One man suggested that it "would be a lot more useful" if the protesters threw themselves, and not their bras, girdles, and makeup, into the trash can.

Nothing—not even the verbal abuse they encountered on the boardwalk—could diminish the euphoria women's liberationists felt as they started to mobilize around their own, rather than other people's, oppression. Ann Snitow speaks for many when she recalls that in contrast to her involvement in the larger, male-dominated protest Movement, where she had felt sort of "blank and peripheral," women's liberation was like "an ecstasy of discussion." Precisely because it was about one's own life, "there was," she claims, "nothing distant about it." Robin Morgan has contended that the Miss America protest "announced our existence to the world." That is only a slight exaggeration, for as a consequence of the protest, women's liberation achieved the status of a movement both to its participants and to the media; as such, the Miss America demonstration represents an important moment in the history of the sixties.

Although the women's liberation movement only began to take shape toward the end of the decade, it was a paradigmatically sixties movement. It is not just that many early women's liberation activists had prior involvements in other sixties movements, although that was certainly true, as has been ably documented by Sara Evans. And it is not just that, of all the sixties movements, the women's liberation movement alone carried on and extended into the 1970s that decade's political radicalism and rethinking of fundamental social organization. Although that is true as well. Rather, it is also that the larger, male-dominated protest Movement, despite its considerable sexism, provided much of the intellectual foundation and cultural orientation for the women's liberation movement. Indeed, many of the broad themes of the women's liberation movement—especially its concern with revitalizing the democratic process and reformulating "politics" to include the personal—

were refined and recast versions of ideas and approaches already present in the New Left and the black freedom movement.

Moreover, like other sixties radicals, women's liberationists were responding at least in part to particular features of the postwar landscape. For instance, both the New Left and the women's liberation movement can be understood as part of a gendered generational revolt against the ultradomesticity of that aberrant decade, the 1950s. The white radicals who participated in these movements were in flight from the nuclear family and the domesticated versions of masculinity and femininity that prevailed in postwar America. Sixties radicals, white and black, were also responding to the hegemonic position of liberalism and its promotion of government expansion both at home and abroad—the welfare/warfare state. Although sixties radicals came to define themselves in opposition to liberalism, their relation to liberalism was nonetheless complicated and ambivalent. They saw in big government not only a way of achieving greater economic and social justice, but also the possibility of an increasingly well-managed society and an ever more remote government.

In this chapter I will attempt to evaluate some of the more important features of sixties radicalism by focusing on the specific example of the women's liberation movement. I am motivated by the problematic ways in which "the sixties" has come to be scripted in our culture. If conservative "slash and burn" accounts of the period indict sixties radicals for everything from crime and drug use to single motherhood, they at least heap guilt fairly equally upon antiwar, black civil rights, and feminist activists alike. By contrast, progressive reconstructions, while considerably more positive in their assessments of the period, tend to present the sixties as if women were almost completely outside the world of radical politics. Although my accounting of the sixties is in some respects critical, I nonetheless believe that there was much in sixties radicalism that was original and hopeful, including its challenge to established authority and expertise, its commitment to refashioning democracy and "politics," and its interrogation of such naturalized categories as gender and race.

Women's discontent with their place in America in the sixties was, of course, produced by a broad range of causes. Crucial in reigniting feminist consciousness in the sixties was the unprecedented number of women (especially married white women) being drawn into the paid labor force, as the service sector of the economy expanded and rising consumer aspirations fueled the desire of many families for a second income. As Alice Kessler-Harris has pointed out, "homes and cars, refrigerators and washing machines, telephones and multiple televisions required higher incomes." So did providing a college education for one's children. These new patterns of consumption were made possible in large part through the emergence of the two-income family as wives increasingly "sought to aid their husbands in the quest for the good life." By 1960, 30.5 percent of all wives worked for wages. Women's growing participation in the labor force also reflected larger structural shifts in the U.S. economy. Sara Evans has argued that the "reestablishment of labor force segregation following World War II ironically reserved for women a large proportion of the new jobs created in the fifties due to the fact that the fastest growing sector of the economy was no longer industry but services." Women's increasing labor force participation was facilitated as well by the growing number of women graduating from college and by the introduction of the birth control pill in 1960.

Despite the fact that women's "place" was increasingly in the paid work force (or perhaps because of it), ideas about women's proper role in American society were quite conventional throughout the 1950s and the early 1960s, held there by a resurgent ideology of domesticity—what Betty Friedan coined the "feminine mystique." But, as Jane De Hart-Mathews has observed, "the bad fit was there: the unfairness of unequal pay for the same work, the low value placed on jobs women performed, the double burden of housework and wage work." By the mid-1960s at least some American women felt that the contradiction between the realities of paid work and higher education on the one hand and the still pervasive ideology of domesticity on the other had become irreconcilable.

Without the presence of other oppositional movements, however, the women's liberation movement may not have developed at all as an organized force for social change. It certainly would have developed along vastly different lines. The climate of protest encouraged women, even those not directly involved in the black movement and the New Left, to question conventional gender arrangements. Moreover, many of the women who helped form the women's liberation movement had been involved as well in the male-dominated Movement. If the larger Movement was typically indifferent, or worse, hostile, to women's liberation, it was nonetheless through their experiences in that Movement that the young and predominantly white and middle-class women who initially formed the women's liberation movement became politicized. The relationship between women's liberation and the larger Movement was at its core paradoxical. If the Movement was a site of sexism it also provided white women a space in which they could develop political skills and self-confidence, a space in which they could violate the injunction against female self-assertion. Most important, it gave them no small part of the intellectual ammunition—the language and the ideas—with which to fight their own oppression.

Sixties radicals struggled to reformulate politics and power. Their struggle confounded many who lived through the sixties as well as those trying to make sense of the period some thirty years later. One of the most striking characteristics of sixties radicals was their ever-expanding opposition to liberalism. Radicals' theoretical disavowal of liberalism developed gradually and in large part in response to liberals' specific defaults—their failure to repudiate the segregationists at the 1964 Democratic National Convention, their lack of vigor in pressing for greater federal intervention in support of civil rights workers, and their readiness (with few exceptions) to support President Lyndon B. Johnson's escalation of the Vietnam War. But initially some radicals had argued that the Movement should acknowledge that liberalism was not monolithic but contained two discernible strands—"corporate" and "humanist" liberalism. For instance, in 1965 Carl Oglesby, an early leader of the Students for a Democratic Society (SDS), contrasted *corporate liberals,* whose identification with the system made them "illiberal liberals," with *humanist liberals,* who he hoped might yet see that "it is this movement with which their own best hopes are most in tune."

By 1967 radicals were no longer making the distinction between humanist and corporate liberals that they once had. This represented an important political shift for early new leftists in particular who once had felt an affinity of sorts with liberalism. Black radicals were the first to decisively reject liberalism, and their move had an enormous impact on white radicals. With the ascendancy of black power many black militants maintained that liberalism was intrinsically paternalistic, and that black liberation required that the struggle be free of white involvement. This was elaborated by white radicals, who soon developed the argument that authentic radicalism involved organizing around one's own oppression rather than becoming involved, as a "liberal" would, in someone else's struggle for freedom. For instance, 1967 Gregory Calvert, another SDS leader, argued that the "student movement has to develop an image of its own revolution . . . instead of believing that you're a revolutionary because you're related to Fidel's struggle, Stokely's struggle, always someone else's struggle." Black radicals were also the first to conclude that nothing short of revolution—certainly not Johnson's Great Society programs and a few pieces of civil rights legislation—could undo racism. As leftist journalist Andrew Kopkind remembered it, the rhetoric of revolution proved impossible for white new leftists to resist. "With black revolution raging in America and world revolution directed against America, it was hardly possible for white radicals to think themselves anything less than revolutionaries." . . .

. . . [S]ixties radicals did (especially over time) appropriate, expand, and recast Marxist categories in an effort to understand the experiences of oppressed and marginalized groups. Thus exponents of what was termed "new working-class theory" claimed that people with technical, clerical, and professional jobs should be seen as constituting a new sector of the working class, better educated than the traditional working class, but working class nonetheless. According to this view, students were not members of the privileged middle class, but rather "trainees" for the new working class. And many women's liberationists (even radical feminists who rejected Marxist theorizing about women's condition) often tried to use Marxist methodology to understand women's oppression. For example, Shulamith Firestone argued that just as the elimination of "economic classes" would require the revolt of the proletariat and their seizure of the means of production, so would the elimination of "sexual classes" require women's revolt and their "seizure of control of reproduction."

If young radicals often assumed an arrogant stance toward those remnants of the Old Left that survived the 1950s, they were by the late 1960s unambiguously contemptuous of liberals. Women's liberationists shared new leftists' and black radicals' rejection of liberalism, and, as a consequence, they often went to great lengths to distinguish themselves from the liberal feminists of the National Organization for Women (NOW). (In fact, their disillusionment with liberalism was more thorough during the early stages of their movement building than had been the case for either new leftists or civil rights activists because they had lived through the earlier betrayals around the Vietnam War and civil rights. Moreover, male radicals' frequent denunciations of women's liberation as "bourgeois" encouraged women's liberationists to distance themselves from NOW.) NOW had been formed in 1966 to push the federal government to enforce the provisions of the 1964 Civil Rights Act outlawing sex discrimination—a paradigmatic liberal agenda focused on public access and the prohibition of employment discrimination. To women's liberation activists, NOW's integrationist, access-oriented approach ignored the racial and class inequities that were the very foundation of the "mainstream" that NOW was dedicated to integrating. In the introduction to the 1970 bestseller, *Sisterhood Is Powerful,* Robin Morgan declared that "NOW is essentially an organization that wants reform [in the] second-class citizenship of women—and this is where it differs drastically from the rest of the Women's Liberation Movement." In *The Dialectic of Sex,* Shulamith Firestone described NOW's political stance as "untenable even in terms of immediate political gains" and deemed it "more a leftover of the old feminism rather than a model of the new." Radical feminist Ti-Grace Atkinson went even further, characterizing many in NOW as only wanting "women to have the same opportunity to be oppressors, too."

Women's liberationists also took issue with liberal feminists' formulation of women's problem as their exclusion from the public sphere. Younger activists argued instead that women's exclusion from public life was inextricable from their subordination in the family and would persist until this larger issue was addressed. For instance, Firestone claimed that the solution to women's oppression was not inclusion in the mainstream, but rather the eradication of the biological family, which was the "tape worm of exploitation."

Of course, younger activists' alienation from NOW was often more than matched by NOW members' disaffection from them. Many liberal feminists were appalled (at least initially) by women's liberationists' politicization of personal life. NOW founder Betty Friedan frequently railed against women's liberationists for waging a "bedroom war" that diverted women from the real struggle of integrating the public sphere.

Women's liberationists believed that they had embarked upon a much more ambitious project—the virtual remaking of the world—and that theirs was the real struggle. Nothing short of radically transforming society was sufficient to deal with what they were discovering: that gender inequality was embedded in everyday life. In 1970 Shulamith Firestone observed that "sex-class is so deep as to be invisible." The pervasiveness of gender inequality and gender's status as a naturalized category demonstrated to women's liberationists the inadequacy of NOW's legislative and judicial remedies and the necessity of thoroughgoing social transformation. Thus, whereas liberal feminists talked of ending sex discrimination, women's liberationists called for nothing less than the destruction of capitalism and patriarchy. As defined by feminists, patriarchy, in contrast to sex discrimination, defied reform. For example, Adrienne Rich contended: "Patriarchy is the power of the fathers: a familial-social, ideological, political system in which men—by force, direct pressure, or through ritual, tradition, law and language, customs etiquette, education, and the division of labor, determine what part women shall or shall not play, and in which the female is subsumed under the male."

Women's liberationists typically indicted capitalism as well. Ellen Willis, for instance, maintained that "the American system consists of two interdependent but distinct parts—the capitalist state, and the patriarchal family." Willis argued that capitalism succeeded in exploiting women as cheap labor and consumers "primarily by taking advantage of women's subordinate position in the family and our historical domination by man."

Central to the revisionary project of the women's liberation movement was the desire to render gender meaningless, to explode it as a significant category. In the movement's view, both masculinity and femininity represented not timeless essences, but rather "patriarchal" constructs. (Of course, even as the movement sought to deconstruct gender, it was, paradoxically, as many have noted, trying to mobilize women precisely on the basis of their gender.) This explains in part the significance abortion rights held for women's liberationists, who believed that until abortion was decriminalized, biology would remain women's destiny, thus foreclosing the possibility of women's self-determination.

Indeed, the women's liberation movement made women's bodies the site of political contestation. The "colonized" status of women's bodies became the focus of much movement activism. (The discourse of colonization originated in Third World national liberation movements but, in an act of First World appropriation, was taken up by black radicals who claimed that African Americans constituted an "internal colony" in the United States. Radical women trying to persuade the larger Movement of the legitimacy of their cause soon followed suit by deploying the discourse to expose women's subordinate position in relation to men. This appropriation represented an important move and one characteristic of radicalism in the *late* 1960s, that is, the borrowing of conceptual frameworks and discourse from other movements to comprehend the situation of oppressed groups in the United States— with mixed results at best. In fact, women's liberationists challenged not only tyrannical beauty standards, but also violence against women's sexual alienation, the compulsory character of heterosexuality and its organization around male pleasure (inscribed in the privileging of the vaginal over clitoral orgasm), the health hazards associate with the birth control pill, the definition of contraception as women's responsibility, and, of course, women's lack of reproductive control. They also challenged the sexual division of labor in the home, employment discrimination, and the absence of quality child-care facilities. Finally, women's liberationists recognized the power of language to shape culture.

The totalism of their vision would have been difficult to translate into a concrete reform package, even had they been interested in doing so. But electoral politics and the legislative and judicial reforms that engaged the energies of liberal feminists did little to animate most women's liberationists. Like other sixties radicals, they were instead taken with the idea of developing forms that would prefigure the utopian community of the imagined future. Anxious to avoid the "manipulated consent" that they believed characterized American politics, sixties radicals struggled to develop alternatives to hierarchy and centralized decision making. They spoke often of creating "participatory democracy" in an effort to maximize individual participation and equalize power. Their attempts to build a "democracy of individual participation" often confounded outsiders, who found Movement meetings exhausting and tedious affairs. But to those radicals who craved political engagement, "freedom" was, as one radical group enthused, "an endless meeting." According to Gregory Calvert, participatory democracy appealed to the "deep anti-authoritarianism of the new generation in addition to offering them the immediate concretization of the values of openness, honesty, and community in human relationships." Women's liberationists, still smarting from their first-hand discovery that the larger Movement's much-stated commitment to egalitarianism did not apply equally to all, often took extraordinary measures to try to ensure egalitarianism. They employed a variety of measures in an effort to equalize power, including consensus decision making, rotating chairs, and the sharing of both creative and routine movement work.

Fundamental to this "prefigurative politics," as sociologist Wini Breines terms it, was the commitment to develop counterinstitutions that would anticipate the desired society of the future. Staughton Lynd, director of the Mississippi Freedom Schools and a prominent new leftist, likened sixties radicals to the Wobblies (labor radicals of the early twentieth century) in their commitment to building "the new society within the shell of the old." According to two early SDSers, "What we are working for is far more than changes in the structure of society and its institutions or the people who are now making the decisions. . . . The stress should rather be on wrenching people out of the system both physically and spiritually."

Radicals believed that alternative institutions would not only satisfy needs unmet by the present system, but also, perhaps, by dramatizing the failures of the system, radicalize those not served by it but currently outside the Movement. Tom Hayden proposed that radicals "build our own free institutions—community organizations, newspapers, coffeehouses—at points of strain within the system where human needs are denied. These institutions become centers of identity, points of contact, building blocks of a new society from which we confront the system more intensely."

Among the earliest and best known of such efforts were the Mississippi Freedom Democratic party and the accompanying Freedom Schools formed during Freedom Summer of 1964. In the aftermath of that summer's Democratic National Convention, Bob Moses [Parris] of the Student Nonviolent Coordinating Committee (SNCC) even suggested that the Movement abandon its efforts to integrate the Democratic party and try instead to establish its own state government in Mississippi. And as early as 1966 SNCC's Atlanta Project called on blacks to "form our own institutions, credit unions, co-ops, political parties." This came to be the preferred strategy as the sixties progressed and disillusionment with traditional politics grew. Rather than working from within the system, new leftists and black radicals instead formed alternative political parties, media, schools, universities, and assemblies of oppressed and unrepresented people.

Women's liberationists elaborated on this idea, creating an amazing panoply of counterinstitutions. In the years before the 1973 Supreme Court decision decriminalizing abortion, feminists established abortion referral services in most cities of any size. Women's liberationists in Chicago even operated an underground abortion clinic, "Jane," where they performed about one hundred abortions each week. By the mid-1970s most big cities had a low-cost feminist health clinic, a rape crisis center, and a feminist bookstore. In Detroit, after "a long struggle to translate feminism into federalese," two women succeeded in convincing the National Credit Union Administration that feminism was a legitimate "field" from which to draw credit union members. Within three years of its founding in 1973, the Detroit credit union could claim assets of almost one million dollars. Feminists in other cities soon followed suit. Women's liberation activists in Washington, D.C., formed Olivia Records, the first women's record company, which by 1978 was supporting a paid staff of fourteen and producing four records a year. By the mid-1970s there existed in most cities of any size a politicized feminist counterculture, or a "women's community."

The popularity of alternative institutions was that at least in part they seemed to hold out the promise of political effectiveness without co-optation. Writing in 1969, Amiri Baraka (formerly LeRoi Jones), a black nationalist and accomplished poet, maintained, "But you must have the cultural revolution. . . . We cannot fight a war, an actual physical war with the forces of evil just because we are angry. We can begin to build. We must build black institutions . . . all based on a value system that is beneficial to black people." . . .

The move toward building counterinstitutions was part of a larger strategy to develop new societies "within the shell of the old," but this shift sometimes had unintended consequences. While feminist counterinstitutions were originally conceived as part of a culture of resistance, over time they often became more absorbed in sustaining themselves than in confronting male supremacy, especially as their services were duplicated by mainstream businesses. In the early years of the women's liberation movement this alternative feminist culture did provide the sort of "free space" women needed to confront sexism. But as it was further elaborated in the mid-1970s, it ironically often came to promote insularity instead—becoming, as Adrienne Rich has observed, "a place of emigration, an end in itself," where patriarchy was evaded rather than confronted. In practice, feminist communities were small, self-contained subcultures that proved hard to penetrate, especially to newcomers unaccustomed to their norm and conventions. The shift in favor of alternative communities may have sometimes impeded efforts at outreach for the women's liberationists, new leftists, and black radicals who attempted it.

On a related issue, the larger protest Movement's great pessimism about reform—the tendency to interpret every success a defeat resulting in the Movement's further recuperation (what Robin Morgan called "futilitarianism")—may have encouraged a too-global rejection of reform among sixties radicals. For instance, some women's liberation groups actually opposed the Equal Rights Amendment (ERA) when NOW revived it. In September 1970 a New York–based group, The Feminists, denounced the ERA and advised feminists against "squandering invaluable time and energy on it." A delegation of Washington, D.C., women's liberationists invited to appear before the senate subcommittee considering the ERA, testified: "We are aware that the system will try to appease us with their [sic] paper offerings. We will not be appeased. Our demands can only be met by a total transformation of society which you cannot legislate, you cannot co-opt, you cannot *control*." In *The Dialectic of Sex,* Firestone went so far as to dismiss child-care centers as attempts to "buy women off" because they "ease the immediate pressure without asking why the pressure is on *women.*"

Similarly, many SDS leaders opposed the National Conference for New Politics (NCNP), an abortive attempt to form a national progressive organization oriented around electoral politics and to launch an antiwar presidential ticket headed by Martin Luther King Jr. and Benjamin Spock. Immediately following NCNP's first and only convention, in 1967, the SDS paper *New Left Notes* published two front-page articles criticizing NCNP organizers. One writer contended that "people who recognize the political process as perverted will not seek change through the institutions that process has created." The failure of sixties radicals to distinguish between reform and reformism meant that while they defined the issues, they often did little to develop policy initiatives around those issues. Moreover, the preoccupation of women's liberationists with questions of internal democracy (fueled in part by their desire to succeed where the men had failed) sometimes had the effect of focusing attention away from the larger struggle in an effort to create the perfect movement. As feminist activist Frances Chapman points out, women's liberation was "like a generator that got things going, cut out and left it to the larger reform engine which made a lot of mistakes." In eschewing traditional politics rather than entering them skeptically, women's liberationists, like other sixties radicals, may have lost an opportunity to foster critical debate in the larger arena.

If young radicals eschewed the world of conventional politics they nonetheless had a profound impact upon it, especially by redefining what is understood as "political." Although the women's liberation movement popularized the slogan "the personal is political," the idea that there is a political dimension to personal life was first embraced by early SDSers who had encountered it in the writings of C. Wright Mills. Rebelling against a social order whose public and private spheres were highly differentiated, new leftists called for a reintegration of the personal with the political. They reconceptualized apparently personal problems—specifically their alienation from a campus cultural milieu characterized by sororities and fraternities, husband and wife hunting, sports, and careerism, and the powerlessness they felt as college students without a voice in campus governance or curriculum—as political problems. Thus SDS's founding Port Huron Statement of 1962 suggested that for an American New Left to succeed, it would have to "give form to . . . feelings of helplessness and indifference, so that people may see the political, social, and economic sources of their private troubles and organize to change society." Theirs was a far more expansive formulation of politics than what prevailed in the Old Left, even among the more renegade remnants that had survived into the early sixties. Power was conceptualized as relational and by no means reducible to electoral politics.

By expanding political discourse to include personal relations, new leftists unintentionally paved the way for women's liberationists to develop critiques of the family, marriage, and the construction of sexuality. (Of course, nonfeminist critiques of the family and sexual repressiveness were hardly in short supply in the 1950s and 1960s, as evidenced by *Rebel without a Cause, Catcher in the Rye,* and Paul Goodman's *Growing Up Absurd,* to mention but a few.) Women's liberationists developed an understanding of power's capillarylike nature, which in some respects anticipated those being formulated by Michel Foucault and other poststructralists. Power was conceptualized as occupying multiple sites and as lodging everywhere, even in those private places assumed to be the most removed from or impervious to politics—the home and, more particularly, the bedroom.

The belief of sixties radicals that the personal is political also suggested to them its converse—that the political is personal. Young radicals typically felt it was not enough to sign leaflets or participate in a march if one returned to the safety and comfort of a middle-class existence. Politics was supposed to unsettle life and its routines, even more, to transform life. For radicals the challenge was to discover, underneath all the layers of social conditioning, the "real" self unburdened by social expectations and conventions. Thus, SNCC leader Stokely Carmichael advanced the slogan, "Every Negro is a potential black man." Shulamith Firestone and Anne Koedt argued that among the "most exciting things to come out of the women's movement so far is a new daring . . . to tear down old structures and assumptions and let real thought and feeling flow." Life would not be comfortable, but who wanted comfort in the midst of so much deadening complacency? For a great many radicals, the individual became a site of political activism in the sixties. In the black freedom movement the task was very much to discover the black inside the Negro, and in the women's liberation movement it was to unlearn niceness, to challenge the taboo against female self-assertion.

Sixties radicalism proved compelling to many precisely because it promised to transform life. Politics was not about the subordination of self to some larger political cause; instead, it was the path to self-fulfillment. This ultimately was the power of sixties radicalism. As Stanley Aronowitz notes, sixties radicalism was in large measure about "infus[ing] life with a secular spiritual and moral content" and "fill[ing] the quotidian with personal meaning and purpose." But "the personal is political" was one of those ideas whose rhetorical power seemed to sometimes work against or undermine its explication. It could encourage a solipsistic preoccupation with self-transformation. As new leftist Richard Flacks presciently observed in 1965, this kind of politics could lead to "a search for personally satisfying modes of life while abandoning the possibility of helping others to change theirs." Thus the idea that "politics is how you live your life, not who you vote for," as Yippie leader Jerry Rubin put it, could and did lead to a subordination of politics to lifestyle. If the idea led some to confuse personal liberation with political struggle, it led others to embrace an asceticism that sacrificed personal needs and desires to political imperatives. Some women's liberation activists followed this course, interpreting the idea that the personal is political to mean that one's personal life should conform to some abstract standard of political correctness. At first this tendency was mitigated by the founders' insistence that there were no personal solutions, only collective solutions, to women's oppression. Over time, however, one's self-presentation, marital status, and sexual preference frequently came to determine one's standing or ranking in the movement. The most notorious example of this involved the New York radical group, The Feminists, who established a quota to limit the number of married women in the group. Policies such as these prompted Barbara Ehrenreich to question "a feminism which talks about universal sisterhood, but is horrified by women who wear spiked heels or call their friends 'girls.' At the same time, what was personally satisfying was sometimes upheld as politically correct. In the end, both the women's liberation movement and the larger protest Movement suffered, as the idea that the personal is political was often interpreted in such a way as to make questions of life-style absolutely central.

The social movements of the sixties signaled the beginning of what was come to be known as "identity politics," the idea that politics is rooted in identity. Although some New Left groups by the late 1960s did come to endorse an orthodox Marxism whereby class was privileged, class was not the pivotal category for these new social movements. (Even those New Left groups that reverted to the "labor metaphysic" lacked meaningful working-class participation.) Rather, race, ethnicity, gender, sexual preference, and youth were the salient categories for most sixties activists. In the women's liberation movement, what was termed "consciousness-raising" was the tool used to develop women's group identity.

As women's liberationists started to organize a movement, they confronted American women who identified unambiguously as women, but who typically had little of what Nancy Cott would call "we-ness," or "some level of identification with 'the group called women.'" Moreover, both the pervasiveness of gender inequality and the cultural understanding of gender as a natural rather than a social construct made it difficult to cultivate a critical consciousness about gender even among women. To engender this sense of sisterhood or "we-ness," women's liberationists developed consciousness-raising, a practice involving "the political reinterpretation of personal life." According to its principal architects, its purpose was to "awaken the latent consciousness that . . . all women have about our oppression." In talking about their personal experiences, it was argued, women would come to understand that what they had believed were personal problems were, in fact, "social problems that must become social issues and fought together rather than with personal solutions."

Reportedly, New York women's liberationist Kathie Sarachild was the person who coined the term *consciousness-raising*. However, the technique originated in other social movements. As Sarachild wrote in 1973, those who promoted consciousness-raising "were applying to women and to ourselves as women's liberation organizers the practice a number of us had learned in the civil rights movement in the South in the early 1960s." There they had seen that the sharing of personal problems, grievances, and aspirations—"telling it like it is"—could be a radicalizing experience. Moreover, for some women's liberationists consciousness-raising was a way to avoid the tendency of some members of the movement to try to fit women within existing (and often Marxist) theoretical paradigms. By circumventing the "experts" on women and going to women themselves, they would be able to not only construct a theory of women's oppression but formulate strategy as well. Thus women's liberationists struggled to find the commonalities in women's experiences in order to generate generalizations about women's oppression.

Consciousness-raising was enormously successful in exposing the insidiousness of sexism and in engendering a sense of identity and solidarity among the largely white, middle-class women who participated in "c-r" groups. By the early 1970s even NOW, whose founder Betty Friedan had initially derided consciousness-raising as so much "navel-gazing," began sponsoring c-r groups. But the effort to transcend the particular was both the strength and the weakness of consciousness-raising. If it encouraged women to locate the common denominators in their lives, it inhibited discussion of women's considerable differences. Despite the particularities of white, middle-class women's experiences, theirs became the basis for feminist theorizing about women's oppression. In a more general sense the identity politics informing consciousness-raising tended to privilege experience in certain problematic ways. It was too often assumed that there existed a kind of core experience, initially articulated as "woman's experience." Black and white radicals (the latter in relation to youth) made a similar move as well. When Stokely Carmichael called on blacks to develop an "ideology which speaks to our blackness," he, like other black nationalists, suggested that there was somehow an essential and authentic "blackness."

With the assertion of difference within the women's movement in the 1980s, the notion that women constitute a unitary category has been problematized. As a consequence, women's experiences have become ever more discretely defined, as in "the black female experience," "the Jewish female experience," or "the Chicana lesbian experience." But, as Audre Lorde has argued, there remains a way in which, even with greater and greater specificity, the particular is never fully captured. Instead, despite the pluralization of the subject within feminism, identities are often still imagined as monolithic. Finally, the very premise of identity politics—that identity is the basis of politics—has sometimes shut down possibilities for communication, as identities are seen as necessarily either conferring or foreclosing critical consciousness. Kobena Mercer, a British film critic, has criticized the rhetorical strategies of "authenticity and authentication" that tend to characterize identity politics. He has observed: "if I preface a point by saying something like, 'as a black gay man, I feel marginalized by your discourse,' it makes a valid point but in such a way that preempts critical dialogue because such a response could be inferred as a criticism not of what I say but of what or who I am. The problem is replicated in the familiar cop-out clause, 'as a middle-class, white, heterosexual male, what can I say?' "

The problem is that the mere assertion of identity becomes in a very real sense irrefutable. Identity is presented as not only stable and fixed, but as also insurmountable. While identity politics gives the oppressed the moral authority to speak (perhaps a dubious ground from which to speak), it can, ironically, absolve those belonging to dominant groups from having to engage in a critical dialogue. In some sense, then, identity politics can unintentionally reinforce Other-ness. Finally, as the antifeminist backlash and the emergence of the New Right should demonstrate, there is nothing inherently progressive about identity. It can be, and has been, mobilized for reactionary as well as for radical purposes. For example, the participation of so many women in the antiabortion movement reveals just how problematic the reduction of politics to identity can be.

Accounts of sixties radicalism usually cite its role in bringing about the dismantling of Jim Crow and disfranchisement, the withdrawal of U.S. troops from Vietnam, and greater gender equality. However, equally important, if less frequently noted, was its challenge to politics as usual. Sixties radicals succeeded both in reformulating politics, even mainstream politics, to include personal life, and in challenging the notion that elites alone have the wisdom and expertise to control the political process. For a moment, people who by virtue of their color, age, and gender were far from the sites of formal power became politically engaged, became agents of change.

Given the internal contradictions and shortcomings of sixties radicalism, the repressiveness of the federal government in the late 1960s and early 1970s, and changing economic conditions in the United States, it is not surprising that the movements built by radicals in the sixties either no longer exist or do so only in attenuated form. Activists in the women's liberation movement, however, helped to bring about a fundamental realignment of gender roles in this country through outrageous protests, tough-minded polemics, and an "ecstasy of discussion." Indeed, those of us who came of age in the days before the resurgence of feminism know that the world today, while hardly a feminist utopia, is nonetheless a far different, and in many respects a far fairer, world than what we confronted in 1967.

✖ F U R T H E R   R E A D I N G

Banner, Lois. *Women in Modern America* (1984).
Breines, Wini. *Young, White, and Miserable: Growing Up Female in the Fifties* (1992).
Chafe, William. *Women and Equality* (1977).
Coontz, Stephanie. *The Way We Never Were: American Families and the Nostalgia Trap* (1993).
Costain, Anne N. *Inviting Women's Rebellion* (1992).

Cruikshank, Margaret. *The Gay and Lesbian Liberation Movement* (1992).

De Hart-Mathews, Jane, and Donald Mathews. *The Equal Rights Amendment and the Politics of Cultural Conflict* (1988).

D'Emilio, John. *Sexual Politics, Sexual Communities: The Making of a Homosexual Minority in the United States, 1940–1970* (1983).

D'Emilio, John, and Estelle B. Freedman. *Intimate Matters: A History of Sexuality in America* (1988).

Douglas, Susan J. *Where the Girls Are: Growing Up Female with the Mass Media* (1994).

Duggan, Lisa, and Nan D. Hunter. *Sex Wars: Sexual Dissent and Political Culture* (1995).

Echols, Alice. *Daring to Be Bad: Radical Feminism in America, 1967–1975* (1989).

Ehrenreich, Barbara. *The Hearts of Men* (1983).

Evans, Sara. *Personal Politics: The Roots of Women's Liberation in the Civil Rights Movement and the New Left* (1979).

Ferree, Myra, and Beth Hess. *Controversy and Coalition: The New Feminist Movement,* 2nd ed. (1994).

Fox-Genovese, Elizabeth. *Feminism Is Not the Story of My Life* (1996).

Freeman, Jo. *The Politics of Women's Liberation* (1975).

———, ed. *Social Movements of the Sixties and Seventies* (1983).

Friedan, Betty. *The Feminine Mystique* (1963).

———. *It Changed My Life: Writings on the Women's Movement* (1976).

———. *The Second Stage* (1981).

Ginsberg, Faye. *Contested Lives: The Abortion Debate in an American Community* (1989).

Harrison, Cynthia. *On Account of Sex: The Politics of Women's Issues, 1945–1968* (1988).

Hoff-Wilson, Joan. *Rites of Passage: The Past and Future of the ERA* (1986).

Hooks, Bell. *Ain't I a Woman? Black Women and Feminism* (1981).

Horowitz, Daniel. *Betty Friedan and the Making of "the Feminine Mystique"* (1998).

Jacoby, Kerry N. *Souls, Bodies, Spirits: The Drive to Abolish Abortion Since 1973* (1998).

Jeansonne, Glen. *Women of the Far Right: The Mothers' Movement and World War II* (1996).

Joseph, Gloria, and Jill Lewis. *Common Differences: Conflicts in Black and White Feminist Perspectives* (1981).

Klatch, Rebecca. *Women of the New Right* (1987).

Koedt, Anne, Ellen Levine, and Anita Rapone, eds. *Radical Feminism* (1973).

Luker, Kristin. *Abortion and the Politics of Motherhood* (1984).

May, Elaine Tyler. *Homeward Bound: American Families in the Cold War Era* (1988).

Meyerowitz, Joanne, ed. *Not June Cleaver: Women and Gender in Postwar America* (1994).

Mintz, Steven and Susan Kellogg. *Domestic Revolutions: A Social History of American Family Life* (1988).

Mohr, James. *Abortion in America* (1980).

Morgan, Robin, ed. *Sisterhood Is Powerful* (1970).

Nicholson, Linda, ed. *The Second Wave: A Reader in Feminist Theory* (1997).

Rupp, Leila, and Verta Taylor. *Survival in the Doldrums: The American Women's Rights Movement, 1945 to 1960s* (1987).

Snitow, Ann, et al., eds. *Powers of Desire: The Politics of Sexuality* (1983).

Sommers, Christina Hoff. *Who Stole Feminism? How Women Have Betrayed Women* (1994).

Umansky, Lauri. *Motherhood Reconceived: Feminism and the Legacies of the Sixties* (1996).

Vance, Carol, ed. *Pleasure and Danger: Exploring Female Sexuality* (1984).

Wandersee, Winifred. *On the Move: American Women in the 1970s* (1988).

Richard M. Nixon, Watergate,

and the Crisis

of the "Imperial" Presidency

※

The arrest on June 17, 1972, of five men inside the headquarters of the Democratic National Committee in Washington, D.C.'s Watergate apartment complex began a dramatic episode in the history of the modern presidency. Before the scandal was over, President Richard Nixon would be forced to resign, many of his principal aides and advisers would be convicted of unlawful activities, and many of the heretofore secret workings of the government would be exposed for public inspection.

In the aftermath of the break-in, Nixon and his closest advisers had worked hard to cover up the involvement of White House aides and officials of the Committee for the Re-Election of the President (CREEP). In the short run, they succeeded. The break-in did not become a major issue in the 1972 campaign, and Nixon won a resounding personal victory over his Democratic challenger, Senator George McGovern. But the cover-up came unraveled the following year, and along with it not just the role of the White House in the break-in but a whole chain of illegal and unethical activities on the part of Nixon's aides and campaign workers, ranging from spying on rival candidates to undertaking elaborate efforts to disrupt their campaigns. The investigation into the break-in and cover-up, moreover, spawned a series of subsidiary investigations into illegal activities on the part of the FBI, the CIA, the Internal Revenue Service, and other government agencies. Public reaction to Watergate became a major factor in the election of Democrat Jimmy Carter to the presidency in 1976.

In attempting to explain Watergate, most contemporary commentators stressed Nixon's personality and the venality of those around him. Others saw in the scandal symptoms not just of personal corruption but of a grave crisis in the postwar presidency. Since the administration of Franklin D. Roosevelt, presidential power had steadily grown. From the beginning of the Cold War, the U.S. government had become increasingly embroiled in covert and illegal activities abroad. It had also become more and more involved in the often illegal surveillance of its own citizens and in the disruption of dissident political activity. Nixon's defenders correctly noted that many of the activities with which his administration was charged had precedents in the actions of previous presidents. Yet notable differences distinguished the Nixon White House's policies from those of his predecessors. Indeed, not only did Nixon and his supporters harass their political opponents with techniques previously reserved primarily for foreign foes or left-wing dissidents, but they did so on a scale that was without precedent in American history.

✖ D O C U M E N T S

Much of the discussion about Watergate has inevitably focused on Nixon's character and personality. Document 1 presents portions of a highly revealing interview with the president on December 20, 1972, shortly after the conclusion of his successful campaign for reelection. Among the activities unearthed during the Watergate investigation was an attempt by the Nixon White House to identify prominent critics and punish them by having the Internal Revenue Service audit their taxes, by denying them federal contracts or licenses, or by otherwise targeting them for harassment. In Document 2, White House counsel John W. Dean III writes to aide John D. Ehrlichman on August 16, 1971, about "how we can use the available federal machinery to screw our political enemies." Lists of White House "enemies" would subsequently be compiled and discussed with the president. In the course of the Watergate investigation, Nixon was compelled to turn over the audiotapes of White House meetings that he had secretly recorded. In Document 3, taped on the morning of June 23, 1972, Nixon and a top adviser, H. R. Haldeman, discuss the Watergate break-in and ways in which to prevent its investigation from implicating the White House.

The investigation of Watergate by a select committee of the U.S. Senate revealed not only the extent of the White House's involvement in the break-in and in other illegal activities but also its efforts to cover up that involvement. In Document 4, the chair of the select committee, Democratic senator Sam J. Ervin Jr. of North Carolina, summarizes the committee's findings. These conclusions in turn led to hearings before the House Judiciary Committee, which recommended that Nixon be impeached. Faced with the threat of impeachment, Nixon resigned. Document 5 records the president's farewell remarks to his cabinet and members of White House staff. Vice President Gerald Ford, who became president upon Nixon's resignation, promptly pardoned the former president, thus sparing him from criminal proceedings.

1. Richard M. Nixon on Being President, 1972

I've been fortunate, I have not had to miss a day because of illness [in response to a question about his health]. I thought that was some kind of a record but I find that Truman beat it except he didn't do it in an elected four-year term. So, I'm the first four-year president who hasn't missed a day in office providing I make it to January 20. I've been blessed with a strong physical makeup, probably as a result of inheritance. You know, I've never had a headache in my life and my stomach never bothers me. I believe in the battle, whether it's the battle of a campaign or

"An Interview with Richard Nixon" by Saul Pett from the *Boston Sunday Globe*, January 14, 1973. Reprinted with permission of the Associated Press.

the battle of this office, which is a continuing battle. It's always there wherever you go. I, perhaps, carry it more than others because that's my way.

It's important to live like a Spartan, . . . to have moderate eating and drinking habits. That's not to say I don't enjoy a good time. But the worst thing you can do in this job is to relax, to let up. One must have physical and mental discipline here. This office as presently furnished probably would drive President Johnson up the wall. He liked things going on. He kept three TV sets here. I have none here or in my bedroom. I find to handle crises the most important qualities one needs are balance, objectivity, an ability to act coolly. . . .

People probably think the President was jumping up and down, barking orders, at those times [referring to his decisions to invade Cambodia in 1970, and to bomb North Vietnam and mine Haiphong Harbor in 1972]. Actually, I have a reputation for being the coolest person in the room. In a way I am. I have trained myself to be that. The great decisions in this office require calm.

I could go up the wall watching TV commentators. I don't. I get my news from the news summary the staff prepares every day and it's great; it gives all sides. I never watch TV commentators or the news shows when they are about me. That's because I don't want decisions influenced by personal emotional reactions.

The major weakness of inexperienced people is that they take things personally, especially in politics and that can destroy you. . . . Years ago, when I was a young congressman, things got under my skin. Herblock the cartoonist got to me. . . . But now when I walk into this office I am cool and calm. I read the news summary and get both sides. That's important because there are so many emotional issues these days, such as the war and busing and welfare. But I never allow myself to get emotional. Now, there are Congressmen and Senators who cut me up, Fulbright, for example. But when he comes here, we're the best of friends, at least, I feel I am.

Now, it's not true that I don't feel emotional or pay attention to what others feel. But the most important thing I can do is to make decisions for the long run. Vietnam, for example. Now, we're having a difficult time. Things don't seem as bright as they did. So, we've had to continue the May 8 policy to bomb the North. We will obtain the right kind of peace but we won't get it because of artificial deadlines, such as the election or Christmas or the inaugural.

Now when Henry Kissinger comes in here in the morning and brings up what Scotty Reston and the other columnists are saying, I tell him, "Henry, all that matters is that it comes out all right. Six months from now, nobody will remember what columnists wrote." Decision makers can't be affected by current opinion, by TV barking at you and commentators banging away with the idea that World War III is coming because of the mining of Haiphong. Nor can decisions be affected by the demonstrators outside.

I find that getting away from the White House, from the Oval Office, from that 100 yards that one walks every day from the President's bedroom to the President's office or the extra 50 yards across to the EOB, getting away gives a sense of perspective which is very, very useful.

One constantly has the problem of either getting on top of the job or having the job get on top of you. I find that up here on top of a mountain it is easier for me to get on top of the job, to think in a more certainly relaxed way . . . also in a way in which one, if not interrupted either physically or personally in any other way, can think objectively with perception. . . .

I'll probably do better in the next four years having gone through a few crises in the White House, having weathered them and learned how to handle them coolly and not subjectively. I probably am more objective—I don't mean this as self-serving—than most leaders. . . . When you're too subjective, you tend to make mistakes.

In speeches or press conferences or interviews you have to be up and sharp. You can't be relaxed. The Redskins were relaxed in their last game of the regular season and they were flat and they got clobbered. You must be up for the great events. Up but not up tight. Having done it so often, I perhaps have a finer honed sense of this. But you can overdo it, overtrain and leave your fight in the dressing room.

When I came into office, I'd been through enough—those shattering defeats in 1960 and 1962, and then those eight years in the wilderness, the way DeGaulle and Churchill were. The result was I was able to confront tough problems without flapping. I don't flap easily. An individual tends to go to pieces when he's inexperienced. . . . Now, there are just not many kinds of tough problems I haven't had to face one way or another. In that respect, the fact that my political career required a comeback may have been a blessing.

Well, the greatest pleasure [in winning reelection to the presidency] was the kick the young people Tricia and Julie and Pat got out of it. Those defeats in 1960 and 1962 were so traumatic for them. To most women, things look black or white; a man tends to roll with events. Oh sure, I took it pretty hard myself. But then there was 1968 and 1972 capped it all, despite all that talk about a one-term presidency. After four years of the most devastating attacks on TV, in much of the media, in editorials and columns, and then all that talk in the last two or three weeks of the campaign of the gap narrowing . . . and then whap! A landslide, 49 states, 61 percent of the vote! You'd think I'd be elated then. But it has always been my experience that it doesn't really come to that. But the family—David and Eddie [sons-in-law] kept running to me in the Lincoln Sitting Room with the results. They were so excited they made me feel excited. Then, after my TV talk here and at the Shoreham Hotel and staying up for the California returns . . . Well, you're so drained emotionally at the end, you can't feel much. . . . You'd think that just when the time comes, you'd have your greatest day. But there is this letdown.

Now, there are some people leaving the administration and some staying. I try to recharge them. There can never be a letdown in this office. That's the danger of a landslide. I want everyone to have a new charge, a new sense of challenge. . . . There are those who say there are no restraints on a President if he doesn't have to run again. This is really a fatuous and superficial analysis of the presidency. . . . Individuals who serve here do not serve to get reelected but to do great things. And they could be even greater when you don't have to worry about reelection.

Now, what we want to do, we want everybody to think the challenge is just as great. The leader has to whip them up. The team goes just as far as the leader, as the quarterback and coach, and I am both.

2. White House Counsel John W. Dean III
Presents the "Enemies List," 1971

[John W. Dean III to John D. Ehrlichman]   August 16, 1971

CONFIDENTIAL

MEMORANDUM

SUBJECT: *Dealing with our Political Enemies*

This memorandum addresses the matter of how we can maximize the fact of our incumbency in dealing with persons known to be active in their opposition to our Administration. Stated a bit more bluntly—how we can use the available federal machinery to screw our political enemies.

After reviewing this matter with a number of persons possessed of expertise in the field, I have concluded that we *do not* need an elaborate mechanism or game plan, rather we need a good project coordinator and full support for the project. In brief, the system would work as follows:

•   Key members of the staff (e.g., [Charles] Colson, Dent Flanigan, [Patrick] Buchanan) should be requested to inform us as to who they feel we should be giving a hard time.
•   The project coordinator should then determine what sorts of dealings these individuals have with the federal government and how we can best screw them (e.g., grant availability, federal contracts, litigation, prosecution, etc.).
•   The project coordinator then should have access to and the full support of the top officials of the agency or department in proceeding to deal with the individual.

I have learned that there have been many efforts in the past to take such actions, but they have ultimately failed—in most cases—because of lack of support at the top. Of all those I have discussed this matter with, Lyn Nofziger appears the most knowledgeable and most interested. If Lyn had support he would enjoy undertaking this activity as the project coordinator. You are aware of some of Lyn's successes in the field, but he feels that he can only employ limited efforts because there is a lack of support.

As a next step, I would recommend that we develop a small list of names—not more than ten—as our targets for concentration. Request that Lyn "do a job" on them and if he finds he is getting cut off by a department or agency, that he inform us and we evaluate what is necessary to proceed. I feel it is important that we keep our targets limited for several reasons: (1) a low visibility of the project is imperative; (2) it will be easier to accomplish something real if we don't over expand our efforts; and (3) we can learn more about how to operate such an activity if we start small and build.

John W. Dean III to John Ehrlichman, August 16, 1971, in *Hearings,* Senate Select Committee on Presidential Campaign Activities, vol. 4 (Washington, D.C.: GPO, 1973), 1689–1690.

3. President Nixon Discusses the Watergate Break-in with Aide H. R. Haldeman, 1972

June 23, 1972, from 10:04 to 11:39 A.M.

[Assistant to the President] Haldeman Okay—that's fine. Now, on the investigation, you know, the Democratic break-in thing, we're back to the—in the, the problem area because the FBI is not under control, because [FBI Director L. Patrick] Gray doesn't exactly know how to control them, and they have, their investigation is now leading into some productive areas, because they've been able to trace the money, not through the money itself, but through the bank, you know, sources—the banker himself. And, and it goes in some directions we don't want it to go. Ah, also there have been some things, like an informant came in off the street to the FBI in Miami, who was a photographer or has a friend who is a photographer who developed some films through this guy, [Bernard L.] Barker [later convicted in the Watergate break-in], and the films had pictures of Democratic National Committee letter head documents and things. So I guess, so it's things like that that are gonna, that are filtering in. [Former Nixon Attorney-General and at the time head of Nixon's re-election effort, John N.] Mitchell came up with yesterday, and John Dean [Counsel to the President] analyzed very carefully last night and concludes, concurs now with Mitchell's recommendation that the only way to solve this, and we're set up beautifully to do it, ah, in that and that . . . the only network that paid any attention to it last night was NBC . . . they did a massive story on the Cuban [Barker and others of those caught at the Watergate were Cubans and had worked for the CIA in the 1960s]. . . .

Haldeman That the way to handle this now is for us to have [Deputy Director, Central Intelligence, Vernon] Walters call Pat Gray and just say, "Stay the hell out of this . . . this is ah, business here we don't want you to go any further on it." That's not an unusual development, . . .

President Um huh.

Haldeman . . . And, uh, that would take care of it.

President What about Pat Gray, ah, you mean he doesn't want to?

Haldeman Pat does want to. He doesn't know how to, and he doesn't have, he doesn't have any basis for doing it. Given this, he will then have the basis. He'll call Mark Felt in, and the two of them . . . and Mark Felt wants to cooperate because . . .

President Yeah.

Haldeman He's ambitious . . .

President Yeah.

Haldeman Ah, he'll call him in and say, "We've got the signal from across the river to, to put the hold on this." And that will fit rather well because the FBI agents who are working the case, at this point, feel that's what it is. This is CIA.

President But they've traced the money to 'em.

Haldeman Well they have, they've traced to a name, but they haven't gotten to the guy yet.

U.S. v. John N. Mitchell et al., transcript of a recording of a meeting between President Nixon and H. R. Haldeman in the Oval Office (June 23, 1972). National Archives.

President Would it be somebody here?

Haldeman Ken Dahlberg.

President Who the hell is Ken Dahlberg?

Haldeman He's ah, he gave $25,000 in Minnesota and ah, the check went directly in to this, to this guy Barker.

*Presiden*t Maybe he's a . . . bum.

President He didn't get this from the committee though, from [Nixon re-election committee's finance chief, Maurice] Stans.

Haldeman Yeah. It is. It is. It's directly traceable and there's some more through some Texas people in—that went to the Mexican bank which they can also trace to the Mexican bank . . . they'll get their names today. And (pause)

President Well, I mean, ah, there's no way . . . I'm just thinking if they don't cooperate, what do they say? They they, they were approached by the Cubans. That's what Dahlberg has to say, the Texans too. Is that the idea?

Haldeman Well, if they will. But then we're relying on more and more people all the time. That's the problem. And ah, they'll stop if we could, if we take this other step.

President All right. Fine.

Haldeman And, and they seem to feel the thing to do is get them to stop?

President Right, fine.

Haldeman They say the only way to do that is from White House instructions. And it's got to be to [Director of Central Intelligence, Richard] Helms and, ah, what's his name . . .? Walters.

President Walters.

Haldeman And the proposal would be that [Assistant to the President for Domestic Affairs, John D.] Ehrlichman (coughs) and I call them in

President All right, fine.

Haldeman and say, ah . . .

President How do you call him in, I mean you just, well, we protected Helms from one hell of a lot of things.

Haldeman That's what Ehrlichman says.

President Of course, this is a, this is a Hunt, you will—that will uncover a lot of things. You open that scab there's a hell of a lot of things and that we just feel that it would be very detrimental to have this thing go any further. This involves these Cubans, [E. Howard Hunt, a former CIA operative then working for Nixon's re-election campaign] Hunt, and a lot of hanky-panky that we have nothing to do with ourselves. Well what the hell, did Mitchell know about this thing to any much of a degree?

Haldeman I think so. I don't think he knew the details, but I think he knew.

President He didn't know how it was going to be handled though, with Dahlberg and the Texans and so forth? Well who was the asshole that did? (Unintelligible) Is it [G. Gordon Liddy, a former CIA agent employed by the Nixon White House and re-election committee] Liddy? Is that the fellow? He must be a little nuts.

Haldeman He is.

President I mean he just isn't well screwed on is he? Isn't that the problem?

Haldeman No, but he was under pressure, apparently, to get more information, and as he got more pressure, he pushed the people harder to move harder on . . .

President Pressure from Mitchell?

Haldeman Apparently.

President Oh, Mitchell, Mitchell was at the point that you made on this, that exactly what I need from you in on the—

Haldeman Gemstone [an early plan for a "dirty-tricks" operation which evolved into the Watergate break-in operation], yeah.

President All right, fine. I understand it all. We won't second-guess Mitchell and the rest. Thank God it wasn't [Special Assistant to the President, Charles] Colson.

Haldeman The FBI interviewed Colson yesterday. They determined that would be a good thing to do.

President Um hum. . . .

Haldeman An interrogation, which he did, and that, the FBI guys working the case had concluded that there were one or two possibilities, one, that this was a White House, they don't think that there is anything at the Election Committee, they think it was either a White House operation and they had some obscure reasons for it, non political, . . .

President Uh huh. . . .

Haldeman Colson, yesterday, they concluded it was not the White House, but are now convinced it is a CIA thing, so the CIA turnoff would . . .

President Well, not sure of their analysis, I'm not going to get that involved. I'm (unintelligible).

Haldeman No sir. We don't want you to.

President You call them in. . . . Good. Good deal. Play it tough. That's the way they play it and that's the way we are going to play it.

Haldeman O.K. We'll do it. . . .

President When you get in these people . . . when you get these people in, say: "Look, the problem is that this will open the whole, the whole Bay of Pigs thing, and the President just feels that" ah, without going into the details . . . don't, don't lie to them to the extent to say there is no involvement, but just say this is sort of a comedy of errors, bizarre, without getting into it, "the President believes that it is going to open the whole Bay of Pigs thing up again. And, ah because these people are plugging for, for keeps and that they should call the FBI in and say that we wish for the country, don't go any further into this case," period!

4. Senator Sam J. Ervin on Watergate, 1974

President Nixon entrusted the management of his campaign for reelection and his campaign finances to the Committee for the Re-Election of the President, which was headed by former Attorney General John N. Mitchell, and the Finance Committee To Re-Elect the President, which was headed by former Secretary of Commerce, Maurice Stans. Since the two committees occupied offices in the same office building in Washington and worked in close conjunction, it seems proper to call them for ease of expression the Nixon reelection committees.

Senate Select Committee on Presidential Campaign Activities, *Final Report* (Washington, D.C.: GPO, 1974), 1098–1101.

Watergate was a conglomerate of various illegal and unethical activities in which various officers and employees of the Nixon reelection committees and various White House aides of President Nixon participated in varying ways and degrees to accomplish these successive objectives:

1. To destroy, insofar as the Presidential election of 1972 was concerned, the integrity of the process by which the President of the United States is nominated and elected.
2. To hide from law enforcement officers, prosecutors, grand jurors, courts, the news media, and the American people the identities and wrongdoing of those officers and employees of the Nixon reelection committees, and those White House aides who had undertaken to destroy the integrity of the process by which the President of the United States is nominated and elected.

To accomplish the first of these objectives, the participating officers and employees of the reelection committees and the participating White House aides of President Nixon engaged in one or more of these things:

1. They exacted enormous contributions—usually in cash—from corporate executives by impliedly implanting in their minds the impressions that the making of the contributions was necessary to insure that the corporations would receive governmental favors, or avoid governmental disfavors, while President Nixon remained in the White House. A substantial portion of the contributions were made out of corporate funds in violation of a law enacted by Congress a generation ago.
2. They hid substantial parts of these contributions in cash in safes and secret deposits to conceal their sources and the identities of those who had made them.
3. They disbursed substantial portions of these hidden contributions in a surreptitious manner to finance the bugging and the burglary of the offices of the Democratic National Committee in the Watergate complex in Washington for the purpose of obtaining political intelligence; and to sabotage by dirty tricks, espionage, and scurrilous and false libels and slanders the campaigns and the reputations of honorable men, whose only offenses were that they sought the nomination of the Democratic Party for President and the opportunity to run against President Nixon for that office in the Presidential election of 1972.
4. They deemed the departments and agencies of the Federal Government to be the political playthings of the Nixon administration rather than impartial instruments for serving the people, and undertook to induce them to channel Federal contracts, grants, and loans to areas, groups, or individuals so as to promote the reelection of the President rather than to further the welfare of the people.
5. They branded as enemies of the President individuals and members of the news media who dissented from the President's policies and opposed his reelection, and conspired to urge the Department of Justice, the Federal Bureau of Investigation, the Internal Revenue Service, and the Federal Communications Commission to pervert the use of their legal powers to harass them for so doing.
6. They borrowed from the Central Intelligence Agency disguises which E. Howard Hunt used in political espionage operations, and photographic equipment which White House employees known as the "Plumbers" and their hired confederates

used in connection with burglarizing the office of a psychiatrist which they believed contained information concerning Daniel Ellsberg which the White House was anxious to secure.

7. They assigned to E. Howard Hunt, who was at the time a White House consultant occupying an office in the Executive Office Building, the gruesome task of falsifying State Department documents which they contemplated using in their altered state to discredit the Democratic Party by defaming the memory of former President John Fitzgerald Kennedy, who as the hapless victim of an assassin's bullet had been sleeping in the tongueless silence of the dreamless dust for 9 years.

8. They used campaign funds to hire saboteurs to forge and disseminate false and scurrilous libels of honorable men running for the Democratic Presidential nomination in Democratic Party primaries.

During the darkness of the early morning of June 17, 1972, James W. McCord, the security chief of the John Mitchell committee, and four residents of Miami, Fla., were arrested by Washington police while they were burglarizing the offices of the Democratic National Committee in the Watergate complex to obtain political intelligence. At the same time, the four residents of Miami had in their possession more than fifty $100 bills which were subsequently shown to be a part of campaign contributions made to the Nixon reelection committees.

On September 15, 1972, these five burglars, E. Howard Hunt, and Gordon Liddy, general counsel of the Stans committee, were indicted by the grand jury on charges arising out of the bugging and burglary of the Watergate.

They were placed on trial upon these charges before Judge John Sirica, and a petit jury in the U.S. District Court for the District of Columbia in January 1973. At that time, Hunt and the four residents of Miami pleaded guilty, and McCord and Liddy were found guilty by the petit jury. None of them took the witness stand during the trial.

The arrest of McCord and the four residents of Miami created consternation in the Nixon reelection committees and the White House. Thereupon, various officers and employees of the Nixon reelection committees and various White House aides undertook to conceal from law-enforcement officers, prosecutors, grand jurors, courts, the news media, and the American people the identities and activities of those officers and employees of the Nixon reelection committees and those White House aides who had participated in any way in the Watergate affair.

Various officers and employees of the Nixon reelection committees and various White House aides engaged in one or more of these acts to make the concealment effective and thus obstruct the due administration of justice:

1. They destroyed the records of the Nixon reelection committees antedating the bugging and the burglary.

2. They induced the Acting Director of the FBI, who was a Nixon appointee, to destroy the State Department documents which E. Howard Hunt had been falsifying.

3. They obtained from the Acting Director of the FBI copies of scores of interviews conducted by FBI agents in connection with their investigation of the bugging

and the burglary, and were enabled thereby to coach their confederates to give false and misleading statements to the FBI.

4. They sought to persuade the FBI to refrain from investigating the sources of the campaign funds which were used to finance the bugging and the burglary.

5. They intimidated employees of the Nixon reelection committees and employees of the White House by having their lawyers present when these employees were being questioned by agents of the FBI, and thus deterred these employees from making full disclosures to the FBI.

6. They lied to agents of the FBI, prosecutors, and grand jurors who undertook to investigate the bugging and the burglary, and to Judge Sirica and the petit jurors who tried the seven original Watergate defendants in January 1973.

7. They persuaded the Department of Justice and the prosecutors to take out-of-court statements from Maurice Stans, President Nixon's chief campaign fundraiser, and Charles Colson, Egil Krogh, and David Young, White House aides, and Charles Colson's secretary, instead of requiring them to testify before the grand jury investigating the bugging and the burglary in conformity with the established procedures governing such matters, and thus denied the grand jurors the opportunity to question them.

8. They persuaded the Department of Justice and the prosecutors to refrain from asking Donald Segretti, their chief hired saboteur, any questions involving Herbert W. Kalmbach, the President's personal attorney, who was known by them to have paid Segretti for dirty tricks he perpetrated upon honorable men seeking the Democratic Presidential nomination, and who was subsequently identified before the Senate Select Committee as one who played a major role in the secret delivery of hush money to the seven original Watergate defendants.

9. They made cash payments totaling hundreds of thousands of dollars out of campaign funds in surreptitious ways to the seven original Watergate defendants as hush money to buy their silence and keep them from revealing their knowledge of the identities of the officers and employees of the Nixon reelection committees and the White House aides who had participated in the Watergate.

10. They gave assurances to some of the original seven defendants that they would receive Presidential clemency after serving short portions of their sentences if they refrained from divulging the identities and activities of the officers and employees of the Nixon reelection committees and the White House aides who had participated in the Watergate affair.

11. They made arrangements by which the attorneys who represented the seven original Watergate defendants received their fees in cash from moneys which had been collected to finance President Nixon's reelection campaign.

12. They induced the Department of Justice and the prosecutors of the seven original Watergate defendants to assure the news media and the general public that there was no evidence that any persons other than the seven original Watergate defendants were implicated in any way in any Watergate-related crimes.

13. They inspired massive efforts on the part of segments of the news media friendly to the administration to persuade the American people that most of the members of the Select Committee named by the Senate to investigate the Watergate were biased and irresponsible men motivated solely by desires to exploit the matters they investigated for personal or partisan advantage, and that the allegations in

the press that Presidential aides had been involved in the Watergate were venomous machinations of a hostile and unreliable press bent on destroying the country's confidence in a great and good President.

One shudders to think that the Watergate conspiracies might have been effectively concealed and their most dramatic episode might have been dismissed as a "third-rate" burglary conceived and committed solely by the seven original Watergate defendants had it not been for the courage and penetrating understanding of Judge Sirica, the thoroughness of the investigative reporting of Carl Bernstein, Bob Woodward, and other representatives of a free press, the labors of the Senate Select Committee and its excellent staff, and the dedication and diligence of Special Prosecutors Archibald Cox and Leon Jaworski and their associates.

5. President Nixon's Farewell, 1974

Members of the Cabinet, members of the White House Staff, all of our friends here:
     I think the record should show that this is one of those spontaneous things that we always arrange whenever the President comes in to speak, and it will be so reported in the press, and we don't mind, because they have to call it as they see it.
     But on our part, believe me, it is spontaneous.
     You are here to say goodby to us, and we don't have a good word for it in English—the best is *au revoir.* We will see you again.
     I just met with the members of the White House staff, you know, those who serve here in the White House day in and day out, and I asked them to do what I ask all of you to do to the extent that you can and, of course, are requested to do so: to serve our next President as you have served me and previous Presidents—because many of you have been here for many years—with devotion and dedication, because this office, great as it is, can only be as great as the men and women who work for and with the President.
     This house, for example—I was thinking of it as we walked down this hall, and I was comparing it to some of the great houses of the world that I have been in. This isn't the biggest house. Many, and most, in even smaller countries, are much bigger. This isn't the finest house. Many in Europe, particularly, and in China, Asia, have paintings of great, great value, things that we just don't have here and, probably, will never have until we are 1,000 years old or older.
     But this is the best house. It is the best house, because it has something far more important than numbers of people who serve, far more important than numbers of rooms or how big it is, far more important than numbers of magnificent pieces of art.
     This house has a great heart, and that heart comes from those who serve. I was rather sorry they didn't come down. We said goodby to them upstairs. But they are really great. And I recall after so many times I have made speeches, and some of them pretty tough, yet, I always come back, or after a hard day—and my days usually have run rather long—I would always get a lift from them, because I might be a little down but they always smiled.

Public Papers of the Presidents of the United States: Richard M. Nixon, 1969–74, vol. 1 (Washington, D.C.: GPO, 1975), 630–632.

And so it is with you. I look around here, and I see so many on this staff that, you know, I should have been by your offices and shaken hands, and I would love to have talked to you and found out how to run the world—everybody wants to tell the President what to do, and boy, he needs to be told many times—but I just haven't had the time. But I want you to know that each and every one of you, I know, is indispensable to this Government.

I am proud of this Cabinet. I am proud of all the members who have served in our Cabinet. I am proud of our sub-Cabinet. I am proud of our White House Staff. As I pointed out last night, sure, we have done some things wrong in this Administration, and the top man always takes the responsibility, and I have never ducked it. But I want to say one thing: We can be proud of it—5½ years. No man or no woman came into this Administration and left it with more of this world's goods than when he came in. No man or no woman ever profited at the public expense or the public till. That tells something about you.

Mistakes, yes. But for personal gain, never. You did what you believed in. Sometimes right, sometimes wrong. And I only wish that I were a wealthy man—at the present time, I have got to find a way to pay my taxes—*[laughter]*—and if I were, I would like to recompense you for the sacrifices that all of you have made to serve in government.

But you are getting something in government—and I want you to tell this to your children, and I hope the Nation's children will hear it, too—something in government service that is far more important than money. It is a cause bigger than yourself. It is the cause of making this the greatest nation in the world, the leader of the world, because without our leadership, the world will know nothing but war, possibly starvation or worse, in the years ahead. With our leadership it will know peace, it will know plenty.

We have been generous, and we will be more generous in the future as we are able to. But most important, we must be strong here, strong in our hearts, strong in our souls, strong in our belief, and strong in our willingness to sacrifice, as you have been willing to sacrifice, in a pecuniary way, to serve in government.

There is something else I would like for you to tell your young people. You know, people often come in and say, "What will I tell my kids?" They look at government and say, sort of a rugged life, and they see the mistakes that are made. They get the impression that everybody is here for the purpose of feathering his nest. That is why I made this earlier point—not in this Administration, not one single man or woman.

And I say to them, there are many fine careers. This country needs good farmers, good businessmen, good plumbers, good carpenters.

I remember my old man. I think that they would have called him sort of a little man, common man. He didn't consider himself that way. You know what he was? He was a streetcar motorman first, and then he was a farmer, and then he had a lemon ranch. It was the poorest lemon ranch in California, I can assure you. He sold it before they found oil on it. *[Laughter]* And then he was a grocer. But he was a great man, because he did his job, and every job counts up to the hilt, regardless of what happens.

Nobody will ever write a book, probably, about my mother. Well, I guess all of you would say this about your mother—my mother was a saint. And I think of her, two boys dying of tuberculosis, nursing four others in order that she could take care of my older brother for 3 years in Arizona, and seeing each of them die, and when they died, it was like one of her own.

Yes, she will have no books written about her. But she was a saint.

Now, however, we look to the future. I had a little quote in the speech last night from T. R. [Theodore Roosevelt]. As you know, I kind of like to read books. I am not educated, but I do read books—*[laughter]*—and the T. R. quote was a pretty good one.

Here is another one I found as I was reading, my last night in the White House, and this quote is about a young man. He was a young lawyer in New York. He had married a beautiful girl, and they had a lovely daughter, and then suddenly she died, and this is what he wrote. This was in his diary.

He said, "She was beautiful in face and form and lovelier still in spirit. As a flower she grew and as a fair young flower she died. Her life had been always in the sunshine. There had never come to her a single great sorrow. None ever knew her who did not love and revere her for her bright and sunny temper and her saintly unselfishness. Fair, pure, and joyous as a maiden, loving, tender, and happy as a young wife. When she had just become a mother, when her life seemed to be just begun and when the years seemed so bright before her, then by a strange and terrible fate death came to her. And when my heart's dearest died, the light went from my life forever."

That was T. R. in his twenties. He thought the light had gone from his life forever—but he went on. And he not only became President but, as an ex-President, he served his country, always in the arena, tempestuous, strong, sometimes wrong, sometimes right, but he was a man.

And as I leave, let me say, that is an example I think all of us should remember. We think sometimes when things happen that don't go the right way; we think that when you don't pass the bar exam the first time—I happened to, but I was just lucky; I mean, my writing was so poor the bar examiner said, "We have just got to let the guy through." We think that when someone dear to us dies, we think that when we lose an election, we think that when we suffer a defeat that all is ended. We think, as T. R. said, that the light had left his life forever.

Not true. It is only a beginning, always. The young must know it; the old must know it. It must always sustain us, because the greatness comes not only when things go always good for you, but the greatness comes and you are really tested, when you take some knocks, some disappointments, when sadness comes, because only if you have been in the deepest valley can you ever know how magnificent it is to be on the highest mountain.

And so I say to you on this occasion, as we leave, we leave proud of the people who have stood by us and worked for us and served this country.

We want you to be proud of what you have done. We want you to continue to serve in government, if that is your wish. Always give your best, never get discouraged, never be petty; always remember, others may hate you, but those who hate you don't win unless you hate them, and then you destroy yourself.

And so, we leave with high hopes, in good spirit, and with deep humility, and with very much gratefulness in our hearts. I can only say to each and every one of you, we come from many faiths, we pray perhaps to different gods—but really the same God in a sense—but I want to say for each and every one of you, not only will we always remember you, not only will we always be grateful to you but always you will be in our hearts and you will be in our prayers.

Thank you very much.

✖ E S S A Y S

Most early accounts of Watergate, such as Jonathan Schell's *Time of Illusion* (1976) and J. Anthony Lukas's *Nightmare: The Underside of the Nixon Years* (1976, 1988), were highly critical of Nixon and the many members of his administration who had participated in the Watergate break-in, the campaign of "dirty tricks" that preceded it, or the cover-up that followed. Watergate, they argued, was the product of both the swollen powers of a Cold War "imperial presidency" and of the criminal conduct of Nixon and his retainers. While many conservatives preferred to ignore Watergate, a few, such as James A. Nuechterlein, the editor of the conservative journal *First Things,* sought to defend the former president. In the first essay, Nuechterlein argues that Nixon's abuse of executive power had deep roots in the actions of his Democratic predecessors and that although Watergate was "an ugly and unforgivable business," it was used unfairly by partisan critics to tar "everything and everyone associated with the Nixon administration." In the second essay, historian Stanley I. Kutler of the University of Wisconsin notes that those who would minimize or dismiss the importance of Watergate have focused narrowly on the break-in itself, ignoring the many abuses of power that preceded it and the widespread and deliberate obstruction of justice that followed. Watergate remains, he concludes, the central drama of the Nixon presidency.

Escaping Watergate: A Revisionist View of the Nixon Presidency

JAMES A. NUECHTERLEIN

Few of us by now can muster the will to wallow any further in Watergate. However we feel about Richard Nixon and the series of events that brought him down, we want above all to be done with both of them. Watergate has so overwhelmed contemporary political consciousness that we feel at once saturated with the lessons of the scandal and yet unsure precisely what they might mean for us. Our conceptual faculties benumbed under the continuing avalanche of Watergate literature— memoirs, recountings, analyses, and sermonizings—we feel it difficult to sort out what the event's significance finally consists in. In any case, we prefer to hear no more about it all just now.

Yet there are reasons for resisting the mood of stupefied exhaustion. There is still learning to be done from Watergate, and it may be, in fact, that we are only now getting far enough removed from the details of the scandal to begin to take proper measure of its meaning. Only as we begin to distance ourselves from the event can we get past the stage of conditioned response and automatic judgment in

"Watergate: Toward a Revisionist View" by James A. Nuechterlein. Reprinted from *Commentary,* August 1979 by permission; all rights reserved. Reprinted by permission of *Commentary* and the author.

our reaction to accounts of it. Two recent memoirs by participants in the crisis—John J. Sirica and Maurice H. Stans—help us ponder aspects and nuances of Watergate that might previously have registered only partially or perhaps even not at all.

Before new lessons concerning Watergate can be absorbed, however, a number of old ones will first have to be unlearned. It is probably inevitable that any major event will occasion a good deal of earnest nonsense. Watergate certainly has.

There is, in the first instance, the matter of significance. Historians and political analysts have a natural inclination to assume that significant events must have significant meanings. Watergate suggests that this is not necessarily so. There was not more there than met the eye. The scandal had momentous political effects, but its circumstances were essentially banal, and it left little in the way of usable lessons or enduring implications. Watergate may by now be the most overinterpreted event of modern times; it simply will not bear the weight of the portentous meanings that have been attached to it. We have learned from it again the venerable lessons that politics should not be conducted as warfare and that we need to elect to high office those who understand that there are certain things that decent men simply do not do. Those are useful reminders, but they require us neither to reconstruct our political system nor to reorder our moral values.

It is perhaps most useful to view Watergate as constituting, in symbolic terms, the last act of the 60s. The scheme issued from an administration enveloped in a state-of-siege mentality, and that mentality grew out of the fevered and polarized political climate of the decade following the assassination of John F. Kennedy. By the end of Nixon's first term, the President and his advisers had become the victims of their ideological preconceptions. Convinced that the message of their accomplishments was being distorted or ignored by hostile media and agitated by left-wing approval of and even participation in leaks of national-security information—some important, some not—they conjured up from within their White House fortress a nightmare vision of a nation deceived and endangered by a radical minority. And they proceeded to act on the basis of that vision.

When politics is war, it is necessary, as in all combat situations, to gather intelligence on the enemy's strategy and tactics. There has never been any good evidence that Nixon knew in advance about the Watergate break-in, and there is probably no reason to doubt his continuing denials. But neither is there any reason to suppose that he would have objected if he had known, except possibly on grounds of prudence.

The cover-up—in which of course Nixon was involved, and virtually from the beginning—followed naturally from the failure of the break-in. There was no plot as such, simply the instinctive behavior of men caught in an incredible blunder, trying to extricate themselves in any way they could. The immediate and automatic decision to deny any higher authorization for the burglary led inexorably, one step after another, to the making of a quagmire. Nixon's own summary observation is self-serving but not inaccurate: "We . . . all simply wandered into a situation unthinkingly, trying to protect ourselves from what we saw as a political problem." The cover-up was sordid and inexcusable, but it was not—as it has been variously depicted—an inevitable product of the imperial Presidency, a function of some peculiarly American preoccupation with ambition, success, and power, or a grand conspiracy against constitutional government.

Much of the initial interpretative gas over Watergate is already dissipating. President Carter's inability to get much of anything at all that he wants from Congress, for example, makes it painfully obvious that we are in no present danger of a runaway Presidency. Carter's particular problems aside, it has been clear to most observers for a very long time that our constitutional arrangements are such that national leadership must come from the President. The Congress is simply not constructed to provide coherent direction to the nation in either foreign or domestic affairs. (A fascinating and relevant statistic: there are now, by recent count, 152 subcommittee chairmen among the members of the House of Representatives.) The Nixon White House undoubtedly misused its powers, but the primary lesson of Watergate remains that we need a vigilant public and honorable leaders, not a reshuffling of the constitutional division of powers.

If the imperial Presidency has lost currency as a Watergate theme, the idea of the scandal as a commentary on the deadline of American morality seems still to have lingering attractions. From the very beginning, our public moralists seized on Watergate as a symbol of the nation's predilection for whoring after false gods. The first of the Watergate conspirators to break into print, Jeb Magruder, deputy director to John Mitchell on the Committee to Reelect the President (CRP), informed us in the title of his memoir that his had been *An American Life,* and he went on to wonder whether the Watergate crimes did not "somehow reflect larger failures in the values" of American society: "I think that I and many members of my generation placed far too much emphasis on our personal ambitions, on achieving success, as measured in materialistic terms, and far too little emphasis on moral and humanistic values." The Reverend William Sloane Coffin Jr. summarized Magruder's involvement with Watergate as "an all-American experience." There was, we were meant to see, significance here.

Perhaps. Recognition of human frailty is always salutary in a society still resistant to notions of original sin. More particularly, it is difficult not to be appalled by the narcissistic preoccupation of a John Dean with vulgar success, particularly in his measuring of it: fast sports cars, lots of women, impressive office furnishings. (Dean, of course, like all the other born-again ex-Watergaters, assures us that "everything is different now.")

Nonetheless, we might well hesitate to blame Watergate on the traditional demons of personal ambition and desire for success. The old bitch goddess gets blamed for so much in general that one begins to wonder if she is responsible for anything in particular. We can safely assume that most major political figures in America—or anywhere else—are overachievers greatly attracted to power and success. Few such men, however, are normally implicated, at least to our knowledge, in criminal conspiracies. The men at the heart of Watergate crimes—Nixon, Mitchell, H. R. Haldeman, John Ehrlichman—obviously wore ethical blinders, but the fundamental problem lay with their public values, not their private moral ones. They had already achieved success and power, and neither materialism nor personal ambition had anything significant to do with their deliberations over Watergate.

Which brings us to the third of the conventional interpretations of Watergate: how close we all came to the loss of our constitutional liberties. There is, of course, considerable evidence that the Nixon administration frequently did step over the line of legitimate behavior: excessive wiretaps; the extra-legal plumbers unit; the Huston intelligence plan; the break-in at the office of Daniel Ellsberg's psychiatrist; attempts to manipulate the CIA and FBI; Watergate itself. Charles Colson at the height of his influence appears to have been a genuinely sinister figure, and too many other men in the Nixon White House, trembling under Haldeman's ultimate and recurring threat, "If you can't get the job done, we'll find someone who can," acted in ways that violated private and public decency. Moreover, the hardball politics was initiated and encouraged at the very top.

But this quite real problem of abuse of executive power has frequently been inflated out of reasonable proportion. One does not in any way have to accept Nixon's various *tu quoque* defenses as exculpation for his crimes to concede that in fact it did not all start with Watergate. It is an exaggeration to argue, as some have done, that the kind of constitutional improprieties Nixon indulged in had constituted standard operating procedure for most administrations since Franklin D. Roosevelt, but it cannot be denied that he was, in a number of areas, armed with considerable precedent. Nixon was chief of presidential sinners, but he was neither the first nor the only one. We have the Nixon tapes; it is probably just as well, from what we already know, that we don't have the Roosevelt, Kennedy, or Johnson ones.

Nor should it be forgotten that, as already noted, Nixon acted in part out of a genuine, if exaggerated, concern for national security. He cynically and egregiously invoked national-security concerns in the Watergate cover-up, where, of course, they were entirely irrelevant, but that was not always the case. Henry Kissinger and Nixon alike had become legitimately concerned over the effect of leaks of confidential information on the conduct of American foreign policy. Nixon's may have been the paranoid style, but, as the saying goes, paranoids do have enemies.

It is virtually impossible to raise these points without seeming to excuse or at least minimize Watergate. Yet it is worth taking that risk if only in an attempt to counter the still widespread assumption that the Nixon administration came close to undermining the American Constitutional system. That assumption found its classic expression a few years back in the widely popular television mini-series, *Washington: Behind Closed Doors,* in which the Nixonesque President, along with all his other sins, contemplates the suspension of national elections. That particular piece of hysteria had originally arisen among the more febrile elements of the radical Left during Nixon's first term, and yet it appeared again, only now blithely mingled in with all the things Nixon *had* done (or had ever been suspected of doing) in a program watched, and considered as truth, by millions of Americans. And the Nixon of that series, who is the Nixon large numbers of people have been led to believe is the genuine article, *could* have suspended national elections. What Nixon did was bad enough that we do not need to attribute to him intentions he never had, and Watergate by itself was bad enough—stupid, criminal, and inexcusable enough—that we do not need to make of it more than it was.

If many of the received lessons of Watergate appear on examination to be trivial, exaggerated, or even downright misleading, there are other aspects of the affair that deserve closer attention than they have so far attracted. The recent memoirs by Sirica and Stans help us to consider these less obvious lessons of the scandal, though not entirely in the ways that the authors intended.

When Maurice H. Stans summarizes his Watergate experience as *The Terrors of Justice,* we immediately suspect hyperbole, if not dissimulation. Yet looked at dispassionately—at least so far as the official record can establish it—his is a genuinely harrowing tale. Ponderously detailed, awkwardly written and organized, this book nonetheless largely persuades, so long, that is, as it sticks to the details of the author's experiences.

Prior to Watergate, Stans had one of those Horatio Alger careers so common in the catalogues of American experience that we forget how significant and impressive they are. Born to children of immigrants in very modest circumstances in Shakopee, Minnesota, in 1908, Stans rose, through ambition, talent, and hard work, to the very top of the accounting profession before entering public life. Having served in the Eisenhower administration, he developed a strong case of Potomac fever (his term) and decided by the mid-60s to attach himself to Richard Nixon's star as his most likely route back to Washington. His special talent was that of fund-raiser, and he took on that role for Nixon, first in the 1962 race for the governorship of California, and later and more enthusiastically in the 1968 campaign for presidential nomination and election. As with everything else that he took on in his career, Stans was good at his job (Dean has said that he was the only member of the administration "who could have tutored Bob Haldeman on efficiency") and Nixon rewarded him with the position of Secretary of Commerce. Indeed, Stans had been too good at his job, and when it came time for the bid for election to a second term, Nixon put such heavy pressure on him that Stans, against his own real wishes, resigned his cabinet position in early 1972 to become finance chairman of CRP.

There, of course, disaster struck. Since he was the man in charge of the money, it seemed obvious to investigators—and to the media—that Stans must have known something about the uses of the funds that were raised first to finance the Watergate break-in and later to aid in the cover-up. Yet the record seems clear that he did not. Stans insisted from the outset on a clear separation of duties within CRP between the finance and campaign committees: his committee would raise and disburse the funds, but it was not its job to judge or verify the uses to which the campaign committee felt the monies should be put. If expenditures were properly authorized by a member of the campaign committee, the finance committee would meet them. And within the finance operation, Stans put his own energies to raising money; he left it to the treasurer of his committee, Hugh Sloan Jr. to pay it out.

Thus the money for Watergate was paid out by Sloan to G. Gordon Liddy on the authorization of Magruder, Mitchell's deputy director. Liddy was so secretive concerning the money's purposes that Sloan complained to Stans; Stans checked with Mitchell, who assured him, without going into detail, that the payment was legitimate; and Stans told Sloan to pay the money. Stan's only involvement with the cover-up was a payment of $75,000 on June 29, 1972 to Herbert Kalmbach for purposes that Kalmbach assured Stans were legitimate, but which turned out to be part of the payoffs to insure the silence of the Watergate burglars. On none of this are we required to accept Stans's word. The Watergate prosecutors never charged Stans with involvement in any aspect of Watergate, and none of the conspirators has ever suggested that he was part of their operations. We might wonder in a few instances why he did not raise more questions than he apparently did (it would seem naive to suppose that he did not harbor certain suspicions), but we have no good reason to doubt his absolute denial of criminal knowledge or action.

Even as the actual record began to emerge, however, the media continued to tell the story of Watergate as if Stans had somehow been at the center of things. Although he was never officially charged with involvement, there is still because of that coverage a widespread public assumption that Stans was in some vague manner part of the Watergate scandal.

That assumption blends into the wider and near universal belief that the entire Nixon fund-raising operation in 1972 was one great sinkhole of corruption. The range of corrupt practices charged against the operation Stans headed has been astonishingly broad: that the Nixon campaign received enormous illegal gifts from foreign sources, such as the Shah of Iran; that CRP fund-raisers, armed with lists of corporations in trouble with government agencies, went about exchanging promises of help for large contributions; that government contracts were promised in exchange for generous gifts to the campaign; that government jobs, especially ambassadorships, were in effect sold to the highest bidders (one potential contributor, assuming that was in fact the ways things operated, bluntly asked Stans, "How much for Luxembourg?"; Stans tells us he informed the man that Luxembourg was not for sale); that CRP urged contributors to pay in cash in order that *quid pro quo* dealings and other corrupt operations would be harder to trace; that a massive "laundering" operation was carried on by the committee to hide the sources of contributions; that an "enemy list" of those who had refused to contribute was kept for later retaliatory action by the administration.

All of these charges, Stans tells us, came under exhaustive scrutiny and investigation by the office of the Watergate special prosecutor. None of them, he insists, resulted in the laying of any criminal charges, much less the securing of any convictions:

> Insofar as the Nixon money-raising in 1972 was concerned, there were only a handful of nonwillful technical violations, and these were less significant individually and in the aggregate than similar oversights and violations by a number of other candidates who were not prosecuted.
>
> That was the surviving sum and substance of all of the alleged financial corruption in the 1972 Nixon campaign. Not a single proven case of corrupt action. No favors granted. No contracts awarded. No cases fixed. No ambassadorships sold. No illegal contributions from foreigners. No overseas laundries. No illegal solicitations. No list of companies in trouble with the government. No enemy lists. No fund-raising by government officials. No extortion or coercion. No intentional circumvention of the law in a single instance. That is precisely what the Department of Justice, the Special Prosecutor, and the courts found.

Stans seems justified in describing the five counts of which he was finally convicted—and fined $1,000 per count—as "technical violations." There were two charges of *non-willful* receipt of illegal corporate contributions and three charges of late reporting of contributions and payments. None of them, as described in detail by Stans, appears to have involved anything more than a minor and insignificant infraction of election-financing laws, and it seems clear that the violations would, under ordinary circumstances, simply have been ignored. Stans reluctantly pleaded guilty to these misdemeanors in 1975, he says, rather than face a protracted, expensive, and debilitating trial in a District of Columbia court which he feared would still be operating in an inflamed climate of opinion. One senses that a part of him now deeply regrets that decision.

Stans's reluctance to face a trial is easily understandable in the circumstances. He had already endured a trial in New York in 1974 in which he and Mitchell faced charges of conspiracy, obstruction of justice, and perjury in connection with receipt of a $200,000 campaign contribution in 1972 from financier Robert Vesco, supposedly in exchange for helping Vesco with an investigation of his activities by the Securities and Exchange Commission. The jury, faced with what Tom Wicker of the *New York Times* described as "clearly a weak case" for the prosecution, acquitted the defendants on all counts.

Stans cherishes that acquittal, but, as already noted, he knows that millions of Americans will remain forever persuaded that, if only in some indefinable way, he was nonetheless "mixed up in Watergate." That is his anguish, and it is impossible upon reading this memoir not in some measure to share it with him. It could be, of course, that he has not told us the full truth, that there are elements, of moral guilt especially, which he has not fully confronted. That, I must add, is not my reading of the book, and in any case—moral guilt or not—Stans does seem fully to have established that he was legally innocent of any significant wrongdoing in the variety of matters that have been gathered under the Watergate umbrella, and that he nonetheless became subject to an extraordinary and vicious campaign of smear and slander.

Stans lays out his case in excruciating and repetitive detail; he specifies what seems to him scores of instances of unfair treatment at the hands of investigators, prosecutors, district attorneys, politicians, public-interest groups, publishers, reporters, and editorialists. The massive misreporting of his situation by the media—some of it malicious, much of it simply ignorant an unprofessional—gets the most careful and, by any standard, devastating attention. Yet for all his sense of grievance and outrage, Stans maintains a restrained and dignified tone. Given all that he endured, he appears surprisingly free of bitterness and desire for vengeance. Moved at times to the edge of despair, he managed throughout his ordeal to hold on to his equanimity, largely through massive doses of old-fashioned American positive thinking. (During the Vesco trial, for example, Stans and his wife attended a variety of church services, "choosing among those listed in the Saturday papers the sermons with the most reassuring titles." By this process, the Stanses found themselves in frequent attendance at the Marble Collegiate Church listening to Dr. Norman Vincent Peale.)

Stans desires the exoneration of history, the reclaiming, as he told the Senate Watergate Committee, of "my good name." But that is not the limit of his intentions. He believes there are lessons in Watergate that transcend his own case. He wants, in fact, though he does not say so directly, to begin the process of Watergate revisionism.

Some of his arguments make good sense. He shows, for example, that much of the post-1972 passion for campaign reform, which climaxed in the passage of the Federal Election Campaign Act of 1974, stemmed from a misreading of the Watergate experience. He dismisses the argument that the break-in occurred because the Republicans had so much money lying around they could indulge nasty impulses that a tighter budget would have required them to resist: "Watergate happened because some persons in authority wanted it to happen; in one way or another they would have financed it, law or no law, surplus or no surplus."

More broadly, he argues that the 1974 law, which provided for government financing of presidential elections and which placed ceilings both on individual contributions and on campaign expenditures, swept through Congress on a wave of indignation, over massive corruption in the financing of the 1972 Nixon campaign that, on this book's showing, never occurred. Those violations that did take place, Stans says, were covered under existing law, and he makes a persuasive case that the pre-Watergate campaign act of 1971, which did not limit expenditures but which did require disclosure of all contributions over $100, offered sufficient safeguards against improper financial influence on elections and on political behavior. He takes some consolation from the Supreme Court decision of 1975 which threw out the provisions of the new law limiting expenditures. As for the remaining limits on individual contributions, Stans's reminder that "special-interest money" is not restricted to large personal contributions should recommend itself to reformers currently exercised over the excessive influence of "single-interest" voting groups.

An ill-considered campaign reform law is not, however, in Stans's view, the worst of the results of the Watergate affair. For him, the great untold story of Watergate is that the "terrors of justice" descended not only on Maurice Stans but on countless others who became victims of the "hysteria" of the times. Stans does not deny that Watergate involved real crimes—though he thinks they have been "exaggerated"—but the whole weight of the book is to emphasize the wrongdoings not of the conspirators but of those who, in their eagerness to expose the crimes of Watergate, trampled on the rights and reputations of the innocent.

To Stans, the Watergate investigation stands in the tradition of Salem, frontier vigilante justice, racial lynchings, and the McCarthyism of the 50s; it was, he charges, a witch-hunt, "where accusation was taken for guilt and association with Richard Nixon's administration or reelection campaign was grounds for accusation." Watergate, in fact, "was in most respects a vastly greater and more far-reaching inquisition than anything that had gone before." These themes have eagerly been seized on by ideologues of the Right; the review in *Human Events,* for example, hailed the book for offering, at long last, the beginning of the "real history" of the scandal. This real history, the reviewer suggested, will expose the "official version" of Watergate as "a monstrous, unconscionable distortion of the truth" and reveal the actual record of "a reign of media and government terror unparalleled in American history."

Such a view of Watergate involves, of course, a monumental loss of proportion and lack of perspective. It is simply perverse to summarize the affair as an instance of the McCarthyism of the Left. There are witch-hunts and witch-hunts (as Stans rather lamely concedes at the end of his Salem/Watergate analogy) and we can distinguish among them only by asking certain necessary questions: Were there witches present? What was their nature? Were the weapons chosen to fight them appropriate to the occasion? It is in the face of such questions that an identification of Watergate with McCarthyism disintegrates.

In Watergate there were real witches; they had to be exorcised; and the weapons devised to combat them, while sometimes put to crude or illegitimate uses, were not fundamentally inappropriate. McCarthy had a real enemy (despite what many cold-war revisionists suggest), but he fought Communism largely in the wrong place and with weapons that disabled more innocent than guilty. The innocents of Watergate—and Stans has shown us that there were some—were not, as were the innocents of McCarthyism, the central element in the story. That they were incidental victims does not make their experience less tragic, but neither does that experience rightfully figure as the heart of the matter. In the end, of course, McCarthy's excesses badly discredited the anti-Communist cause. (He had considerable help, it should be noted, from those who, either out of willful ignorance or malicious intent, collapsed all anti-Communism into McCarthyism.) It is unlikely that Stans or anyone else will be able to persuade future generations that the pursuit of the truth of Watergate was so flawed in procedure as to suggest doubts concerning its purposes.

Keeping these distinctions in mind, we can nonetheless assess the *elements* of McCarthyism that did, in fact, creep into the Watergate investigations. One can fully believe that Richard Nixon and his associates deserved everything they got and still acknowledge that the investigation which brought them down included avoidable instances, official and unofficial, of false accusation, abuse and harass-ment, misrepresentation, and character assassination. There *were* occasions when the affair took on, as Stans says, a "Roman circus atmosphere" and there were too many assumptions of guilt by association. Genuinely innocent men suffered real injuries: loss of friends, loss of income, loss of reputation. Opportunistic politicians and social critics used the weapon of Watergate to settle old scores and to advance their ideological interests. Reporting and analysis by the media too often exceeded the bounds of fair comment. People who should have made it their business to dis-courage the populist fantasies concerning tyranny and corruption that Watergate inevitable bred instead fostered and nourished them. The Watergate investigation did what it had to do—uncover the crimes of the Nixon administration—but in the process it also did unnecessary damage to civil liberties and to political civility. It would be wrong to argue that partially discreditable means invalidated legitimate ends, but the cause neither of justice nor of historical accuracy would be served by denial of the tainted means.

The tangled conflict between means and ends presents itself in acute form in consideration of the role of Judge John J. Sirica in the Watergate affair. The ad-vertising for *To Set the Record Straight* describes Sirica as the "one true hero" of Watergate. That view matches the popular perception, but careful analysis of the record suggests that Sirica was a more ambiguous sort of hero than his publishers imagine. Sirica did play a critical part in uncovering the facts of the scandal. The cover-up began to fall apart with James McCord's letter to the judge after the initial burglary trial indicating his willingness to break silence about the conspiracy (though there may well be exaggeration in Sirica's claim that without McCord's letter the case "would never have been broken"). Yet doubts arise concerning Sirica's actions during the first Watergate trial and its aftermath, doubts which his memoir does not dispel.

In the pages of this book, Sirica frequently comes across as a kind of Harry Truman of the judiciary. As Truman did, Sirica clearly thinks of himself as a plain man without supposing for a moment that he is only an ordinary one. Sensitive concerning his limited education (he finished high school at night, skipped college, and only got through law school on the third try after earlier dropping out twice), Sirica, like Truman, compensates for educational deficiencies with brisk decisive-ness, firm self-confidence (perhaps not always fully felt), and an uncomplicated assurance that problems can be solved and moralities secured without excessive cerebration, equivocation, or concern with customary rules of procedure. Such a personality is not at home with intellectual uncertainty or moral ambiguity. It is qualities like these that helped Harry Truman make the most momentous political decisions without tortuous agonizing, but sometimes also without sufficient reflection. It is a similar cast of mind that allowed Sirica relentlessly to pursue the deeper truths of Watergate, with little apparent concern—then or now—that in so doing he occasionally bent the rules of judicial behavior.

Sirica's vigorous desire for natural justice and his untroubled sense of right and wrong persuaded him from the outset to use the burglary trial to get at the "truth" of Watergate hidden behind the simple facts of the break-in. His reputation in Washington legal circles as "Maximum John" did not at all hurt his efforts to find that truth. Sirica's reputation, combined with his clear indication of frustration and anger during the course of the trial that those behind the burglary were avoiding detection, no doubt inclined McCord to the view that honesty was, with this judge at least, a prudential policy. It was just four days before he was due to be sentenced that McCord decided to confide in Sirica.

Both before and after McCord broke, Sirica went to considerable lengths to bring the full story of Watergate to the surface. Unsatisfied with the prosecution's efforts to get at the higher-ups behind the burglary, he subjected Hugh Sloan, treasurer of CRP, to intense questioning concerning the origins and intended purposes of the money Sloan had handed over to Liddy. In the course of the questioning, Sirica made abundantly clear his suspicion that Sloan was telling less than the full truth. But Sirica's questioning of Sloan turns out to have added nothing substantial to what had already been revealed in the court record; its only significant effect was to impugn the honesty, before the court and the nation, of a man who, as Sirica himself now admits, had not lied. Yet Sirica feels no need in any way to apologize for his actions in the Sloan interrogation. He has, he says, "no regrets" over his action during the trial: "The more I think about it, the more I believe that it was the proper course to take and in fact the only course to take. . . . Simply stated, I had no intention of sitting on the bench like a nincompoop and watching the parade go by."

Sirica also used sentencing procedure both as a deterrent and as a method of getting behind the cover-up. Thus in March 1973 he sentenced Liddy to a $40,000 fine and up to 20 years in jail (at several points Sirica reveals the strong dislike he had developed for the "smart-alecky, cocky" Liddy); with the other break-in defendants, he issued "provisional" sentences of 35 to 40 years, on the understanding that those sentences would be reduced if the defendants cooperated with the continuing Watergate grand jury and with the Senate Watergate Committee. Again, Sirica appears entirely unable to understand the "great furor" created by his use of draconian discretionary sentencing in order to coerce testimony on the larger questions related to the case. Federal statutes allow for the provisional sentencing procedure, and Sirica does not find it necessary to meet objections that that procedure was inappropriate in these circumstances. He does insist that he at no time meant to follow through on the threat implicit in the provisional sentences: "I never had any intention whatsoever of putting those men in jail for thirty to forty years," he says.

That is reassuring, but it still does not meet the question of the propriety of making the threat in the first place. (Eight months later, Sirica did issue final, lesser sentences to all the defendants except Liddy.)

In assessing the judge's actions in the break-in trial, it is necessary to keep in mind that the prosecutors had their own plans for breaking the cover-up. Sirica himself notes U.S. Attorney Earl Silbert's intention, once he had obtained convictions in the break-in, to give grants of immunity to the burglars and haul them all back before the Watergate grand jury "to give the full story behind the break-in."

One need not be in any measure an apologist for the Watergate criminals to raise questions over Sirica's behavior. Reviewing Sirica's memoir in the *New Republic,* Joseph L. Rauh Jr., a former national chairman of Americans for Democratic Action and a prominent civil-rights, civil-liberties, and labor lawyer, pointedly notes the statement of the American Bar Association that "the only purpose of a criminal trial is to determine whether the prosecution has established the guilt of the accused as required by law, and the trial judge should not allow the proceedings to be used for any other purpose." Observing that Sirica not only allowed but himself used the proceedings for "other purposes," Rauh concludes that "there was no warrant for Sirica to go beyond his proper judicial role":

> And the statement of the Court of Appeals, in affirming the burglary convictions, that Sirica's conduct of the trial "was in the highest tradition of his office as a federal judge," is more a commentary on anti-Watergate hysteria than a justification for Sirica's misuse of judicial power. This same hysteria brought spokesmen for the greatest civil-liberties organization in the history of the nation (American Civil Liberties Union) . . . to applaud Sirica's conduct. But all of this cannot alter the end-justifies-the-means philosophy that surrounded Sirica's actions.

In the course of his book, Sirica delivers himself of some gratuitous pronouncements on the character and fate of Richard Nixon that are worth noting. At one point, he discloses that had Nixon refused to turn over the tapes to the court, he would have found the President in contempt and forced compliance by levying large daily fines, because, he says, "I knew the President loved money." Sirica also announces that Nixon should not have been pardoned, but should have been indicted and tried, and had he been convicted in Sirica's court, "I would have sent him to jail." To the argument that Nixon could not have been tried because the proceedings would have dragged on for months or even years, disrupting the country, Sirica replies that any such delays would only have come from the defendant himself, and he proceeds to a truly bizarre comparison:

> Nixon's tactic was really the same as the tactic behind the behavior of the Black Panthers and others who in those years disrupted their trials by yelling and throwing things and screaming insults at the judge. Nixon's threatened uproar would have taken the more genteel form of legalistic objections and emotional appeals for sympathy, but that made him no different from the others. The only difference between them was that Nixon got away with it.

The argument here is doubly peculiar. In the first place, even granting that Nixon by his actions in Watergate invited a kind of permanent open season on himself, it still seems excessive to anticipate and criticize behavior on his part that never occurred. He surely has enough real sins to account for that it is not necessary to create imaginary ones for him. Beyond that, it seems incredible that a federal district judge could be so injudicious as to find no distinction between tearing up a courtroom and making "legalistic objections."

It is in connection with Richard Nixon that Watergate issues the greatest challenge to our capacity for reasonable judgment. The problem, of course, involves not Nixon's role in Watergate itself—judgments are all too easy to make there—but relating Watergate to our larger conclusions concerning the Nixon Presidency. It will always be impossible to think of Nixon without thinking of the scandal that drove him from office, but severe distortion results when, as is often currently the case, everything in the Nixon years is viewed *sub specie* Watergate. It is probably still too early to establish the necessary distinctions, but the process ought to start soon. (A good place to begin, incidentally, is with Nixon's own memoirs, which are considerably more useful and revealing than many critics have suggested.)

Those who hope to see Nixon given his due will do well to avoid the approach taken in *The Terrors of Justice*. Stans makes ritual concessions concerning the evils of Watergate, but he still finds it hard to take them all that seriously. The break-in was, he acknowledges, a crime, but it was only "a very minor one except for the political repercussions that followed it" (which is a little like saying that the striking of the iceberg by the *Titanic* was insignificant except for the sinking that followed it). In his handling of the affair, Nixon "stumbled over a molehill," and it still seems to Stans tragically unfair that because of Nixon's "clumsy handling of a small incident" it became possible for a coalition of "opportunistic politicians, an aggressive and hostile media, ambitious prosecutors, and organized 'public-interest' groups" to combine to bring down the administration. The worst that Stans can bring himself to say about Nixon and Watergate is that Nixon was a President "who tried too hard."

It is clearly unacceptable to plead for justice for the Nixon administration on the grounds that Watergate did not make any difference or that it was not the President's fault. Watergate was an ugly and unforgivable business, and Nixon's tragic destiny was of his own making. What the liberals, the commentators, and all the rest of his ancient enemies could not have done to him, Nixon did to himself—and to all of us (particularly those who shared, in varying degrees, in his administration's aims and purposes).

The only path to historical rehabilitation for Richard Nixon will be the recognition that there was more to his administration than Watergate. Stans is unconvincing as an apologist, but he becomes more persuasive when he suggests that there were a great many people who, because they lost their emotional and intellectual balance or because they harbored ideological purposes, unfairly decided after Watergate that everything and everyone associated with the Nixon administration were irredeemable corrupt. Watergate became a symbol of total depravity, and too many people who should have known better swept together under the Watergate umbrella, without discrimination, all that the Nixon people had ever touched. That was unfair; more important, it was historically inaccurate. It is at this point that historical revisionism on Watergate might fruitfully begin.

The Inescapability of Watergate

STANLEY I. KUTLER

"In the past few days," Richard Nixon told the nation on the evening of August 8, 1974, he had realized that he no longer had "a strong enough political base in the Congress" to maintain himself in office. The President's contention that he had to resign merely because he had lost his political base sounded the *leitmotif* for his last campaign—his struggle for the grace and favor of history. That political base was Nixon's to lose, yet his remarks implied that he had been the victim of a political conspiracy. He mentioned the Watergate "matter" only once.

Nixon's apologia alarmed his old nemesis Wright Patman, Chairman of the House Banking Committee. The morning after the speech, he wrote to House Judiciary Committee Chairman Peter Rodino, urging that the committee complete its investigation into Nixon's presidential conduct. Patman told Rodino it was imperative to preserve all the documents and tapes and to ensure that nothing was lost as a result of the presidential transition.

Patman understood the stakes. He suspected that "in the coming weeks and months, there will be some who will attempt to distort the record, [to] misconstrue events, and to cloud the real issues." Watergate had been a "wrenching experience," he told Rodino, but nothing would be learned if the record were incomplete or distorted. He urged that the committee secure additional White House tapes and publish them. Patman had correctly complained on other occasions that the available tape transcripts revealed nothing of White House discussions between September 15, 1972, and February 28, 1973.

The thought of remaining in the limelight apparently was too much for Rodino. He had been a reluctant warrior from the outset. Now, with almost unseemly haste, he retreated to his familiar obscurity—and shut down the House impeachment inquiry. No one challenged him; Patman again found himself abandoned and isolated. Meanwhile, Rodino had given aid and comfort to Nixon's embarrassed supporters, one of whom had begged Leon Jaworski to put an "immediate end" to this "mess," and allow everyone to "quickly forget about it and go on about their business."

Nixon himself was more than ready to go about the business of refurbishing his historical reputation. What he said when he resigned, and what he did after that, signaled his campaign to capture the soul of history. Gerald Ford, never known for stern judgments of his contemporaries, remarked that Nixon's resignation-eve statement on his loss of political support dodged the real issue. Nixon, he complained, had failed to offer any note of contrition, refusing to "take that final step." Surely, Nixon had no desire for such finality. A contentious man, so self-consciously struggling to emulate Theodore Roosevelt's "man in the arena," Nixon simply could not couple the shame of resignation with the obscurity that public penance might bring. Wright Patman could but ponder the future implications of Rodino's decision to bow out. What, indeed, would history say?

Before and after his resignation, Nixon and his supporters either minimized Watergate or ignored it altogether. In May 1974 Nixon told Rabbi Baruch Korff that Watergate was the "thinnest scandal" in American history. Although embattled by that scandal near the end of his tenure, Nixon suggested to Alexander Haig that a failure to respond to a North Korean attack on an American reconnaissance plane in 1969 "was the most serious misjudgment of my Presidency, including Watergate." He assured his fallen aide, Charles Colson, that Colson's "dedicated service" to the nation would be remembered after Watergate had "become only a footnote in history." At an October 1973 press conference, Nixon anticipated his theme of victimization when he denounced his congressional and media opponents as spiteful enemies who sought to reverse "the mandate of 1972." Just after the resignation, David Eisenhower, the former President's son-in-law, said that in fifteen years, Watergate would "look pretty small." The President, Eisenhower said, had "simply acquiesced in the non-prosecution of aides who covered up a little operation into the opposition's political headquarters"—hardly something to be taken seriously. In an April 1988 television appearance, Nixon repeated the "footnote" thesis but added that his delay in bombing North Vietnam was the biggest mistake of his presidency.

If he could not reduce Watergate to banality, to something commonplace, Nixon's fallback position always was to insist that no wrong had occurred. "When the President does it, that means that it is not illegal," he told television interviewer David Frost in May 1977, in the first of many self-orchestrated "comebacks." He referred to the "political" (not criminal) activities that led to his resignation. Following the broadcast of the Frost interviews, a Gallup poll found that 44 percent of those who watched were more sympathetic toward Nixon than they had been, while 28 percent felt less so. Yet Nixon's early venture into revisionism and vindication failed dismally. Nearly three-quarters of the viewing audience believed he had been guilty of an obstruction of justice, and nearly as many thought he had lied during the Frost interviews themselves.

Fifteen years after the Watergate break-in, Nixon loyalists faithfully echoed their leader's interpretation. At a 1987 conference, H. R. Haldeman resurrected the "third-rate burglary" pronouncement of June 1972, calling it the work of "stupid" Nixon supporters. If the problem had been "handled" within the White House staff structure from the outset," he said, the matter would have been contained—as if John Dean had ever worked for someone other than H. R. Haldeman. In a televised 1984 memoir, one which Nixon and his staff carefully controlled, the former President called the break-in a "botched" job, a "misdemeanor" that his enemies had turned into the "crime of the century." In 1988, Patrick Buchanan dismissed the Watergate events as "Mickey Mouse misdemeanors," evidently forgetting that felonies, as well as stupidity, followed the Watergate break-in. "A child of ten would have been able to figure out that it wasn't a sensible thing for [Nixon] to do, to try that cover-up," observed Richard Helms, no stranger to clandestine affairs. It was "one of the stupidest things that anybody could have done."

Those who would minimize or dismiss Watergate focused on the break-in of Democratic headquarters, an event of which the President and his closest staff members pled total ignorance, and at the same time avoided any discussion of the abuses of power that preceded the burglary and the obstruction of justice that followed it. Those acts, which are part of the Watergate story, run like a seamless web throughout the Nixon presidency, and while they constituted the focus of the impeachment proceedings, they were ignored in the interpretation imposed by the former President. William Ruckelshaus, a victim of the Saturday Night Massacre, had a different stake in the interpretation of Watergate, but one more in accord with the facts: "[T]he break-in was trivial but what happened afterwards was not trivial. It was profound." And Leon Jaworski, who perhaps understood Nixon's stonewalling better than anyone, brusquely noted: "To deny impeachable acts and criminal wrongdoing is untruthful. . . . They cannot be erased by the belated efforts of the man who created them." Jaworski had enthusiastically supported Nixon's re-election bid in 1972; his later judgment gave the lie to Nixon's bald claim that he had been undone by political enemies.

Revisionism perhaps is as inevitable as death and taxes, and the Watergate affair deserves some, to be sure. Contemporary commentator Nicholas von Hoffman, for example, shrewdly warned of the dangers of history written only from the perspective of the winners. The uncritical fascination with Judge John Sirica and his transformation into a neo-folk idol; the press's excessive claims for its role; the lynch-mob mentality of what von Hoffman called the "monotone" media; and some questionable prosecutorial tactics suggests topics that deserve more critical scrutiny. But that kind of revisionism is quite different from one that proceeds from the premise that "everyone" had engaged in abuses of power, that obstruction of justice was a matter of "national security," and that Nixon's actions pale into insignificance against the achievements of his Administration. Such attitudes come close to validating Voltaire's dictum that history is a pack of tricks the living play upon the dead.

How shall we remember Richard Nixon?

The movie is Woody Allen's *Sleeper* (1973); the scene is set in the year 2073; several people, apparently anthropologists, are watching old videotapes of Richard Nixon:

> *Doctor* Some of us have a theory that he might once have been President of the United States, but that he did something horrendous. So that all records—everything was wiped out about him. There is nothing in the history books, there are no pictures on stamps, on money. . . .
>
> *Miles Monroe* He actually was President of the United States but I know whenever he used to leave the White House, the Secret Service would count the silverware.

That, of course, was at the height of the Watergate affair. In the years that followed, Nixon regularly presented himself as an elder statesman and as a knowing political handicapper; still, for many, he remained a comic figure, a butt of derision, constantly forced back into private retreat as the barbs and jokes resonated. But the *Sleeper* lines about forgetting have a ring of painful reality. We are, to some extent, in danger of forgetting—not forgetting Richard Nixon, but forgetting what he did and what he symbolized to his contemporaries. History, after all, is not just what the present wishes to make of the past for its own purposes; present-mindedness has its own alphabet of sins. Historians are entitled to weigh the past by the measure of the evidence of long-term consequences, and they must weigh by the standards of the past, not those of their own time. Yet as Leon Jaworski cautioned, they must not uncritically accept the judgments of the actors themselves.

Memories proved short in some cases. The upper echelon of the co-called media "lynch mob," the American Society of Newspaper Editors, who had heard Nixon proclaim "I am not a crook" in 1973, welcomed him to their annual meeting in 1984 with a standing ovation. The former President expressed surprise that he had been asked so few Watergate questions. Two years later, *Newsweek* reported that when asked what he considered Watergate's greatest lesson, Nixon replied: "Just destroy all the tapes." Yet two weeks afterward, the same periodical proclaimed Nixon "rehabilitated," and featured him on its cover over the caption, "He's back." One scholar argued that Nixon might be the greatest domestic president of the twentieth century—a notion first advanced by John Ehrlichman—and described Watergate as only a "dim and distant curiosity" which eventually would be seen as "a relatively insignificant event." Worse yet, treatment of Watergate ran the danger of trivialization, as when the *Today* television show interviewed Gordon Liddy for his views on the Soviet Union or when Jeb Magruder was selected to chair an ethics commission. Typically, media fascination with personality rather than with substance served to keep "the slippery former president" alive as a public figure, political writer David Broder noted, "when he ought to be living out his life in private and in disgrace."

The Nixon revisionism attempted to inflict a collective national amnesia on historians, the media, and our political leadership regarding Watergate. Watergate at times seemed lost in the mists of history, an odd fate for an event that consumed and convulsed the nation and tested the constitutional and political system as it had not been tested since the Civil War. But, in truth, once out of the White House, Richard Nixon commanded attention precisely because of his indissoluble links to Watergate, a connection indelibly engraved on our history. When asked in 1968 how he envisioned the first line of his *New York Times* obituary, Nixon replied: "'He made a great contribution to the peace of the world.'" Twenty years later, he told reporters: "History will treat me fairly. Historians probably won't[,] because most historians are on the left, and I understand that"—resorting to a familiar refrain and technique. Then he asked that he be remembered most for his China initiative.

Nixon certainly will be remembered for his role in world affairs. He will receive heavy measures of both praise and criticism, and historians of both the Right and Left probably will cross sides in unpredictable ways. It might never have occurred to Richard Nixon that so-called leftist historians helped rehabilitate Herbert Hoover. Whatever historians do, however, no "fair" history of the Nixon era can overlook the centrality of Watergate. Textbooks a century from now will inevitably speak of Richard Nixon as the first president to resign because of scandals. His achievements will get their due, as different generations weigh them, favorably or unfavorably, but they probably will not rival Watergate for historical attention.

Henry Kissinger contemptuously dismissed the political and media assault on the Nixon Administration as an "American extravaganza," something profoundly distasteful to him as a longtime admirer of the ordered past of nineteenth-century Europe. "Extravaganza," indeed; not every president has stood in danger of impeachment. Neither Nixon nor we can escape Watergate. Its history demands our serious attention; it was neither trivial nor insignificant. It raised important, painful questions about American political behavior and the American political system, questions that speak to the traditions and structure of American life. Whether the actors in the drama of Watergate confronted those questions successfully or unsuccessfully, directly or passively, honestly or conveniently, will be the subject for history. That is the significant, inescapable importance of Watergate.

The wars of Watergate are rooted in the lifelong political personality of Richard Nixon. His well-documented record of political paranoia, his determination to wreak vengeance on his enemies, and his overweening concern with winning his own elections, rather than with the fortunes of his colleagues or with the substance of policy, animated the thoughts and actions of his aides, who fulfilled his wishes.

The period is also bounded by much more than a burglary in 1972 and a resignation in 1974. The fall of Richard Nixon was the last act in a decade-long political melodrama that haunted the American stage, beginning with the civil rights movement and John F. Kennedy's assassination. War and unprecedented social protest about the war and other complex problems in American life followed and eventually culminated in Watergate. To that extent, Richard Nixon was the last casualty.

Richard Nixon cannot be separated from Watergate, however valiant his efforts. In time, Haldeman, Ehrlichman, Mitchell, Colson, Dean, Butterfield, Haig, and the other supporting players in the Watergate drama will fade into the same well-deserved obscurity as have their counterparts in other historical scandals. Ultimately, we leave behind the spear carriers, what the poet Coleridge called the Ancient Mariner's "strange and ghastly crew." But Nixon himself will remain as the one indisputably unforgettable and responsible actor.

President Nixon and his defenders have claimed that in the Watergate affair he behaved no differently from other presidents. Watergate emerged "exactly how the other side would have played it," Nixon said in 1977. It was all "politics pure and simple." With even less plausibility, he justified the crimes of Watergate as an outgrowth of the "end-justifies-the-means mentality of the 1960s." The long answer to all that is that *not* everyone did it. The short answer is that others' behavior is beside the point. Sam Ervin impatiently dismissed Nixon's plea: "Murder and theft have been committed since the earliest history of mankind, but that fact has not made murder meritorious or larceny legal." The Nixon rationalization rested on a claim that he was an unfortunate victim of time and place and deserves to be considered entirely apart from Watergate. Still, there is no dodging the fact that Watergate happened and he was found culpable.

Egil Krogh, who engineered and illegal break-in on Nixon's behalf, confessed that his work, "as official Government action, . . . struck at the heart of what the Government was established to protect, which is the . . . rights of each individual." His mission had not been designed to protect national security but to gain material to discredit Daniel Ellsburg *[sic]*. Charles Colson similarly later admitted that "the official threats" to individual rights were wrong and had to be stopped. Yet the President himself repeatedly had initiated and encouraged those threats, and then had sacrificed his closest political subordinates to conceal his own involvement in their abuses of power and obstructions of justice. "I abdicated my moral judgments and turned them over to someone else," Ehrlichman confessed to Judge Sirica. Watergate gives us cause to ponder anew Alexander Hamilton's query in *Federalist I* whether in this nation, men would establish "good government from reflection and choice, or whether they are forever destined to depend for their political constitutions, on accident and force."

Richard Nixon discovered that the nation would tolerate an imperial president, but not an imperious one. Centuries of British and American constitutional experience have dictated limitations on executive power. However necessarily powerful the presidency may be in a fragile, dangerous world, however indispensable presidential action may seem for the nation's security and well-being, the practiced traditions of constitutionalism and the rule of law still count for much.

The Watergate wars offered eloquent testimony that the nation had a serious commitment to the rule of law. Our tradition has been that of a nation of laws, not of men only; a nation of orderly means and processes, not of burglars or imperious executives and their compliant servants. That tradition is the essence of American constitutionalism. John Ehrlichman—and Richard Nixon—suffered irreparable damage when Ehrlichman so cavalierly brushed aside Senator Herman Talmadge's concern for the security of home and person. Men are not angels, Madison said, and we wisely have fenced them in with constitutional prescriptions for the restraint of power. The legal order, as Alexander Bickel wrote at the time of Watergate, required "not a presumed, theoretical consent, but a continuous actual one, born of continuous responsibility." Rulers cannot legitimately impose a rule of law on the ruled unless they themselves will submit to it.

"[L]et us begin by committing ourselves to the truth, to see it like it is and tell it like it is, to find the truth, to speak the truth and to live the truth. That's what we will do," Richard Nixon told his fellow Republicans when they nominated him for the presidency in 1968. "Truth will become the hallmark of the Nixon Administration," Herbert Klein told reporters several weeks after the election. But lies became the quicksand that engulfed Nixon, estranged him from his natural political allies, and eventually snapped the fragile bond of trust between leaders and led that binds government and the people. Nixon's lies brought him to the dock and cost him his presidency. "I have impeached myself," he confessed in 1977.

Political language can conceal the truth, as George Orwell and others have noted. Often truth is concealed with a knowing wink between the political leader and his audience, and much of it is concealed in the language of symbolic politics. Richard Whalen, a one-time Nixon adviser and speechwriter, described how Nixon confined his conservative instincts to private company, while publicly positioning himself to the left—where, he believed, the votes were. "You don't know how to lie," Nixon told an early political associate. "If you can't lie, you'll never go anywhere." But for Nixon, lies led ultimately to a disgraceful resignation. At Republican leadership meetings throughout 1973 and 1974, Nixon's allies pleaded with him to "get it all out on the table." Nixon would say there was no more. But with repeated new disclosures, even those most steadfast among his supporters reached the point where, Congressman Barber Conable recalled, "you didn't believe anything." And still Nixon would insist, "it's all out there." The President informed Republican National Chairman George Bush, "George, I'm telling the truth." But the tape revelations reportedly devastated Bush; lying, a friend said, just was "not in George Bush's book."

Nixon confronted Democratic majorities in Congress throughout his presidency, a fact which doubtless contributed mightily to his sense of peril. But a numerical majority dictates organizational control, not necessarily ideological dominance. Friendly Southern Democrats and Republican loyalists regularly eased Nixon's path through his first term. Conflicts existed, to be sure, but he was not a President denied. The domestic achievements that Nixon and Ehrlichman claimed with such pride offer ample testimony to the President's success with Congress. The unfolding events in 1973 and 1974 weakened Nixon's support base in Congress, and the

President's lies, deceit, "stonewalling"—to use the popular phrase of Watergate—eventually destroyed it.

The Saturday Night Massacre convinced many that Nixon had something to hide. The exposure of the taping system betrayed a sinister side to the White House. The 18½-minute tape gap, the incorrect transcripts, and the President's shifting explanations inexorably chipped away at his credibility. The Republican and Southern Democratic members of the House Judiciary Committee watched the President descend the slippery slope away from truth, convinced that he had lied. Repeated sentiments such as he expressed in August 1973—"That was and that is the simple truth"—were seen as hollow and perverse. The Republican loyalists on the House Judiciary Committee realized the irreparable damage of Nixon's lying. After the release of the "smoking gun" transcripts, they expressed amazement and dismay that for so long he had suppressed the truth about his role in Watergate; consequently, they sadly noted, the truth "could not be unleashed without destroying his presidency."

William Buckley thought that presidents must on occasion violate laws, but he judged that Nixon's denials of his actions magnified the violations. For Buckley, the denials, not Nixon's lawbreaking, constituted the President's "real" crimes. Nixon repeatedly promised the "truth," an old refrain that echoed the "Checkers" speech of 1952 when he said that the "best thing is to tell the truth." Barry Goldwater did not share Buckley's brief for moral relativism. "Truth is the foundation of a stable society," he insisted. "Its absence was the crux of Nixon's failure." With biting contempt, Goldwater read the indictment: Nixon had lied to his family, his friends, his political supporters in and out of Congress, the nation, and the world. "Tell the truth," Goldwater told Nixon when he visited the former President in his San Clemente exile in 1975. When he wrote his memoirs thirteen years later, Goldwater was still waiting for the truth from Richard Nixon.

Because he lied, Richard Nixon lost his political base. That deceit was intended to obscure the overwhelming evidence that he *had* abused power and he *had* obstructed justice. The actions of the President and his men were serious. More than seventy persons were convicted or offered guilty pleas as a consequence of the Age of Watergate. These included several Cabinet officers, two Oval Office aides, and numerous presidential assistants. Revisionism, to be whole, must produce more than pardons at the bar of history; it must produce the necessary exculpatory evidence.

Nixon's deeds as well as his own words, on tape, in public, and in his memoirs, convicted him. "I brought myself down. I gave them a sword. And they stuck it in," he bitterly observed. But he reminded us of what he was: "And, I guess, if I'd been in their position, I'd have done the same thing." Resignation, he once said, meant that he was guilty, and it would weaken the presidency he so cherished. For two years, he had resisted cooperation in the name of "preserving the presidency"—meaning, of course, himself. But in the end, he willingly sacrificed the presidency in order to save the President.

Political philosophers since the ancient Greeks have sought to understand the links between politics and ethical behavior—"virtue," as eighteenth-century men were fond of calling it. They agreed at least, Dwight Macdonald once wrote, "that there is some connection between ethics and politics and there is a problem involved." They all, he observed, rejected the "simplistic" view, so congenial to the "pragmatic" American mind, that there was no connection and no problem.

The eagerness of Nixon and his supporters to dismiss his misdeeds because "everyone does it" perversely twisted the conservative political tradition to which they subscribed, a tradition that rests upon virtue and morality. As the impeachment inquiry reached its climax, Congressman William Cohen recognized that perversion as he wondered how we had moved from the *Federalist Papers* of the 1780s to the Nixon tapes of the 1970s. Alexander Hamilton and James Madison, who had few illusions about human nature, nevertheless understood that leadership must rest on something other than covering up crimes or scheming to punish alleged enemies.

Americans idealize their presidents and hence expect them to meet the highest moral standards. People demand leaders better than themselves; such is the stuff of "heroes." Nixon's "tricky" image was one he never escaped. Watergate reinforced, and then confirmed, that image.

Competence and expertise were not enough to protect Richard Nixon. The President symbolizes "legitimacy, continuity, and morality"; Nixon tarnished the symbol, and it cost him dearly. What is clear, above all, is that the country had come together on the fundamental proposition that virtue mattered, that some ethical standard applied in political life. Thomas Jefferson once remarked that the whole art of government consists in being honest. George Washington, who gave a "Farewell Address" in 1796 far different from Nixon's, said that virtue and morality formed the "necessary spring of government" and were "indispensable supports" for political prosperity. "The mere politician," Washington insisted, "ought to respect and cherish them." Washington and the cherry tree myth are deeply ingrained in American civil religion. Richard Nixon never understood. Nearly a decade after he resigned, he wrote: "Virtue is not what lifts great leaders above others." But even those words of self-incrimination pale next to the most fateful ones he ever uttered: "I hereby resign."

⋙ *F U R T H E R   R E A D I N G*

Ambrose, Stephen. *Nixon: The Education of a Politician, 1913–1962* (1987).
Arnold, Peri. *Making the Managerial Presidency* (1986).
Ball, Howard. *"We Have a Duty": The Supreme Court and the Watergate Tapes Litigation* (1990).
Ben-Veniste, Richard, and George Frampton Jr. *Stonewall: The Real Story of the Watergate Prosecution* (1977).
Bernstein, Carl, and Bob Woodward. *All the President's Men* (1974).
———. *The Final Days* (1976).
Brodie, Fawn. *Richard Nixon: The Shaping of His Character* (1981).
Cannon, James. *Time and Chance: Gerald Ford's Appointment with History* (1994).
Chester, Lewis, Godfrey Hodgson, and Bruce Page. *An American Melodrama* (1969).
Dash, Samuel. *Chief Counsel* (1976).
Dean, John. *Blind Ambition* (1976).
———. *Lost Honor* (1982).
Dent, Harry. *The Prodigal South Returns to Power* (1978).
Ehrlichman, John. *Witness to Power: The Nixon Years* (1982).

Emery, Fred. *Watergate: The Corruption of American Politics and the Fall of Richard Nixon* (1994).

Ervin, Sam. *The Whole Truth: The Watergate Conspiracy* (1980).

Evans, Roland Jr., and Robert Novak. *Nixon in the White House* (1974).

Fisher, Louis. *Constitutional Conflicts Between the President and Congress* (1985).

Haldeman, H. R. *The Ends of Power* (1978).

Halpern, Paul J., ed. *Why Watergate?* (1975).

Harward, Donald W., ed. *Crisis in Confidence: The Impact of Watergate* (1974).

Hersh, Seymour. *The Price of Power: Kissinger in the Nixon White House* (1983).

Hodgson, Godfrey. *All Things to All Men: The False Promise of the Modern American Presidency* (1980).

Hoff, Joan. *Nixon Reconsidered* (1994).

Hougan, Jim. *Secret Agenda: Watergate, Deep Throat, and the CIA* (1984).

Jaworski, Leon. *Confession and Avoidance: A Memoir* (1979).

———. *The Right and the Power: The Prosecution of Watergate* (1976).

Kelley, Clarence. *Kelley: The Story of an FBI Director* (1987).

Kissinger, Henry. *White House Years* (1979).

———. *Years of Upheaval* (1982).

Klein, Herbert G. *Making it Perfectly Clear* (1980).

Kleindienst, Richard. *Justice: The Memoirs of an Attorney General* (1985).

Kutler, Stanley I. *The Wars of Watergate: The Last Crisis of the Nixon Presidency* (1990).

———. ed. *Abuse of Power: The New Nixon Tapes* (1977).

Lang, Gladys Engel, and Kurt Lang. *The Battle for Public Opinion: The President, the Press, and the Polls During Watergate* (1983).

Lowi, Theodore J. *The Personal President: Power Invested, Promise Unfulfilled* (1985).

Lukas, J. Anthony. *Nightmare: The Underside of the Nixon Years* (1976, 1988).

McGinniss, Joe. *The Selling of the President* (1970).

McQuaid, Kim. *The Anxious Years: America in the Vietnam-Watergate Era* (1989).

Magruder, Jeb Stuart. *An American Life* (1974).

Mazo, Earl. *Nixon: A Political and Personal Portrait* (1959).

Morris, Roger. *Richard Milhous Nixon: The Rise of an American Politician* (1990).

———. *Uncertain Greatness: Henry Kissinger and American Foreign Policy* (1977)

Nathan, Richard P. *The Plot That Failed: Nixon and the Administrative Presidency* (1975).

Nixon, Richard. *RN: The Memoirs of Richard Nixon* (1978).

Olmsted, Kathryn. *Challenging the Secret Government: The Post-Watergate Investigations of the CIA and FBI* (1996).

Parmet, Herbert. *Richard Nixon and His America* (1990).

Powers, Richard Gid. *Secrecy and Power: The Life of J. Edgar Hoover* (1986).

Powers, Thomas. *The Man Who Kept the Secrets: Richard Helms and the CIA* (1979).

Safire, William. *Before the Fall* (1975).

Schell, Jonathan. *The Time of Illusion* (1976).

Schlesinger, Arthur Jr. *The Imperial Presidency* (1973).

Sirica, John J. *To Set the Record Straight* (1979).

Spear, Joseph C. *Presidents and the Press: The Nixon Legacy* (1984).

Stans, Maurice. *The Terrors of Justice* (1984).

Sundquist, James L. *The Decline and Resurgence of Congress* (1981).

Theoharis, Athan, and John Stuart Cox. *The Boss: J. Edgar Hoover and the Great American Inquisition* (1986).

White, Theodore H. *Breach of Faith: The Fall of Richard Nixon* (1975).

———. *The Making of the President, 1968* (1969).

Wills, Garry. *Nixon Agonistes: The Crisis of the Self-Made Man* (1970).

C H A P T E R
12

The Reagan Revolution
and After: Politics and
Political Economy in
the New Era

※

The presidency of Ronald Reagan frequently has been termed a revolution, not only by Reagan and his supporters but by critics as well. Yet if there is seemingly widespread consensus that the Reagan years somehow constituted a revolution, there has been far less agreement as to that revolution's extent and character, the degree of its success or failure, whether or not it was truly Reagan's, or what it may bode for the future. If nothing else, the Reagan "revolution" produced major changes in the country's leadership, its public policy, and its political agenda. These changes are at the very least comparable with those associated with the Democratic presidencies of John F. Kennedy and Lyndon B. Johnson during the 1960s, and, in the view of some, approach even the transformation in politics and public life wrought during the New Deal and Cold War presidencies of Franklin D. Roosevelt and Harry S Truman.

As journalists and political scientists have noted, the Reagan years were marked by the continued decomposition of the old New Deal Democratic coalition forged by Roosevelt during the 1930s and by the growing ascendancy of the Republican party at the national level. Despite Democratic control of the House of Representatives (and the Senate, too, after 1986), Reagan secured passage of a series of major legislative initiatives. Through his power of appointment, moreover, he reshaped the nation's courts. He became the first president since Dwight D. Eisenhower to complete two terms in office successfully. Perhaps most important, he exercised a profound influence over the country's political agenda, molding the issues and terms of political debate throughout the decade. The succession of Vice President George Bush to the White House in 1988 confirmed the Republican party's national strength,

449

although the Democrats retained control of both houses of Congress and indeed increased their margins in the 1990 off-year elections.

The economic changes of the Reagan era have been no less dramatic. Reagan entered the White House pledged to stem inflation, lower taxes, reduce government spending, and cut federal regulation of the economy. He succeeded in many of these efforts, although not always in ways that he and his supporters had predicted and not necessarily in ways that produced all the benefits that they claimed would follow. He halted inflation through the classic Republican strategy of high interest rates and the cold bath of a major recession. He lowered taxes, especially on the well-to-do, although it is unclear whether this reduction spurred increased investment or only fueled an orgy of conspicuous consumption by the rich. He presided over a wave of deregulation during which regulatory structures in place for decades were eliminated or radically revised. Whether deregulation has heightened competition and lowered prices as its proponents predicted remains unclear. Finally, and perhaps ironically, Reagan conspicuously failed to reduce government spending. Indeed, steep increases in defense costs, coupled with lower taxes, contributed to the largest annual deficits in American history. In the short run, these policies paid rich political dividends: a huge military buildup without cuts in entitlements such as Social Security and Medicare, combined with a tax cut that left many Americans with more money for private consumption. In the long run, Reagan's programs spawned an enormous increase in the nation's indebtedness that would be paid for by Americans for generations to come.

Reagan's success as president must also be understood, however, in light of the powerful tensions coursing through American society and culture during the 1970s and 1980s: the polarizing impact of race, the reemergence of Christian conservatism in politics, and the ambivalent revolt against modernity. Race was perhaps the single most important force driving political realignment, as white southern Democratic conservatives and blue-collar ethnics continued to shift their allegiance from the Democratic to the Republican party. Reagan also appealed to conservative Christians, whose political mobilization became one of the decade's defining characteristics. Indeed, much of his success as a national leader seemed to derive from a paradox: on the one hand, Reagan was himself the product of a technologically progressive, corporate, and media-driven modern culture; on the other hand, he continually evoked the images of an earlier, premodern America of individualism and traditional values. There can be no doubt that in doing so he deftly captured the ambivalence felt by many Americans.

Reagan's triumph—or, more accurately, the triumph of the forces he represented—exerted a powerful influence on the presidents who followed him. George Bush inherited both the successes and failures of the Reagan administration, including a set of contradictory economic policies that led to recession and spiraling deficits. Bill Clinton shrewdly capitalized on these in a campaign that emphasized domestic concerns. "It's the economy, stupid," proclaimed a key Clinton adviser. As president, Clinton pursued a moderately conservative course, emphasizing deficit reduction, welfare reform, free trade, and the continued deregulation of the economy. As the twentieth century drew to a close, Democrats and Republicans alike jostled to position themselves in the mainstream of American politics. Vice President Al Gore, like Clinton a "New Democrat," hailed the administration's success in promoting the longest economic expansion in postwar history and touted his leadership of an initiative to "reinvent" government. George W. Bush, son of the former president, stole a page from both his father and Bill Clinton by seeking the center with what he called "compassionate conservatism."

By 1979 the Democratic administration of President Jimmy Carter was beset by a host of problems, many of which Carter had inherited but few of which he had successfully resolved. Chief among them were an economy wracked by inflation and high unemployment, and an energy crisis that was in part the product of the explosive politics of the Middle East and that signaled the end of an era of cheap energy. In Washington, D.C., political gridlock had set in, virtually paralyzing the efforts of either Congress or the administration to act decisively. In his July 15, 1979, speech to the nation (Document 1), Carter addressed not only the problems of economics and energy but also the larger crisis of confidence that he believed pervaded the nation. Republican presidential candidate Ronald Reagan skillfully capitalized on the economic and political failures of the Carter administration, as is clear from his September 9, 1980, campaign speech before the International Business Council (Document 2). Although Carter and Reagan alike invoked traditional American values, Carter, reflecting the chastened mood of the 1970s, had emphasized sacrifice and restraint, while Reagan, in what would become the dominant themes of the 1980s, stressed economic growth and renewal.

In the 1988 presidential campaign, Vice President George Bush embraced the policies of the Reagan years. In his inaugural address as president (Document 3), however, Bush sought to move toward the center, celebrating the Republican triumph while promising to create a "kinder" and "gentler" America. Bill Clinton defeated Bush in 1992, only to be ambushed two years later by Republican conservatives led by House Speaker Newt Gingrich. Announcing the "Contract with America" (Document 4), Republicans in 1994 won control of both houses of Congress for the first time since 1952. Clinton deftly turned the Republican victory to his own advantage, depicting the new congressional leaders as partisan extremists. At the same time, he captured conservative issues such as deficit reduction and welfare reform and made them his own (Document 5). Although liberals were dismayed by Clinton's abandonment of traditional liberalism (Document 6), the president's strategy paid rich political dividends in 1996, when he easily defeated Republican Robert Dole. Indeed, not even the salacious scandal involving the president and the young White House intern Monica Lewinsky could shake the president's personal popularity.

1. President Jimmy Carter and the Crisis of the American Spirit, 1979

It's clear that the true problems of our Nation are much deeper—deeper than gasoline lines or energy shortages, deeper even than inflation or recession. And I realize more than ever that as President I need your help. So, I decided to reach out and listen to the voices of America.

I invited to Camp David people from almost every segment of our society— business and labor, teachers and preachers, Governors, mayors, and private citizens. And then I left Camp David to listen to other Americans, men and women like you. It has been an extraordinary 10 days, and I want to share with you what I've heard.

Jimmy Carter, Address to the Nation, *Weekly Compilation of Presidential Documents* (July 20, 1979): 1235–1241.

First of all, I got a lot of personal advice. Let me quote a few of the typical comments that I wrote down.

This from a southern Governor: "Mr. President, you are not leading this Nation—you're just managing the Government."

"You don't see the people enough any more." . . .

"Don't talk to us about politics or the mechanics of government, but about an understanding of our common good."

"Mr. President, we're in trouble. Talk to us about blood and sweat and tears."

"If you lead, Mr. President, we will follow."

Many people talked about themselves and about the condition of our Nation. This from a young woman in Pennsylvania: "I feel so far from government. I feel like ordinary people are excluded from political power."

And this from a young Chicano: "Some of us have suffered from recession all our lives." . . .

And I like this one particularly from a black woman who happens to be the mayor of a small Mississippi town: "The big-shots are not the only ones who are important. Remember, you can't sell anything on Wall Street unless someone digs it up somewhere else first."

This kind of summarized a lot of other statements: "Mr. President, we are confronted with a moral and a spiritual crisis."

Several of our discussions were on energy, and I have a notebook full of comments and advice. I'll read just a few.

"We can't go on consuming 40 percent more energy than we produce. When we import oil we are also importing inflation plus unemployment."

"We've got to use what we have. The Middle East has only 5 percent of the world's energy, but the United States has 24 percent."

And this is one of the most vivid statements: "Our neck is stretched over the fence and OPEC has a knife."

"There will be other cartels and other shortages. American wisdom and courage right now can set a path to follow in the future."

This was a good one: "Be bold, Mr. President. We may make mistakes, but we are ready to experiment." . . .

These 10 days confirmed my belief in the decency and the strength and the wisdom of the American people, but it also bore out some of my long-standing concerns about our Nation's underlying problems.

I know, of course, being President, that government actions and legislation can be very important. That's why I've worked hard to put my campaign promises into law—and I have to admit, with just mixed success. But after listening to the American people I have been reminded again that all the legislation in the world can't fix what's wrong with America. So, I want to speak to you first tonight about a subject even more serious than energy or inflation. I want to talk to you right now about a fundamental threat to American democracy.

I do not mean our political and civil liberties. They will endure. And I do not refer to the outward strength of America, a nation that is at peace tonight everywhere in the world, with unmatched economic power and military might.

The threat is nearly invisible in ordinary ways. It is a crisis of confidence. It is a crisis that strikes at the very heart and soul and spirit of our national will. We can see this crisis in the growing doubt about the meaning of our own lives and in the loss of a unity of purpose for our Nation.

The erosion of our confidence in the future is threatening to destroy the social and the political fabric of America.

The confidence that we have always had as a people is not simply some romantic dream or a proverb in a dusty book that we read just on the Fourth of July. It is the idea which founded our Nation and has guided our development as a people. Confidence in the future has supported everything else—public institutions and private enterprise, our own families, and the very Constitution of the United States. Confidence has defined our course and has served as a link between generations. We've always believed in something called progress. We've always had a faith that the days of our children would be better than our own.

Our people are losing that faith, not only in government itself but in the ability as citizens to serve as the ultimate rulers and shapers of our democracy. As a people we know our past and we are proud of it. Our progress has been part of the living history of America, even the world. We always believed that we were part of a great movement of humanity itself called democracy, involved in the search for freedom and that belief has always strengthened us in our purpose. But just as we are losing our confidence in the future, we are also beginning to close the door on our past.

In a nation that was proud of hard work, strong families, close-knit communities, and our faith in God, too many of us now tend to worship self-indulgence and consumption. Human identity is no longer defined by what one does, but by what one owns. But we've discovered that owning things and consuming things does not satisfy our longing for meaning. We've learned that piling up material goods cannot fill the emptiness of lives which have no confidence or purpose.

The symptoms of this crisis of the American spirit are all around us. For the first time in the history of our country a majority of our people believe that the next 5 years will be worse than the past 5 years. Two-thirds of our people do not even vote. The productivity of American workers is actually dropping, and the willingness of Americans to save for the future has fallen below that of all other people in the Western world.

As you know, there is a growing disrespect for government and for churches and for schools, the news media, and other institutions. This is not a message of happiness or reassurance, but it is the truth and it is a warning.

These changes did not happen overnight. They've come upon us gradually over the last generation, years that were filled with shocks and tragedy.

We were sure that ours was a nation of the ballot, not the bullet, until the murders of John Kennedy and Robert Kennedy and Martin Luther King Jr. We were taught that our armies were always invincible and our causes were always just, only to suffer the agony of Vietnam. We respected the Presidency as a place of honor until the shock of Watergate.

We remember when the phrase "sound as a dollar" was an expression of absolute dependability, until 10 years of inflation began to shrink our dollar and our savings. We believed that our Nation's resources were limitless until 1973 when we had to face a growing dependence on foreign oil.

These wounds are still very deep. They have never been healed.

Looking for a way out of this crisis, our people have turned to the Federal Government and found it isolated from the mainstream of our Nation's life. Washington, D.C., has become an island. The gap between our citizens and our Government has never been so wide. The people are looking for honest answers, not easy answers; clear leadership, not false claims and evasiveness and politics as usual.

What you see too often in Washington and elsewhere around the country is a system of government that seems incapable of action. You see a Congress twisted and pulled in every direction by hundreds of well-financed and powerful special interests.

You see every extreme position defended to the last vote, almost to the last breath by one unyielding group or another. You often see a balanced and a fair approach that demands sacrifice, a little sacrifice from everyone, abandoned like an orphan without support and without friends.

Often you see paralysis and stagnation and drift. You don't like it, and neither do I. What can we do?

First of all, we must face the truth, and then we can change our course. We simply must have faith in each other, faith in our ability to govern ourselves, and faith in the future of this Nation. Restoring that faith and that confidence to America is now the most important task we face. It is a true challenge of this generation of Americans. . . .

All the traditions of our past, all the lessons of our heritage, all the promises of our future point to another path, the path of common purpose and the restoration of American values. That path leads to true freedom for our Nation and ourselves.

2. Presidential Candidate Ronald Reagan Calls for New Economic Policies, 1980

Almost two months ago, in accepting the Presidential nomination of my party, I spoke of the historically unique crisis facing the United States. At that time I said:

> Never before in our history have Americans been called upon to face three grave threats to our very existence, any one of which could destroy us. We face a disintegrating economy, a weakened defense and an energy policy based on the sharing of scarcity. . . .

I'd like to speak to you today about a new concept of leadership, one that has both the words and the music. One based on faith in the American people, confidence in the American economy, and a firm commitment to see to it that the Federal Government is once more responsive to the people.

That concept is rooted in a strategy for growth, a program that sees the American economic system as it is—a huge, complex, dynamic system which demands not piecemeal Federal packages, or pious hopes wrapped in soothing words, but the hard work and concerted programs necessary for real growth.

We must first recognize that the problem with the U.S. economy is swollen, inefficient government, needless regulation, too much taxation, too much printing-press money. We don't need any more doses of Carter's eight- or 10-point programs

---

Excerpts from Ronald Reagan, Speech delivered before the International Business Council (Chicago: September 9, 1980), *Vital Speeches of the Day* 46, no. 24 (October 1, 1980), 738–741.

to "fix" or fine tune the economy. For three and one-half years these ill-thought-out initiatives have constantly sapped the healthy vitality of the most productive economic system the world has ever known.

Our country is in a downward cycle of progressive economic deterioration that must be broken if the economy is to recover and move into a vigorous growth cycle in the 1980s.

We must move boldly, decisively and quickly to control the runaway growth of Federal spending, to remove the tax disincentives that are throttling the economy, and to reform the regulatory web that is smothering it.

We must have and I am proposing a new strategy for the 1980s.

Only a series of well-planned economic actions, taken so that they complement and reinforce one another, can move our economy forward again.

We must keep the rate of growth of government spending at reasonable and prudent levels.

We must reduce personal income tax rates and accelerate and simplify depreciation schedules in an orderly, systematic way to remove disincentives to work, savings, investment, and productivity.

We must review regulations that affect the economy and change them to encourage economic growth.

We must establish a stable, sound, and predictable monetary policy.

And we must restore confidence by following a consistent national economic policy that does not change from month to month.

I am asked: 'Can we do it all at once?' My answer is: 'We must.'

I am asked: 'Can we do it immediately?' Well, my answer is: 'No, it took Mr. Carter three and one-half years of hard work to get us into this economic mess. It will take time to get us out.'

I am asked: 'Is it easy?' Again, my answer is: 'No. It is going to require the most dedicated and concerted peacetime action ever taken by the American people for their country.'

But we can do it, we must do it, and I intend that we will do it.

We must balance the budget, reduce tax rates, and restore our defenses.

These are the challenges. Mr. Carter says he can't meet these challenges; that he can't do it. I believe him. He can't. But, I refuse to accept his defeatist and pessimistic view of America. I know we can do these things, and I know we will.

But don't just take my word for it. I have discussed this with any number of distinguished economists and businessmen, including such men as George Shultz, William Simon, Alan Greenspan, Charles Walker, and James Lynn. The strategy is based on solid economic principles and basic experience in both government and the marketplace. It has worked before and will work again.

Let us look at how we can meet this challenge.

One of the most critical elements of my economic program is the control of government spending. Waste, extravagance, abuse, and outright fraud in Federal agencies and programs must be stopped. The billions of the taxpayers' dollars that are wasted every year throughout hundreds of Federal programs, and it will take a major, sustained effort over time to effectively counter this.

Federal spending is now projected to increase to over $900 billion a year by fiscal year 1985. But, through a comprehensive assault on waste and inefficiency, I am confident that we can squeeze and trim 2 percent out of the budget in fiscal year 1981, and that we will be able to increase this gradually to 7 percent of what otherwise would have been spent in fiscal year 1985.

Now this is based on projections that have been made by groups in the government. Actually I believe we can do even better. My goal will be to bring about spending reductions of 10 percent by fiscal year 1984. . . .

This strategy for growth does not require altering or taking back necessary entitlements already granted to the American people. The integrity of the Social Security System will be defended by my administration and its benefits will once again be made meaningful.

This strategy does require restraining the Congressional desire to "add-on" to every old program and to create new programs funded by deficits.

This strategy does require that the way Federal programs are administered will be changed so that we can benefit from the savings that will come about when, in some instances, administrative authority can be moved back to the states.

The second major element of my economic program is a tax rate reduction plan. This plan calls for an across-the-board, three-year reduction in personal income tax rates—10 percent in 1981, 10 percent in 1982, and 10 percent in 1983. My goal is to implement three reductions in a systematic and planned manner.

More than any single thing, high rates of taxation destroy incentive to earn, to save, to invest. And they cripple productivity, lead to deficit financing and inflation, and create unemployment.

We can go a long way toward restoring the economic health of this country by establishing reasonable, fair levels of taxation.

But even the extended tax rate cuts which I am recommending still leave too high a tax burden on the American people. In the second half of the decade ahead we are going to need, and we must have, additional tax rate reductions. . . .

Another vital part of this strategy concerns government regulation. The subject is so important and so complex that it deserves a speech in itself—and I plan to make one soon. For the moment, however, let me say this:

Government regulation, like fire, makes a good servant but a bad master. No one can argue with the intent of this regulation—to improve health and safety and to give us cleaner air and water—but too often regulations work against rather than for the interests of the people. When the real take-home pay of the average American worker is declining steadily, and 8 million Americans are out of work, we must carefully re-examine our regulatory structure to assess to what degree regulations have contributed to this situation. In my administration there should and will be a thorough and systematic review of the thousands of Federal regulations that affect the economy.

Along with spending control, tax reform, and deregulation, a sound, stable, and predictable monetary policy is essential to restoring economic health. The Federal Reserve Board is, and should remain, independent of the Executive Branch of government. But the President must nominate those who serve on the Federal Reserve Board. My appointees will share my commitment to restoring the value and stability of the American dollar.

A fundamental part of my strategy for economic growth is the restoration of confidence. If our business community is going to invest and build and create new, well-paying jobs, they must have a future free from arbitrary, government action. They must have confidence that the economic "rules-of-the-game" won't be changed suddenly or capriciously.

In my administration, a national economic policy will be established, and we will begin to implement it, within the first 90 days.

Thus, I envision a strategy encompassing many elements—none of which can do the job alone, but all of which together can get it done. This strategy depends for its success more than anything else on the will of the people to regain control of their government. . . .

The time has come for the American people to reclaim their dream. Things don't have to be this way. We can change them. We must change them. Mr. Carter's American tragedy must and can be transcended by the spirit of the American people, working together.

Let's get America working again.

The time is now.

3. President George Bush Seeks a Kinder, Gentler Nation, 1989

I come before you and assume the Presidency at a moment rich with promise. We live in a peaceful, prosperous time, but we can make it better. For a new breeze is blowing, and a world refreshed by freedom seems reborn. For in man's heart, if not in fact, the day of the dictator is over. The totalitarian era is passing, its old ideas blown away like leaves from an ancient, lifeless tree. A new breeze is blowing, and a nation refreshed by freedom stands ready to push on. There is new ground to be broken and new action to be taken. There are times when the future seems thick as a fog; you sit and wait, hoping the mists will lift and reveal the right path. But this is a time when the future seems a door you can walk right through into a room called tomorrow.

Great nations of the world are moving toward democracy through the door to freedom. Men and women of the world move toward free markets through the door to prosperity. The people of the world agitate for free expression and free thought through the door to the moral and intellectual satisfactions that only liberty allows.

We know what works: Freedom works. We know what's right: Freedom is right. We know how to secure a more just and prosperous life for man on Earth: through free markets, free speech, free elections, and the exercise of free will unhampered by the state. . . .

America is never wholly herself unless she is engaged in high moral principle. We as a people have such a purpose today. It is to make kinder the face of the Nation and gentler the face of the world. My friends, we have work to do. There are the homeless, lost, and roaming. There are the children who have nothing, no love and no normalcy. There are those who cannot free themselves of enslavement to whatever addiction—drugs, welfare, the demoralization that rules the slums. There is

George Bush, Inaugural Address, *Weekly Compilation of Presidential Documents* (January 30, 1989): 99–102.

crime to be conquered, the rough crime of the streets. There are young women to be helped who are about to become mothers of children they can't care for and might not love. They need our care, our guidance, and our education, though we bless them for choosing life.

The old solution, the old way, was to think that public money alone could end these problems. But we have learned that that is not so. And in any case, our funds are low. We have a deficit to bring down. We have more will than wallet, but will is what we need. We will make the hard choices, looking at what we have and perhaps allocating it differently, making our decisions based on honest need and prudent safety. And then we will do the wisest thing of all: We will turn to the only resource we have that in times of need always grows: the goodness and the courage of the American people.

And I am speaking of a new engagement in the lives of others, a new activism, hands-on and involved, that gets the job done. We must bring in the generations, harnessing the unused talent of the elderly and the unfocused energy of the young. For not only leadership is passed from generation to generation but so is stewardship. And the generation born after the Second World War has come of age.

I have spoken of a thousand points of light, of all the community organizations that are spread like stars throughout the Nation, doing good. We will work hand in hand, encouraging, sometimes leading, sometimes being led, rewarding. We will work on this in the White House, in the Cabinet agencies. I will go to the people and the programs that are the brighter points of light, and I'll ask every member of my government to become involved. The old ideas are new again because they're not old, they are timeless: duty, sacrifice, commitment, and a patriotism that finds its expression in taking part and pitching in.

We need a new engagement, too, between the Executive and the Congress. The challenges before us will be thrashed out with the House and the Senate. And we must bring the Federal budget into balance. And we must ensure that America stands before the world united, strong, at peace, and fiscally sound. But of course things may be difficult. We need to compromise; we've had dissension. We need harmony; we've had a chorus of discordant voices.

For Congress, too, has changed in our time. There has grown a certain divisiveness. We have seen the hard looks and heard the statements in which not each other's ideas are challenged but each other's motives. And our great parties have too often been far apart and untrusting of each other. It's been this way since Vietnam. That war cleaves us still. But, friends, that war began in earnest a quarter of a century ago, and surely the statu[t]e of limitation has been reached. This is a fact: The final lesson of Vietnam is that no great nation can long afford to be sundered by a memory. A new breeze is blowing, and the old bipartisanship must be made new again. . . .

A President is neither prince nor pope, and I don't seek a window on men's souls. In fact, I yearn for a greater tolerance, and easy-goingness about each other's attitudes and way of life. . . .

Some see leadership as high drama and the sound of trumpets calling, and sometimes it is that. But I see history as a book with many pages, and each day we fill a page with acts of hopefulness and meaning. The new breeze blows, a page turns, the story unfolds. And so, today a chapter begins, a small and stately story of unity, diversity, and generosity—shared, and written, together. . . .

4. The Republican "Contract with America," 1994

The Contract's Core Principles

The Contract with America is rooted in 3 core principles:

Accountability—The government is too big and spends too much, and Congress and unelected bureaucrats have become so entrenched [as] to be unresponsive to the public they are supposed to serve. The GOP contract restores accountability to government.

Responsibility—Bigger government and more federal programs usurp personal responsibility from families and individuals. The GOP contract restores a proper balance between government and personal responsibility.

Opportunity—The American Dream is out of the reach of too many families because of burdensome government regulations and harsh tax laws. The GOP contract restores the American dream.

The Contract

As Republican Members of the House of Representatives and as citizens seeking to join that body we propose not just to change its policies, but even more important, to restore the bonds of trust between the people and their elected representatives.

That is why, in the era of official evasion and posturing, we offer instead a detailed agenda for national renewal, a written commitment with no fine print.

This year's election offers the chance, after four decades of one-party control, to bring to the House a new majority that will transform the way Congress works. That historic change would be the end of government that is too big, too intrusive, and too easy with the public's money. It can be the beginning of a Congress that respects the values and shares the faith of the American family.

Like Lincoln, our first Republican president, we intend to act "with firmness in the right, as God gives us to see the right." To restore accountability to Congress. To end its cycle of scandal and disgrace. To make us all proud again of the way free people govern themselves.

On the first day of the 104th Congress, the new Republican majority will immediately pass the following major reforms, aimed at restoring the faith and trust of the American people in their government:

FIRST, require all laws that apply to the rest of the country also apply equally to the Congress;

SECOND, select a major, independent auditing firm to conduct a comprehensive audit of Congress for waste, fraud, or abuse;

THIRD, cut the number of House committees, and cut committee staff by one-third;

From www.newt.org/contract.htm.

FOURTH, limit the terms of all committee chairs;

FIFTH, ban the casting of proxy votes in committee;

SIXTH, require committee meetings to be open to the public;

SEVENTH, require a three-fifths majority vote to pass a tax increase;

EIGHTH, guarantee an honest accounting of our Federal Budget by implementing zero base-line budgeting.

Thereafter, within the first 100 days of the 104th Congress, we shall bring to the House Floor the following bills, each to be given full and open debate, each to be given a clear and fair vote, and each to be immediately available this day for public inspection and scrutiny.

1. The Fiscal Responsibility Act.   A balanced budget/tax limitation amendment and a legislative line-item veto to restore fiscal responsibility to an out-of-control Congress, requiring them to live under the same budget constraints as families and businesses.

2. The Taking Back Our Streets Act.   An anti-crime package including stronger truth-in-sentencing, "good faith" exclusionary rule exemptions, effective death penalty provisions, and cuts in social spending from this summer's "crime" bill to fund prison construction and additional law enforcement to keep people secure in their neighborhoods and kids safe in their schools.

3. The Personal Responsibility Act.   Discourage illegitimacy and teen pregnancy by prohibiting welfare to minor mothers and denying increased AFDC [Aid to Families with Dependent Children] for additional children while on welfare, cut spending for welfare programs, and enact a tough two-years-and-out provision with work requirements to promote individual responsibility.

4. The Family Reinforcement Act.   Child support enforcement, tax incentives for adoption, strengthening rights of parents in their children's education, stronger child pornography laws, and an elderly dependent care tax credit to reinforce the central role of families in American society.

5. The American Dream Restoration Act.   A $500 per child tax credit, begin repeal of the marriage tax penalty, and creation of American Dream Savings Accounts to provide middle class tax relief.

6. The National Security Restoration Act.   No U.S. troops under UN command and restoration of the essential parts of our national security funding to strengthen our national defense and maintain our credibility around the world.

7. The Senior Citizens Fairness Act.   Raise the Social Security earnings limit which currently forces seniors out of the work force, repeal the 1993 tax hikes on Social Security benefits, and provide tax incentives for private long-term care insurance to let Older Americans keep more of what they have earned over the years.

8. The Job Creation and Wage Enhancement Act.   Small business incentives, capital gains cut and indexation, neutral cost recovery, risk assessment/cost-benefit analysis, strengthening the Regulatory Flexibility Act, and unfunded mandate reform to create jobs and raise worker wages.

9. The Common Sense Legal Reform Act.   "Loser pays" laws, reasonable limits on punitive damages, and reform of product liability laws to stem the endless tide of litigation.

10. The Citizen Legislature Act.   A first-ever vote on term limits to replace career politicians with citizen legislators.

Further, we will instruct the House Budget Committee to report to the floor and we will work to enact additional budget savings, beyond the budget cuts specifically included in the legislation described above, to ensure that the Federal budget deficit will be less than it would have been without the enactment of these bills.

Respecting the judgment of our fellow citizens as we seek their mandate for reform, we hereby pledge our names to this Contract with America.

5. President Bill Clinton Signs a Bill "To End Welfare as We Know It," 1996

The bill I'm about to sign, as I have said many times, is far from perfect, but it has come a very long way. Congress sent me two previous bills that I strongly believe failed to protect our children and did too little to move people from welfare to work. I vetoed both of them. This bill had broad bipartisan support and is much, much better on both counts.

The new bill restores American's basic bargain of providing opportunity and demanding in return responsibility. It provides $14 billion for child care, $4 billion more than the present law does. It is good because without the assurance of child care it's all but impossible for a mother with young children to go to work. It requires states to maintain their own spending on welfare reform and gives them powerful performance incentives to place more people on welfare in jobs. It gives states the capacity to create jobs by taking money now used for welfare checks and giving it to employers as subsidies as incentives to hire people. This bill will help people to go to work so they can stop drawing a welfare check and start drawing a paycheck.

It's also better for children. It preserves the national safety net of food stamps and school lunches. It drops the deep cuts and the devastating changes in child protection, adoption, and help for disabled children. It preserves the national guarantee of health care for poor children, the disabled, the elderly, and people on welfare— the most important preservation of all.

Remarks by the President at the signing of the Personal Responsibility and Work Opportunity Reconciliation Act, Office of the Press Secretary, the White House, August 22, 1996, at http://www.pub. whitehouse.gov/uri-res/I2R?urn:pdi://oma.eop.gov.us/1996/8/22/1.text.1.

It includes the tough child support enforcement measures that, as far as I know, every member of Congress and everybody in the administration and every thinking person in the country has supported for more than two years. . . .

With this bill we say, if you don't pay the child support you owe we'll garnish your wages, take away your driver's license, track you across state lines; if necessary, make you work off what you pay—what you owe. It is a good thing and it will help dramatically to reduce welfare, increase independence, and reenforce parental responsibility. (Applause.) . . .

Today, we are ending welfare as we know it. But I hope this day will be remembered not for what it ended, but for what it began—a new day that offers hope, honors responsibility, rewards work, and changes the terms of the debate so that no one in America ever feels again the need to criticize people who are poor on welfare, but instead feels the responsibility to reach out to men and women and children who are isolated, who need opportunity, and who are willing to assume responsibility, and give them the opportunity and the terms of responsibility. (Applause.) . . .

(The bill is signed.)

Q Mr. President, some of your core constituencies are furious with you for signing this bill. What do you say to them?

The President Just what I said up there. We saved medical care. We saved food stamps. We saved child care. We saved the aid to disabled children. We saved the school lunch program. We saved the framework of support. What we did was to tell the state[s], now you have to create a system to give everyone a chance to go to work who is able-bodied, give everyone a chance to be independent. And we did— that is the right thing to do.

And now, welfare is no longer a political football to be kicked around. It's a personal responsibility of every American who ever criticized the welfare system to help the poor people now to move from welfare to work. That's what I say.

This is going to be a good thing for the country. We're going to monitor it and we're going to fix whatever is wrong with it.

Q What guarantees are there that these things will be fixed, Mr. President, especially if Republicans remain in control of Congress?

The President That's what we have elections for.

6. A Liberal Postmortem on the 1996 Election, 1997

I hate welfare. To be more precise, I hate the welfare system we had until last August, when Bill Clinton signed a historic bill ending "welfare as we know it." It was a system that contributed to chronic dependency among large numbers of people who would be the first to say they would rather have a job than collect a welfare check every month—and its benefits were never enough to lift people out of poverty. In April of 1967 I helped Robert Kennedy with a speech in which he called the welfare system bankrupt and said it was hated universally, by payers and recipients alike. Criticism of welfare for not helping people to become self-supporting is nothing new.

But the bill that President Clinton signed is not welfare reform. It does not promote work effectively, and it will hurt millions of poor children by the time it is fully implemented. . . .

Governor Clinton campaigned in 1992 on the promise to "end welfare as we know it" and the companion phrase "Two years and you're off." He knew very well that a major piece of welfare-reform legislation, the *Family Support Act,* had already been passed, in 1988. As governor of Arkansas he had been deeply involved in the enactment of that law, which was based on extensive state experimentation with new welfare-to-work initiatives in the 1980s, especially *GAIN* in California. The 1988 law represented a major bipartisan compromise. The Democrats had given in on work requirements in return for Republican concessions on significant federal funding for job training, placement activities, and transitional child care and health coverage.

The Family Support Act had not been fully implemented, partly because not enough time had passed and partly because in the recession of the Bush years the states had been unable to provide the matching funds necessary to draw down their full share of job-related federal money. Candidate Clinton ought responsibly to have said that the Family Support Act was a major piece of legislation that needed more time to be fully implemented before anyone could say whether it was a success or a failure.

Instead Clinton promised to end welfare as we know it and to institute what sounded like a two-year time limit. This was bumper-sticker politics— oversimplification to win votes. Polls during the campaign showed that it was very popular, and a salient item in garnering votes. Clinton's slogans were also cleverly ambiguous. On the one hand, as President, Clinton could take a relatively liberal path that was nonetheless consistent with his campaign rhetoric. In 1994 he proposed legislation that required everyone to be working by the time he or she had been on the rolls for two years. But it also said, more or less in the fine print, that people who played by the rules and couldn't find work could continue to get benefits within the same federal-state framework that had existed since 1935. . . .

Candidate Clinton, however, had let a powerful genie out of the bottle. During his first two years it mattered only insofar as his rhetoric promised far more than his legislative proposal actually offered. When the Republicans gained control of Congress in 1994, the bumper-sticker rhetoric began to matter. So you want time limits? the Republicans said in 1995. Good idea. We'll give you some serious time limits. We now propose an absolute lifetime limit of five years, cumulatively, that a family can be on welfare. End welfare as we know it? You bet. From now on we will have block grants. And what does that mean? First, that there will be no federal definition of who is eligible and therefore no guarantee of assistance to anyone; each state can decide whom to exclude in any way it wants, as long as it doesn't violate the Constitution (not much of a limitation when one reads the Supreme Court decisions on this subject). And second, that each state will get a fixed sum of federal money each year, even if a recession or a local calamity causes a state to run out of federal funds before the end of the year.

This was a truly radical proposal. For sixty years Aid to Families with Dependent Children had been premised on the idea of entitlement. "Entitlement" has become a dirty word, but it is actually a term of art. It meant two things in the AFDC program: a federally defined guarantee of assistance to families with children who met the statutory definition of need and complied with the other conditions of the law; and a federal guarantee to the states of a matching share of the money needed to help everyone in the state who qualified for help. (AFDC was never a guarantor of income at any particular level. States chose their own benefit levels, and no state's AFDC benefits, even when coupled with food stamps, currently lift families out of poverty.) The block grants will end the entitlement in both respects, and in addition the time limits say that federally supported help will end even if a family has done everything that was asked of it and even if it is still needy. . . .

This was *the* major milestone in the political race to the bottom. The President had said he was willing to sign legislation that would end a sixty-year commitment to provide assistance to all needy families with children who met the federal eligibility requirements. In the floor debate Senator Edward Kennedy, who voted against the bill, described it as "legislative child abuse." . . .

The game was over. Now no one could ever say again with any credibility that this President is an old liberal.

✖ E S S A Y S

The following essays offer two different, though not necessarily contradictory, assessments of late-twentieth-century politics. In the first essay, political journalist Thomas Byrne Edsall places the Reagan presidency in the context of the continued decline of the New Deal coalition (with its popular base of less wealthy Americans) and the growing ascendancy of a new politics centered on television, campaign financing, political action committees, and lobbyists. The "Reagan Revolution," he contends, was "a revolution led by the affluent." In the second essay, Daniel Yergin and Joseph Stanislaw depict the Reagan Revolution as part of a broader response to the new global era. Both essays raise profound questions about the future of demo-cratic government: Edsall in describing a politics that seemingly combines manipu-lation from above and acquiescence from below, Yergin and Stanislaw by charting the surrender to markets of functions previously discharged by public bodies.

The Mobilization of American Business

THOMAS BYRNE EDSALL

The past twenty years in America have been marked by two central political devel-opments. The first is the continuing erosion of the political representation of the economic interests of those in the bottom half of the income distribution. The second is the growing dominance of the political process by a network of elites that includes fund-raisers, the leadership of interest groups, specialists in the technology and manipulation of elections, and an army of Washington lobbyists and law firms—elites that augment and often overshadow political officeholders and the candidates for office themselves.

The shift in the balance of power has not been accompanied by realignment of the electorate, although the shape and relative strength of the Republican and Democratic parties have changed dramatically.

Twice during the past twenty years, the Republican party has had the opportunity to gain majority status: in the early 1970s, and again after the 1980 election. The first opportunity emerged when the fragile Democratic coalition was fractured by the independent presidential bid of Alabama governor George C. Wallace in 1968. The Democratic party then amplified its own vulnerability four years later with the nomination of Sen. George S. McGovern, Democrat of South Dakota, whose candidacy alienated a spectrum of traditional Democrats from Detroit to Atlanta. This potential Republican opportunity crumbled, however, when the web of scandals known as Watergate produced across-the-board setbacks for the GOP in campaigns ranging from city council contests to the presidency in the elections of 1974 and 1976.

The period from 1978 to 1981 offered even more fertile terrain for the Republican party. Not only had Democratic loyalties dating back to the depression of the 1930s been further weakened during the presidency of Jimmy Carter, with the emergence of simultaneous inflation and high unemployment, but the candidacy of Ronald Reagan provided the Republican party with its first substantial opportunity to heal the fissures that had relegated the GOP to minority status for two generations. In Reagan, the party long identified with the rich found a leader equipped to bridge divisions between the country club and the fundamentalist church, between the executives of the Fortune 500 and the membership of the National Rifle Association. Just as Watergate halted Republican momentum in the early 1970s, however, the severe recession of 1981–82 put the brakes on what had the earmarks of a potential Republican takeover, for the first time since 1954, of both branches of Congress. In the first two years of the Reagan administration, the Republican party captured the Senate by a six-vote margin and, with a gain of thirty-two House seats, acquired de facto control of the House in an alliance with southern Democratic conservatives. The recession, however, resulted in the return of twenty-six House seats to the Democrats in 1982, and with those seats went the chance to establish Republican dominance of the federal government.

As the two parties have gained and lost strength, the underlying alteration of the balance of political power over the past decade has continued in a shift of power among the rich, the poor, and the middle class; among blacks and whites; among regions in the country; and among such major competitors for the federal dollar as the defense and social services sectors.

The past twenty years have, in effect, produced a policy realignment in the absence of a political realignment. The major beneficiaries of this policy realignment are the affluent, while those in the bottom half of the income distribution, particularly those whose lives are the most economically marginal, have reaped the fewest rewards or have experienced declines in their standard of living.

A major factor contributing to this development is the decline of political parties: In the United States, as well as in most democratic countries, parties perform the function of representing major interests and classes. As parties erode, the groups that suffer most are those with the fewest resources to protect themselves. In other words, the continued collapse of the broad representation role of political parties in the United States has direct consequences for the distribution of income.

As the role of parties in mobilizing voters has declined, much of the control over both election strategy and issue selection—key functions in defining the national agenda—has shifted to a small, often interlocking, network of campaign specialists, fund-raisers, and lobbyists. While this element of politics is among the most difficult to quantify, there are some rough measures. For example, there are approximately thirty Republican and Democratic consultants and pollsters, almost all based in Washington, who at this writing are the principal strategists in almost every presidential and competitive Senate race, in addition to playing significant roles in gubernatorial, House, and local referenda contests.

At another level, the years from 1974 to 1984 show a steady growth in the financial dependence of House and Senate candidates on political action committees (PACs), vehicles through which money is transferred from organized interests groups to elected officeholders. In that decade, the PAC share of the total cost of House campaigns went from 17 percent to 36 percent, while individual contributions fell from 73 percent to 47 percent, with the remainder coming from parties, loans, and other sources. For House Democratic incumbents, 1984 marked the first year in which PACs were the single most important source of cash; they provided 47 percent of the total, compared with 45 percent from individuals.

This shift has, in turn, magnified the influence of a group of lobbyists who organize Washington fund-raisers for House and Senate incumbents, among whom are Thomas Hale Boggs Jr., whose clients include the Trial Lawyers Association, the Chicago Board of Options Exchange, and Chrysler; Edward H. Forgotson, whose clients include Enserch Corp., the Hospital Corp. of America, and the Texas Oil and Gas Corp.; Robert J. Keefe, whose clients include Westinghouse and the American Medical Association; and J. D. Williams, whose clients include General Electric Co. and the National Realty Committee. The Washington consulting-lobbying firm of Black, Manafort, Stone, Kelly and Atwater provides perhaps the best example of the range of political and special interests one firm can represent. In 1987, one partner, Charles Black, managed the presidential bid of Rep. Jack Kemp (R-N.Y.); another, Lee Atwater, managed the campaign of Vice-President George Bush; and a third, Peter Kelly, was a principal fund-raiser for the campaign of Sen. Albert Gore (D-Tenn.). At the same time, the firm's clients have included the Dominican Republic, the anti-Communist insurgency in Angola run by Jonas Savimbi, Salomon Brothers, the government of Barbados, the Natural Gas Supply Association, and, briefly, the Marcos government in the Philippines. In addition, the firm has served as principal political consultant to the Senate campaigns of Phil Gramm (R-Tex.), Jesse Helms (R-N.C.), and Paula Hawkins (formerly R-Fla.).

A few general indicators of the scope of lobbying and political party bureaucracies point to the sizable influence small elites can exercise over public policy. In 1986, there were almost 10,000 people employed as registered Washington lobbyists, with 3,500 of these serving as officers of 1,800 trade and professional organizations, including labor unions; another 1,300 were employed by individual corporations, and approximately 1,000 represented organizations ranging from the National Right to Life Association to the Sierra Club. The six major political party committees headquartered in Washington now employ roughly 1,200 people. The creation and expansion of such ideological think tanks as the Heritage Foundation, the Center for National Policy, the Urban Institute, the American Enterprise Institute, the Cato Institute, and the Hoover Institution have established whole networks of influential public policy entrepreneurs specializing in media relations and in targeted position papers. Within a general framework of increasingly monopolized American mass media—both print and electronic—the growth of the Gannett and Los Angeles Times-Mirror chains are examples of an ever greater concentration of power within the media, just as the acquisition of NBC by General Electric has functioned to submerge a major network within the larger goals of the nation's sixth biggest corporation. Staffers acquiring expertise and influence on Capitol Hill, in the executive branch, and throughout the regulatory apparatus routinely travel to the private sector—and sometimes back again—through the so-called revolving door. In effect, an entire class of public and private specialists in the determination of government policy and political strategy has been created—a process replicated in miniature at the state level.

The rise to authority of elites independent of the electorate at large, empowered to make decisions without taking into direct account the economic interests of voters, is part of a much larger shift in the balance of power involving changed voting patterns, the decline of organized labor, a restructuring of the employment market-place, and a transformed system of political competition. This power shift, in turn, has produced a policy realignment most apparent in the alteration of both the *pre-tax* distribution of income and the *after-tax* distribution of income. In both cases, the distribution has become increasingly regressive. The alteration of the pretax distribution of income is the subject of a broad debate in which there are those, particularly critics on the left, who argue that growing regressivity emerges from government policies encouraging weakened union representation and a proliferation of low-wage service industry jobs. On the other side, more conservative analysts contend that changes in the pre-tax distribution result from natural alterations of the marketplace and the workplace, as the United States adjusts to a changing economic and demographic environment. The figures in Table 1, derived from Census Bureau data, indicate

Table 1   Shares of Pre-tax Household Income, by Income Distribution

	YEAR	
	1980	1985
INCOME GROUP	(%)	(%)
Quintile[a]		
Bottom	4.1	3.9
Second	10.2	9.7
Third	16.8	16.3
Fourth	24.8	24.4
Top	44.2	45.7
Top 5%	16.5	17.6

Sources: Bureau of the Census, *Estimating After-Tax Money Income Distribution,* Series P-23, no. 126, issued August 1983; and ibid., *Household After-Tax Income: 1985,* Series P-23, no. 151, issued June 1987.
[a]A quintile is a block of 20% of the population.

changes in the distribution of pretax household income from 1980 through 1985, the most recent year for which data from the census is available.

The data clearly show a growing disparity in the distribution of income. Of the five quintiles, all but those in the top 20 percent have seen their share of household income decline. In addition, most of the gains of the top 20 percent have, in fact, been concentrated in the top 5 percent of the income distribution. The gain of 1.1 percent for the top 5 percent translates into a total of $38.8 billion (in 1987 dollars) more for this segment of the population than if the income distribution had remained constant after 1980. These regressive trends were, moreover, intensified by the tax policies enacted between 1980 and 1985, as demonstrated in Table 2, based on Census Bureau data.

What had been a $38.8 billion improvement in the status of the top 5 percent in pre-tax income over these six years becomes a $49.5 billion gain in after-tax income, while the bottom 80 percent of the population saw larger losses in its share of after-tax income between 1980 and 1985 than it had seen in the case of pre-tax income. These findings are even more sharply delineated in a November 1987 study by the Congressional Budget Office showing that from 1977 to 1988, 70 percent of the population experienced very modest increases in after-tax income or, for those in the bottom 40 percent, net drops, when changes over that period in the federal income tax, the Social Security tax, corporate tax, and excise taxes are taken into account. In contrast, those in the seventy-first to ninetieth percentiles experienced a modest improvement, and those in the top 10 percent significantly improved their standard of living. For those at the very top, the gains have been enormous. Table 3, developed from Congressional Budget Office data, shows that distribution.

What these tables point to is a major redistribution of economic power in the private marketplace and of political power in the public sector, which, in turn, has been reflected in very concrete terms in family income patterns. One of the major characteristics, then, of the post–New Deal period in American politics has been a

---

Table 2   Shares of After-Tax Household Income, by Income Distribution

	YEAR	
INCOME GROUP	1980 (%)	1985 (%)
Quintile[a]		
Bottom	4.9	4.6
Second	11.6	11.0
Third	17.9	17.2
Fourth	25.1	24.7
Top	40.6	42.6
Top 5%	14.1	15.5

Sources: Bureau of the Census, *Estimating After-Tax Money Income Distribution,* Series P-23, no. 126, issued August 1983; and ibid., *Household After-Tax Income,* 1985, Series P-23, no. 151, issued June 1987.

[a]A quintile is a block of 20% of the population.

Table 3   Changes in Estimated Average After-Tax Family Income, by Income Distribution (in 1987 dollars)

INCOME GROUP	1977 AVERAGE INCOME ($)	1988 AVERAGE INCOME ($)	PERCENTAGE CHANGE (+ OR −)	DOLLAR CHANGE (+ OR −)
Decile[a]				
First (poor)	3,528	3,157	−10.5	−371
Second	7,084	6,990	−1.3	−94
Third	10,740	10,614	−1.2	−126
Fourth	14,323	14,266	−0.4	−57
Fifth	18,043	18,076	+0.2	+33
Sixth	22,009	22,259	+1.1	+250
Seventh	26,240	27,038	+3.0	+798
Eighth	31,568	33,282	+5.4	+1,718
Ninth	39,236	42,323	+7.9	+3,087
Tenth (rich)	70,459	89,783	+27.4	+19,324
Top 5%	90,756	124,651	+37.3	+33,895
Top 1%	174,498	303,900	+74.2	+129,402
All groups	22,184	26,494	+9.6	+2,310

Source: Congressional Budget Offices, *The Changing Distribution of Federal Taxes: 1975–1990,* October 1987.
[a]A decile is a block of 10% of the population.

reversal of the progressive redistribution of income that underlay the policies of the administrations of Franklin Roosevelt and Harry Truman.

In the competition between the defense and social welfare sectors, the outcome of a parallel, although more recent, shift in the balance of power can be seen in the years from 1980 through 1987. During this period, the share of the federal budget going to national defense grew from 22.7 percent in 1980 to 28.4 percent in 1987. At the same time, the share of federal dollars collectively going to education, training, employment, social services, health, income security, and housing dropped from 25.5 percent in 1980 to 18.3 percent in 1987.

In many respects, these policy changes reflect the rising strength of the Republican party. In terms of tax policy and the balance of spending between defense and social programs, the Republican party under Ronald Reagan has been the driving force pushing the country to the right. During the past ten years, the Republican party has made substantial gains in the competition for the allegiance of voters, gaining near parity by 1987, reducing what had been a 20- to 25-point Democratic advantage in terms of self-identification to a six- or seven-point edge.

The income distribution trends and the shifts in budget priorities began, however, before the Republican party took over the presidency and the U.S. Senate in 1980. The emergence of a vital, competitive Republican party is less a cause of the changed balance of power in the country than a reflection of the underlying forces at work in the post-New Deal phase of American politics.

Together, these forces—which include the deterioration of organized labor, the continued presence of divisive racial conflict, the shift from manufacturing to service industries, the slowing rates of economic growth, the threat of international competition to domestic production, the replacement of political organization with political technology, and the growing class-skew of voter turnout—have severely undermined the capacity of those in the bottom half of the income distribution to form an effective political coalition.

In tracing the erosion of the left wing of the Democratic party in the United States, it is difficult to overestimate the importance of the collapse of the labor movement. In 1970, the continuing growth in the number of labor union members came to a halt. Unions represented 20.7 million workers that year, or 27.9 percent of the non-agricultural work force. Through 1980, the number of workers represented by unions remained roughly the same, dropping slightly to 20.1 million employees by 1980. At the same time, however, the total work force had grown, so that the percentage of workers who were represented by unions fell to 23 percent in 1980. With the election of Ronald Reagan, however, the decline of organized labor began to accelerate sharply, a process encouraged by Reagan's firing of 11,500 striking PATCO air traffic controllers, and by the appointment of promanagement officials to the National Labor Relations Board and to the Department of Labor. From 1980 to 1986, not only did the share of the work force represented by unions drop from 23 percent to 17.5 percent, but the number of workers in unions began to fall precipitously for the first time in fifty years, dropping by 3.1 million men and women, from 20.1 million to 17 million, in 1986. During the first half of the 1980s, almost all the decline in union membership was among whites employed in private industry.

The decline of organized labor dovetailed with a continuing shift from traditional manufacturing, mining, and construction employment to work in the technology and service industries. From 1970 to 1986, the number of jobs in goods-producing industries, which lend themselves to unionization, grew only from 23.8 million to 24.9 million, while employment in the service industries, which are much more resistant to labor organizing, shot up from 47.3 million to 75.2 million.

The difficulties of organized labor were compounded by the unexpected decision on the part of many of the major corporations in the early 1970s to abandon what had been a form of tacit détente between labor and management, in which Fortune 500 companies kept labor peace through agreements amounting to a form of profit sharing by means of automatic cost-of-living pay hikes. Faced with growing competition from foreign producers—in 1968, car imports exceeded exports for the first time in the nation's history, an unmistakable signal that domestic producers of all goods faced serious foreign competition—major American companies dropped the fundamentally cordial relations that had characterized the largest part of postwar union negotiations. Catching the leaders of organized labor entirely unprepared, these corporations adopted a tough, adversarial approach regarding both pay and fringe benefits, willing to break union shops and to relocate facilities either abroad or in nonunion communities in the South and Southwest.

The decline of organized labor was particularly damaging to the Democratic party because unions represent one of the few remaining institutional links between working-class voters and the Democratic party. The decline of political parties has resulted in the end of the clubhouse tie between the party of Franklin Delano Roosevelt and the blue-collar voters of row- and tract-house neighborhoods throughout the Northeast and Midwest. In addition, it is among these white, blue-collar workers that the racial conflicts within the Democratic party have been the most divisive. Interviews with whites in Dearborn, Michigan, the west-side suburbs of

Birmingham, Chicago, Atlanta, and New Orleans—all communities that have suffered major industrial layoffs and that are either part of or adjoin cities now run by
Democratic black mayors—reveal voters who are disenchanted with the unions that
failed to protect their jobs, and with a local Democratic party no longer controlled
by whites. Race, which previously severed the tie between the white South and the
Democratic party, has, in cities with black mayors, served to produce white Republican voting, not only for president but for local offices that once were unchallenged
Democratic bastions.

These developments, in the 1970s, contributed significantly to the creation of a
vacuum of power within the Democratic party, allowing the party to be taken over,
in part, by its most articulate and procedurally sophisticated wing: affluent, liberal
reformers. This faction capitalized first on the public outcry against police violence
at the Chicago presidential convention in 1968, and then on the Watergate scandals
in the mid-1970s, to force priority consideration of a series of reforms involving
campaign finance, the presidential nominating process, the congressional seniority
system, the congressional code of ethics—and an expansion of the federal role in
regulating the environment, through creation of the Environmental Protection
Agency and new water- and air-pollution standards. The strength of this wing of the
Democratic party subsided during the 1980s, although its leverage within the party
has been institutionalized through the creation of a host of primaries and caucuses
in the presidential selection process, giving disproportionate influence to middle-
and upper-middle-class voters and interests in a party that claims to represent the
nation's working and lower-middle classes. The turnout in primaries and in caucuses
is skewed in favor of the affluent and upper-middle class. In addition, these delegate
selection processes have been contributing factors in the acceleration of the decline
of political organizations in working-class communities.

The Democratic agenda set in the 1970s by the reform wing of the party
was, however, more important for what it omitted and neglected than for what was
included. The ascendancy of the reformers took place just when the fissures within
the Democratic party had become most apparent. In 1968, 9.9 million mostly Democratic voters turned to George C. Wallace, the segregationist-populist governor of
Alabama, and they strayed off the Democratic reservation in 1972 when Nixon beat
McGovern by a margin of 47.2 million votes to 29.2 million. The cultural and ideological gulf that had steadily widened between these voters and the wings of the
Democratic party supporting the antiwar movement, gay rights, women's rights, and
civil rights had reached such proportions in the early and mid 1970s that rapprochement between warring factions was difficult, if not impossible.

The rise to prominence within the Democratic party of a well-to-do liberal-
reform wing worked in other ways to compound the divisions in the party. Relatively
comfortable in their own lives, reformers failed to recognize the growing pressure
of marginal tax rates on working- and lower-middle-class voters. The progressive
rate system of the federal income tax remained effectively unchanged from the
early 1950s through the 1970s, so that the series of sharply rising marginal tax
rates that had originally been designed to affect only the upper-middle class and
rich, began to directly impinge on regular Democratic voters whose wages had
been forced up by inflation. By neglecting to adjust the marginal rate system to
account for inflation, in combination with repeated raising of the highly regressive

Social Security tax, Democrats effectively encouraged the tax revolt of the 1970s which, in turn, provided a critically important source of support to the conservative movement and to the rise of the Republican party. . . .

On the Republican side, the same developments that debilitated the Democratic coalition served to strengthen ascendant constituencies of the Right. For a brief period in the late 1970s and early 1980s, the constituencies and interests underpinning the Republican party had the potential to establish a new conservative majority in the electorate. The tax revolt, the rise of the religious right, the mobilization of much of the business community in support of the Republican party, renewed public support for defense spending, the political-financial mobilization of the affluent, and the development of a conservative economic theory promising growth through lower taxes—all combined to empower the political right to a degree unprecedented since the 1920s.

Proposed tax cuts provided an essential common ground for the right-of-center coalition that provided the core of the Reagan revolution. The combination of corporate tax reductions and individual tax cuts embodied in the 1981 tax bill served to unify a divided business community by providing a shared legislative goal, to strengthen the commitment of the affluent to the Republican party, and to attract white working- and lower-middle-class former Democrats who had seen their paychecks eaten away by inflation-driven higher marginal rates. The tax cut theme was adopted as a central element of the speeches of such religious-right figures as the Rev. Jerry Falwell of the Moral Majority, Ed McAteer of the Religious Roundtable, and the Rev. Marion G. (Pat) Robertson of the Christian Broadcast Network. . . .

This growing political tilt in favor of the affluent is further reflected in voting turnout patterns over the past twenty years. During this period, the class-skewing of voting in favor of the affluent has grown significantly. In the presidential election year of 1964, the self-reported turnout among members of professions associated with the middle and upper classes was 83.2 percent, compared with 66.1 percent among those employed in manual jobs, including skilled crafts, a difference of 17.1 points; by 1980, the spread between the two had grown to 25 points, 73 percent to 48 percent. In the off-year election of 1966, the percentage-point spread in terms of voter turnout between middle-to-upper-class job holders and those employed in manual jobs was 18.1 percent; by 1978, this had grown to a 23.8-percent spread. While overall turnout has been declining, the drop has been most severe among those in the bottom third of the income distribution.

For the Republican party, these turnout trends were a political bonanza, accentuated by trends in the correlation between income and both voting and partisan commitment. Through the 1950s, 1960s, and into the early 1970s, the sharp class divisions that characterized the depression-era New Deal coalition structure gave way to diffuse voting patterns with relatively little correlation between income and allegiance to the Democratic or Republican party. By 1980 and 1982, with the election of Reagan and then the enactment of the budget and tax bills of 1981, the correlation between income and voting began to reemerge with a vengeance. By 1982, the single most important determinant of probable voting, aside from membership in either the Republican or Democratic party, became income, with the Democratic margin steadily declining as one moved up the ladder. The changes in partisan allegiance are shown in Table 5. The numbers in the table are the percentage-point

Table 5   Democratic Party Allegiance, by Income, 1956 and 1984

	PERCENTAGE-POINT ADVANTAGE (+) OR DISADVANTAGE (−)	
INCOME GROUP	1956	1984
Very poor (bottom 10%)	+18	+36
Working and lower-middle class (11–30%)	+22	+29
Middle class (31–60%)	+17	+6
Upper-middle class (61–90%)	+13	0
Affluent (91–100%)	−22	−33

Source: Martin B. Wattenberg, "The Hollow Realignment: Partisan Change in a Candidate-Centered Era" (Paper delivered at the 1985 annual meeting of the American Political Science Association, based on data from the National Election Studies).

Democratic advantage in the income group (+) or the Democratic disadvantage (−). Thus, for example, the very poor were 18 points more Democratic than Republican in 1956, and 36 points more Democratic than Republican in 1984.

In other words, the Reagan years polarized the electorate along sharp income lines. While income made almost no difference in the partisan loyalties of 90 percent of the population in 1956, by 1984 income became one of the sharpest dividing lines between Democrats and Republicans. In 1956, the very poor were only 5 percentage points more likely to be Democratic than the upper-middle class, and 40 points more likely than the affluent top 10 percent of the income distribution. By 1984, however, the spread between the poor and the upper-middle-class reached 36 points, and between the poor and the affluent, 69 points. These income correlations with partisan allegiance were replicated, in part, by actual voting patterns, as shown in Table 6.

These figures accurately describe an electorate polarized by income, but what they mask are the effects of black and white voter participation on the figures. The civil rights movement, and civil rights legislation enacted in the 1960s, enfranchised millions of blacks who, in 1956, were barred from voting. During the twenty-eight years from 1956 to 1984, roughly 4.2 million blacks entered the electorate. During the same period, blacks' allegiance to the Democratic party, which in 1956 held their loyalty by a 34-percentage-point edge, increased to provide an overwhelming 72-percentage-point Democratic edge in 1984. This infusion of black Democratic support sharply increased the low-income tilt of the party: in 1984, the median family income for whites was $28,674, while for blacks it was $15,982.

The Reagan revolution was, at its core, a revolution led by the affluent. The class polarization of voters . . . cut cross the country, but nowhere were the trends stronger than in the South, where a realignment in miniature took place among the white elite. In the 1950s, Democratic allegiance in the South was strongest among the most well-to-do whites, for whom the Democratic party was the vehicle for maintaining the pre-civil rights social structure of the Confederate states. These voters gave the Democratic party their support by a 5 to 1 margin, higher than that of any other income group in the South. By the 1980s, in the aftermath of a civil

Table 6   Republican Percentage of Presidential Vote, by Income, 1956 and 1984

INCOME GROUP	EISENHOWER, 1956 (%)	REAGAN, 1984 (%)
Very poor (bottom 10%)	59	36
Working and lower-middle class (11–30%)	56	43
Middle class (31–60%)	58	57
Upper-middle class (61–90%)	57	64
Affluent (91–100%)	75	75

Source: Martin P. Wattenberg, "The Hollow Realignment: Partisan Change in a Candidate-Centered Era" (Paper delivered at the 1985 annual meeting of the American Political Science Association, based on data from the National Election Studies).

rights movement supported by the Democratic party, these same voters had become the most Republican in the South. "The class cleavage had reversed itself," John R. Petrocik, of UCLA, noted. Whites, particularly white men, have become increasingly Republican as blacks have become the most consistent source of Democratic votes. In the five presidential elections from 1968 to 1984, only one Democrat, Jimmy Carter, received more than 40 percent of the white vote, and by 1984, white, male Protestants voted for Reagan over Mondale by a margin of 74 to 26.

The Reagan revolution would, however, have been a political failure if it had not gained extensive support from voters outside the upper-middle class. In addition to the deep inroads made in previously Democratic working-class communities in northern urban areas, perhaps the single most important source of new support for the Republican party has been the religious Right.

In a far shorter period, voters identifying themselves as born-again Christians radically shifted their voting in presidential elections. Between 1976 and 1984, these voters went from casting a 56-to-44 margin for the Democratic candidate, Jimmy Carter, to one of the highest levels of support of any group for the reelection of President Reagan in 1984: 81 to 19, according to *New York Times*/CBS exit polls. This shift represents, in effect, a gain of eight million voters for the GOP.

As a political resource, support among born-again Christians represents not only a loyal core of voters, but a growing core. In contrast with such mainline churches as the United Methodist Church, the United Church of Christ, and the United Presbyterians, which experienced membership losses from 1970 to 1980, the fundamentalist, evangelical, and charismatic churches have seen their congregations grow at an explosive rate: the Southern Baptist Convention by 16 percent, the Assemblies of God by 70 percent, and Seventh Day Adventists by 36 percent.

The Republican party has, in turn, been the major beneficiary of an internal power struggle taking place within the Southern Baptist Convention, now the largest Protestant denomination. During a ten-year fight, the denomination has been taken over by its conservative wing, believers in the "absolute inerrancy" of the Bible. This wing of the denomination, in turn, has been a leading force within the broader religious Right, as such pastors as Adrian Rogers, James T. Draper Jr., and Charles F. Stanley—all outspoken conservatives—have won the denomination's presidency. The move to the right has been reflected in the ranks of the denomination, producing what amounts to a realignment of the ministry of the Southern Baptist Convention. James L. Guth, of Furman University, found that in just three years, surveys of Southern Baptist ministers showed a remarkable shift from a strong majority in 1981 favoring the Democratic party, 41 to 29, to nearly 70 percent in 1984 favoring the GOP, 66 to 26.

The growth of Republican strength is not, however, confined to evangelical and charismatic Christians, and the party appears to be developing a much broader religious base as part of its core constituency. In one of the most interesting recent analyses of voting trends, Frederick T. Steeper, of Market Opinion Research, and John Petrocik, of UCLA, have found that since 1976, one of the sharpest partisan cleavages emerging among white voters in the electorate is between those who attend church regularly and those who never go to church. This represents a major change from past findings. In the period from 1952 to 1960, there was no statistical difference between the Democratic and Republican loyalties of white churchgoers and nonchurchgoers. By the elections of 1972 and 1976, a modest difference began to appear, with nonchurchgoers 7 percentage points more likely to be Democrats than regular churchgoers. By 1986, however, the spread had grown to a striking 35-point difference, with regular churchgoers identifying themselves as Republicans by a 22-point margin, and with nonchurchgoers identifying themselves as Democrats by a 13-point edge. The partisan spread between churchgoers and nonchurchgoers was most extreme among white Northern Protestants (51 points) and Catholics (52 points). These findings dovetail with studies showing that the memberships of such Establishment, nonevangelical denominations as the Methodists, Episcopalians, Lutherans, and Presbyterians were significantly more supportive of the election of Ronald Reagan than the electorate at large. . . .

Cumulatively, developments over the past twenty years—the deterioration of the labor movement; economically polarized partisanship; the skewing of turnout patterns by income; stagnation of the median family income; the rising importance of political money; the emergence of a Republican core composed of the well-to-do and the religious; the globalization of the economy; and competition from foreign producers—have combined to disperse constituencies and groups seeking to push the country to the left, and to consolidate those on the right. The consequences of that shift are most readily seen in the figures in table 3, which show that 80 percent of the population has experienced a net loss in after-tax income between 1977 and 1988, while the top 5 percent has seen average family income grow by $26,134, and the top 1 percent, by $117,222.

In the long run the prospects are for the maintenance of a strong, conservative Republican party, continuing to set the national agenda on basic distributional issues, no matter which party holds the White House. Barring a major economic catastrophe, or a large-scale international conflict, the basic shift from manufacturing to service industry jobs is likely to continue to undermine the political left in this country, not only for the reasons outlined earlier in this essay, but also by weakening economically—and therefore politically—those in the bottom 40 percent of the income distribution.

In the thirty-year period spanning 1949 to 1979, the number of manufacturing jobs grew by an average of three million a decade, from 17.6 million in 1949, to 20.4 million in 1959, to 24.2 million in 1969, and finally to a high of 26.5 million in 1979. This growth in no way kept pace with the increase in service industry jobs, which shot up from 26.2 million in 1949 to 63.4 million in 1979, but the continuing, if modest, manufacturing expansion provided a partial cushion in an economy going through a major restructuring—a restructuring involving the loss of 950,000 jobs in steel and other metals industries, automobiles, food production, and textiles from 1972 to 1986. From 1979 to 1986, however, the absolute number of manufacturing jobs began to decline, dropping from 26.5 million to 24.9 million, a loss of 1.6 million jobs.

These employment shifts have been particularly damaging to blacks and Hispanics. From 1970 to 1984, in major northern cities, there has been a massive decline in the number of jobs requiring relatively little education—the kind of jobs that provide entry into the employment marketplace for the poor—and a sharp increase in the number of jobs requiring at least some higher education. "Demographic and employment trends have produced a serious mismatch between the skills of inner-city blacks and the opportunities available to them . . . substantial job losses have occurred in the very industries in which urban minorities have the greatest access, and substantial employment gains have occurred in the higher-education-requisite industries that are beyond the reach of most minority workers," according to William Julius Wilson, of the University of Chicago (see Table 7).

While blacks and Hispanics will, at least for the time being, disproportionately bear the burden of this shift in job requirements, the altered structure of the marketplace will work to the disadvantage of the poorly educated of all races. In 1985, there were 30.6 million whites over the age of twenty-five without a high school education—five times the number of blacks without high school degrees (5.9 million) and seven times the number of poorly educated Hispanics (4.4 million). These job market trends will intensify throughout the rest of this century. According to estimates by the Department of Labor, 21.4 million jobs will be created between 1986 and the year 2000, all of which will be in service industries or government, as losses in traditional goods manufacturing industries are unlikely to be fully offset by gains in the technology manufacturing sector. In terms of educational requirements, there will be a significant increase in the proportion of jobs requiring at least one year of college education, no change in the proportion of jobs requiring a high

---

Table 7   Changes in the Combined Number of Jobs, by Employee Education Level, in New York, Philadelphia, Boston, Baltimore, St. Louis, Atlanta, Houston, Denver, and San Francisco, 1970 and 1984

	NUMBER OF JOBS		
MEAN LEVEL OF EMPLOYEE EDUCATION	1970	1984	CHANGE, 1970–84
Less than high school	3,068,000	2,385,000	−683,000
Some higher education	2,023,000	2,745,000	+722,000

Source: Computed from William Julius Wilson, *The Truly Disadvantaged: The Inner City, the Underclass, and Public Policy* (Chicago: University of Chicago Press, 1987), table 2.6, p. 40. The table, in turn, is taken from John D. Kasarda, "The Regional and Urban Redistribution of People and Jobs in the U.S." (Paper presented to the National Research Council Committee on National Urban Policy, National Academy of Sciences, 1986).

school degree, and a sharp decline in the percentage of jobs requiring no high school education.

In effect, trends in the job market through the next ten years will in all likelihood exacerbate the regressive distribution of income that has taken place over the past decade. Under American democracy, those who are unemployed or marginally employed are weakest politically. The decline of traditional political organizations and unions has made significantly more difficult the political mobilization of the working poor, the working class, and the legions of white-collar workers making from $10,000 to $25,000 a year—a universe roughly containing 24.6 million white households, 3.4 million black households, and 2 million Hispanic households. Within this group, providing a political voice becomes even more difficult for those workers with poor educations who have been dispersed from manufacturing employment into cycles of marginal work. While most of those who have lost manufacturing jobs have found full-time employment, such workers have, in the main, seen wages fall and fringe benefits, often including medical coverage, decline or disappear, leaving them even further outside of the American mainstream and even less well equipped to ensure adequate educational levels for their children. When combined with the declining voter turnout rates associated with falling income, these workers have fallen into what amounts to a new political underclass.

The major forces at work in the last two decades of the post-New Deal period are, then, cumulatively functioning to weaken the influence and power of those in the bottom half of the income distribution, while strengthening the authority of those in the upper half, and particularly the authority of those at elite levels. Trends in political competition and pressures in the private marketplace have combined to create a whipsaw action, reversing New Deal policies that empowered the labor movement and reduced disparities between rich and poor. Recent forces, both in the marketplace and in the political arena, have not produced a realignment of the electorate, but, in terms of outcomes, there has been a realignment in public policy—with few forces, short of a downturn in the business cycle, working against the continuing development of a political and economic system in which the dominant pressures will be toward increased regressivity in the distribution of money and in the ability to influence the outcome of political decisions.

Democrats and Republicans Forge
a New Political Economy

DANIEL YERGIN AND JOSEPH STANISLAW

The redefinition of the relationship between state and marketplace has been less dramatic in the United States than elsewhere because, while government did expand after World War II as in other countries, it did not do so through state ownership. If the great expansion of government activity in the United States was based originally upon the notion of market failure, then the redefinition of the relationship of state and marketplace reflected a shift in attitudes—toward less confidence in the ability of governments to correct market failures and more confidence in the ability of markets to sort things out themselves. Yet how much of this shift represented mainly a change in language and beliefs? And how much did it reflect a real redrawing of the frontier between government and the marketplace?

The United States was always thought to be the true homeland of capitalism in the Manichaean contest between communism and capitalism. It was considered the land of entrepreneurship, innovation, risk taking, opportunity, and the "creative destruction" of the market. Yet government was hardly absent. Whereas intervention in other countries often took the form of the state ownership, its characteristic form in the United States was regulation. And the United States also developed a large and growing welfare state and system of entitlements. As a result, the battle in the United States was—and still is—being played out in the arenas of regulation, taxation and spending, the welfare state, and (although less visibly) privatization. Regulation itself is going in two directions. One direction is toward less economic intervention in markets. The other is toward more intervention to uphold social values. Overall, however, the nation has waged battles over fiscal discipline that parallel those in most countries on the eve of the twenty-first century. The struggle began two decades ago.

The Outsider

When Ronald Reagan won the Republican presidential nomination in 1980, he seemed so much on the political fringe that during the convention, there were intense semisecret negotiations about making former president Gerald Ford his vice-presidential running mate. But Ford was not to be a normal vice president. He was to have far-reaching responsibilities as a kind of copresident with responsibility for foreign affairs and the budget. He would also be "super executive of the office of the President." As proof of the seriousness of the initiative, none other than the master negotiator himself, Henry Kissinger—along with the master of money Alan Greenspan—represented Ford, and by extension the Republican establishment, in the discussions. . . .

Yet the very fact that this bizarre idea was considered underlined how unreliable and inexperienced Reagan was deemed to be despite his having been governor of California, the nation's most populous state (at the time there were 20 million inhabitants) for eight years, compared to Jimmy Carter's four years as governor of Georgia (which had a population of 4.5 million). But Reagan was regarded as outside the mainstream of American politics, a genial figure from the far right. He was an ideologue using a vocabulary made obsolete by Franklin Roosevelt's New Deal. He talked about rolling back government and cutting programs; he promoted free enterprise and celebrated the magic of the market. That was understandable if one was a spokesman for General Electric, or even the successor to the "Old Prospector" as the host of the television series *Death Valley Days*—as Reagan had been in his final years as an actor—before going into politics. But surely that was not the kind of rhetoric that was expected of a president of the United States.

Reagan liked to say that he did not mind being underestimated. It gave him an advantage. As it turned out, Ronald Reagan and his presidency did change the language of American politics, and he helped to set in motion a struggle to redefine the relationship of state and marketplace.

"Mugged by Reality"

Ideas created the context for Reaganism. In this, the Chicago School loomed very large. The skepticism generated by the economic difficulties of the 1970s helped to enlarge further the growing influence of the Chicago economists, who argued that government was the problem, not the solution. But the Chicago School was hardly alone in this. Harvard's Martin Feldstein, who served for a time as the head of Reagan's Council of Economic Advisers, and others did major work assessing the costs, in terms of lost investment and initiative, imposed by high tax rates. The public-choice theories emanating from the University of Virginia provided an influential explanation for government's problems—that special interests turned government activities to their own benefit. There also emerged a group of writers and economists who quickly became known as "supply-siders." This group fervently believed that inflation was society's principal enemy, that the best way to fight inflation was by controlling the money supply, and that the international currency system should be based upon fixed rates, ideally gold. But the most famous concept associated with supply-side was the notion that the revenues lost through tax cuts would be more than made up by the additional tax revenues flowing in as a result of higher growth rates.

If various groups of economists dislodged assumptions about the way America was working, a second set of ideas would provide a parallel political, social, and even cultural critique that bolstered the redefinition: neoconservatism. This movement emerged in the United States in the late 1960s and early 1970s. Its cadres, numbering only a few dozen at first, were disillusioned liberals—in the words of one of the leaders of the movement, Irving Kristol, "liberals mugged by reality." Many had migrated from far on the left—from youthful Marxism of one kind or another. Kristol himself observed that he did not mind being tagged as an ex-Trotskyite fifty years after the fact because he had first met his wife at a meeting of young Trotskyites in Brooklyn.

Neoconservatism had been energized into existence in response to the "counter-cultural" explosion and the youth rebellion of the late 1960s, the New Left and student assaults on universities, and the celebration of militancy and radicalism. The enemies of the neoconservatives were not only socialism, Marxism, communism, and statism. Another enemy was the dominant American liberal ethos, which they believed had so permeated politics, the media, and universities as to be almost unchallengeable. The neoconservatives became convinced that liberalism spawned laxity, decay, and moral decline and that, ultimately, it would mean the degeneration of the United States. They criticized ambitious government programs for failing to deliver what they promised, for creating cultures of dependency, and for making things worse instead of better. They based many of their most potent arguments on the law of unintended consequences. Public housing, for example, created slums instead of eliminating them and, in the process, bulldozed what had been affordable housing for lower-income working people. The "neocons," as they came to be known, were also reacting against "third worldism," which portrayed the United States as the source of the ills afflicting developing nations, the exploiter of the third world and purveyor of oppression, and the blighter of human aspiration—in contrast to the benignity of socialism and the Soviet Union. Tying it all together in the minds of the neocons was what they saw as the liberal predilection for guilt and self-flagellation, and the liberal culture of apology and quest for absolution, all of which led to disastrous policies at home and surrender abroad.

. . . Though not easy to pin down, the influence of neoconservatism was considerable. It redefined the boundaries of political debate. It provided a new set of ideas for conservatives. "The weakness of liberal social policy was becoming evident," recalled Kristol. "We gave conservatives a way of critiquing social and economic policies. Part of the impact arose from the peculiarity that we were a group of social scientists, not literary intellectuals, who came up with studies that Congress could understand and that the media could not dismiss merely as the work of New York intellectuals." . . .

The neoconservatives called for a shrinking of government. With increasing vigor, they also offered an optimistic and confident affirmation of capitalism and the marketplace. Norman Podhoretz, the editor of *Commentary,* once suggested to Kristol that, since the word *capitalism* was somewhat "besmirched," he should instead write about *free enterprise* or *free markets*. Kristol would not budge. In his view, "the fight to rehabilitate the reputation of the system would be incomplete unless its name was rescued from discredit as well." As he later added, "That's the word. Use it."

"We had no economist in the original group around *The Public Interest,*" said Kristol. "I was not then a great admirer of Chicago. I was still a liberal, a skeptical liberal. What happened was that around 1980, the free-market school of thought and the noeconservative school of thought fused. Maybe Reagan did it."

The irony was that the market system, as it was then, looked increasingly impaired. But under the influence of conservative economics and the neoconservative social critique, a profound change began to take place in views about the role of the American government. The process would take a long time. It really began with a crisis that preceded the Reagan administration: the inflationary turmoil of the late 1970s. As it had in the other industrial countries, that crisis signaled the weakness of the prevailing economic system and brought about its eventual transformation.

The Central Banker

The White House swearing-in ceremony on August 6, 1979, was unusually sober. Inflation was rising to levels never seen before in modern America, frighteningly high levels. It seemed to have become embedded in the very fibers of the country. Confidence was ebbing. Three weeks before, President Jimmy Carter had proclaimed a national "crisis of confidence" and had fired members of his cabinet. The move was meant to show resolve and steady the nation, but instead it further rattled the country. Carter appointed a new Treasury secretary, businessman William Miller, which in turn meant that the president had to fill Miller's former position—the chairmanship of the Federal Reserve Board. It would be a critical choice, for the Fed, which by statute operates as the nation's independent central bank, had a decisive role in the war on inflation. But whom to appoint? Carter was told that Paul Volcker, a longtime monetary expert and at the time president of the

New York Federal Reserve, had the necessary capabilities and reputation to provide financial backbone. In fact Carter had never heard of Volcker, but he was desperate to restore some modicum of confidence and authority to the management of the economy. That was how Volcker ended up in the East Room of the White House. Considering the subsequent impact that his policies would have on the economy and their contribution to the outcome of the 1980 presidential election, Carter may later have wished that he had never heard of Volcker at all.

But on that August day Volcker knew exactly what his task was, even if he did not know exactly how to achieve it. "We are face-to-face with economic difficulties really unique in our experience," he said, suitably glum-faced at the swearing-in. "And we have lost that euphoria that we had fifteen years ago, that we knew all the answers to managing the economy." His mission was, he put it later, "to slay the inflationary dragon." If he failed, the consequences could either be a Latin American-style permanent inflation or another Great Depression. The political consequences could be even worse and would threaten the very foundations of American democracy. He was absolutely convinced of one other thing: Gradualism and half measures would not work.

At a White House tea party after the swearing-in, Volcker confided to a reporter, "I'm boring. It's the job of all central bankers to be as boring as possible." That was an exceedingly harsh self-appraisal for the man who would wage war on inflation and, against very high odds, win—and, in the process, set the United States on a new economic course.

Volcker was cut out for the part. At six-foot-seven, with a cigar often jammed into the corner of his mouth, he had been an unmistakable figure on the international financial circuit for years. It was said that he was the only man who could talk down to you and over your head at the same time. If somewhat shy, he was also self-confident and commanding, with considerable technical and political skills, a strong intuitive feel for markets, and a widely recognized integrity. In most of his career he was a public servant, and he lived a life of probity. His family remained in New York City, to which he returned on weekends, while during the week he lived in a small Washington apartment cluttered with old newspapers and fishing flies. Once a week, he packed up his laundry in a suitcase and took it to get washed at his daughter's house in northern Virginia. His personal style was enigmatic. Well schooled over the years in the tools of central banking, including the importance of surprise and secrecy, Volcker had perfected a talent for obfuscation and the central banker's mumble, which mixed profundities and banalities and non sequiturs in such a way as to be deliberately indecipherable. . . .

As chairman of the Fed, Volcker was determined to extinguish the inflationary expectations that gripped the United States—what had become, as he called it, the national "bet on inflation." His weapon was a modified monetarism. Instead of explicitly setting interest rates (the price of money), the Fed would control the actual supply (or quantity) of money by managing bank reserves. It was a blunt weapon. But Volcker saw no choice. The effects were dramatic. As the Fed restricted the money supply, interest rates shot up, to 20 percent and above. The economy slowed and then contracted, falling into the deepest recession since the Great Depression. Unemployment rose to as high as 10 percent, houses went unsold, companies struggled with liquidity problems, cars sat on dealers' lots. The slump was—along with the Iran hostage crisis—a major factor in Ronald Reagan's defeat of Jimmy Carter in 1980. After Reagan's election, the Fed, and Volcker in particular, continued to be a prime target for angry politicians, who feared the political backlash. Yet Reagan himself never quite attacked Volcker. "People in the White House and Treasury put pressure on Reagan, but they could never get Reagan to criticize me," Volcker said. "Slight musings, yes. But Reagan had this visceral feeling that fighting inflation was a good thing." On the subject of conquering inflation, Reagan would say to his secretary of state, George Shultz, "If not us, who? If not now, when?"

Meanwhile, public anger against Volcker and the Fed mounted. Farmers surrounded the Federal Reserve building to protest the high interest rates. Auto dealers sent in coffins with car keys to symbolize the vehicles that went unsold because of high interest rates. Volcker himself would read heartbreaking letters that people wrote to him—about how they had saved for years to buy a house for their parents, but now, because of the high rates, could not. He was deeply upset by these letters, but he still saw no choice. If inflation were not stamped out, there would be a much greater collapse. And he was convinced that, at last, he had support for tackling inflation head-on. "There was a sense that you wouldn't have won a majority of voters but you would have won a lot of votes," he said. "People were scared. Something had to be done. But none of us quite understood how tough it would be. Some things we never expected. Interest rates of twenty percent! Who ever expected twenty percent interest rates? But you get caught up in the process, and you can't let go. You don't want to let go. Letting up, giving up—that was not in my psychology."

It took three years. By the summer of 1982, the conquest of inflation was in sight. In fact, inflation that year would fall below 4 percent. Volcker's singular achievement was to conquer inflation at a time when defeatism was rampant. He set the United States on a new economic course. The risks of not succeeding were often on his mind. So was history. Once confronted with the accusation that he was behaving like a German central banker, he replied, "I don't take that as criticism. That's a compliment. I'm in pretty good company there."

Beyond Tax-and-Spend

Thanks to Volcker's efforts, monetary restraint was obtained quite early in the course of the Reagan administration. And Reagan's unwavering stance in the air traffic controllers' strike of 1981 helped change the tone of labor relations, indirectly contributing to the muting of inflationary psychology. But there was still fiscal policy to be dealt with—the ways that government raised its revenues and the ways that it chose to spend them. The rise of welfare demands, entitlements, and obligations toward the middle class, the poor, and especially the elderly made spending politically necessary as a source of votes. The problem, of course, was how to finance the outlays.

Ronald Reagan's advisers came to office with the intention of cutting both taxes and spending. But they soon found out that it was easier to achieve the first of these objectives than the second. The reason was simple: politics. It was popular to cut taxes. And taxes did come down substantially. The top marginal rate was reduced from 70 percent to 28 percent, the tax base was broadened, and many deductions and loopholes were eliminated. But it was unpopular to cut spending, and the Democratic

Congress bridled at the extent of the cuts that the president proposed. Reagan did not take on middle-class entitlements. He also spared the Defense Department from the ax, and indeed initiated, over the course of his two terms, major increases in defense expenditures, including the "Star Wars" space defense program.

Some in the Reagan camp were optimistic, despite the failure to cut total government spending. They were the advocates of what traditional Republican economist Herbert Stein—echoing the music of the day—called "punk" supply-side economics, which made sweeping assertions that reductions in tax revenues resulting from tax cuts would be more than made up for by higher tax revenues generated by economic growth. It did not turn out that way. Because spending did not come down with taxes—and indeed defense spending went up sharply—and because the tax cuts did not feed back into the economy to the extent hoped, both the federal debt and the annual deficit ballooned; and in 1981–82, the economy was in a deep recession. In September 1982, in its first effort to repair the damage, the Reagan administration followed the "largest tax cut in history" with the "largest tax increase in history." But there was no catching up. By the end of Reagan's first term, the supply-side logic was discredited in the eyes of many, and the inability to bring taxes and spending down together stood in marked contrast to Volcker's victory over inflation. David Stockman, Reagan's first director of the Office of Management and Budget, left the administration dejected, disillusioned with supply-side economics, and chastened by the realities of the political process. Failure to achieve fiscal-policy change, he argued, was a clear vindication of the "triumph of politics"—of entitlements over austerity, and of the enduring pork-barrel tradition of American legislation over any cold economic logic. "I joined the Reagan Revolution as a radical ideologue," he wrote. "I learned the traumatic lesson that no such revolution is possible."

The triumph of politics and what Stockman called the "fiscal error" that went with it spawned a new monster, which would come to occupy center stage in policy debate: the deficit and the federal debt. Between the beginning and the end of the Reagan presidency, the annual deficit almost tripled. So did the gross national debt—from $995 billion to $2.9 trillion. Or, as Reagan and Bush administration official Richard Darman put it, "In the Reagan years, more federal debt was added than in the entire prior history of the United States."

There simply was no quick cure to the scale of spending. In the minds of some, however, there was another logic to tax cuts: Reduce taxes and government revenue, and eventually the pain and scale of deficits—and the threat of national bankruptcy—would force a retrenchment of government spending. That thought was not restricted to fervent supply-siders, and ultimately it would end up true. But not for some years, and certainly not during the Reagan years.

When George Bush took office in 1989, the annual deficit stood at $152 billion. Taxes could not be raised substantially for devastatingly powerful political reasons—as Bush found out when his retreat from his solemn "read my lips" campaign promise of "no new taxes" became his most damaging political liability. There was no choice but to contain spending. And luckily, international events afforded a good opportunity to start tackling the problem. The fall of the Berlin Wall and the crumbling of the Soviet empire made possible a tapering-off in defense spending. Still, this was not enough. Owing to the recession of the early 1990s, tax revenues fell, and in 1992, as Bush was ending his term, the deficit peaked at $290 billion.

By that time, out-and-out fiscal conservatives, proud to call themselves such, had gained ground in both major parties. The ideas that underpinned the "Reagan revolution" had acquired much wider resonance. "Tax and spend"—after all, the two basic functions of any fiscal policy—became a pejorative term, an epithet to avoid. On the Democratic side, a group calling themselves New Democrats criticized the traditional Democratic approach, and came to influence more and more of the party's agenda.

One of their best-known figures was the governor of Arkansas, Bill Clinton, who springboarded to the presidency. The division between Democrats ran right through his administration. Treasury Secretary Lloyd Bentsen and Robert Rubin, head of the the newly established National Economic Council, were convinced that the best way to promote economic growth was by reducing the deficit. That would bring down long-term interest rates. It would do so directly; it would also do so by engendering confidence in the bond market that the deficit really was being tackled, which would reduce the inflation premium in interest rates. And lower rates would be the best stimulus to investment-led growth, much better than the traditional Keynesian spending stimulus. In fact, any gains from a stimulus package would be more than offset by the higher interest rates with which the market would respond. In this, they were much in accord with Alan Greenspan, who had succeeded Volcker as chairman of the Federal Reserve Board in 1987, and who had watched the swelling deficits with increasing dismay. Greenspan was convinced that the continuing growth of deficits not only would mean higher taxes and slower growth but could well end in catastrophe. The traditional liberals among Clinton's officials and advisers were appalled. Clinton had not fought the election, they argued, to promote "Republican economics." The Democrats were betraying their traditional constituencies in order to pamper the rich. They wanted stimulus programs, increased government spending, and higher taxes, especially on the upper income. But Clinton had already made his choice. "During the transition," recalled Rubin, now Treasury secretary, "the president expressed his unequivocal commitment to making the deficit his priority." The deficit was enemy number one. That meant that spending would have to be restrained.

The president went all out in 1993 for a deficit reduction program that involved both spending cuts and some tax increases. The political battle was, as one participant put it, "murderous." The program just squeaked through Congress; Vice-President Al Gore had to break a tie in the Senate. "I said at the time that we would only get lower rates if the market believed in the deficit reduction," Rubin later said. "How long would it take for that to happen? The markets believed in our deficit reduction program, more quickly than I had thought they might." Passage of the program in August 1993 indeed proved to be the turning point. The bond market became persuaded that the deficit would be reduced. Long-term rates started down, and the economy moved into a state of reasonable economic growth and low inflation.

Yet this reorientation did not happen in a political vacuum. It was given high visibility by the 1992 third-party presidential bid of Ross Perot. The drive for spending cuts gained immensely in popularity in the early 1990s, culminating in the Contract with America, the Republicans' capture of both houses of Congress, and the ascendancy of Newt Gingrich. The confrontation between Clinton's Democratic administration and the brash Republican crusaders of the 104th Congress and the resulting government shutdown shifted the center in American economic policy. The Republicans used the specter of a prolonged battle over a balanced budget amendment to galvanize debate on current spending. They challenged virtually every area of traditionally "untouchable" government expenditure. They even proposed shutting down or merging entire executive departments, eliminating cabinet positions in the process. All this made the budget the chief focus of relations between the White House and the Congress. Overruling his more liberal advisers, Clinton adopted the principle of the proposed changes, including the balanced budget. But he stopped short of going as far as the Republicans advocated. That maneuver—which became known as triangulation—deprived them of much of their agenda.

The battle over the budget shifted the center of American economic policy, even of American politics. The ease—in relative terms—with which budget deals have been made since then shows how much this center has grown.

Though not well recognized, the economic recovery and expansion actually began in the Bush administration. But subsequent deficit reduction was central to its continuation—an acknowledgment, among other things, that the United States, no less than an emerging-market nation, is judged every day by the capital markets. As Rubin explained, "The threshold issue had to be the deficit and how quickly you can gain credibility with the markets, since ultimately it's interest rates that drive the economy."

The speed with which the deficit came down—from almost 5 percent of GDP in 1992 to less than 1 percent in 1997—has surprised almost everybody. During the 1993 budget battle, both the administration and the Congressional Budget Office predicted that the 1997 deficit would be over $200 billion. It came in at only a tenth of that, $22.6 billion, the lowest level since the early 1970s. How did this dramatic turnaround come about? Partly through reductions in spending (primarily from defense), partly through higher taxes, and certainly through the flow of additional tax revenues generated by a strong economy. Whatever the reasons, the result is, as economist Benjamin Friedman put it, "a great achievement, and there is plenty of credit to go around." The next stage became the battle over what to do with an anticipated surplus—whether to pass it on to the public through tax cuts, or use it to chip away at the $5.7 trillion national debt, or spend it. All that assumes, of course, that there would be no recession along the way that would reduce tax revenues and require increased transfer payments. In the meantime, at least one downside to the falling deficit has been detected. "The deficit is disappearing so fast," mused one senator, in 1997, "that we may not be able to take complete credit for the decline." By 1998, the deficit had turned into a surplus of 70 billion.

The deficit reduction was not, however, matched by a corresponding reduction in the growth of entitlement spending. This leaves a major challenge ahead. "Demographic forces will require adjustments starting a decade into the next century," in the words of Roger Porter of the Center for Business and Government at Harvard. "We can begin making these changes now and phase them in gradually, or we can wait and face much more wrenching adjustments." . . .

A Delayed Revolution

It had taken more than a decade and a half from Ronald Reagan's election to dilute the Keynesian imprint on government policy: to steady monetary policy, and to significantly restrain spending and taxation in ways that both parties could discuss and compromise on. The substance of the Reagan revolution was realized well after Reagan's passing from the political scene and well after the logic of supply-side economics had been discredited. It was not, therefore, the revolution the Reaganites had had in mind. But it was no less a revolution in its long-term effects, for it saw the government painfully but genuinely reducing its scope of intervention in the economy.

That applied to regulation as well. Ever since the New Deal, America had placed much of its confidence, in terms of overseeing the economy and avoiding abuses, in its web of regulatory agencies, combined with the powerful judicial antitrust tradition. From the mid-1930s until the mid-1970s the system did not change much. The regulators and the courts played their appointed roles. They came to resemble each other in procedure and style. But from 1975 onward, regulation began to change—drastically. In many areas, America experienced so-called deregulation—meaning the withdrawal of many regulatory restrictions over economic activity, although often with the requirement that new ones be devised as well. Yet in some other areas—particularly health, safety, the environment, employee and consumer rights, and affirmative action—there has been a great deal of new regulation. In some cases, the balance is ambiguous or still shifting. All in all, however, regulation remains a central means for government in the United States to effect major changes in the way the market, and individuals, behave.

From Capture to Competition

Economic regulation emerged with the establishment of the Interstate Commerce Commission in 1887. Over the next several decades, the rationales for such regulation were progressively elaborated. They included the promotion of economic development, equity and fairness, the requisite counterbalance to monopolies, and the provision of economically affordable universal services. From the New Deal onward, market imperfections and failures became a dominating rationale. And in the postwar years, government presence came to be felt in almost every economic enterprise.

Though the Reagan administration arrived with a promise to roll back economic regulation, the process had actually begun in the Ford and Carter administrations, in the middle and late 1970s. By then there was already a well-articulated critique of economic regulation, the result of the attention that economists and other social scientists had been devoting to the subject for a decade and a half. The Chicago School had been at the forefront, owing to the critique of American-style regulation by George Stigler. Stigler had spent much of the 1960s plowing through mountains of data on electric power regulation, stock exchange rules, and antitrust cases. "My findings were often surprising," he said. "The regulation of electric utilities did not help residential users; the regulation of stock issues did not help the widows and orphans who bought these issues."

From these findings came Stigler's famous theory of "regulatory capture." He concluded that the regulated firm always knew more about its own activities than the regulator could find out, and could use this information advantage to shift regulation in its favor. Entrenched regulation had come to serve the firms it was once meant to restrain. Later, students of Stigler would extend this theory to explore how special-interest groups and lobbies could take over the process. Because it challenged the notion that regulation could serve and protect an abstract, impartial public interest, Stigler's theory of regulatory capture was a head-on challenge to James Landis's ideal of disinterested regulation. On the contrary, Stigler argued, it was all too "interested." . . .

With the passage of time, competition increasingly came to be seen as preferable to regulation. The very concept of natural monopoly—the economic name for a situation where multiple suppliers would lead to higher, not lower, costs—was questioned. If people who were now prevented from doing so really wanted to get into a business, and could feasibly do so even if only on a small scale, then the market would not, in fact, be a natural monopoly. Instead, it would be "contestable"—that is, subject to competition. And perhaps competition could better serve the objective that regulation was supposed to achieve. The results would be lower costs to consumers. . . .

. . . In 1974, Senator Edward Kennedy became chairman of a newly created subcommittee on "administrative practice and procedure." For chief counsel, he brought down Stephen Breyer, a Harvard Law School professor, who had worked in the Watergate investigation. At Kennedy's request, Breyer came up with a list of possible investigations for the subcommittee. One of the items, airline regulation, interested Breyer the most. Kennedy checked it off. And that is how deregulation began in the United States.

"Plums" and "Dogs"

Breyer taught antitrust and administrative law at Harvard. He believed in free markets and in ensuring that they worked through competition. Indeed, he could not understand the rationale for regulating markets that were structurally competitive. "Why regulate something," he asked, "if it can be done better by the market?". . .

Airline regulation offered a particularly tempting target. The Civil Aeronautics Board (CAB) had been established in 1938 to deal with what was described at the time as "near chaos" and "uneconomic, destructive competition and wasteful duplication of services" in U.S. aviation. The issue then was the rampant instability of the fledgling airline industry. The specific problem was airmail. The contracts let by the post office for airmail provided subsidies for the new business, and companies that were desperate to win those contracts wildly undercut each other in their bids. Losers accused the post office of favoritism. Regulation was introduced to bring some order to what was seen as a public service, both to meet the nation's needs and—at a time when war was on the horizon—to ensure stability in a civilian aviation industry that would be a very important foundation for military power.

What resulted, as the years passed, was a government-run cartel based upon a symbiotic relationship between regulator and regulatee, a system characterized by the allocation of what had become known as "plums" and "dogs." The CAB decided what tickets would cost on all routes, which meant that all airlines charged the same price on the same route. The CAB also decided who could fly the various interstate routes. This was the deal: Airlines would agree to provide unprofitable service along some routes—the dogs—for instance, to smaller cities. In turn, they would be compensated with high-volume, profitable routes—the plums. The CAB conducted lengthy and tedious public hearings, very much in the Brandeisian tradition and without much relation to the actual economics of the business. Then the commissioners would retire to a private room, make their decisions, and hand out the plums and the dogs.

"The CAB was supposed to be protecting the public," said Breyer. "But regulation was leading to higher prices. It spent 95 percent of its time keeping prices from being too low instead of pushing to get them lowered." The Kennedy hearings, in Breyer's mind, unfolded almost like a symphony. They were, he said, "beautiful. Everything emerged in detail just as the score had predicted." The hearings demonstrated how the system prevented competition and thus denied the public the price benefits that would otherwise result.

Yet it was one thing to so demonstrate the flaws of the system; it was quite another to change it in the face of the entrenched opposition by most of the airline industry. In the aftermath of the hearings, President Ford's CAB began to explore how to implement deregulation, but the Ford administration lasted only two and a half years. The Carter administration picked up the theme. The attack on regulation was thereafter led by an economist who was not at all part of the Chicago School. Indeed, he was a liberal Democrat in everything but, as it turned out, economic theory.

"Marginal Costs with Wings"

Something of a prodigy, Alfred Kahn graduated from New York University summa cum laude at age eighteen and then went on to Yale for his Ph.D. in economics, which he obtained at age twenty-four. Endowed with a quick mind and a passion for Gilbert and Sullivan operettas, he enjoyed playing with words, sometimes quite slyly. A professor of economics at Cornell University, he published his masterwork *The Economics of Regulation* at the right time, in 1970. It has been described as the "most influential work ever written on the subject."

The problem with so much regulation, said Kahn, was that it did not reflect the realities of the marketplace, and prevented price from doing its essential job. He explained, "The only economic function of price is to influence behavior—to elicit supply and to regulate demand." But much regulation seemed to do just the opposite—it sent signals quite at variance with the realities of supply and demand. Regulators often did not seem to understand the economics of the industries they were regulating—or the economic consequences of their own decisions. The guiding star of regulation, Kahn said, should be marginal cost pricing—that is, prices should be determined by the cost of providing one additional unit of whatever the good or service. . . .

Kahn had little patience with the hearing process. "Due process in the fashioning of economic policy," he protested, "is not the same as due process in criminal trial." But one would not know that from the way the CAB operated. He was amazed by the kind of questions the CAB was forced to consider: "May an air taxi acquire a fifty-seat plane? May a supplemental carrier carry horses from Florida to somewhere in the Northeast? May a carrier introduce a special fare for skiers that refunds the cost of their ticket if there is no snow?" And one of the most momentous questions of all: "May the employees of two financially affiliated airlines wear similar-looking uniforms?" All this—and much more—was being decided by government regulators. "Is there any wonder," said Kahn, "that I ask myself every day: Is this action necessary? Is this what my mother raised me to do?"

His major assault on the system was to allow flexibility in pricing, which meant discount fares. By the summer of 1978, over half of coach-class miles were being flown on "peanut," supersaver, and other discount fares. Kahn personally fielded many irate complaints. When Senator Barry Goldwater, the 1964 Republican presidential candidate and author of the best-selling *Conscience of a Conservative,* wrote him to complain about unpleasant conditions aboard now-packed flights, Kahn replied that this was the inevitable consequence of breaking up a "cartel-like regime." He added, "When you have further doubts about the efficiency of a free market system, please do not hesitate to convey them to me. I also warmly recommend some earlier speeches and writings of one Senator Barry Goldwater." When a friend wrote him about how unpleasant it had been to sit next to a hippie on a flight, Kahn replied, "Since I have not received any complaints from the hippie, I assume the distaste was not reciprocated."

Kahn's biggest battles were with the airlines and groups that had grown up with regulation and did not want it changed. In one hearing, former astronaut Frank Borman, president of Eastern Airlines, was seeking to clarify the advantages of different types of aircraft. "I really don't know one plane from another," Kahn shot back. "To me they are all marginal costs with wings." In October 1978, airline deregulation became law: The plums and dogs were gone. Airlines were free to set fares competitively. They could decide whether to enter or exit markets and routes. And entry was now open to new companies. The CAB itself went out of business in 1985. Safety remained the province of the Federal Aviation Administration.

This was deregulation—the first major rolling back of the New Deal system. And how did it work out? It is estimated that on average, air travelers in 1996 paid 26 percent less for trips than they would have if regulation had stayed in place—although business travelers are clearly disadvantaged compared to leisure travelers. Some of the most established carriers have gone bankrupt, although some operated through bankruptcy and came out on the other side. Instead of ten trunk (i.e., major) carriers in the United States, there are now six. In the early years of deregulation smaller cities and towns either lost their air service (especially jets) or were threatened with such loss. Commuter airlines stepped into the breach, replacing one or two jet touchdowns a day with much more frequent small-plane service. One of the unanswered questions is what effect the loss of jet service has had on economic development in smaller cities and towns. But in the larger context, airline deregulation did mark a turning point, a reversal of the regulatory thrust of the preceding forty years and a turn to the market. . . .

For Whom the Bell Tolls

The biggest regulated company of all was AT&T—the country's largest enterprise, with over 1 million employees—which provided the bulk of telephone services, local and long distance, in the United States. Other companies, like General Telephone and Electric, competed around the edges. AT&T's operation was based on the idea of a natural monopoly; and its regulation, on the preservation of the public good. . . .

AT&T provided everything, from the long-distance service to the equipment in the house. And it delivered a very high quality of service. If a subscriber had a problem, the truck would speedily arrive, the problem would be traced and rectified, and there was no squabbling over jurisdiction. "By comparison to any other national network," observed regulatory historian Richard Vietor, "there is no question that this system worked best—measured by penetration, technical quality, or price." AT&T also jealously guarded its monopoly. "Foreign attachments" were not permitted anywhere. Thus the phone company effectively fought off the competitive challenge posed by the Hush-a-Phone, a sort of small cuplike attachment put around the mouthpiece to increase the privacy of the speaker. Using any foreign attachment meant risking the cutoff of one's phone service.

The system was settled and accepted. Only the most adventurous, and perhaps even foolhardy, would dare to challenge AT&T's formidable position—and expend the time and effort so doing. And it took such a character, William McGowan, a consultant-turned-entrepreneur, who started his attack from the fringes in the late 1960s and pursued it resolutely thereafter. McGowan had grasped a golden opportunity when the founders of a firm called Microwave Communications, Inc. (later just MCI) came to him for advice about securing finance for their venture to connect trucks on the St. Louis–Chicago run by microwave signal. Instead of giving them advice, he bought control of the firm.

McGowan embarked on a crusade to undermine AT&T's monopoly. The first step was to win approval from the FCC for its long-distance private-line service. After six years of interminable hearings, filings, appeals, and rehearings—during which it almost went under—MCI won approval from the FCC to establish its service. The vote among the commissioners was a close four to three. One of those who voted yes explained that he was looking "for ways to add a little salt and pepper of competition to the rather tasteless stew or regulatory protection that this Commission and Bell have cooked up." McGowan continued his campaign against AT&T in the courts. At times, it seemed that pursuing lawsuits was the company's only vocation—as the in-house joke went, the company was " a law firm with an antenna on the roof." But McGowan's perseverance would pay off.

McGowan may have done more than anybody else to upset the longstanding regulatory system. But it was technological change that really undermined AT&T's monopoly and the regulatory system that went with it. The problem was no longer a little cup like the Hush-a-Phone. It was the computer age. The development of computing technology and the tremendous growth in data transmission eroded the traditional concept of long distance, creating new demands by customers and new incentives for competition. Private networks were developing rapidly to meet the demands of large users and data flow. There was no longer any clear difference between switching equipment and data processing. Technological progress was generating a growing pressure on the AT&T monopoly. More and more people were doubting the validity of the existing system, which in any event was eroding. Moreover, it had become very clear that long-distance rates subsidized local rates; that recognition provided an incentive for large corporate users to seek ways around the monopoly in order to get cheaper rates for their long-distance and data services.

AT&T sought to resist the pressure for change. "What do we believe?" the chairman of AT&T rhetorically asked a convention of state utility regulators. "We believe

. . . that the public interest . . . cannot help but be impaired by the duplication . . . that will inevitably result from the further encroachment of competition. . . . There is something right about the common carrier principle. There is something right about regulation. And, given the nature of our industry, there is something right about monopoly—regulated monopoly." The message may have rung with a clear tone since the turn of the century, but it did not ring true anymore. The Justice Department filed an antitrust suit against AT&T in 1974. Federal judge Harold Greene took responsibility for the case. The trial opened in 1981. Judge Greene rejected AT&T's motion for dismissal, commenting that the government had presented evidence that "the Bell System has violated the antitrust laws in a number of ways over a lengthy period of time." Concluding that the company was cornered, management made the decision to accept the breakup of the company. The consequence—the result of almost two years of negotiation between the company and the Department of Justice—was "the biggest, most complex restructuring in the history of business." The company was divided into separate "local" (i.e., regional) companies—the Baby Bells—and a long-distance-only company, the successor AT&T, which now competes in the United States against MCI (merged into MCI Worldcom, an even more recent upstart giant), Sprint, and a host of others, and is also competing in markets around the world. . . .

Where the Money Is

The New Deal's regulatory legacy is also being reassessed in the financial sector. "Our approach is not deregulation but sensible regulatory reform," said Eugene Ludwig, who, as comptroller of the currency, between 1993 and 1998 oversaw a major part of the national banking system. One of the first things that Franklin Roosevelt did when he became president in 1933 was declare a "bank holiday"—temporarily shutting their doors to prevent runs—and ever since the New Deal, the financial sector has been heavily regulated. The range of control is extraordinarily broad—from the Glass-Steagal legislation, which until recently forbade overlap between commercial and investment banks, to the requirement that the federal government approve every new automated teller machine—a process that typically, for each ATM, requires thirty-five steps and takes thirty-seven days. The Office of the Comptroller has been reviewing every single one of its seventy-two regulations. "We want to hold up everything to the light," said Ludwig "and ask: Does it make sense? Add value? How much does it matter? Is the burden worth the benefit? Some of the regulations didn't make sense when they were first put in place."

That things can go wrong was underlined by the severe crisis that hit the savings and loan industry in the late 1980s and early 1990s. That crisis was the result of both partial deregulation and what Paul Volcker called "a failure of regulation and supervision." Restrictions were lifted on the interest rates that these institutions could pay for deposits and on what they could invest those deposits in. This led them, in Volcker's words, into "temptation—they could make bigger mistakes than otherwise." But deposits were guaranteed by the federal government, meaning that the savings and loans could take ever-larger risks with a sense of impunity. Government examiners might well have blown the whistle, but executives of savings and loans, big political contributors, applied intense political pressure to avert exposure of the risks. It was only when massive bankruptcy and default were at hand that the full extent of the scandal became apparent. Taxpayers ended up stuck with the tab for a $300 billion bailout. The crisis also left a renewed sense of sobriety about the complexity of regulation in the financial sector.

"The trick in regulation," Ludwig said, "is to get the right balance. There is pretty clear evidence that some of the financial unraveling of the 1980s occurred because of regulatory mistakes. On the other hand, there are knaves and fools, and you can't rely entirely on the market itself. The financial system does benefit from a certain amount of oversight and supervision. Some participants will go way out on the bell curve toward high risk in pursuit of high rewards. Regulation helps to push back toward the center, and ensures that a high risk/reward ratio for individuals does not lead to contagion or a systemic crisis. The financial system is different from other sectors because of its centrality to the economy. It can be manipulated. You don't get a run on Toys "Я" Us because of rumors about Barbie. You can get a run on a bank. Illegal activities can lead to insolvency. There's more of a stake in keeping the financial sector honest than there is, for instance, in cosmetics."

But the biggest deregulation yet is still very much in the process of unfolding. It is transforming an industry that is the most capital intensive in the world and is bigger than airlines and telecommunications combined—electric power. Nothing else is as emblematic of deregulation. It touches everyone—and everyone's monthly bills. . . .

Social Regulation: Expanding Its Reach

If the general trend in economic regulation is toward greater reliance on the market, somewhat the opposite is happening in the realm of what is called social-value regulation, which encompasses such areas as environmental, antidiscrimination, and workplace regulation. In these realms, the "fourth branch of government" is having a bigger and bigger say. Every administration since Richard Nixon's, whether Democrat or Republican, has declared that there is too much regulation and that it needs serious pruning. But the trend has been the opposite—a vast expansion in the fourth branch, resulting in what has been described by critics as the "criminalization of just about everything." It is very difficult to gain an overall view of the ever-growing edifice of social-value regulation; only those who are touched by this or that part of the regulatory system know it is there. To confuse matters further, the debates are passionate. Emotions run very high, driven by notions of justice and fairness, of safety and risk, and differing fundamentally on facts and theory. There is also, at least in the view of some, an ideological difference.

Whatever the point of view, risk regulation—involving health, safety, and the environment—suffers from what Stephen Breyer, now a Supreme Court Justice, calls "regulatory gridlock." . . . [I]n the late 1960s and early 1970s that a new spirit of activism initiated a great growth in regulatory activities, at the federal, state, and local levels. Both EPA—the Environmental Protection Agency—and OSHA—the Occupational Safety and Health Administration—were established during the Nixon administration. Pollution—dirty air in cities, dirty water in the nation's lakes and streams—spawned a host of new requirements. Progress has been enormous. It is now possible to fish and swim in the Hudson River. A new car rolling off the assembly line in Detroit in 1997 produced only 5 percent as much pollution as a car built during the early 1970s. Los Angeles is the city that made smog famous. Yet, despite an increase in population of more than 30 percent in Los Angeles since then, the air is 36 percent cleaner.

Overall, the environment in the United States and other industrial countries is much cleaner that it was two decades ago. This has been achieved by a combination of regulation and activism, along with technological innovation and intellectual redefinition. Yet at the same time, the system of environmental regulation that has evolved is increasingly seen as cumbersome, inflexible, and overly prescriptive. Among other reasons, this happens because the Congress writes extremely detailed statutory instructions. Instead of general guidelines and goals, "command and control" regulation tends to be imposed in very defined ways, which deters innovation and efficiency. Moreover, regulations have a habit of growing topsy-turvy. Governmental micromanagement is endemic, further reducing the potential for technological innovation and creativity. Science is often at the center of dispute, and priorities often result from the unpredictable interplay of press, public, special-interest groups, politicians, and what Breyer calls "pseudo-science," rather than some ranking of risk and urgency. In the words of Breyer, "We have substituted fear of the market with fear of what goes up the chimney."

He points to the challenge of building flexibility into regulation. "It is always a problem to get discretion into the process so that the regulator can apply a reasonable amount of cautious regulation. Because no one trusts anyone else, there is less discretion, more rules, more rigid results. The only way to improve this regulation is to give administrators more discretion. But Congress writes the rules to prevent discretion. If there is too much discretion, there is a risk of abusing it. If you stop discretion, you get rules and rigidity. It's always true. The challenge is to find balance between rules and discretion."

Critics of the current system worry about its rationality and the "last five—or ten—percent problem." Remediating 90 or 95 percent of a pollution problem can be done in an efficient, cost-effective fashion. The last 5 or 10 percent—purity— is an almost unachievable goal, and one that diverts resources from more pressing needs. "The drive for perfectionism has created a very big mess," said Justice Breyer. In his recent book *Breaking the Vicious Circle: Toward Effective Risk Regulation,* he cited a case he presided over when he was a federal judge. The case involved a ten-year battle to force the cleanup of a toxic waste dump in New Hampshire: "The site was mostly cleaned up. All but one of the private parties had settled. The remaining private party litigated the cost of cleaning up the last little bit, a cost of about $9.3 million to remove a small amount of highly diluted PCBs and 'volatile organic compounds' (benzene and gasoline components) by incinerating the dirt. How much extra safety did this $9.3 million buy? The forty-thousand-page record of this ten-year effort indicated (and all parties seemed to agree) that, without the extra expenditure, the waste dump was clean enough for children playing on the site to eat small amounts of dirt for 70 days each year without significant harm. Burning the soil would have made it clean enough for the children to eat small amounts daily for 245 days per year without significant harm. But there were no dirt-eating children playing in the area, for it was a swamp. Nor were dirt-eating children likely to appear there, for future building seemed unlikely. The parties also agreed that at least half of the volatile organic chemicals would likely evaporate by the year 2000. To spend $9.3 million to protect non-existent dirt-eating children is what I mean by the problem of the 'last 10 percent.'"

The entire system struggles with the fundamental issue of how to assess and measure risk. One way is to analyze the balance between the costs of a regulation and the benefits achieved, but the results of such cost-benefit analysis have been mixed. The vexing matter of the cost of lives saved demonstrates the difficulties. The range is so wide as to veer into the meaningless. It is estimated that the ban on flammable pajamas for children came out to less than $1 million per life saved. By contrast, a more recent rule limiting exposure to formaldehyde works out to an estimated $93 billion per life saved.

A new approach is evolving to bring greater flexibility and efficiency to environmental protection. It is the application of economic incentives and market mechanisms to solve problems, which supplants traditional bureaucratic methods. Clearly, this is the frontier for ecology in the United States. "After twenty-five years, we are moving into a new generation of environmentalism," explained Daniel Esty, director of the environmental law program at Yale University and former assistant EPA administrator. "Rather than command-and-control, it will be market-based." This emerges from dissatisfaction with the rigidities of regulatory command-and-control systems and a quest for greater effectiveness—along with an overall greater openness to market solutions in the United States than in the past.

This new approach is most evident in the emergence of "emissions trading" as a way to promote better air quality. Under a system known as tradable rights, a company acquires from the government, either by purchase or as a grant, a permit to emit a certain amount of pollution. It can either emit pollution up to that point or sell all or part of its allotment to other companies and clean up some of its own emissions. One consequence is that the government controls the overall allowable pollution in a certain region, but the market portions it out. As a result, environmental quality is optimized for the entire region rather than on a company-by-company or facility-by-facility basis. Although experiments with such market approaches actually began in the late 1970s, they became successfully institutionalized only with the Clean Air Act Amendment of 1990.

The record so far is very encouraging. Indeed, in the words of Daniel Dudek of the Environmental Defense Fund, the results have been "spectacular" in terms of demonstrating "the power of market forces to produce environment benefits"—as measured in "superior environmental performance, lower cost and a ramping back of otherwise intrusive relationships between regulators and business." Total emissions have been reduced much more rapidly, and at much lower cost than had been anticipated. "What other environmental program can show such dramatic performance in so short a time?" asked Dudek. This kind of approach—providing incentives and allowing choice—is also encouraging innovation in a way that overwritten, highly directive regulations cannot. Market-based systems have one other very promising characteristic: They have the potential to reduce the adversarial conflict between environmentalists and industry and, instead, provide a framework for collaborating on solutions. Can market-based systems work across borders? That will be tested by the attempts to create an international system to respond to global-climate-change concerns.

The "Rights Explosion"

Social regulation has also been mounting since the 1960s in what has been called the rights explosion. This is particularly evident in the expanding definitions of discrimination, which, it is argued, should be corrected through various requirements, tests, and penalties. In turn, all of these have increased. The most prominent rights initiative is affirmative action, the legacy of the civil rights movement, which now inflames opinion on both sides of a very bitter debate. To proponents, affirmative action is a method of correcting past wrongs, creating opportunities where they have been denied, and confronting the persistence of race and gender discrimination. Opponents argue that by submerging people into special-interest groups, the programs run counter to equality of opportunity, brand beneficiaries as inferior, prevent people from being judged on their merits, and depend upon controversial definitions of racism and sexism. Contention has increased as quotas and other methods devised to correct one fundamental problem—racial inequality—have been extended to a host of other issues and as new values are set against traditional meritocracy. The explosion of rights has bred a proliferation of rules and of agencies to administer them.

There are many other examples of the ways in which government is extending its regulation and control over the marketplace. The constraints in the processes of hiring and firing are a notable example. In hiring someone, an employer is proscribed from asking about such things as the age of the applicant, his or her marital or family or even health status, for any one of these might be considered a basis of discrimination. Yet critics maintain that all those are reasonable questions in order to get to know applicants and make a judgment about whether or not to hire them. It is also very risky for an employer to provide anything more than the most banal reference for a former employee. Companies are now advised to restrict references to the "former employee's job title and starting and ending dates of employment." Otherwise, they open themselves to being sued.

The direct impact of social-value regulation and legislation is much accentuated by the peculiar American phenomenon of "adversarial legalism"—lawsuits. This form of litigation has been described by Pietro Nivola, a senior fellow at the Brookings Institution, as not merely a "means of resolving personal disagreements" but also as "institutions of governance or social regulation." He explained: "A civil jury that levies millions in punitive damages against a maladroit business is addressing more than a private matter. Much like an injunctive order from the Consumer Product Safety Commission or the Equal Employment Opportunity Commission, the civil verdict supposedly serves the public purpose of deterring some perceived threat to society." An eighty-two-year-old woman sued McDonald's after she burned herself by spilling hot coffee bought from a drive-through line. The jury found that McDonald's was willfully negligent for serving coffee that was too hot and awarded her $2.9 million to send a message (the judgment was subsequently reduced). Universities have grown accustomed to expect lawsuits charging discrimination by professors who do not get tenure. Even corporate results provide a platform for litigation. A company that may have created hundreds of new jobs is vulnerable when it goes public. For if its share price falls because of a poor quarter, the company may well end up in the defendant's chair.

The drive to encourage litigation has been deliberate. The 1991 Civil Rights Act greatly stiffened penalties, promoted punitive damages, allowed claims for emotional injury, and increased attorneys' fees. All this was in line with the act's explicit purpose, in the words of Philip Howard, "to encourage private citizens to sue" because "the principle of antidiscrimination is as important as the principle that prohibits assaults, batteries and other intentional injuries to people." Thus, Congress envisions each employee as deputized to act as a "private attorney general to vindicate these precious rights."

At least one major objective of the new legislation is being achieved: Employment discrimination litigation is mushrooming. Indeed, the regulation/litigation system is expanding so fast that Federal District Judge Stanley Sporkin has warned that "the federal courts are becoming flooded with employment cases." He added, "We are becoming the personnel czars of virtually every one of this nation's public and private companies."

✕ *F U R T H E R   R E A D I N G*

Ackerman, Frank. *Reaganomics* (1982).

Allen, Charles F. *The Comeback Kid: The Life and Career of Bill Clinton* (1992).

Barnet, Richard J. *The Lean Years: Politics in the Age of Scarcity* (1980).

Berman, William. *America's Right Turn: From Nixon to Bush* (1994).

Blumenthal, Sidney, and Thomas Byrne Edsall, eds. *The Reagan Legacy* (1988).

Blumenthal, Sidney. *The Rise of the Counter-Establishment: From Conservative Ideology to Political Power* (1986).

Boyer, Paul, ed. *Reagan as President* (1990).

Broder, David S. *Changing of the Guard* (1980, 1981).

Cannon, Lou. *President Reagan: The Role of a Lifetime* (1991).

Carter, Jimmy. *Keeping Faith* (1982).

Dallek, Robert. *Ronald Reagan and the Politics of Symbolism* (1984).

D'Souza, Dinesh. *Ronald Reagan: How an Ordinary Man Became an Extraordinary Leader* (1997).

Duffy, Michael. *Marching in Place: The Status Quo Presidency of George Bush* (1992).

Edsall, Thomas Byrne, with Mary D. Edsall. *Chain Reaction: The Impact of Race, Rights, and Taxes on American Politics* (1991).

Ferguson, Thomas, and Joel Rogers. *Right Turn: The Decline of the Democrats and the Future of American Politics* (1986).

Ginsberg, Benjamin, and Martin Shefter. *Politics by Other Means* (1990, 1999).

Greenberg, Stanley B., and Theda Skocpol, eds. *The New Majority: Toward a Popular Progressive Politics* (1997).

Himmelstein, Jerome L. *To the Right: The Transformation of American Conservatism* (1990).

Hodgson, Godfrey. *The World Turned Right Side Up: A History of the Conservative Ascendancy in America* (1996).

Hoeveler, J. David Jr. *Watch on the Right: Conservative Intellectuals in the Reagan Era* (1991).

Isikoff, Michael. *Uncovering Clinton: A Reporter's Story* (1999).

Johnson, Haynes. *Sleepwalking Through History: America in the Reagan Years* (1991).

Jordan, Hamilton. *Crisis: The Last Year of the Carter Presidency* (1982).

Kaufman, Burton I. *The Presidency of Jame Earl Carter, Jr.* (1993).

Lash, Jonathan. *A Season of Spoils: The Story of the Reagan Administration's Attack on the Environment* (1984).

Lawrence, David G. *The Collapse of the Democratic Presidential Majority* (1998).

Levy, Frank. *The New Dollars and Dreams* (1999).

Lind, Michael. *The Next American Nation: The New Nationalism and the Fourth American Revolution* (1995).

Lowi, Theodore J., and Benjamin Ginsberg. *Embattled Democracy: Politics and Policy in the Clinton Era* (1997).

Mervin, David. *George Bush and the Guardianship Presidency* (1996).

Mills, Nicolaus. *The Triumph of Meanness: America's War Against Its Better Self* (1997).

Morris, Edmund. *Dutch: A Memoir of Ronald Reagan* (1999).

Parmet, Herbert S. *George Bush: The Life of a Lone Star Yankee* (1997).

Piven, Frances Fox, and Richard A. Cloward. *The Breaking of the American Social Compact* (1997).

Philips, Kevin. *The Politics of Rich and Poor: Wealth and the American Electorate in the Reagan Aftermath* (1990).

Ribuffo, Leo. *Right Center Left: Essays in American History* (1992).

Rosenstiel, Tom. *Strange Bedfellows: How Television and the Presidential Candidates Changed American Politics, 1992* (1993).

Sabato, Larry J., ed. *Toward the Millennium: The Elections of 1996* (1996).

Schmertz, Eric J., et al. *Ronald Reagan's America* (1997).

Sexton, Patricia Cayo. *The War on Labor and the Left* (1991).

Stefancic, Jean, Richard Delgado and Mark Tushnet. *No Mercy: How Conservative Think Tanks and Foundations Changed America's Social Agenda* (1997).

Stephanopoulos, George. *All Too Human: A Political Education* (1999).

Stockman, David A. *The Triumph of Politics* (1986).

Vogel, David. *Fluctuating Fortunes: The Political Power of Business in America* (1989).

Wier, Margaret, ed. *The Social Divide; Political Parties and the Future of Activist Government* (1998).

Wills, Garry. *Reagan's America: Innocents at Home* (1987).

Woodward, Bob. *The Choice: How Clinton Won* (1996).

C H A P T E R
13

The Empire Strikes Back: Ronald Reagan and the End of the Cold War

✕✕✕

In the wake of the U.S. experience in Vietnam, Richard Nixon and Jimmy Carter alike sought to engineer what some have called America's "retreat from empire"— a scaling back of the rampant globalism of the Kennedy and Johnson years and the beginnings of détente with the Soviet Union and China. In contrast, Ronald Reagan campaigned for the White House on a platform that promised to restore American leadership in world affairs. Reagan and his supporters initially denounced the Soviet Union in vintage Cold War terms as an "evil empire" and pledged to rebuild U.S. military strength. Under Reagan the United States embarked on a massive military buildup, first in more or less conventional weapons and then through "Star Wars," the highly controversial Strategic Defense Initiative (SDI), which proposed to defend the United States with a high-tech "umbrella" of costly and sophisticated electronic weapons. The United States also pursued a new interventionism, especially in the Caribbean, where the Reagan administration invaded the tiny island of Grenada and launched a "covert" campaign to overthrow the left-wing Sandinista government of Nicaragua. Reagan's revival of Cold War patriotism touched a popular nerve, perhaps best symbolized by the flag waving and chants of "We're Number One" by Americans at the 1984 summer Olympic Games in Los Angeles. By 1986, nevertheless, the administration was in deep trouble. Massive military spending, coupled with reduced taxes, sent the nation's indebtedness skyrocketing. The Iran-contra scandal, meanwhile, revealed that the president and his top advisers were clearly implicated in an illegal attempt to trade arms for hostages and divert the proceeds to the U.S.-sponsored "contras"—and anti-Sandinista guerrilla army—in Nicaragua.

The administration abruptly changed course during the final two years of Reagan's term. The president abandoned Cold War confrontation for a new pragmatism that included the Intermediate-range Nuclear Forces (INF) Treaty with the Russians and progress toward a more comprehensive reduction of all nuclear weapons. Much of this change owed to developments that neither Reagan nor most Americans anticipated—the growing economic paralysis of the Soviet

*Union, the rapid dismantling of its empire in Eastern Europe, and the rise of
Mikhail Gorbachev and a new leadership dedicated to sweeping political and economic reforms. Some saw in these developments a vindication of Reagan's policies.
The United States, they claimed, had won the Cold War. Others viewed the shift as
a happy coincidence. Ronald Reagan, the "Teflon President," had lucked out again.
Still others saw in these developments an end not only to the Cold War but to an
entire era in world history.*

*Yet if the Cold War had ended, the many conflicting interests and impulses on
which it had for a time imposed an order of a sort remained and in fact began to
reassert themselves. In the Middle East, the euphoria of the new post-Cold War era
was quickly shattered by the Iraqi invasion of Kuwait in August 1990 and by the
Persian Gulf War in which U.S.-led forces easily crushed the Iraqis. Although
President George Bush proclaimed his commitment to the establishment of a new
world order, neither the character of that new order nor America's role in it were at
all clear. Indeed, even as he called for the use of force to defend "our jobs, our way
of life, our own freedom, and the freedom of friendly countries around the world,"
liberals and conservatives alike scrambled to reconstruct their understanding of
American foreign policy.*

₩ D O C U M E N T S

In a June 8, 1982, speech to the British House of Commons, excerpts from which are
reprinted in Document 1, President Reagan invoked the image of the U.S.S.R. as a
threatening "evil" empire and called for expanded U.S. military power. Document 2, a
graph drawn from public sources, traces the rise in military spending during the Reagan
administration. Document 3, excerpted from the 1987 report of the congressional
committees investigating the Iran-contra affair, describes the covert and illegal activities
of Oliver North and other White House officials who sought to sell arms to Iran in return
for money and the release of hostages, and then to divert the proceeds to support the
U.S.-backed contra rebels in Nicaragua. In a December 1988 speech to the United
Nations, Soviet president Mikhail Gorbachev outlined a new and peaceful course for
relations between the Soviet Union and the United States (Document 4). In Document 5,
the editors of the *New York Times,* summarizing nearly two months of discussion and
debate on the paper's op-ed page, announced on April 2, 1989, that the Cold War was
over. As the Cold War ended, however, debate focused increasingly on the future of the
postwar era. In Document 6, excerpted from a joint address to Congress following
the Iraqi invasion of Kuwait, President George Bush announced his administration's
goal of establishing a new world order.

1. President Ronald Reagan Denounces the
Soviet Union as an "Evil" Empire, 1982

We're approaching the end of a bloody century plagued by a terrible political
invention—totalitarianism. Optimism comes less easily today, not because democracy is less vigorous, but because democracy's enemies have refined their instruments
of repression. Yet optimism is in order because day by day democracy is proving

Public Papers of the Presidents of the United States: Ronald Reagan, 1981–89 (Washington: GPO,
1984), 359–362.

itself to be a not at all fragile flower. From Stettin on the Baltic to Varna on the Black Sea, the regimes planted by totalitarianism have had more than thirty years to establish their legitimacy. But none—not one regime—has yet been able to risk free elections. Regimes planted by bayonets do not take root.

The strength of the Solidarity movement in Poland demonstrates the truth told in an underground joke in the Soviet Union. It is that the Soviet Union would remain a one-party nation even if an opposition party were permitted because everyone would join the opposition party. . . .

Historians looking back at our time will note the consistent restraint and peaceful intentions of the West. They will note that it was the democracies who refused to use the threat of their nuclear monopoly in the forties and early fifties for territorial or imperial gain. Had that nuclear monopoly been in the hands of the Communist world, the map of Europe—indeed, the world—would look very different today. And certainly they will note it was not the democracies that invaded Afghanistan or suppressed Polish Solidarity or used chemical and toxic warfare in Afghanistan and Southeast Asia.

If history teaches anything, it teaches self-delusion in the face of unpleasant facts is folly. We see around us today the marks of our terrible dilemma—predictions of doomsday, antinuclear demonstrations, an arms race in which the West must, for its own protection, be an unwilling participant. At the same time we see totalitarian forces in the world who seek subversion and conflict around the globe to further their barbarous assault on the human spirit. What, then, is our course? Must civilization perish in a hail of fiery atoms? Must freedom wither in a quiet, deadening accommodation with totalitarian evil?

Sir Winston Churchill refused to accept the inevitability of war or even that it was imminent. He said, "I do not believe that Soviet Russia desires war. What they desire is the fruits of war and the indefinite expansion of their power and doctrines. But what we have to consider here today while time remains is the permanent prevention of war and the establishment of conditions of freedom and democracy as rapidly as possible in all countries."

Well, this is precisely our mission today: to preserve freedom as well as peace. It may not be easy to see; but I believe we live now at a turning point.

In an ironic sense Karl Marx was right. We are witnessing today a great revolutionary crisis, a crisis where the demands of the economic order are conflicting directly with those of the political order. But the crisis is happening not in the free, non-Marxist West but in the home of Marxism-Leninism, the Soviet Union. It is the Soviet Union that runs against the tide of history by denying human freedom and human dignity to its citizens. It also is in deep economic difficulty. The rate of growth in the national product has been steadily declining since the fifties and is less than half of what it was then.

The dimensions of this failure are astounding: a country which employs one-fifth of its population in agriculture is unable to feed its own people. Were it not for the private sector, the tiny private sector tolerated in Soviet agriculture, the country might be on the brink of famine. These private plots occupy a bare 3 percent of the arable land but account for nearly one-quarter of Soviet farm output and nearly one-third of meat products and vegetables. Overcentralized, with little or no incentives, year after year the Soviet system pours its best resources into the making of instruments of destruction. The constant shrinkage of economic growth combined with the growth of military production is putting a heavy strain on the Soviet people. What we see here is a political structure that no longer corresponds to its economic base, a society where productive forces are hampered by political ones.

The decay of the Soviet experiment should come as no surprise to us. Wherever the comparisons have been made between free and closed societies—West Germany and East Germany, Austria and Czechoslovakia, Malaysia and Vietnam—it is the democratic countries that are prosperous and responsive to the needs of their people. And one of the simple but overwhelming facts of our time is this: of all the millions of refugees we've seen in the modern world, their flight is always away from, not toward the Communist world. Today on the NATO line, our military forces face east to prevent a possible invasion. On the other side of the line, the Soviet forces also face east to prevent their people from leaving.

The hard evidence of totalitarian rule has caused in mankind an uprising of the intellect and will. Whether it is the growth of the new schools of economics in America or England or the appearance of the so-called new philosophers in France, there is one unifying thread running through the intellectual work of these groups—rejection of the arbitrary power of the state, the refusal to subordinate the rights of the individual to the superstate, the realization that collectivism stifles all the best human impulses. . . .

Chairman Brezhnev repeatedly has stressed that the competition of ideas and systems must continue and that this is entirely consistent with [a] relaxation of tensions and peace.

Well, we ask only that these systems begin by living up to their own constitutions, abiding by their own laws, and complying with the international obligations they have undertaken. We ask only for a process, a direction, a basic code of decency, not for an instant transformation.

We cannot ignore the fact that even without our encouragement there has been and will continue to be repeated explosion against repression and dictatorships. The Soviet Union itself is not immune to this reality. Any system is inherently unstable that has no peaceful means to legitimize its leaders. In such cases, the very repressiveness of the state ultimately drives people to resist it, if necessary, by force.

While we must be cautious about forcing the pace of change, we must not hesitate to declare our ultimate objectives and to take concrete actions to move toward them. We must be staunch in our conviction that freedom is not the sole prerogative of a lucky few but the inalienable and universal right of all human beings. So states the United Nations Universal Declaration of Human Rights, which, among other things, guarantees free elections.

The objective I propose is quite simple to state: to foster the infrastructure of democracy, the system of a free press, unions, political parties, universities, which allows a people to choose their own way to develop their own culture, to reconcile their own differences through peaceful means.

This is not cultural imperialism; it is providing the means for genuine self-determination and protection for diversity. Democracy already flourishes in countries with very different cultures and historical experiences. It would be cultural condescension, or worse, to say that any people prefer dictatorship to democracy. Who would voluntarily choose not to have the right to vote, decide to purchase government propaganda handouts instead of independent newspapers, prefer government to worker-controlled unions, opt for land to be owned by the state instead of those who till it, want government repression of religious liberty, a single political party instead of a free choice, a rigid cultural orthodoxy instead of democratic tolerance and diversity?

Since 1917 the Soviet Union has given covert political training and assistance to Marxist-Leninists in many countries. Of course, it also has promoted the use of violence and subversion by these same forces. Over the past several decades, West European and other social democrats, Christian democrats, and leaders have offered open assistance to fraternal, political, and social institutions to bring about peaceful and democratic progress. Appropriately, for a vigorous new democracy, the Federal Republic of Germany's political foundations have become a major force in this effort.

We in America now intend to take additional steps, as many of our allies have already done, toward realizing this same goal. The chairmen and other leaders of the national Republican and Democratic party organizations are initiating a study with the bipartisan American Political Foundation to determine how the United States can best contribute as a nation to the global campaign for democracy now gathering force. They will have the cooperation of congressional leaders of both parties, along with representatives of business, labor, and other major institutions in our society. I look forward to receiving their recommendations and to working with these institutions and the Congress in the common task of strengthening democracy throughout the world.

It is time that we committed ourselves as a nation—in both the public and private sectors—to assisting democratic development. . . .

What I am describing now is a plan and a hope for the long term—the march of freedom and democracy which will leave Marxism-Leninism on the ash heap of history as it has left other tyrannies which stifle the freedom and muzzle the self-expression of the people. And that's why we must continue our efforts to strengthen NATO even as we move forward with our zero-option initiative in the negotiations on intermediate-range forces and our proposal for a one-third reduction in strategic ballistic missile warheads.

Our military strength is a prerequisite to peace, but let it be clear we maintain this strength in the hope it will never be used, for the ultimate determinant in the struggle that's now going on in the world will not be bombs and rockets but a test of wills and ideas, a trial of spiritual resolve, the values we hold, the beliefs we cherish, the ideals to which we are dedicated.

The British people know that, given strong leadership, time, and a little bit of hope, the forces of good ultimately rally and triumph over evil. Here among you is the cradle of self-government, the Mother of Parliaments. Here is the enduring greatness of the British contribution to mankind, the great civilized ideas: individual liberty, representative government, and the rule of law under God.

I've often wondered about the shyness of some of us in the West about standing for these ideals that have done so much to ease the plight of man and the hardships of our imperfect world. This reluctance to use those vast resources at our command reminds me of the elderly lady whose home was bombed in the blitz. As the rescuers moved about, they found a bottle of brandy she'd stored behind the staircase, which was all that was left standing. And since she was barely conscious, one of the workers pulled the cork to give her a taste of it. She came around immediately and said, "Here now—there now, put it back. That's for emergencies."

Well, the emergency is upon us. Let us be shy no longer. Let us go to our strength. Let us offer hope. Let us tell the world that a new age is not only possible but probable.

During the dark days of the Second World War, when this island was incandescent with courage, Winston Churchill exclaimed about Britain's adversaries, "What kind of people do they think we are?" Well, Britain's adversaries found out what extraordinary people the British are. But all the democracies paid a terrible price for allowing the dictators to underestimate us. We dare not make that mistake again. So, let us ask ourselves, "What kind of people do we think we are?" And let us answer, "Free people, worthy of freedom and determined not only to remain so but to help others gain their freedom as well."

Sir Winston led his people to great victory in war and then lost an election just as the fruits of victory were about to be enjoyed. But he left office honorably and, as it turned out, temporarily, knowing that the liberty of his people was more important than the fate of any single leader. History recalls his greatness in ways no dictator will ever know. And he left us a message of hope for the future, as timely now as when he first uttered it, as opposition leader in the Commons nearly twenty-seven years ago, when he said, "When we look back on all the perils through which we have passed and at the mighty foes that we have laid low and all the dark and deadly designs that we have frustrated, why should we fear for our future? We have," he said, "come safely through the worst."

Well, the task I've set forth will long outlive our own generation. But together, we too have come through the worst. Let us now begin a major effort to secure the best—a crusade for freedom that will engage the faith and fortitude of the next generation. For the sake of peace and justice, let us move toward a world in which all people are at last free to determine their own destiny.

2. U.S. Military Spending, 1980–1990: A Graphic

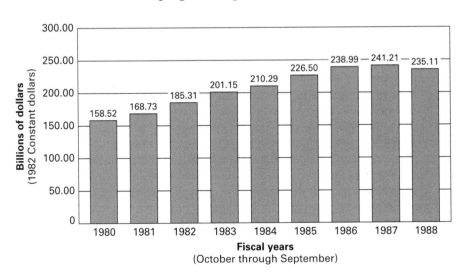

Statistics compiled by David Murphy, University of Maryland, College Park, from government statistics.

3. A Congressional Committee
Reports on "Irangate," 1987

The full story of the Iran-Contra Affair is complicated, and, for this Nation, profoundly sad. In the narrative portion of this Report, the Committees present a comprehensive account of the facts, based on 10 months of investigation, including 11 weeks of hearings.

But the facts alone do not explain how or why the events occurred. In this Executive Summary, the Committees focus on the key issues and offer their conclusions. Minority, supplemental, and additional views are printed in Section II and Section III.

Summary of the Facts

The Iran-Contra Affair had its origin in two unrelated revolutions in Iran and Nicaragua.

In Nicaragua, the long-time President, General Anastasio Somoza Debayle, was overthrown in 1979 and replaced by a Government controlled by Sandinista leftists.

In Iran, the pro-Western Government of the Shah Mohammed Riza Pahlavi was overthrown in 1979 by Islamic fundamentalists led by the Ayatollah Khomeini. The Khomeini Government, stridently anti-American, became a supporter of terrorism against American citizens.

United States policy following the revolution in Nicaragua was to encourage the Sandinista Government to keep its pledges of pluralism and democracy. However, the Sandinista regime became increasingly anti-American and autocratic; began to aid a leftist insurgency in El Salvador; and turned toward Cuba and the Soviet Union for political, military, and economic assistance. By December 1981, the United States had begun supporting the Nicaraguan Contras, armed opponents of the Sandinista regime.

The Central Intelligence Agency (CIA) was the U.S. Government agency that assisted the Contras. In accordance with Presidential decisions, known as Findings, and with funds appropriated by Congress, the CIA armed, clothed, fed, and supervised the Contras. Despite this assistance, the Contras failed to win widespread popular support or military victories within Nicaragua.

Although the President continued to favor support of the Contras, opinion polls indicated that a majority of the public was not supportive. Opponents of the Administration's policy feared that U.S. involvement with the Contras would embroil the United States in another Vietnam. Supporters of the policy feared that, without U.S. support for the Contras, the Soviets would gain a dangerous toehold in Central America.

Congress prohibited Contra aid for the purpose of overthrowing the Sandinista Government in fiscal year 1983, and limited all aid to the Contras in fiscal year 1984 to $24 million. Following disclosure in March and April 1984 that the CIA

U.S. Congress, *Report of the Congressional Committees Investigating the Iran-Contra Affair* (Washington, D.C.: GPO, 1987), 3–11.

had a role in connection with the mining of the Nicaraguan harbors without adequate notification to Congress, public criticism mounted and the Administration's Contra policy lost much of its support within Congress. After further vigorous debate, Congress exercised its Constitutional power over appropriations and cut off all funds for the Contras' military and paramilitary operations. The statutory provision cutting off funds, known as the Boland Amendment, was part of a fiscal year 1985 omnibus appropriations bill, and was signed into law by the President on October 12, 1984.

Still, the President felt strongly about the Contras, and he ordered his staff, in the words of his National Security Adviser, to find a way to keep the Contras "body and soul together." Thus began the story of how the staff of a White House advisory body, the NSC, became an operational entity that secretly ran the Contra assistance effort, and later the Iran initiative. The action officer placed in charge of both operations was Lt. Col. Oliver L. North.

Denied funding by Congress, the President turned to third countries and private sources. Between June 1984 and the beginning of 1986, the President, his National Security Adviser, and the NSC staff secretly raised $34 million for the Contras from other countries. An additional $2.7 million was provided for the Contras during 1985 and 1986 from private contributors, who were addressed by North and occasionally granted photo opportunities with the President. In the middle of this period, Assistant Secretary of State A. Langhorne Motley—from whom these contributions were concealed—gave his assurance to Congress that the Administration was not "soliciting and/or encouraging third countries" to give funds to the Contras because, as he conceded, the Boland Amendment prohibited such solicitation.

The first contributions were sent by the donors to bank accounts controlled and used by the Contras. However, in July 1985, North took control of the funds and—with the support of two National Security Advisers (Robert McFarlane and John Poindexter) and, according to North, [CIA] Director [William] Casey—used those funds to run the covert operation to support the Contras.

At the suggestion of Director Casey, North recruited Richard V. Secord, a retired Air Force Major General with experience in special operations. Secord set up Swiss bank accounts, and North steered future donations into these accounts. Using these funds, and funds later generated by the Iran arms sales, Secord and his associate, Albert Hakim, created what they called "the Enterprise," a private organization designed to engage in covert activities on behalf of the United States.

The Enterprise, functioning largely at North's direction, had its own airplanes, pilots, airfield, operatives, ship, secure communications devices, and secret Swiss bank accounts. For 16 months, it served as the secret arm of the NSC staff, carrying out with private and non-appropriated money, and without the accountability or restrictions imposed by law on the CIA, a covert Contra aid program that Congress thought it had prohibited.

Although the CIA and other agencies involved in intelligence activities knew that the Boland Amendment barred their involvement in covert support for the Contras, North's Contra support operation received logistical and tactical support from various personnel in the CIA and other agencies. Certain CIA personnel in Central America gave their assistance. The U.S. Ambassador in Costa Rica, Lewis Tambs, provided his active assistance. North also enlisted the aid of Defense

Department personnel in Central America, and obtained secure communications equipment from the National Security Agency. The Assistant Secretary of State with responsibility for the region, Elliott Abrams, professed ignorance of this support. He later stated that he had been "careful not to ask North lots of questions."

By Executive Order and National Security Decision Directive issued by President Reagan, all covert operations must be approved by the President personally and in writing. By statute, Congress must be notified about each covert action. The funds used for such actions, like all government funds, must be strictly accounted for.

The covert action directed by North, however, was not approved by the President in writing. Congress was not notified about it. And the funds to support it were never accounted for. In short, the operation functioned without any of the accountability required of Government activities. It was an evasion of the Constitution's most basic check on Executive action—the power of the Congress to grant or deny funding for Government programs.

Moreover, the covert action to support the Contras was concealed from Congress and the public. When the press reported in the summer of 1985 that the NSC staff was engaged in raising money and furnishing military support to the Contras, the President assured the public that the law was being followed. His National Security Adviser, Robert C. McFarlane, assured Committees of Congress, both in person and in writing, that the NSC staff was obeying both the spirit and the letter of the law, and was neither soliciting money nor coordinating military support for the Contras. . . .

The NSC staff was [thus] already engaged in covert operations through Secord when, in the summer of 1985, the Government of Israel proposed that missiles be sold to Iran in return for the release of seven American hostages held in Lebanon and the prospect of improved relations with Iran. The Secretaries of State and Defense repeatedly opposed such sales to a government designated by the United States as a supporter of international terrorism. They called it a straight arms-for-hostages deal that was contrary to U.S. public policy. They also argued that these sales would violate the Arms Export Control Act, as well as the U.S. arms embargo against Iran. The embargo had been imposed after the taking of hostages at the U.S. Embassy in Tehran on November 4, 1979, and was continued because of the Iran-Iraq war.

Nevertheless, in the summer of 1985 the President authorized Israel to proceed with the sales. The NSC staff conducting the Contra covert action also took operational control of implementing the President's decision on arms sales to Iran. The President did not sign a Finding for this covert operation, nor did he notify the Congress.

Israel shipped 504 TOW anti-tank missiles to Iran in August and September 1985. Although the Iranians had promised to release most of the American hostages in return, only one, Reverend Benjamin Weir, was freed. The President persisted. In November, he authorized Israel to ship 80 HAWK anti-aircraft missiles in return for all the hostages, with a promise of prompt replenishment by the United States, and 40 more HAWKs to be sent directly by the United States to Iran. Eighteen HAWK missiles were actually shipped from Israel in November 1985, but no hostages were released.

In early December 1985, the President signed a retroactive Finding purporting to authorize the November HAWK transaction. That Finding contained no reference to improved relations with Iran. It was a straight arms-for-hostages Finding. National Security Adviser Poindexter destroyed this Finding a year later because, he testified, its disclosure would have been politically embarrassing to the President.

The November HAWK transaction had additional significance. The Enterprise received a $1 million advance from the Israelis. North and Secord testified this was for transportation expenses in connection with the 120 HAWK missiles. Since only 18 missiles were shipped, the Enterprise was left with more than $800,000 in spare cash. North directed the Enterprise to retain the money and spend it for the Contras. The "diversion" had begun.

North realized that the sale of missiles to Iran could be used to support the Contras. He told Israeli Defense Ministry officials on December 6, 1985, one day after the President signed the Finding, that he planned to generate profits on future arms sales for activities in Nicaragua. . . .

In February 1986, the United States, acting through the Enterprise, sold 1,000 TOW's to the Iranians. The U.S. also provided the Iranians with military intelligence about Iraq. All of the remaining American hostages were supposed to be released upon Iran's receipt of the first 500 TOW's. None was. But the transaction was productive in one respect. The difference between what the Enterprise paid the United States for the missiles and what it received from Iran was more than $6 million. North directed part of this profit for the Contras and for other covert operations. Poindexter testified that he authorized this "diversion."

The diversion, for the Contras and other covert activities, was not an isolated act by the NSC staff. Poindexter saw it as "implementing" the President's secret policy that had been in effect since 1984 of using nonappropriated funds following passage of the Boland Amendment.

According to North, CIA Director Casey saw the "diversion" as part of a more grandiose plan to use the Enterprise as a "stand-alone," "off-the-shelf," covert capacity that would act throughout the world while evading Congressional review. To Casey, Poindexter, and North, the diversion was an integral part of selling arms to Iran and just one of the intended uses of the proceeds.

In May 1986, the President again tried to sell weapons to get the hostages back. This time, the President agreed to ship parts for HAWK missiles but only on condition that all the American hostages in Lebanon be released first. A mission headed by Robert McFarlane, the former National Security Adviser, traveled to Tehran with the first installment of the HAWK parts. When the mission arrived, McFarlane learned that the Iranians claimed they had never promised to do anything more than try to obtain the hostages' release. The trip ended amid misunderstanding and failure, although the first installment of HAWK parts was delivered.

The Enterprise was paid, however, for all of the HAWK parts, and realized more than an $8 million profit, part of which was applied, at North's direction, to the Contras. Another portion of the profit was used by North for other covert operations, including the operation of a ship for a secret mission. The idea of an off-the-shelf, stand-alone covert capacity had become operational. . . .

The sale of arms to Iran was a "significant anticipated intelligence activity." By law, such an activity must be reported to Congress "in a timely fashion" pursuant to Section 501 of the National Security Act. If the proposal to sell arms to Iran had been reported, the Senate and House Intelligence Committees would likely have joined Secretaries Shultz and Weinberger in objecting to this initiative. But Poindexter recommended—and the President decided—not to report the Iran initiative to Congress.

Indeed, the Administration went to considerable lengths to avoid notifying Congress. The CIA General Counsel wrote on January 15, 1986, "the key issue in this entire matter revolves around whether or not there will be reports made to Congress." Shortly thereafter, the transaction was restructured to avoid the pre-shipment reporting requirements of the Arms Export Control Act, and place it within the more limited reporting requirements of the National Security Act. But even these reporting requirements were ignored. The President failed to notify the group of eight (the leaders of each party in the House and Senate, and the Chairmen and Ranking Minority Members of the Intelligence Committees) specified by law for unusually sensitive operations.

After the disclosure of the Iran arms sales on November 3, 1986, the American public was still not told the facts. The President sought to avoid any commitment on the ground that it might jeopardize the chance of securing the remaining hostages' release. But it was impossible to remain silent, and inaccurate statements followed. . . .

While the President was denying any illegality, his subordinates were engaging in a coverup. Several of his advisers had expressed concern that the 1985 sales violated the Arms Export Control Act, and a "cover story" had been agreed on if these arms sales were ever exposed. After North had three conversations on November 18, 1986, about the legal problems with the 1985 Israeli shipments, he, Poindexter, Casey, and McFarlane all told conforming false stories about the U.S. involvement in these shipments. . . .

In light of the destruction of material evidence by Poindexter and North and the death of Casey, all of the facts may never be known. The Committees cannot even be sure whether they heard the whole truth. . . . But enough is clear to demonstrate beyond doubt that fundamental processes of governance were disregarded and the rule of law was subverted.

The common ingredients of the Iran and Contra policies were secrecy, deception, and disdain for the law. A small group of senior officials believed that they alone knew what was right. They viewed knowledge of their actions by others in the Government as a threat to their objectives. They told neither the Secretary of State, the Congress, nor the American people of their actions. When exposure was threatened, they destroyed official documents and lied to Cabinet officials, to the public, and to elected representatives in Congress. They testified that they even withheld key facts from the President.

The United States Constitution specifies the process by which laws and policy are to be made and executed. Constitutional process is the essence of our democracy and our democratic form of Government is the basis of our strength. Time and again we have learned that a flawed process leads to bad results, and that a lawless process leads to worse.

4. Soviet Leader Mikhail Gorbachev Charts a New Direction for the U.S.S.R., 1988

The Soviet Union's role in world affairs is well known. In view of the revolutionary restructuring that is taking place in our country—perestroika—which has a tremendous potential for promoting peace and international cooperation, we are particularly interested today in being understood correctly. . . .

What will humanity be like as it enters the 21st century? Thoughts about this already very near future are engaging people's minds. While we look forward to the future with the anticipation of change for the better, we also view it with alarm.

Today, the world is a very different place from what it was at the beginning of this century, and even in the middle of it. And the world and all of its components keep changing.

The emergence of nuclear weapons was a tragic way of stressing the fundamental nature of these changes. Being the material symbol and the bearer of the ultimate military force, nuclear weapons at the same time laid bare the absolute limits to this force.

Humankind is faced with the problem of survival, of self-protection, in all its magnitude.

Profound social changes are taking place.

In the East and in the South, in the West and in the North, hundreds of millions of people, new nations and states, new public movements and ideologies have advanced to the foreground of history.

The striving for independence, democracy, and social justice manifests itself, in all its diversity and with all its contradictions, in broad and frequently turbulent popular movements. The idea of democratizing the entire world order has grown into a powerful social and political force.

At the same time, the revolution in science and technology has turned economic, food, energy, ecological, information, and demographic problems, which only recently were of a national or regional character, into global problems.

The newest techniques of communications, mass information, and transport have made the world more visible and more tangible to everyone. International communication is easier now than ever before.

Nowadays, it is virtually impossible for any society to be "closed". That is why we need a radical revision of the views on the totality of problems of international cooperation, which is the most essential component of universal security.

The world economy is becoming a single entity, outside of which no state can develop normally, regardless of its social system or economic level.

All this calls for creating an altogether new mechanism for the functioning of the world economy, a new structure of the international division of labour.

World economic growth, however, is revealing the contradictions of the traditional type of industrial development and its limitations. The expansion and deepening of industrialization is leading to an ecological catastrophe.

Mikhail Gorbachev, "U.S.S.R. Arms Reduction: Rivalry into Sensible Competition," *Vital Speeches of the Day* vol. 54 (December 7, 1988), 229–236.

But there are many countries with insufficiently developed industry and some that are not yet industrialized. Whether these countries will follow the old technological patterns in their economic development or be able to join the search for ecologically clean industries is one of the biggest problems.

Another problem is the growing gap between the industrialized nations and most of the developing countries, which is presenting an increasingly serious threat on a global scale.

All these factors make it necessary to look for a fundamentally new type of industrial progress that would be in accordance with the interests of all peoples and states. . . .

In thinking all this over, it becomes clear that we have to look for ways together to improve the international situation, to build a new world—that is, if we are going to take into consideration the lessons of the past, the realities of the present, and the objective logic of world development.

If this is really true, it would be worthwhile to reach an understanding on the basic and genuinely universal principles of this search, and the prerequisites for it.

It is evident, in particular, that force or the threat of force neither can nor should be instruments of foreign policy. This mainly refers to nuclear arsenals, but not to them alone. All of us, and first of all the strongest of us, have to practice self-restraint and renounce the use of force in the international arena. . . .

5. The *New York Times* Announces the End of the Cold War, 1989

The cold war of poisonous Soviet-American feelings, of domestic political hysteria, of events enlarged and distorted by East-West confrontation, of almost perpetual diplomatic deadlock is over.

The we-they world that emerged after 1945 is giving way to the more traditional struggles of great powers. That contest is more manageable. It permits serious negotiations. It creates new possibilities—for cooperation in combating terrorism, the spread of chemical weapons, and common threats to the environment, and for shaping a less violent world.

True, Europe remains torn in two; but the place where four decades of hostility began is mending and changing in complicated patterns. True, two enormous military machines still face each other around the world; but both sides are searching for ways to reduce the burdens and risks. Values continue to clash, but less profoundly as Soviet citizens start to partake in freedoms.

The experts who contributed to a two-month series on the Op-Ed page called "Is the Cold War Over?" agreed, with variations in emphasis and definition, that Soviet-American relations are entering a new era. They differed over whether Mikhail Gorbachev can last and whether his policies can outlast him, and over how much the West can or should do to help him and what to ask in return. But these questions are the stuff of genuine policy debate, not grist for old ideological diatribes.

In his four years of power, what has Mikhail Gorbachev done to bring about this reconsideration of the cold war?

A great deal, as Jeremy Stone of the Federation of American Sciences rightly pointed out. Mr. Gorbachev has pushed Yasir Arafat toward renouncing terrorism and accepting Israel, supported political settlements in Angola and Cambodia, pulled out Soviet troops from Afghanistan, agreed to vastly disproportionate cuts in medium-range missiles, and pledged significant unilateral reductions in Soviet forces in Central Europe.

At home, Mr. Stone said properly, the Soviet leader is introducing economic decentralization, allowing Soviet nationalities to assert their separate identities, encouraging free speech, and experimenting with elections. These measures give hope for a more open Soviet society and Government. And, as Graham Allison of Harvard's Kennedy School pointed out, this has been the very goal of America's containment policy.

But what if Mr. Gorbachev is ousted? Couldn't his successors readily reverse his actions?

Frank Carlucci argued that it's too early to foretell Mr. Gorbachev's fate or judge whether he or his successors might not simply change policies. The former Defense Secretary argued that Soviet policy is in a transitional phase.

Dimitri Simes of the Carnegie Endowment for International Peace, on the other hand, convincingly made the case that the changes occurring in the Soviet Union are of a more fundamental nature. Whoever leads the Soviet Union, he argued, would have little choice but to respond to Moscow's current economic and political weaknesses and follow the Gorbachev path.

Mr. Simes rightly argued that the debate in the Soviet Union revolves around the scope and pace of change, not the need for change. And there is little evidence that Mr. Gorbachev's foreign and military policies are under attack. Moscow simply does not have the resources for costly global challenges.

If the Soviet Union is in such bad shape, why not squeeze hard for concessions?

William Luers, a former U.S. diplomat, offered one reason. He warned against humiliating Mr. Gorbachev in ways that would unite a proud nation against the West. Ed Hewitt of the Brookings Institution provided another: Soviet leaders still have sufficient economic strength and foreign policy options to make life easier or harder for the West.

These cautions have to be kept in mind. But the West should not shy away from driving hard bargains. That can be done, as Ronald Reagan demonstrated, without destroying relations.

What should Western policy be?

Zbigniew Brzezinski correctly argued that the West needs a strategy to deal with "the gravity of the challenge and the magnitude of the opportunity." But the West would tie itself in knots if it followed his advice to "insist that any substantial assistance be reciprocated by reforms that institutionalize economic and political pluralism."

On the contrary, the West cannot manage Soviet reforms any more than it can "save" Mr. Gorbachev. It can reinforce and encourage reforms when Western interests are also at stake—by providing credits and technology on a modest and safe scale and by easing restrictions on trade. The point is for the West to rid itself of self-made restraints on expanding economic relations so that decisions can be made on a case-by-base basis.

The prospect of such economic openings and the diminishing Soviet threat are likely to give freer play to conflicts among Western industrialized powers, according to Edward Luttwak of the Center for Strategic and International Studies. He was exactly right in urging Western leaders to "act now to construct a new system of economic cooperation that would stand on its own and not lean on the imperatives of resisting" Moscow.

No one seems to have a good answer about the division of Europe, always the most dangerous East-West question. Michael Mandelbaum of the Council on Foreign Relations offered as good a prescription as anyone. He looked toward superpower talks to bring about sovereign nations in Eastern Europe and special arrangements for the two Germanys.

The Bush Administration seems less attentive to these issues and more preoccupied with Mr. Gorbachev's seizing headlines worldwide. It would do better to think of him as part of the solution, not the problem, as Richard Ullman of Princeton University counseled. "Who takes the initiative," he wrote, "matters less than the result."

The Administration now nears the completion of its East-West policy review. Hints dribble out about senior officials worrying that Mr. Reagan was too friendly with Mr. Gorbachev and too eager for arms control. That's self-defeating talk. The treaty eliminating medium-range missiles in Europe represents a substantial victory for the West. Similarly, Mr. Bush and the country would gain by early completion of a treaty to cut intercontinental-range missiles and bombers.

None of the contributors recommended cosmic disarmament agreements, and Mr. Bush would be right to avoid them. But he would be flat wrong not to exploit Moscow's willingness to compromise on cutting troops in Europe and otherwise reduce the costs and risks of security.

It would also be unfortunate if the Bush team worried too much about its right flank and tried to prove that it can out-tough Mr. Reagan. That would drain them of the imagination and boldness necessary to go beyond the cold war. Presidents Bush and Gorbachev have the opportunity of the century to refocus energies and resources from sterile conflicts onto common threats to mankind.

6. President George Bush Proclaims a New World Order, 1990

We gather tonight, witness to events in the Persian Gulf as significant as they are tragic. In the early morning hours of August 2nd, following negotiations and promises by Iraq's dictator Saddam Hussein not to use force, a powerful Iraqi army invaded its trusting and much weaker neighbor, Kuwait. Within 3 days, 120,000 Iraqi troops with 850 tanks had poured into Kuwait and moved south to threaten Saudi Arabia. It was then that I decided to check that aggression.

"Address to Congress on Persian Gulf Crisis," 11 September, 1990, *Public Papers of the Presidents of the United States: George Bush, 1990* (Washington, D.C.: GPO, 1991), Book II, 1218–1222.

At this moment, our brave servicemen and women stand watch in that distant desert and on distant seas, side-by-side with the forces of more than 20 other nations.

Tonight, I want to talk to you about what's at stake—what we must do together to defend civilized values around the world and maintain our economic strength at home.

The Objectives and Goals

Our objectives in the Persian Gulf are clear; our goals defined and familiar.

- Iraq must withdraw from Kuwait completely, immediately, and without condition.
- Kuwait's legitimate government must be restored.
- The security and stability of the Persian Gulf must be assured.
- American citizens abroad must be protected.

These goals are not ours alone. They have been endorsed by the UN Security Council five times in as many weeks. Most countries share our concern for principle, and many have a stake in the stability of the Persian Gulf. This is not, as Saddam Hussein would have it, the United States against Iraq. It is Iraq against the world.

We stand today at a unique and extraordinary moment. The crisis in the Persian Gulf, as grave as it is, also offers a rare opportunity to move toward a historic period of cooperation. Out of these troubled times, our fifth objective—a new world order—can emerge; a new era—freer from the threat of terror, stronger in the pursuit of justice, and more secure in the quest for peace, an era in which the nations of the world, East and West, North and South, can prosper and live in harmony.

A hundred generations have searched for this elusive path to peace, while a thousand wars raged across the span of human endeavor. Today, that new world is struggling to be born, a world quite different from the one we have known, a world where the rule of law supplants the rule of the jungle, a world in which nations recognize the shared responsibility for freedom and justice, a world where the strong respect the rights of the weak.

This is the vision that I shared with President Gorbachev in Helsinki. He and other leaders from Europe, the gulf, and around the world understand that how we manage this crisis today could shape the future for generations to come.

The test we face is great—and so are the stakes. This is the first assault on the new world that we seek, the first test of our mettle. Had we not responded to this first provocation with clarity of purpose, if we do not continue to demonstrate our determination, it would be a signal to actual and potential despots around the world.

America and the world must defend common vital interests. And we will. America and the world must support the rule of law. And we will. America and the world must stand up to aggression. And we will. And one thing more; in the pursuit of these goals, America will not be intimidated.

Vital issues of principles are at stake. Saddam Hussein is literally trying to wipe a country off the face of the earth. We do not exaggerate. Nor do we exaggerate when we say Saddam Hussein will fail.

Vital economic interests are at risk as well. Iraq itself controls some 10% of the world's proven oil reserves. Iraq plus Kuwait controls twice that. An Iraq permitted to swallow Kuwait would have the economic and military power, as well as the arrogance, to intimidate and coerce its neighbors—neighbors that control the lion's share of the world's remaining oil reserves. We cannot permit a resource so vital to be dominated by one so ruthless. And we won't.

Recent events have surely proven that there is no substitute for American leadership. In the face of tyranny, let no one doubt American credibility and reliability. Let no one doubt our staying power. We will stand by our friends. One way or another, the leader of Iraq must learn this fundamental truth.

Our interest, our involvement in the gulf is not transitory. It predated Saddam Hussein's aggression and will survive it. Long after all our troops come home—and we all hope it is soon, very soon—there will be a lasting role for the United States in assisting the nations of the Persian Gulf. Our role then—to deter future aggression. Our role is to help our friends in their own self-defense, and, something else, to curb the proliferation of chemical, biological, ballistic missile, and, above all, nuclear technologies.

Let me also make clear that the United States has no quarrel with the Iraqi people. Our quarrel is with Iraq's dictator and with his aggression. Iraq will not be permitted to annex Kuwait. That is not a threat; that is not a boast; that is just the way it is going to be.

✸ E S S A Y S

As the Cold War gave way to a new and uncertain era in international affairs, historians and other foreign-policy experts hastened to explain the legacy of the Reagan era. In the first essay, diplomatic historian John Lewis Gaddis of Yale University offers a favorable assessment of Reagan's policies, praising him for "hanging tough" and for helping to bring about "the most dramatic improvement in U.S.-Soviet relations . . . since the Cold War began." In the second essay, political scientists Richard Ned Lebow and Janice Gross Stein argue that the Soviet Union collapsed of its own internal contradictions and that, if anything, Reagan's policies prolonged the Cold War. The last essay, the conclusion of American University Professor William M. LeoGrande's richly detailed account of U.S. policy in Central America, presents a critical assessment of the deadly "low intensity conflicts" waged throughout the region during the Reagan years.

Ronald Reagan's Cold War Victory

JOHN LEWIS GADDIS

The time has come to acknowledge an astonishing development: during his eight years as president, Ronald Reagan has presided over the most dramatic improvement in U.S.-Soviet relations—and the most solid progress in arms control—since the Cold War began. History has often produced unexpected results, but this one surely sets some kind of record.

"Hanging Tough Paid Off" by J. L. Gaddis, from *The Bulletin of the Atomic Scientists,* January/February 1989. Reprinted by permission of *The Bulletin of the Atomic Scientists,* copyright 1999 by the Educational Foundation for Nuclear Science, 6042 South Kimbark, Chicago, Ill. 60637, USA. A one year subscription is $28.

Reagan was not an enthusiast for arms control before entering the White House: indeed his 1976 and 1980 campaigns appeared to reject that enterprise altogether in favor of a simpler search for national security through military superiority over the Soviet Union. That arms control has not only survived but prospered under his leadership ought to make us take a fresh look, both at the administration he headed and at the arms control process itself as it has traditionally been understood.

That process had taken on several distinctive characteristics by the end of the 1970s:

Pessimism. It is now almost forgotten (perhaps even by themselves) that Richard Nixon and Henry Kissinger had originally portrayed the SALT [Strategic Arms Limitation Treaty] I negotiations as a way to reduce the effects of America's military decline, stemming from a Soviet strategic buildup in the mid-1960s, to which the United States, because of the Vietnam War, had at first been too distracted and then too divided to respond. Arms control carried with it the tacit assumption that, in this situation, SALT was, at best, a way of minimizing the damage. Coincident but unrelated events had reinforced, by the end of the 1970s, the association of arms control with visions of U.S. military inferiority. These developments included the energy crisis and ensuing double-digit inflation; the erosion of presidential authority that began with Watergate and continued under Ford and Carter; the collapse of old allies in Iran and Nicaragua; and, most dramatically, the juxtaposition of American ineffectiveness in the Tehran hostage crisis with apparent Soviet purposefulness in invading Afghanistan.

Complexity. The Partial Test Ban Treaty of 1963 took 10 days to negotiate and fills just over two pages in the Arms Control and Disarmament Agency's published version. SALT I took two-and-a-half years to negotiate; the text is 18 pages. The unratified SALT II Treaty required almost seven years to negotiate; the resulting text and accompanying statements fill 31 pages of text. With arms control agreements becoming so complex that the experts themselves—to say nothing of average citizens—were finding them difficult to understand, it was reasonable to begin to wonder by the end of the 1970s how one would actually know whether they coincided with the national interest, or how to be sure that the Soviets understood them in precisely the same way.

Insularity. As the SALT process became more complex it appeared to take on a life of its own, insulated from outside events. Despite increasingly detailed provisions for verification, arms control still depended to a considerable extent upon trusting the Soviets. But that was becoming harder to do. After 1975 Moscow openly violated the Helsinki Agreement's human rights provision; indirect military intervention in Angola, Somalia, and Ethiopia suggested at a minimum an unwillingness to cooperate with the West in managing regional conflicts; the Kremlin appeared determined to push the limits of SALT I as far as possible as it continued its buildup of strategic weapons. Yet the SALT II negotiations proceeded, apparently unaffected by these less than reassuring signs.

Illogic.   The SALT process seemed to be based on two propositions generally accepted within the arms control community, but that laymen found less and less plausible when tested against the simpler standards of common sense. One was implied in the very term "arms control"; why not "arms reduction"? And why did "strategic arms limitation" agreements seem to do so little actual "limiting"? The other had to do with the assertion that safety could come only through vulnerability, and that defense, therefore, at lease in the nuclear realm, was bad. However rational the experts may have found these precepts, they did not appear rational to the average citizen, and as the nuclear standoff showed signs of stretching endlessly into the future, people became uncomfortable with them.

Whether these criticisms of arms control were fair is not the point. What is important is the skill with which Ronald Reagan focused on them during his campaigns for the presidency. And even more important was the way he incorporated them, after January 1981, into a new approach to arms control that would in time, and against conventional wisdom, produce impressive results. The principal means by which he accomplished this were as follows:

Rebuilding Self-Confidence.   There are rare moments in history when public moods reverse themselves almost overnight. One occurred in March 1933, when Franklin Roosevelt replaced Herbert Hoover in the White House; another took place in Great Britain in May 1940, when Winston Churchill became prime minister; still another occurred in Western Europe in June 1947, when Secretary of State George C. Marshall announced the economic recovery plan that came to bear his name. The mood reversal that followed Reagan's January 1981 inauguration was by no means as dramatic as these, but it occurred: long before the new administration had completed its military buildup, before Paul Volcker and the Federal Reserve Board had checked inflation, and before OPEC's [Organization of Petroleum Exporting Countries] disarray had turned the energy crisis into an oil glut, the *perception* had become widespread that events were beginning to break Washington's way. And that made a big difference.

It has since become commonplace to criticize Reagan for having placed greater emphasis on imagery than on substance during his years as president. But leadership begins with the creation of self-confidence, and that—as Roosevelt, Churchill, and Marshall all knew—is a psychological process depending less upon the rational calculation of tangible gains than upon the ability to convince people that however bad things may be at the moment, time is on their side. Reagan managed during his first months in office to project—and therefore to instill—a degree of self-confidence that went well beyond anything his predecessor had achieved. Without that shift from pessimism to optimism, much of what followed could hardly have taken place.

Spooking the Soviets.   The second element in the Reagan strategy proceeded logically from the first—to persuade the Kremlin that time was working against it. Nor was it so difficult to do, because events were beginning to demonstrate precisely this: Afghanistan was revealing the costs of what Paul Kennedy has called "strategic overstretch;" "Solidarity" had brought Poland to the edge of open rebellion; economic stagnation was becoming a serious problem inside the Soviet Union; and an increasingly sclerotic Kremlin leadership was responding to these difficulties with near catatonic immobility. In one sense, Reagan was lucky to have come into office at a trough in American fortunes and a peak in those of the Soviets. Things could not get much worse, and were likely to get better. But more than luck is involved in the ability to recognize that such trends are under way, and to capitalize upon them. Reagan's leadership proved decidedly superior to Carter's in that respect.

Several subsequent Reagan administration actions sought to reinforce the idea that time no longer favored Moscow. The U.S. military buildup was launched with the intention of so straining an already inefficient economy that the Soviet leadership would have little choice but to make substantial concessions on arms control. Similar intentions lay behind the Strategic Defense Initiative [SDI]. The vision of a shift from deterrence to a defense based on American technological superiority would, it was thought, shock the Soviets into contemplating for the first time significant reductions in their own long-range strategic forces.

At the same time, the administration was skillfully defusing both the U.S. nuclear freeze movement and opposition to the deployment of Pershing II and cruise missiles in Western Europe by calling for actual *reductions* in nuclear weapons, and by holding out, through SDI, the prospect of ultimately making them obsolete altogether. To the extent that the Soviets had counted on such groups to constrain administration freedom of action—and they almost certainly had—the effect again was to demonstrate that time was no longer on Moscow's side.

Negotiation from Strength. A third element in the Reagan strategy was the principle that negotiations should take place only from a position of strength. The idea dates from the Truman administration's military buildup following the outbreak of the Korean War. Over the years it had come to be understood as a way of evading negotiations altogether, since "strength" was so relative a concept that one might never actually attain it and since adversaries would presumably never negotiate from "weakness." There was reason to believe, at the outset of the Reagan years, that this devious approach was alive and well. Presidential subordinates gleefully put forward "killer" proposals for arms control talks, while the Pentagon swallowed huge military appropriations without any indication that "strength" was about to be achieved.

An important characteristic of Reagan's leadership, however, was that he was *not* devious; when he spoke of the possibility that a military buildup might actually lead to reductions in strategic weapons, he appears to have meant precisely what he said. He also understood, perhaps instinctively, a point George Kennan had been arguing: that the arms control process had become too complex while producing too little, and that the only way to rebuild a domestic consensus in support of it was to hold out clear, simple, and sweeping objectives, such as a 50 percent cut in strategic weapons on both sides.

With the 1984 elections coming up and with indications that Congress would resist further defense budget increases, it could be argued that the administration had little choice but to appear to seek negotiations with the Soviets. Certainly some Reagan advisers felt that negotiations so protracted as to produce no results were almost as desirable as having no negotiations at all. But what many of Reagan's subordinates did not understand—and what those who seek to explain what subsequently happened will have to comprehend—is that while the president may have shared their conservatism, he did not share their cynicism. For him the only question was with whom to negotiate.

Responding to Gorbachev.   It is difficult to see that much could have been accomplished in this respect until a functional Soviet leadership had been established. That happened in March 1985, and a fourth element in the Reagan strategy soon emerged, which was to acknowledge Mikhail Gorbachev as a new kind of Soviet leader whose chief priority was internal reform, and with whom one could, in the realm of external affairs, find common interests.

The White House was therefore ready to respond when Gorbachev began modifying long-standing Soviet positions on arms control in a way quite consistent with what the Reagan strategy had anticipated. Neither critics on the left, who had favored negotiations for their own sake, nor those on the right, who had sought negotiation from strength, were in any position to object. The long-stalemated arms control process suddenly accelerated, producing by the final year of the Reagan administration not only an Intermediate-range Nuclear Forces (INF) Treaty that contained unprecedented Soviet concessions on asymmetrical reductions and on-site verification, but substantial progress as well toward agreement on deep cuts in long-range strategic systems, and at least the possibility of a grand compromise that would delay if not defer altogether the deployment of SDI.

There were, to be sure, deficiencies in the Reagan strategy. Characteristically, the president found it easier to think of SDI as he had advertised it—as a first step toward abolishing nuclear weapons altogether—than as the successful bargaining chip it turned out to be. This created an opportunity for Gorbachev to endorse nuclear abolition by the year 2000 and thus to align himself with the president against Reagan's own skeptical advisers. There were few signs of progress toward conventional arms limitation, or toward restricting nuclear testing. Little thought had been given to how the United States might respond if the relaxation of controls that perestroika required were to produce actual rebellions among Soviet nationality groups, or within Eastern Europe. And almost no thought appeared to have been given to the relationship between national security and national solvency—an issue to which Gorbachev himself seemed keenly attuned.

Still, the clock on the front cover of the *Bulletin* was set back, a year ago, for the first time since 1972. That symbolic act ought to make us think critically—and without preconceptions—about how we got to that point. It was not by means of arms control as traditionally practiced: the old SALT process would never have survived the Reagan administration's insistence on asymmetrical reductions instead of symmetrical limitations, on intrusive rather than remote verification, and on the virtues of strategic defense as opposed to mutual vulnerability. Strength this time did lead to negotiations, bargaining chips did produce bargains, and "hanging tough" did eventually pay off.

The Soviets deserve much of the credit for what happened. They made most of the concessions, a pattern not likely to be repeated often in the future. It was the Reagan administration, however, that assessed correctly the potential for Soviet concessions. And because of the way it came about, this new approach to arms control has won firmer domestic support within the United States than the SALT process ever did; witness the caution both sides showed in not making it an issue during the otherwise hotly contested 1988 presidential election. How valid the approach will be in years to come remains to be seen, but as Reagan leaves office it would be uncharitable—and historically irresponsible—to begrudge the strategic vision of an administration once thought by many of us to have had none at all.

Reagan and the Russians

RICHARD NED LEBOW AND JANICE GROSS STEIN

Shortly after the Berlin Wall was torn down, prominent political leaders and commentators concluded that the U.S. military buildup under President Ronald Reagan had won the Cold War. "We were right to increase our defense budget," Vice President Dan Quayle announced. "Had we acted differently, the liberalization that we are seeking today throughout the Soviet bloc would most likely not be taking place." Even Tom Wicker, a *New York Times* columnist with impeccable liberal credentials, reluctantly conceded that the Strategic Defense Initiative (SDI) and the Reagan buildup "seemed to impress the Soviets as a challenge that they might not be able to meet."

Hanging tough paid off. Forty years of arms competition, so the argument goes, brought the Soviet economy to the brink of collapse. The Vatican's Secretary of State, Agostino Cardinal Casaroli, said, "Ronald Reagan obligated the Soviet Union to increase its military spending to the limits of insupportability." When the Soviet Union could no longer afford the competition, its leaders decided to end the Cold War. A modified version of this argument holds that the American military buildup simply worsened the Soviet economic quandary; it was the straw that broke the camel's back. Neither the strong nor the weak version of the proposition that American defense spending bankrupted the Soviet economy and forced an end to the Cold War is sustained by the evidence.

The Soviet Union's defense spending did not rise or fall in response to American military expenditures. Revised estimates by the Central Intelligence Agency indicate that Soviet expenditures on defense remained more or less constant throughout the 1980s. Neither the military buildup under Jimmy Carter and Reagan nor SDI had any real impact on gross spending levels in the U.S.S.R. At most SDI shifted the marginal allocation of defense rubles as some funds were allotted for developing countermeasures to ballistic defense.

If American defense spending had bankrupted the Soviet economy, forcing an end to the Cold War, Soviet defense spending should have declined as East-West relations improved. CIA estimates show that it remained relatively constant as a proportion of the Soviet gross national product during the 1980s, including Gorbachev's first four years in office. Soviet defense spending was not reduced until 1989 and did not decline nearly as rapidly as the overall economy.

To be sure, defense spending was an extraordinary burden on the Soviet economy. As early as the 1970s some officials warned Leonid Brezhnev that the economy would stagnate if the military continued to consume such a disproportionate share of

"Reagan and the Russians" by Richard Ned Lebow and Janice Gross Stein, in *Atlantic Monthly,* (February 1994). Reprinted by permission of Richard Ned Lebow and Janice Gross Stein.

resources. The General Secretary ignored their warnings, in large part because his authority depended on the support of a coalition in which defense and heavy industry were well represented. Brezhnev was also extraordinarily loyal to the Soviet military and fiercely proud of its performance. Soviet defense spending under Brezhnev and Gorbachev was primarily a response to internal political imperatives—to pressures from the Soviet version of the military-industrial complex. The Cold War and the high levels of American defense spending provided at most an opportunity for leaders of the Soviet military-industrial complex to justify their claims to preferential treatment. Even though the Cold War has ended and the United States is no longer considered a threat by the current Russian leadership, Russian defense spending now consumes roughly as great a percentage of GNP as it did in the Brezhnev years.

The Soviet economy was not the only economy burdened by very high levels of defense spending. Israel, Taiwan, and North and South Korea have allocated a disproportionate share of resources to defense without bankrupting their economies. Indeed, some of these economies have grown dramatically. A far more persuasive reason for the Soviet economic decline is the rigid "command economy" imposed by Stalin in the early 1930s. It did not reward individual or collective effort; it absolved Soviet producers from the discipline of the market; and it gave power to officials who could not be held accountable by consumers. Consequently much of the investment that went into the civilian sector of the economy was wasted. The command economy pre-dated the Cold War and was not a response to American military spending. The Soviet Union lost the Cold War, but it was not defeated by American defense spending.

Former Soviet officials insist that Gorbachev's decisions to withdraw Soviet forces from Afghanistan and to end the arms race were made despite the Reagan buildup and SDI. In 1983 Gorbachev, then the youngest member of the politburo, visited Canada and spent long hours in private conversation with Aleksandr Yakovlev, then the ambassador in Ottawa. The two men talked openly for the first time about the deep problems that the Soviet Union faced and the urgent need for change. To their mutual surprise they agreed on the folly of the Soviet intervention in Afghanistan and the necessity of ending the Cold War before it led to catastrophe for both superpowers. Both men hoped to reduce the burden of military spending in the U.S.S.R. and thus free resources for domestic reform and renewal.

By the time Gorbachev became General Secretary, in March of 1985, he was deeply committed to domestic reform and fundamental changes in Soviet foreign policy. "I, like many others," he observed recently, "knew that the U.S.S.R. needed radical change. If I had not understood this, I would never have accepted the position of General Secretary." Within a month of assuming office he attempted to signal his interest in arms control to the United States by announcing a unilateral freeze on the deployment of Soviet intermediate-range missiles in Europe. The deployment of the SS-20, Yakovlev explains, was a " stupid and strange policy" that defied logical explanation. Yakovlev considered the deployment illogical and self-defeating before President Reagan announced SDI and the buildup of American military forces. He and Gorbachev were "united" on this issue.

Gorbachev felt free to make a series of proposals for deep cuts in his country's nuclear arsenal because he was confident that the United States would not attack the Soviet Union. In conversation with his military advisers he rejected any plans that were premised on war with the West. Since he saw no threat of attack by the

United States, Gorbachev was not intimidated by the military programs of the Reagan Administration. "These were unnecessary and wasteful expenditures that we were not going to match," he told us. If both superpowers were to avoid the growing risk of accidental war, they had to make deep cuts in their strategic forces. "This was an imperative of the nuclear age."

Reagan's commitment to SDI made it more difficult for Gorbachev to persuade his officials that arms control was in the Soviet interest. Conservatives, some of the military leadership, and spokesmen for defense-related industries insisted that SDI was proof of America's hostile intentions. In a contentious politburo meeting called to discuss arms control, Soviet armed forces chief of staff Marshal Sergei Akhromeyev angrily warned that the Soviet people would not tolerate any weakening of Soviet defenses, according to Oleg Grinevsky, now Russia's ambassador to Sweden. Yakovlev insists that "Star Wars was exploited by hardliners to complicate Gorbachev's attempt to end the Cold War."

President Reagan continued to regard the Soviet Union as an "evil empire" and remained committed to his quest for a near-perfect ballistic-missile defense. To break the impasse, Gorbachev tried at the two leaders' summit meeting in Reykjavik to convince Reagan of his genuine interest in ending the arms race and restructuring their relationship on a collaborative basis. For the first time, the two men talked seriously about eliminating all their countries' ballistic missiles within ten years and significantly reducing their arsenals of nuclear weapons. Although the summit produced no agreement, Reagan became "human" and "likable" to Gorbachev and his advisers, and the President, convinced of Gorbachev's sincerity, began to modify his assessment of the Soviet Union and gradually became the leading dove of his Administration. The Reykjavik summit, as Gorbachev had hoped, began a process of mutual reassurance and accommodation. That process continued after an initially hesitant George Bush became a full-fledged partner.

The Carter-Reagan military buildup did not defeat the Soviet Union. On the contrary, it prolonged the Cold War. Gorbachev's determination to reform an economy crippled in part by defense spending urged by special interests, but far more by structural rigidities, fueled his persistent search for an accommodation with the West. That persistence, not SDI, ended the Cold War.

Reagan and Central America

WILLIAM M. LEOGRANDE

For decades, Central America had been a backwater of U.S. foreign relations, a region so unimportant that Washington often assigned its least promising diplomats there. Then suddenly, in the 1980s, the United States became so obsessed with the small countries of the isthmus that they dominated not just hemispheric policy, but all of foreign policy. Central America occasioned the most bitter domestic political debate since Vietnam and ignited a scandal that rivaled Watergate. How could the United States have become so alarmed about such a small place?

In part, it was an accident of timing. Ronald Reagan came to Washington in 1981 determined to restore America's global stature by taking the offensive in the Cold War. At that very moment, the accumulated grievances from decades of social inequality and political repression in Central America exploded in revolutionary violence. Historically, Washington had sided with the region's elites, subordinating democracy and human rights to the exigencies of national security and stability. The revolutionaries, most of them Marxists, saw the United States as an imperialist nemesis and looked to Washington's global adversaries for support.

To Reagan, the Marxist ideological bent of Central America's radicals and their willingness to solicit Soviet aid branded them as enemies. Urged on by Secretary of State Alexander Haig, Reagan declared Central America the place to draw the line against the expansion of Soviet influence in the Third World, a test case of Washington's assertive new foreign policy. Over the next eight years, U.S. policy never wavered from the core premise that Central America's wars were Cold War battles that Washington could not afford to lose. "Central America is the most important place in the world," Jeane Kirkpatrick solemnly avowed in 1981.

In this Manichean struggle between good and evil, anything short of victory amounted to defeat. Negotiated solutions were not good enough; you could not negotiate with Communists, administration officials said repeatedly. You could not bargain with the devil. In El Salvador, the objective was to prevent the Salvadoran guerrillas from seizing power by force, or gaining any share of power at the bargaining table. In Nicaragua, administration hard-liners were not content with containment. They wanted to reverse Communism in the Third World, and Nicaragua became the test case for the Reagan Doctrine.

Reagan's political appointees tended to be committed ideologies of the Republican right, eager to unleash the military power of the United States, both overtly and covertly, in hopes of rolling back the "Evil Empire" at the periphery. Not everyone in the government shared this zest for fomenting "low intensity conflicts." Foreign policy professionals generally saw the Reagan Doctrine as reckless. Pragmatic by instinct, they tended to be more cautious about embroiling Washington in multiple brushfire wars around the world.

The balance of power between pragmatists and hard-liners shifted to and fro as Reagan's staff played musical chairs through two secretaries of state, two UN ambassadors, four White House chiefs of staff, and six national security advisers. But despite having more government experience and foreign policy expertise than most of the hard-liners, pragmatists (such as Thomas Enders, Deane Hinton, Philip Habib, and George Shultz) could never quite get the upper hand. In the end, the hard-liners always prevailed, even after their chieftains (Alexander Haig, William Clark, Jeane Kirkpatrick, William Casey, John Poindexter, and Caspar Weinberger) departed, because they accurately reflected the emotional commitment of the president himself. Ronald Reagan was the premier hard-liner, pursuing victory in Central America as single-mindedly as Ahab pursued the whale.

Did Washington Win This Time?

How successful was Ronald Reagan's policy? Assessments were as sharply divergent in hindsight as they were when the policy was first formulated. Conservatives were quick to credit the president with having saved Nicaragua from the Sandinistas and El Salvador from the guerrillas of the Farabundo Martí National Liberation Front (FMLN). Liberals retorted that both the Nicaraguan elections and the Salvadoran peace accord were produced by diplomacy, not the military initiatives favored by Reagan. Both were half right.

During the protracted debates over contra aid, the conservatives warned that the Sandinistas were Communists who would never hold a free election or surrender power peacefully; they could be driven out only at the point of a bayonet. If liberal Democrats refused to give the contras military aid, conservatives insisted, they were condemning the Nicaraguan people to the "the endless darkness of Communist tyranny." When liberals replied that diplomacy was more likely to produce Sandinista concessions, conservatives derided them for the foolish prattle of weaklings. As it turned out, the hard-liners were wrong on every count—wrong about the consequences of ending military aid to the contras, wrong about the efficacy of diplomacy, and wrong about the Sandinistas' willingness to accept free elections. Had the hard-liners prevailed, continuing contra aid, Nicaragua would have remained a garrison state at war.

On the other hand, liberals were reluctant to acknowledge that the duress Ronald Reagan and the contras inflicted on Nicaragua was the main reason the Sandinistas held an election in 1990 and lost it. The contras never came close to winning a military victory, but the war and Washington's financial pressure destroyed the Nicaraguan economy. Had the Nicaraguan economy been in better shape, perhaps the Sandinistas would not have felt compelled to change their constitution and advance the electoral timetable by almost a year. Had the economy been in better shape, perhaps they would not have lost.

A certain unintended symbiosis emerged from the bitter battles between liberals and conservatives over Nicaragua. When the Iran-contra revelations led Congress to halt military aid, the White House had to shift policy away from relying exclusively on the ineffectual exile army. Unable to continue the war, President Bush had no alternative but to accept a diplomatic approach as outlined in the Esquipulas peace process. To Bush's great surprise, it worked.

But Washington's strategy carried a heavy price for Nicaraguans. Some 30,000 died in the contra war—proportionate to population, this was more than the United States lost in the Civil War, World War I, World War II, Korea and Vietnam *combined.* Over a hundred thousand Nicaraguans were turned into refugees. Millions suffered economic privation as real wages fell 90 percent, inflation spun out of control, and unemployment afflicted a third of the labor force. Even with international help, it would take a generation for the Nicaraguan economy to recover. In official Washington, these costs were downplayed amid the euphoria of the Sandinistas' defeat. But if Ronald Reagan wanted credit for having saved Nicaragua, he also had to take responsibility for having destroyed much of it in the process.

In El Salvador, too, the verdict on U.S. policy was mixed. As in Nicaragua, Reagan failed to win a military victory. Despite over a billion dollars in military aid, the Salvadoran armed forces could not defeat the guerrillas. While the two sides fought to a stalemate, some 80,000 people died, most of them innocent civilians killed by the military and the government's security forces, armed and bankrolled by Washington. Three billion dollars in U.S. economic aid prevented El Salvador's economy from collapsing like Nicaragua's, but the war still took its toll—over a billion dollars in lost production and destroyed infrastructure, another billion lost to capital flight. In 1991, though the Salvadoran economy was growing at a healthy 3.5 percent rate, a third of the population was unemployed and 90 percent lived in poverty, not earning enough to adequately feed a family of four.

Yet Washington succeeded in denying the guerrillas victory, which they almost certainly would have won in the early 1980s if the Salvadoran government had not received massive U.S. aid. By giving the government the wherewithal to avoid defeat, the Reagan administration met its minimum objective. When the two sides finally sat down to negotiate an end to the war, the FMLN won key concessions from the armed forces, but they received no guaranteed share of political power in return for laying down their arms.

Could a similar outcome have been attained in the early 1980s if the Reagan administration had been willing to accept a diplomatic settlement? Both the guerrillas and the armed forces still thought they could win the war then, so finding sufficient common ground to sustain a settlement would have been difficult. Nevertheless, the possibility of a negotiated settlement was visible as early as 1981. Sobered by the failure of their "final" offensive, the guerrillas made their first serious peace proposal that year—a proposal similar in many regards to the agreement signed a decade later. Christian Democrats in the government were disposed to begin talks in 1981, but the army wouldn't let them. Mexico and the Socialist International were prepared to press the guerrillas to make compromises for peace, and European Christian Democrats were willing to do the same with the government. The missing piece was the United States. Only Washington had the power to force the Salvadoran military to make to concessions necessary to stop the war, but the Reagan administration had no interest in a negotiated settlement. Only after a decade of inconclusive combat was Washington willing to acknowledge that military victory was unattainable. Once the United States put itself squarely behind the negotiating process, the armed forces fell into line, albeit grudgingly.

In El Salvador, even more than in Nicaragua, congressional opposition forced changes in the president's policy that ultimately helped it succeed. To win aid increases from Congress, Reagan embraced José Napoleón Duarte despite conservatives' initial suspicions about the Christian Democrats' "communitarianism." The certification requirements imposed by Congress in 1981 forced the administration to pay attention to agrarian reform and human rights, despite Reagan's initial instinct to downplay both. Although the facts of Reagan's certifications were questionable, the need to certify led the administration to pressure the Salvadoran regime into undertaking real change, if only to make the semi-annual ordeal of certification less onerous. Eventually, U.S. pressure produced significant reductions in the number of political murders. That, in turn, created enough political space for the reemergence of an unarmed, dissident politics—an essential first step in the process of moving El Salvador's conflict off the battlefield and into the political arena. Toward the end of the war, Congress's decision to cut military aid by 50 percent in 1991 and the threat to cut it even further in 1992 compelled the Bush administration to support a compromise peace agreement.

In the end, Washington neither won nor lost the wars in Central America; it grew tired of fighting them and, with the waning of the Cold War, settled for diplomatic solutions not fundamentally different from ones it had resisted for years.

The Past Is Prologue

"Too often in our history, we have turned our attention to Latin America in times of crisis, and we have turned our backs when the crisis passed," said Deputy Secretary of State Clifford Wharton in early 1993. "That is shortsighted and self-defeating. This administration will not make that mistake." Wharton was giving the first Latin American policy address of Bill Clinton's presidency. But the circumstances belied the message. Wharton was standing in for Secretary of State Warren Christopher, who had been scheduled to give the speech, but was called to Europe on more urgent business—conferring with NATO about the escalating war in Bosnia. The history of U.S.–Latin American relations was ever thus: until a Latin country erupted in crisis, someplace else was always more important. As the wars that swept Central America in the 1980s subsided, Washington's attention drifted away, Wharton's brave rhetoric notwithstanding.

Nothing was a better indicator than the foreign assistance budget. In the mid-1990s, scarce foreign aid dollars flowed away from Central America, toward Eastern Europe and the former Soviet states. For fiscal year (FY) 1998, President Clinton requested just $169 million in economic assistance for all of Central America—down 86 percent from the peak level of $1.2 billion in 1985. Military assistance virtually disappeared; none of the Central American countries were slated for any in FY 1996, other than a few hundred thousand dollars in military training funds—a total of just $1.6 million regionwide.

Costa Rica "graduated" from AID programs in 1996 and thus was slated for no economic assistance at all. Nicaragua and El Salvador suffered dramatic declines in aid despite the danger that economic difficulties could undermine their fragile democratic institutions. Nicaragua, which received almost $300 million in 1990 after the Sandinistas lost the election, was slated for just $24 million in FY 1998. El Salvador, which received almost $500 million annually in the late 1980s and $230 million as recently as 1993, was slated for just $35 million.

For Central Americans, Washington's shifting priorities came as a shock. After the tumultuous 1980s, when U.S. foreign policy seemed to hinge on events in Central America, the disinterest of the 1990s was disquieting. "It is as though a hurricane passed through," a Honduran businessman said, "and all that is left is the bad aftermath"—an aftermath that the United States expected the Central Americans to clean up themselves.

Vital Interests and the War at Home

Washington's abrupt loss of interest in Central America suggested that perhaps it had not been quite so "vital" to U.S. national security as Ronald Reagan proclaimed. No doubt the Soviet Union saw the region as a point of vulnerability for the United States in the 1980s and was happy to stir up trouble there. But the Soviets were never eager for a direct confrontation with Washington in its own backyard, where all the geostrategic advantages lay with the United States. They were reluctant to supply the Salvadoran guerrillas with arms and gave the Sandinistas significant military aid only after the contra war began. Moreover, the Soviets were always stingy with economic assistance; their financial help fell well below what the Sandinistas needed to prevent economic decay. Much as the Soviets may have enjoyed seeing Washington squirm in Central America, they had no interest in paying for another Cuba. Such an adventure was just too expensive.

But the Reaganites were reacting as much to the symbolic threat posed by the Soviet Union as to the actual threat. Here was a region, close to home, where the United States had traditionally held sway. Suddenly, it was rising in rebellion against regimes that historically aligned themselves with Washington, rebellions led by insurgents who identified ideologically with the rival superpower. Could the United States defend its interests in Central America, or would this region, like Southeast Asia before it, slip into the orbit of the enemy? And if the erosion of American power and influence could not be halted there, in our own backyard, where would it end?

The memory of Vietnam was fresh when Central America erupted in revolution. To conservative Republicans, the Vietnam syndrome was the Achilles' heel of American national security. Could they reestablish an activist, interventionist posture or would liberal Democrats ratify the nation's post-Vietnam reluctance to entangle itself in other people's insurgencies? If the advocates of intervention could not maintain domestic support for the use of force abroad, the United States would be unable to meet the Soviet challenge in the Third World, with catastrophic consequences.

Liberal Democrats thought Reagan was exaggerating the threat to U.S. security posed by the upheavals in Nicaragua and El Salvador, just as President Lyndon B. Johnson had exaggerated the importance of Vietnam. As Reagan became more and more committed to the Salvadoran regime and the Nicaraguan contras, Democrats worried that the president was taking America down another slippery slope. Unlike the Cold War liberals, who stifled their doubts about Johnson's war, the Democrats of the 1980s were determined to use the power of Congress to prevent "another Vietnam" in Central America.

That was something Ronald Reagan would not tolerate. The Reagan Republicans refused to acknowledge the legitimacy of congressional activism in international affairs. To them, foreign policy was the president's job, and he would brook no interference. Washington itself had become a crucial front in every brushfire war. The struggle for Central America was more likely to be lost in the halls of Congress than on the battlefields of the region itself—just as the war in Vietnam had been lost in Washington, according to conservative mythology. Convinced that the global stakes were enormous, the Reaganites were determined to prevail over congressional resistance by any means necessary.

Add to these high stakes a slightly conspiratorial mentality, a touch of the paranoid style in American politics, and some conservatives became convinced that domestic opposition was being fueled clandestinely by America's global enemies. To them, the line between loyal opposition and treason became indistinct. The epic struggle between good and evil was no longer simply the United States versus the Soviet Union. Some of "us" had joined "them," or acted as if they had, which amounted to the same thing. The battle lines were no longer drawn along national boundaries, but between Democrats and Republicans, between liberals and conservatives, between Congress and the White House. One result was the corrosion of civility in the foreign policy debate, epitomized by the Republican right's incessant red-baiting of opponents. Another was the erosion of the rule of law caused by the executive branch's flagrant flouting of statutes that did not comport with policy.

From Reagan's first weeks in office, he treated Congress as an adversary to be subdued. To evade congressional scrutiny of his aid program for El Salvador, he invoked presidential emergency powers to send military assistance without congressional approval. When Congress imposed certification requirements on aid, he blithely certified that things were getting better regardless of the facts. When Congress refused to fund police training for the Salvadoran security forces, Reagan went ahead anyway, using the regular military aid program and pretending the police were actually regular military units. He refused to comply with laws governing the deployment of U.S. military advisers to El Salvador and Honduras, and he used the CIA to send U.S. soldiers into covert combat in El Salvador and Nicaragua without complying with the War Powers Resolution. When Congress refused to fund the construction of new military bases in Honduras, the Pentagon built them anyway under the cover of military exercises.

Nowhere was Reagan's contempt for Congress more manifest than on the issue of contra aid. From the beginning, administration officials lied to Congress about the real intent of the not-so-secret war against Nicaragua. Despite repeated assurances, the operation was never aimed at interdicting arms smuggled from Nicaragua to the Salvadoran guerrillas. When Congress passed the Boland amendment to halt contra aid, the administration simply ignored the law, using every artifice to continue the war—rerouting money from the Pentagon, soliciting funds from foreign countries, and diverting profits from Iranian arms sales. And through it all, administration officials lied about what they were doing—publicly, privately, repeatedly, and egregiously.

From 1983 on, the White House's secret efforts on behalf of the contras were carried out by a clandestine foreign policy apparatus under the Orwellian code name Project Democracy. By setting up this secret network, the Reagan administration subverted the constitutional balance between the branches of government and thereby posed a greater threat to democracy in the United States than Nicaragua ever could. Moreover, when the Iran-contra scandal revealed how deceitful the White House had been, neither Reagan nor most of the responsible officials were contrite. On the contrary, they defended their actions as necessary to defeat Communism in Central America—an imperative that took precedence over telling the truth to Congress or obeying the law. Most Republicans endorsed this rationale, praising the inauguration of the new Imperial Presidency.

In point of fact, the Democrats were much less implacable foes of Reagan's Central America policy than one would think from reading the president's speeches. Liberals in Congress tried mightily to block Reagan from taking the nation down a path they believed led to disaster, but they were not in full command of their party. On foreign policy issues, conservative southern Democrats invariably sided with

Reagan, often giving him an ideological majority that rendered the Democrats' partisan majority meaningless. At critical junctures—the 1984 House votes on military aid to El Salvador and the 1985 and 1986 House votes on contra aid—divisions among the Democrats handed victory to the White House.

Despite consistent public opposition to Reagan's policy, Democratic leaders in Congress were slow to mobilize the party to challenge the president precisely because the issue exacerbated the Democrats' internal ideological split. Some Democratic leaders were themselves ambivalent about the policy. Jim Wright opposed Reagan on Nicaragua more effectively than anyone—so much so that angry Republicans attacked him mercilessly and drove him from the Speaker's chair in 1989. But Wright supported the president on El Salvador. Senate Democratic leader Robert Byrd vacillated between support and opposition, never taking an active role in the Central America debate, wishing it would simply go away. But even among Democrats who consistently opposed Reagan's policy, many were reluctant to stand up to the popular president for fear they would be tarred with having lost Central America to Communism. Senator Joseph McCarthy was thirty years dead, but his ghost was still enough to give Democrats a fright.

In short, Congress largely failed in its institutional responsibility to serve as a check on executive behavior. Democrats were reluctant to protest too vehemently or look too closely at what the White House was doing, even when they knew it was improper; Republicans made transparently partisan excuses for their president. The foreign policy process would have been healthier had Democrats brought more backbone to it and Republicans brought more conscience.

The press and public also proved imperfect bulwarks against executive malfeasance. Except for a few investigative journalists who gave Reagan headaches, most of the media reported the Central America story from the official point of view. Administration efforts at elaborate public relations campaigns to manage the press or, failing that, to intimidate it succeeded more often than not.

Throughout Reagan's eight years in the White House, polls showed that a large majority of the public opposed every aspect of his Central American policy. In fact, administration officials suffered from a Vietnam syndrome of their own— the fear that direct military action might trigger the sort of mass public opposition that made the war in Vietnam untenable. Significant organized grassroots opposition to Reagan's policy from the religious community and the peace movement foreshadowed what might happen if direct involvement produced significant U.S. casualties. But so long as U.S. troops stayed out, most voters paid little attention to Central America, and the White House could ignore the polls.

One lesson of the experience in Central America was that values expressed in policies abroad invariable seep into politics at home. The only way to assure that foreign policy remains consistent with American values is to subject it to the same close public scrutiny and debate as domestic policy. Although the foreign policy process has become more open than in the heyday of the Imperial Presidency, it was not democratic enough to prevent Ronald Reagan from disregarding the law. Congress, the press, and—most especially—the voting public need to pay more attention to foreign affairs, not less. Only their vigilance can hold presidents to account when ideological certainty convinces them that they alone understand the national interest and that the ends of securing it justify the means.

Like Vietnam, the Central American crisis ended without policymakers reaching any consensus about how the United States should deal with similar conflicts in the future. To be sure, with the end of the Cold War, those issues seemed less compelling. Third World struggles that Washington once viewed as proxy wars with Moscow ceased to have any larger meaning, and successful interventions elsewhere—in Grenada, Panama, and the Persian Gulf—boosted America's confidence in its ability to go to war and win.

Yet much of the Third World, Latin America not excepted, still holds the tinder for social upheaval—privileged classes and political elites unresponsive to the majority's demands for democracy and social justice. If the past is any guide, the United States is unlikely to stand aloof from such conflicts, especially in its own backyard. Although the imperative of superpower rivalry is gone, other interests—in immigration, narcotics interdiction, oil supplies, humanitarian aid, or "promoting democracy"—tend to pull Washington in. And like Banquo's ghost, the questions raised first in Vietnam and again in Central America will reappear: What national interests are compelling enough to justify the use of force abroad; how can we use force in ways consistent with the laws of war and our own sense or moral decency; and how can we do it without undermining the foundations of our own democracy?

In the end, Central America proved not to be another Vietnam, at least not in the way that people feared in 1981. Neither the worst nightmare of the conservative Republicans—a Communist Central America toppling dominoes from Panama to Mexico—nor those of the liberal Democrats—a quagmire on our doorstep—came to pass. Washington avoided the slippery slope in part just by knowing it was there.

We went to war in Central America to exorcise the ghosts of Vietnam and to renew the national will to use force abroad. These imperatives, more than the Soviet threat, Fidel Castro's menace, or the Nicaraguan and Salvadoran revolutions, shaped U.S. policy—how it was conceived, struggled over, and executed. Central America's misfortune lay in being the stage upon which this American drama was played out.

✴ *F U R T H E R   R E A D I N G*

Barnet, Richard J. *The Alliance* (1983).

Beschloss, Michael R., and Strobe Talbot. *At the Highest Levels: The Inside Story of the End of the Cold War* (1993).

Bialer, Seweryn, and Michael Mandelbaum, eds. *Gorbachev's Russia and American Foreign Policy* (1988).

Booth, John A., and Thomas W. Walker. *Understanding Central America* (1990).

Boswell, Terry, and Albert Bergesen, eds. *America's Changing Role in the World System* (1987).

Brzezinski, Zbigniew K. *The Grand Chessboard: American Primacy and Its Geostrategic Imperatives* (1998).

Bush, George H. W., and Brent Scowcroft. *A World Transformed* (1998).

Calleo, David P. *Beyond American Hegemony* (1987).

Chomsky, Noam. *Towards a New Cold War* (1982).

Coleman, Kenneth M., and George C. Herring, eds. *The Central American Crises* (1985).

Crothers, Thomas. *In the Name of Democracy: U.S. Foreign Policy Toward Latin America in the Reagan Years* (1991).

Dalby, Simon. *Creating the Second Cold War* (1990).

Dallek, Robert. *Ronald Reagan and the Politics of Symbolism* (1984).

Demuth, Christopher C. *The Reagan Doctrine and Beyond* (1988).

Destler, I. M., et al. *Our Own Worst Enemy* (1984).

Dumbrell, John. *American Foreign Policy: Carter to Clinton* (1997).

Dunlop, John B. *The Rise of Russia and the Fall of the Soviet Empire* (1993).

Freedman, Lawrence, and Efraim Karsh. *The Gulf Conflict, 1990–1991: Diplomacy and War in the New World Order* (1995).

Gaddis, John Lewis. *The Long Peace* (1987).

———. *The United States and the End of the Cold War* (1992).

Garthoff, Raymond. *Détente and Confrontation: American-Soviet Relations from Nixon to Reagan* (1985).

———. *The Great Transition: American-Soviet Relations and the End of the Cold War* (1995).

George, Alexander, et al., eds. *U.S.-Soviet Security Cooperation* (1988).

Gilpin, Robert. *The Political Economy of International Relations* (1987).

Glynn, Patrick. *Closing Pandora's Box: Arms Races, Arms Control, and the History of the Cold War* (1992).

Halliday, Fred. *The Making of the Second Cold War* (1983, 1986).

Hogan, Michael J., ed. *The End of the Cold War* (1992).

Hough, Jerry F. *Russia and the West* (1988).

Hyland, William, ed. *The Reagan Foreign Policy* (1987).

Klare, Michale T. *Beyond the "Vietnam Syndrome": U.S. Interventionism in the 1980s* (1981).

Klare, Michale, and Peter Kornbluh, eds. *Low Intensity Warfare: Counterinsurgency, Proinsurgency, and Antiterrorism in the Eighties* (1988).

LaFeber, Walter. *Inevitable Revolutions: The United States in Central America* (1983).

Lebow, Richard Ned, and Janice Gross Stein. *We All Lost the Cold War* (1994).

Lebow, Richard Ned, and Thomas Risse-Kappen, eds. *International Relations Theory and the End of the Cold War* (1995).

Leiken, Robert S. and Barry M. Rubin, eds. *The Central American Crisis Reader* (1987).

LeoGrande, William M. *Our Own Backyard: The United States in Central America, 1977–1992* (1998).

Lundestad, Geir, and Odd Arne Westad, eds. *Beyond the Cold War* (1993).

Mandelbaum, Michael. *Reagan and Gorbachev* (1987).

Mead, Walter R. *Mortal Splendor: The American Empire in Transition* (1987).

Morley, Morris H. *Crisis and Confrontation: Ronald Reagan's Foreign Policy* (1988).

Nisbet, Robert. *The Present Age* (1987).

Nye, Joseph S. *Bound to Lead: The Changing Nature of American Power* (1990).

Oberdorfer, Don. *From the Cold War to a New Era: The United States and the Soviet Union, 1983–1991* (1998).

Paterson, Thomas G. *Meeting the Communist Threat: Truman to Reagan* (1988).

Quandt, William B. *Camp David: Peacemaking and Politics* (1986).

Rodman, Peter. *More Precious Than Peace: Fighting and Winning the Cold War in the Third World* (1994).

Rodrik, Dani. *Has Globalization Gone Too Far?* (1997).

Rubin, Barry M. *Paved with Good Intentions: The American Experience and Iran* (1980).

Sanders, Jerry W. *Peddlers of Crisis: The Committee on the Present Danger and the Politics of Containment* (1983).

Schoultz, Lars. *National Security and United States Policy Toward Latin America* (1987).

Smith, Gaddis. *Morality, Reason, and Power: American Diplomacy in the Carter Years* (1986).

Talbot, Strobe. *Deadly Gambits* (1984).

———. *Endgame: The Inside Story of SALT-II* (1979).

———. *The Master of the Game: Paul Nitze and the Nuclear Peace* (1988).

———. *The Russians and Reagan* (1984).

Wohlforth, William C., ed. *Witnesses to the End of the Cold War* (1997).

Wolfe, Thomas W. *The SALT Experience* (1979).

Woodward, Bob. *Veil: The Secret Wars of the CIA, 1981–1987* (1987).

CHAPTER
14

Brave New World:
The United States
and the Global Era

XX

As the 1900s gave way to the new millennium, it became increasingly clear that a new era in American (and world) history had begun. The old era had been dominated by the Cold War struggle between the United States and the Soviet Union. The new era was defined by the rise of a new global economy that had begun to transform not only the ways in which business was conducted but also the ways in which the world's peoples lived, worked, and governed themselves. Global communication, trade, and capital flow all grew more rapidly than either national or international political systems could fully comprehend or control. The world's wealth also grew rapidly, raising global living standards while at the same time creating stark new inequalities. Global (mostly American) culture increasingly penetrated many of the world's most remote localities. Although none of these developments was entirely new (the late nineteenth and early twentieth centuries also had been marked by a dramatic increase in international trade and communication), the speed, scope, and pervasiveness of these trends defined a new era.

In the old postwar era, international relations were dominated by the bipolar conflict of the United States and the Soviet Union. By contrast, the new era was characterized by a series of seemingly divergent tendencies. While the advance of global capitalism threatened to undermine both nations and nationalism, the end of the Cold War also released a wave of long-suppressed national and even tribal passions. The United States was unquestionably the most powerful nation in the world, but its power was limited and Americans themselves seemed unsure about the role their country should play in the new era. What goals and values should drive U.S. foreign policy? How should economic and strategic interests be balanced against humanitarian concerns? What role should force play? Some argued that as the largest stakeholder in the new era, the United States must be willing to use economic, political, and even military force to sustain the new global system. "The hidden hand of the market will never work without the hidden fist," proclaimed New York Times *columnist Thomas Friedman. "Without America on duty, there will be no America*

Online." Many sharply disagreed. Some saw increased global integration as a threat to American living standards and national sovereignty. Others questioned whether the United States could (or should) play the role of imperial policeman.

In the United States, the new global era was marked by the emergence of what some called a "new economy"—an economy marked not only by the continuing shift from manufacturing to services but also by heightened competition, rapid innovation, increased organizational flexibility, and more fluid capital and labor markets. The introduction of new computer technologies radically changed patterns of work and consumption, while deregulation, accompanied by widespread corporate restructuring, transformed the face of American business. The U.S. economy, which in the 1970s had faltered and stagnated, entered the longest period of sustained growth since World War II. As the twentieth century ended, the country seemed awash in a rising tide of computers, cell phones, and sport-utility vehicles.

There were downsides to the new economy as well. While the economy of the old postwar order had been characterized by stability and security, the new economy was marked by almost continuous change. In the 1950s, many blue-collar and white-collar workers could realistically anticipate lifetime employment by a single company. By the 1990s, students graduating from college were told to expect as many as six to seven careers, much less jobs, over the course of their working lives. Moreover, the benefits of the new economy were distributed with startling inequality, reversing the trend toward greater equality that had prevailed from World War II through the 1960s. The power of organized labor was greatly reduced, and with it labor's share of increased productivity. The rich became much richer—by the end of the century, the top 1 percent of U.S. households possessed more wealth than the bottom 95 percent—while almost 35 million people remained below the poverty line of about $13,000 a year income for a three-person family. For many, remaining in the middle class required two incomes, mounting consumer debt, and long commutes that left less and less time for family and friends. Enthusiasts argued that the U.S. economy had entered a "long boom," but more sober-minded critics warned of an impending reckoning.

The rapid diffusion of new technologies, especially in communications and biotechnology, was accompanied by growing uneasiness over how these new technologies might reshape people's lives. While millions joined the rush to shop online, others worried about new breaches in the walls that had once separated families from the marketplace. The rapid spread of genetically engineered foods boosted America's much-vaunted agricultural productivity even higher, although consumers both in the United States and abroad worried over the impact of such foods on health and the environment. The successful mapping of the human genome promised breathtaking new advances in medical science but also prompted disturbing ethical questions that Americans had never before confronted. Uncontrolled economic growth, many feared, posed an irreparable threat to the global environment.

The old postwar order had seemed relatively homogeneous. Immigration restriction, together with two world wars and the Great Depression, had closed America's borders to immigration, and fifty years of assimilation had blurred many of the differences that had characterized the American people at the beginning of the twentieth century. By contrast, the new era was fueled in part by a "fourth wave" of immigrants, whose arrival began a transformation of the nation's demographics rivaling that which had occurred during the late nineteenth and early twentieth centuries. Indeed, demographers predicted that non-Hispanic whites would become a minority in the United States by the mid-twenty-first century. Some conservatives greeted this prospect with near hysteria, clamoring for immigration restriction, an end to bilingual education, and the establishment of English as the nation's official language. Some liberals worried about the "disuniting" of America and diminished opportunities for the native-born poor and working class. Others, drawing on the traditions of America's own immigrant origins, sought to create a new and more diverse national identity.

The politics of the old era had been shaped in large measure by the Democratic New Deal coalition that had emerged during the 1930s. But the Democrats had been deeply divided from the beginning, and the old coalition disintegrated in the late 1960s and 1970s amid turmoil over civil rights and Vietnam. In the 1980s, the Republicans sought to mobilize a coalition of both social and business conservatives but failed to weld these two divergent groups into a cohesive political base. During the 1990s, so-called New Democrats led by President Bill Clinton, sought to replace the party's older industrial and agricultural bases with a new, if unwieldy, coalition of women, minorities, social liberals, and technological progressives. Both parties paid obeisance to older voters, whose ranks were swollen by aging baby boomers; both sought to position themselves with younger voters from Generation X, as the children of the baby boomers were sometimes called; and both tried to come to terms with the ways in which globalization was reorganizing the contours of domestic politics. Moreover, by the end of the century, politics itself seemed increasingly dominated by lobbyists, campaign consultants, and the media, and growing numbers of Americans, seemingly alienated from or indifferent to the political process, refused even to vote. Here, too, the old era had given way to a new one, the precise character of which was not yet clear.

✖ E S S A Y S

The closer we approach the present, the more difficult it becomes to distinguish an "essay" from a "document." Thus, in this final chapter, we present four selections, each of which offers a perspective on globalization and the new economy. No one of these essays should be accepted uncritically. Each of them should be subjected to thoughtful criticism. The first selection, by Robert D. Atkinson and Randolph H. Court, describes the "new economy" of the 1990s. Atkinson and Court are staff members of the Progressive Policy Institute, an arm of the Democratic Leadership Council (DLC), which was closely identified with the Clinton administration. In this selection, they defend the concept of the new economy against both left-wing critics and free-market enthusiasts. In the second essay, "Jihad vs. McWorld," Rutgers University political scientist Benjamin R. Barber explores some of the cultural and political consequences of the new global economy: the powerful, homogenizing spread of global (mostly American) culture; the reactive nationalism or "tribalism" of those resisting the onrush of international markets; and the erosion of nation-states and with it, in his view, a growing threat to democratic self-government. In the third essay, Ronald Takaki, a professor of ethnic studies at the University of California, at Berkeley, explores the complex racial and ethnic demography created both by earlier waves of immigration (including the forced "immigration" of African Americans) and by the renewal of immigration into the United States during the last several decades of the twentieth century.

In the fourth and final selection, Professor of Communication Michael Schudson of the University of California, San Diego, joins the debate begun by Yale sociologist Robert Bellah, Harvard political scientist Robert Putnam, and others over the quality of

American civic life at the end of the twentieth century. Has citizenship been replaced by consumption in the "fast world" of the new century? Has government (and political democracy itself) become irrelevant in a world ruled by distant markets? Has individualism eroded the bonds of community? As the new millennium begins, these questions and others like them will challenge not only Americans, but people throughout the world.

The "New Economy" of the 1990s

ROBERT D. ATKINSON AND RANDOLPH H. COURT

The U.S. economy is undergoing a fundamental transformation at the dawn of the new millennium. Some of the most obvious outward signs of change are in fact among the root causes of it: revolutionary technological advances, including powerful personal computers, high-speed telecommunications, and the Internet. The market environment facilitated by these and other developments in the last decade and a half has been variously labeled the "information economy," "network economy," "digital economy," "knowledge economy," and the "risk society." Together, the whole package is often simply referred to as the "New Economy."

The story of how businesses are changing in today's economy has been told and retold with such frequency in recent years that it has become something of a cliché: the new rules of the game require speed, flexibility, and innovation. New, rapidly growing companies are selling to global markets almost from their inception, and established companies are being forced to reinvent their operations to stay competitive in the new terrain. This is the part of the New Economy that was born in Steve Jobs' and Steve Wozniak's garage, at Bell Labs, Xerox PARC, and in the trunk of Michael Dell's car. It is Silicon Valley: Netscape, Yahoo!, and the next Big Thing. And of course it is Microsoft, with a market capitalization now second only to General Electric's.

But this New Economy is about more than high technology and the frenetic action at the cutting edge. Most firms, not just the ones actually producing technology, are organizing work around it. The New Economy is a metal casting firm in Pittsburgh that uses computer-aided manufacturing technology to cut costs, save energy, and reduce waste. It is a farmer in Nebraska who sows genetically altered seeds and drives a tractor with a global satellite positioning system. It is an insurance company in Iowa that uses software to flatten managerial hierarchies and give its workers broader responsibilities and autonomy. It is a textile firm in Georgia that uses the Internet to take orders from customers around the world.

It is also as much about new organizational models as it is about new technologies. The New Economy is the Miller brewery in Trenton, Ohio, which produces 50 percent more beer per worker than the company's next-most-productive facility, in part because a lean, 13-member crew has been trained to work in teams to handle the overnight shift with no oversight.

Yet while the social and political implications of this New Economy are clearly vast, our system for tracking economic progress—the set of indicators we

"The 'New Economy' of the 1990s," by Robert D. Atkinson and Randoph H. Court. Introduction to "The New Economy Index: Understanding America's Economic Transformation" (Policy Report, 1998). By permission of Progressive Policy Institute. www.ppionline.org

use as a gauge—has not kept up with the pace of evolution. Our statistical system was essentially established to measure a stable economy with most of the output in agriculture and manufactured goods. Until the Great Depression, economic indicators were often measures of natural resources and commodity production: the number of bales of cotton produced, hogs raised, steel ingots melted. (Even today, the United States spends three times more on agricultural statistics than on national income statistics, according to MIT economist Lester Thurow.) After the New Deal and the creation of federal statistical agencies, our economic indicators began to focus on monetary measures related to managing the business cycle. For example, significant effort is made to track the gross domestic product (GDP), inflation and changes in the money supply, business inventories, and consumer purchases thought to affect the business cycle, such as housing and autos. (The first 15 pages of the Congressional Joint Economic Committee's monthly "Economic Indicators" are devoted to these sorts of indicators of the business cycle. It is not until the sixteenth page that the report gets to arguably the most important indicator of economic well-being: productivity.)

The purpose of this report is to draw on a new set of indicators, gathered from existing public and private data, to examine some of the key characteristics of the New Economy. We have divided these indicators into three groups. The first group tracks some of the elemental structural changes that collectively mark the transition to the New Economy: industrial and occupational change, globalization, the changing nature of competition and economic dynamism, and the progress of the information technology (IT) revolution. The second group examines the implications of this transition for working Americans: what is happening to incomes and economic growth, jobs, and employment dynamics. The third group assesses the nation's performance in terms of three main foundations for growth in the New Economy: the pace of transition to a digital economy, investment by business and government in technology and innovation, and progress on the development of education and skills.

Structural Transformation

Beyond the technological advances, what is actually new about the so-called New Economy? In one respect, nothing. We still work at jobs for a living, and we still buy, sell, and trade products and services, just like we always have. As Federal Reserve Chairman Alan Greenspan has noted, the heart of the economy is, as it always has been, grounded in human nature, not in any new technological reality. In Greenspan's analysis,

> The way we evaluate assets, and the way changes in those assets affect our economy, do not appear to be coming out of a set of rules that is different from the one that governed the actions of our forebears. . . . As in the past, our advanced economy is primarily driven by how human psychology molds the value system that drives a competitive market economy. And that process is inextricably linked to human nature, which appears essentially immutable and, thus, anchors the future to the past.

Nonetheless, Greenspan and other economists agree that some of the key rules of the game are changing, from the way we organize production, to our patterns of trade, to the way organizations deliver value to consumers. . . .

The United States is ahead of the curve in a number of areas. Here, one of the most noticeable structural changes in the New Economy is the degree to which dynamism, constant innovation, and adaptation have become the norm. One of the keys to the recent strong U.S. economic performance has been the country's ability to embrace these changes. Nearly three quarters of all new jobs are being created by 350,000 new fast-growing "gazelle" firms (companies with sales growth of at least 20 percent per year for four straight years). Almost a third of all jobs are now in flux (either being born or dying, added or subtracted) every year. This churning of the economy is being spurred by new technology, but also by increasing competition, a trend that is in turn partly a product of increasing globalization. Between 1970 and 1997, U.S. imports and exports grew three and a half times faster than GDP in 1992 dollars.

Another striking structural characteristic of the New Economy is occupational change. Between 1969 and 1995, virtually all the jobs lost in the production or distribution of goods have been replaced by jobs in offices. Today, almost 93 million American workers (which amounts to 80 percent of all jobs) do not spend their days making things—instead, they move things, process or generate information, or provide services to people.

The Challenge Ahead

Is all of this turbulence, change, and complexity temporary, simply the byproduct of the transition from the Industrial Age to an information era? Or are these intrinsic and permanent aspects of the New Economy? The Progressive Policy Institute believes that the latter is true and that the challenge now is to learn how to manage and govern in an era of sustained and constant innovation and adaptation.

Some see the emergence of the New Economy as disruptive and threatening. Others celebrate it uncritically, ignoring the social strains created by its constant change and uneven distribution of costs and benefits, and rejecting any role for government. PPI subscribes to a third view, embracing the inherent new possibilities born of unleashed entrepreneurial energy for technological and economic progress, while supporting policies that foster growth and innovation, and equip all Americans with the tools they need to succeed. The New Economy is not an end in itself, but the means to advance larger progressive goals: new economic opportunities and higher living standards, more individual choice and freedom, greater dignity and autonomy for working Americans, stronger communities, and wider citizen participation in public life.

Today, though the foundations for the New Economy are in place, widespread benefits haven't yet been realized. Despite job growth, low unemployment, and other notable signs of economic progress—and despite gushing press accounts of fabulous new wealth and opportunities—a central paradox of the emerging New Economy is that the 1980s and 1990s have seen productivity and per capita GDP growth rates languish in the 1.25 percent range, while income inequality has grown. Our challenge is to create a progressive economic policy framework that will encourage a new era of higher growth, while promoting and enabling a broad-based prosperity that produces the widest possible winner's circle.

Old economic policy, shaped by the Great Depression, largely focused on creating jobs, controlling inflation, and managing the business cycle. The New Economy brings new concerns. Technology, as well as a highly competent Federal

Reserve policy, may have lessened the importance and severity of the domestic business cycle. We have shown that we can create jobs—over nine million of them in the first five years of the Clinton Administration. And there is general agreement that in the new global economy, with increased competition and technology, the risk of inflation is reduced. The real challenge of economic policy now is to support and foster continued adaptation, including policies that lead to a fully digital economy characterized by continuous, high levels of innovation and a highly educated and skilled workforce.

The nascent transformation to a digital economy, where an increasing share of economic value is a product of electronic means, has the potential to usher in a new period of sustained higher productivity and wage growth in America. Most of the indicators of the transformation to a digital economy forecast steady progress. Computing and telecommunications costs have been falling dramatically, and the U.S. Internet economy is projected to be worth $350 billion by 2001 (when nearly 40 percent of U.S. households are projected to be online). But realizing the digital economy's potential will depend in part on regulatory, tax, and procurement policies—at all levels of government—aimed first at not hindering, and where possible at fostering this transformation. Government also clearly has a role to play in spurring the transformation by encouraging the electronic delivery of public services, though it has taken little more than baby steps in the right direction at this point.

New Economy economists like Paul Romer, Richard Nelson, and Rob Shapiro have focused on knowledge, technology, and learning as keys to economic growth and have begun to focus on how policy can actually affect innovation. A consensus has emerged that investments to develop and commercialize research and technology play a major role in increased standards of living for Americans. However, indicators of innovation and investment suggest cause for concern. In the last five years, federal support for both basic and applied research has fallen precipitously. Industry investment in basic research has also declined. Similarly, over the last decade the stock of machinery and equipment that American workers use to be productive has fallen as a share of GDP.

Education is another economic foundation area showing a lack of sufficient progress. Corporate expenditures on employee training have fallen in the 1990s as a share of GDP. Meanwhile, K–12 performance has simply failed to keep up with the pressing need for a skilled workforce, in spite of continued increases in education spending. We need a set of policies to ensure that American companies have the skilled workers they need to be productive, and that American workers have the skills they need to navigate, adapt, and prosper in the New Economy.

The New Economy puts a premium on what Nobel Laureate economist Douglas North calls "adaptive efficiency"—the ability of institutions to innovate, continuously learn, and productively change. In the old economy, fixed assets, financing, and labor were principal sources of competitive advantage for firms. But now, as markets fragment, technology accelerates, and competition comes from unexpected places, learning, creativity, and adaptation are becoming the principal sources of competitive advantage in many industries. Enabling constant innovation has become the goal of any organization committed to prospering, and should also become the goal of public policy in the New Economy.

PPI believes that a progressive innovation-oriented policy framework for the New Economy should rest on four pillars:

1. Investment in new economic foundations, specifically education, training, and scientific and technological research.
2. Creation of an open and flexible regulatory and trade regime that supports growth and innovation, including policies that support the IT revolution.
3. Development of policies to enable American workers to have the tools they need to navigate, adapt, and prosper in a continually changing economic environment.
4. Reinvention—and digitization—of government to make it fast, responsive, and flexible.

In summary, if we are to ask workers to take the risks inherent in embracing the New Economy, we must equip them with the tools to allow them to prosper and cope with change and uncertainty. If we fail to invest in a knowledge infrastructure—world-class education, training, science, and technology—our enterprises will not have the skilled workers and cutting-edge tools they need to grow and create well-paying jobs. And if Industrial Age government does not transform itself into Information Age government, it will become an inefficient, anachronistic institution, impeding rather than advancing progress.

Keys to the Old and New Economies

ISSUE	OLD ECONOMY	NEW ECONOMY
ECONOMY-WIDE CHARACTERISTICS		
Markets	Stable	Dynamic
Scope of competition	National	Global
Organizational form	Hierarchical, bureaucratic	Networked
INDUSTRY		
Organization of production	Mass production	Flexible production
Key drivers of growth	Capital/labor	Innovation/knowledge
Key technology driver	Mechanization	Digitization
Source of competitive advantage	Lowering cost through economies of scale	Innovation, quality, time-to-market, and cost
Importance of research/innovation	Low–moderate	High
Relations with other firms	Go it alone	Alliances and collaboration
WORKFORCE		
Policy goal	Full employment	Higher real wages and incomes
Skills	Job-specific skills	Broad skills and cross-training
Requisite education	A skill or degree	Lifelong learning
Labor-management relations	Adversarial	Collaborative
Nature of employment	Stable	Marked by risk and opportunity
GOVERNMENT		
Business-government relations	Impose requirements	Encourage growth opportunities
Regulation	Command and control	Market tools, flexibility

Nine Myths About the New Economy

Almost everyone now agrees that the U.S. economy has undergone fundamental changes in the last 15 years, whether or not they refer to these changes as constituting a New Economy. However, too often the discussion on either end of the political spectrum has been driven by inaccurate assessments and selective choices of data—in short, by New Economy myths.

For many on the left, the New Economy represents a new threat to economic justice and social cohesion. These New Economy pessimists emphasize—and exaggerate—the downsides of the New Economy, while underestimating the benefits. They blame technology and globalization for downsizing, stagnant wages, growing inequality, and environmental degradation. Sometimes this leads to internally contradictory positions. They claim that if companies install technology, workers are laid off, but if companies don't install technology, they are milking profits and not reinvesting to raise wages. Pessimists correctly point out that economic change creates losers as well as winners, but their preferred solution is too often to slow or stop the processes of change. Thus, they prescribe trade protection, top-down regulation, and spending on outdated industrial-era bureaucratic programs. Their "land of milk and honey" is made up of large organizations with stable employment, stable markets, and stable competition, which are unrealistic expectations in the context of the fundamental trends in the New Economy.

For many on the right, the dawn of a digital era automatically means the twilight of government. These New Economy optimists emphasize—and exaggerate—the upsides of the New Economy, while overlooking its problems. While viewing it correctly as an era with great possibilities for growth and creativity, some on the right seek the elimination of virtually all regulation of technology, oppose government funding of research and development (excluding defense), and argue that government should simply "get out of the way," a stance that leaves Americans to fend for themselves during a difficult, often wrenching transition. Their "land of milk and honey" is made up of small firms and individual entrepreneurs in dynamic markets; higher income inequality that encourages hard work; a vastly reduced role for government, including reduced roles in technology, education, and skill development; and little effort to expand the winner's circle so that all Americans share in the benefits.

New Economy Pessimists' Myths

MYTH #1 The New Economy has facilitated the dramatic deindustrialization of America.
REALITY *Manufacturing has not disappeared, it has been reinvented.*
Between 1987 and 1996, inflation-adjusted manufacturing output in the United States increased 27 percent. But because of investments in technology, training, and new forms of work organization, U.S. firms were able to improve productivity even faster, which meant that manufacturing employment declined by only 1.4 percent.

MYTH #2 In the New Economy, globalization and corporate greed have combined to produce stagnant wages for most American workers.
REALITY *Slow growth in real wages is a result of slow growth in economy-wide productivity.*
While income inequality is linked to technological change, immigration, and the decline of unionism, total wage income in the economy is tied to productivity growth. From 1963 to 1973, business productivity grew 35 percent while wages grew 31 percent. Between 1985 and 1995, productivity grew 9 percent, while wages grew only 6 percent. Without faster productivity growth, faster wage growth is impossible. Some argue that wages have stagnated because corporate profits grew. In fact, if all of the increase in the share of national income going to corporate dividends went instead to wages, the latter would have increased only marginally faster between 1978 and 1997—20 percent instead of 16 percent.

MYTH #3 In the New Economy, most new jobs are low-wage jobs.
REALITY *Low-wage jobs are growing, but higher-wage jobs are growing even faster.*
Between 1989 and 1998, high-paying jobs grew 20 percent, while low-paying jobs grew 10 percent. Middle-paying jobs showed no growth.

MYTH #4 Technological change kills more jobs than it creates.
REALITY *Technology changes the composition of jobs and raises productivity and incomes, but it does not raise the natural rate of unemployment. On the contrary, the dynamic New Economy has reduced unemployment rates to a 25-year low.*
New technologies (e.g., tractors, disease resistant crops, etc.) spurred the decline in agricultural jobs. However, as food became cheaper (American consumers spend less of their income on food than any other nation) consumers spent their increased real income on other things (e.g., cars, appliances, entertainment), creating employment in other sectors. The 30-year low for unemployment after the wave of corporate downsizing and technology introduction makes it clear that technology doesn't reduce the total number of jobs in the economy. As new information technologies begin to raise productivity growth rates, this same positive dynamic will continue, leading to higher incomes, not fewer jobs.

MYTH #5 Corporate reengineering has meant the downsizing of large numbers of middle class, managerial jobs.

REALITY *In the last nine years, three million new managerial jobs have been added (14.8 million in 1989 to 18 million in 1998).*

Despite the fact that New Economy organizations flatten hierarchies, the New Economy spurs greater demand for more managers who focus on quality, innovation, design, marketing, and finance.

New Economy Optimists' Myths

MYTH #1 The U.S. economy is in the midst of [an] unprecedented economic boom that began in the early 1980s.

REALITY *Growth in per capita GDP, productivity, and wages since the 1980s have lagged behind growth rates in the 1960s and early 1970s.*

While job growth was stronger in the 1980s and 1990s than in the 1960s and 1970s, productivity and per capita GDP grew about half as fast.

MYTH #2 Income inequality is not a serious problem.

REALITY *Between 1980 and 1996, real incomes went up 58 percent for the wealthiest 5 percent of American households, but less than 4 percent for the lowest 60 percent.*

Household income inequality has increased and has made it more difficult for many Americans to achieve the American dream. The strength of America's economy has historically been that most Americans have felt that they can prosper if they get an education, work hard, and play by the rules. If this compact is broken, our social fabric will start to disintegrate.

MYTH #3 The dispersing tendencies of the New Economy mean the death of large corporations and the twilight of government.

REALITY *Large corporations and government are reinventing themselves and still play key roles in the economy, to say the least.*

Because information technology lets firms reach larger markets and take advantage of economies of scale, the average size of firms in the New Economy is growing, not shrinking. Moreover, just as the Internet did not mean the end of large companies like IBM, it also does not bode the end of government. Rather, it creates a requirement that governments re-engineer themselves to be faster, more flexible, and smarter.

MYTH #4 In the New Economy, a significantly growing share of the workforce are *[sic]* self-employed entrepreneurs.
REALITY *Entrepreneurs represent about the same share of the workforce as ever.*
Between 1975 and 1994, self-employment as a share of total employment remained level at approximately 8.7 percent (10.6 million workers)—an all-time low.

Jihad vs. McWorld

BENJAMIN R. BARBER

Just beyond the horizon of current events lie two possible political futures—both bleak, neither democratic. The first is a retribalization of large swaths of humankind by war and bloodshed: a threatened Lebanonization of national states in which culture is pitted against culture, people against people, tribe against tribe—a Jihad in the name of a hundred narrowly conceived faiths against every kind of interdependence, every kind of artificial social cooperation and civic mutuality. The second is being borne in on us by the onrush of economic and ecological forces that demand integration and uniformity and that mesmerize the world with fast music, fast computers, and fast food—with MTV, Macintosh, and McDonald's, pressing nations into one commercially homogenous global network: one McWorld tied together by technology, ecology, communications, and commerce. The planet is falling precipitantly apart *and* coming reluctantly together at the very same moment.

These two tendencies are sometimes visible in the same countries at the same instant: thus Yugoslavia, clamoring just recently to join the New Europe, is exploding into fragments; India is trying to live up to its reputation as the world's largest integral democracy while powerful new fundamentalist parties like the Hindu nationalist Bharatiya Janata Party, along with nationalist assassins, are imperiling its hard-won unity. States are breaking up or joining up: the Soviet Union has disappeared almost overnight, its parts forming new unions with one another or with like-minded nationalities in neighboring states. The old interwar national state based on territory and political sovereignty looks to be a mere transitional development.

The tendencies of what I am here calling the forces of Jihad and the forces of McWorld operate with equal strength in opposite directions, the one driven by parochial hatreds, the other by universalizing markets, the one re-creating ancient subnational and ethnic borders from within, the other making national borders porous from without. They have one thing in common: neither offers much hope to citizens looking for practical ways to govern themselves democratically. If the global future is to pit Jihad's centrifugal whirlwind against McWorld's centripetal black hole, the outcome is unlikely to be democratic—or so I will argue.

"Jihad vs. McWorld" by Benjamin R. Barber. Published originally in *Atlantic Monthly* March 1992 as an introduction to *Jihad vs. McWorld* (Ballantine paperback, 1996), a volume that discusses and extends the themes of the original article.

McWorld, or the Globalization of Politics

Four imperatives make up the dynamic of McWorld: a market imperative, a resource imperative, an information-technology imperative, and an ecological imperative. By shrinking the world and diminishing the salience of national borders, these imperatives have in combination achieved a considerable victory over factiousness and particularism, and not least of all over their most virulent traditional form—nationalism. It is the realists who are now Europeans, the utopians who dream nostalgically of a resurgent England or Germany, perhaps even a resurgent Wales or Saxony. Yesterday's wishful cry for one world has yielded to the reality of McWorld.

The Market Imperative.   Marxist and Leninist theories of imperialism assumed that the quest for ever-expanding markets would in time compel nation-based capitalist economies to push against national boundaries in search of an international economic imperium. Whatever else has happened to the scientistic predictions of Marxism, in this domain they have proved farsighted. All national economies are now vulnerable to the inroads of larger, transnational markets within which trade is free, currencies are convertible, access to banking is open, and contracts are enforceable under law. In Europe, Asia, Africa, the South Pacific, and the Americas such markets are eroding national sovereignty and giving rise to entities—international banks, trade associations, transnational lobbies like OPEC and Greenpeace, world news services like CNN and the BBC, and multinational corporations that increasingly lack a meaningful national identity—that neither reflect nor respect nationhood as an organizing or regulative principle.

The market imperative has also reinforced the quest for international peace and stability, requisites of an efficient international economy. Markets are enemies of parochialism, isolation, fractiousness, war. Market psychology attenuates the psychology of ideological and religious cleavages and assumes a concord among producers and consumers—categories that ill fit narrowly conceived national or religious cultures. Shopping has little tolerance for blue laws, whether dictated by pub-closing British paternalism, Sabbath-observing Jewish Orthodox fundamentalism, or no-Sunday-liquor-sales Massachusetts puritanism. In the context of common markets, international law ceases to be a vision of justice and becomes a workaday framework for getting things done—enforcing contracts, ensuring that governments abide by deals, regulating trade and currency relations, and so forth.

Common markets demand a common language, as well as a common currency, and they produce common behaviors of the kind bred by cosmopolitan city life everywhere. Commercial pilots, computer programmers, international bankers, media specialists, oil riggers, entertainment celebrities, ecology experts, demographers, accountants, professors, athletes—these compose a new breed of men and women for whom religion, culture, and nationality can seem only marginal elements in a working identity. Although sociologists of everyday life will no doubt continue to distinguish a Japanese from an American mode, shopping has a common signature throughout the world. Cynics might even say that some of the recent revolutions in Eastern Europe have had as their true goal not liberty and the right to vote but well-paying jobs and the right to shop (although the vote is proving easier to acquire than consumer goods). The market imperative is, then, plenty powerful; but, notwithstanding some of the claims made for "democratic capitalism," it is not identical with the democratic imperative.

The Resource Imperative.   Democrats once dreamed of societies whose political autonomy rested firmly on economic independence. The Athenians idealized what they called autarky, and tried for a while to create a way of life simple and austere enough to make the polis genuinely self-sufficient. To be free meant to be independent of any other community or polis. Not even the Athenians were able to achieve autarky, however: human nature, it turns out, is dependency. By the time of Pericles, Athenian politics was inextricably bound up with a flowering empire held together by naval power and commerce—an empire that, even as it appeared to enhance Athenian might, ate away at Athenian independence and autarky. Master and slave, it turned out, were bound together by mutual insufficiency.

The dream of autarky briefly engrossed nineteenth-century America as well, for the underpopulated, endlessly bountiful land, the cornucopia of natural resources, and the natural barriers of a continent walled in by two great seas led many to believe that America could be a world unto itself. Given this past, it has been harder for Americans than for most to accept the inevitability of interdependence. But the rapid depletion of resources even in a country like ours, where they once seemed inexhaustible, and the maldistribution of arable soil and mineral resources on the planet, leave even the wealthiest societies ever more resource-dependent and many other nations in permanently desperate straits.

Every nation, it turns out, needs something another nation has; some nations have almost nothing they need.

The Information-Technology Imperative.   Enlightenment science and the technologies derived from it are inherently universalizing. They entail a quest for descriptive principles of general application, a search for universal solutions to particular problems, and an unswerving embrace of objectivity and impartiality.

Scientific progress embodies and depends on open communication, a common discourse rooted in rationality, collaboration, and an easy and regular flow and exchange of information. Such ideals can be hypocritical covers for power-mongering by elites, and they may be shown to be wanting in many other ways, but they are entailed by the very idea of science and they make science and globalization practical allies.

Business, banking, and commerce all depend on information flow and are facilitated by new communication technologies. The hardware of these technologies tends to be systemic and integrated—computer, television, cable, satellite, laser, fiber-optic, and microchip technologies combining to create a vast interactive communications and information network that can potentially give every person on earth access to every other person and make every datum, every byte, available to every set of eyes. If the automobile was, as George Ball once said (when he gave his blessings to a Fiat factory in the Soviet Union during the Cold War), "an ideology on four wheels," then electronic telecommunication and information systems are an ideology at 186,000 miles per second—which makes for a very small planet in a very big hurry. Individual cultures speak particular languages; commerce and science increasingly speak English; the whole world speaks logarithms and binary mathematics.

Moreover, the pursuit of science and technology asks for, even compels, open societies. Satellite footprints do not respect national borders; telephone wires penetrate the most closed societies. With photocopying and then fax machines having infiltrated Soviet universities and *samizdat* literary circles in the eighties, and computer modems having multiplied like rabbits in communism's bureaucratic warrens thereafter, *glasnost* could not be far behind. In their social requisites, secrecy and science are enemies.

The new technology's software is perhaps even more globalizing than its hardware. The information arm of international commerce's sprawling body reaches out and touches distinct nations and parochial cultures, and gives them a common face chiseled in Hollywood, on Madison Avenue, and in Silicon Valley. Throughout the 1980s one of the most-watched television programs in South Africa was *The Cosby Show.* The demise of apartheid was already in production. Exhibitors at the 1991 Cannes film festival expressed growing anxiety over the "homogenization" and "Americanization" of the global film industry when, for the third year running, American films dominated the awards ceremonies. America has dominated the world's popular culture for much longer, and much more decisively. In November of 1991 Switzerland's once insular culture boasted best-seller lists featuring *Terminator 2* as the No. 1 movie, *Scarlett* as the No. 1 book, and Prince's *Diamonds and Pearls* as the No. 1 record album. No wonder the Japanese are buying Hollywood film studios even faster than Americans are buying Japanese television sets. This kind of software supremacy may in the long term be far more important than hardware superiority, because culture has become more potent than armaments. What is the power of the Pentagon compared with Disneyland? Can the Sixth Fleet keep up with CNN? McDonald's in Moscow and Coke in China will do more to create a global culture than military colonization ever could. It is less the goods than the brand names that do the work, for they convey life-style images that alter perception and challenge behavior. They make up the seductive software of McWorld's common (at times much too common) soul.

Yet in all this high-tech commercial world there is nothing that looks particularly democratic. It lends itself to surveillance as well as liberty, to new forms of manipulation and covert control as well as new kinds of participation, to skewed, unjust market outcomes as well as greater productivity. The consumer society and the open society are not quite synonymous. Capitalism and democracy have a relationship, but it is something less than a marriage. An efficient free market after all requires that consumers be free to vote their dollars on competing goods, not that citizens be free to vote their values and beliefs on competing political candidates and programs. The free market flourished in junta-run Chile, in military-governed Taiwan and Korea, and, earlier, in a variety of autocratic European empires as well as their colonial possessions.

The Ecological Imperative.   The impact of globalization on ecology is a cliché even to world leaders who ignore it. We know well enough that the German forests can be destroyed by Swiss and Italians driving gas-guzzlers fueled by leaded gas.

We also know that the planet can be asphyxiated by greenhouse gases because Brazilian farmers want to be part of the twentieth century and are burning down tropical rain forests to clear a little land to plough, and because Indonesians make a living out of converting their lush jungle into toothpicks for fastidious Japanese diners, upsetting the delicate oxygen balance and in effect puncturing our global lungs. Yet this ecological consciousness has meant not only greater awareness but also greater inequality, as modernized nations try to slam the door behind them, saying to developing nations, "The world cannot afford *your* modernization; ours has wrung it dry!"

Each of the four imperatives just cited is transnational, transideological, and transcultural. Each applies impartially to Catholics, Jews, Muslims, Hindus, and Buddhists; to democrats and totalitarians; to capitalists and socialists. The Enlightenment dream of a universal rational society has to a remarkable degree been realized—but in a form that is commercialized, homogenized, depoliticized, bureaucratized and, of course, radically incomplete, for the movement toward McWorld is in competition with forces of global breakdown, national dissolution, and centrifugal corruption. These forces, working in the opposite direction, are the essence of what I call Jihad.

Jihad, or the Lebanonization of the World

OPEC, the World Bank, the United Nations, the International Red Cross, the multinational corporation . . . there are scores of institutions that reflect globalization. But they often appear as ineffective reactors to the world's real actors: national states and, to an ever greater degree, subnational factions in permanent rebellion against uniformity and integration—even the kind represented by universal law and justice. The headlines feature these players regularly: they are cultures, not countries; parts, not wholes; sects, not religions; rebellious factions and dissenting minorities at war not just with globalism but with the traditional nation-state. Kurds, Basques, Puerto Ricans, Ossetians, East Timoreans, Quebeçois; the Catholics of Northern Ireland, Abkhasians, Kurile Islander Japanese, the Zulus of Inkatha, Catalonians, Tamils, and, of course, Palestinians—people without countries, inhabiting nations not their own, seeking smaller worlds within borders that will seal them off from modernity.

A powerful irony is at work here. Nationalism was once a force of integration and unification, a movement aimed at bringing together disparate clans, tribes, and cultural fragments under new, assimiliationist flags. But as Ortega y Gasset noted more than sixty years ago, having won its victories, nationalism changed its strategy. In the 1920s, and again today, it is more often a reactionary and divisive force, pulverizing the very nations it once helped cement together. The force that creates nations is "inclusive," Ortega wrote in *The Revolt of the Masses.* "In periods of consolidation, nationalism has a positive value, and is a lofty standard. But in Europe everything is more than consolidated, and nationalism is nothing but a mania. . . ."

This mania has left the post–Cold War world smoldering with hot wars; the international scene is little more unified than it was at the end of the Great War, in Ortega's own time. There were more than thirty wars in progress last year, most of them ethnic, racial, tribal, or religious in character, and the list of unsafe regions doesn't seem to be getting any shorter. Some new world order!

The aim of many of these small-scale wars is to redraw boundaries, to implode states and resecure parochial identities: to escape McWorld's dully insistent imperatives. The mood is that of Jihad: war not as an instrument of policy but as an emblem of identity, an expression of community, an end in itself. Even where there is no shooting war, there is fractiousness, secession, and the quest for ever smaller communities. Add to the list of dangerous countries those at risk: In Switzerland and Spain, Jurassian and Basque separatists still argue the virtues of ancient identities, sometimes in the language of bombs. Hyperdisintegration in the former Soviet Union may well continue unabated—not just a Ukraine independent from the Soviet Union but a Bessarabian Ukraine independent from the Ukrainian republic; not just Russia severed from the defunct union but Tatarstan severed from Russia. Yugoslavia makes even the disunited, ex-Soviet, nonsocialist republics that were once the Soviet Union look integrated, its sectarian fatherlands springing up within factional motherlands like weeds within weeds within weeds. Kurdish independence would threaten the territorial integrity of four Middle Eastern nations. Well before the current cataclysm Soviet Georgia made a claim for autonomy from the Soviet Union, only to be faced with its Ossetians (164,000 in a republic of 5.5 million) demanding their own self-determination within Georgia. The Abkhasian minority in Georgia has followed suit. Even the good will established by Canada's once promising Meech Lake protocols is in danger, with Francophone Quebec again threatening the dissolution of the federation. In South Africa the emergence from apartheid was hardly achieved when friction between Inkatha's Zulus and the African National Congress's tribally identified members threatened to replace European's racism with an indigenous tribal war. After thirty years of attempted integration using the colonial language (English) as a unifier, Nigeria is now playing with the idea of linguistic multiculturalism—which could mean the cultural breakup of the nation into hundreds of tribal fragments. Even Saddam Hussein has benefited from the threat of internal Jihad, having used renewed tribal and religious warfare to turn last season's mortal enemies into reluctant allies of an Iraqi nationhood that he nearly destroyed.

The passing of communism has torn away the thin veneer of internationalism (workers of the world unite!) to reveal ethnic prejudices that are not only ugly and deep-seated but increasingly murderous. Europe's old scourge, anti-Semitism, is back with a vengeance, but it is only one of many antagonisms. It appears all too easy to throw the historical gears into reverse and pass from a Communist dictatorship back into a tribal state.

Among the tribes, religion is also a battlefield. ("Jihad" is a rich word whose generic meaning is "struggle"—usually the struggle of the soul to avert evil. Strictly applied to religious war, it is used only in reference to battles where the faith is under assault, or battles against a government that denies the practice of Islam. My use here is rhetorical, but does follow both journalistic practice and history.) Remember the Thirty Years War? Whatever forms of Enlightenment universalism might once have come to grace such historically related forms of monotheism as Judaism, Christianity, and Islam, in many of their modern incarnations they are parochial rather than cosmopolitan, angry rather than loving, proselytizing rather than ecumenical, zealous rather than rationalist, sectarian rather than deistic, ethnocentric rather than universalizing. As result, like the new forms of hypernationalism, the new expressions of religious fundamentalism are fractious and pulverizing, never integrating. This is religion as the Crusaders knew it: a battle to the death for souls that if not saved will be forever lost.

The atmospherics of Jihad have resulted in a breakdown of civility in the name of identity, of comity in the name of community. International relations have sometimes taken on the aspect of gang war—cultural turf battles featuring tribal factions that were supposed to be sublimated as integral parts of large national, economic, postcolonial, and constitutional entities.

The Darkening Future of Democracy

These rather melodramatic tableaux vivants do not tell the whole story, however. For all their defects, Jihad and McWorld have their attractions. Yet, to repeat and insist, the attractions are unrelated to democracy. Neither McWorld nor Jihad is remotely democratic in impulse. Neither needs democracy; neither promotes democracy.

McWorld does manage to look pretty seductive in a world obsessed with Jihad. It delivers peace, prosperity, and relative unity—if at the cost of independence, community, and identity (which is generally based on difference). The primary political values required by the global market are order and tranquillity, and freedom—as in the phrases "free trade," "free press," and "free love." Human rights are needed to a degree, but not citizenship or participation—and no more social justice and equality than are necessary to promote efficient economic production and consumption. Multinational corporations sometimes seem to prefer doing business with local oligarchs, inasmuch as they can take confidence from dealing with the boss on all crucial matters. Despots who slaughter their own populations are no problem, so long as they leave markets in place and refrain from making war on their neighbors (Saddam Hussein's fatal mistake). In trading partners, predictability is of more value than justice.

The Eastern European revolutions that seemed to arise out of concern for global democratic values quickly deteriorated into a stampede in the general direction of free markets and their ubiquitous, television-promoted shopping malls. East Germany's Neues Forum, that courageous gathering of intellectuals, students, and workers which overturned the Stalinist regime in Berlin in 1989, lasted only six months in Germany's mini-version of McWorld. Then it gave way to money and markets and monopolies from the West. By the time of the first all-German elections, it could scarcely manage to secure three percent of the vote. Elsewhere there is growing evidence that *glasnost* will go and *perestroika*—defined as privatization and an opening of markets to Western bidders—will stay. So understandably anxious are the new rulers of Eastern Europe and whatever entities are forged from the residues of the Soviet Union to gain access to credit and markets and technology—McWorld's flourishing new currencies—that they have shown themselves willing to trade away democratic prospects in pursuit of them: not just old totalitarian ideologies and command-economy production models but some possible indigenous experiments with a third way between capitalism and socialism, such as economic cooperatives and employee stock-ownership plans, both of which have their ardent supporters in the East.

Jihad delivers a different set of virtues: a vibrant local identity, a sense of community, solidarity among kinsmen, neighbors, and countrymen, narrowly conceived.

But it also guarantees parochialism and is grounded in exclusion. Solidarity is secured through war against outsiders. And solidarity often means obedience to a hierarchy in governance, fanaticism in beliefs, and the obliteration of individual selves in the name of the group. Deference to leaders and intolerance toward outsiders (and toward "enemies within") are hallmarks of tribalism—hardly the attitudes required for the cultivation of new democratic women and men capable of governing themselves. Where new democratic experiments have been conducted in retribalizing societies, in both Europe and the Third World, the result has often been anarchy, repression persecution, and the coming of new, noncommunist forms of very old kinds of despotism. During the past year, Havel's velvet revolution in Czechoslovakia was imperiled by partisans of "Czechland" and of Slovakia as independence entities. India seemed little less rent by Sikh, Hindu, Muslim, and Tamil infighting than it was immediately after the British pulled out, more than forty years ago.

To the extent that either McWorld or Jihad has a *natural* politics, it has turned out to be more of an antipolitics. For McWorld, it is the antipolitics of globalism: bureaucratic, technocratic, and meritocratic, focused (as Marx predicted it would be) on the administration of things—with people, however, among the chief things to be administered. In its politico-economic imperatives McWorld has been guided by laissez-faire market principles that privilege efficiency, productivity, and beneficence at the expense of civic liberty and self-government.

For Jihad, the antipolitics of tribalization has been explicitly antidemocratic: one-party dictatorship, government by military junta, theocratic fundamentalism—often association with a version of the *Führerprinzip* that empowers an individual to rule on behalf of a people. Even the government of India, struggling for decades to model democracy for a people who will soon number a billion, longs for great leaders; and for every Mahatma Gandhi, Indira Gandhi, or Rajiv Gandhi taken from them by zealous assassins, the Indians appear to seek a replacement who will deliver them from the lengthy travail of their freedom.

The Confederal Option

How can democracy be secured and spread in a world whose primary tendencies are at best indifferent to it (McWorld) and at worst deeply antithetical to it (Jihad)? My guess is that globalization will eventually vanquish retribalization. The ethos of material "civilization" has not yet encountered an obstacle it has been unable to thrust aside. Ortega may have grasped in the 1920s a clue to our own future in the coming millennium.

> Everyone sees the need of a new principle of life. But as always happens in similar crises—some people attempt to save the situation by an artificial intensification of the very principle which has led to decay. This is the meaning of the "nationalist" outburst of recent years. . . . things have always gone that way. The last flare, the longest; the last sigh, the deepest. On the very eve of their disappearance there is an intensification of frontiers—military and economic.

Jihad may be a last deep sigh before the eternal yawn of McWorld. On the other hand, Ortega was not exactly prescient; his prophecy of peace and internationalism came just before blitzkrieg, world war, and the Holocaust tore the old order to bits.

Yet democracy is how we remonstrate with reality, the rebuke our aspirations offer to history. And if retribalization is inhospitable to democracy, there is nonetheless a form of democratic government that can accommodate parochialism and communitarianism, one that can even save them from their defects and make them more tolerant and participatory: decentralized participatory democracy. And if McWorld is indifferent to democracy, there is nonetheless a form of democratic government that suits global markets passably well—representative government in its federal or, better still, confederal variation.

With its concern for accountability, the protection of minorities, and the universal rule of law, a confederalized representative system would serve the political needs of McWorld as well as oligarchic bureaucratism or meritocratic elitism is currently doing. As we are already beginning to see, many nations may survive in the long term only as confederations that afford local regions smaller than "nations" extensive jurisdiction. Recommended reading for democrats of the twenty-first century is not the U.S. Constitution or the French Declaration of Rights of Man and Citizen but the Articles of Confederation, that suddenly pertinent document that stitched together the thirteen American colonies into what then seemed a too loose confederation of independent states but now appears a new form of political realism, as veterans of Yeltsin's new Russia and the New Europe created at Maastricht will attest.

By the same token, the participatory and direct form of democracy that engages citizens in civic activity and civic judgment and goes well beyond just voting and accountability—the system I have called "strong democracy"—suits the political needs of centralized communities as well as theocratic and nationalist party dictatorships have done. Local neighborhoods need not be democratic, but they can be. Real democracy has flourished in diminutive settings: the spirit of liberty, Tocqueville said, is local. Participatory democracy, if not naturally apposite to tribalism, has an undeniable attractiveness under conditions of parochialism.

Democracy in any of these variations will, however, continue to be obstructed by the undemocratic and antidemocratic trends toward uniformitarian globalism and intolerant retribalization which I have portrayed here. For democracy to persist in our brave new McWorld, we will have to commit acts of conscious political will—a possibility, but hardly a probability, under these conditions. Political will requires much more than the quick fix of the transfer of institutions. Like technology transfer, institution transfer rests on foolish assumptions about a uniform world of the kind that once fired the imagination of colonial administrators. Spread English justice to the colonies by exporting wigs. Let an East Indian trading company act as the vanguard to Britain's free parliamentary institutions. Today's well-intentioned quick-fixers in the National Endowment for Democracy and the Kennedy School of Government, in the unions and foundations and universities zealously nurturing contacts in Eastern Europe and the Third World, are hoping to democratize by long distance. Post Bulgaria a parliament by first-class mail. Fed Ex the Bill of Rights to Sri Lanka. Cable Cambodia some common law.

Yet Eastern Europe has already demonstrated that importing free political parties, parliaments, and presses cannot establish a democratic civil society; imposing a free market may even have the opposite effect. Democracy grows from the bottom up and cannot be imposed from the top down. Civil society has to be built from the inside out. The institutional superstructure comes last. Poland may become democratic, but then again it may heed the Pope, and prefer to found its politics on its Catholicism, with uncertain consequences for democracy. Bulgaria may become democratic, but it may prefer tribal war. The former Soviet Union may become a democratic confederation, or it may just grow into an anarchic and weak conglomeration of markets for other nations' goods and services.

Democrats need to seek out indigenous democratic impulses. There is always a desire for self-government, always some expression of participation, accountability, consent, and representation, even in traditional hierarchical societies. These need to be identified, tapped, modified, and incorporated into new democratic practices with an indigenous flavor. The tortoises among the democratizers may ultimately outlive or outpace the hares, for they will have the time and patience to explore conditions along the way, and to adapt their gait to changing circumstances. Tragically, democracy in a hurry often looks something like France in 1794 or China in 1989.

It certainly seems possible that the most attractive democratic ideal in the face of the brutal realities of Jihad and the dull realities of McWorld will be a confederal union of self-autonomous communities smaller than nation-states, tied together into regional economic associations and markets larger than nation-states—participatory and self-determining in local matters at the bottom, representative and accountable at the top. The nation-state would play a diminished role, and sovereignty would lose some of its political potency. The Green movement adage "Think globally, act locally" would actually come to describe the conduct of politics.

This vision reflects only an ideal, however—one that is not terribly likely to be realized. Freedom, Jean-Jacques Rousseau once wrote, is a food easy to eat but hard to digest. Still, democracy has always played itself out against the odds. And democracy remains both a form of coherence as binding as McWorld and a secular faith potentially as inspiriting as Jihad.

America as a New World "Borderland"

RONALD TAKAKI

The Civil Rights Revolution . . . was unable to correct the structural economic foundations of racial inequality. While the laws and court orders prohibited discrimination, they failed to abolish poverty among blacks. African Americans had won the right to sit at a lunch counter and order a hamburger, but many of them did not have the money to pay for their meal. Blacks were told that the law now prohibited discrimination in employment, but they also saw that jobs for them were scarce. The desperation was especially acute in the inner cities of the North. "You know the average young person out here don't have a job, man, they don't have anything to do," a black in Harlem explained angrily in the early 1960s. "You go down to the employment agency and you can't get a job. They have you waiting all day, but you can't get a job." Young blacks of the inner cities knew the playing field was not level. "Those who are required to live in congested and rat-infested

From *A Different Mirror* by Ronald Takaki. Copyright © 1993 by Ronald Takaki. By permission of Little, Brown and Company (Inc.).

homes," scholar Kenneth Clark noted in *Dark Ghetto,* "are aware that others are not so dehumanized. Young people in the ghetto are aware that other young people have been taught to read, that they have been prepared for college, and can compete successfully for white-collar, managerial, and executive jobs." One of these alienated blacks predicted in 1962: "When the time comes, it is going to be too late. Everything will explode because the people they live under tension now; they are going to a point where they can't stand it no more." This point was dramatically reached in Los Angeles during the long hot summer of 1965.

"The fire bombs of Watts blasted the civil rights movement into a new phase," declared Martin Luther King. Ultimately, the struggle to realize the American Dream had to advance beyond antidiscrimination laws and confront what King called the "airtight cage of poverty." The underlying economic basis of racial inequality was a far more elusive and formidable foe than the lynch mobs and police attack dogs. "Jobs are harder and costlier to create than voting rolls," King explained. "The eradication of slums housing millions is complex far beyond integrating buses and lunch counters." This harsh reality of urban squalor and despair was reflected in the jagged mirrors of every northern ghetto. "I see a young Negro boy," King wrote in 1963. "He is sitting on a stoop in front of a vermin-infested apartment house in Harlem. The stench of garbage is in the halls. The drunks, the jobless, the junkies are shadow figures of his everyday world."

This impoverished and depressing world was familiar to Malcolm X. "I don't see any American dream," he declared in 1964; "I see an American nightmare." Growing up in the ghettos of the North, Malcolm Little had pursued a life of drugs and crime. Arrested and found guilty of burglary, he was given an eight-year sentence. As Malcolm X later explained, his "high school" had been the "black ghetto of Roxbury" in Boston, his "college" the "streets of Harlem," and his graduate school the "prison." While serving time, he was converted to Elijah Muhammad's Nation of Islam. As a leader of the Black Muslims, Malcolm X advocated a separatist ideology and mocked King for his belief in integration as well as his strategy of nonviolence. Like David Walker, who had issued his revolutionary appeal in the early nineteenth century, Malcolm X advised blacks to use violence to defend their rights. As the struggle for racial justice shifted from the South to the urban North, Malcolm X's message exposed the failure of the Civil Rights Movement to address the problems of joblessness and poverty. Even Martin Luther King began to feel the despair. Four years after the March on Washington where he had passionately described his "dream," he confessed: "I watched that dream turn into a nightmare as I moved through the ghettos of the nation and saw black brothers and sisters perishing on a lonely island of poverty in the midst of a vast ocean of material prosperity, and saw the nation doing nothing to grapple with the Negroes' problem of poverty." After the Watts riot and his encounter with the "other America" of the ghetto, as historian James H. Cone noted, King more clearly and painfully understood "something of the world that created Malcolm X."

The Civil Rights Movement was hitting the walls of inequality based on class as well as race—what King called the "inseparable twins" of economic injustice and racial injustice. Beginning in the 1960s, black America became deeply splintered into two classes. On the one hand, the black middle class experienced gains: the percentages of families earning $25,000 or more (in 1982 dollars) increased from

10 percent in 1960 to 25 percent in 1982, and the number of blacks in college nearly doubled between 1970 and 1980 (from 522,000 to over a million). On the other hand, there emerged what has been called a "black underclass." The distressing situation of this group can be measured by the persistence of intergenerational poverty, the increasing unemployment rates for young blacks, and the dramatic rise of black female-headed families. Between 1960 and 1980, the percentage of such families doubled, reaching 40 percent, compared to an increase from 8 to 12 percent for white families. While blacks composed only 12 percent of the American population in 1980, they constituted 43 percent of all welfare families.

The context for this deteriorating condition for African Americans extended far beyond the borders of the ghetto. Between 1960 and 1980, the baby boomers of post–World War II entered young adulthood. During these years, the country's total population increased by a quarter, but the eighteen- to twenty-four-year old group had nearly doubled. There were simply more workers entering the labor force: between 1970 and 1980, the labor force grew by 24 million, compared to only 13 million for the previous decade. The sudden entry of this age cohort into the labor market was accompanied by a sharp rise in unemployment—from 2.8 million in 1968 to 7.6 million in 1980. Meanwhile, families supported by Aid to Families with Dependent Children (AFDC) grew from 1.4 million to 3.5 million. Significantly, unemployment rose faster and in greater numbers than AFDC families. Thus, contrary to the claims of pundits like Charles Murray as well as politicians like Ronald Reagan, families were being pushed onto welfare rolls by unemployment, not simply pulled there by welfare benefits. The push was especially felt by young workers: for the age group twenty- to twenty-four-year-olds, unemployment jumped from 8 to 11 percent for white men and from 13 to 22 percent for black men. "By now my wife was pregnant," said John Godfrey. "And I was unemployed. . . . So push came to shove. We went down to welfare. I needed medical protection for her and the baby. It was a sobering experience. I felt—I don't know how to put it into words— I was totally disgusted with myself. I felt I had failed myself, because I was unable to take care of myself and my family.

Soaring unemployment for black men was accompanied by rising welfare enrollments for black women with children. The majority of black mothers on AFDC were young—under thirty years old. They had extremely limited possibilities of finding black men with incomes capable of supporting families. According to sociologist William Julius Wilson's "male marriageable pool index," 72 percent of the black men between ages twenty and twenty-four in 1980 were either unemployed, employed only part-time, or working full-time but earning below poverty wages. For white men in the same age cohort, the rate was only 36 percent. Wilson's model was based on the assumption that the family would be a two-parent unit and that wives would be financially dependent on their husbands. But for black women, the problem of welfare dependency also resulted from gender inequality in the labor market. Like women in general, they found themselves crowded into so-called female-dominated occupations such as low-wage clerical and sales jobs. Some of these occupations, such as secretarial work, required training, but they did not pay "comparable worth"—what male-dominated jobs with similar requirements paid. Consequently, women with children to support often discovered that working did not pay enough to cover child care and living expenses. Therefore, they had no choice but to depend on AFDC in order to make ends meet. Black women were especially disadvantaged in the labor market and more dependent on welfare because of their lower levels of education and job skills. . . .

Moreover, the employment situation of both black women and men has been devastated by recent major changes in the economy. The movement of plants and offices to the suburbs during the last three decades has isolated urban blacks from many places of employment: in 1980, 71 percent of them lived in central cities, whereas 66 percent of whites resided in suburbs. Illustrating the dynamic interaction of the suburbanization of production, unemployment, and welfare, Chicago lost 229,000 jobs and enrolled 290,000 new welfare recipients in the sixties, while its suburbs gained 500,000 jobs. Meanwhile, blacks have also been suffering from the effects of the "deindustrialization of America." Due to the relocation of production in low-wage countries like South Korea and Mexico, some 22 million American workers lost their jobs between 1969 and 1976. "The decline in blue-collar employment hit black men especially hard," sociologist Andrew Hacker reported. "Blacks have been severely hurt by deindustrialization," William Julius Wilson explained, "because of their heavy concentration in the automobile, rubber, steel, and other smokestack industries."

During the two world wars and the labor-organizing drives of the 1930s, blacks were able to find higher-paying jobs in the industrial sector. Opportunities continued after World War II. "I remember when you could quit one job one day and go out the next day and get a better job making more money," said Lawrence Hunter, referring to the bountiful employment situation in Milwaukee in the 1950s. The forty-eight-year-old machinery operator added: "You could go to a foundry and get a job any day. It was hard-bull work, but if push came to shove there was a job for you."

But suddenly, beginning in the late 1960s, push came to shove, and many blacks found themselves out of work. One of these black workers was Jimmy Morse. After working for U.S. Steel in Gary, Indiana, for thirty years, he voluntarily retired in 1983 rather than wait for the imminent layoff. His monthly retirement pay totaled $552.63, which did not pay all his bills. "Now, you get the light bill outta there," he explained in 1986. "You get the water bill outta there. Buy some food outta that plus $131 we get in food stamps. You're about $40 short." Asked about looking for other work, he replied that he was fifty-one years old and was unwilling to commute to Chicago for $3.75 an hour. During the 1970s, the region around Gary had lost 65,000 manufacturing jobs, including 12,000 at U.S. Steel. "Foreign steel was takin' our man-hours away from us," Morse said. "And it ain't no racial thing either. That blue-eyed soul brother is catchin' jes' as much hell as I'm catching." Actually, black workers were catching more than their share of hell. In the ranks of this new army of displaced workers was a disproportionately large number of blacks. A study of 2,380 firms which were shut down in Illinois between 1975 and 1978 found that while blacks constituted only 14 percent of the state's work force, they totaled 20 percent of the laid-off laborers. Of the black workers displaced between 1979 and 1984, only 42 percent were able to secure new employment. The macroeconomic developments of plant shutdowns and economic relocations rather than the growth of the welfare state help explain why blacks have been "losing ground" and why many of them have become "truly disadvantaged."

Staring at the boarded-up factories, many young blacks have been unable to get even their first jobs—work experience essential for acquiring skills as well as self-esteem. One of them, Darryl Swafford, grew up around Gary. Unemployed and dependent on food stamps, he had the same dream as most Americans: "I always had that goal, working in the mill. Have a home, a big car. But now there's no mill and I'm down. Just trying to make it, trying to survive." Many of the jobs available to young blacks have been in the fast-food services like Burger King and McDonald's. But these jobs pay very low wages and lead nowhere. "They treat you like a child on those minimum-wage jobs," complained Danny Coleman, who had worked in a fast-food restaurant. "And there is no way you can make it on that kind of salary. It is just a dead end." Young workers like Coleman have been facing an economy that says: Let them flip hamburgers.

Meanwhile, African-American "failure" has been contrasted with Asian-American "success." In 1984, William Raspberry of the *Washington Post* noted that Asian Americans on the West Coast had "in fact" "outstripped" whites in income. Blacks should stop blaming racism for their plight, he argued, and follow the example of the self-reliant Asian Americans. In 1986, *NBC Nightly News* and *McNeil/Lehrer Report* aired special news segments on Asian Americans and their achievements. *U.S. News & World Report* featured Asian-American advances in a cover story, and *Newsweek* focused a lead article on "Asian Americans: A 'Model Minority,'" while *Fortune* applauded them as "America's Super Minority."

But in their celebration of this "model minority," these media pundits have exaggerated Asian-American "success." Their comparisons of incomes between Asians and whites fail to recognize the regional locations of the Asian-American population. Concentrated in California, Hawaii, and New York, most Asian Americans reside in states with higher incomes but also higher costs of living than the national average: in 1980, 59 percent of all Asian Americans lived in these three states, compared to only 19 percent for the general population. The use of "family incomes" has been very misleading, for Asian-American families have more persons working per family than white families. Thus, the family incomes of Asian Americans indicate the presence of more workers in each family rather than higher individual incomes. Actually, in terms of personal incomes, Asian Americans have not reached equality.

While many Asian Americans are doing well, others find themselves mired in poverty: they include Southeast-Asian refugees such as the Hmong and Mien as well as immigrant workers trapped in Chinatowns. Eighty percent of the people of New York Chinatown, 74 percent of San Francisco Chinatown, and 88 percent of Los Angeles Chinatown are foreign-born. Like the nineteenth-century Chinese immigrants in search of Gold Mountain, they came here to seek a better life. But what they found instead was work in Chinatown's low-wage service and garment industries: 40 to 50 percent of the workers in the Chinatowns of San Francisco and Los Angeles and almost 70 percent of the New York Chinatown laborers are crowded into such occupations.

Most of these workers do not have a high school degree and lack English-language skills. Fifty-five percent of the residents of New York Chinatown do not speak English well or at all. "This does not mean that they are not trying to learn," explained Peter Kwong, who has worked as a community organizer for fifteen years.

"In fact, there are at least two dozen English-language schools in the community. . . . Thousands of working people squeeze time out from their busy schedules to attend classes. However, the real problem is that they do not have the opportunity to use English on the job or with other Chinese immigrants. They soon forget the scant English they have learned." . . .

The myth of the Asian-American "model minority" has been challenged, yet it continues to be widely believed. One reason for this is its instructional value. For whom are Asian Americans supposed to be a "model"? Shortly after the Civil War, southern planters recruited Chinese immigrants in order to pit them against the newly freed blacks as "examples" of laborers willing to work hard for low wages. Today, Asian Americans are again being used to discipline blacks. If the failure of blacks on welfare warns Americans in general how they should not behave, the triumph of Asian Americans affirms the deeply rooted values of the Protestant ethic and self-reliance. Our society needs an Asian-American "model minority" in an era anxious about a growing black underclass. Asian-American "success" has been used to explain the phenomenon of "losing ground"—why the situation of the poor has deteriorated during the last two decades while government social services have expanded. If Asian Americans can make it on their own, conservative pundits like Charles Murray are asking, why can't other groups? Many liberals have joined this chorus. In 1987, CBS's *60 Minutes* presented a glowing report on the stunning achievements of Asian Americans in the academy. "Why are Asian Americans doing so exceptionally well in school?" Mike Wallace asked and quickly added, "They must be doing something right. Let's bottle it." Wallace then suggested that failing black students should try to pursue the Asian-American formula for academic success.

Betraying a nervousness over the seeming end of the American Dream's boundlessness, praise for this "super minority" has become society's most recent jeremiad—a call for a renewed commitment to the traditional virtues of hard work, thrift, and industry. After all, it has been argued, the war on poverty and affirmative action were not really necessary. Look at the Asian Americans! They did it by pulling themselves up by their bootstraps. For blacks shut out of the labor market, the Asian-American model provides the standards of acceptable behavior: blacks should not depend on welfare or affirmative action. While congratulating Asian Americans for their family values, hard work, and high incomes, President Ronald Reagan chastised blacks for their dependency on the "spider's web of welfare" and their failure to recognize that the "only barrier" to success was "within" them. . . .

The global context of the Cold War has also conditioned immigration from what had been the Soviet Union. Refugees fleeing from religious oppression, Jews have been arriving in America again. The collapse of communism in Eastern Europe and Russia has unleashed a new wave of anti-Semitism, and many Jews have been afraid of what will happen to them. "Anti-Semitism and all the other old national hatreds were never really extinguished by Communism, merely frozen in time," James E. Young noted in his review of Charles Hoffman's recently published study of the Jews of Eastern Europe in the post-Communist era. "When the thaw came, the traditional conflicts bloomed with a vengeance, picking up exactly where they left off 45 years ago." The unraveling of Communist controls has given freedom to old, pent-up nativist passions. "The country is experiencing a process of 'decivilization,'" explained a Moscow lawyer in 1990. "The layers of civilization are being peeled off, and underneath there is this ugliness, including fascism and anti-Semitic hatred. Jews are trying to get out of Russia as fast as they can." An old Jewish man in a village near Minsk told two American visitors: "It's time now. We have to go. It wouldn't be safe for us to stay." Ironically, he was not religiously Jewish. For lunch he served ham. Prohibited from practicing their religion, many Jews are Jewish mainly in terms of their ethnic origins. "The last of the [Jewish] culture-bearers were executed 40 years ago," explained Aleksandr Z. Burakovsky, chair of the Kiev Sholom Aleichem Society. "Schools, synagogues, libraries were all abolished." Aleksandr A. Shlayen, director of the Babi Yar Center, added: "They started to beat the Jewishness out of Jews a long time ago, under the czars."

But, though many Jews in what had been the Soviet Union might not feel a strong identity as Jews, they have encountered hatred from neighbors and fellow citizens. In schools, Jewish children have been beaten and called names. Resentment has spread to the workplace: professional Jews have been experiencing discrimination in employment. Graffiti on walls have warned: "Jews get out." "My husband wanted to emigrate, but I didn't want to leave," recounted a young Jewish woman. "My parents are old and need to be cared for. I also thought of myself as a Soviet citizen." But many people saw her as a "Jew," and the harassment became "awful." Seeking sanctuary, half a million Jews have fled to Israel and also to America.

Recently, 40,000 Soviet Jews have been entering the United States annually, and altogether they total over 200,000. Like the Jewish immigrants of the late nineteenth century, they have been selling their houses and furniture, giving away almost everything, and leaving with only what they can carry wrapped in bedspreads or packed in suitcases. After their arrival, they have had to start all over again. Describing the plight of a Jewish refugee family, Barbara Budnitz of Berkeley, California, explained: "These people have nothing. I offered them an old desk. They said they wanted it, but what they really needed was a bed." Many of these refugees had been engineers in the old country, but here they have been suffering from unemployment. Lacking English language skills and possessing technical knowledge that has limited transferability, many have been forced to find jobs as apartment managers, janitors, or even as helpers at McDonald's. According to Barbara Nelson of the Jewish Family Services in Oakland, California, about 80 percent of the Jewish refugee families have been compelled to seek welfare support.

Still the Jews are glad to be in America where there is religious freedom. "My five-year-old daughter is attending school at the synagogue—something she could not do in the Ukraine," explained Sofiya Shapiro, who came with her family in 1991. "I am glad she can get to know Jewish tradition." Indeed, many of the refugees are learning about Judaism for the first time in their lives. But like the Jewish immigrants of earlier times, the recent refugees are hopeful this country will offer them an opportunity to begin again. "That's what America is," commented Budnitz. "We need to keep it that way."

America's continuing allure has also been as a place for a fresh economic start. This has been particularly true for the recent arrivals from Ireland. Like the nineteenth-century Irish immigrants fleeing hunger and the ravages of the potato famine, these recent newcomers have been pushed by grim economic conditions at home: in 1990, unemployment in Ireland was a staggering 18 percent. Seeking work in America, many have entered illegally in the past decade. Undocumented

Irish workers have been estimated to total as many as 120,000. "It's an anonymous floating population," stated Lena Deevy, director of the Irish Immigration Reform Movement office in Boston. "It's like counting the homeless." These illegal aliens constitute what one of them described as "an underclass," forced to take "the crummiest jobs at the lowest wages." The 1987 Immigration Reform Act, which made it unlawful for employers to hire undocumented workers, has created economic and social borders for many Irish. "You can't apply for a job," explained an Irish waitress who came to Boston in 1986. "You can't answer a want ad [because of the 1987 law]. It's all word of mouth." Undocumented Irish workers have to keep a low profile, she added: "My social life is limited to the Irish sector. I can't talk to Americans—you just have to tell too many lies." Director Deevy described their nervousness: "It's like living on the edge. There's a lot of fear" that someone "will squeal to the INS [Immigration and Naturalization Service]." In 1990, a new immigration law provided for the distribution of 40,000 green cards to be awarded by lottery, with 16,000 of them reserved for Irish. "I plan to fill out at least a thousand applications," said Joanne O'Connell of Queens, New York, as she looked forward to this "Irish Sweepstakes."

Most of today's immigrants, however, come from Asia and Latin America. Over 80 percent of all immigrants have been arriving from these two regions, adding to America's racial diversity—a reality charged with consequences for our nation's work force. By the year 2000, there will be more than 21 million new workers. They will be 44 percent white, 16 percent black, 11 percent Asian and other groups, and 29 percent Hispanic. A preview of the significance of this racial diversity in the twenty-first century can be seen in California. There, Hispanics, composed mostly of Mexican Americans, number 4.5 million, or approximately 20 percent of the state's population. Many of them are recent newcomers, pulled here again by dreams of El Norte. Compared to the Anglos, the Hispanics are young. In 1985, they represented 32 percent of the youth (aged birth to fifteen years) and only 8 percent of the elderly (sixty-five years and over), compared to 52 percent and 83 percent for Anglos. The number of Hispanics entering the work force will increase, while Anglos will continue to constitute a large majority of the elderly.

"What does all this portend for the future work force?" asked David Hayes-Bautista and his co-authors in their seminal study *The Burden of Support: Young Latinos in an Aging Society.* They noted that in 1980, working-age Anglos had an educational level of 13.5 years, while laborers in general had 12.9 years. But Hispanics, with a high school dropout rate of 60 percent, lagged behind with only 10.4 years. Hayes-Bautista calculated that if the 1980 differentials remained the same, the increase of Hispanics in the work force would decrease the overall educational level of the working population to only 12.1 years. "That the labor force of 2030 would actually be less educated than in 1980 is bad enough," he observed; "it would be particularly serious if, as seems certain, a more-educated, better-prepared labor force will be required for a high-tech future."

Clearly, the educational level of Hispanics should be raised to meet the needs of the future California economy. But in 1983, California was forty-fifth of all states in per capita spending on education. Is the largely Anglo population of today, Hayes-Bautista asked, willing to commit a sufficient portion of its economic pie to an investment in Hispanic youth?

The need to educate minority youth and prepare them to enter the work force suddenly became an urgent issue during the 1992 racial explosion in Los Angeles. "It took a brutal beating, an unexpected jury verdict, and the sudden rampage of rioting, looting, and indiscriminate violence to bring this crisis [of urban America] back to the forefront," *Business Week* reported. "Racism surely explains some of the carnage in Los Angeles. But the day-to-day living conditions with which many of America's urban poor must contend is an equally compelling story—a tale of economic injustice." This usually conservative magazine pointed out that "the poverty rate, which fell as low as 11% in the 1970s, moved higher in the Reagan years and jumped during the last couple of years. Last year, an estimated 36 million people—or about 1.47% of the total population—were living in poverty."

South Central Los Angeles has come to symbolize the plight of poor blacks trapped in inner cities. "South Central Los Angeles is a Third World country," declared Krashaun Scott, a former member of the Los Angeles Crips gang. "There's a South Central in every city, in every state." Describing the desperate conditions in his community, he continued: "What we got is inadequate housing and inferior education. I wish someone would tell me the difference between Guatemala and South Central." This comparison graphically illustrates the squalor and poverty present within one of America's wealthiest and most modern cities. Like a Third World country, South Central Los Angeles is also extremely volatile. A gang member known as Bone explained that the recent violence was "not a riot—it was a class struggle. When Rodney King asked, 'Can we get along?' it ain't just about Rodney King. He was the lighter and it blew up."

What exploded was anguish born of despair. "What happens to a dream deferred?" asked Langston Hughes in Harlem during the 1920s.

> Does it dry up
> Like a raisin in the sun?
> . . . Or does it explode?

But what happens when there are no dreams? Plants have been moving out of central Los Angeles into the suburbs as well as across the border into Mexico and even overseas to countries like South Korea. Abandoned inner-city factories, which had employed many of the parents of these young blacks, are now boarded up, like tombs. In terms of manufacturing jobs, South Central Los Angeles has become a wasteland. Many young black men and women nervously peer down the corridor of their futures and see no possibility of full-time employment paying above minimum wage, or any jobs at all. The unemployment rate in this area is 50 percent—higher than the national rate during the Great Depression.

"Once again, young blacks are taking to the streets to express their outrage at perceived injustice," *Newsweek* reported, "and once again, whites are fearful that The Fire Next Time will consume them." But this time, the magazine noticed, the situation was different from the earlier riot: the recent conflict was not just between blacks and whites. "The nation is rapidly moving toward a multiethnic future," *Newsweek* reported, in which Asians, Hispanics, Caribbean islanders, and many other immigrant groups compose a diverse and changing social mosaic that cannot be described by the old vocabulary of race relations in America." The terms "black" and "white," *Newsweek* concluded, no longer "depict the American social reality."

At the street level, black community organizer Ted Watkins observed: "This riot was deeper, and more dangerous [than the 1965 uprising]. More ethnic groups were involved." Watkins had witnessed the Watts rebellion, an expression of black fury;

since then, he had watched the influx of Hispanics and Koreans into South Central Los Angeles. Shortly after the 1992 explosion, social critic Richard Rodriguez reflected on the significance of these changes: "The Rodney King riots were appropriately multiracial in this multicultural capital of America. We cannot settle for black and white conclusions when one of the most important conflicts the riots revealed was the tension between Koreans and African Americans." He also noted that "the majority of looters who were arrested . . . turned out to be Hispanic." Out of the Los Angeles conflict came a sense of connectedness. "Here was a race riot that had no border," Rodriguez wrote, "a race riot without nationality. And, for the first time, everyone in the city realized—if only in fear—that they were related to one another."

Beyond this awareness was another lesson: the need for all of us to become listeners. "A riot," Martin Luther King asserted, "is the language of the unheard." As Americans watched the live television coverage of the violence and destruction in Los Angeles, the cry of the ghetto could be heard everywhere. "I think good will come of [the riot]," stated Janet Harris, a chaplain at Central Juvenile Hall. "People need to take off their rose-colored glasses," she added, "and take a hard look at what they've been doing. They've been living in invisible cages. And they've shut out that world. And maybe the world came crashing in on them and now people will be moved to do something."

The racial conflagration in Los Angeles violently highlighted America's economic problems. Racial antagonisms in Los Angeles and cities across the country are being fueled by a declining economy and rising general unemployment. One of the major causes for our economic downturn has been the recent deescalation of the U.S.-Soviet conflict: our economy has become so dependent on federal military spending that budget cuts for defense contractors have led to massive layoffs, especially in the weapons-producing states such as Massachusetts, Texas, and California. This economic crisis has been fanning the fires of racism in American society: Asian Americans have been bashed for the "invasion" of Japanese cars, Hispanics accused of taking jobs away from "Americans," and blacks attacked for their dependency on welfare and the special privileges of affirmative action.

Still, there are new prospects for change and progress. The end of the Cold War has given us the opportunity to shift our resources from nuclear weapons development to the production of consumer goods, which could help revitalize the American economy, making it more competitive with Japan and Germany. "It's as though America just won the lottery," the *New York Times* editorialized exuberantly in March 1990. "With Communism collapsing, the United States, having defended the free world for half a century, now stands to save a fortune. Defense spending could drop by $20 billion next year and $150 billion a year before the decade ends. "This tremendous resource can now be directed into the consumer goods economy. What is needed, proposed Ann Markusen of Rutgers University, is "an independent Office of Economic Conversion, designed to be self-liquidating by the year 2000 and accountable to the President."

In the wake of the Cold War, the United States is perched on the threshold of a new era of economic expansion. To meet the research needs of the military over the last half century, the government has educated and supported an impressive array of brilliant engineers and scientists. "These wizards of the cold war comprise the greatest force of scientific and engineering talent ever assembled," observed journalist

William J. Broad in 1992. "Over the decades this army of government, academic, and industry experts made the breakthroughs that gave the West its dazzling military edge." Released from military R&D, they now have the opportunity to give the United States an economic edge in the consumer goods market. Under the guidance of a comprehensive national industrial strategy, giant American corporations like Rockwell International, Grumman, Northrup, Martin Marietta, and Lockheed could now start designing and producing "smart" consumer goods rather than "smart" bombs. A growing demand for labor in a revitalized economy, combined with the rebuilding of the manufacturing base in inner cities as well as education and job training programs funded by the "peace dividend," could help to bring minority workers into the mainstream economy without making white laborers feel threatened. These needed economic changes face formidable difficulties, however. The tremendous federal debt incurred under President Reagan could dissipate the dividend generated by military budget reductions. Automation and the suburbanization of production could continue to shut out workers, especially minority laborers. The labor market has been internationalized, and American corporations could continue to relocate their production facilities in low-wage countries like Indonesia and Mexico, rendering millions of American workers superfluous. Nonetheless, the decomposition of the Soviet Union and the end of its military threat have given us new options for economic development. . . .

By viewing ourselves in a mirror which reflects reality, we can see our past as undistorted and no longer have to peer into our future as through a glass darkly. The face of our cultural future can be found on the western edge of the continent. "California, and especially Los Angeles, a gateway to both Asia and Latin America," Carlos Fuentes observed, "poses the universal question of the coming century: how do we deal with the Other?" Asked whether California, especially with its multiethnic society, represented the America of the twenty-first century, Alice Walker replied: "If that's not the future reality of the United States, there won't be any United States, because that's who we are." Walker's own ancestry is a combination of Native American, African American, and European American. Paula Gunn Allen also has diverse ethnic roots—American Indian, Scotch, Jewish, and Lebanese. "Just people from everywhere are related to me by blood," she explained, "and so that's why I say I'm a multicultural event. . . . It's beautiful, it's a rainbow. . . . It reflects light, and I think that's what a person like me can do." Imagine what "light" a "multicultural event" called America can reflect. America has been settled by "the people of all nations," Herman Melville observed over a century ago, "all nations may claim her for their own. You can not spill a drop of American blood, without spilling the blood of the whole world." Americans are not "a narrow tribe"; they are not a nation, "so much as a world." In this new society, Melville optimistically declared, the "prejudices of national dislikes" could be "forever extinguish[ed]."

But, as it has turned out, Melville was too sanguine. As our diversity is increasingly recognized today, it is accompanied by even more defensive denial, grim jeremiads of the Allan Blooms about the "closing of the American mind," and demagogic urgings of the Patrick Buchanans to take back "our cities, our culture, and our country." But who, in this case, are "we"? Such a backlash is defining our diversity as a "cultural war," a conflict between "us" and "them." Reflecting a traditional

Eurocentrism that remains culturally hegemonic, this resistance is what is really driving the "disuniting of America."

America's dilemma has been our resistance to ourselves—our denial of our immensely varied selves. But we have nothing to fear but our fear of our own diversity. "We can get along," Rodney King reassured us during an agonizing moment of racial hate and violence. To get along with each other, however, requires self-recognition as well as self-acceptance. Asked whether she had a specific proposal for improving the current racial climate in America, Toni Morrison answered: "Everybody remembers the first time they were taught that part of the human race was Other. That's a trauma. It's as though I told you that your left hand is not part of your body." In his vision of the "whole hoop of the world," Black Elk of the Sioux saw "in a sacred manner the shapes of all things in the spirit, and the shape of all shapes as they must live together like one being." And he saw that the "sacred hoop" of his people was "one of many hoops that made one circle, wide as daylight and as starlight, and in the center grew one mighty flowering tree to shelter all the children of one mother and one father." Today, what we need to do is to stop denying our wholeness as members of humanity as well as one nation.

As Americans, we originally came from many different shores, and our diversity has been at the center of the making of America. While our stories contain the memories of different communities, together they inscribe a larger narrative. Filled with what Walt Whitman celebrated as the "varied carols" of America, our history generously gives all of us our "mystic chords of memory." Throughout our past of oppressions and struggles for equality, Americans of different races and ethnicities have been "singing with open mouths their strong melodious songs" in the textile mills of Lowell, the cotton fields of Mississippi, on the Indian reservations of South Dakota, the railroad tracks high in the Sierras of California, in the garment factories of the Lower East Side, the canefields of Hawaii, and a thousand other places across the country. Our denied history "bursts with telling." As we hear America singing, we find ourselves invited to bring our rich cultural diversity on deck, to accept ourselves. "Of every hue and caste am I," sang Whitman. "I resist any thing better than my own diversity."

A Gathering of Citizens

MICHAEL SCHUDSON

Citizenship in the United States has not disappeared. It has not even declined. It has, inevitably, changed.

Past models of citizenship have not vanished as newer models became ascendant. The legacy of a colonial citizenship built on social hierarchy survives in the deference old families command and the traditions of public service they sometimes nurture. It endures in the trust people place in individuals who have a visible record of public service, personal integrity, charitable giving, and mentorship and sponsorship of younger leaders. It persists in the framework of our government in the ways that the constitutional machinery sifts raw opinion through deliberative legislative processes.

Similarly, the nineteenth-century citizenship of mass political participation carries on into our own day. Political parties, popular social movements, the social honor that citizens of every rank accrue for active participation in their communities, and the widespread obeisance in political rhetoric to public opinion, "the people," and majority rule all testify to the permanent contribution of mass democracy to modern politics. As for the Progressive Era ideal of the informed citizen, it, too, exerts enormous influence. It is the lamp held aloft by journalists committed to their profession, it directs civic education in and out of the schools, and it still dominates public understanding of civic obligation at election time. Even as rights-consciousness places the courtroom alongside the polling place in the practice of public life, and opens the political like a Pandora's box to cover a vastly expanded range of meanings, earlier visions of politics and citizenship survive and even prosper.

The successive coats that laminate our political ideals and practices have transformed citizenship profoundly. The United States has come from an era dominated by gentlemen to one dominated by parties, to one in which many groups and interests not only compete for political power but also contend with one another to define what powers are political. With such dramatic changes in who is free to participate in politics, what means are available for political participation, and what domains of human endeavor fall within the political, it would be remarkable if one could quickly sum up the changing quality of civic life as rise or fall. But many critics over the past two decades have made a case that the American story is, at least in the past half century, one of decline; civic life has collapsed. "By almost all the available evidence, we are witnessing a widespread turning away from public life," wrote the political philosopher Hanna Pitkin in 1981. Public life is disappearing," the editors of *Harper's* declared in 1990, and many heartily agreed. Evidence is everywhere: the decline of parties; the fiscal impoverishment of cities strangled by suburbs; the dwindling of newspaper readership; disappearing trust in government and nearly all other major institutions; shrinking voter turnout; citizens' paltry knowledge of national and international affairs; the lack of substance in political campaigns; the decline of conversation and the informal gathering places where it is said to have flourished; the fear of street crime that keeps people behind their locked doors; the spread of scandal as a political issue—and more. The general point, it seems, has scarcely to be argued; the only question is what to do about it.

Yet intellectuals have complained that "we no longer have citizens" at least since 1750, when Jean-Jacques Rousseau penned those words in Geneva. Pick your appropriate quotation from Tocqueville in 1840, E. L. Godkin in the 1890s, Walter Lippmann in the 1920s, or political scientists and sociologists in the 1950s and you will find the theme sounded again. In 1979, President Jimmy Carter worried out loud about moral and civic decline in his "malaise" speech; in 1985, a concern with American moral decline was vividly renewed as sociologist Robert Bellah and his colleagues, in their widely discussed *Habits of the Heart,* criticized the ways liberal individualism had narrowed the American political imagination. Energetic discussion in American history, political science, and law in the 1970s and 1980s looked to eighteenth-century "civic republicanism" as a superior alternative to liberalism or socialism for our own day.

All the social criticism of privatized citizens and the various solutions offered to renew or reawaken their public involvement took a new turn and gained new substance with the recent writings of Robert Putnam. In 1993, Putnam, a Harvard political scientist, published a study of Italian democracy that argues, on the basis of considerable historical evidence, that the parts of Italy that best nurture local political democracy are distinguished not by economic standing or class cohesion or other likely variables but by long-standing traditions of active voluntary associations. The number of choral societies, soccer teams, and bird-watching clubs in a region in the late nineteenth century turned out to be the best predictor of the late-twentieth-century success of the region in self-government. Tocqueville was alive and well and dining on pasta.

This work gained broader attention when Putnam published a brief but clever and provocative paper that tried to make a related case for the United States. This essay, "Bowling Alone," like the Italian study, focused on the importance to democracy of "social capital." What sustains viable democratic politics is the underlying strength of social bonds that people can draw on to propel them into and sustain them in civic affairs. Voluntary organizational involvement, from bowling leagues to the PTA, are the signs of community health. They provide the social resources and the civic training that citizens need to make democracy tick. Putnam shows that membership in organizations from the League of Women Voters to the Red Cross to business clubs like the Rotary, Lions, Elks, and Jaycees have fallen off dramatically in the past twenty-five years. The "Bowling Alone" title refers to the fact that the number of people who go bowling has remained constant over twenty-five years but the number enrolled in bowling leagues has declined sharply—in other words, people bowl, as ever, but they do not do so as part of organized social life. (It was not long before a wry critic pointed to the extraordinary growth of soccer participation in the same period and titled his article "Kicking in Groups.")

As always, the most decisive index of decline is voter turnout. People who became eligible to vote in 1968 or later have had turnout rates sharply lower than those who came to voting age between the 1930s and 1964. In 1972, post–New Deal generation citizens with less than a high school education had a turnout rate of 41 percent, whereas 62 percent of New Deal generation citizens with the same level of education voted. With a high school degree, 83 percent of the New Deal generation voted, 55 percent of the post–New Deal. With some college, the figures were 88 percent and 79 percent, respectively. By 1992, the disparity between the generations in voter turnout remained huge, except for those with some college.

Other measures present a somewhat more complicated picture. For instance, where Putnam reported PTA membership down from twelve million in 1964 to five million in 1982, the Roper Center for Public Opinion Research found that in 1969 only 16 percent of people surveyed had ever attended a school board meeting, whereas 39 percent did so in 1995. Charitable financial contributions from those who itemize their returns declined from 1960 to 1980, but there was also a self-reported increase in volunteer activities from 1965 to 1981. Putnam himself discovered that an error in calculation had led him to overestimate the decline in the number of organizations people belong to.

Even so, a lot of substantial civic organizations have clearly lost members. Putnam's data, drawn from the best national surveys that have repeated the same questions to the general public every few years, is simply more thorough than any alternatives anyone else has provided. His data can be supplemented with still other evidence that points in the same direction. Alexander Astin and his colleagues at UCLA have gathered data annually in a national survey of college freshmen from 1966 to the present. In 1966, 58 percent of college men and women held "keeping up to date with political affairs" an essential or important objective, but only 33 percent of men and 27 percent of women made the same affirmation by 1996. Attitudes toward service rather than toward politics showed more modest change, but in the same downward direction: in 1966, 59 percent of the men judged it essential or important to "help others who are in difficulty," sliding very slowly to 53 percent in 1996, while for women the slippage was from 80 percent (the single most important objective for women in that year) to 70 percent (in second place, behind "be well off financially" at 72 percent).

It may be that Putnam has not counted all that should be counted. Does the survey data in which people report how many organizations they belong to truly reflect the social capital he seeks to measure? For instance, what about the millions of people who go to commercial health clubs, often making friends there and developing an informal group life? Should this activity be counted as contributing to social capital? In an earlier generation after all, some of the kinds of people who now go to the commercial fitness center probably joined the Y or the Elks for no purpose but to use their gyms and steam rooms. Today they would be unlikely to list the family fitness center as an organization they belong to; yesterday they would have listed the Y. The market has expanded in useful ways and serves needs that associational life once catered to. Other kinds of organizational life, from soccer leagues (that no adults, after all, would identify as organizations they belong to—it is their children who belong) to neighborhood watch meetings or block associations (that no adults would be likely to list as full-fledged associations or organizations of which they are members) have taken up some of the slack of associational life.

Assume that the problems of measuring organizational involvement could be resolved and that the results show a decline in significant individual engagement in associational activity. This seems to me plausible, indeed, likely. The burden of proof at this point in the debate rests with Putnam's critics, not with Putnam. However, even if Putnam's data holds up, it would still be premature to infer from it a decline in civic participation. The reason, as the last chapter suggested, is that civic participation now takes place everywhere. It exists in the microprocesses of social life. In the cultural shift from the informed citizen model of the Progressive Era to the rights-regarding citizens of the present day, a dimension of citizenship has come to color everything. Whatever the measures on social capital may finally show, it will still be the case that individual political activity in the past quarter century has actually risen. It could scarcely be otherwise when the idea of citizenship has colonized so many of the territories of private life that once were beyond its jurisdiction.

Citizens still exercise citizenship as they stand in line at their polling places, but now they exercise citizenship in many other locations. They have political ties not only to elected public officials in legislatures but also to attorneys in courtrooms and organized interest groups that represent them to administrative agencies. Moreover, they are citizens in their homes, schools, and places of employment.

Women and minorities self-consciously do politics just by turning up, so long as they turn up in positions of authority and responsibility in institutions where women and minorities were once rarely seen. They do politics when they walk into a room, anyone's moral equals, and expect to be treated accordingly. The gay and lesbian couples in Hawaii in 1991 or in Vermont in 1997 are political when they try to be legally married (and, of course, so are their opponents in Congress and the twenty-five states that have passed laws to bar recognition of such marriages). Others do politics when they wear a "Thank You For Not Smoking" button or when they teach their children to read nutritional labeling at the supermarket or when they join in class action suits against producers of silicon breast implants, Dalkon shields, or asbestos insulation.

The changes that have made the personal political have been profound, arguably more so than the slackening of voter turnout, the decline in PTA membership, the decreasing willingness of college freshmen to affirm political obligations and political convictions, or television's incursion into living rooms and bedrooms. What also has invaded the household is talk—talk between husband and wife as equals, political talk between husband and wife, political talk even between parents and children, no doubt often prompted by the television news or even the outrageous TV magazine or talk shows. And the language of this talk is a public language that, within it, bears the seeds of rights-consciousness and its premises of moral equality. There is evidence of this in, for instance, the ways that even women who claim no allegiance to feminism and no interest in politics have come to use terms like "male chauvinist" in their everyday language. There is evidence of it also in the ways that ordinary Americans from all walks of life address their congressional representatives in letters—which they do, as it happens, with more frequency than ever before.

It is hard to fully credit the 1990s rhetoric of decline when it is so easy to recall almost the same language from the 1950s. I remember, from my own growing-up, David Riesman's *The Lonely Crowd* on my parents' bookshelf along with William Whyte's *Organization Man* and Sloan Wilson's novel *The Man in the Gray Flannel Suit,* and other popular statements that condemned American conformity, complacency, and mediocrity. The pursuit of private material gain was widely condemned. I remember listening to the rabbi at my synagogue in Milwaukee attack my elders for failing to participate in community and religious life. He called his congregants "cardiac Jews" because they were Jewish "in their hearts" but not in their participation in the life of the Jewish community.

Much of the alarm at the time was pegged to the Cold War and the need to stand up the forces of evil in the world. Americans not only lacked community, it was said, they lacked courage. They were without role models, heroes, and wisdom. What they did not lack was trust in major institutions. In retrospect, they had far too much of it. They trusted a Cold War government that tested radioactive fallout on unwitting citizens, welfare bureaucrats who told the poor they were not eligible for benefits they were qualified for, registrars of voters who denied the franchise to blacks in the South who could not explain complex clauses of the Constitution, doctors who kept from patients the knowledge they were dying or concealed the risks of elective surgery, teachers who told parents their children could not learn because they were retarded (when they were not) or because their skin was not white. Perhaps they even trusted too much in marriage and the family, with a higher percentage of the population marrying than ever before, and at younger ages, and with more children spaced more closely together, reversing a long-term decline in fertility. Divorce rates declined, too, bucking a historical trend upward. Could the nuclear family satisfy all the demands made of it?

A society cannot long endure without basic social trust, nor can a democracy survive without well-organized and well-institutionalized distrust. Because of distrust, we have a Bill of Rights; because of distrust, we have checks and balances; because of distrust, we are enjoined as citizens to be watchful.

Reviewing the broad contours of the 1950s should breed skepticism about contemporary exclamations of moral degradation. What sense are we to make of today's critique when examined alongside the lamentations from the 1950s about the apathetic Americans, the suburbanites David Riesman characterized as "seldom informed, rarely angry, and only spasmodically partisan" or the citizens C. Wright Mills judged politically "inactionary" and "out of it"? These thinkers wrote at exactly the moment when the World War II generation that Putnam has called the "long civic generation" was in command, social capital was supposedly at its height, and the television virus had not yet spread. The rhetoric of decline should send up a red flag; for the socially concerned intellectual, it is as much an off-the-rack rhetoric as is a rhetoric of progress for the ebullient technocrat.

How could we know if citizenship and community are in decline? What kinds of measures might we look to, recognizing, of course, that the question is far too general to admit of any simple index?

The most familiar measure has been voter turnout—the percentage of citizens eligible to vote who do so has declined in the past generation. This is a relevant measure, indeed, in part because voting is an act not only of citizen participation but also of general faith in the political system. Voting is an instrumental act to elect one candidate and not another, but it is also a mass ritual, and failure to engage in it suggests declining fervor for the religion of democracy. A decline in turnout is, on its face, a worrisome sign. On the other hand, high voter turnout is not necessarily a sign of civic health. An analyst would have to examine not only what percentage of the eligible electorate vote but also who is eligible to vote (the number doubled with woman's suffrage in 1920 and rose again after the Civil Rights Acts of 1964 and 1965 were passed and enforced) and what the act of voting means. The turnout decline since the 1960s is scarcely conclusive in itself. The high turnout figures of the nineteenth century, as I have argued, do not reveal that the civic health of America's party period was glowing; neither do recent low turnout figures indicate fatal illness.

A second measure would be people's expressed trust in government and other leading social institutions. Here, too, there has been a substantial decline; people are much less likely in the 1990s than in the 1960s to tell pollsters they "trust in" the president, the Congress, the medical profession, the military, the Supreme Court, business, unions, universities, or the news media. Still, as I have suggested, there can be too much trust as well as too little, and the baseline measures of trust from the 1950s and early 1960s surely reflected a moment of unusual consensus in American life held together by Cold War paranoia, middle-class complacency, postwar affluence, and the continuing denial of a voice in public life to women and minorities. Some of the skepticism about major institutions today is amply warranted. Skepticism can be healthy. Some of today's skepticism is in a grand old

American tradition that distrusts all politics and politicians. Then again, some of it seems to express a deeper alienation or aimlessness, especially among the young. But in the crude measures we have, there is no distinguishing a healthy inclination to question authority from a depressed withdrawal in which it is impossible to place faith in anyone or anything.

A third plausible measure of civic health would be the stock of social capital as measured by people's membership in and connection to social groups in which they can and do participate. As Putnam has argued well, this is an important measure. Still, it is difficult to know how to weigh it against the growth of individual choice, which is its flip side. Let me offer an example. The Roman Catholic Church in America has long been a powerful institution in community-building, especially among the urban, immigrant working-class Catholics who for a century were the core of its membership. The Catholic parish was disciplined by the priest who had enormous power in prescribing norms of behavior for everyday life. His authority was exercised through a dense network of youth groups, fraternal organizations, parish sports teams, choirs, women's clubs, and, of course parochial schools and the church itself. More than for Protestants or Jews, Catholic adherence to church was also involvement in a neighborhood. In the 1950s, rental listings for homes and apartments in cities like Philadelphia and Chicago were categorized *by parish.* In the 1960s, the Catholic Church, like the rest of America, experienced profound changes, but more so. Pope John XXIII called the Second Vatican Council together in 1962, the first such council since 1870. The report of Vatican II, issued in 1965, declared that the church should adapt itself to modernity, dissent within the church could be tolerated, religious freedom should be prized, and the liturgy should be revised to make it more comprehensible to parishioners and more participatory. The Mass in Latin was now in English, the priest who had faced the wall and prayed silently now led the congregation in prayer; the once silent congregation now sang hymns, shook hands, and stood rather than knelt.

Vatican II was an authoritative statement that questioned authority. It had far-reaching consequences. The traditional deference of the laity to the clergy in the conduct of the church declined. As Catholics, both laity and clergy, participated actively in the civil rights movement, lay parishioners, nuns, and seminarians all were "imbued with new notions of 'rights'" and explicitly compared their lack of power or their ghettoization within the church to the condition of blacks in American society. When Vatican II was followed in 1968 by *Humanae vitae,* Pope Paul VI's encyclical that reaffirmed the prohibition on birth control, millions of Catholics were at least confused, and many of them felt betrayed, by a church they had believed was modernizing. Both clergy and laity protested, some by leaving the church or their vocations. There were 181,000 women in religious orders in 1966 and 127,000 by 1980, and the downward trend was the same for men. Even for those who remained, clerical leadership changed as lay leaders came to take a larger and larger role in church governance. The church became increasingly pluralistic: "There is no longer one way to do theology, to worship at Mass, to confess sin, or to pray. There are various ways of being Catholic, and people are choosing the style that best suits them." As Catholics moved to the suburbs, the link between parish, church, ethnicity, and personal identity did not break down, but it did to a degree break apart. Suburban Catholics are not Protestants and retain, as Andrew

Greeley has argued, a distinctive Catholic "imagination," but the locus of authority about what it is to be Catholic has gravitated further from the church and closer to the household than a generation ago.

Was the old way better? Did the authoritarian structure that held together a parish community provide a stronger basis for self-fulfillment and a rich public life than the new structure that offered the individual more choice, autonomy, and power? The Catholic Church is, of course, only one example of the kind of institution that built social capital in the old days, and it is obviously an example of a particularly rigid and hierarchical cast. Yet it is one of the fundamental constituents of twentieth-century American society, the strength of its community life a major source of the strength of urban machine politics, the Democratic Party, and the union movement. Its broad influence seems much more important in this context than its atypicality, and its transformation reveals starkly that the trade-off between community and individualism is also a trade-off between hierarchy and egalitarianism, between authoritarian codes and democratic ones, between unitary, rigid ways of living and pluralistic ones, between imposition and individual choice. There are costs to the decline of traditional authority in the church, patriarchal family, party machine, and settled elites of community life. The costs are grounds for regret, nostalgia, and a variety of imaginative efforts at renewal, but few people find them grounds for turning back.

Voting, social trust, and social membership are the three most familiar measures of civic health, and the three most familiar bases on which it is argued that the present has slipped from a more desirable past. Other measures might be given consideration, too. A fourth measure is the quality of public discourse. Critics look at daytime talk shows, or listen to Howard Stern or Rush Limbaugh, or read pornography or scurrilous political gossip on the Internet, or feel assaulted by the public use of words that a generation ago could be heard only in locker rooms and not on television, or observe the reduction of political speeches to catchphrases that might win the attention of broadcast journalists committed to ever shorter sound bites. Can this be judged anything but degradation?

I do not have an answer here, but on this measure, too, there is another side of the story. The greater openness and rawness of public talk that produced raunchy talk shows also produced *All in the Family, Maude,* and *Ellen* in entertainment and programs like *60 Minutes* in television news. All of these programs share with their more disparaged and tasteless cousins a frank and aggressive style, a quest for transgression, and a pushing of the limits of conventional civility. Meanwhile, a serious argument can be made that ordinary Americans have better access to solid news reporting and analysis today than they did in 1960 or 1965. Journalists are less complacent in general; more individual journalists have become expert and ambitious contributors to public dialogue with magazine essays, long newspaper pieces, and nonfiction books; our leading newspapers reach many more people than ever through national editions and their own wire services (notably the *New York Times, Washington Post,* and *Los Angeles Times);* national network news is more sophisticated than a generation ago even if local television news is increasingly a moral desert; and in some major cities and regions there are today exponents of the best journalism the country has produced where none existed in 1960—I think of Chicago, Washington D.C., and Los Angeles.

A fifth measure: how great is the disparity between rich and poor? Related to this: is there an economic bottom below which society by private and public efforts will not allow people to fall? Prosperity as such is no measure of civic life, nor is it apparent what level of economic inequality might endanger the public good. But there is a quality of care for the poor, lacking which a society has clearly failed. The United States remains a reluctant welfare state, never fully committed to seeing economic equality or even a baseline minimum economic subsistence as an obligation of the state. Even so, a smaller percentage of the population lives in poverty today than in 1960, although the percentage was higher in 1990 than in 1980.

One must consider quality as well as quantity in the disparity between rich and poor. It is important to know not only how great is the gap between those at the top and those at the bottom but how hopeless the world appears from the bottom. Do economic and social inequalities take on a castelike form? How well can one predict the economic or social life-chances of an infant from the economic status, skin color, age, and marital status of his or her mother? If these predictions are becoming easier, then on this measure public life is getting worse.

Sixth, is the capacity of the least advantaged groups in society to make their voices heard in the political process increasing or decreasing? And what of less advantaged groups, say, blue-collar workers? If the power of unions is declining, as certainly it is, and if the Democratic Party is correspondingly less responsive to working-class concerns, has a large segment of the population lost its clearest access to political power?

Finally, is the reach of state-guaranteed rights increasing or decreasing? If it is increasing, then public life is improving in that public responsibility is growing and the range of human actions in which publicly accountable language is brought to bear is enlarging. Of course, state-guaranteed rights increase only because people believe that state or private power has violated the fundamental autonomy of individuals—the government has quartered its soldiers in your house without permission, the police have searched your house or person without a warrant, your school board has expelled you from school because your religious beliefs forbid you to salute the flag, your husband beats you, your employer threatens you for refusing sexual favors, your public transportation has not accommodated your wheelchair. If none of these things ever happened, then there would be no requirement of state-protected rights. But the existence of state-protected rights is a force for keeping these violations from happening or, at least, for calling people to account when they do. By this measure, it can scarcely be doubted that public life has improved in the past generation.

Public life can be measured by the inclusiveness of public deliberations. The more people among the total population who are eligible to should the burden of public decision-making and who are equipped to do so, the better the public life of a society. By this measure, certainly, the United States after 1920 has a better public life than at any earlier time, and the United States after 1965 has a better public life than at any earlier time. To the extent that certain senseless discriminations, apart from limitations on voting, are struck down—for instance, discrimination in employment or housing on the basis of sexual orientation—this also helps to fully empower citizens to speak and participate. By this measure, American society is better since *Romer* v. *Evans* (1995) struck down Colorado's anti-homosexual state constitutional amendment than it was before. To the extent that the poor and the oppressed whose voices have commonly been excluded from public deliberation today a least have institutionalized surrogates in public interest associations, law firms, foundations, and other organizations, there is progress rather than decline.

How is American public life doing today on these seven measures? Voter turnout offers troubling evidence of decline. Polling that indicates a lessening of trust in major institutions is a much more equivocal measure of civic health. We do not know what it means. How does the answer people give to an abstract question about their level of trust relate to actual behavioral indices of trust—compliance with the Internal Revenue Service or willingness to defer to the authority of a medical doctor, a government bureaucrat, a school administrator, or a court order? Nor do we know what the optimal level of trust would be. Surely it would be deeply troubling if 100 percent of the people placed "a great deal" of faith in the president, the Congress, big business, labor, medicine, universities, or the media. But is 75 percent the right level? Or 50 percent? Or 25 percent?

I do not think that trust, so far as polls are able to measure it, is an intelligible indicator of anything. What then, about social capital? Is declining membership in important civic organizations a clear sign of declining social health? I think a reasonable observer must be agnostic on this one. The decline in organizational solidarity is truly a loss, but it is also the flip side of a rise in individual freedom, which is truly a gain. Assessments of the state of public discourse must likewise reckon with its double-edged character. On the down side, public talk has clearly grown more harsh, more crude, and more uncivil over the past several decades. On the up side, however, public discourse is more honest and more inclusive of a wide range of persons and topics that the late, lamented "civility" excluded. These two measures seem to have an inherently paradoxical quality; the very social changes that give good reason for regret also give good reason for satisfaction.

As for the disparity between the most and lest advantaged citizens, a straight-line trend seems hard to find. This measure seems to be very sensitive to party politics, so a society that grew more kind and just in the 1960s and 1970s became notably less so in the Reagan eighties, and only under President Bill Clinton has it begun to inch back toward decency.

Regarding the measures of political inclusion and protection for individual rights, Americans are unquestionably better off in the past quarter century than at any prior moment in our history. There are ups and downs here, too, but the 1960s and 1970s saw the emergence of a consensus that, though assaulted and even shaken, has not surrendered the field. It is, on the contrary, our new foundation.

By my count, then, there is a clear decline on one measure, clear progress on two others, a mixed verdict on three, and a judgment that one measure (trust) is thus far too faulty a concept to use. To summarize all of this as amounting to a decline in civic well-being is, to put it kindly, premature.

Of course, this is no more than a provisional thought-experiment, not a definitive assessment of the state of the nation. We do not truly know how to measure change on these seven dimensions, nor do we know how to weigh one dimension against another. . . .

Is the glass of citizenship, of political democracy, of membership in a moral community of equals entitled to the rights and responsibilities of self-government half empty or half full? If this is a question about a three centuries' stretch of history or even a half century's expanse, and not an attitude survey on the politics of the moment, then the answer is easy. For women, wage laborers, racial, ethnic, sexual preference, or religious minorities, the poor, and the elderly, progress toward genuine inclusion in the past half century has been extraordinary. A significant part of that progress came in the 1960s and 1970s, far-reaching and unsettling enough that society is still reacting and adjusting to the changes wrought in those years. Progress or decline is not the real question. All that is required to criticize the present state of affairs is to know that some serious injustices persist, that some remediable conditions that limit human possibility lie before us, and that resources for reconstituting ourselves can be found. Injustices and exclusions remain, especially in the bifurcation of society into the relatively comfortable and the abjectly poor. We do not need to beat ourselves with the stick of the past. . . . We will not recover our heritage by hiding behind it, nor will we relinquish it by facing the present as honestly as we can.

✖ F U R T H E R   R E A D I N G

Abbate, Janet. *Computers: Inventing the Internet* (2000).

Bagby, Meredith. *Rational Exuberance: The Influence of Generation X on the New American Economy* (1999).

Easton, Nina. *Gang of Five: Leaders at the Center of the Conservative Crusade* (2000).

Coontz, Stephanie. *The Way We Really Are: Coming to Terms With America's Changing Families* (1998).

De Long, J. Bradford. "What 'New' Economy?" *Wilson Quarterly* (Autumn, 1998).

Garreau, Joel. *Edge City: Life on the New Frontier* (1992).

Kelly, Kevin. *Out of Control: The New Biology of Machines, Social Systems and the Economic World* (1994).

Kelley, Robin D. G. *Yo' Mama's Disfunktional!: Fighting the Culture Wars in Urban American* (1998).

Levy, Frank. *The New Dollars and Dreams* (1999).

Lind, Michael. *The Next American Nation: The New Nationalism and the Fourth American Revolution* (1995).

Mills, Nicolaus. *The Triumph of Meanness: America's War Against Its Better Self* (1997).

Nolan, James L., Jr. *The Therapeutic State: Justifying Government at Century's End* (1998).

Piven, Frances Fox, and Richard A. Cloward. *The Breaking of the American Social Compact* (1997).

Putnam, Robert D. *Bowling Alone: The Collapse and Revival of American Community* (2000).

Ritzer, George. *The McDonaldization of Society: An Investigation into the Changing Character of Contemporary Social Life* (1996).

Roberts, Paul Craig, and Lawrence M. Stratton. *The Tyranny of Good Intentions: How Prosecutors and Bureaucrats Are Trampling the Constitution in the Name of Justice* (2000).

Schudson, Michael. *The Good Citizen: A History of American Civil Life* (1998).

Schrag, Peter. *Paradise Lost: California's Experience, America's Future* (1998).

Schwarz, John E. "The Hidden Side of the New Economy," *Atlantic Monthly* (October, 1998).

Stein, Harry. *How I Accidently Joined the Vast Right Wing Conspiracy (And Found Inner Peace)* (2000).

Stiroh, Kevin. "Is There a New Economy?" *Challenge* (July/August, 1999).

Winner, Langdon. "Cyberlibertarian Myths and the Prospects for Community," (1997).